Sight
Sound
Motion

From the Wadsworth Series in Broadcast and Production

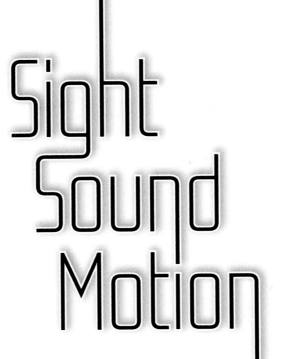

Sight Sound Motion

Applied Media Aesthetics

6th Edition

Herbert Zettl

San Francisco State University

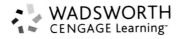

WADSWORTH
CENGAGE Learning

Australia • Brazil • Japan • Korea • Mexico • Singapore • Spain • United Kingdom • United States

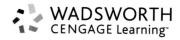

Sight Sound Motion:
Applied Media Aesthetics, Sixth Edition
Herbert Zettl

Senior Publisher: Lyn Uhl

Publisher: Michael Rosenberg

Associate Development Editor: Megan Garvey

Assistant Editor: Jillian D'Urso

Editorial Assistant: Erin Pass

Media Editor: Jessica Badiner

Marketing Manager: Bryant Chrzan

Marketing Coordinator: Darlene Macanan

Marketing Communications Manager:
    Christine Dobberpuhl

Senior Content Project Manager: Michael Lepera

Art Director: Linda Helcher

Print Buyer: Justin Palmeiro

Permissions Editor: Bob Kauser

Production Service/Compositor: Ideas to Images

Text Designer: Gary Palmatier, Ideas to Images

Photo Manager: Mandy Groszko

Cover Designer: Gary Palmatier, Ideas to Images

Cover Image: Vasily Kandinsky, *Dominant Curve*
    (Courbe dominante) (April 1936), oil on canvas,
    50⅞" × 76½" (129.2 × 194.3 cm). Solomon R.
    Guggenheim Museum, New York. Solomon R.
    Guggenheim Founding Collection [45.989].
    © 2009 Artists Rights Society (ARS), New York/
    ADAGP, Paris.

For product information and technology assistance, contact us at
Cengage Learning Customer & Sales Support, 1-800-354-9706

For permission to use material from this text or product, submit all requests online at **www.cengage.com/permissions**
Further permissions questions can be emailed to
permissionrequest@cengage.com

Library of Congress Control Number: 2009940268
ISBN-13: 978-0-495-80296-9
ISBN-10: 0-495-80296-4

Wadsworth
20 Channel Center Street
Boston, MA 02210
USA

Cengage Learning is a leading provider of customized learning solutions with office locations around the globe, including Singapore, the United Kingdom, Australia, Mexico, Brazil, and Japan. Locate your local office at **international.cengage.com/region**

Cengage Learning products are represented in Canada by Nelson Education, Ltd.

For your course and learning solutions, visit **www.cengage.com**

Purchase any of our products at your local college store or at our preferred online store **www.ichapters.com**

Printed in the United States of America
1 2 3 4 5 6 7   13 12 11 10 09

To all who see virtue in optimizing the aesthetics of visual communication.

Brief Contents

Contents

2

The First Aesthetic Field: Light   18

3

Structuring the First Aesthetic Field: Lighting   36

4

The Extended First Field: Color   52

5

Structuring Color: Function and Composition   70

6

The Two-dimensional Field: Area   80

7

The Two-dimensional Field: Forces Within the Screen   102

Structuring the Two-dimensional Field: Interplay of Screen Forces   128

9

The Three-dimensional Field: Depth and Volume 154

10

Structuring the Three-dimensional Field: Screen Volume and Effects 176

11

Building Screen Space: Visualization 202

12

The Four-dimensional Field: Time   228

13

The Four-dimensional Field: Motion   252

14

Structuring the Four-dimensional Field: Timing and Principal Motions   272

15

The Five-dimensional Field: Sound   294

16

Structuring the Five-dimensional Field: Sound Structures and Sound/Picture Combinations   318

17

Visual Narrative:
The Syntax of Continuity Editing   352

18

Visual Narrative:
The Syntax of Complexity Editing 378

About the Author

HERBERT ZETTL TAUGHT FOR 40 YEARS IN THE BROADCAST AND Electronic Communication Arts Department at San Francisco State University. His research emphases were, and still are, media aesthetics and video production. While at San Francisco State, he headed the Institute of International Media Communication (IIMC). The IIMC facilitates international visitors through the auspices of the U.S. State Department's International Information Programs and the San Francisco International Diplomacy Council, sponsors international visiting scholars, and gives occasional international summer workshops for television professionals. Dr. Zettl is one of the founders of the Annual Visual Communication Conference, a national conference for visual communication scholars. He received the California State Legislature Distinguished Teaching Award in 1966, and in 2004 he received the Distinguished Education Service Award of the Broadcast Education Association.

Prior to joining the San Francisco State University faculty, Dr. Zettl worked at several professional television stations, including KPIX, the CBS affiliate in San Francisco, where he was a producer-director. He participated in numerous CBS and NBC network television productions, such as Edward R. Murrow's *Person to Person* and several network specials. He is a member of the prestigious Silver Circle of the National Academy of Television Arts and Sciences (NATAS), Northern California Chapter, for his outstanding contributions to the television profession. He is also a member of NATAS Broadcast Legends.

Dr. Zettl has been a visiting professor at Concordia University in Montreal, Canada; Heidelberg University in Heidelberg, Germany; and the Institute for Television and Film in Munich, Germany. For one year he served as resident director in Germany for California State University students at Heidelberg and Tübingen Universities. For several years he consulted as an academic specialist with broadcast institutions in various countries, frequently under the auspices of the U.S. State Department's International Information Programs. He also acted as consultant to a number of universities and professional broadcast institutions in North and South America, Europe, the Middle East, Africa, Asia, and Southeast Asia.

In his seminar on experimental production, Dr. Zettl spearheaded various experimental television productions, such as dramas for simultaneous multiscreen and inductive narrative presentation techniques.

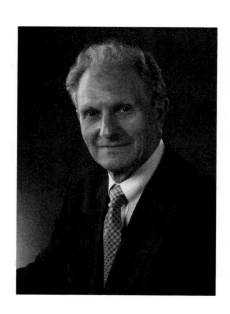

Herbert Zettl, PhD

He has presented many papers on media aesthetics and video production for a variety of academic and professional media conventions both in this country and abroad. He has also published numerous articles, many of which were translated into foreign languages and/or published abroad. His other books on television production and aesthetics, all published by Cengage Learning, include: *Television Production Handbook,* 10th ed., 2009; *Television Production Workbook,* 10th ed., 2009; *Video Basics 6,* 2010; and *Video Basics Workbook 6,* 2010. *Television Production Handbook, Sight Sound Motion,* and *Video Basics* have been translated into several foreign languages (including Spanish, Greek, Chinese, and Korean) and are used in key television production centers and universities around the world.

Dr. Zettl developed with the Cooperative Media Group an interactive multimedia program, *Zettl's VideoLab 2.1,* published by Cengage Learning in 1995. This CD-ROM contained basic information on video production and interactive simulated production exercises. It won the Macromedia People's Choice Award and the following 1995 New Media Invision Awards: Gold Medal in the Best Higher Education category and Silver Medals in the Best Use of Video and Best Continuing Education categories. From *A/V Video* magazine, it won the Silver Medal, Best Product in Education and Training, 1995; and from the National Educational Media Network, the Bronze Apple Award, 1996. The new DVD edition of *Zettl's VideoLab 3.0* has subsequently been released by Cengage Learning and includes several new features and a new module on switching.

Preface

THE NEW VIDEO TECHNOLOGY, WHICH LETS YOU PRODUCE HIGH-QUALITY images and sound with relatively inexpensive equipment, puts more pressure on you to match this technical quality with equally high aesthetic standards. For example, the many screen sizes and aspect ratios of large digital movie screens, high-definition home video screens, various computer monitors, and tiny mobile media displays require not only new framing and compositional principles but new sound considerations as well. In this context applied media aesthetics has gained new prominence and urgency.

Despite the ever-increasing automation of digital cinema and video equipment, you are still in charge of making aesthetic decisions. More so, you can no longer rely solely on instinct when framing a shot or adding music to your video track but must acquire the knowledge and the skill to select and apply on a regular basis those aesthetic elements that translate significant ideas into maximally effective messages. *Sight Sound Motion* will help you in this task.

When analyzing video programs and film, you must learn to recognize and evaluate the established production standards as well as the new ways aesthetic elements are used. For example, the jump cut, extreme high-contrast lighting, or color and sound distortion can be either purposeful aesthetic effects to intensify the message or gross production mistakes. By knowing what aesthetic tools you have at hand and how to use them in the context of the screen event, you will have little trouble deciding whether the effects were done intentionally or out of ignorance.

The text also provides a basis for the study of media literacy—an educational discipline that has become an essential prerequisite for producers as well as consumers of media programs. Unfortunately, such studies usually concentrate on the literal content of the program but ignore its aesthetic envelope. Any textual analysis that ignores media aesthetics misses the very essence of how we actually perceive Web pages, video programs, and films.

Sight Sound Motion describes the major aesthetic image elements—light and color, space, time/motion, and sound—and how they are used in electronic media. These elements are discussed in the context of the five principal aesthetic fields: light and color, two-dimensional space, three-dimensional space, time/motion, and sound. This organization allows you to scrutinize each individual aesthetic element while at the same time maintaining an overview of how they all interact contextually.

Features

Although the basic aesthetic principles of the five aesthetic fields do not change with the advancement of technology, their applications do. I have therefore emphasized certain areas that have become especially important in digital video and digital cinema.

Screen size   In today's digital video world, you will have to be an expert miniature painter as well as one for huge outdoor advertising panels. This text contains valuable information about how to compose effective shots for the tiny mobile media display as well as the large screens in motion picture theaters.

Aspect ratio   Although the wide-screen aspect ratios of high-definition television and standard motion pictures are similar, much video is still watched on the traditional 4 × 3 screen and on mobile media displays with various aspect ratios. You will find information about how to compose effective shots within the different aspect ratios. The simulated screen images in this text are shown in both the 4 × 3 and the 16 × 9 formats.

Inductive sequencing   The inductive approach to the visual narrative by showing a series of close-ups rather than moving from master shot to close-up has become a fundamental prerequisite for telling a story effectively on the small screen. In combination with surround sound, the inductive visual approach has also become an effective technique for creating high-energy sequences on the large movie screen.

Stereoscopic projection   The aesthetic effects of stereoscopic three-dimensional projection and how they differ from the traditional 3D simulation on the screen are explored.

Visual narrative   The chapters on the five-dimensional field—chapter 15, Sound, and chapter 16, Sound Structures and Sound/Picture Combinations—precede the editing chapters. The last two chapters deal more specifically with the narratives and the syntax of continuity and complexity editing.

Pedagogy

As in the previous edition, this sixth edition of *Sight Sound Motion* incorporates several pedagogical devices for optimal learning.

REFERENCES AND TERMS

To facilitate learning, this text contains various types of redundancy.

Chapter summaries   The chapter summaries recapitulate the main ideas in each chapter for quick review.

References   Although the numerous notes at the end of each chapter are not essential for understanding the text, they identify the significant research and can serve as a useful guide for further study of media aesthetics. The specific titles and examples are chosen for how well they illustrate or support a specific media aesthetic concept rather than whether they are currently popular. As an instructor, you are encouraged to contribute your own material whenever it is deemed more appropriate and effective than the ones mentioned in the text.

Cross-references   The text includes frequent references to how a specific aesthetic principle in one field operates contextually in another or several other fields.

Glossary   All the fundamental media aesthetic terms are defined in the glossary and appear in ***bold italic*** in the chapter text in the context in which they are defined. Like the vocabulary of a foreign language, knowledge of these terms is an essential prerequisite to communication about media aesthetics. Realize that some of the less familiar terms, such as *vector,* are used in this book not to test the reader's patience but because they are more precise than the ones commonly used. Perusing the glossary before reading the text may facilitate understanding of the various concepts.

Ancillaries

Three ancillaries were designed to aid in the teaching and the understanding of *Sight Sound Motion:* a fully revised and updated *Instructor's Manual; Zettl's Video-Lab 3.0* interactive DVD-ROM; and online music files that let you listen to the musical examples in chapter 16. Each example appears in written form so that you can follow the notes while hearing them.

Instructor's Manual   The *Instructor's Manual* contains suggestions for classroom demonstrations, exercises, and discussions and includes a battery of tests. It is intended as a guide, not a dictum. The demonstrations do not require top-of-the-line equipment—they can be done with a small camcorder and a low-end videocassette recorder—but they can also be staged somewhat more effectively in a multicamera studio setup. Ideally, the *Instructor's Manual* should stimulate the instructor to come up with maximally effective ways to make the connection between media aesthetic principles and their applications. The *Instructor's Manual* is available for download at:

www.cengage.com/rtf/zettl/ssm6e

If you require assistance, please contact your local sales representative.

Zettl's VideoLab 3.0   This interactive DVD-ROM combines the basic television production techniques with some of the fundamental principles of media aesthetics. It is truly interactive: the student can zoom in and out, turn on lighting instruments, mix sounds, and edit together certain shots and see the results immediately. An extensive quiz feature and instant access to the glossary reinforce learning. The DVD-ROM can be used as a convenient way to help students acquire or reinforce basic video and film production techniques and to illustrate aesthetic concepts that need to be shown in motion. The *Instructor's Manual* refers to the relevant sections of *Zettl's VideoLab 3.0* for each chapter of *Sight Sound Motion.*

Music examples   To actually listen to all the major musical examples in chapter 16, go to *http://zettl-ssm.com.* The examples are listed at the left of the page by the figure number referenced in the chapter. Each example appears in musical notation so that you can follow the notes or, if you don't read music, the vector directions while listening to it.

Acknowledgments

I would like to thank first and foremost the people who were directly responsible for this sixth edition of *Sight Sound Motion:* the Cengage Team of Michael Rosenberg, publisher; Megan Garvey, editor; Jillian D'Urso, assistant editor; Ed Dodd, development editor; Mandy Groszko, photo manager; and Erin Pass, editorial assistant; and the Ideas to Images team of Gary Palmatier, art director and project manager; Elizabeth von Radics, copy editor; Ed Aiona, photographer; Mike Mollett, proofreader; and Edwin Durbin, indexer. I am especially fortunate because Gary and Elizabeth are not only experts in bookmaking and editing but also extremely well versed in electronic media—by avocation and education. Ed Aiona's pictures are always worthy of a coffee-table book edition. Some of John Veltri's pictures proved so distinguished that they have endured several editions. He deserves much praise.

I am also greatly indebted to the five reviewers of the previous edition of *Sight Sound Motion* for their valuable comments: Dr. Peter B. Gregg, University of Minnesota; JC Barone, Western Connecticut State University; Hamid Khani, San Francisco State University; William A. Adams, Clarion University; and William Deering, University of Wisconsin. Special credit must go to Hamid Khani and to Peter Gregg of the University of Minnesota, whose detailed analyses and suggestions led to a major reshuffling of the final chapters. The insightful questions by Daniel Miller of the University of Oregon during an interview also led to a sharpening of some concepts. As always, Nikos Metallinos of Concordia University, Montreal, stood by me with valuable advice whenever needed.

A big thank-you for the people in the various photographs who gave their time and talent to make this book more visual: Noah Aiona, Martin Aichele, Stephen Angeles, Gloria Ariche, Mathew Baker, Shibani Battiya, Hoda Baydoun, Kent Beichley, Brian Biro, Eric Blackburn, Kelly Briley, George Caldas, William Carpenter, Neela Chakravartula, Brandon Child, Laura Child, Rebecca Child, Lori Clark, Janine Clarke, Joseph Consins, Jon Corralejo, Carletta Currie, Lauren Dunn, Jon Dutro, Askia Egashira, Chaim Eyal, Tammy Feng, Derek Fernandez, Karyna Fuentes, Kelly Gavin, Ian Grimes, Rebecca Hayden, Joshua Hecht, Janellen Higgins, Nicolina Higgins, Abroo Kahn, Akiko Kajiwara, Hamid Khani, Philip Kipper, Kimberly Kong, Surya Kramer, Jason Kuczenski, Rinkhen Lama, Antonio Leigh, Joshua Lopez, Orcun Malkoclar, Teri Mitchell, Maki Mizutani, Meg Mizutani, Ben Nam, Andre Nguyen, Einat Nov, Jennyvi Olaes, Gary Palmatier, Dimitry Panov, David Park, Ildiko Polony, Logan Presnell, Rachel Rabin, Jon Rodriquez, Robert Salcido, Reyna Sandoval, Philip Siu, Kate Slater, Taneka Smothers, Renee Stevenson, Coleen Sullivan, Jairo Vargas, Selene Veltri, Amy Vylecka, Eboni Warnking, Athena Wheaton, Carey Wheaton, Gabriel Wheaton, Jim Wheaton, Erina Yamamoto, Gloria Yamoto, and Daniel Dunping Zheng.

A big hug for my wife, Erika, who once again gave unqualified support to my working on this project. In fact, this time she refrained from asking me how many more chapters I have yet to do after my initial toil with chapter 1.

Herbert Zettl

Prologue

THIS BOOK GIVES YOU THE TOOLS TO CLARIFY, INTENSIFY, AND INTERPRET events for television, computer, and film presentation. In effect, it teaches you how to apply the major aesthetic elements to manipulate people's perceptions. Because media consumers are largely unaware of the power of media aesthetics, they must and do trust your professional judgment and especially your good intentions.

Irrespective of the scope of your communication—a brief news story, an advertisement, or a major dramatic production—your overriding aim should be to help people attain a higher degree of emotional literacy, the ability to see the world with heightened awareness and joy. All of your aesthetic decisions must ultimately be made within an ethical context—a moral framework that holds supreme the dignity and the well-being of humankind.

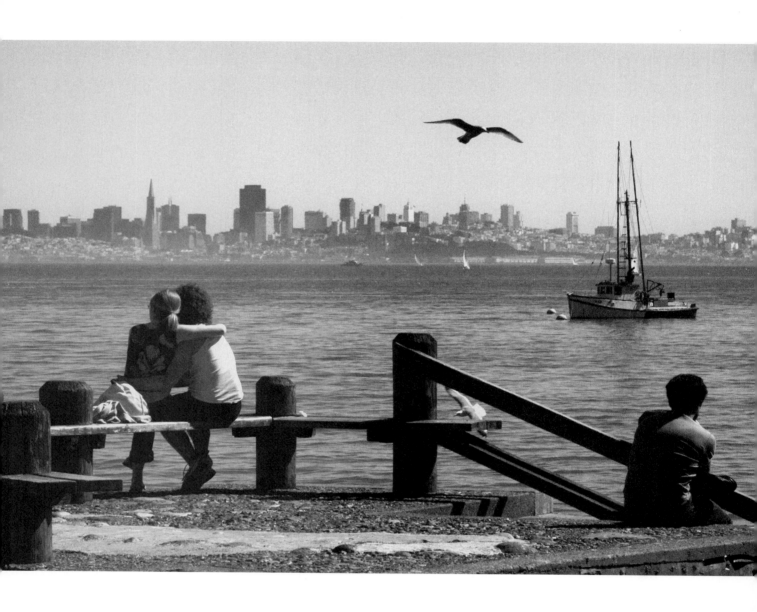

Applied Media Aesthetics

CONSCIOUSLY OR NOT, YOU MAKE MANY AESTHETIC CHOICES EVERY DAY. When you decide what to wear, arrange stuff on your desk, or choose what flowers to put on the dinner table, or even when you judge the speed or distance of your car relative to other cars while driving, you are engaging in basic perceptual and aesthetic activities. Even the everyday expression "I know what I like" requires aesthetic judgment.

When you select a certain picture to put on your wall, choose a specific color for your car, or look through the viewfinder of a camera, you are probably more conscious of making an aesthetic decision. This kind of decision-making, as any other, requires that you know what choices are available and how to make optimal decisions with a minimum of wasted effort. Painting your bathroom first red, then pink, then orange only to discover that off-white is in fact the best color would be not only expensive and time-consuming but also cumbersome and frustrating.

As a responsible media communicator, you must go beyond everyday reflexes and approach creative problems with educated judgment. You must also develop a heightened sense of vision to recognize the universal needs and desires of human beings and learn how to give such vision significant form so that you can share it with all of us.[1] Applied media aesthetics helps you in this formidable task. If not communicated effectively, even significant vision subsides into an insignificant dream. Despite the enormous changes that the digital revolution has brought about in video and film production hardware, software, and production methods, the basic media aesthetic principles still stand. In fact, because of the vastly increased choices in digital audio and video manipulation, media aesthetics has become an indispensable tool for structuring content.

To provide you with some overview of applied media aesthetics and a background for its study, we focus on six major areas: applied media aesthetics: definition, applied aesthetics and art, applied aesthetics and contextual perception, the power of context, the medium as structural agent, and applied media aesthetics: method.

Applied Media Aesthetics: Definition

Applied media aesthetics differs from the traditional concept of aesthetics in three major ways. First, we no longer limit aesthetics to the traditional philosophical concept that deals primarily with the understanding and the appreciation of beauty and our ability to judge it with some consistency. Nor do we consider aesthetics only to mean the theory of art and art's quest for truth. Applied media aesthetics considers art and life as mutually dependent and essentially interconnected.

The major functions of media aesthetics are based on the original meaning of the Greek verb *aisthanomai* ("I perceive") and the noun *aisthetike* ("sense perception").[2] ***Applied media aesthetics*** is not an abstract concept but a process in which we examine a number of media elements, such as lighting and sound, how they interact, and our perceptual reactions to them. Second, the media—in our case primarily video and film (including digital cinema) and, to a lesser extent, Web images—are no longer considered neutral means of simple message distribution but essential elements in the aesthetic communication system. Third, whereas traditional aesthetics is basically restricted to the analysis of existing works of art, applied media aesthetics serves not only the analyses of the various forms of media productions but their synthesis—their creation—as well.

In contrast to traditional aesthetic theories, you can apply almost all media aesthetic principles and concepts discussed in this book to a variety of media production tasks. A thorough understanding of media aesthetic principles will also help you adjust relatively easily to the new and always changing production requirements of various digital media. Finally, the criteria of applied media aesthetics let you employ formative evaluation, which means that you can evaluate the relative communication effectiveness of the aesthetic production factors step-by-step while your production is still in progress.

Applied Aesthetics and Art

Applied aesthetics emphasizes that art is not an isolated object hidden away in a museum and that aesthetic experiences are very much a part of everyday life. Whatever medium you choose for your expression and communication, art is a process that draws on life for its creation and, in turn, seems necessary, if not essential, for living life with quality and dignity. We need art to educate our emotions. Even if you are not in the process of creating great works of art, you are nevertheless constantly engaged in myriad aesthetic activities that require perceptual sensitivity and judgment. But if ordinary life experiences are included in the process of art, how are you to distinguish between aesthetic processes that we call "art" and those that are not art? Is every aspect of life, every perceptual experience we have, art? No. Ordinary daily experiences may be full of wonder, but they are not art—not yet, in any case. But they do have the potential of serving as raw material for the process of aesthetic communication that we call art.

ART AND EXPERIENCE

What, then, is the deciding element that elevates an ordinary life experience to the realm of art? The critical factor is you—the artist—or a group of artists, such as the members of a video or film production team, who perceive, order, clarify, intensify, and interpret a certain aspect of the human condition for themselves or, in the case of media communication, for a specific audience.

Philosopher Irwin Edman pioneered a new aesthetic concept almost a century ago that stresses the close connection between art and life. He wrote: "So far from having to do merely with statues, pictures, symphonies, art is the name for

Irwin Edman (1896–1954) was a philosopher and a professor of philosophy at Columbia University. His main theme in his teaching and writing was to connect, rather than isolate, art with the ordinary aspects of life.

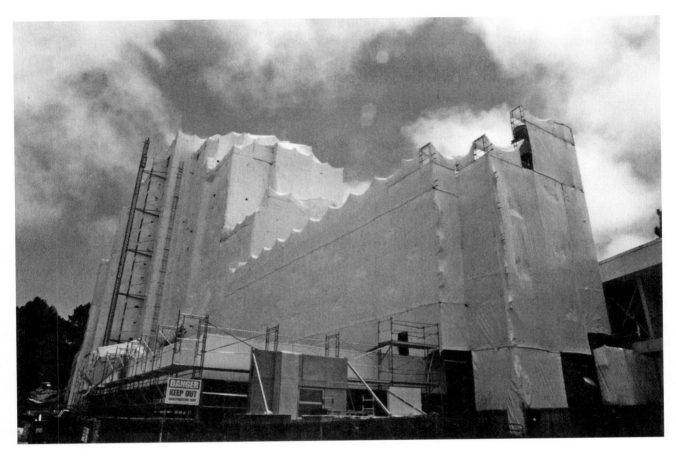

1.1 Art and Life

Within the contextualistic framework, we can draw aesthetic experience from all aspects of life. By giving "line and composition" to even a relatively ordinary scene, like the renovation of a college dormitory, an artist can help us perceive its inherent beauty.

that whole process of intelligence by which life, understanding its own conditions, turns these into the most interesting or exquisite account."[3] This process presupposes that life is given "line and composition" and that the experience is clarified, intensified, and interpreted. "To effect such an intensification and clarification of experience," Edman says, "is the province of art."[4] From this perspective, events that some may consider ugly or utilitarian have as much chance of becoming an aesthetic experience as a beautiful sunset. **SEE 1.1**

This process of clarification, intensification, and interpretation is also the province of applied media aesthetics. Whenever you look through the viewfinder of a camera to compose a shot, arrange some visual elements on a computer screen, or edit a film or video sequence, you are engaged in the creative act of clarifying, intensifying, and interpreting some event for a particular audience.

Applied Aesthetics and Contextual Perception

We perceive our world not in terms of absolutes but rather as changing contextual relationships. When we look at an event, we are constantly engaged in judging one aspect of it against another aspect or another event. A car is going fast because another one is going slowly or because it moves past a relatively stationary object. An object is big because another one is smaller. The beam from the same flashlight looks pitifully dim in the midday sun but bright and powerful in a dark room.

When you drive a car, your perceptual activities work overtime. You are constantly evaluating the position of your car relative to the surroundings as well as the changes in the surroundings relative to your car. No wonder you feel tired after even a short drive through the city during rush hour. When you sit perfectly still and stare at a stationary object, such as a table, your eyes nevertheless move constantly to scan the object. You then fuse the many, slightly different views together into a single image of the table, much as a well-edited sequence of various camera angles becomes a cohesive unit.

How, then, can we ever make sense of our multiple views of a changing world with its onslaught of sensations? Our mental operating system encourages a considerable perceptual laziness that shields us from input overload. We all develop habitual ways of seeing and hearing that make us focus on and notice only a small portion of what is actually there. We screen out most of the sensations that reach our eyes and ears, and we stabilize and simplify as much as possible what we do perceive.[5]

STABILIZING THE ENVIRONMENT

Our perceptual mechanisms are designed to simplify and stabilize our surroundings as much as possible so that they become manageable. We tend to cluster certain event details into patterns and simple configurations, perceive the size of an object as constant regardless of how far away we are from it, and see the same color regardless of the actual color variations when part of the object is in the shade. Another of our automatic, "hardwired" perceptual stabilizers is the *figure/ ground principle*, whereby we order our surroundings into foreground figures that lie in front of, or move against, a more stable background.[6]

SELECTIVE SEEING AND SELECTIVE PERCEPTION

Most of us tend to notice especially those events, or event details, that we want to see or are used to seeing. In our habitual ways of seeing, we generally select information that agrees with how we want to see the world. This type of *selective seeing*—frequently but not too accurately called *selective perception*—is like selective exposure to information. Once we have made up our minds about something, we seem to expose ourselves mostly to messages that are in agreement with our existing views and attitudes, ignoring those messages that would upset our deeply held beliefs.[7] We also choose to look at things we like to see and are especially interested in, and we ignore those that mean little to us. **SEE 1.2**

Although such cue reductions can clarify and intensify an event for us, they can also create problems. For example, we often see and hear only those details of an experience that fit our prejudicial image of what the event should be and ignore the ones that interfere with that image. The don't-confuse-me-with-evidence joke aptly mirrors this attitude. We then justify our questionable selection process by pointing out that the event details selected were, indeed, part of the actual occurrence. For example, if you have come to believe (perhaps through advertising or a recommendation) that the Shoreline Café has a nice atmosphere and serves excellent food, a friendly waiter may be enough evidence to verify your positive image, even if the restaurant's food is actually quite awful. By looking only at what we want to see rather than at all there is to see, we inevitably gain a somewhat distorted view of the world.

Selective perception, on the other hand, is much more automatic; in most cases, we have no control over it. For example, if you are talking to a friend in a streetcar, you are probably not aware of most of the other sounds surrounding you, unless they start interfering with your conversation or are especially penetrating, such as a police siren or a crash. When you see somebody wearing a white shirt,

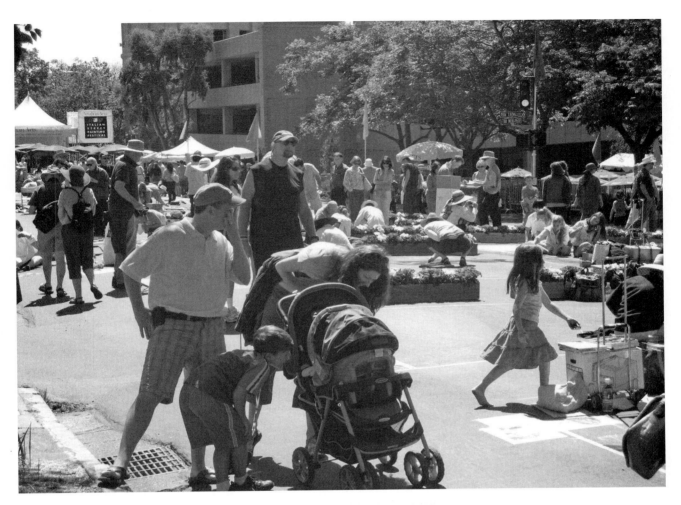

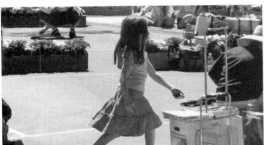

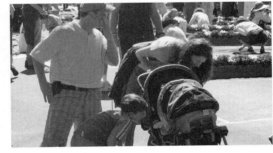

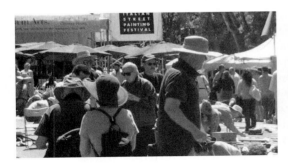

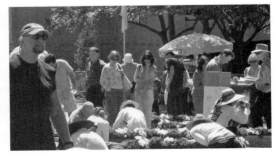

1.2 Selective Seeing

We tend to see events or event details that fit our perceptual expectations or that interest us highly.
Each of us sees an event from his or her own point of view and according to a specific experiential context.

you will perceive the same white, regardless of whether the person is standing in bright sunlight or in the shade. Your book pages will not look bluish when you read under a fluorescent light instead of the normal incandescent indoor lighting. Although a video camera would make such distinctions quite readily, you would have trouble seeing them, especially if you weren't looking for them. Your selective perception shields you from seeing too many varieties of shades and colors so that you can keep your environment relatively stable.

The Power of Context

Many of our perceptions are guided if not dictated by the event **context**. When context is imposed by the event itself, such as a snowstorm in May, you have little control over it. Such a context is sometimes called a "bottom-up" context. If you now decide to pitch your tent rather than abandon your backpacking trip, you are establishing a new event context—the setting up of the tent. This new context is called "top-down" because it is based on the intentionality of your actions, the putting up of the tent.

Sometimes we interpret an event by a virtual context that we form through our experience and our knowledge of how the world works or ought to work, and even through our prejudices.[8] At other times we react to contextual cues more viscerally, on a gut level, without much thought about it. Because we engage our cognitive faculties in the first situation, we call this the associative context. The second context is based more on an immediate, nonrational emotional reaction and is therefore called the aesthetic context.[9]

ASSOCIATIVE CONTEXT

One of the more important top-down contexts is the associative context. It consciously establishes and applies a code that dictates, at least to some extent, how you should feel about and interpret what you see. Here is a simple example of an associative context. Assume that you are to write down quickly the names of major U.S. television networks:

ABC NBC CBS CNN FOX

Now we change the context to helping a child learn to write numbers from 11 to 15.

11 12 13 14 15

Take another look at the network names and the numbers. You may have noticed that the *B* in *CBS* and the *13* in the number series are very similar. In fact, they are identical.[10] Obviously, the associative context has had a powerful influence on the radically different perceptions of an identical sensation. The power of the context is so strong that you will probably find it difficult to see a *13* in the network context and a *B* in the numbers. Going against the established context is almost as hard as nodding your head affirmatively while uttering "no" or shaking your head sideways while saying "yes." **SEE 1.3**

Another example of associative context shows how we may react to the immediate world we have constructed around us and how this world is definitely culture-bound. **SEE 1.4 AND 1.5**

What is your initial reaction to the two advertisements? Whereas you might respond positively to the eggs-for-sale sign and even buy some eggs if convenient, you would probably not be eager to sign up for your first flying lesson with the Affordable Flights Company. Why? Because our experience tells us that awkward

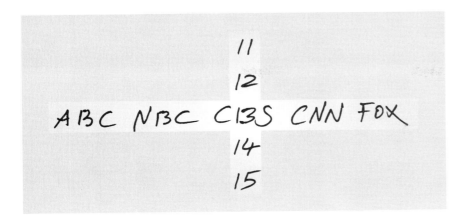

1.3 Associative Context

In the context of the horizontal row, the symbol at the center of this intersection is read as the letter *B*. In the context of the vertical row, the identical symbol is read as the number *13*.

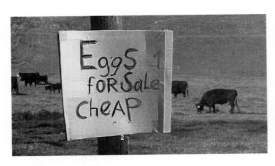

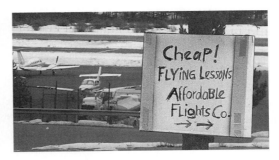

1.4 Eggs for Sale

If convenient, would you respond to this sign and buy some eggs? Justify your action.

1.5 Cheap Flying Lessons

Would you respond to this advertisement and take some flying lessons from the Affordable Flights Company? Justify your decision.

hand lettering may be appropriate in the context of a small, family-run, charmingly inefficient operation that occasionally sells surplus eggs; but in the context of aviation, the sloppy hand-lettered sign is not a good indicator of reliability, efficiency, and safety. You are now comparing, however unintentionally or even subconsciously, what you see with your previous experiences and prejudices.

AESTHETIC CONTEXT

When confronted with an aesthetic context, our perceptual processes are so immediate and forceful that we respond to certain stimuli in predictable ways even when we know that we are being perceptually manipulated. The many well-known optical illusions are good examples.[11] **SEE 1.6A AND 1.6B**

Even if you try vigorously to resist the idea of aesthetic manipulation, you cannot help but perceive the center circle in figure 1.6a as smaller than the one in figure 1.6b although in reality they are exactly the same size. The contextual circles make you perceive the central circles as being different sizes whether you like it or not. When surrounded by small circles, the central circle appears larger than it does when surrounded by larger circles.

Sufficient consistency exists in human perceptual processes so that we can predict with reasonable accuracy how people will respond to specific aesthetic stimuli and contextual patterns regardless of where they grew up. To test this, the next time you invite a friend to visit, move some of your pictures a little so that they hang slightly crooked, then watch your friend. Most likely, he or she will adjust the pictures so that they hang straight again. Your friend's action is a predictable

1.6 Optical Illusion

Although we may know that the center circles in this Ebbinghaus figure are identical, we still perceive the center circle in (a) as smaller than the one in (b). The large surrounding circles in (a) make the center circle look relatively small, and the small surrounding circles in (b) make the center circle appear relatively large.

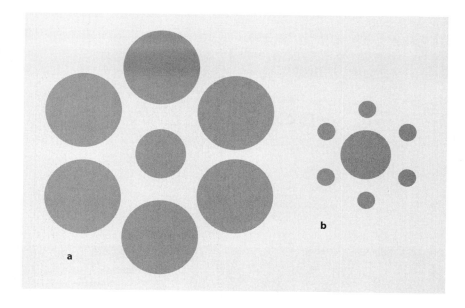

1.7 Tilted Horizon

We automatically perceive a tilted horizon line as a relatively unstable event. This car seems to travel precariously fast around the turn.

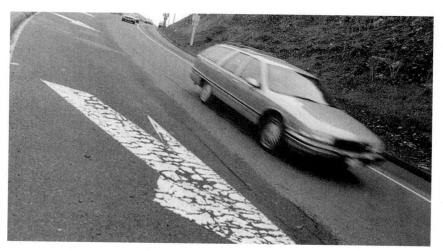

response to a powerful aesthetic stimulus: the disturbance of strong horizontals and verticals, of standing upright on level ground. You apply the same principle when you cant the camera to make a scene look more dynamic. **SEE 1.7**

As you know, certain lighting, colors, and especially types of music can have an immediate emotional effect on you. They all sidestep our rational faculties and therefore play a big role in establishing an aesthetic context.

But if we seek only information that reinforces our personal projection of reality and are so readily manipulated by context, how can we ever attain a relatively unbiased view of the world? The fine arts have tried for centuries to break this vicious circle. Although we may still be tied to our automatic perceptual processes and stabilizing cue reductions, all art leads, at least to some extent, to counter this automatization, to see events from various points of view and shift from glance to insight. While we may perceive a shirt as uniformly white, in a painting the artist may not only see but exaggerate the various colors reflected off the white shirt—all this so that we too can share the beauty of this world.

Significant video productions and films, regardless of genre, can and should do the same. Depending on where you put a camera or microphone, and what field of view or camera angle you select, your viewers have no choice but to share your point of view. You can prod them to see an event from different perspectives and advance them from "looking at" to "looking into." In essence, you can help viewers educate their way of seeing, if not their perceptions. **SEE 1.8**

Before you can expect to help viewers become more sensitive to their surroundings and unlearn, at least to some degree, their habitual ways of seeing, you will have to acquire a degree of aesthetic literacy that allows you to perceive the complexities, subtleties, and paradoxes of life and to clarify, intensify, and interpret them effectively for an audience.[12]

The Medium as Structural Agent

Even when your primary function in talking to someone is to communicate certain information, your behavior exerts considerable influence on how a specific message is received. It certainly makes a difference to the message recipient whether you smile or frown when extending the familiar how-do-you-do greeting. The smile will show that you are, indeed, glad to see the other person or that your message is a pleasant one; a scowl would signal the opposite. You, as the communication medium, have now become a part of the structuring of the message. Well-known communication scholar Marshall McLuhan proclaimed almost half a century ago that "the medium is the message."[13] With this insightful overstatement, he meant that the medium, such as television or film, occupies an important position not only in distributing the message but also in *shaping* it.

Despite overwhelming evidence of how important the medium is in shaping the message, many prominent communication researchers remain more interested in analyzing the content of the literal message than in the combined effect of the message and the medium as a structural agent.[14] In their effort to keep anything from contaminating their examination of mass-communicated content, they consider the various media as merely neutral channels through which the all-important messages are squeezed. Their analysis would reveal only your how-do-you-do greeting but ignore your smile or scowl. Gerhard Maletzke was one of the first significant mass communication scholars in Europe to advocate that it may not be only cultural or aesthetic preference that influences the shaping of the message but especially the *Zwang des Mediums* (the force of the medium). This concept was convincingly reinforced almost four decades later by Lev Manovich for new media, specifically various computer interfaces.[15] Although this concept is obvious to the people who actually do the productions, it is, unfortunately, still neglected by many media scholars. This apparent lack of medium awareness stems from the very beginnings of systematic mass communication studies, where the influence of the medium on the message was almost totally ignored.[16] **SEE 1.9**

If you have ever tried to make oil paints or clay do what you wanted them to do, you will readily admit that the medium is not neutral by any means. In fact, it has a decisive influence on the final outcome of your creative efforts. Even if you intend to communicate the same message, you will have to go about it in different ways depending on whether, for example, you design the message for wide-screen digital cinema, standard video, or a cell-phone display.

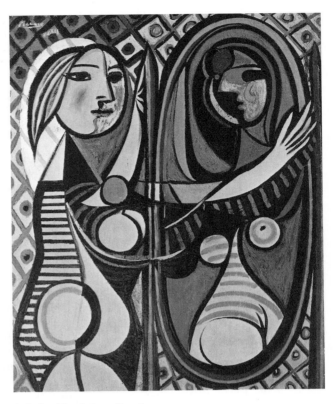

1.8 Looking into an Event

As in the classic Japanese film *Rashomon,* which shows one event from the perspectives of several different people, some paintings permit a variation of viewpoints and "looking into" the event. In this work by Picasso, we see the girl from straight on; we also see her profile and her reflection, representing her other self. Thus we perceive several layers of her existence.

Pablo Picasso (1881–1973) *Girl Before a Mirror,* Boisgeloup (March 1932), oil on canvas, 64" × 51¼". Gift of Mrs. Simon Guggenheim. Location: The Museum of Modern Art, New York, NY, USA. Digital Image © The Museum of Modern Art/Art Resource, NY./© 2009 Estate of Pablo Picasso/Artists Rights Society (ARS), New York.

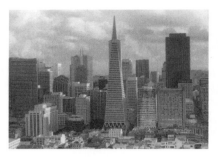

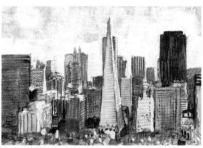

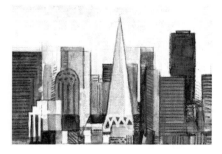

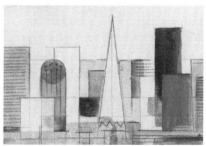

1.10 Deductive Abstraction

In the deductive approach to abstraction, we move from photographic realism to the essential qualities of the event.

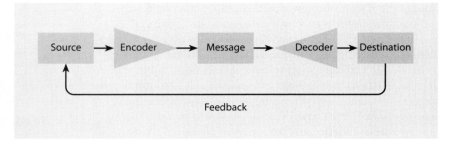

1.9 Early Communication Model

This model suggests that the communication process goes from idea to message and from message to recipient. It ignores the medium as a factor in the communication process.

The encoding (production) as well as the decoding (reception) of the message are, to a considerable extent, a function of the technical and aesthetic potentials and requirements of the medium. Exactly how media (video, film, the computer screen, and especially the tiny cell-phone display) shape or must shape the message for a specific viewer response is the subject of applied media aesthetics.

Throughout this book you will find references to video, television, film, and computer images. *Video* is intended to be the more inclusive term and generally includes all kinds of video productions, including television. *Television* is sometimes singled out, however, especially when discussed as broadcast television in connection with a specific transmission mode (such as live versus recorded), reception situation, or program genre. *Film* includes traditional motion pictures, whose recording medium is the photo-chemical film, as well as digital cinema that uses digital production and projection devices.

Applied Media Aesthetics: Method

The method of presenting applied media aesthetics is loosely based on Leonardo da Vinci's *Notebooks,* in which he describes the "Ten Attributes of Sight Which All Find Expression in Painting." Rather than deductively analyze a specific painting, da Vinci describes inductively the perceptual attributes that all paintings have to deal with: darkness and brightness, substance and color, form and place, and so forth.[17] More specifically, applied media aesthetics is modeled after the theories and the practices of Russian painter and teacher Wassily Kandinsky. For Kandinsky abstraction did not mean reducing a realistic scene down to its essential formal elements. **SEE 1.10** Rather, it meant an inductive process of building a scene by

Wassily Kandinsky (1866–1944) was a painter and a teacher at the Bauhaus. The Bauhaus (literally, "building house" or, more appropriate, "house for building") was founded by the well-known architect and artist Walter Gropius in Weimar, Germany, in 1919. Besides Kandinsky, members of the Bauhaus included such eminent artists as Paul Klee, Johannes Itten, Oskar Schlemmer, and László Moholy-Nagy. The Bauhaus developed a unique style for everyday objects, such as furniture, dishes, and tools, by following to its limits the basic credo: form follows function. Its approach to educational theories was a thorough examination of such basic elements as light, space, movement, and texture. The Bauhaus was forced to close in 1933 as part of Adolf Hitler's drive to rid German culture of all "degenerate art." Later, Moholy-Nagy transferred the Bauhaus to Chicago, where it became the School of Design and, later, the Institute of Design, but it never reached the prominence of its forerunner, the Bauhaus.[18]

combining the "graphic elements"—the fundamental building blocks of painting, such as points, lines, planes, color, texture, and so forth—in a certain way.[19] **SEE 1.11**

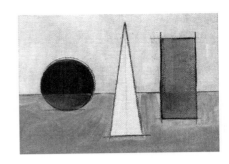

Following this approach, he was not limited by what was there in the world around him; instead he could extend his vision to what he felt *ought* to be there— the construction of a new world.

As you can see, the final outcome of the deductive and inductive abstraction processes is the same, but the deductive world was reduced to its basic aesthetic elements, the inductive one built by them.

Fundamental Image Elements

In a similar inductive way, I have identified and isolated five fundamental and contextual *image elements* of video and film: light and color, two-dimensional space, three-dimensional space, time/motion, and sound.[20] This book examines the aesthetic characteristics and potentials of these five elements and how we can structure and apply them within their respective aesthetic fields. This analysis is an essential prerequisite to understanding their contextual and expressive functions. Once you know the aesthetic characteristics and potentials of these fundamental image elements, you can study how they operate in the context of a larger aesthetic field and combine them knowledgeably into patterns that clarify, intensify, and effectively communicate a significant experience. A thorough grasp of the five image elements will help you establish an aesthetic vocabulary and language unique to the medium of your choice—a language that will enable you to speak with optimum clarity, impact, and personal style.

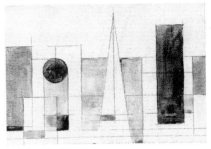

ANALYSIS AND SYNTHESIS

As an analysis tool, the use of the image elements differs considerably from the traditional methods of media analysis, such as semiotics and rhetorical media criticism. Rather than analyze video and film as mostly narrative "texts" to discover how their signs function and ultimately create higher meaning, media aesthetics investigates how their fundamental image elements—light, space, motion, and sound—function within specific contexts and how they contribute to how we feel. As pointed out previously, the great advantage of applied media aesthetics over other media analysis techniques is that all its theories can be directly applied not only to media analysis but also, if not especially, to media synthesis, or the creation of media events—the production process.

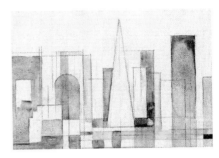

CONTENT

You may wonder at this point what happened to the story content in all this discussion of fundamental aesthetic elements. Is not content—some form of human experience—the most fundamental of all aesthetic elements? Don't we first need an event, or some basic story idea, before we can shape it to fit the various medium and audience requirements? The answer to both of these questions is, of course, yes. But it is valuable to realize that a good idea by itself does not necessarily make for effective media communication. You must learn how to develop and mold an idea so that it fits the medium's technical as well as aesthetic production and reception requirements. This molding process, called *encoding*, presupposes a thorough knowledge of such production tools as cameras, lenses, lighting, audio, and so forth as well as applied aesthetics, such as selective focus, the proper framing of a shot, the use of color, the selection of music, and the sequencing of various parts of a scene.

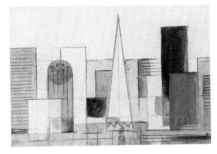

1.11 Inductive Abstraction

In the inductive approach to abstraction, we study the formal elements of painting, or of video and film, and then arrange those elements to express the essential quality of an event. In this case, we combine lines, circles, and areas to build up (inductively) the essence of a cityscape.

This so-called formalistic approach to applied media aesthetics is similar to the study of production techniques. In both cases, we learn the tools and the techniques before putting them to work in different contexts for a variety of communication purposes. Concern about significant literal content is not unimportant; it is merely premature. The study of vocabulary and the parts of speech does not preclude a respect for literature, but it is an essential prerequisite for writing the great American novel.

Once you have a strong grasp of applied media aesthetics, you can select those elements and techniques that are most appropriate and maximally effective for shaping specific ideas. More important, you will gain the opportunity to combine aesthetic elements in nontraditional ways so that your viewers can perceive the world with fresh eyes and ears and from a new and unique perspective. Conversely, the requirements and the potentials of applied media aesthetics could also generate new ideas—content that might otherwise have remained dormant. Your familiarity with the formal elements of applied media aesthetics and their respective fields will enable you to exercise your creativity to its fullest.

Responsibility

As you now know, the basic purpose of applied media aesthetics is to clarify, intensify, and interpret events for a specific audience. Although such processes are designed to help the audience see the world from a new perspective and experience it in heightened ways, they also imply a direct and calculated manipulation of the audience's perceptions. Even when producing a simple commercial, you are purposely exploiting the feelings, the emotions, and ultimately the behaviors of your viewers. Worse, although the recipients of your aesthetically clarified and intensified messages may realize that they are being manipulated, they are usually not quite sure how. For example, alert viewers will usually recognize blatantly biased editing, but they may remain largely unsuspecting when manipulated through subtle means such as color, lens distortions, lighting effects, or contextual background sounds.

An anesthetized patient on the operating table and the aesthetically illiterate video or film viewer have much in common. Both have little control over what is happening to them, and both must trust the skills, the judgment, and, above all, the good intentions of someone else. Thus the surgeon and the media producer bear a heavy responsibility. One penetrates human beings with a scalpel whereas the other uses highly charged, keenly calculated aesthetic energy. This is why you, as a media communicator, must make all your decisions within the context of established ethics—within a basically moral frame of reference.[21]

As a mass communicator who daily influences millions of unsuspecting people, or as a video artist with an audience of a few friends, acceptance of such responsibility is a major job prerequisite. Skill alone is not enough. First and foremost you must bring to the job a genuine concern and respect for your audience. And you must be prepared to bear responsibility for your actions.

As consumers of media communication, we cannot escape similar responsibilities. If we want to guard against irresponsible persuasion and take an active part in making media communication more beneficial to our fellow human beings, even as consumers we must learn as much as we can about the methods of media aesthetics.

Once we learn how lighting or sound can influence our perceptions and emotions, we are less susceptible to blind persuasion. We will be able to identify aesthetic techniques and the reasons for their use, enabling us to analyze the message for its true communication value, judge the mediated event's relative bias, and ultimately preserve our freedom of choice. Such media literacy will help us experience with heightened awareness and joy the mediated world on the screen as well as the real world in which we live.

When applied media aesthetics has become the common province of both the communication producer and the consumer, the imprudent use of media will become less of a problem. Both will find it easier to trust the other and to treat each other with the respect and the dignity worthy of our global community.

SUMMARY

Applied media aesthetics differs from traditional aesthetics in three major ways: rather than being concerned primarily with beauty and the philosophy of art, applied aesthetics deals with a number of aesthetic phenomena, including light and color, space, time/motion, and sound, and our perceptual reactions to them.

The media (video, film, and computers) themselves play an important part in shaping the message. Whereas traditional aesthetics is used primarily for analysis, media aesthetics can be applied to both analysis and synthesis—production.

In the framework of applied media aesthetics, every aspect of life has the potential to become art and serve as raw material for aesthetic processes, so long as it is clarified, intensified, and interpreted for an audience by the artist.

Common to all perceptions is our innate urge to stabilize our environment and the practice of selective seeing and perception.

To cope with the onslaught of changing stimuli and to make our environment more manageable, our mental operating system establishes perceptual filters and has us perceive stable patterns rather than unrelated event detail.

We tend to select information that agrees with how we want to see the world and to screen out other data that might interfere with our constructs. Such habitual cue reductions tend to make us perceptually lazy and can even lead to prejudiced perceptions.

We perceive an event relative to the context in which it occurs. The bottom-up context is a given over which we have little control. As media people we have no choice but to work within it. The top-down context is intentional and in our control throughout the production process. In media aesthetics we stress the associative context, which calls up a cognitive framework in which we judge what we see by our experience and prejudices. It is definitely culture-bound. The aesthetic context, on the other hand, is independent of a cultural frame of reference. We seem to perceive certain contextual stimuli in much the same way, irrespective of cultural upbringing or experience.

Applied media aesthetics places great importance on the influence of the medium on the message. The medium itself acts as an integral structural agent.

The method of presenting applied media aesthetics is an inductive one: rather than analyze existing video program fare and films, we isolate the five fundamental image elements of video and film, examine their aesthetic characteristics and potentials, and structure them in their respective aesthetic fields. These elements are: light and color, two-dimensional space, three-dimensional space, time/motion, and sound. We thus do not take the traditional literal content (ideas to be encoded) as an essential pre- or co-requisite to the discussion of the formal image elements. Rather we consider the study of the image elements to be the essential prerequisite to the proper shaping of ideas and events into messages.

Because the process of clarification, intensification, and interpretation of events is based on the selection and the specific use of aesthetic elements, the recipient's perceptions are indirectly and, more often, directly manipulated. Such aesthetic manipulation must always occur and be evaluated within a framework of basic ethics. To facilitate effective communication, the consumers as well as the producers of media communication have the responsibility to learn as much as possible about applied media aesthetics and its communicative power.

N O T E S

1. See Stuart W. Hyde, *Idea to Script: Storytelling for Today's Media* (Boston: Allyn and Bacon, 2003), pp. 6–7, 18–33. See also László Moholy-Nagy, *Vision in Motion* (Chicago: Paul Theobald, 1947, 1965), pp. 42–45; and Ellen Langer, *Mindfulness* (Reading, N.Y.: Addison-Wesley, 1989).

2. The word *anesthetic* suggests that we are bereft of all aesthetics, that our perceptions are dulled or totally shut off so that we no longer receive any stimuli, even physical ones.

3. Irwin Edman, *Arts and the Man* (New York: W. W. Norton, 1967), p. 12. First published in 1928.

4. Edman, *Arts and the Man,* p. 12.

5. Robert Ornstein, *Multimind: A Way of Looking at Human Behavior* (Cambridge, Mass.: Malor Books, 2003), pp. 25–29.

6. Bruce E. Goldstein, *Sensation and Perception,* 8th ed. (Belmont, Calif.: Wadsworth, 2010), pp. 108–9.

7. The idea of selective exposure is broadly based on the theory of cognitive dissonance, advanced by Leon Festinger in his *A Theory of Cognitive Dissonance* (Evanston, Ill.: Row, Peterson, 1957). Basically, the theory states that we try to reduce dissonance by seeking out comments and other information that support—are consonant with—the decisions we have made.

8. Malcolm Gladwell describes in detail how a specific top-down context (dangerous neighborhood) can lead to the most tragic events (an innocent person being shot). See the chapter "Seven Seconds in the Bronx: The Delicate Art of Mind Reading" in his *Blink* (New York: Little, Brown, 2005), pp. 189–97.

9. Herbert Zettl, "Contextual Media Aesthetics as the Basis for a Media-literacy Model," *Journal of Communication* 48, no. 1 (1998): 86–89. You may also encounter the term *contextualism* to describe the associative and aesthetic contexts, but contextualism can also refer to a specific branch of philosophy. Basically, as a philosophical term, *contextualism* means that we should evaluate art within its historical epoch and according to what the artist felt while creating it. All events, or "incidents of life," are relative and must be understood within their cultural contexts. Very much in the sense of a television docudrama, such incidents of life are interconnected and alive and spontaneous in their present, regardless of when they happened. See Stephen C. Pepper, *Aesthetic Quality: A Contextualistic Theory of Beauty* (New York: Charles Scribner's Sons, 1938). Also see Stephen C. Pepper, *The Basis of Criticism in the Arts* (Cambridge, Mass.: Harvard University Press, 1945); Stephen C. Pepper, *World Hypotheses* (Berkeley: University of California Press, 1942, 1970); and Lewis Edwin Hahn, *A Contextualistic Theory of Perception,* University of California Publications in Philosophy, vol. 22 (Berkeley: University of California Press, 1939).

    A more modern representative of contextualistic aesthetics is Hans-Georg Gadamer. Although he calls the basis for his aesthetic theory *hermeneutical epistemology,* he nevertheless represents the contextualistic point of view. See his *Truth and Method* (New York: Seabury Press, 1975). His basic credo is that understanding (*Verstehen*) can occur only within the context of everyday living and that we interpret art not outside of our actual experiential context but very much within it.

    See also Keith DeRose, *The Case for Contextualism: Knowledge, Skepticism, and Context,* vol. 1 (New York: Oxford University Press, 2010). Duncan McCorquodale (ed.) demonstrates in his book *Education and Contextualism: Architects Design Partnership* (London: Black Dog, 2008) how contextualism can be applied to various architectural projects.

In this book I use *contextualism* to mean that all events we perceive are greatly influenced by their context. It also stresses the interconnection of the major aesthetic fields of applied media aesthetics: light and color, space, time/motion, and sound. Finally, it helps organize the discussion of the great variety of aesthetic elements in each field and their influence and dependence on one another.

10. This perceptual set is based on the B/13 experiment by Jerome S. Bruner and A. L. Minturn in their "Perceptual Identification and Perceptual Organization," *Journal of General Psychology* 53 (1955): 21–28.

11. This figure is based on the classic Ebbinghaus illusions as published in various books on visual illusion. See Richard Zakia, *Perception and Imaging,* 3d ed. (Boston: Focal Press, 2007), p. 190.

12. Being literate, or the term *literacy* in this context, does not mean the ability to read and write but rather having achieved proficiency and polish in some area of knowledge. *Media literacy* refers to a basic knowledge of how, for example, video structures pictures and sound for specific purposes. See Paul Messaris, *Visual Literacy: Image, Mind, and Reality* (Boulder, Colo.: Westview Press, 1994).

13. Marshall McLuhan, *Understanding Media: The Extensions of Man* (New York: McGraw-Hill, 1964), p. 314. Also see Eric McLuhan and Frank Zingrone (eds.), *Essential McLuhan* (New York: Basic Books, 1995), pp. 151–61.

14. Compare the convincing argument that it is the information systems in general and the media specifically that shape media content rather than the other way around. Some of the classic arguments are published in Joshua Meyrowitz, *No Sense of Place* (New York: Oxford University Press, 1985), pp. 13–16.

15. See Gerhard Maletzke, *Psychologie der Massenkommunikation* (Psychology of Mass Communication) (Hamburg: Verlag Hans-Bredow-Institut, 1978), pp. 98–100. Also see Lev Manovich, *The Language of New Media* (Cambridge, Mass.: MIT Press, 2002), pp. 94–115.

16. Wilbur Schramm, one of the pioneers of mass communication research, and others adapted this communication model from the basic model of information theory published by Claude Shannon and Warren Weaver in 1949. See Wilbur Schramm and Donald F. Roberts (eds.), *The Process and Effects of Mass Communication,* rev. ed. (Urbana: University of Illinois Press, 1971), pp. 22–26.

17. Edward McCurdy (ed.), *The Notebooks of Leonardo da Vinci* (Old Saybrook, Conn.: Konecky and Konecky, 2003), p. 874.

18. One of the most comprehensive books on the Bauhaus is Hans M. Wingler, *The Bauhaus,* trans. by Wolfgang Jabs and Basil Gilbert (Cambridge, Mass.: MIT Press, 1979).

19. Wassily Kandinsky, *Point and Line to Plane,* trans. by Howard Dearstyne and Hilla Rebay (New York: Dover, 1979). This work was originally published as *Punkt und Linie zu Fläche* in 1926 as the ninth in a series of 14 Bauhaus books edited by Walter Gropius and László Moholy-Nagy.

20. Herbert Zettl, "Essentials of Applied Media Aesthetics," in *Media Computing: Computational Media Aesthetics,* ed. by Chitra Dorai and Svetha Venkatesh (Boston: Kluwer Academic, 2002), pp. 11–38.

21. Louis Alvin Day, *Ethics in Media Communications,* 5th ed. (Belmont, Calif.: Wadsworth, 2005). See also Herbert Zettl, "Back to Plato's Cave: Virtual Reality," in *Communication and Cyberspace,* 2nd ed., ed. by Lance Strate, Ron Jacobson, and Stephanie Gibson (Creskill, N.J.: Hampton Press, 2003), pp. 99–111.

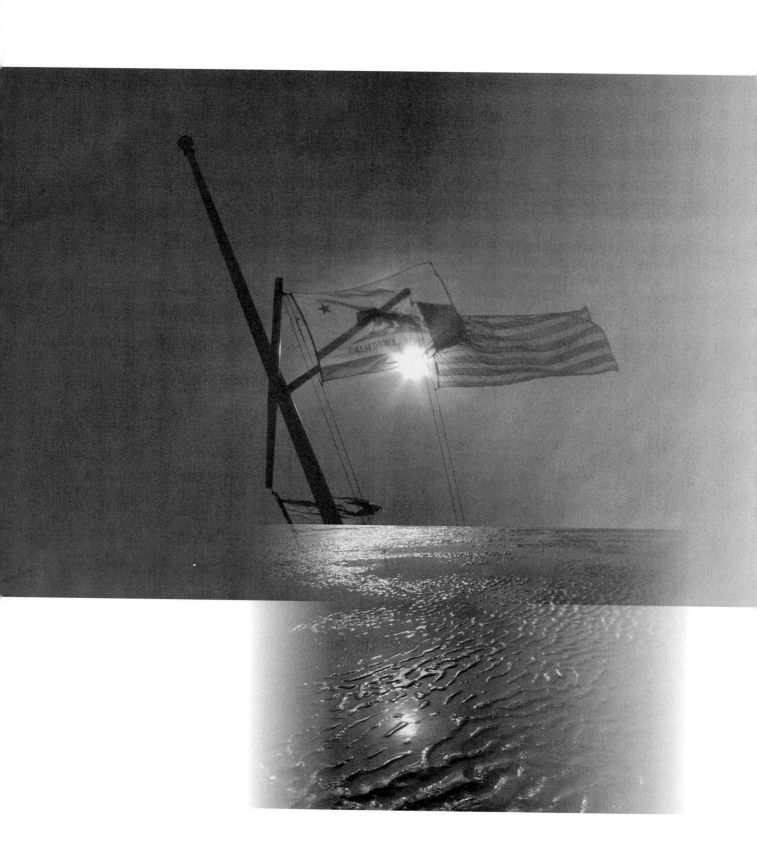

The First Aesthetic Field: Light

LIGHT IS ESSENTIAL TO LIFE. IT IS NECESSARY FOR MOST THINGS TO GROW. It is the key element of visual perception, and it orients us in space and time. It also affects our emotions. Light is the agent that makes things visible. When we look at our surroundings, we receive a multitude and a variety of light reflections. Each reflection has a certain degree of light intensity and complexity. The intensity variations appear to us as light or dark areas—as light and shadow—and the complexity as color.

Of course, we perceive light reflections as actual things. Most likely, we do not say, "I see the light variations that are reflected off these different surfaces." Rather we say, "This is an automobile." Often we conceive light to be the property of the objects themselves.[1] We speak of light and dark hair, a red ball, a green frog, a bright sky.

Video and film, as well as computer images, are pure light shows. In contrast to the theater, for example, where light is used simply to make things visible onstage and to set a mood, the final images on the movie screen and on electronic screens consist of light. The *materia* of the theater—the stuff that makes theater—is people and objects in the real space and time of the stage. The *materia* of television and film, however, is light. The control of light is therefore paramount to the aesthetics of television and film. *Lighting*, then, is the deliberate manipulation of light and shadows for a specific communication purpose. When creating computer images, such manipulation of light and shadows is more akin to painting, where you simulate light with light-colored paint and make shadows with darker paint. With computers you paint light and shadows with pixels.

Before you try to manipulate light and shadows and use them creatively, you need to familiarize yourself with the nature of light, lighting purposes and functions, the nature of shadows, and the outer and inner orientation functions of lighting.

The Nature of Light

Light is a form of radiant energy. It consists of separate bits of energy—energy particles—that behave commonly as electromagnetic waves. It makes up a part of the total electromagnetic spectrum, which includes such other magnetic energy

2.1 Visibility of Light
We see light only at its source and when it is reflected.

waves as radio waves, X-rays, satellite transmissions, and the waves in your microwave oven that heat up your coffee.

So-called white sunlight consists of a combination of light waves that are visible as various colors. When white sunlight is bent by a prism, it separates into a spectrum of clearly discernible hues: red, orange, yellow, green, blue, and violet. **SEE COLOR PLATE 1**

Because we can see the colors, that is, the various electromagnetic waves, *light* is usually defined as "visible radiant energy." Actually, light is invisible: we can see it only at its source or when it is reflected. **SEE 2.1** For example, a beam of light that shoots across a clean room or studio remains invisible to our eyes and to the camera unless the light hits a reflecting agent, such as dust, smoke, an object, or a person.

If there were not a reflecting atmosphere, the sky would appear always dark, and you could see the stars even during the day. In deep space the astronauts see a black sky even in sunlight. If our surroundings did not reflect light, we would live in total darkness, much as if there were no light at all.

Lighting Purposes and Functions

Lighting is the deliberate control of light and shadows. The basic purpose of lighting is to manipulate and articulate our perception of the environment. It can also establish an aesthetic context for our experiences, a framework that tells us how we should feel about a certain event. Lighting helps us, or makes us, see and feel in a specific way.

Through lighting we can articulate our outer space/time environment and our inner environment—our emotions. Lighting reveals what objects look like, where they are located, and what surface textures they have. It also influences how we feel about a person or an event. Very much like music, lighting seems able to bypass our usual cognitive perceptual screens—our rational faculty with its critical judgment—and affect us directly and immediately. Because lighting helps articulate our outer and inner environments, it has outer and inner orientation functions. Both functions depend to a great extent on the proper control of shadows. Let's take a closer look at shadows before discussing the specific orientation functions of lighting.

The Nature of Shadows

Ordinarily, we are not aware of shadows; we take them for granted. We readily accept the harsh and distinct shadows on a sunny day, the soft shadows on an overcast day, and the virtual absence of shadows under fluorescent lights. Only occasionally do we become more conscious of shadows. For example, we seek the shade when the sun gets too hot during an outdoor picnic, we shift the reading lamp so that the shadow of our head or hand does not fall directly on the page, or we might chuckle when our shadow shows us an especially distorted image of ourselves.

When you are engaged in clarifying and intensifying an event through lighting, however, you become very aware of shadows and learn to use them for specific orientation tasks. It is not the basic illumination that clarifies and intensifies the shape and the texture of people and things—it is the shadows. You will find that in critical lighting situations, you often need more lighting instruments for controlling the shadows than for making things visible.

Let's look at an example. **SEE 2.2A** Both objects look like simple white discs; both are lighted with highly diffused light (by using floodlights), rendering them practically shadowless and revealing little more than their basic contour.[2] As soon as you use a more directional light source, such as a Fresnel spotlight, and place it somewhat to the side of the object, you have no trouble distinguishing between the two. **SEE 2.2B** Because the directional light produces dense shadows, you can now see that the left object is a white ball and not a disc. But the object on the right remains evenly lighted, without any shadows. It looks like, and indeed is, a disc.

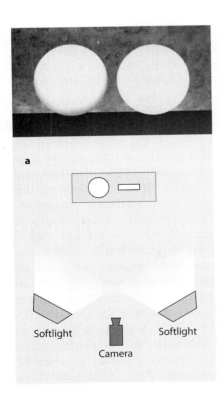

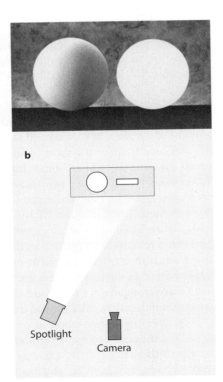

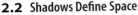

2.2 Shadows Define Space

a When objects are lighted "flat" with a highly diffused light source, such as a scoop or softlight, we see nothing more than two flat discs.

b With a more directional light source, such as a Fresnel or ellipsoidal spotlight, placed somewhat to the side of the object, we see that the object on the left is a sphere and the one on the right a flat disc.

2.3 Shadows Define Shape and Location

The attached shadows give us additional information about the true shape of the object (the hollow cone). The cast shadow tells us where the object is relative to its surroundings.

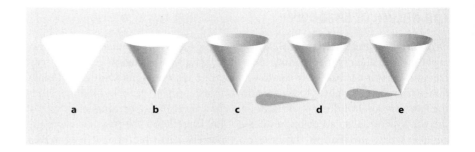

a   b   c   d   e

Now look at the next figure. **SEE 2.3A–2.3E** Without any shadows (figure 2.3a), we perceive only the basic contour of the object—an inverted triangle with a curved top—but the true spatial nature of the object and its location relative to its environment remain ambiguous. As soon as we attach a shadow (b), pretending that the main light source is coming from the right, we perceive the object as rounded and three-dimensional. An additional shadow on the top of the object (c) reveals that the object is a cone and that it is hollow. The cone's shadow that is cast on another surface tells us where the cone is in relation to the horizontal surface (a table) directly underneath it (d); according to this shadow, the cone obviously floats above the table. The shadow in (e) is connected to the tip of the cone; we now see the cone as touching the table. Thus the initial spatial ambiguity has been drastically reduced by the various shadows.

ATTACHED AND CAST SHADOWS

If you take another look at figure 2.3, you will probably notice that some shadows are attached to the cone and others are relatively independent of it. An equally astute observer, Leonardo da Vinci, called these two types of shadows *attached* and *cast.*

Attached shadows   An ***attached shadow*** is ***inevitably*** fixed to its object. No amount of wiggling or turning will remove the shadow from the object, assuming you keep it under the same lighting conditions. The attached shadow helps reveal the basic form of an object, but it can also fool you into perceiving what you normally expect to see. **SEE 2.4A AND 2.4B** Figure 2.4a shows an ornament that protrudes; figure 2.4b shows one that is indented. The major clues for such perceptions are the attached shadows. Now turn your book upside down and take another look. Figure 2.4a now shows an indented ornament, and figure 2.4b, a protruding one. Why? Because through lifelong experience, we assume that light comes from above rather than from below, so we expect the attached shadows to appear in the upper part of an indentation and the lower part of a protrusion. This perceptual habit is so strong that we will readily accept a change in the actual appearance of the object rather than the assumed direction of illumination.

If the proper perception of protrusions and indentations is crucial, you must light the object steeply from above to place strong attached shadows where we expect them to be. This type of space articulation is especially important for painters and graphic artists, who must suggest protrusions and indentations on a flat surface by painting in prominent attached shadows. Attached shadows help us primarily with interpreting an object's basic shape and texture.

Cast shadows   Whereas the attached shadow is always part of the actual object and is virtually glued to the side that is turned away from the light, the ***cast shadow*** always falls on something, in this case the road. **SEE 2.5** Other examples

> **Leonardo da Vinci** (1452–1519), considered the most gifted genius of the Italian Renaissance, was equally versed as a painter, an architect, a designer, and an inventor.

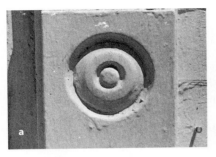

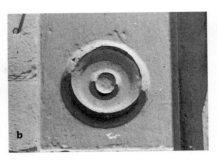

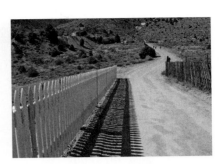

2.4 Attached Shadow Reversal

a In this ornament the attached shadow is at the top of the circles. Because we naturally expect light to be coming from above, we see this ornament first to indent, then to protrude, then to indent and protrude again.

b This is the same ornament as in (a) except it is turned upside down. Now you will probably perceive the exact opposite: a protrusion first, then an indentation, another protrusion, then another indentation. By turning the book upside down, the ornaments will reverse once more.

2.5 Cast Shadow: Object-connected

This shadow of the fence is no longer part of the fence but cast by the strong spotlight of the sun onto the road.

of cast shadows are the shadow of a power pole that stretches across the street, the shadow of a tree that falls on the grass beneath it and provides a cool spot for a picnic, or an airplane's shadow moving across the landscape. Most cast shadows show a distorted shape of an object. **SEE 2.6** As you can see in figure 2.6, the long distorted shadows that are cast onto the smooth tiles of the plaza are independent of the group of five people with their backs to the late-afternoon sun. You can take a photograph of their cast shadows without showing them in the picture.

Another example of the independence of cast shadows is making shadow pictures on a brightly lighted wall. You can admire the cast shadows of your creations without ever looking at your hand. Although the shadows are projected onto the wall, they are not part of the wall and disappear as soon as you drop your hand.

Cast shadows help us locate an object relative to its surroundings. **SEE 2.7** As you can see, the cast shadow indicates whether the object rests on the table or is suspended above it. Notice how the cast shadow becomes independent of the object and gets fuzzier at the edges as the object moves farther away from the table. **SEE 2.8**

Contrary to the attached shadow, which is inevitably fixed to its object, a cast shadow may be connected to the object that causes it or be totally free of it. **SEE 2.9** A cast shadow that is still connected to its object is called object-connected;

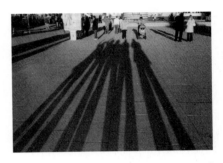

2.6 Cast Shadows: Object-disconnected

These cast shadows no longer connect to the people causing them.

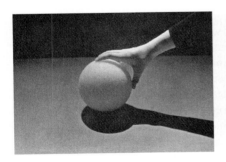

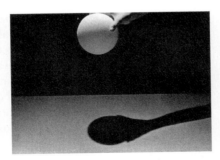

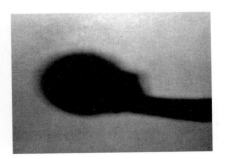

2.7 Cast Shadow: Object-connected

Cast shadows can reveal whether objects rest on another surface (in this case, a table) or are separate from it. Notice here that the shadow is still object-connected. The white ball rests on the table (and on its own shadow).

2.8 Cast Shadow: Object-disconnected

Now that the object no longer rests on the table, the cast shadow has become object-disconnected. In contrast to the attached shadow, which remains on the object, the cast shadow is now independent of it.

2.9 Cast Shadow: Independent

The farther away the ball moves from the table, the fuzzier its cast shadow appears. Such interpretations of cast shadows are crucial for computer-generated images.

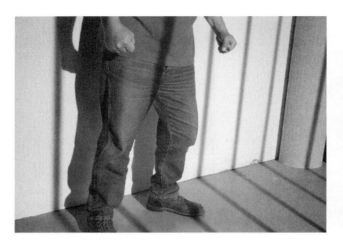

2.10 Cast Shadows Suggest Locale

Cast shadows are sometimes used to suggest a certain location, such as a prison, which isn't actually shown.

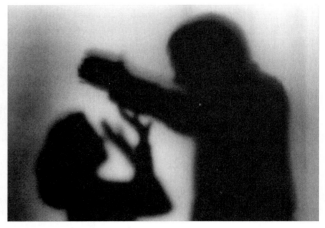

2.11 Cast Shadows Add Drama

We can use cast shadows to create or emphasize a dramatic event.

one that is seen independent of its object is called object-disconnected. Note that object-connected cast shadows are not the same as attached shadows. In contrast to attached shadows, cast shadows become disconnected from the object as soon as you move it away from the surface on which it is resting. Figure 2.9 shows a good example: when the ball is lifted from the table, the cast shadow becomes object-disconnected; the attached shadow, however, remains on the ball.

Although we are normally unaware of or unconcerned about cast shadows, we continually make spatial judgments by perceiving their general shape, intensity, and direction and are readily influenced by their dramatic implications and impact. Cast shadows can help break up large, monotonous surfaces and give an area more visual variety and interest. They can suggest a specific locale, add drama to an event, and even help tell time. **SEE 2.10 AND 2.11** The discussion of outer and inner orientation functions later in this chapter includes more specific information about the two types of shadows.

Not all cast shadows are desirable. The infamous microphone boom or camera shadow on someone's face or on the living room wall is an ever-present menace during large studio productions. So are the multiple cast shadows in a scene that simulates illumination by sunlight or a single table lamp. When you see the lone lost and thirsty hero cast three long shadows onto the hot desert sand while desperately trying to make radio contact, you needn't worry about him: he will have plenty of time to get a glass of water while the studio crew is resetting the lights to simulate the illumination coming from a single sun.

The distinction between attached and cast shadows is important not only in critical video and film lighting but also in creating scenes with a graphics generator or in working out computer-generated designs. Although ultimately linked logically, attached and cast shadows require separate and careful attention during the design phase. For example, you need to have attached shadows change positions on the object when the object moves relative to the (usually virtual) light source or when the light source moves relative to the object.

As you can see in figures 2.7 to 2.9, a cast shadow must also get larger and less dense when the object moves away from the surface on which the shadow is cast (or smaller and denser as the object moves toward such a surface). The constantly changing cast shadows are an important indicator of position change when you move through a virtual-reality environment. Just make sure that when simulating a light source, your 3D software has both types of shadows move accordingly.

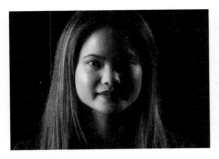

2.12 Fast Falloff
Spotlights, which have a highly directional beam, produce fast falloff. Note that the light side and the dark attached-shadow side differ greatly in brightness. This results in high-contrast lighting.

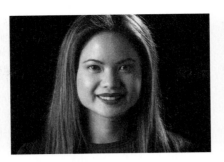

2.13 Slow Falloff
A highly diffused floodlight produces slow falloff. There is little brightness contrast between the illuminated side and the shadow side. The attached shadow has become transparent.

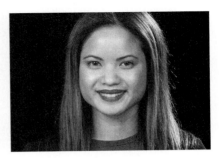

2.14 Elimination of Falloff
When both sides are equally bright, there is no falloff: there is no longer a discernible shadow side, and the picture looks flat.

FALLOFF

We use the term ***falloff*** to mean two different yet related light/shadow relationships: the brightness contrast between the light and shadow sides of an object, and the rate of change from light to shadow.[3]

Contrast   If the brightness contrast between the lighted side of an object and the attached shadow is high, the falloff is *fast*. This means that the illuminated side is relatively bright, and the attached shadow is dense and dark. **SEE 2.12** If the brightness contrast is low, the resulting falloff is *slow*. **SEE 2.13** In figure 2.13 the brightness difference between the illuminated side and the attached-shadow side is relatively small. In extremely flat lighting, no contrast at all shows between the so-called illuminated and shadow sides. In this case, falloff no longer exists. **SEE 2.14** Because most flash photography illuminates the subject directly from the front, both sides are often equally bright. Such elimination of the light/shadow contrast—and with it the falloff—results in the typically flat image of such snapshots.

Change   Calling falloff "fast" or "slow" makes more sense when applied to the rate of change between light and dark. **SEE 2.15** Look, for example, at the tops of the steps in figure 2.15: they are exposed to the sun and are very bright, but they suddenly turn into dense attached shadows at the risers. Such an abrupt change from light to shadow represents extremely fast falloff. Conversely, you automatically interpret such fast falloff on a surface as an edge.

Now imagine yourself moving, like Spider-Man, across the rounded surface of a domed building. You will move from bright sunlight to a hint of a shadow until you reach a dense area of attached shadow at the far side of the rounded building. Because such a change from light to dense shadow is much more gradual than on the steps, the falloff on a curved surface is slow. **SEE 2.16** If the falloff on a curved surface is exceptionally fast, we have a tendency to perceive the rounded surface as an edge. To emphasize the rounded surface, you need to slow the falloff.

Controlling falloff   You can control falloff by using highly directional or diffused light for the basic illumination and by manipulating the amount of fill light.[4] The directional beam of a spotlight (or the sun) causes sharp contrast between the illuminated area and the dense attached shadow. The resulting falloff is fast. Floodlights, on the other hand, produce slow falloff. The highly diffused and more omnidirectional spread of a floodlight not only illuminates the side of the object

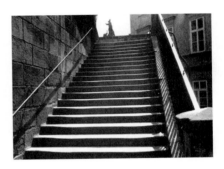

2.15 Fast Falloff: Edge
The lighting on these steps shows fast falloff. The change from light to dark is sudden, signifying a sharp edge or corner.

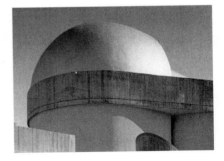

2.16 Slow Falloff: Curved Surface
The light on the surface falls off gradually into its attached shadow. The surface of this building is obviously curved.

that is oriented toward the light but also "floods" the shadow side, rendering the attached shadow more or less transparent.

If the directional light source produces falloff that is too fast, with attached shadows so dense that you can no longer discern any detail (as in figure 2.12), you need to slow down the falloff to some degree. Slowing falloff means rendering the attached shadows somewhat transparent and reducing the contrast between light and shadow areas (see figure 2.13). You control such "contrast falloff" through various amounts of fill light. The more fill light you use, the more transparent the attached shadows become and the less contrast there is between light and dark.

Instead of using the customary fill-light instrument to slow down falloff, you can use simple reflectors. They are often used in outdoor shooting to make the sunlight do double duty—to work as both a key light and a fill light.[5] When shooting outdoors many video camera operators prefer a foggy day to a brightly sunlit one. The fog acts as a giant diffuser of sunlight, producing soft, slow-falloff lighting with highly transparent shadows.

You may have noticed that it is not the illuminated side that tells us whether the light is "hard" (produced by spotlights) or "soft" (produced by floodlights) but rather the speed of the falloff and the density of the shadows. When looking at a close-up of the illuminated side of a face or an object, you can't really tell whether the light used was a spotlight or a floodlight. When seeing fast falloff and dense shadows, however, you will immediately know that a hard (spot) light was used. When the falloff is slow and the shadows are transparent, a soft (diffused) light was used.

Outer Orientation Functions: How We See an Event

Lighting orients us in space. It shows us what an object looks like: whether it is round or flat and has rough or smooth surfaces and round or sharp edges. It can also show us where the object is in relation to other things. It lets us know whether it is day or night, morning or noon, summer or winter. The use of lighting to articulate the outer environment is known as outer orientation. Thus we can identify three principal functions: spatial, tactile, and time.

SPATIAL ORIENTATION

Lighting reveals the basic shape of an object and where it is located relative to its environment. The principal light source—the key light—and the attached shadows carry the major burden of fulfilling the basic shape function. The cast shadow indicates where the object is: whether it sits on a table or floats above it, whether it is close to the wall or away from it. Under certain circumstances, a cast shadow can give you a rough idea of what the object that caused the shadow looks like.

TACTILE ORIENTATION

Lighting for tactile orientation is very closely related to lighting for spatial orientation. Actually, texture is a spatial phenomenon because a texture, when sufficiently enlarged, resembles the peaks and valleys, ridges and crevasses of a rugged mountain range. The only difference is that lighting for space is done primarily to orient us better visually, whereas lighting for texture is supposed to appeal to our haptic sense—our sense of touch. As in lighting for spatial orientation, control of falloff is of the utmost importance.

To demonstrate the importance of falloff in texture, let us assume that the wrinkles and the folds in a backdrop or curtain represent an enlarged surface texture. If you point a spotlight at the wrinkled side of a backdrop and direct

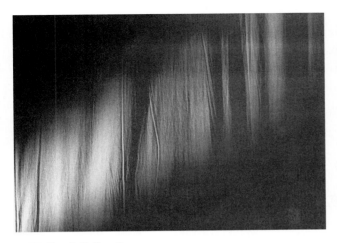

2.17 Fast Falloff on Cyc

When a directional light hits a cyclorama (backdrop) from the side, the texture—wrinkles and folds—shows up prominently.

2.18 Slow Falloff on Cyc

When the very same area of the backdrop is illuminated with diffused light from the front, the backdrop looks taut and wrinkle-free.

the beam so that it hits the backdrop from the side, you will produce prominent, fast-falloff, attached shadows; the wrinkles will be greatly emphasized. **SEE 2.17** When illuminating the identical area directly from the front with a soft floodlight, however, the falloff is slowed down so drastically that the attached shadows become all but invisible to the camera. The backdrop now lacks texture and therefore looks taut. **SEE 2.18**

The same principle applies to lighting a face. You can use falloff control either to emphasize the texture of a face (wrinkles or beard stubble) or to de-emphasize it and make the skin look taut and smooth. Thus, if you have to light the face of a rugged adventurer, you go for fast falloff. In our society we seem to associate a man's experience and masculinity, if not virility, with a moderate amount of wrinkles. **SEE 2.19** This is not so with women, however. We seem to believe that women's faces should look reasonably smooth regardless of age and experience. To emphasize the smoothness of a woman's face, you obviously light for slow falloff. **SEE 2.20** How slow the falloff should be (which translates into how much fill light you use) depends on the specific message you want to convey. For example, if you need to demonstrate the effectiveness of a new skin cream, you light the model's face with extremely slow or no falloff. But to intensify a woman's exhaustion after surviving a bad fall while rock climbing, you light for relatively fast falloff.

As adults we sometimes forget that our tactile, or haptic, sense is a very important (if not the most direct) means of perceiving our environment, of experiencing the nature of the objects around us. As infants we tend to learn as much, if not more, about our environment by touching as by looking, smelling, or listening. Only gradually, and after many warnings from our parents not to touch this or that, do we finally manage to drive the tactile sense underground. But the many do-not-touch signs in stores and especially in museums suggest that apparently we would still like to touch objects to get to know them better and to enrich our experience.

Johannes Itten, who taught the famous Basic Course at the Bauhaus in Weimar, Germany, from 1919 to 1923, put great emphasis on the study of textures. One of the texture exercises in the Basic Course involved making long boards on which a variety of materials with different consistency (steel wool, wood, cotton) were glued. The students would then run their fingers over these textures with their eyes closed. Itten found that through such systematic exercises, the students' sense of touch improved to an amazing degree. In turn the students learned to appreciate texture as an important design element as well as an orientation factor to the materials used. Itten stated that through such texture exercises the students developed a real "design fever."[6]

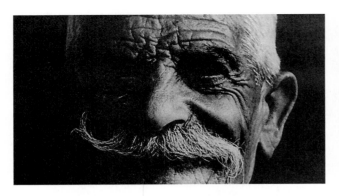

2.19   Fast Falloff: Facial Texture Emphasized

Highly directional hard spotlights hitting the face from a steep angle create fast falloff. The facial texture—the wrinkles, ridges, and hollows—is accentuated.

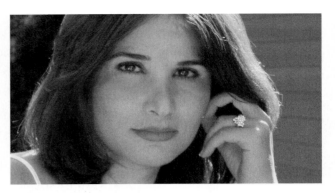

2.20   Slow Falloff: Facial Texture Reduced

When you want the skin to look smooth and wrinkle-free, you need to reduce, rather than emphasize, facial texture.

TIME ORIENTATION

Control of light and shadows also helps viewers determine the time and even the seasons. In its most elementary application, lighting can show whether it is day or night. More specific lighting can indicate the approximate hour of the day or at least whether it is early morning, high noon, or evening. With certain subtle color changes, you can also suggest whether it is winter or summer.

Day and night   In general, daytime lighting is bright and nighttime lighting is less so. Because we are used to seeing everything around us during the day but not at night, we keep the sky or background illuminated to indicate daytime. **SEE 2.21** We leave it dark or only partially illuminated for nighttime. **SEE 2.22** A daytime scene needs a great amount of all-around light with everything brightly illuminated, including the background. Nighttime lighting needs more specific and more selective fast-falloff illumination. Note that nighttime lighting does not mean "no light" but rather highly selective light with a minimum of spill. The light must also come from an obvious source, such as the moon or a streetlamp.

You can use the same lighting principle for indicating day or night indoors. For a daytime interior, light so that the background is bright and the rest of the interior is bathed in slow-falloff illumination. **SEE 2.23** For nighttime the back-

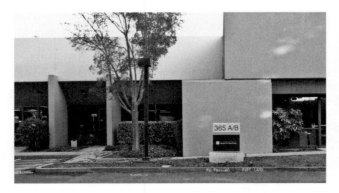

2.21   Outdoor Illumination: Day

In this daylight scene, the sky and the walls of the building are light. All recessed areas (doors and windows) are in the shade and therefore dark.

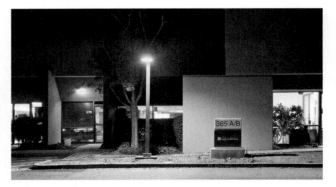

2.22   Outdoor Illumination: Night

In this night shot, the sky is dark as are all areas that are not illuminated by the street lamp. Because the lights are on inside the building, the windows appear light.

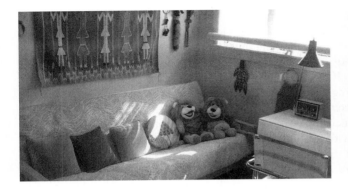

2.23 Indoor Lighting: Day

In this daylight interior scene, the window area (covered by a translucent shade) is brightly illuminated, with highlights spilling onto the sofa. The overall interior lighting is rather flat, with soft, slow-falloff shadows.

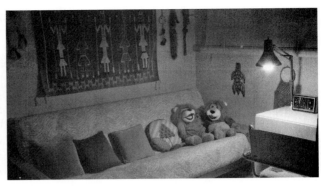

2.24 Indoor Lighting: Night

In the nighttime lighting of the same interior scene, the window shade is obviously dark, with the main light source (the desk lamp) turned on. The shadows have fast falloff. The illumination of the wall hanging drops off toward the top, suggesting a room ceiling. Note that the action areas (lions' corner and desk) are almost equally bright in both lighting setups.

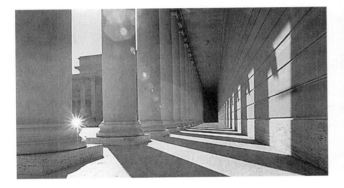

2.25 Cast Shadows Tell Time

Long cast shadows tell us that the sun is in an early-morning or late-afternoon position. At noon cast shadows are optimally short. In this picture the long cast shadows were produced by the early-morning sun.

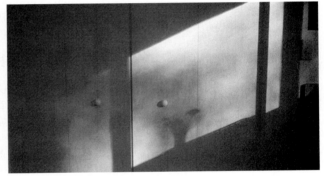

2.26 Slice of Light

An angled slice of light on the background can substitute for a cast shadow as a time indicator.

ground is predominantly dark, and the lighting in the rest of the interior becomes more selective. **SEE 2.24** In daytime lighting, the lamp is turned off and the window is light. In nighttime lighting, the lamp is on but the window is dark.

Clock time The common indicator of clock time is the length of cast shadows. As shown in figures 2.6 and 2.25, the early-morning or late-afternoon sun causes long cast shadows. **SEE 2.25** At high noon shadows are very short. Outdoors such shadows are usually cast along the ground. This is of little help, however, because the camera rarely shoots wide enough for us to see the shadows on the ground. You must therefore produce cast shadows somewhere in the background, such as on the wall of a building, so that the camera can see them even in fairly tight shots.

The same shadow requirement holds for shooting indoors. Rather than have the cast shadows fall on the studio floor, you should devote a fair amount of background lighting to producing cast shadows, or even slices of light, that cut across the background at the desired angle. Though illogical, we readily seem to substitute a slice of light for a cast shadow. **SEE 2.26** If clock time is critical to the plot, you may want to reinforce the lighting with other, less subtle cues, such as somebody saying, "Oh, it's five o'clock already," or by briefly intercutting a close-up of a clock. In any case, the lighting must correspond with such additional cues.

Also ensure that all of the background cast shadows are consistent with the attached shadows. If the window of the room is the primary light source, with illumination coming from the left, attached and cast shadows should be on the opposite side. Because the indoor lighting setup usually requires several instruments, most of which come from somewhat different directions and angles, you can easily end up with a variety of cast shadows falling in different directions. For example, the hand that turned on the single light bulb in the cheap motel room should not cast multiple shadows on the wall. You must keep all distracting cast shadows out of camera range and show only one prominent cast shadow that falls opposite the primary light source.

Seasons   Generally, the winter sun is weaker and colder than the summer sun, so the light representing the winter sun should be slightly more bluish. The winter sun also strikes the earth's surface from a fairly low angle, even at noon; this makes cast shadows in winter longer and not quite so dense. A slightly diffused light beam helps create softer winter shadows. Because snow reflects a moderate amount of diffused light, the falloff is somewhat slower than in a similar outdoor scene without snow.[7]

Inner Orientation Functions: How We Feel About an Event

So far we have explored outer orientation functions of lighting: light and shadows manipulated to articulate the outer environment. You now know the aesthetic principles of lighting to show what an object looks like, what texture it has, and where it is located in space and time. Such articulation is a major factor in structuring screen space. But you can also use light to articulate the *inner* environment—that of our feelings and emotions—a lighting function we call inner orientation.

The specific inner orientation functions of lighting are: establishing mood and atmosphere, above- and below-eye-level key-light position, predictive lighting, and the use of light and lighting instruments as dramatic agents.

ESTABLISHING MOOD AND ATMOSPHERE

Much like music, lighting can have an intuitive effect, influencing our emotions directly. Some lighting makes us feel happy, some sad, and some uncomfortable or even frightened. The two major aesthetic lighting techniques for establishing mood and atmosphere are high-key and low-key lighting, and above- and below-eye-level key-light position.

High-key lighting   This kind of lighting has nothing to do with the position or the intensity of the principal illuminating source, called the key light. Nor does it mean that the key light shines down on the scene from above. *High-key lighting* means that the scene has an abundance of bright, usually slow-falloff illumination and a light background. Television news sets and interview areas, game shows, and many situation comedies have high-key illumination. High-key lighting reflects normalcy and or upbeat feeling. **SEE 2.27**

Low-key lighting   The fast-falloff illumination of *low-key lighting* is highly selective, usually leaving the background as well as part of the scene predominantly dark. This type of lighting has less overall light and fewer light sources than high-key lighting. Scenes that deal with caves, medieval dungeons, submarine

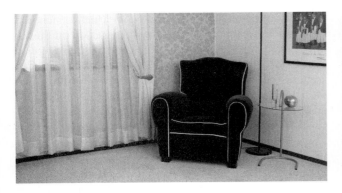

2.27 High-key Lighting
This lighting technique is bright and generally nonspecific. It has a high overall light level, slow or no falloff, and usually a light background.

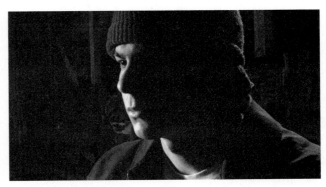

2.28 Low-key Lighting
This scene has a low overall light level with selective lighting. The lighting has fast falloff with dense shadows and a dark background.

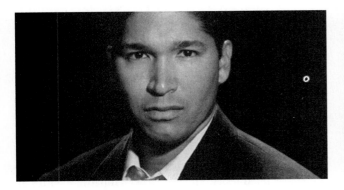

2.29 Above-eye-level Lighting
When the principal light source, the key light, comes from above eye level, the shadows are below the protrusions and above the indentations, as expected. We perceive normalcy.

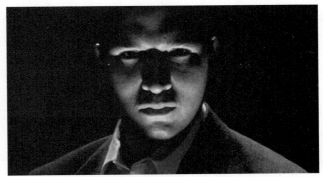

2.30 Below-eye-level Lighting
When the light source strikes the face from below, the shadows are exactly opposite of their expected positions. We are immediately disoriented. We affix to this outer disorientation an inner disorientation: the face appears unusual, ghostly, and frightening.

interiors, or nighttime exteriors or interiors normally call for low-key lighting. Whereas high-key lighting is "up," low-key lighting is "down." There is hardly a crime or mystery show that does not use some form of low-key lighting. **SEE 2.28**

ABOVE- AND BELOW-EYE-LEVEL KEY-LIGHT POSITION

These positions are, indeed, meant to tell where the key light is located. As stated earlier, we usually expect the principal light source to come from above the object, producing attached shadows underneath protrusions. This normal lighting is achieved by having the key light illuminate a person from *above eye level*. Note that *eye level* refers to the eyes of the subject or the middle portion of the object lighted. As soon as the principal light source strikes the face from *below eye level* (sometimes called reverse modeling), the attached shadows reverse vertically and are exactly opposite their expected positions. Because we are so used to seeing the light come from above eye level, such a shadow reversal affixes to the outer disorientation an inner disorientation, which translates into surprise, suspicion, or fear. This lighting technique, sometimes called horror lighting, is as blatant as it is effective. **SEE 2.29 AND 2.30**

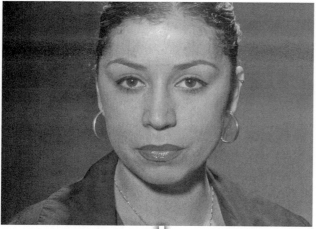

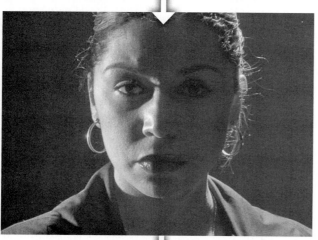

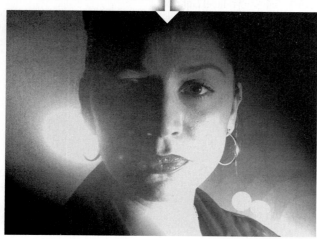

2.31 Predictive Lighting

The lighting change in this picture series increases the tension of the event and suggests a somewhat ominous outcome for the woman.

Whom would you trust more as a news anchor, a computer salesman, or an attorney—the person on the left or the one on the right? Most of us would probably opt for the person on the left (figure 2.29). Why? Because when seeing the lighting effect in figure 2.30, we probably would not take the time to trace the cause of the person's strange appearance to a below-eye-level key-light position and the subsequent vertical reversal of the attached shadows; we would simply label the person as weird, dangerous, or at best untrustworthy. This seemingly minor position change of the key light has a decisive influence on our perception of the person's credibility if not character. Worse, we have a tendency to extend such unexamined aesthetic manipulations of appearance to the person's entire behavior and psychological makeup.

PREDICTIVE LIGHTING

The ***predictive lighting*** technique helps to portend, however subtly, a coming event. Light that changes from high-key to low-key, from general to specific, from above eye level to below eye level or, more obviously, a flashing light, can signal how the event will go. **SEE 2.31** The lighting changes from a normal slow-falloff lighting to a fast-falloff lighting, with the key light moving quickly from camera-left to camera-right, past the person, to a partial background lighting. Such drastic lighting changes give the viewer a strong clue to some unpleasant future event, even if the lighted character may be unaware of it. As in all good drama, we now know something the character doesn't, and we either empathize with her predicament or anticipate her deserved doom.

Similar predictions of trouble are possible when you change the lighting of a party from high-key to low-key while maintaining the seemingly happy and innocent mood of the festivities, with all other aesthetic devices remaining the same. By reversing this procedure and changing from "down" to "up" lighting, you can predict the happy ending (the famous ray of light), even if the other aesthetic elements are still signaling disaster.

You can also use moving light sources in predictive lighting. You may have seen some version of a scene in which the night watchman discovers that something is not quite right in Building 47, which houses top-secret documents. We see him getting up, looking left and right, and turning on his flashlight. We see the flashlight beam creeping nervously down the long, dark hallway until it finally reveals—you guessed it—the broken lock, the open file cabinets, and papers strewn all over the floor.

As with any application of contextual aesthetics, predictive lighting rarely operates alone; it usually works

We can learn a great deal about lighting from classic black-and-white motion pictures. Lacking color, the lighting of black-and-white films had to be especially expressive. For example, **Federico Fellini** (1920–1993) used light as a dramatic agent with great virtuosity in his timeless films *La Dolce Vita* and *8½*.

In *La Dolce Vita,* he shows a television remote unit covering the events of an alleged miracle. Young children claim to have seen Holy Mary descend from heaven and heard her speak to them. There is a great amount of confusion. Fellini cuts in close-ups of lighting instruments being turned on, shining their cold, controlled light beams over the highly emotional, ecstatic crowd. To counterpoint even more the discrepancy between the emotionally charged crowd, which represents the uncritical world of blind faith, and the analytical and soulless modern age, as symbolized by the lighting instruments and the cameras, he shows a tight close-up of a huge Fresnel lens bursting in the first seconds of a chilling downpour.

In *8½* Fellini uses many lighting instruments arranged in large circles, illuminating the representatives of humanity who, following the director's orders, march willingly like circus clowns within the lights' periphery. The lighting instruments and the light, which occasionally shines directly into the camera, are a strong reminder that when properly "enlightened," we may discover that we are all part of a big cosmic joke that some superior power occasionally plays on us. Unless we embrace humanity and "join the show," we remain alienated from the circus of life and face an empty existence.

in conjunction with appropriate sounds, suspenseful music, and the like. In fact, oncoming changes of events are more commonly introduced by predictive sounds than predictive lighting. Flashes of white light, accompanied by a generous amount of *whoosh* sound effects, are some of the less subtle examples of predictive lighting and sound.

LIGHT AND LIGHTING INSTRUMENTS AS DRAMATIC AGENTS

You can use the light source itself as an effective ***dramatic agent***—an element that operates as an aesthetic intensifier in a scene. By showing the actual light source—the sun, a spotlight, or a flashlight—you can intensify the scene, assuming that it is set up properly for such intensification. Well-known, and often well-worn, examples are the close-up of the flashing red and blue lights on top of a police car, the flashing lights of a rock concert, or the searchlight from a prison tower that, by shining into the camera, not only searches for the escapees on the prison grounds but also ruthlessly invades your personal space and privacy as a viewer. The dim overhead lights in a garage or the on/off blinking motel sign are other examples of using lighting as a dramatic agent. Movies about extraterrestrials depend heavily on light as a dramatic agent. The creatures from space are usually introduced and dismissed as mysterious light beams, regardless of their eventual metamorphosis or whether they turn out to be friend or foe.

S U M M A R Y

Light is what orients us in space and time and influences how we feel about a thing, a person, or an event. The areas that need special attention when dealing with light are the nature of light, lighting purposes and functions, the nature of shadows, and the outer and inner orientation functions of lighting.

Light is a form of radiant energy that commonly behaves as electromagnetic waves. Perceptually, light is invisible except at its source and when it is reflected by an object.

Lighting is the deliberate control of light and shadows. Through lighting we can articulate our outer space/time environment and our inner environment—our emotions. These outer and inner orientation functions of lighting (how we see and feel) are primarily dependent on the proper control of shadows.

There are two types of shadows, attached and cast. The attached shadow is inevitably fixed to its object on the opposite side of the principal light source. The cast shadow is independent and may be connected to its object or disconnected from it. The attached shadow reveals the basic form of the object; the cast shadow tells where the object is in relation to its surroundings.

Falloff is the brightness contrast between the light and shadow sides of an object. The term also refers to the relative rate of change from light to dark (shadow). Slow falloff means that the illuminated side and the shadow side have very little brightness contrast or that the change from light to shadow area is gradual. Fast falloff means that the illuminated side and the shadow side have a great brightness contrast and that the change from light to shadow is abrupt.

The outer orientation functions of lighting include spatial, tactile, and time. The spatial orientation functions are to reveal the basic shape of the object and its location relative to its environment. The tactile orientation function means that fast-falloff lighting is employed to reveal and emphasize the object's surface texture and that slow- or no-falloff lighting is used to reduce or eliminate texture. Time orientation is achieved primarily by controlling the relative brightness of the background and the length and the angle of cast shadows. A light background suggests daylight; a dark background, nighttime. Long cast shadows suggest early morning or late afternoon; short shadows suggest high noon. The winter sun is weaker and slightly more bluish than the summer sun.

The inner orientation functions of lighting include establishing mood and atmosphere, above- and below-eye-level key-light position, predictive lighting, and the use of light and lighting instruments as dramatic agents. Mood and atmosphere are affected by low- and high-key lighting as well as by above-eye-level and below-eye-level lighting. High-key lighting has an abundance of light, and the distribution of the light is nonspecific; the falloff is slow. With low-key lighting, the overall light level is low and the lighting illuminates specific areas; the falloff is fast. An above-eye-level key-light position places attached shadows in a normal position; a below-eye-level key-light position reverses them vertically into an abnormal position. We usually interpret below-eye-level lighting as frightening or dangerous.

Predictive lighting refers to a lighting change that portends an upcoming event. One type of predictive lighting is a moving light source, such as a night watchman's flashlight, that reveals something.

Light and lighting instruments can be used as dramatic agents: the light is used directly as an aesthetic intensifier. The flashing lights during a rock concert or the flashing lights on a police car are examples of such intensifiers.

NOTES

1. Rudolf Arnheim, *Art and Visual Perception: A Psychology of the Creative Eye, The New Version* (Berkeley: University of California Press, 1974), p. 305.

2. Herbert Zettl, *Television Production Handbook,* 10th ed. (Belmont, Calif.: Wadsworth, 2009), p. 160.

3. Herbert Zettl, *Video Basics 6* (Boston: Wadsworth, 2010), pp. 157–61.

4. Zettl, *Video Basics 6,* pp. 177–78.

5. Zettl, *Television Production Handbook,* pp. 237–38.

6. Johannes Itten, *Design and Form: The Basic Course at the Bauhaus,* trans. by John Maas (New York: Van Nostrand Reinhold, 1963).

7. Ross Lowell, *Matters of Light and Depth* (New York: Lowel-Light Manufacturing, 1999), pp. 92–96. See also Blain Brown, *Motion Picture and Video Lighting,* 2nd ed. (Burlington, Mass.: Focal Press, 2008), pp. 76–80.

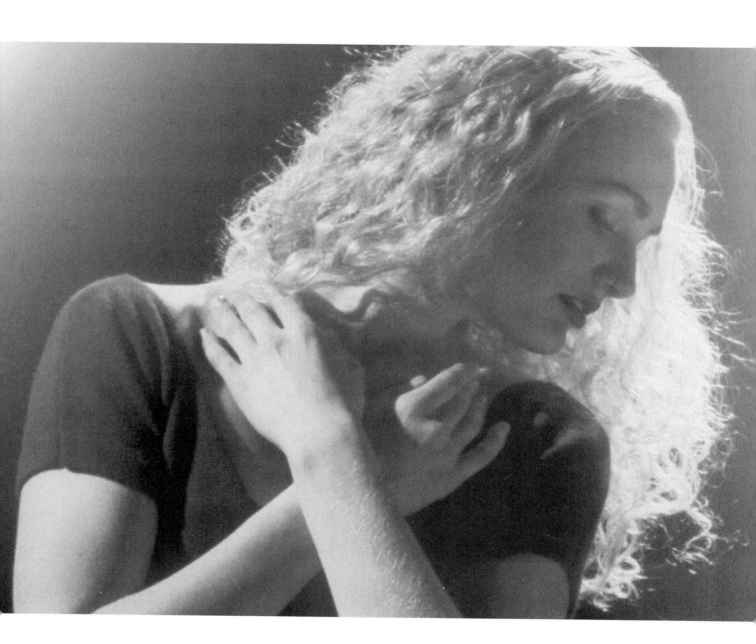

Structuring the First Aesthetic Field: Lighting

L IGHTING IS THE DELIBERATE CONTROL OF LIGHT AND SHADOWS TO fulfill specific aesthetic objectives relating to outer and inner orientation. This chapter on structuring the first aesthetic field includes a discussion of the major types and functions of lighting. You should realize, however, that these lighting types and functions are not etched in stone and are often adjusted to suit a certain theme or communication objective. They also depend on the application of other aesthetic elements, such as music. The specific functions of lighting frequently do, and should, overlap when applied to video productions or films.

All lighting shows up on the screen as an interplay of light and shadow, regardless of whether the light is colored. As you recall, some scenes need fast-falloff lighting with deep and pronounced attached and cast shadows. Others call for much softer slow-falloff lighting with highly transparent shadows. The lighting type that emphasizes highly contrasting light and shadow areas is called chiaroscuro lighting. The type that de-emphasizes the light/dark contrast is called flat lighting. Most chiaroscuro and flat-lighting techniques are relatively simple variations of the standard photographic principle.

Standard Lighting Techniques

The standard photographic lighting technique is known as the *photographic principle* or *triangle lighting*. This refers to the triangular arrangement of key, back, and fill lights, with the back light opposite the camera and directly behind the object, and the key and fill lights on opposite sides of the camera and to the front and the side of the object (see figure 3.3).

The *key light* is the principal source of illumination. It reveals the basic shape of the object or event. **SEE 3.1** The *back light* separates the figure from the background and provides sparkle. **SEE 3.2** The *fill light* controls falloff. **SEE 3.3**

In an expanded lighting setup, there are three additional light sources. The *side light* comes from the side of the object, acting as an additional fill light and providing contour. **SEE 3.4** The *kicker*, which comes from the back, is usually from below and off to one side. The kicker is an extension of the back light and rims the object from below what the back light can reach. **SEE 3.5** The *background light*,

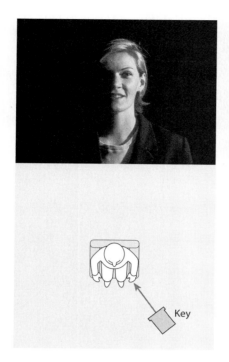

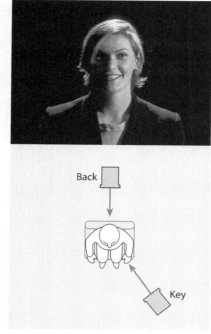

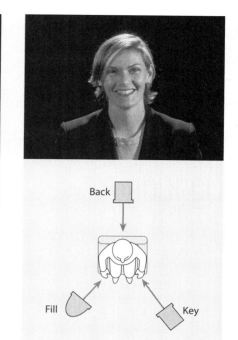

3.1 Key Light

Key light: principal source of illumination (normally a directional spot).

3.2 Key Light and Back Light

Back light: rims top and separates subject from background (normally a directional spot).

3.3 Key, Back, and Fill Lights

Fill light: controls falloff (normally a floodlight).

or set light, illuminates the background, which can be an actual set of an interior or some kind of backdrop. **SEE 3.6**

Chiaroscuro Lighting

Chiaroscuro (pronounced "key-aura-skoor-o") is an Italian word meaning "light/dark" (*chiaro* = light; *oscuro* = dark). Chiaroscuro lighting borrowed its name and technique from the chiaroscurists of the Mannerist (post-Renaissance) and Baroque periods (roughly 1530 to 1650), who emphasized fast-falloff, high-contrast "lighting" in their paintings. Chief among them are the Italian painter **Michelangelo Merisi da Caravaggio** (1573–1610), who is commonly considered the father of the chiaroscuro school, and the Dutch painter **Rembrandt van Rijn** (1606–1669), who brought the chiaroscuro technique to perfection.

Chiaroscuro lighting means lighting for fast falloff and for light/dark contrast. The basic aim of this type of lighting is to articulate space, to clarify and intensify the three-dimensional property of things and the space that surrounds them, and to give the scene an expressive quality. Chiaroscuro lighting creates volume and gives drama to a scene.

ANALYSIS OF CHIAROSCURO LIGHTING

Let's briefly analyze a chiaroscuro scene and see how the lighting contributes to our outer and inner orientation, that is, to how we see the event and how we feel about it. **SEE 3.7**

You probably feel that the scene (*Spanish Wake* by the late American master photographer W. Eugene Smith) is dramatic and emotionally involving. This emotional reaction is due in large measure to its highly charged subject matter—women mourning the death of a patriarch—but also the chiaroscuro treatment of the lighting. This photograph fulfills most of the functions of chiaroscuro lighting, which adds to the drama and the intensity of the event.

Light source and overall illumination   The light source seems to come from a single direction—the upper left. Although the actual photograph was taken with a flash that was positioned camera-left, we assume that the illumination originates

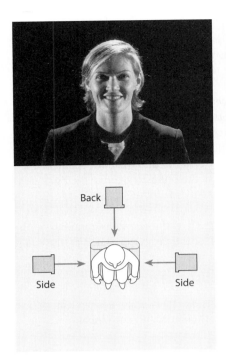

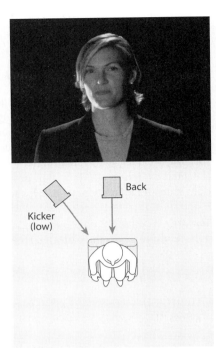

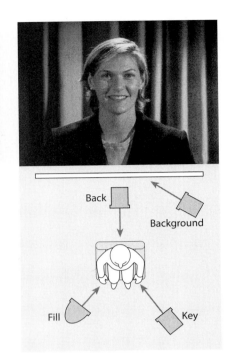

3.4 Back and Side Lights

Side light: directional spotlight coming from the side.

3.5 Kicker and Back Light

Kicker: directional spot from the back, off to one side, usually from below.

3.6 Standard Triangle with Added Background, or Set, Light

Background light: background or set illumination (often by spots).

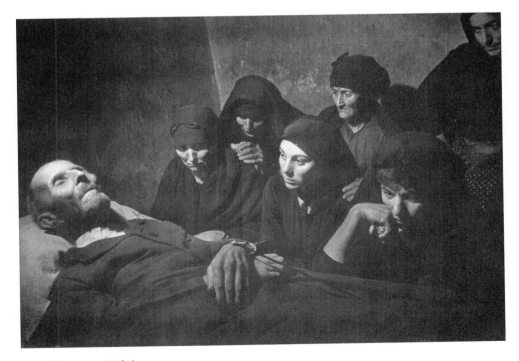

3.7 Chiaroscuro Lighting

In this photograph we can see major elements of chiaroscuro lighting: selective illumination (faces, hands, and part of the background); a low-key effect (background is predominantly dark, and the overall light level is low); and fast-falloff lighting with distinct, dense attached shadows.

W. Eugene Smith, *Spanish Wake* (1951). Courtesy of W. Eugene Smith/Blackstar.

from candles or a small window. It is highly specific, illuminating some parts of the scene while leaving others purposely dark. The overall illumination is low-key: the background is relatively dark, the overall light level is low, and the lighting is selective.

Shadow distribution and falloff   The scene shows a fine example of fast-falloff lighting. The lighted areas change abruptly into dense attached shadows, telling us once again that the illumination source is highly directional. The faces of the people appear stark and sculpted, reflecting death and the expression of intense sorrow. The dark areas (shadows and black clothes) dominate the scene and are accented by light areas. In a high-key scene, the opposite occurs: the light areas dominate and are only occasionally accented by shadows.

Texture   The highly directional light source and the fast falloff emphasize the texture of the faces, the clothing, the beard of the deceased, and even the walls.

FUNCTIONS OF CHIAROSCURO LIGHTING

Chiaroscuro lighting should perform some or all of these major aesthetic functions: organic, directional, spatial/compositional, thematic, and emotional.

Organic function   The lighting should look organic, that is, approximate as closely as possible the actual illumination source shown in the scene, such as a candle, a window, a table lamp, or the sun. If the only illumination source is a candle, the lighting should look as though the scene were in fact illuminated by a single flame. You may be able to accomplish this by using a single light or, more often, by having the principal light source (key light) come from the "organic" direction (the direction of the light source in the scene) so that the attached and cast shadows are in their appropriate places—opposite the principal light source. In lighting for video, however, you will rarely get a satisfactory effect by simply duplicating the actual light source shown in a scene. In other words, a single candle may not yield enough light to create the lighting effect of a single candle. But there is no harm in starting out with a candle or at least with as few lighting instruments as possible before adding more.[1]

If you were asked to reproduce the scene of the painting *The New Born Child* by Georges de La Tour, how would you light it? **SEE 3.8** Would you just hand one of the women a single candle and let it go at that? It's certainly worth a try, but you may find that a single candle simply does not produce enough light to effect such strong illumination as is shown in the picture.

Even with highly light-sensitive video cameras, the lack of adequate baselight (overall light level) and the high contrast might contribute to picture "noise" (snowlike electronic interference) in the large shadow areas, especially in the background.[2] By looking at the painting more closely, you will undoubtedly discover that the light is coming not just from a single source. For example, the background light in the upper-left corner cannot possibly come from the candle.

The following figure shows a possible lighting setup that simulates the illumination in the La Tour painting. **SEE 3.9** When duplicating the lighting setup, start with one candle. If the effect is similar to the one in the painting, you are done. If you need more light in different places, add one instrument at a time. Figure 3.9 shows a lighting setup that has probably more instruments than you need. Note that you can always use reflectors in place of the fill lights.

Directional function   You can use light to direct the viewer's attention to certain picture areas. In figure 3.7 the lighting guides you to the women's faces and the patriarch's face. In figure 3.8 the light directs your attention to the women's faces

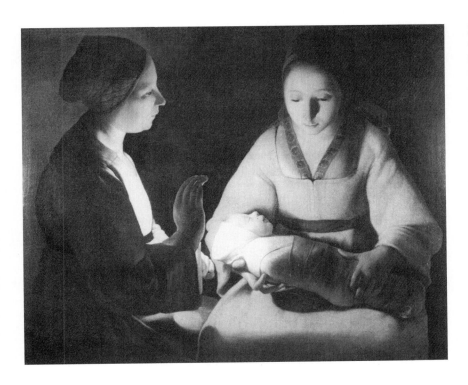

3.8 Functions of Chiaroscuro Lighting

The principal functions of chiaroscuro lighting are clearly identifiable in this reproduction of a La Tour painting: *organic function*—the light seems to radiate from a single candle hidden behind the woman's hand; *directional*—our eyes are led to the women's faces and ultimately to the newborn child; *spatial/compositional*—note the light-against-dark and dark-against-light illumination that sets off the figures from the dark background as well as the balanced distribution of light and dark picture areas.

Georges de La Tour, French (1593–1652) *The New Born Child* (ca. 1640s), oil on canvas. Musée des Beaux Arts, Rennes, France/Bridgeman Art Library, London/SuperStock.

and ultimately to the child. Whereas this function is very important for theater lighting, painting, still photography, and sometimes even for large-screen movies, it is less critical in video, where we are much more readily guided by close-up shots than strategically placed points of illumination.

Spatial/compositional function   The light (high-energy) and dark (low-energy) areas should be distributed within the frame in such a way that they balance one another (see figure 3.8). The distribution of light and dark also contributes to a definition of volume, contour, and foreground and background planes. Note how in figure 3.8 the light profile of the woman on the left is set off against a dark background, while her darker headdress and clothing are contrasted against a

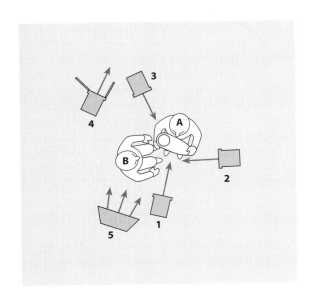

3.9 Lighting Setup for La Tour's *The New Born Child*

Lighting instruments and major functions: (1) key light for woman A: focused spot; (2) key light for woman B: focused spot; (3) back light/kicker for baby and woman B's torso: focused spot; (4) background light camera-left: flooded spot (right barn door prevents spill into center); (5) baselight to raise level and to slow falloff on woman B: softlight.

slightly lighter background. Such light-against-dark and dark-against-light variations are favorite lighting techniques for defining foreground and background in static scenes.

Thematic function   Lighting should emphasize the theme or story of the scene. The lighting in figures 3.7 and 3.8 clearly emphasizes the eternal themes of death and birth. The death theme in figure 3.7 is communicated by the light on the dead patriarch and the faces of the mourning women. In figure 3.8 the lighting focused on the two women and the newborn child seems to suggest that the infant is itself part of the light source. All other aspects are deliberately kept dark and thus de-emphasized.

Emotional function   Though closely related to the thematic function, the emotional function of chiaroscuro lighting is to affect our feelings directly regardless of the actual subject matter of the scene. Most often these two functions operate in unison. In both figures 3.7 and 3.8, the lighting determines a dominant mood and reflects the strong emotions that prevail in both scenes—one of deep sorrow and anguish, the other of wonderment and joy. Both have drama. But, although both lighting setups use chiaroscuro techniques, the tragedy of death in *Spanish Wake* is intensified through extremely fast falloff and the light concentrated on the dead patriarch and the faces of the mourners. In *The New Born Child,* the falloff is somewhat slower, underscoring a more gentle, less dramatic event.

All major functions of chiaroscuro lighting clearly operate harmoniously in both pictures: the lighting obviously contributes to the clarification, intensification, and interpretation of the scenes.

Specific Chiaroscuro Lighting Types

Rembrandt and cameo are two distinct types of chiaroscuro lighting. Both are used in a great variety of ways, usually displaying only part of their primary characteristics.

REMBRANDT LIGHTING

The major characteristic of **Rembrandt lighting** is its selectivity: only specific areas are carefully illuminated while others are kept purposely under- or unlighted. The falloff is fast, but there is enough fill light to render the attached shadows somewhat transparent. The background, although generally dark, is at least partially illuminated to outline and set off the figures or to fulfill other orientation functions.

When you look at Rembrandt's *Old Woman Reading,* you can clearly see the basic characteristics of the lighting type bearing his name. **SEE 3.10** Only some areas are illuminated (the woman's blouse, her face, and her hands) while others are kept relatively dark. The falloff is fast, but the shadows are reasonably translucent. The book itself, acting as an efficient reflector, seems to emit light, although we do not actually see its illuminated side. The background is dark, but it is still carefully illuminated to set off the contour of the foreground figure. Such separation of background and foreground is especially important because Rembrandt did not simulate any back lighting.[3]

CAMEO LIGHTING

Cameo lighting is chiaroscuro lighting pushed to its extreme. As a direct imitation of the cameo stone, in which a white figure is sharply set off against a dark background, **cameo lighting** illuminates the foreground figures while leaving the

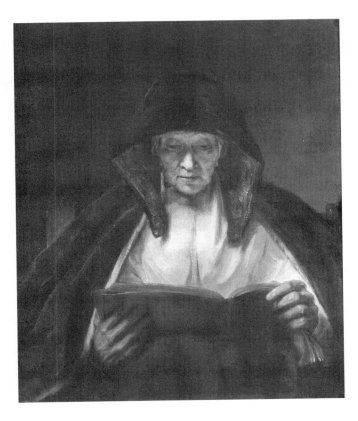

3.10 Rembrandt Lighting

The most widely applied type of chiaroscuro, Rembrandt lighting has selective illumination, transparent shadows, fairly fast falloff, and carefully placed background illumination. It is lighting for volume and drama.

Rembrandt van Rijn, *Old Woman Reading* (1631). Courtesy of the Duke of Buccleuch. Photograph by Tom Scott.

background totally dark. **SEE 3.11 AND 3.12** Cameo lighting is highly directional, producing fast falloff with dense attached and sharply defined cast shadows. The cast shadows are usually visible only on the lighted floor areas or occasionally on the performers themselves. **SEE 3.13**

The high concentration of light on the performers and the lack of scenery should make cameo lighting an ideal video production technique. Unfortunately, this has proven not to be the case. The highly directional nature of the lighting makes it difficult for performers to move without stepping out of the precisely

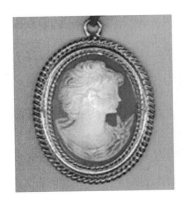

3.11 Cameo Stone

In a typical cameo, the light figure is sharply set off against a dark background.

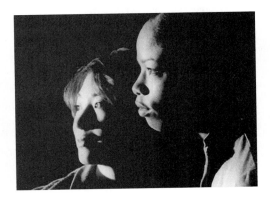

3.12 Cameo Lighting

In this cameo scene, the two actors are sharply set off against a dark background very much like the figure in an actual cameo stone. Note the extremely fast falloff and the dark, unlighted background. A cameo scene has no scenery.

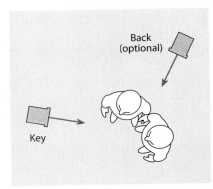

3.13 Cameo-lighting Setup

A cameo-lighting setup normally uses spotlights for the key light and the (optional) back light. Sometimes a kicker is added. There are no fill lights or background lights.

defined light pools. Also, if the audio pickup is by boom microphone, you may find it hard to prevent boom shadows from falling across the actors' faces. Such high-contrast lighting is also difficult to handle even for high-quality video cameras. If the camera is adjusted for the brightly illuminated areas, the dense shadow areas tend to turn uniformly black and become subject to video noise. If adjusted to the dark areas, the light areas overload the camera circuits and look overexposed or "bloom" unnaturally bright. Extreme light/dark contrast also tends to distort color somewhat, especially in the shadow areas.[4]

The most serious problem with cameo lighting, however, is its visual intensity. Even if this stark and focused lighting were matched by an equally dramatic performance, the pictures would still look strangely theatrical and often removed from the television reality to which we have become accustomed.

Flat Lighting

The opposite of chiaroscuro lighting is ***flat lighting***, which uses highly diffused light that seems to come from all directions. It has very slow falloff and such highly transparent attached and cast shadows that we usually do not notice them. Except for a strong backlight, flat lighting does not reveal any particular light source. **SEE 3.14 AND 3.15**

FUNCTIONS OF FLAT LIGHTING

Although flat lighting is often done for optimal visibility or expediency, it can nevertheless fulfill several important aesthetic functions.

Visibility   Contrary to chiaroscuro lighting, where much of the picture detail is purposely hidden in deep shadows, flat lighting shows the whole scene more or less equally illuminated. If the background is bright and the entire scene is bathed in light, you have flat, high-key lighting. Flat lighting is ideal for continuous action, making it possible for cameras to shoot from a variety of angles without having to worry about distracting shadows and thus affords performers maximum mobility.

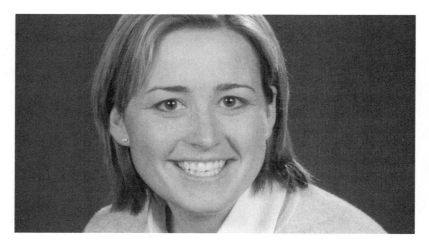

3.14 Flat Lighting
Note how in this scene the light does not come from a particular direction or source; it is simply there. The shadows are so transparent that we are not aware of them. Flat lighting has slow or, more often, no falloff.

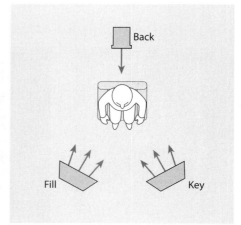

3.15 Flat-lighting Setup
A flat-lighting setup normally uses softlights or reflectors for both the key and the fill functions. The back light, however, is always a spot.

But while we can see a maximum of picture detail with flat lighting, the slow falloff reduces the texture and the three-dimensionality of things and renders them oddly flat (see figure 2.14). Extremely flat lighting can lead to serious disorientation, very much like total darkness. Sometimes, when the highly diffused light of an overcast day robs a snowy landscape of all shadows, and the white ground seems to blend into an equally white sky, skiers and mountain climbers experience a "whiteout" even without a snowstorm. Without any space-defining shadows, they lose all sense of direction and are no longer able to see, but only feel, whether they are moving up- or downhill. You may have had a similar disorienting experience when driving in heavy fog or standing in a television studio whose chroma-key backdrop is made to blend into the studio floor through uniform color and illumination.

Technically, the video camera likes flat lighting because little contrast exists between light and shadow areas. Lacking prominent shadows, there is no danger of color distortion or blooming (overloading the white areas), but the absence of shadows takes away important spatial orientation clues. Flat lighting *looks* flat, and it is uninteresting unless used to serve a specific aesthetic purpose.

Thematic and emotional functions   In flat lighting the thematic and emotional functions are so intertwined that we can discuss them together. Flat lighting can suggest efficiency, cleanliness, truth, fun, and an upbeat mood. News sets are always lit with flat lighting, not just to make the newscasters appear wrinkle-free but also to assure us of the "enlightened" accuracy of the news.

Flat lighting can also convey mechanization, depersonalization, or disorientation. For example, if you want to emphasize the theme of a high-tech operation and impress the viewer with its efficiency, you might do well by lighting the computer room flat rather than chiaroscuro. But you might also inevitably communicate the metamessage (the latent message that may not consciously be perceived by the viewer) that this environment is devoid of human warmth and compassion. If you need to intensify the feeling of a prisoner's isolation in an interrogation room, you could use totally flat lighting in a white room to simulate the disorienting whiteout discussed earlier. The shadowless environment prompts the viewer to empathize with the prisoner's isolation, his being in nothingness, probably more so than if he had been placed in the traditional chiaroscuro-lighted cell with the strong light source shining into his eyes.

On the other hand, high-key flat lighting can also express energy and enthusiasm. Game shows and many situation comedies are illuminated by flat lighting—apt signifiers of the energetic and pleasant superficiality of such events. Sometimes sitcoms play in cramped quarters, such as living rooms, small offices, or restaurants, or they have action that happens at night. In such cases, moderate chiaroscuro lighting is obviously more appropriate to fulfill the organic functions, but it should not be so heavy that it detracts from the comedic action.

Let's apply these theories and assume that you must light the set of a hospital corridor so that it first suggests to the viewer that the hospital is rundown and inefficient and then, without changing anything in the set itself, relight it to indicate that it is clean and highly professional. Which type of lighting would you use for the rundown hospital and which for the clean and efficient one?

Chiaroscuro is the most appropriate choice for the first assignment, and flat lighting for the second. Why? Because the many prominent shadow areas that stripe the corridor through chiaroscuro lighting inevitably provoke a response in the viewer that the hospital is so poor it cannot afford adequate lighting; it must be old because it obviously has too few windows that are also too small; it lacks adequate ventilation; it is likely to be untidy and dirty; it is a firetrap because we can't see where we are going; and the rest of the hospital, including its staff, must be just as antiquated.

Leonardo da Vinci preferred an overcast sky while painting. Under even, diffused light, the colors are less distorted than in bright sunlight with deep shadows. This is also why, traditionally, studio windows are oriented toward the north: the light inside remains more even throughout the day than if the studio were subjected to direct, changing sunlight.

One specific flat-lighting technique is sometimes called limbo. In *limbo* lighting, the background is evenly illuminated and the object in front of it is lighted with the standard photographic principle. Actually, limbo refers more specifically to a staging rather than a lighting technique. For example, if you are asked to set up a commercial display "in limbo," you need not light specifically for it. It simply means that you push the commercial display in front of a plain, neutral background (usually light colored) so that the emphasis is on the product and not on the environment.

With flat lighting, however, everything changes. Due to the profuse amount of shadowless illumination and the increased visibility, we are now inclined to feel that the corridor and so the entire hospital is clean and germ-free; nothing is hidden in dark corners; it has big windows and is therefore modern throughout; it is a place where we can easily find our way around; and its staff and doctors must be equally bright and efficient.

Silhouette Lighting

Silhouette lighting falls into neither the chiaroscuro nor the flat category, yet it has characteristics of both. It is chiaroscuro because of its extreme light/dark contrast, and it is flat because it emphasizes contour rather than volume and texture. So far as lighting technique is concerned, *silhouette lighting* is the exact opposite of cameo: in cameo we light the figure and not the background; in silhouette we light the background and not the figure.[5]

Obviously, you light only those scenes in silhouette that gain by emphasizing contour. A sharp, jagged jazz dance or ballet section, in which contour is of the essence, calls for silhouette lighting. **SEE 3.16** Romantic scenes take on a certain prominence when shown in silhouette. You can also use silhouette lighting to conceal a person's identity. If you're interviewing someone who has good reason to remain incognito, or you show a man cautiously sneaking into a house through the bedroom window, silhouette lighting would be an effective dramatic agent.

On the other hand, always be aware of unintentional silhouette effects. A field reporter positioned against a sun-drenched white wall will certainly be shown in an unflattering silhouette, especially if no reflector or additional lighting is used to offset the strong background light. A similar problem exists if you want to photograph someone on a sunny beach against the ocean. The water, reflecting the sunlight, acts like a giant background light, illuminating the background so much that the person standing on the beach looks underlighted and, for most camera positions, unlighted. To avoid such problems, you may want to shoot beach scenes on an overcast day (thus reducing the glare of the sea and the extreme contrast), shoot against the land rather than the water, or put the subjects in the diffused shade of a beach umbrella. If available, you may offset the silhouette effect by putting additional fill light on the subject with large reflectors or, in big production, with giant lighting instruments.

3.16 Silhouette Lighting

Notice that this lighting is the exact opposite of cameo. In silhouette lighting, the background is lighted and the figures in front remain unlighted. Silhouette lighting shows contour but no volume or texture. It emphasizes the outline of things.

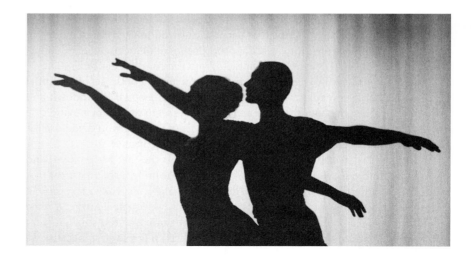

3.17 Overview of Chiaroscuro- and Flat-lighting Techniques

Type	Source, illumination area	Illumination level	Falloff, shadow distribution
Rembrandt	Spotlights with barn doors. Carefully placed background lights. Specific area lighting— selective illumination but fill light for making shadows transparent.	Low-key. Selectively illuminated figures. Illuminated yet generally dark background.	Fast falloff. Transparent shadows.
Cameo	Directional spots. Directional fill on subject. Back light. Dark background. Minimum of spill, especially on background.	Low-key. Illuminated figures only. Dark background.	Fast falloff. Dense shadows.
Flat	Highly diffused floodlights (scoops and softlights). Nonselective, omnidirectional illumination. Light is fairly evenly distributed.	High-key. Generally bright illumination with light background.	Slow falloff. Highly transparent shadows or no perceivable shadows.
Silhouette	Evenly lighted bright background (floodlights). No illumination on foreground figures.	High on background. No illumination on foreground figures.	No shadows, but figures appear as black, contoured cutouts.

The table above gives a brief overview of chiaroscuro- and flat-lighting techniques. **SEE 3.17** Bear in mind that this table represents only the most basic approaches to lighting aesthetics. These approaches do, however, lend themselves readily to a great number of modifications that may be required by various lighting assignments.

Media-enhanced and Media-generated Lighting

All photographic arts (still photography, film, and video) can enhance, change, or simulate lighting effects through manipulation by the medium. If you still use photographic film, you can affect colors or the brightness contrast through filters as well as in the processing phase. In digital photography and video, these variables can be manipulated with the camera controls, electronic enhancement equipment, and computer software. Video allows further electronic manipulation by viewers, who may adjust, or misadjust, the brightness, contrast, and color controls of their television sets.

For example, you can easily change the appearance of a chiaroscuro scene by turning down the contrast control and turning up the brightness control. You end up with a washed-out picture with the original lighting setup no longer recognizable. You can increase falloff by simply turning up the contrast control as high as it will go.

Most of the media-controlled lighting effects are achieved through digital special-effects equipment or computer programs. In computer-generated images, all lighting effects are synthetic and, like in painting, totally independent of actual external light and lighting techniques. Most computer graphics programs let you simulate light sources and their resulting attached and cast shadows. Because the shadows are independent of the light source, you can place the attached shadow anywhere on the object and create Escher-like paradoxes in which cast and attached shadows contradict each other in direction or relative to the virtual principal light source. Other computer programs offer a wide choice of special effects,

3.18 **Solarization**

A solarization effect occurs when the positive and negative images of the same subject are combined. The black lines indicate where the two images meet. It can imply an extreme heat or radiation effect.

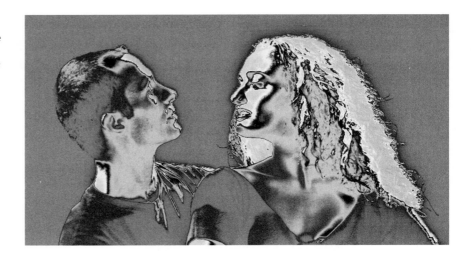

such as extremely fast falloff, flat lighting, spotlight effects (where one area of the picture is illuminated by the typical spotlight circle), *solarization* (by combining the positive and negative images of the same subject), and *posterization* (reducing the brightness values of an image to only a few steps).[6]

Some effects, such as solarization, not only show a lighting change but suggest a structural change as well. **SEE 3.18** Progressive solarization can express intense heat or some sort of radiation. To show someone dying—the ultimate structural change—you need no longer resort to the traditional graphic Hollywood versions of expiring heroes. You can show a close-up of the person and, through progressive solarization, disintegrate the structure of the image and, with it, the person. You should realize, however, that such powerful effects need to be applied with discretion. If used inappropriately, too frequently, or for too long, they can quickly turn against you and deflate rather than intensify the emotional impact of the scene.

Single- and Multicamera Lighting

Although basic lighting principles apply to all the photographic arts, certain operational differences exist between lighting for the single camera (such as film or single-camera video productions) and for multicamera video productions that sometimes influence, if not dictate, a particular lighting technique.

SINGLE-CAMERA LIGHTING

Single-camera lighting is also called film lighting or film-style lighting because it is most commonly used in film production. Lighting for single-camera productions is set up for discontinuous, short-duration action. In film and single-camera video productions, each scene, if not each shot, is lighted separately, and lighting control is extremely high. Because all movements of actors, cameras, microphones, and so forth are carefully planned in advance—a process known as blocking—the lighting instruments can be placed on the studio floor or on the floor of the remote location. Shadow control is improved by barn doors (metal flaps attached to the front of the lighting instrument) and by gobos and flags (small transparent or solid pieces of metal, plastic, or cloth panels) that are placed in front of the instrument to partially block its beam, preventing it from hitting certain areas.

MULTICAMERA LIGHTING

Lighting for multiple cameras that cover a scene simultaneously from a variety of angles is necessarily less precise. ***Multicamera lighting*** must satisfy the different points of view of the cameras as well as the continuous, long-duration action of performers in interviews, game shows, situation comedies, talk shows, or song-and-dance routines. To accommodate the continuous camera and people traffic, the lighting instruments must be suspended from the studio ceiling, with only a minimum of instruments on the floor. Because of the continuously shifting points of view, some instruments that function as key lights become fill lights, side lights, or even back lights.

The Aesthetic Edge: Unusual Lighting

Now that you have become an astute observer of lighting for photographic media, you've probably noticed that many films and dramatic television series use lighting techniques that seem to fly in the face of what you just learned to be the norm. For example, you may see a scene in which the characters are lighted only with extremely fast-falloff side lights rather than the traditional lighting triangle. **SEE 3.19** Or you may see a person turning the shadow side, rather than the key-lighted side, of his face toward the camera. **SEE 3.20** Sometimes one person may be silhouetted against a very bright background while talking to someone else. **SEE 3.21**

Didn't the LD (lighting director) and the DP (director of photography) know any better? Of course they did. They were giving the scene a creative edge, an added intensification through unusual lighting. They used the occasional "wrong" lighting to make you take notice or to emphasize the style of the show. But this doesn't mean you should excuse poor lighting as simply "an aesthetic edge." As with all other production techniques, you need to know and understand the rules before you have license to break them.

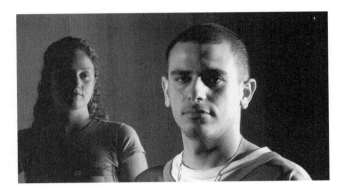

3.19 Harsh Side Light
Fast-falloff side lighting can be used to heighten or predict a dramatic situation.

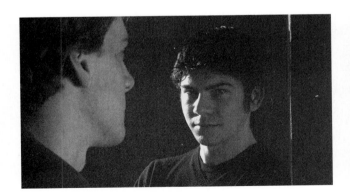

3.20 Shadow Side Toward Camera
You can intensify a dramatic scene by lighting faces so that their shadow sides, rather than their key-lighted sides, face the camera.

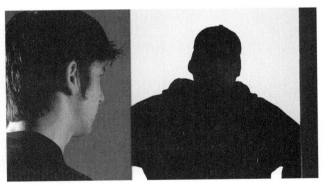

3.21 Partial Silhouette Lighting
An interesting lighting effect can be achieved by having a person appear partially, or temporarily, in silhouette.

SUMMARY

The photographic lighting principle, or triangle lighting, consists of a key light (principal light source), a fill light (opposite the camera from the key), and a back light (behind the subject).

The two principal lighting techniques are chiaroscuro and flat. Chiaroscuro lighting emphasizes contrasting light and shadow areas and has fast falloff. Flat lighting has slow falloff, and the shadows are highly transparent or simply not perceivable by the camera.

Both lighting types have specific functions. The major functions of chiaroscuro lighting are organic (to make the scene look realistic), directional (to lead the eye to specific picture areas), spatial/compositional (to define space and contribute to a balanced pictorial composition), thematic (to emphasize the theme or the story being told), and emotional (to establish or emphasize a mood). The major function of flat lighting is to provide optimal visibility, but it can also have thematic and emotional functions.

The specific chiaroscuro lighting techniques are Rembrandt and cameo. The characteristics of Rembrandt lighting are selectivity and fairly fast falloff. Cameo lighting illuminates only the subject, with the background remaining unlighted.

Flat lighting is highly diffused with extremely slow falloff. It is nonselective, and its light seems to come from all directions, rendering the attached shadows highly transparent or virtually invisible. Flat lighting is normally high-key, implying high energy, efficiency, and cleanliness but also mechanization and depersonalization.

Silhouette lighting is a hybrid of chiaroscuro and flat lighting. It shows unlighted figures against a bright, evenly illuminated background. The lighting makes the figures appear flat and dark but accentuates their contour.

Media-enhanced and media-generated lighting effects refer to the manipulation of the lighting by the medium itself. Media-enhanced effects include manipulations in the processing of photographic film or, in electronic images, with computer software. Computer-generated images can simulate a variety of lighting effects and create such special effects as extremely fast falloff, flat lighting, spotlight effects, solarization, and posterization.

Single-camera lighting for film and video (film-style) affords maximum control because each scene or shot is set up and lighted separately. Many television studio shows, however, require multicamera setups for continuous action. In this case, lighting is for overlapping action areas, a technique that decreases considerably the aesthetic control of lighting.

Sometimes unusual lighting is used as an intensification device—as an aesthetic edge.

N O T E S

1. Ross Lowell, *Matters of Light and Depth* (New York: Lowel-Light Manufacturing, 1999), pp. 66–69.

2. Herbert Zettl, *Television Production Handbook,* 10th ed. (Belmont, Calif.: Wadsworth, 2009), pp. 232–33.

3. See art books that have good reproductions of paintings by Rembrandt, Caravaggio, La Tour, and other chiaroscuro painters. You will find that these artists did not use a back-light effect. The back light was made prominent in photographic lighting techniques.

4. Zettl, *Television Production Handbook,* p. 89.

5. Zettl, *Television Production Handbook,* pp. 228–29.

6. For electronic and computer effects, see the latest user's guides to computer graphics programs, such as Adobe Photoshop. They give myriad examples of computer-generated lighting and color effects. To see how a computer program synchronizes virtual light sources with resulting shadows, look at the Lighting module of *Zettl's VideoLab 3.0* DVD-ROM (Belmont, Calif.: Wadsworth, 2004).

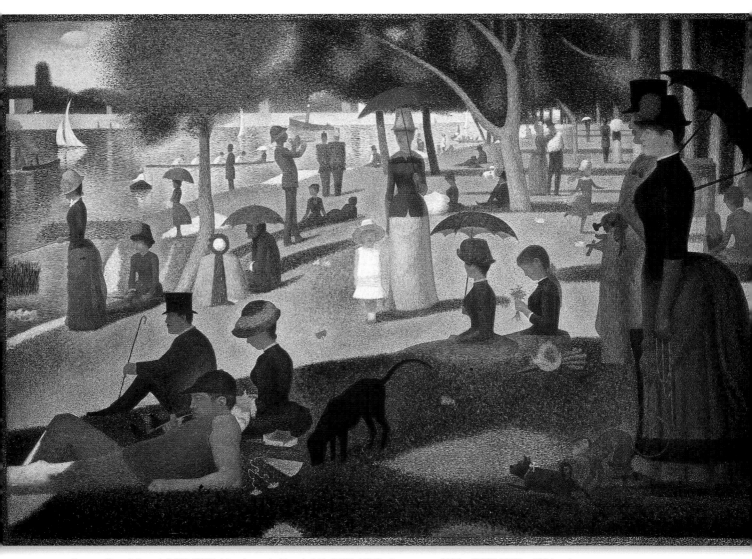

Georges Seurat, French (1859–1891) *A Sunday on La Grande Jatte* (1884–1886), oil on canvas, 81¾" × 121¼" (207.5 × 308.1 cm).
Helen Birch Bartlett Memorial Collection, 1926.224, Reproduction, The Art Institute of Chicago.

The Extended First Field:
Color

OLOR ADDS A NEW DIMENSION TO EVERYTHING. IT BRINGS EXCITEMENT and joy, makes us more aware of the world around us, and helps us organize our environment. A child likes to play with a red ball more than with a gray one. The colored lights at a rock concert push the high energy of the music even higher. In purchasing a car, many people feel that its color is as important as its performance. When we dress ourselves or decorate our living quarters, we make sure that the colors work together. We admire red tulips that stand out against the green of a lawn. We stop when the traffic light turns yellow or red—and we go on green. Every day, consciously or not, we make judgments based on color.

Although most of our daily activities are influenced by color, color perception has remained a challenging subject. We know that colors are generated by the wavelengths of the light spectrum and that red colors emit a longer wavelength than blue colors do. But simply measuring light frequencies will not necessarily tell us the colors we actually see. The reason for this is that colors are extremely relative. A color does not remain stable under all conditions but changes in different contexts. A particular blue, for example, looks darker or lighter depending on whether it is painted on a highly reflective surface, such as porcelain, or an absorbent one, such as cloth. The same blue will also look different depending on the other colors that surround it or on how much and what kind of light falls on it. Worse, you and I may perceive colors differently yet react to a certain color similarly because we have simply learned to do so.[1]

Despite this relativity of color, we have gathered enough working knowledge to describe and even predict how most of us will perceive and react to certain colors and color combinations. In this chapter we look at what color is, how we perceive color, how we mix color, the relativity of color, colors and feelings, and color energy.

What Is Color?

Color is the property of light, not of objects or liquids. We can see colors when our eyes receive light of a certain wavelength or, more realistically, a mixture of wavelengths that is reflected off objects or transmitted through fluids. When white light, such as the one emitting from a reading lamp or the sun, is divided by a prism, you see the familiar rainbow colors ranging from red to purple. These rainbow colors are called spectral colors because their wavelengths fall into the visible electromagnetic spectrum. Note that the waves of the visible spectrum are not colored; our visual perception mechanism simply translates them that way. **SEE COLOR PLATE 1**

How We Perceive Color

Before you can effectively use color in video and film production, or in the design of content for Internet streaming, you should acquaint yourself not only with the basic physiological processes of how we see color but also—and more so—with the factors that influence our aesthetic color perception.

BASIC PHYSIOLOGICAL FACTORS

The lens of the eye focuses light on the light-sensitive cells of the retina, which comprises a combination of cones and rods. Both cones and rods react to a light stimulus but in different ways. The cones need more light to fire than the rods do and are not equally receptive to all colors. One group of cones is more sensitive to the short waves that make up blue. A second group responds to the medium-length waves of green, and a third to the long waves of the red end of the spectrum. Because most colors we encounter are mixtures of various wavelengths, all three groups are in action in bright light. Each of the cones fires its own signal, which results in a high-resolution image of the colored object.

The rods do not respond equally across the color spectrum and are, for all practical purposes, colorblind. They jump into action when it gets dark. They help us see even when the cones give up for a lack of adequate light. This is why you don't see much color in dim moonlight but still see some things around you. Because some of the rods gang up under very low illumination to deliver a strong enough signal for the brain to process, we see a slightly fuzzier image than with the cones, which fire individually.

Before the brain can make us see color, or adapt our vision to a certain level of darkness, the cones and rods must send their signals to neurons (nerves), which process the signals and code them into simpler ones. This encoding process is similar to changing analog into digital signals to make them more robust (less borderline). Finally, these less ambiguous signals are sent to the brain to interpret—like a television receiver—the various signals as colors.[2] **SEE 4.1**

4.1 Color Perception

The object reflects parts of the light spectrum and absorbs the rest. The reflected light is focused by the lens of the eye onto the retina—the cones and the rods. The cones are for bright daylight vision and therefore also receive the reflected light that makes up the color. The rods help us see when the light is dim but are virtually colorblind. The combined signals are sent to the brain, which interprets it as a particular color or shades of gray.

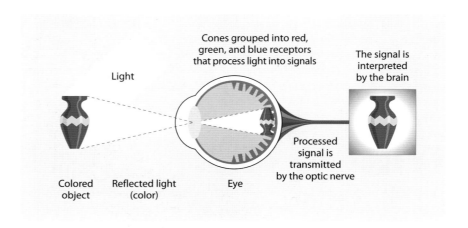

Light

Cones grouped into red, green, and blue receptors that process light into signals

The signal is interpreted by the brain

Colored object

Reflected light (color)

Eye

Processed signal is transmitted by the optic nerve

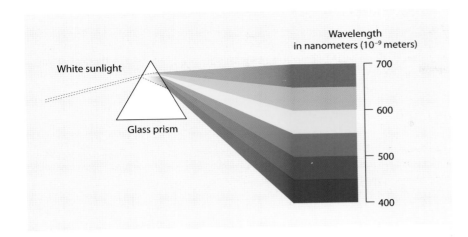

CP1 The Visible Spectrum

When we shine a beam of sunlight through a prism (diamonds or water drops create a similar effect), we see a series of colors ranging from red to violet. These rainbow colors are called spectral colors because their wavelengths fall into the visible electromagnetic spectrum. This means we can see them as rainbow colors.

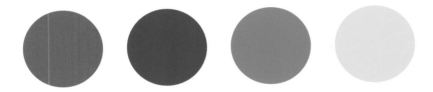

CP2 Hue

Hue describes the color itself. Red, blue, green, and yellow are color hues.

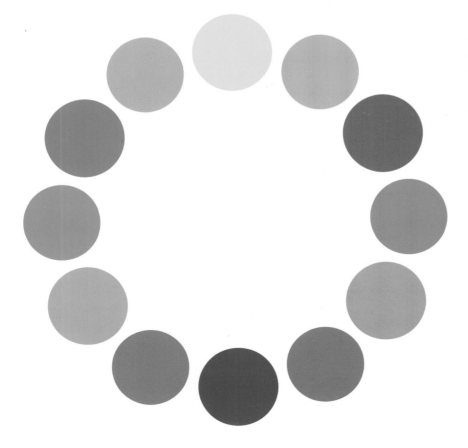

CP3 Hue Circle

The hue circle arranges the major hues in a circle (red, yellow, green, and blue) and how they change from one to the other. When moving counterclockwise, you can see how the reds change to yellow, to green, to blue, and back to red again.

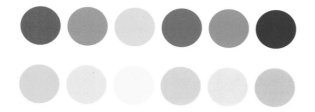

CP4 High and Low Saturation

Saturation describes the color richness. The colors in the first row are highly saturated; the colors in the second row are less saturated. Saturation is sometimes called chroma (Greek for "color"). This is why colors with a hue are called chromatic colors. White, gray, and black have no chroma (actual color saturation) and are therefore called *achromatic colors.*

CP5 Desaturation

When a color is desaturated with white light (or white pigment), it looks more washed out and gets lighter.

CP6 Maintaining Brightness During Desaturation

The upper strip shows the gradual desaturation of an orange hue by mixing in more and more of the same gray. When the strip is photographed in black-and-white, all degrees of saturation show the same gray. The desaturated hue does not get lighter or darker.

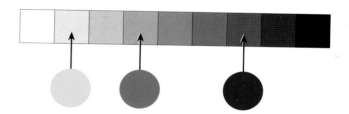

CP7 Brightness

Brightness, or value, indicates how light or dark a color appears in a black-and-white photograph. The brightness of a color depends on how much light it reflects. Black-and-white television produces images that vary in brightness only. Brightness is called lightness when it refers to how bright we *perceive* an object to be.

CP8 Color Models

All color models show a range of hues, saturation, and brightness.

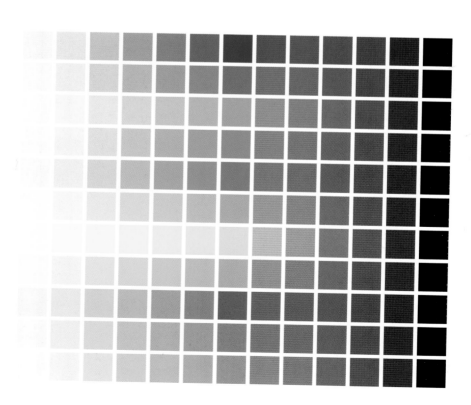

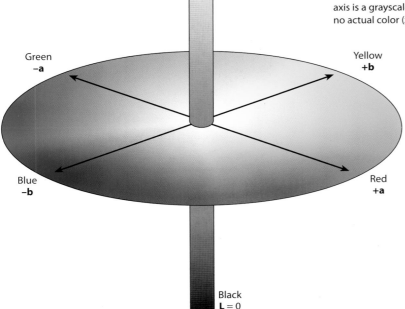

CP9 L*a*b Color Model

L*a*b color consists of a luminance or lightness component (*L*), which we call brightness, and two chromatic components: the *a* component (from green to red) and the *b* component (from blue to yellow). In this color model, the major hues are arranged in a circle. The farther away a color is from the achromatic axis, the more saturated it is. The model's axis is a grayscale (the brightness variations). Because a grayscale has no actual color (zero saturation), it is called the achromatic axis.

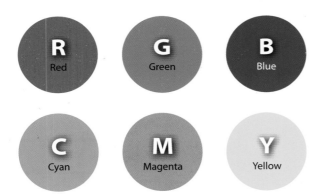

CP10 Additive and Subtractive Primary Colors

The additive (light) primaries are red, green, and blue (RGB).

The subtractive (paint) primaries are cyan, magenta, and yellow (CMY).

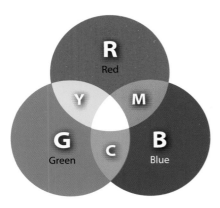

CP11 Additive Color Mixing

Imagine that these three light primaries are produced with three slide projectors containing a red, a green, and a blue slide. If you add green to the red light, you get yellow. If you add blue instead, you get magenta. If you add green and blue together, you get cyan. If you add all three light primaries together, you get white. If you turn all projectors off, obviously you get black. If you now put each projector on a separate dimmer, you can produce a great number of different hues by varying the light intensity of any—or all—of the projectors.

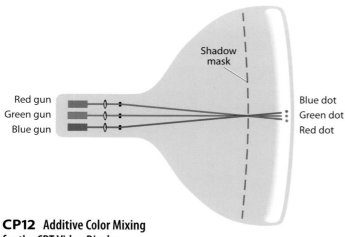

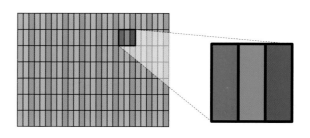

CP12   Additive Color Mixing for the CRT Video Display

The standard cathode ray tube color television receiver has three electron guns, each responsible for either the red, the green, or the blue signal. Each beam is assigned to either a red, green, or blue color pixel (color dot or rectangle).

CP13   Additive Color Mixing in Flat-panel Displays

Flat-panel video displays also use the RGB additive mixing principle but use no electron guns to activate the individual RGB pixels. The LCD screen has tiny shutters (liquid crystals) for each pixel that let a back light shine through or block it. The plasma panel operates similarly to a fluorescent light and activates the RGB pixels with an electrically charged gas. In all systems the RGB pixels don't mix but simply light up in various configurations.

CP14   Color Mixing in Pointillist Painting

Much like color mixing in video, the painting theory of the pointillists is based on our capacity to mix colors in the mind. Pointillists, such as French painter Georges Pierre Seurat, built their paintings and color schemes by juxtaposing thousands of individual dots, all consisting of a few basic colors of varying saturation. Seen from a distance, the color dots blend into a wide variety of rich hues.

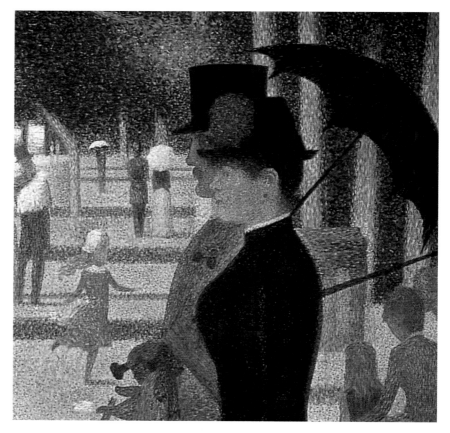

Detail. Georges Seurat, French (1859–1891) *A Sunday on La Grande Jatte* (1884–1886), oil on canvas, 81¾" × 121¼". (207.5 × 308.1 cm). Helen Birch Bartlett Memorial Collection, 1926.224, Reproduction, The Art Institute of Chicago.

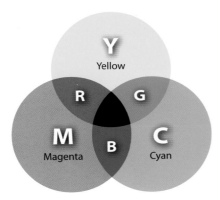

CP15 Subtractive Color Mixing

When all three subtractive primary filters overlap, we get black; they swallow one another's light until no light is passed. Note that where two subtractive colors overlap, they produce an additive primary.

CP16 Color Vibrations

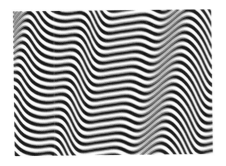

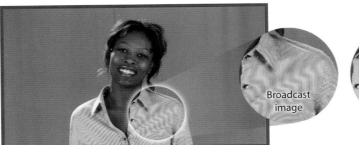

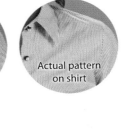

a When intended, color vibrations can provide an exciting visual experience. In video, however, they are often unintentional and undesirable. They happen when the video camera looks at narrow, highly contrasting patterns, such as thin stripes and checkered or herringbone designs.

b The narrow stripes on this actor's shirt create a highly colorful, albeit undesirable, moiré pattern.

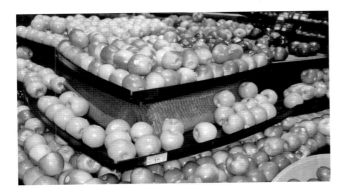

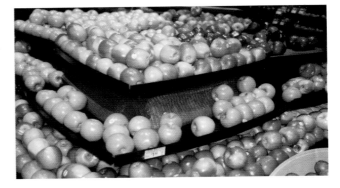

CP17 Informational Function of Color

Color tells us more about a scene; we simply get more information from a color picture than we do from a black-and-white one.

CP18 Identification by Color

The informational function of color is especially important when we have to identify and discriminate among things, such as the specific wires in a telephone cable. The color coding enables us to match the right wires at both ends of the cable.

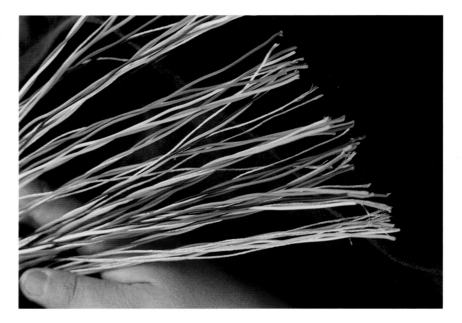

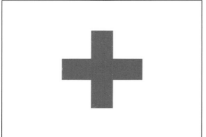

CP19 Color Symbolism

The Red Cross emblem is so widely known throughout the world that it has become an almost universal symbol.

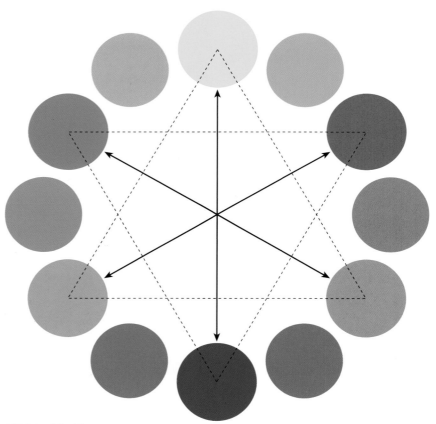

CP20 Color Harmony

Traditional, although not always accurate, rules suggest that colors harmonize best when they are close to each other on the hue circle, on opposite sides of it, or on the tips of an equilateral triangle superimposed on it.

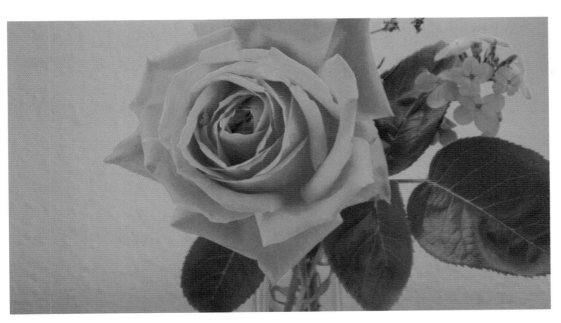

CP21 High- and Low-energy Color Distribution
One of the most effective ways of combining high- and low-energy colors is to set off a high-energy color against a low-energy background.

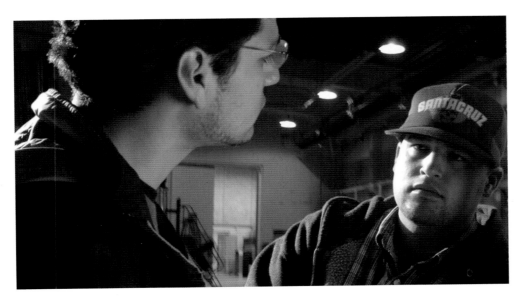

CP22 Color Distortion
The colors of this scene are purposely given a green tint, which, in concert with high-contrast lighting, heightens its dramatic impact.

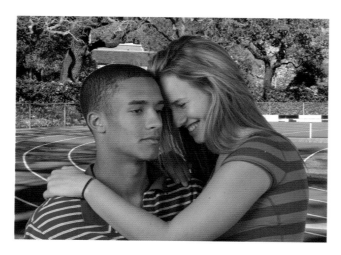

CP23 Normal Color Saturation

The normally saturated colors in this picture give us more information about the event but do not necessarily intensify it.

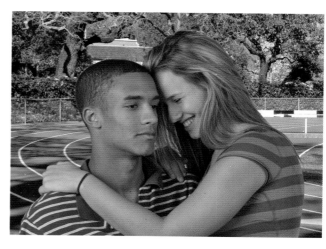

CP24 Desaturation of Colors

When the colors are desaturated, the scene becomes more low-definition and so more emotionally accessible. The desaturated colors do not prevent us from looking into the event.

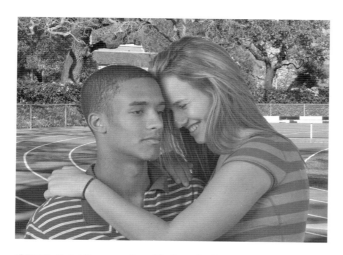

CP25 Total Desaturation: Black-and-white Image

We can achieve further low-definition by eliminating color altogether. In black-and-white the outer event often serves as an extension of the inner event.

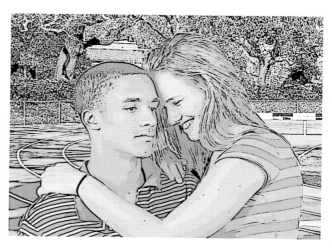

CP26 Low-definition Rendering

When the black-and-white image is further reduced in definition, we are not only permitted but often compelled to deal with an inner reality. Low-definition images force us to mentally fill in the missing parts and thereby become involved in the event.

Fortunately, in the context of the extended first field, we need not concern ourselves with the exact nature and processes of neural interaction that change light frequencies into colors. We can focus on the factors that influence our actual aesthetic perception of color and how to use it in our quest for the clarification, intensification, and interpretation of a mediated event.

BASIC AESTHETIC PERCEPTION FACTORS

When we look at colored objects, we can detect three basic color sensations: the color itself—red, green, or blue; the color strength—whether a red is deep and undiluted or looks faded and washed out; and how light or dark it appears to us. These three basic color sensations we call **color attributes**.[3]

Color attribute: hue   *Hue* describes the colors you see in the rainbow and all the variations among them. Hue helps you classify colors so that, when asked to buy red roses, you won't come home with yellow ones. Only the colors of the spectrum are pure hues. Most colors we see are impure, which means that they combine several wavelengths and are further modified by the degree to which they are washed out by white light or how light and dark they appear relative to white and black. Our whole color perception is based on only four hues: red, yellow, green, and blue. The color chips you see in a hardware or paint store give you some idea of the variety of possible hues. The many subtle colors that lie, for example, between red and purple or between blue and green, and all the color chips you see in a paint store, are part of the hue classification system. How these colors relate to one another and move from one hue to another is demonstrated by the *hue circle*.   **SEE COLOR PLATES 2 AND 3**

As you will learn later in this chapter, all the colors on a computer or television screen are created with only three hues: red, green, and blue, usually labeled **RGB**. So why does the computer ask you whether you would like to see hundreds, thousands, or even millions of colors? Even if you choose a million colors, the computer is not prepared to offer a palette that contains literally millions of hues; what "millions of colors" refers to is a mathematical process by which each pixel is generated and identified by a specific combination of hues, saturation, and brightness.[4] If you were to use a calculator to figure all the possible combinations of the three color attributes, you would get into the millions without trying very hard. Can you really see millions of colors? Yes and no. If the computer displayed any single one of these color combinations, you could recognize it and tell whether it was bluish, reddish, greenish, or yellowish, light or dark. But if some of these combinations were placed right next to each other, you would probably have a hard time distinguishing between two adjacent colors.

Color attribute: saturation   *Saturation*, sometimes called *chroma* (Greek for "color"), describes the relative strength or purity of a color. A highly saturated color looks rich; a color with low saturation looks washed out.   **SEE COLOR PLATE 4** Technically, saturation represents the amount of white light (or white, gray, or black paint) mixed into the hue. White, gray, and black have no chroma and are therefore called **achromatic**. When you hear of **chromatic** colors, you should think of colors with hue: blue, green, yellow, and so forth, whereas the achromatic "colors" are white, gray, and black. But in our everyday color terminology, we call white, gray, and black "color" much like red and blue.

When you use white to desaturate a particular color, such as a deep red, it turns progressively pink and lighter until all the color (red or pink) is gone and the resulting desaturated color is white. Obviously, the desaturated color moves up on

The various types of desaturation may have their own names. You may find that sometimes hue change through desaturation with white is called *tint;* with black, *shade;* and with its corresponding gray, *tone.*

the brightness scale. This means that a color that is desaturated with white light or paint will inevitably get lighter. When you desaturate the same color with black, the red changes to a maroon and eventually turns black. Because the desaturation agent is black, the original achromatic gray of the red color will move down on the brightness scale toward the black end. **SEE COLOR PLATE 5** If you were to desaturate the same color by mixing in more and more of a specific gray, however, the brightness value would not change. If you were now to photograph such a gradual desaturation with black-and-white film, the various stages of desaturation would show the same gray. **SEE COLOR PLATE 6**

Color attribute: brightness   Also called value, or lightness, **brightness** is how light or dark we perceive a color to be. There are actually two types of brightness. One measures the amount of light reflected off a colored surface. You use a light meter to get the reflected-light reading. If you were to measure the amount of light reflected off a bright yellow tablecloth in an outdoor lunch setting, you would get a high brightness reading. If you were to use the same tablecloth in a studio setting with a normal amount of illumination, say, 150 foot-candles (fc), it would reflect considerably less light. Consequently, the light meter would measure a much lower light level than in the outdoor scene. But would you now perceive the tablecloth as considerably darker than when you looked at it in the outdoor setting? Probably not. Most likely you would see the brightness of the tablecloth as still very high, especially when compared with the surrounding set. This condition of perceiving, rather than measuring, relative brightness is usually called **lightness**. You judge lightness with your eyes; you measure brightness with a light meter.

To avoid unnecessary confusion at this stage, we will stick with the term *brightness* as the name for the third color attribute, regardless of whether we are dealing with the actual amount of reflected light or our perception of it. What you should realize is that your subjective judgment of whether a color is too dark or too bright by looking at the video monitor is often more useful in lighting than relying solely on a light meter reading. **SEE COLOR PLATE 7**

GRAYSCALE

Black-and-white, or monochrome, video or film shows only achromatic colors, which are various steps of brightness. These steps are carefully charted by **grayscale** steps.[5] The more steps of gray there are between white and black, the more differentiated the various grays will be. This means we can see shadows not as uniformly dark but in various degrees of transparency. Similarly, the light areas will have more differentiated bright areas rather than "blooming" into a uniformly bright and overexposed white area.

The minimal brightness steps that a video camera and a monitor should be able to deliver are measured on a grayscale. In standard color video, we normally work with nine or 12 such brightness, or grayscale, steps, including television white (a little off-white) and television black (not pitch black). A good video camera is, of course, capable of delivering considerably more brightness steps, with a high-end high-definition television (HDTV) camera approaching those of film. The grayscale for each pixel in a typical computer graphics display has a range of 256, starting with black (brightness value 0), 254 shades of gray, and ending with white (brightness value 256).

COLOR MODELS

In an attempt to standardize the color attributes and show their basic interrelation, color theorists have devised **color models**. Although such models may differ in arrangement, they all present an array of hues and degrees of saturation and brightness.[6] **SEE COLOR PLATE 8**

Color models are especially helpful when dealing with computer programs for graphics or editing. The computer will undoubtedly ask you which kind of hue you intend to use and its specific degree of saturation and brightness. The model that shows most clearly the interrelationships among the three color attributes—hue, saturation, and brightness—has the hues arranged in a circle in their spectral, or rainbow, order. The central axis is the brightness scale, or achromatic axis with zero saturation, which is nothing more than a vertical grayscale. The degree of saturation is indicated by how far away the hue is from the center. The hue farthest from the center has the highest degree of saturation; it is, after all, farthest away from being diluted by the corresponding gray. The closer the hue moves to the achromatic axis, the grayer it gets, and when it reaches the achromatic axis, the color is completely desaturated. The color is now without hue.[7] **SEE COLOR PLATE 9**

COMPATIBLE COLOR

Technically, compatible color means that any color video signal must be encoded in such a way that it can be received and reproduced by a black-and-white television set. Aesthetically, it means that the colors used in a scene have enough brightness contrast that they will show up on the monochrome video screen as distinctly different shades of gray. If two contrasting, highly saturated hues, such as red and green, have the same brightness, they will photograph as the same gray. This means you wouldn't be able to distinguish between them in black-and-white video.

Why bother with compatibility when black-and-white video is practically extinct except for industrial use, and almost all movies are produced in color? Besides the compatibility just mentioned, there are several other reasons. First, the lightness and darkness elements give the picture its definition. As you recall it is the shadows that emphasize texture and provide an image with depth and the illusion of volume. Chiaroscuro painters often used subtle hues and equally subtle differences in saturation, yet they relied heavily on extreme variations in brightness. Second, a black-and-white rendering produces a higher-resolution picture than a color one. This is why you can focus more easily with a black-and-white viewfinder than with a color one. Third, as you will see later in this chapter, a monochrome scene has its very own aesthetic that is quite different from a colored one.

To ensure that a scene has colors with enough brightness difference, glance at it quickly while squinting. If the whole scene looks uniformly pale or dark, you need to use colors with greater brightness differences. If it looks contrasting, the compatibility is good.

How We Mix Color

You probably discovered during your finger-painting days that by mixing red and green paints, you got a dirty brownish color. Having graduated to the finer art of studio lighting, you may be surprised to find that by shining a red and a green light on the same target area you get an amazingly clear and bright yellow. This dramatic difference occurs because we are dealing with two separate and distinct color-mixing principles: additive and subtractive mixing.

Additive color mixing means shining, or adding, colored lights on top of each other. Subtractive color mixing means mixing paints or combining color filters to absorb, or subtract, certain color frequencies so that only a specific color is reflected back. Whether you work with additive or subtractive mixing, you need only three basic colors to produce a wide range of other colors. These basic colors are called the ***primaries***. **SEE COLOR PLATE 10**

ADDITIVE COLOR MIXING

The primaries for additive mixing are red, green, and blue, often referred to as additive primaries, light primaries, or simply RGB. In ***additive color mixing***, we aim red light, green light, and blue light at the same target area; by adding these three colored lights in various intensities, we can achieve a great variety of hues.

Additive mixing with colored light   Let's do some additive mixing by putting a red slide in one slide projector, a green slide in a second projector, and a blue one in a third and overlapping them partially on a screen. What colors will you get? **SEE COLOR PLATE 11** The red-green overlap produces a bright yellow; the red-blue overlap produces a bluish red, called magenta; and the blue-green overlap yields a greenish blue, called cyan. The spot where they all overlap looks white. If you now were to dim one or the other slide projector, you could produce a great variety of colors. Video and computers use the same additive-mixing principle: by generating the three primaries and displaying them on the screen in tightly spaced RGB clusters or tri-colored pixels, they can produce all the hues you see on the screen.

Additive mixing in video   Color television works on the same principle. The white light that enters the camera is split by mirrors or prisms into the three additive, or light, primaries: red, green, and blue. These three colors represent the three color signals that are processed and finally sent to the home receiver. Although almost all video is displayed on some kind of flat-panel screen, it is easier to explain additive mixing when using the old-fashioned CRT (cathode ray tube) of a standard television set. In such a television receiver, the RGB color signals activate three electron guns, each of which shoots its beam at its assigned color dots on the inside surface of the television screen. One beam is responsible for the red dots, another for the green dots, and another for the blue dots that line the inside of the screen.[8] **SEE COLOR PLATE 12** By changing the intensity of either or all of the beams, you can achieve the great variety of colors you see on the screen.

The three electron guns operate on the same principle as the three slide projectors. When the red and green guns fire and the blue one doesn't, you get yellow. When the red and blue guns fire but not the green one, you get magenta. When the blue and green guns fire but not the red one, you get cyan. The black-and-white images on a color video screen are actually produced by the red, green, and blue electron guns all firing in unison at equally varying intensities. When all three guns fire at maximum strength, you perceive white; when they don't fire at all, you perceive black. When they fire at only half power, you see a middle gray.[9] Although the flat-panel displays for video and computers work on different display principles, they too use RGB color primaries for additive mixing.

Note that no actual additive mixing (shining one colored light on top of another) takes place on the video screen. The video screen simply displays the three pure additive primaries side-by-side. Because the RGB pixels or clusters of colored dots are very small and lie close together, you need to be only a short distance away from the screen to have them mix into various wavelengths that our eye/brain mechanisms readily translate into colors. On some color video screens, you can actually see the RGB dot clusters by looking through a magnifying glass. **SEE COLOR PLATE 13** This experiment works best while watching a black-and-white television program during which, as you have just learned, all three RGB primaries are activated together at equal intensities. Whereas you see the individual color dots in the magnified section, the non-magnified dots seem farther away and, therefore, appear already mixed into various grays.

The color mixing in paintings of the pointillists is based on the same principle. Rather than mix paint into various hues (as in subtractive mixing) before putting them on the canvas, the pointillists painted thousands of discrete dots, all consisting of a few basic hues. Seen from a distance, the pure hues blend into each other very much like the colors on the video screen. **SEE COLOR PLATE 14**

Complementary colors   You may have heard of complementary light colors that eliminate each other when mixed additively. For example, if you were to additively mix a blue light with a yellow light, you would not get the customary green as you would when mixing paint; you would get *white* light. And, as you have just learned, you also get white when mixing red, green, and blue lights. In effect, when complementary colors are mixed additively, they eliminate their hue. All three types of cones (the receptors in the eye for long, medium, and short light waves) are stimulated in the same way. When they all fire simultaneously at equal intensity, the brain interprets this as white. Yes, as you just read, a similar process occurs when the three RGB electron guns in a video receiver fire their electron beams with equal intensity. What you perceive is a white screen. Color models normally show complementary colors on opposite sides of the hue circle (see color plate 3).

SUBTRACTIVE COLOR MIXING

Now your finger-painting experience applies. When mixing paint you are engaged in subtractive color mixing. Why? Because the paints, when mixed, filter each other out; in fact, each paint has built-in color filters that block any other frequencies (hues) from reaching your eye except the one whose hue you see. While we may be very happy with a red ball, the ball might not be so happy: the color it bears is the very one that the ball rejected and reflected back to your eyes.

Technically, *subtractive color mixing* involves filtering out, or subtracting, from white light all colors except the one it displays. If you want red, use a filter that prevents all other colors from reaching the eye except red. The red ball has such a filter built-in; so has red paint. Blue paint subtracts from the total light spectrum (white) everything except blue, which it reflects back. By combining two or more such filters (or by mixing paint), you can again achieve a wide variety of hues. A painter's palette is ample proof of such color variations.

Instead of the red, green, and blue colors that are the primaries for additive mixing, you now need the red-absorbing cyan (bluish green), the green-absorbing magenta (bluish red), and the blue-absorbing yellow. As you know, inkjet printers use the three subtractive primaries (CMY) to create their colors. They add black for brightness variations and to achieve higher picture definition. In color photography (including film), these primary colors are created by filters in the film that subtract the unwanted colors and transmit the colors as seen by the lens. Most painters call these subtractive primaries blue (for cyan), red (for magenta), and yellow.

When mixing subtractive primaries, you get the additive primaries: by overlapping magenta and yellow filters, you get red; cyan and yellow make green; and cyan and magenta mix into blue. **SEE COLOR PLATE 15** When you combine all three subtractive primaries, you get black. Instead of adding various light frequencies, as in additive mixing, the three filters now prevent one another's colors from passing.

MIXED MIXING

When lighting a set with colored lights (instruments that have color filters attached to them to produce a colored light), you may encounter additive *and* subtractive color mixing. When you shine red and green lights on a white or off-white background, you get yellow. But what would happen if you shone a red light on a green apple? Would the apple turn yellow? No, the apple would look nearly black. Why? Because the red light contains no green, the apple has nothing to reflect back. All but a few stray frequencies are absorbed by the apple. If all frequencies were absorbed, the apple would indeed look black.

What would happen if an actor wore a yellow dress in a romantic scene that uses bluish light to simulate moonlight? Would her dress turn green? No, the dress would take on a gray color—similar to what you would see in actual moonlight. In this case, the blue filters in the lights absorb most of the yellow light; little or no yellow is reflected back from the dress. Contrary to the apple example, this gray/yellow effect is desirable in the moonlit scene.

This mixed-mixing effect of color filters comes in handy for controlling brightness in black-and-white photography. For example, if you want to have a light blue, such as the sky, come out a relatively dark gray (low end of the brightness scale) in the black-and-white print, when taking the picture use a filter that blocks some of the blue light. A medium yellow filter would do the trick. Similarly, a light-green filter will make reddish skin tones appear as a slightly dark, suntan-like gray. The following table gives an overview of the most common color filters in black-and-white photography. **SEE 4.2**

Relativity of Color

As helpful as the theoretical color models are for standardizing the appearance of color and making it more manageable in video and film, they cannot account for all the variables that could influence our color perception. One and the same red may look lighter or darker, purple or even black, bright or dull, strong or weak, depending on what kind of light or how much light falls on it, on what colors surround it, and even on whether we know what kind of red it should be. Of the many factors that influence how we perceive colors, the six most relevant are light environment, surface reflectance, color temperature, surrounding colors, color juxtaposition, and color constancy.

LIGHT ENVIRONMENT

Colors change depending on how much and what kind of light falls on the object or scene.

Minimum amount of light   Because color is basically filtered and reflected light, we need to ensure a certain amount of light so that some of it can be reflected by the object after partial absorption. With adequate light a colored object can reflect enough of the rejected light so that we can see its actual color. But when we gradually reduce illumination, these objects reflect less and less light, and the colors begin to lose their hue. Like the baselight requirement of the video camera or film, objects also have a minimum illumination requirement to show their true colors. A full moon, for example, may emit enough light so that you can distinguish between objects or even read a newspaper, but there is simply not enough light to reflect back the actual colors of illuminated objects. A moonlit scene is therefore

4.2 Color Filters for Black-and-white Photography

Scene	Effect	Filter
Sky and clouds	Heightened cloud effect, yet natural	Medium yellow
	Dark sky, white clouds	Orange
	Very dark sky, very bright white clouds; dramatic	Red
	Extreme contrast: black sky, brilliant white clouds; special effect (night scene)	Dark red
Fog (landscape)	Foreground pieces appear quite dark; silhouette against soft, light-gray background	Blue
Haze (landscape)	Reduces atmospheric haze	Medium yellow
Flowers and grass (colorful landscape)	More contrast between flowers and grass; bright flowers against dark grass	Medium yellow
Snow	Heightened contrast between light and dark (accentuates ridges)	Medium yellow
	Exaggerated contrast (ski goggles are usually medium yellow or orange to accentuate for the skier imperfections in the snow)	Orange
People (portraits)		
Outdoors	Accentuated skin tones but natural looking	Light green
Indoors	Suntan	Light green
	Light yet accentuated skin tones	Medium yellow

strangely colorless. Why then do we see so much bluish light used when simulating a moonlit scene? One is convention. Rather than show drab grays, a bluish tone simply looks better. Another, more scientific explanation is that moonlight is, after all, reflected sunlight. As such it contains a fair amount of the original bluishness—the high color temperature—of sunlight. (We explain color temperature later in this section.)[10] Still another justification is that in the relatively dark moonlight, our eyes must shift from the color receptors (cones), which can easily handle the longer, reddish frequencies of bright light, to the brightness receptors (rods), which are more sensitive to the short, bluish frequencies of dim light.[11] Despite the low light level, however, a moonlight scene still has fast falloff. Besides the bluish tint, you need to use chiaroscuro lighting when simulating moonlight in the studio.

Too much light   Too much light can distort colors just as much as too little can. When you flood a colored object with light, it no longer reflects back only the rejected light frequencies, which make up its color, but also most of the white light that falls on it. Consequently, all that the camera picks up is an overabundance of light that it translates into an extremely bright spot with little or no hue or picture detail. This blooming effect occurs frequently when shooting in bright sunlight without a brightness-reducing neutral density (ND) filter.

SURFACE REFLECTANCE

Whether a colored object reflects too much or too little light depends partly on the amount of light that falls on it but primarily on how much light the surface of the object reflects. A mirror reflects almost all the light that falls on it, whereas a velvet cloth absorbs most of it. This means you need much less light to bring out the colors of a polished object than those of an object with a more textured, light-absorbing surface. If, for example, you stand too close to a blue chroma-key backdrop, a white shirt or a starched cotton blouse will inevitably pick up the reflection and turn bluish. You may not see this color change, but the camera will surely pick it up. To counteract this reflection, you can place a yellow or amber gel in front of the back light. As you recall, the yellow light will mix with the blue reflection into a harmless gray. When using a green chroma-key backdrop, you need a bluish-red light to eliminate such a reflection. In this case, a magenta rather than a yellow filter for the back light will do the job.

COLOR TEMPERATURE

Our color perceptions are also influenced by the kind of light under which we experience them. Although we speak of "white light," no light we ordinarily see is pure white. Some so-called white light has a reddish tinge; other white light is bluish. Even the "white" sunlight changes color. At midday sunlight has an extremely bluish tinge; during sunrise or sunset, it is much more reddish. This relative reddishness or bluishness of white light is measured by *color temperature* in Kelvin degrees (usually expressed as *K* in lighting lingo).[12]

The more bluish the light, the higher the color temperature; the more reddish the light, the lower the color temperature. The ordinary tungsten light bulb in your home has a more reddish white light and therefore a lower K value than does normal fluorescent lighting. Note that color temperature has nothing to do with physical temperature—how hot or cool the light bulb or fluorescent tube feels. The fluorescent tube may feel much cooler than the ordinary incandescent lamp, but bluish fluorescent light still has a higher color temperature than an ordinary incandescent lamp. For indoor lighting the standard is 3,200K; for the more bluish outdoor lighting, the standard is the higher 5,600K.

Because these variations in white light show up prominently as reddish (low K) or bluish (high K) white, you need to adjust the video camera so that the video display of a white card or shirt looks, indeed, white. This is done by white-balancing the camera. During such a *white balance*, the three primary color

The color temperature standard for indoor lighting is 3,200K, and the standard for outdoors is 5,600K. Through excessive dimming of both types of instruments, the color temperature is lowered and skin colors turn reddish. On a clear, sunny day, the color temperature of outdoor light can be much too high (bluish) for the video camera's electronic white-balance circuits to handle. In this case, you must use the color filters on the camera's filter wheel to lower the color temperature to the 5,600K norm. You can use indoor lights outdoors, but you must raise the 3,200K light to the 5,600K standard. You do this by attaching a light-blue gel (sheet of colored plastic) in front of the instrument, by using a dichroic filter, or by using lamps that have the outdoor (5,600K) rating.

channels (red, green, and blue) are balanced against one another so that, when combined, they produce the white of the actual object regardless of the K value of the illumination.[13] Film stock has these color corrections built-in. Because outdoor light usually has a much higher color temperature than indoor light, outdoor film has a reddish filter to compensate for the bluishness of outdoor light; indoor film has a bluish filter that compensates for the reddish indoor light. If you use an outdoor film with indoor illumination, the pictures will have a noticeable reddish tinge; if you shoot outside with indoor film, the scene is bound to be washed in blue. When using colored lights to intentionally distort colors, as in a musical number or crime scene, you need to white-balance for normal illumination; otherwise a light color palette will look surprisingly distorted.

SURROUNDING COLORS

The way we perceive a color is also greatly influenced by the surrounding colors. Sometimes, if a color is set off against a dark background, it looks lighter than its real brightness value. The same color may practically disappear in front of a similarly colored background. Sometimes the foreground color may take on the tinge of the background color.

Similar colors It seems obvious that when you use the same color for the foreground object as for the background, you will have a hard time seeing the object. Such problems can arise in routine television shows, however, where you may have no control over what a guest wears. If, for example, a guest wears a suit of the same beige color as the background of the interview set, you may experience some difficulty even with high-quality cameras. One of the quickest solutions to such problems is to reduce the intensity of the background (set) lights and increase the intensity of the back lights. The reduction of the background light will lower the background brightness and increase the contrast between foreground and background; the back lights will rim the foreground people or objects and further separate background and foreground.

Wearing blue in front of a blue backdrop for chroma keying or any other blue-screen process has even more dire consequences. During the key all blue areas—including the blue dress, suit, or tie—are replaced by the background image being keyed, such as a weather map. You may see only the hands and the face of the talent moving mysteriously in front of the map. The same is true when green is used for the chroma-key backdrop and you wear a green outfit. As hilarious as such unintentional visual effects may be, they do reduce the effectiveness of communication.[14]

Contrast As stated earlier, similarity of hue and brightness between foreground and background leads to poor pictures; so does too much contrast between foreground and background. Putting a highly reflecting bright object in front of a black or dark-blue background may result in a contrast that exceeds the technical capabilities of the video camera, thereby either overexposing the light areas or making the shadows uniformly dark and dense. The more brightness steps a camera and the display system can deliver, the better the picture will look. The subtle differences in brightness contribute significantly to the so-called film look. This should not prevent you from lighting a dramatic scene with very fast falloff, however, even at the risk of making the attached shadows dense or causing some color distortion.

COLOR JUXTAPOSITION

When juxtaposing highly saturated complementary colors, such as red and green, in a single graphic rendering or a static camera shot, you run the risk of causing "color vibrations." Somehow the two colors seem to compete for attention, pushing the opposite hue to a point of becoming an artifact, an undesirable color distortion.

Similar color vibrations are caused by narrow, highly contrasting patterns, such as a thinly striped black-and-white dress or a herringbone jacket. These artifacts are called *moiré effects;* they are caused when the scanning frequency competes with the light/dark contrast of the pattern.

Some painters—Isia Leviant, for example—create designs to deliberately generate such vibrations and an impression of movement.[15] But when they occur on scenery or the performer's clothing, such moiré effects are highly undesirable. **SEE COLOR PLATE 16** Sometimes such vibration effects can bleed through the entire picture. Unless you want to create these effects intentionally, in a dance number for instance, beware of thinly striped scenery or drapery, and tell performers to avoid clothes with highly contrasting patterns.

BRIGHTNESS AND COLOR CONSTANCY

Just for a moment, move this book from the light into a shaded area. Do you still see black letters on a white page? Of course you do. But if you were now to measure the actual brightness of the white page, it would be considerably less than when the book was in the light. Your mental operating system tried to stabilize the situation as much as possible and made you perceive the white as white and the black as black regardless of the actual amount of light reflected. This stabilization by your brain is called *brightness constancy* or lightness constancy.

Now take a yellow pencil and move it from the light into the shade. Is it still the same yellow as before? Yes, it is; at least it *appears* to be the same yellow. If you were now to do an accurate painting of the pencil, you would probably be surprised at how much the yellows differ from each other, although in the finished painting the pencil appears again to be of uniform color. Why? As mentioned previously, your perception is guided not only by what you actually see (the retinal stimulus) but also by your mental operating system, which tries to stabilize the environment as much as possible and have you perceive a uniform yellow regardless of the variations of the actual colors the pencil reflects. In the case of color, such stabilization is called *color constancy*.

Unfortunately, the color camera (video or film) knows nothing about color constancy and mental operating systems. Through close-ups it can readily divorce an object from its context and record the colors it actually sees. If you were now to take a close-up of the pencil and pan the camera from the lighted portion to the shadow portion, the color camera would faithfully reproduce the differences in brightness and hue. The same problem occurs when you follow a football player running from a sun-flooded part of the field into a dense shadow area. Unless you work with high-end cameras, the player's red jersey might turn dark purple and leave a red trail in the shadow areas. You perceive a white shirt as white even if part of it reflects the bluish light streaming through a window and another part reflects the orange tint of the low color temperature of an indoor fill light. But because the camera makes no such perceptual adjustments, it faithfully shows a bluish shirt on the window side and an orange-tinted shirt on the fill-light side.

You can avoid most color constancy problems by having all your lighting instruments operate with the same color temperature and all cameras properly white-balanced.

Colors and Feelings

Colors, or particular color groups, seem to influence our perceptions and emotions in specific ways. Certain colors seem warmer than others; some appear closer or more distant. A baby is apt to overreach a blue ball because it seems farther away than it really is, and underreach a red ball because it seems closer. A box painted with a warm color seems heavier than the same-weight box painted a cooler color. In a room bathed in red light, we seem to feel that time moves more slowly; in one illuminated by cooler light, time seems to go a little faster. Some colors seem high-energy and excite us; others seem low-energy and calm us down.

Although consistency in such observations is commonplace, we still don't have enough hard scientific data to permit valid and reliable correlations or generalizations. The problem with such perceptual effects is that they are contextual—they rarely if ever occur in isolation; instead they usually operate in the context of other aesthetic variables. Also, these color effects seem to show up best in a positively predisposed context, that is, in a field in which most other elements display similar tendencies.

WARM AND COLD COLORS

It is generally assumed that red is warm and blue is cold. Thus we have a tendency to consider warm all colors of the red (long wave) end of the spectrum and consider cold all colors of the blue (shorter wave) end. This generalization, however, is inaccurate. We experience certain blues as warm, and some reds seem rather cold.

Rudolf Arnheim, perception psychologist and art theorist (1904–2007), suggests that it is not the main color that determines the warm/cold effect but rather the color of the slight deviation from the main hue. Thus a reddish blue looks warm and a bluish red seems cold.[16] You can most readily see the relative warmth or coldness of a single color by looking at different yellows. Cold yellows have a definite bluish tint; warm yellows, a more orange one.

Warm reds and other warm colors seem to produce more excitement than cold blues or other cold colors. Assuming similar degrees of saturation and brightness, warm colors seem more active than cold colors. Highly saturated warm colors can make us feel "up," whereas cold colors of less saturation can dampen our mood so we feel "down." The traditional green room of a theater is supposed to make us feel calm and relaxed. The intense reds of some nightclubs and the yellows and oranges of fast-food restaurants are meant to produce the opposite effect.

Note that the psychological property of color, which we call warm and cold, has nothing to do with color temperature—the relative reddishness and bluishness of white light—but rather with whether a color has a reddish tint (warm) or a bluish tint (cold).

Color Energy

Color energy is the relative aesthetic impact a color has on us. A color's energy depends on its hue, saturation, and brightness attributes; the size of the color area; and the relative contrast between foreground and background colors.

When looking at hues, warm colors usually have more energy than cold ones. Colors that show up high on the brightness scale, such as a bright yellow, have higher energy than those low on the brightness scale, such as a dull brown.

4.3 Aesthetic Energy of Colors

Attribute	Variable	Energy
Hue	Warm	High
	Cold	Low
Brightness	High	High
	Low	Low
Saturation (major attribute)	High	High
	Low	Low
Area	Large	High
	Small	Low
Contrast	High	High
	Low	Low

It is the saturation of a color that especially contributes to its energy. When equal in saturation, a warm red obviously has more impact on us than a cold blue. But if the red is desaturated, the saturated cold blue becomes the more energetic color. In general, high saturation means high energy, and low saturation means low energy.

As for color area, large areas usually carry more energy than small ones. This assumes, however, that they are of similar saturation. A large field of red on a computer screen is "louder" and commands more attention than a small red dot.

Colors have more energy when set off against a background of contrasting brightness than against a background of similar brightness. A bright yellow has more energy against a dark-purple background than against a white one. Even achromatic (no saturation) white and black can have high energy, especially if set off against contrasting backgrounds.

High-energy colors are more active than low-energy colors. For instance, the high-energy red of a sports car seems to fit our concept of power and speed, and a red ball promises more fun than a white one. Apparently, we are quite willing to associate the relative color energy with a product that displays the particular hue. **SEE 4.3**

The advantage of translating colors into **aesthetic energy** is that you can integrate the effects of color more readily with other aesthetic elements, which, when working in concert, can produce a variety of overall emotional effects. Best of all, this knowledge allows you to generate color composition in moving images. Such applications of color energies are explored more thoroughly in chapter 5.

SUMMARY

Colors are generated by specific waves from the visible light spectrum. When white light (sunlight) is divided by a prism, we see the spectral, or rainbow, colors ranging from red to violet. Objects do not possess color; they merely reflect back the colored light frequencies they are unable to absorb. Liquids filter out certain frequencies and transmit them as a color.

The basic physiological factors of color perception are that our eyes pick up the light reflected off an object and focus this on the retina. The retina consists of cones and rods. Cones need a fair amount of light to encode the various wavelengths (short, medium, and long) into a color signal. The rods are virtually color blind but spring into action when the light gets dim. The signals from both cones and rods are then transmitted to the brain, where they are decoded into color sensations.

The basic aesthetic perception factors include three major attributes (sensations) of color as well as compatible colors. The three attributes of color are hue, saturation, and brightness. Hue describes the color itself, for example, whether an object is red, blue, yellow, or green. Saturation describes the color richness or strength. A deep, rich blue is highly saturated; the same hue that looks washed out has a low saturation. Brightness indicates the amount of reflected light, or how light or dark a color would appear in a black-and-white photograph. Brightness is measured with the grayscale. Lightness is how we perceive relative light and dark differences. The interrelation of these three color attributes is standardized in a variety of color models.

In media aesthetics, color compatibility means that the various colors in a scene have enough brightness contrast so that they will show up on a monochrome video screen as distinct shades of gray.

We can mix colors additively or subtractively. Additive mixing refers to the adding of the three light primaries (colored light): red, green, and blue (RGB). Video and computer displays work on the additive-mixing principle, whereby pixels can emit one of the three additive light primaries of various brightness. Our optical system mixes these primaries into various colors.

Subtractive mixing refers to filtering certain light frequencies from the light that falls on an object. The object absorbs—filters out—all frequencies except the one that produces the color you see on the object. The three primary filters are cyan (greenish blue), magenta (bluish red), and yellow. When all these filters overlap, they absorb one another's light (frequencies) and therefore produce black. Paints and photographic film work on the subtractive mixing principle.

Colors are relative, that is, we perceive the same color differently under various conditions. The six most relevant factors that influence how we perceive colors are light environment, surface reflectance, color temperature, surrounding colors, color juxtaposition, and brightness and color constancy.

If there is too little light, an object will not reflect back the true colors. When the environment has too much light, the colors look washed out. Highly reflective objects need less light for proper color renditions than highly light-absorbent objects.

Colors change depending on color temperature—the relative reddishness or bluishness of white light. Normal indoor light is reddish and therefore has a relatively low color temperature. Outdoor light and normal fluorescent lighting have a bluish tint and therefore a relatively high color temperature.

If a color is surrounded by a similar color, it loses its prominence. All color pictures should have enough brightness contrast to show up well even on a black-and-white monitor.

Color vibrations are caused by juxtaposing highly saturated complementary colors (usually colors that lie opposite on the hue circle) and narrow-striped, highly contrasting patterns. Such patterns may cause a moiré effect, which shows up on the video screen as pulsating color vibrations.

Brightness, or lightness, constancy means that once we have established which is white or black, we perceive white or black even if the white measures less reflectance than the black.

Color constancy means that we perceive an object as uniformly colored even if part of the object is shaded, greatly influencing its hue and brightness. When the object is isolated from its context, the camera will faithfully display the color differences and make us disengage our aptitude for perceptual color constancy.

Colors can influence our feelings in specific ways. We perceive some colors as warm, others as cold. The relative warmth or coldness of a color is a function not so much of its main hue (such as red or blue) but of the secondary hue that is mixed into the main color. For example, we tend to perceive a bluish red as cold and a reddish blue as warm.

Color energy refers to the relative aesthetic impact a color has on us. The energy depends on the hue, saturation, brightness, size of the color area, and contrast between foreground and background. Of these variables, saturation is the most influential in determining color energy.

N O T E S

1. George Mather, *Foundations of Perception* (Hove and New York: Psychology Press, 2006), pp. 332–37. See also Bruce E. Goldstein, *Sensation and Perception*, 8th ed. (Belmont, Calif.: Wadsworth, 2010), pp. 217–20.

2. The picture resolution of rods and cones is just the opposite from what you may know about camera viewfinders. Black-and-white viewfinders produce usually a sharper image than the foldout color monitor panels. See Herbert Zettl, *Video Basics 6* (Boston: Wadsworth, 2010), p. 60.

3. Goldstein, *Sensation and Perception*, pp. 203-26. See also the classic book on color theory by Ralph Evans, *The Perception of Color* (New York: John Wiley and Sons, 1974). He distinguishes among five color attributes: hue, saturation, brightness, lightness, and brilliance (p. 94).

4. In computer graphics programs, this combination of hue, saturation, and brightness values determines color, or pixel, depth. It measures the fidelity of color for each pixel. The normal range of color information in computer displays is from 1 to 24 bits per pixel. A color depth of 1 bit has 2 levels of information: black and white. A color depth of 8 bits has 8 levels of color information, which translates into 2^8, or 256 color values per pixel. A color depth of 24 has 2^{24}, which amounts to 16,777,216 color values per pixel.

5. Herbert Zettl, *Television Production Handbook*, 10th ed. (Belmont, Calif.: Wadsworth, 2009), pp. 301–2.

6. One of the popular early but enduring color models was devised by American painter Albert H. Munsell (1858–1918). It is appropriately called the Munsell color system. Twenty basic hues make up the hue circle. The brightness axis (which he called the value axis) is divided into nine steps, ranging from black to white. The saturation is uneven, depending on how much the basic hue can be saturated. The individual hue branches are numbered, as are the brightness steps and the saturation squares. Thus the appearance of a color can be specified precisely; a 5Y 8/10 means a fairly warm yellow, rather light (almost to the top of the brightness scale), and highly saturated (12 steps away from the brightness axis). For a good reproduction of the Munsell model, see Conrad Mueller and Mae Rudolph (eds.), *Light and Vision* (New York: Time-Life Books, 1966), pp. 116–17. For other color models, see *www.handprint.com/HP/WCL/color7.html* and *http://javaboutique.internet.com/ColorFinder*.

7. The L*a*b model was adopted from the Munsell arrangement of the three color attributes by the CIE (Commission Internationale d'Eclairage). See color plate 9.

8. Zettl, *Video Basics 6*, pp. 37–38.

9. You can do your own RGB channel mixing with the interactive CD-ROM *Virtual Lab* by Bruce Goldstein, chapter 9: "Perceiving Color." This CD is part of his *Sensation and Perception,* 8th ed.

10. Zettl, *Television Production Handbook,* pp. 217–18.

11. This change is generally known as the *Purkinje shift.* See "The Purkinje Shift" in Mather, *Foundations of Perception,* pp. 215–16. See also Gerald Millerson, *The Technique of Lighting for Television and Film,* 3rd ed. (Boston and London: Focal Press, 1991), pp. 261–65; see moonlight rod shift.

12. Zettl, *Television Production Handbook,* pp. 217–18.

13. Zettl, *Television Production Handbook,* pp. 81–82.

14. Zettl, *Television Production Handbook,* pp. 284–86.

15. Study some of the more widely reproduced paintings by Bridget Riley and Isia Leviant. You will find reproductions in books on kinetic or optical art, a mathematically themed form of abstract art.

16. Rudolf Arnheim, *Art and Visual Perception: A Psychology of the Creative Eye, The New Version* (Berkeley: University of California Press, 1974), p. 369.

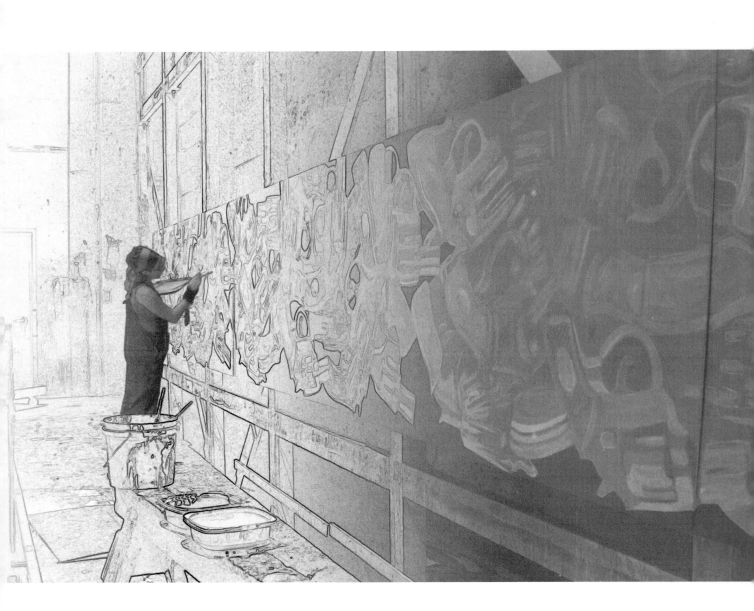

Structuring Color: Function and Composition

S TRUCTURING COLOR MEANS TO USE COLOR FOR A SPECIFIC PURPOSE in the overall quest to clarify and intensify a media-transmitted event. To do this effectively, you will need to acquire some insight into the principal functions of color: informational, compositional, and expressive.

Informational Function of Color

The informational function of color is to tell us more about an event than would be possible without color, to help us distinguish among things, and to use specifically designed color codes. For instance, a color reproduction usually gives more information about an event than a black-and-white rendering. **SEE COLOR PLATE 17** The colors not only make the event more realistic but also give specific information about its conditions: you can easily distinguish the red apples from the green ones; and, if you happen to know something about apples, you can now tell what kind they are.

In medicine the diagnostician must rely heavily on the informational function of color; a difference in color may signal health or sickness. It goes without saying that in medical photography (still, video, film, and computer display), accurate color renditions are an absolute must.

Colors help us distinguish among objects and establish an easy-to-read code: the red rose, the girl in the yellow dress, the fellow with the blue coat. The many wires in a telephone cable are color coded so that each wire can be easily identified and matched at both ends of the cable. **SEE COLOR PLATE 18** Mapmakers, meteorologists, and weathercasters use color codes that enable us to read a variety of data quickly and accurately. We also know that observance of the red-yellow-green color code in a traffic light can literally be a matter of life and death.

Within the context of the informational function of color, our primary task is to make one color as distinguishable as possible from the next. Considerations concerning *color harmony*—hues with balanced energy that go well together—remain secondary. Our main objective in the informational function of color is clarity.

This informational function is rendered meaningless in black-and-white (monochrome) pictures. Monochrome video is color-blind and responds only to differences in brightness. As viewers we cannot identify an object by its color or distinguish among various hues unless other cues, such as screen position or relative lightness or darkness of the objects, are given.

5.1 Black-and-white Video Is Color-blind

The informational function of color is meaningless in black-and-white images. We cannot tell which of the four buttons is the green one.

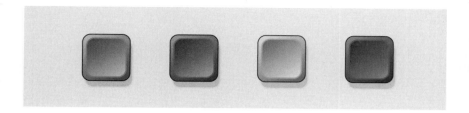

Assume that one of the buttons in figure 5.1 is green and that you have to press only the green one to save the world from disaster. Which would you press? **SEE 5.1**

If you pressed the first button on the left, you are still able to read this. If you pressed any other, you don't have to worry about color theory any longer—you have just blown up the earth. Fortunately, monochrome images are used much more for establishing or reflecting a certain mood than for distinguishing among similar objects. We address the aesthetic functions of monochrome images later in this chapter.

COLOR SYMBOLISM

For centuries people have used color to symbolize events, beliefs, and behavior. Color can symbolize life, death, hate, and faith, but such symbolic associations are learned and therefore are not uniform among all peoples. These associations are subject to people's habits, values, traditions, and myths, which vary considerably from culture to culture and from period to period. For example, some cultures use black as the color of mourning whereas others use white and even pink.[1] Such expressions as *blacklist, black sheep, blue blood, blue movie, feeling blue, purple joke, greenhorn, yellow coward, red-light district,* and *to be in the red or the black*—all are examples of color symbolism that apply in English-speaking countries. Translated into other languages, such color-oriented phrases often change or lose their meaning. For example, to be "blue" in German does not mean to be sad or even of royal blood; it means to be heavily intoxicated.

Color symbolism also changes with the experiential context. As a religious symbol, white signifies purity, joy, and glory; but in war it means surrender. Nevertheless, certain symbols have found almost worldwide acceptance, such as the Red Cross insignia and certain traffic signs. **SEE COLOR PLATE 19** In some countries red can have political significance or it can simply mean good luck.

When you use color symbolically, make sure that you firmly establish the context within which you use the symbolic associations and especially ensure that a majority of your audience is familiar with the symbolism used. A red rose is the universal symbol of beauty and love, but it may well be the rose rather than its color that has the true significance. A symbol with an unknown referent serves no purpose whatsoever. Beware of unexplained or obscure color symbolism, especially in video, film, and computer presentations. Contrary to a painting or a novel, which yields readily to close and prolonged examination, moving screen events are not easily revocable for closer study; their color symbolism must therefore reveal its meaning instantaneously.

The problem with symbolic color is obvious: an understated color symbol may remain undetected and thus ineffective; an overstated one may prove too obvious to the sensitive viewer. For example, having the bad guy in a cowboy movie wear a black hat and the good guy a white one has become such a hackneyed symbol that it is now used as an effective comic device.

If you establish a new symbolic color/event relationship, you must provide the audience with enough clues to learn this new association.

Sergei Eisenstein (1898–1948) in *The Film Sense* devotes a whole section (No. 3: "Color and Meaning") to the symbolic use of color. But, inadvertently, his essay reveals more about the problems of precise symbolic associations through color than about the informational function of symbolic color itself.[2]

Compositional Function of Color

Colors contribute greatly to the general form of the screen image. As in a painting, colors help define certain screen areas; that is, they emphasize some areas and de-emphasize others. We may select a certain color as the focal point in the screen area and then distribute the other colors accordingly to achieve a balanced pictorial composition. Or we may choose certain colors or color combinations that will help produce a predetermined overall energy level. Using colors for such purposes represents the compositional function of color.

Generally, we aim at a harmonious color combination—a juxtaposition of colors that go well together. This means that we should be able to detect certain color relationships that yield to the perception of a dynamic yet unified pattern. In an effective color composition, colors are no longer random; each has a purpose.

Advice on which colors go together or harmonize well is readily available in paint-store pamphlets and painting manuals. These resources usually tell you that colors harmonize best when they are next to each other on the hue circle, on opposite sides of the hue circle (which makes them complementary colors), or on the tips of an equilateral triangle superimposed on the hue circle.
SEE COLOR PLATE 20

In practice in video and film, such formulas are of little use. The intended color composition can easily be upset by the relative color temperature of the lighting, the initial color setup in the camera, the color setting of the display monitor, any colored lights shining on the scene, and the moving subject or camera. The primary factor that makes stable color composition so difficult is movement: in front of the camera or of the camera itself, and even a change of field of view. Certain colors that look pleasingly balanced in a long shot can fight one another in medium or close-up shots.

Should you give up now and simply forget about color composition? Not at all, but in video and film you simply need a different approach than the usual formulas.

COLOR ENERGY

Rather than try to identify hues that go well together, you will do much better by translating colors into color energies and then bringing the various energies into either balance or purposeful conflict.[3] As discussed in chapter 4, the **_color energy_** is principally determined by saturation level: highly saturated warm colors carry more aesthetic energy than do desaturated cold colors (see figure 4.3).

The most common compositional practice is to have small areas of high-energy colors set off against large areas of low-energy background colors. **SEE COLOR PLATE 21** This color distribution is probably the arrangement you have in your home. Many people have walls that are painted in low-energy colors (off-white, beige, light blue, pink, and so forth) to serve as a unifying element for the more high-energy colors of such accessories as plants, rugs, pillows, and paintings.

Such an energy distribution of color works especially well in scene design and costuming. Generally, you should try to keep large set areas in a uniform, low-energy color scheme but then accent with high-energy accessories, such as bright curtains, pillows, upholstery, flowers, rugs, and the like. This gives you more control over the total effect irrespective of the various camera points of view.

Painting a background a high-energy color tends to reduce the energy of the more active foreground. Worse, it assaults our senses so much that we tend to protect ourselves with sensory filters that, in time, cause us to ignore the colors altogether. High-energy color backgrounds also make it difficult to maintain visual continuity in postproduction editing.

Likewise, you can keep the general color scheme of the costumes somewhat conservative but then energize the scene with colorful, high-energy costume accessories, such as scarves, hats, belts, and the like.

When dealing with the compositional function of color, you can incorporate color energies into the constantly changing aesthetic energy field more readily than if you were dealing solely with the relationships of hues. As a matter of fact, when balancing color energies rather than hues, you may discover exciting new color combinations that defy tradition but aid our quest for an intensified experience.

If you now had to design a color scheme for a fast, high-energy dance number for a music video, for example, how would you ensure some color balance during the dance? Rather than worry about the specific colors of the dancers' costumes or the background scenery, you should first decide on the general distribution of high- and low-energy color areas. A good start would be to think, once again, of a low-energy background and high-energy colors for the dancers. Regardless of whether you shoot the dance wide or close-up or from a variety of angles, the high-energy colors of the dancers and their movements will be effectively set off against a low-energy background.

Best of all, the low-energy background will provide you with color continuity, which, as mentioned, is especially important for extensive postproduction editing. With a fairly uniform background color, the editor will have little trouble matching the various shots even if the foreground colors of the dancers differ widely from shot to shot. If the background were painted in multiple high-energy colors, the editor would find it extremely difficult to achieve even modest color continuity from shot to shot. Also, a high-energy background and a high-energy foreground would vie for the viewer's attention in each shot, clearly a formidable and unproductive setup for a fast dance number.

The Aesthetic Edge: Expressive Function of Color

As soon as we have video equipment and film stock that can accurately reproduce the actual colors around us, we distort them again to gain an aesthetic edge—to heighten the expressive quality of an event. The expressive function of color is to make us feel a specific way: colors can express the essential quality of an object or event, add excitement and drama, and help establish a mood. As you can see, we are no longer content with reproducing the colors of a scene but rather aim to manipulate colors for aesthetic intensification.

EXPRESSING THE ESSENTIAL QUALITY OF AN EVENT

Picture for a moment your favorite sports car. What color is it? Now visualize a luxury limousine. What color do you give the limo? You probably assigned the sports car the color red and the limousine black, gray, or perhaps silver. The high-energy red expresses the power of the car, its mobility, and the fun of driving it. The low-energy colors of the limousine appropriately reflect the quiet elegance and understated wealth we associate with such a vehicle. How would you feel if a doctor performing surgery wore red and orange and the operating room was painted in pink candy stripes?

Package designers are careful to choose colors for their products that we associate most readily with their essential quality. A gold-striped purple box seems entirely fitting for a spicy perfume but somewhat inappropriate for toothpaste. In connection with perfume, purple and gold suggest elegance, forbidden love, or secret passion; in connection with toothpaste, they signal bad taste. If the essential quality of the product is softness (such as hand lotion or bathroom tissue), we expect the color of the product to convey this quality. Desaturated pastel colors are the most fitting in this case. Strong spices, on the other hand, are best expressed by vibrant, highly saturated colors. A dark, warm brown or a neutral off-white seems to express the objective, unbiased judicial activity in a courtroom more readily than a bright, highly saturated red. A soothing, desaturated green appropriately reflects the cool, efficient activity of an operating room.

Here again it is not so much the color itself—the hue—that we associate with the quality of the object or event but the color energy. In the bustling, noisy, and emotional environment of a carnival, high-energy colors are well suited to express the event's fun and joyful nature; but we tend to associate the cool, rational activity of a laboratory most readily with low-energy, cold colors.

ADDING EXCITEMENT AND DRAMA

Colors can add excitement and drama to an event. The colorful uniforms of a marching band, the brightly hued costumes of flamenco dancers, the red and blue flashing lights of police cars, the colored lights in a rock concert, the changing hues of a sunset or sunrise—all are examples of how colors excite us and dramatically intensify an event. A scene bathed in warm colors can communicate a glowing feeling of affection and compassion. Cold-colored scenes may indicate mystery, sadness, sorrow, or disillusionment. Postproduction and special-effects software make it easy to change the colors of a scene or parts of a scene. You may find that a greenish or bluish tint heightens a scene's drama and suspense, especially when coupled with appropriate sound effects. **SEE COLOR PLATE 22**

> The expressive function of colored light was recognized long ago by the artisans who crafted the stained-glass windows of the Gothic cathedrals of Europe.

Such colorization is often applied to commercials, some of which are bathed in warm- or cold-colored light or use a predominant color scheme. For example, you may find that an ad for a hearty hamburger is primarily warm colors, whereas a commercial for a thirst-quenching soft drink may show a preponderance of cold colors.

The advantage of colorization software is that you can run through a great number of experiments in a relatively short time without elaborate lighting and camera setups. Once you are satisfied with a particular color effect, you can apply it in film and video production or in Web design.

Color as principal event You can use color not only as an additional element of an event but also as the event itself. Laser light shows, gallery exhibits of colored fluorescent tubes, and abstract paintings that have as their subject bold color areas are examples of using color as the basic *materia* of the event. To express someone's intense moments of rage or love, you could, for example, project red flashes over the entire screen.

Contrary to abstract painting, the many attempts by video artists to use color as the primary event, however, have not proven highly successful. Although temporarily exciting, most of these experiments do not seem to communicate the depth of feeling and significance we expect from art. Perhaps we have become so accustomed to seeing color used as a supplementary element within a scene that using it as the primary event does not hold our attention for long. In other words, we may be delighted by the juxtaposition of two high-energy colors such as yellow and red when they appear in a realistic picture—such as two small children in yellow raincoats carrying a bright red plastic umbrella—but not when we see just two abstract color areas jostling for dominance.

Nevertheless, the various computer paint programs on the market offer exciting possibilities in the art of electronic painting. Some screen savers apply the tenet of color as principal event by producing a variety of moving and changing color patterns.

Some of the early studies of color/sound relationships were done by **Sir Isaac Newton** (1642–1727) in the early part of the eighteenth century. They were continued by Jesuit priest and mathematician **Louis-Bertrand Castel** who, in 1714, constructed the first color organ.[4] Like Newton, physicist **Hermann L. F. von Helmholtz** (1821–1894) tried to establish an analogy between the color spectrum and the notes of a musical scale.[5] In the first decade of the twentieth century, Russian composer **Aleksandr N. Scriabin** (1872–1915) used a "light-clavier" to accompany the music of his 1910 composition *Prometheus: The Poems of Fire*. A few years later, **Thomas Wilfrid** built his own "clavilux," an instrument that projected patterns of light onto a screen with the rhythm of the music. Other pioneers—such as **Adrian Bernard Klein**, who published a treatise on the expressive function of color, *Colour-Music: The Art of Light*, as early as 1927; and **László Moholy-Nagy**[6] (see chapter 1) and **Gyorgy Kepes**,[7] with their Bauhaus-inspired light experiments in the 1920s and 1930s—were all forerunners of laser light shows. In the 1950s and 1960s, **Norman McLaren** produced hand-painted films of colored patterns that matched the music on the sound track; later, however, he returned to matching filmically manipulated movements of dancers to music.[8]

Color and sound combinations   Combining color and sound seems a natural thing to do. Aesthetically, we seem to react similarly to color and sound. Think of how we use musical terms to describe colors and how we use color terminology to describe musical sounds. We speak of shrill and loud colors or of harmonic and dissonant color combinations. We also talk about warm sounds, blue notes, and colorful cadenzas.

Many attempts to match colors and sounds in an aesthetic system, however, have largely failed. The problem is that although individual notes might correspond to specific colors in feeling and aesthetic energy, combinations of notes, as in a chord, rarely match similar combinations of assigned colors. A chord is quite different from the sum of its individual tonal components. The same is true of color. A color pattern has an expressive quality that differs, sometimes vigorously, from the way each individual color feels. Matching color and sound *patterns* by their relative aesthetic energies rather than by individual notes and hues might be the most sensible approach to this problem. Again, translating color and sound patterns into certain types of vector combinations may assist you in matching colors and sound. Vectors are discussed in chapter 7.

ESTABLISHING MOOD

The expressive quality of color, like music, is an excellent vehicle for establishing or intensifying the mood of an event. This application of color requires particular attention to the relative warmth or coldness of the color and its overall aesthetic energy. Generally, you can easily attach similar labels to the mood of a scene: there may be a high-energy hot scene or a low-energy warm scene; there may be a high-energy cold scene or a low-energy hot scene or any combination thereof. By using the color energy table (see figure 4.3), you can easily find the color or color combination that fits harmoniously the feeling of the event. High-energy warm colors certainly suggest a happier mood or a more forceful event than do low-energy cold colors. As with all uses of color, however, innumerable variations to this admittedly gross generalization are possible and are successfully applied.

For example, you can intensify a scene just as readily by using a color palette that acts as a counterpoint to the other aesthetic elements in the event. An especially violent scene, for example, may gain intensity when presented in a cool, low-energy color scheme. Warm, bright colors, on the other hand, can become a chilling counterpoint to a death scene. Whether to use colors harmonically (high-energy event matched with high-energy colors) or contrapuntally (low-energy event matched with high-energy colors) depends to a great extent on the context of the total event, your communication intent, and your overall presentation style.

DESATURATION THEORY

Although bright, highly saturated colors are well suited to enhance an external high-energy scene, such as a football game, a lively dance, or an automobile race, they can also prevent us from getting caught up and involved in a quiet and intimate screen event. Showing in highly saturated basic colors an intimate love scene, a wounded soldier lying helplessly on a battlefield, or the silence of internal rage between two people may well hinder rather than further the emotional depth of the event. Saturated colors can make such internal events, or **inscapes**, too external, luring the viewer into looking *at* rather than *into* the event. This is one of the problems with showing a tragic event in HDTV colors on a large screen. The vivid, highly saturated HDTV colors are apt to make us realize that we are, indeed, only watching TV pictures, giving us a ready excuse for not getting too emotionally involved in the event itself.

The *desaturation theory* asserts that one way of reducing the blunt and brazen impact of high-energy colors in a quiet, introspective scene is to lessen their saturation, give them a monochrome tint, or omit color altogether. To portray the internal condition of an event means to penetrate outer reality—to make the viewers supply some of their own emotional energy to the communication process. Color on recognizable images (people and objects) emphasizes their appearance; thus our attention is directed toward the outer, rather than the inner, reality of an event. But when we render the scene more low-definition through desaturation of color, by applying a monochrome tint, or through posterization, solarization, or soft-focus effects,[9] the event becomes more transparent. It also makes the audience apply psychological closure, that is, fill in the missing elements of the low-definition images. In this way viewers will inevitably get more involved in the event than if they were looking at high-definition color images.[10]

SEE COLOR PLATES 23–26

When to use color—or when not to use it—should no longer present too difficult a problem for you. If color, even when used expressively, prevents you from perceiving an event in all its depth and subtleties, use black-and-white. If color helps clarify and intensify an event, use it. A death scene is most likely more effective in black-and-white than in living color. Obviously, if colors are necessary for providing information about an event, black-and-white will not suffice. If you are after sheer excitement and spectacle, color is a must. A football game shot in black-and-white will certainly look less thrilling than when presented in high-energy colors.

Generally, the more intimate and internal an event becomes, the more you can treat outer reality low-definition. The more low-definition the outer reality should be, the less important color becomes. Color intensifies landscape, not necessarily inscape.

COLORIZING FILM

Some time ago there were passionate debates about colorizing classic black-and-white movies. The proponents of colorizing claimed that it made the films more attractive and realistic. The opponents asserted that any colorization would inevitably destroy the films' aesthetic integrity.

Now you have at least one aesthetic theory that you can apply when reading in a film history book about the arguments of whether colorizing old black-and-white movies with digital paint programs was a good idea. If the film is a typical *landscape* movie, whose scenes are mostly external (galloping horses, battle scenes, car chases, sports spectaculars), color will most often intensify the screen events. In any case, it certainly would not harm the intended effect of the film. If, however, the movie is primarily concerned with inscape, with scenes that deal with deep and intense human emotions, color may well keep us from experiencing the empathetic involvement, thus destroying the film's intended effect.

We also need to question ethically as well as aesthetically the practice of colorization. Do we have the right to tamper with the finished work of an artist? In the television business, the answer is yes. Since the beginning of transmitting motion pictures via television, we have been editing films to fit the mores, time requirements, and aspect ratio of the television medium. This "editing for television" practice hardly raised an eyebrow among filmmakers and the television audience. Squeezing a wide-screen movie onto a relatively small television set that has a differently proportioned picture area is, as you will read in chapter 6, an equally severe tampering with the film's original construct. Colorization, it seems, represents no more serious an aesthetic intrusion.

One could also argue that many films would probably have been shot in color had color been available at the time. But what about films that were deliberately

The films of Swedish filmmaker **Ingmar** (Ernst) **Bergman** (1918–2007), often treating man's search for God, are usually studies of human loneliness and anguish. They include *The Seventh Seal* (1956), *The Silence* (1963), *Cries and Whispers* (1972), *Autumn Sonata* (1978), and *Fanny and Alexander* (1983) for which he won an Academy Award. He also wrote the screenplays for *The Best Intentions* (1992) and *Sunday's Children* (1993). His relentless probing of the internal condition of human beings would have made him a superior director of television drama. Unfortunately, he never really took advantage of this medium, nor the medium of him. His *Scenes from a Marriage*, a six-episode television series, was the notable exception and showed his brilliance as a television director.

shot in black-and-white to intensify the internal events? In Ingmar Bergman's *The Silence* and Woody Allen's *Manhattan,* for example, colorization becomes a blatant, if not irresponsible, mutilation of the film.[11]

TELEVISION COMMERCIALS

If thematically appropriate, black-and-white television commercials are good examples of the desaturation theory. More than a mere attention-getting device, the black-and-white pictures entice us to colorize the scene in our heads and thus move psychologically closer to the event. We are made to *feel* what is going on in the commercial rather than to cognitively observe it. When, at the end of the commercial, parts of the scene or the entire scene finally appears in color, we seem oddly relieved. We are now permitted to switch back from the more demanding internal mode of perception to the customary external one, from looking *into* the event to looking *at* it.

SUMMARY

Structuring color means to use color for a specific purpose. Color has three principal functions: informational, compositional, and expressive.

The informational function of color is to tell us more about an object or event or to give it symbolic meaning. Color can help render a scene more realistically and also help us distinguish among objects and establish an identification code. The symbolic use of color is part of its informational function, but symbolic associations are learned; to be effective the symbolism used must be known to the audience.

The compositional function of color is to help define certain screen areas and to bring the energies of pictorial elements into a balanced yet dynamic interplay. The traditional techniques of color composition—in which colors are said to harmonize best if they are close together, directly opposite each other, or in a triangular configuration on the hue circle—are of little value in video and film unless they are used for environmental shots, such as interior or exterior scenery. The constant movement of camera and object and the selective point of view of the camera normally render such compositional rules impractical. A more effective way of dealing with color balance and composition in the moving image is to translate the various colors into color energies and then distribute the energies within the video or film picture area so that they contribute to an overall balanced pattern. To achieve this we usually keep the background colors low-energy (less saturated) and the foreground colors high-energy (highly saturated).

The expressive function of color is to make us feel a specific way. Colors can express the essential quality of an object or an event; designers choose colors for product packaging that we associate with certain feelings and attitudes. Color can provide drama and excitement, such as the colorful uniforms of a sports team, the flashing red or blue light on an ambulance, or the colored lights of a carnival. The expressive quality of color can easily set or intensify a specific mood. Generally, warm, high-energy colors suggest a happy mood; and cold, low-energy colors evoke a somber mood.

Color can also be used as the event itself. In this case, color is no longer a part of what is happening—it is the principal subject. Laser light shows, fluorescent tubes of different colors arranged in patterns, and certain types of abstract painting are examples of this. Although relatively easy to produce with the aid of computers, video presentations that feature abstract color patterns have not proved successful as a popular form of expression. We experience similar problems when trying to combine color and sound. Individual colors and sounds can be matched quite easily, but clusters of color and sound harmony (chords) defy such integration.

The desaturation theory suggests that by desaturating, even to the point of omitting chromatic colors altogether, we can entice the viewer to participate in the event—to look *into* rather than merely *at* it. Such desaturation is especially successful when we need to reveal or intensify an inscape, or internal event. In this case, the low-definition color (subdued, desaturated color scheme or single hue) and especially the low-definition black-and-white renderings de-emphasize the outer appearance of things and draw attention to the inner reality of the event. The less concerned we are about outer reality, the less important color becomes. Given this as an aesthetic context, colorizing film that was originally shot in black-and-white seems less offensive if the major portion of the film deals with external action and outer reality. But if the film depicts deep emotions and an inner reality, color will probably work against the film's aesthetic intent.

Black-and-white video commercials are a direct application of the desaturation theory. Such total desaturation renders the event low-definition, which forces the viewer into psychological involvement.

NOTES

1. My colleague Gregory Gutenko, of the University of Missouri at Kansas City, sees an important connection between culture and the color of mourning by pointing out that the colors of mourning are basically rooted in the prevailing philosophy of a particular culture. He says that the "void" of the black color resonates in cultures that see death as emptiness and loss, whereas the "positive but featureless" white color is preferred by cultures that see death "as eternal true self from which the temporal and transitory 'writings' of ego and experience have been erased." This clearly points to the difficulty, if not the impossibility, of using specific symbols for media content that is intended for a global audience.

2. Sergei Eisenstein, *Film Form and The Film Sense,* ed. and trans. by Jay Leyda (New York: World, 1957), pp. 113–53. This edition consists of two books paginated separately; this reference is to the second volume, *The Film Sense.*

3. When you deal with color energies in pictorial composition, you are actually working with vectors and the structure of the vector field. Compare the discussions of vectors in chapters 7, 8, 11, and 13.

4. Conrad Mueller and Mae Rudolph (eds.), *Light and Vision* (New York: Time-Life Books, 1966), pp. 130–31.

5. You can find good examples of op art on the Internet, such as at: *www.artcyclopedia.com/history/optical.html* and *www.columbusmuseum.org/media/optic.*

6. László Moholy-Nagy, *Vision in Motion* (Chicago: Paul Theobald, 1947, 1965).

7. Gyorgy Kepes performed many experiments with light and color when he was head of the Light and Color Department of the Institute of Design in Chicago in the late 1930s and later as a professor of visual design at the Massachusetts Institute of Technology.

8. Terence Dobson, *The Film Work of Norman McLaren* (Bloomington: Indiana University Press, 2007).

9. Herbert Zettl, *Television Production Handbook,* 10th ed. (Belmont, Calif.: Wadsworth, 2009), p. 288.

10. Marshall McLuhan, *Understanding Media: The Extensions of Man* (New York: McGraw-Hill, 1964), pp. 321–22. One of McLuhan's main theories about television's intimacy is that the medium is "low-definition" and that viewers therefore get more involved in the presentation than if they were to see the event on the high-definition cinema screen.

11. The by-now-classic 1979 film *Manhattan* by Woody Allen was deliberately shot in black-and-white to magnify the emotional intensity of the complex romantic relationships among a TV writer and his neurotic friends.

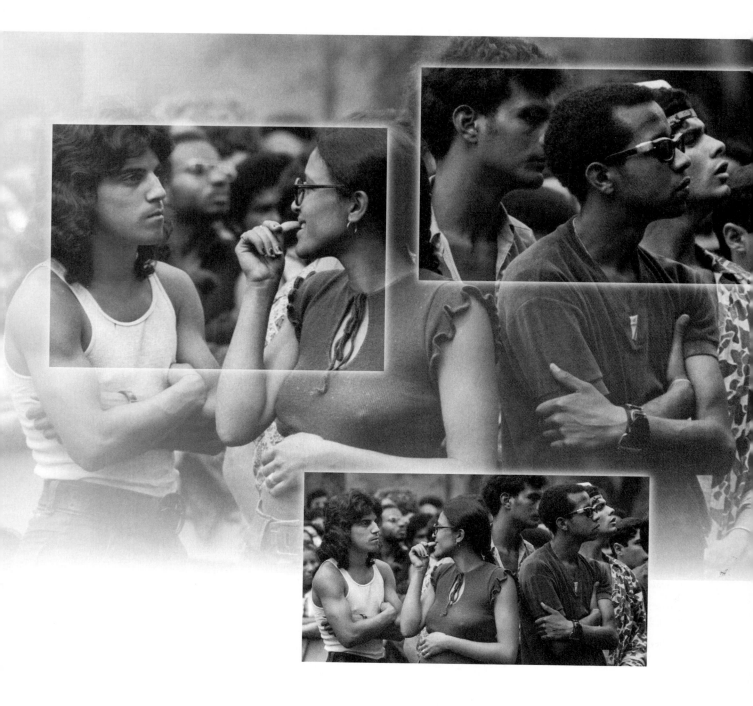

The Two-dimensional Field: Area

THE SCREEN PROVIDES YOU WITH A NEW, CONCENTRATED LIVING SPACE—a new field for presenting media events. It helps you tame space. You are no longer dealing with the real, amorphous space we walk through and live in every day but with screen space. The viewfinder in a video or digital cinema camera and the various screens on which the media event is projected have definite, fixed borders that define the new aesthetic playing field. You must now clarify and intensify an event within the confines of this new space. Boris Uspensky's insightful comment about the frame in painting applies equally to the video screen: "The frame is the borderline between the internal world of the representation and the world external to the representation."[1]

This chapter examines the structural factors of screen space: aspect ratio and the aesthetics of object size and image size.

Aspect Ratio

Aspect ratio is the relationship of screen width to screen height. As a painter or still photographer, you have free choice in the basic orientation of your picture frame: you may want a frame that is taller than it is wide for the picture of a skyscraper, or a horizontally oriented format for the wide expanse of a desert landscape. You may even choose a round or an irregularly shaped boundary. In video, film, or computer displays, you do not have this format flexibility. The various video and motion picture screens may differ in size and aspect ratio, but the only flexibility is within the screen, not of the screen itself.

HORIZONTAL ORIENTATION

The standard video, film, and computer screens are horizontally oriented. Why?

One reason could be that our peripheral vision is greater horizontally than vertically.[2] But this does not mean that we actually see much more at the sides of our head than what is above or below it, especially because we can look up and down just as easily as sideways. Even if the screen is small enough that it is reflected in full at our retina, we can't see all of its content by simply staring at it. Our eyes must constantly cut from one spot to another in a picture before we can make sense of what we see.[3] A wide screen will not eliminate such a scanning process. It will, however, allow us to use our peripheral vision to become aware of what is going on at the sides of the screen before deciding to actually look at it.

A more compelling reason for the horizontal screen is that we normally live and operate on a horizontal plane. In the context of our everyday pursuits, the world is flat. Gravity makes it relatively easy for us to stay and move on a horizontal plane but rather difficult to conquer vertical space. To travel 200 miles over land is nothing special; to cover the same distance vertically is a supreme achievement. A 600-foot-high tower is a structural adventure; a 600-foot-long building is simply large.

STANDARD ASPECT RATIOS

The two aspect ratios most prevalent in video production are the traditional 4×3 and the HDTV 16×9. Standard television and many computer screens took over the traditional 4×3 aspect ratio of early motion pictures. Regardless of their size, they are all 4 units wide by 3 units high. This aspect ratio is also expressed as 1.33:1—for every unit in height, there are 1.33 units in width. **SEE 6.1**

The digital video screens, usually called HDTV television screens regardless of whether they are high- or low-definition, have a wide-screen aspect ratio of 16×9, or 1.78:1. **SEE 6.2** The aspect ratio of the standard wide screen of motion pictures is 5.55×3, or 1.85:1. **SEE 6.3**

The Panavision 35 or Cinemascope format has a very wide, wraparound aspect ratio of 7×3, or 2.39:1. To distinguish it from the older and slightly narrower Cinemascope aspect ratio of 2.35:1, the movie pros call the wider version the 240 ("two-four-O") format. **SEE 6.4**

Most U.S. films are shot and projected in the 1.85:1 *wide-screen format*. The newer, wider Panavision aspect ratio requires an anamorphic lens to stretch the squeezed film frame for projection on the ultrawide screen.

The aspect ratios of mobile video devices (cell phones and mini camcorders) differ widely to serve a variety of multimedia functions, such as texting, framing a shot during video capture, or displaying graphics, tables, and text. Some have a single fixed window in the upper part of the device that can display a variety of differently proportioned images; others have a larger screen whose aspect ratio is a skinny vertical one when held upright and a wide one when turned sideways. As a stretched vertical aspect ratio (from top to bottom), the screen can display vertical vistas or be divided into a number of individual picture spaces; as a horizontal one, it can display wide-screen scenes and, especially, wide texting. **SEE 6.5–6.7**

6.1 Standard Television, Computer, and Classic Movie Screen Aspect Ratio

All standard television screens, computer screens, and the classic motion picture screen have an aspect ratio of 4×3, which means that they are 4 units wide by 3 units high. The 4×3 aspect ratio is also expressed as 1.33:1—for every unit in height, there are 1.33 units in width.

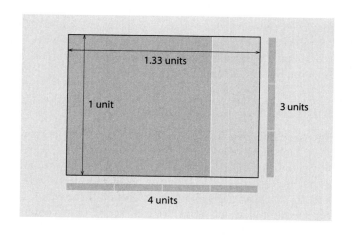

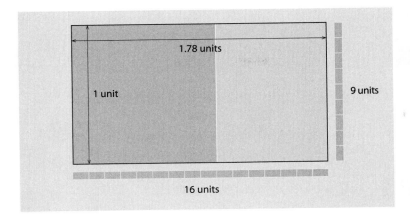

6.2 HDTV Aspect Ratio

The HDTV screen aspect ratio is 16 × 9, or 1.78:1, making this screen more horizontally stretched than the traditional television screen. The HDTV aspect ratio can accommodate wide-screen movie formats without much picture loss at the sides. Many standard digital cameras can switch between the 4 × 3 and the 16 × 9 aspect ratios.

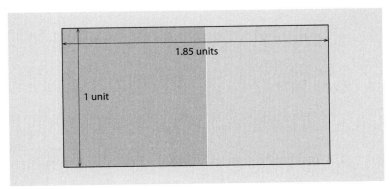

6.3 Wide-screen Motion Picture Aspect Ratio

The aspect ratio of wide-screen motion pictures is 5.55 × 3, or 1.85:1. This ratio provides a horizontally stretched vista and is the standard film aspect ratio in the United States.

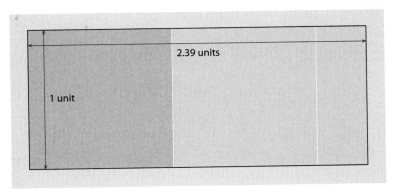

6.4 Panavision 35 Motion Picture Aspect Ratio

The aspect ratio of the Panavision film format is 7 × 3, or 2.39:1, which gives a wider panoramic view than the standard wide-screen format.

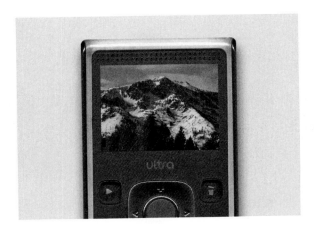

6.5 Mini Camcorder

There are several mobile video devices whose screens have the classic 4 × 3 aspect ratio.

6.6 Vertical Aspect Ratio

When held upright, this mobile video device can display images in a relatively large screen with a vertical aspect ratio. It can display tall objects or stacked information.

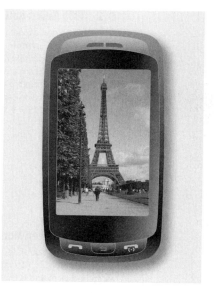

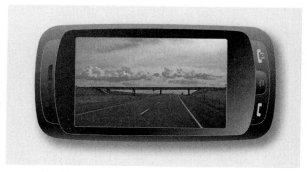

6.7 Horizontal Aspect Ratio

When turned sideways, the same screen becomes a display area with a wide-screen aspect ratio.

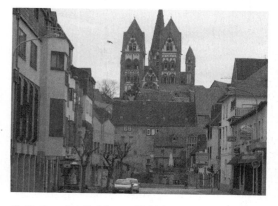

6.8 Framing Height and Width in a Single Shot

In the 4 × 3 aspect ratio, the difference between width and height is not so noticeable as to unduly emphasize one screen dimension over the other. It accommodates both horizontal vistas and vertical objects.

FRAMING IN THE 4 × 3 ASPECT RATIO

The 4 × 3 standard for film was established as early as 1889. There is still some controversy, if not confusion, about just why this aspect ratio became the standard.[4] Be that as it may, when you look at this standard not from a technical but from an aesthetic point of view, the reason for this screen format is not so baffling.

The advantage of the 4 × 3 aspect ratio is that the difference between screen width and screen height is not pronounced enough to emphasize one dimension over the other. **SEE 6.8** You can frame a horizontally oriented scene without too much wasted vertical screen space, and a vertical scene without worrying too much about how to fill the sides of the screen. **SEE 6.9 AND 6.10**

The 4 × 3 aspect ratio is especially appropriate for the close-up (CU) and extreme close-up (ECU) framing of a person. In the CU or medium shot (MS), the person seems to be comfortably placed in the 4 × 3 frame; but in the 16 × 9 frame, the subject in the medium shot seems somewhat lost in the wide-screen video space. **SEE 6.11 AND 6.12**

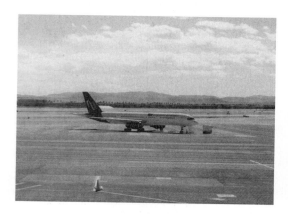

6.9 Framing a Horizontal View

The 4 × 3 aspect ratio can easily accommodate a horizontally oriented vista.

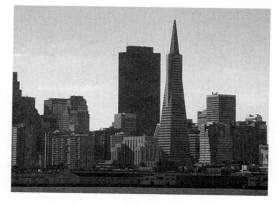

6.10 Framing a Vertical View

Even a vertically oriented scene can be easily framed within the 4 × 3 aspect ratio.

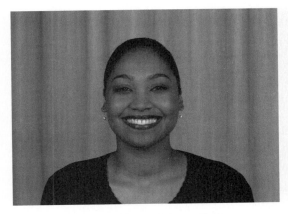

6.11 Framing a CU in the 4 × 3 Aspect Ratio

The 4 × 3 aspect ratio allows us to frame a close-up of a person without crowding the frame or leaving unused screen space.

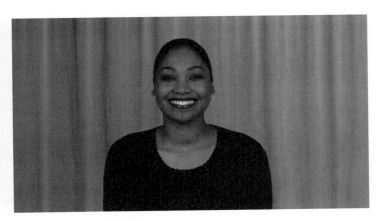

6.12 Framing an MS in the 16 × 9 Aspect Ratio

When framing a medium shot, there is much unused space on both sides of the screen (called dead zones), so the person seems oddly lost in video space.

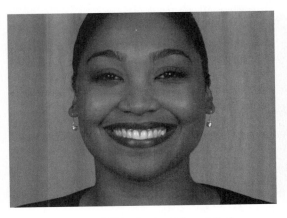

6.13 Framing an ECU in the 4 × 3 Aspect Ratio

The 4 × 3 aspect ratio can accommodate an extreme close-up without leaving undesirable screen space at the sides.

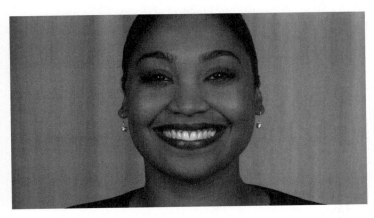

6.14 Framing an ECU in the 16 × 9 Aspect Ratio

When framing a close-up or an extreme close-up in the HDTV aspect ratio, we are again left with a considerable amount of unused screen space on either side of the subject. Also, the person looks somewhat squeezed by the low ceiling of the frame.

The extreme close-up of the person looks properly intensified when placed in the 4 × 3 aspect ratio but loses intensity in the 16 × 9 frame because of the "dead zones," of leftover screen space on either side. **SEE 6.13 AND 6.14** These dead zones are especially noticeable on the larger HDTV screens.

FRAMING IN THE 16 × 9 ASPECT RATIO

Why, then, did the motion picture and HDTV standards committees opt for the wider aspect ratio? One of the initial reasons was certainly film's desire to compete with television and to engulf us in spectacle—something difficult for standard television to achieve.[5] In the meantime directors and camera operators have learned how to use the wide screen effectively for intimate scenes as well. Still, it is the landscape shots in which the wide-screen format shines. As discussed in chapter 4, the term *landscape* includes environmental shots, such as actual landscapes as well as city streets, sports arenas, and interiors.

6.15 **Framing a Wide Vista in the 16 × 9 Aspect Ratio**

The wide 16 × 9 aspect ratio is ideally suited to show the long row of people waiting for the bus. In a narrower frame, the picture would lose its charm.

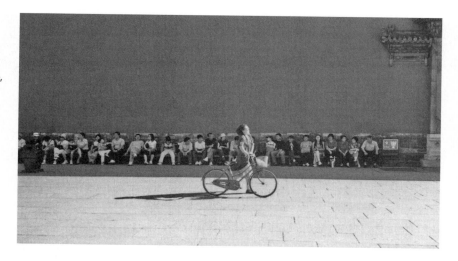

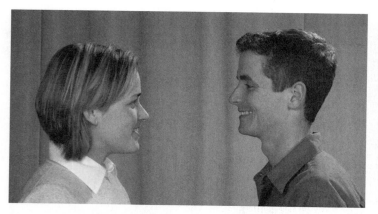

6.16 **Framing of Two Dialogue Partners in the 16 × 9 Aspect Ratio**

On the wide HDTV screen, you can easily frame a head-on medium shot of two people facing each other. The two people can stand at a comfortable distance without being too close to each other.

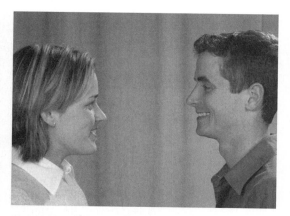

6.17 **Framing of Two Dialogue Partners in the 4 × 3 Aspect Ratio**

On the narrower standard television screen, the same setup is difficult to frame. Note how the two people are partially cut by the screen edges. The empty screen center becomes especially prominent.

Although the 4 × 3 aspect ratio can frame horizontal scenes as well as vertical ones, it is obviously not as adept at showing wide vistas. No matter how hard you try, you will find it difficult to show a long row of people queued horizontally or to overwhelm your audience with the great expanse of the ocean, the majestic power of the Grand Canyon, or the intensity of a sold-out football stadium. **SEE 6.15**

On a much smaller scale, it easier to show people standing or sitting across from each other in a conversation in the wide aspect ratio than on the smaller 4 × 3 screen. There is enough lateral space to have the people at a comfortable distance from each other. When duplicating the shot on the small screen, you usually end up with both conversation partners seemingly glued to the edges of the screen with a definite aesthetic hole in screen-center. On the wide screen, the people have more personal space, more breathing room. **SEE 6.16 AND 6.17**

The wide aspect ratio also allows you to establish a specific setting, such as a street scene, a restaurant, or a living room, in a single long shot. **SEE 6.18** It also gives you more room for lateral (screen-left or screen-right) motion without having to pan with the camera. Such flexibility is greatly appreciated by television

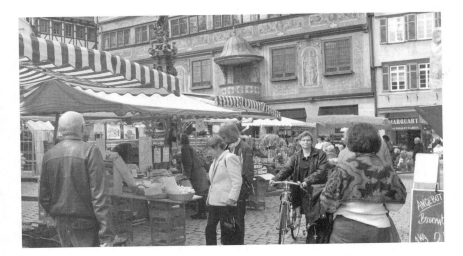

6.18 Establishing a Scene
With the wide screen, you can establish a scene without having to go to an extreme long shot.

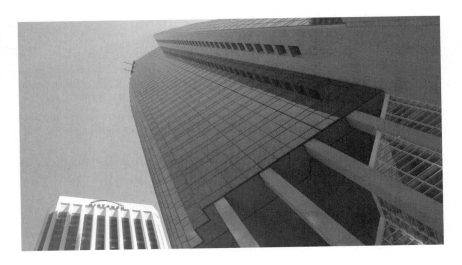

6.19 Framing Vertical Vistas
A vertical vista, such as a tall building, is difficult to fit into the wide HDTV screen. One solution is to frame it diagonally.

directors when blocking multicamera productions, such as soap operas and other serial dramas.[6] Lateral motion is relatively ineffective on the small 4 × 3 screen, but it can have powerful effects on the wider 16 × 9 screen.

Framing tall objects such as towers, high-rise buildings, and trees in the wide-screen aspect ratio always presents a problem. On long shots you end up with an inordinate amount of space to fill on both sides. When using closer shots, you need to decide to show either the top or the bottom of the tall object. Such problems are usually solved by tilting the object and placing it on the screen diagonal, by shooting from below and looking up with the camera, or by slowly tilting up or down with the camera. **SEE 6.19** Another way is to create a vertical aspect ratio within the wide screen, which is the subject of the following discussion.

Flexible Aspect Ratio

We cannot alter the physical aspect ratio of a video, movie, or computer screen, but we can rearrange the screen space itself to create a variety of horizontal landscape and vertical portrait formats. The most immediate task is to accommodate wide-screen HDTV and film images into the 4 × 3 screen of the standard television set and to fit the 4 × 3 images of standard video into the wide-screen format. A similar problem exists when placing the standard video and wide-screen HDTV and film aspect ratios into the various small mobile video displays.

Regardless of the aspect ratio of the video screen, we can create secondary frames within the principal screen.

MATCHING ASPECT RATIOS

So far the problem has been to make the 16 × 9 movie images fit the 4 × 3 television screen. But with the increasing number of wide-screen TV sets in use, we face the reverse dilemma when trying to show material that has been produced in the traditional 4 × 3 format.

Windowboxing   The simplest way to accommodate a 4 × 3 picture in an HDTV aspect ratio is to reduce the size of the picture and place it in the center of the wide-screen frame, with the leftover space of the 16 × 9 frame surrounding it. This technique is called *windowboxing*, although the 4 × 3 image looks more like a picture with a matte around it than a window. The problem with such a framing is, of course, the reduced size of the 4 × 3 image.   **SEE 6.20**

Pillarboxing   Fitting a full-sized 4 × 3 image in the middle of a 16 × 9 screen is called *pillarboxing*. When using this method, the 4 × 3 picture is simply inserted into the center of the wider screen so that the top and the bottom of its frame coincide with the 16 × 9 picture space. The leftover empty sides of the screen are blanked with vertical bars, often called side bars or dead zones. These side bars are vertical and look like pillars, hence the term pillarboxing.   **SEE 6.21**

Letterboxing   *Letterboxing* is used to make a wide-screen presentation, such as a 1.85:1 movie or 16 × 9 (1.78:1) digital video, fit a 4 × 3 (1.33:1) screen or some kind of vertical mobile video display.

A wide-screen letterbox is created by showing the whole width and height of the original format and masking the top and the bottom of the screen with black, white, or colored bars.   **SEE 6.22**

You may also see motion pictures windowboxed on the HDTV screen, which makes little sense, especially because the wide-screen HDTV format was developed in large part to accommodate motion pictures without cropping. Such

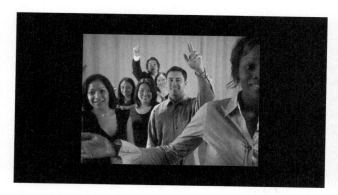

6.20 Windowboxing

Maintaining the aspect ratio of the original image but reducing it in size and then placing it in the center of the primary (usually 16 × 9) screen is called windowboxing.

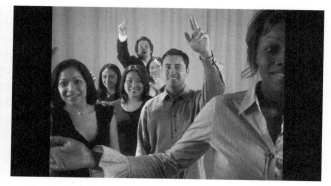

6.21 Pillarboxing

Fitting a 4 × 3 format into a 16 × 9 aspect ratio leaves empty bands on both sides of the screen. This change of aspect ratio is called pillarboxing.

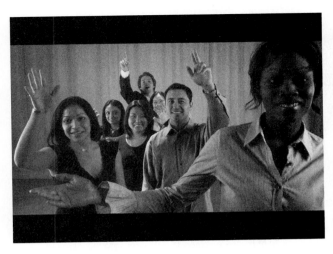

6.22 Letterboxing

When showing a full frame of a wide-screen image on the standard television screen, we must leave borders on the top and the bottom of the screen. This change of aspect ratio is called letterboxing.

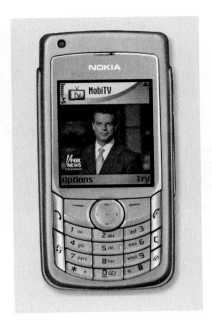

**6.23
Letterboxing on
Mobile Video Display**

The vertical format of this mobile video display is changed to a 4 × 3 video format through letterboxing. Note that the so-called dead zones are quite alive with written information.

maneuvers are performed not for aesthetic reasons, however, but for technical ones. A smaller image saves bandwidth, which allows more information to be transmitted or squeezed onto recording media.

Because the small display of mobile multimedia phones may be square or even vertical, letterboxing is the typical way of adjusting the display to accommodate the 4 × 3 format of standard television or the 16 × 9 format of HDTV or wide-screen movies. Often the dead zones are quite alive with lettering, which sometimes relates to what is displayed on the screen or shows unrelated text messages. **SEE 6.23**

You will find that on a fairly large screen, such aspect ratio accommodations do not do too much damage to the overall aesthetic intent and usually preserve the integrity of the original production. On a small screen, however, the letterboxed or pillarboxed images shrink so much that they inevitably lose most or all of their landscape impact. Realize, however, that such a loss of aesthetic energy is more a function of the small screen size than the manipulation of aspect ratios.

Cutting, stretching, and squeezing More drastic ways of making wide-screen images fit the aspect ratio of standard video is to simply crop the wide-screen image on either side. If the film or video was shot with standard television in mind, not much is lost. A good director will have kept most of the important action screen-center and more of the decorative material, which Peter Ward calls "visual fluff," on the extreme sides.[7] If the movie or video was shot explicitly for the wide screen, however, such a technique is quite intrusive. You become especially aware of this crude method of amputating picture information when letters or words from titles, credits, or subtitles are missing. When you enlarge the standard 4 × 3 television image to fill the sides of a wide-screen television receiver, you inevitably lose headroom and cut off some feet at the bottom of the screen.

A relatively simple way to address this problem is to digitally stretch or squeeze the image to fit a specific aspect ratio without the telltale dead zones on the sides or on the top and the bottom of the screen. Unfortunately, when stretching the 4 × 3 image to fit the wide screen, the people on-screen instantly gain at least 25 pounds and vertical objects look wider than in the original. All

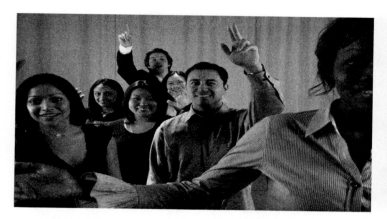

6.24 Digital Stretching

Sometimes the 4 × 3 image is digitally stretched to make it fit the 16 × 9 HDTV aspect ratio. The unfortunate consequence of this simple solution is that objects lose their normal proportions: people look chubby, horizontal lines get longer, and vertical lines get wider.

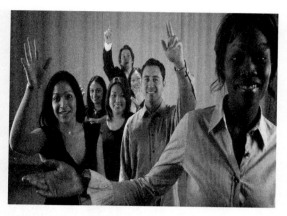

6.25 Digital Squeezing

To fit the wide-screen 16 × 9 image into the standard 4 × 3 aspect ratio, the image is sometimes digitally squeezed. People look thinner and taller, and objects look vertically stretched.

horizontal lines get wider, as well. **SEE 6.24** When squeezing a wide-format image into a 4 × 3 aspect ratio without the dead zones, the people and vertical objects get thinner, and the horizontal lines get shorter. **SEE 6.25** These stretching and squeezing methods become especially noticeable when there is written material on the screen. We as viewers may eventually accept such aesthetic anomalies if we are told often enough that this is the new and fashionable look of high-tech picture manipulation.

One of the more sophisticated and costly techniques for adapting a wide-screen presentation to normal television is the *pan-and-scan* process, whereby the more important portions of the wide-screen frame are scanned and made to fit the 4 × 3 aspect ratio of the standard video screen.

To satisfy the aesthetic requirements of the tiny displays of mobile media, various techniques have been developed to "repurpose" visual content.[8] This means that a series of shots is analyzed for various aesthetic criteria and then reedited so that they will show up effectively on the small screen. This is much more frequently a matter of resizing content or highlighting the area of interest, however, than of changing the aspect ratio.

Whatever technique is employed, such a recomposition of each frame is as much an aesthetic intrusion as re-editing the entire movie. It is therefore much easier for you to frame each shot with the "4 × 3 protect" in mind, which means to keep, at least for the time being, the central action more or less confined to the 4 × 3 aspect ratio.

ASPECT RATIOS OF MOBILE VIDEO MEDIA

Although the viewing screens of mobile video devices have different aspect ratios, all must be able to accommodate the 4 × 3 and 16 × 9 formats. Much like the larger screens of television sets, the small screen of the mobile video media use letter- and pillarboxing for displaying content framed in one or the other aspect ratio.

Because of the small size of the mobile video displays, the difference between the two aspect ratios is hardly noticeable. In any case, the aesthetic consequences of such space manipulation are minimal. For example, the extended width of a large 16 × 9 screen is definitely superior to the 4 × 3 format when showing a typical landscape shot, such as a city skyline, a mountain range, or a river. As

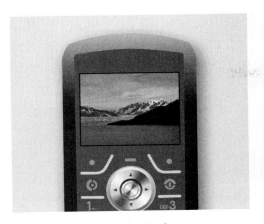

6.26 4 × 3 Mobile Video Display

The small 4 × 3 screen of a mobile video device can show a landscape but not carry its emotional impact.

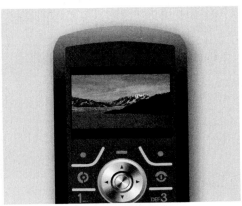

6.27 16 × 9 Mobile Video Display

Although the shot now captures the full 16 × 9 aspect ratio, the difference in size from the 4 × 3 ratio is so minute that it will not make us feel the landscape any more intensely.

mentioned earlier, the extended screen width intensifies the landscape character of a horizontally oriented scene. On the small screen, however, the difference in screen size is so minute that it fails to cause such an affective response. We may *see* a slight difference in how much of the scene is captured by the shot, but we won't *feel* it. **SEE 6.26 AND 6.27**

SECONDARY FRAMES

Since the early days of the motion picture, directors have attempted to change the fixed aspect ratio of the screen whenever the pictorial content demanded it. Especially in the era of silent film, when story and concepts had to be communicated by visual means only, attempts were made to break out of the static 4 × 3 aspect ratio.

Artificial masking   D. W. Griffith used masking during a spectacular battle scene in his 1916 film *Intolerance*. By blacking out both sides of the screen, he created a secondary frame and changed the fundamentally horizontal aspect ratio to a vertical one. This vertical orientation greatly intensified a soldier's fall from high atop the walls of Babylon. Yes, he used the pillarboxing technique long before the digital age. **SEE 6.28**

American film producer and director **D. W. (David Wark) Griffith** (1875–1948) was the innovator of several filmic techniques, such as using various camera positions to change the field of view (long shots and close-ups) and the angle from which the event was filmed. His *Birth of a Nation* (1915) established the feature-length film.

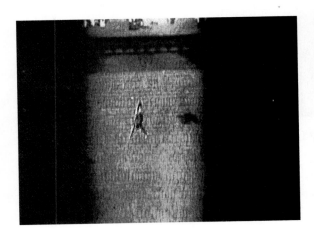

6.28 Changing Aspect Ratio Through Artificial Masking

One of the more successful masking effects occurred in 1916 in the spectacular battle scene in D. W. Griffith's *Intolerance*. To intensify a soldier's fall from high atop the walls of Babylon, Griffith changed the horizontal aspect ratio to a vertical one by masking both sides of the screen. Obviously, pillarboxing is nothing new.

6.29 **Changing Aspect Ratio Through Organic Masking**

Rather than artificially block out the sides of the wide movie screen to change its aspect ratio, we can use scenic elements such as trees or buildings as masking devices. In this case, the foreground buildings change the horizontal aspect ratio to a vertical one that dramatizes the high-rise building.

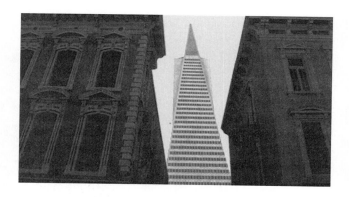

Organic masking A less obvious method of masking is filling the sides of the screen with natural scenic elements, such as buildings, trees, or furniture. This technique is especially effective when framing close-ups or vertical scenes within the wide aspect ratio. **SEE 6.29**

SCREENS WITHIN THE SCREEN

You can create a secondary frame of any aspect ratio within the principal frame and simply leave the space around the secondary frame empty (or color it in some way to suggest a common background). This is one of the favorite ways in advertising to draw attention to the central message. **SEE 6.30**

Today the use of different aspect ratios within the main frame is common in video presentations, especially in news and advertisements. Through the use of digital video effects equipment, we can easily create separate and discrete picture areas within the television frame, each carrying a different static or moving image. **SEE 6.31**

By displaying multiple images with their own aspect ratios on the principal video screen, you are able to show simultaneous yet spatially separated events or relate various subjects or points of view in a single shot. Note, however, that such displays do not change or expand the original aspect ratio of the screen. **SEE 6.32**

However you look at it, a divided screen cannot replace the effect of an expanded field through multiple screens. We discuss this distinction in chapter 8.

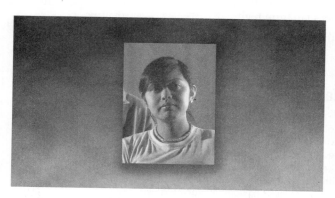

6.30 **Secondary Frame Within the Principal Frame**

A secondary frame within the main video display can have a variety of aspect ratios. In this case, the secondary frame has a vertical orientation. This is similar to windowboxing, but the secondary frame does not have to be centered.

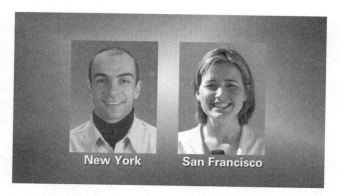

6.31 **Changing Aspect Ratio with Secondary Frames**

Through digital video effects, we can create many secondary picture areas within the video display. Both secondary frames have a different aspect ratio from the principal 16 × 9 screen.

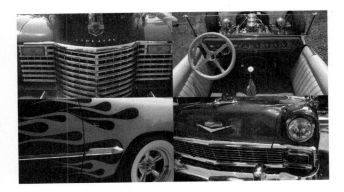

6.32 **Split Screen**
So long as we are aware of the actual screen borders, the four separate screen areas divide the major display but do not expand it as would separate smaller screens.

Moving camera   A moving camera, of course, can easily overcome the basic restrictions of the fixed aspect ratio. To show the height of a tower, for example, you can start with a close-up of the bottom of the tower and then gradually tilt up to reveal its top. Panning sideways, you can reveal an equally wide horizontal vista. Such gradual revelations are often more dramatic than a long shot of the same scene.

The Aesthetics of Size

When you watch a movie first on a large screen in the theater and then on a small video screen, do you see giants on the large screen and Lilliputians on the small screen? Of course not. As with color constancy, which makes us see colors as uniform despite variations, our perception is guided by *size constancy*, which means that we perceive people and their environments as normal sized regardless of whether they appear in a long shot or a close-up on a large movie screen or a small video screen, or whether we are relatively close to or far away from the screen. So long as we know by experience how large or small an object should be, we perceive it as its normal size regardless of screen size, relative image size, or perceived object distance. As you will see, however, the physical size of the screen does have a great influence on how we perceive its projected images.

To learn more about the aesthetics of size, we take a closer look at two important factors: object size and image size.

> Size constancy is truly a contextual phenomenon. It is the context within which we see an object that supplies us with the necessary clues for perceiving the object's actual shape and size. In the absence of other clues, it is the perceived distance that keeps the size of an object constant.

Object Size

How do you know how big an object that appears on a video or movie screen really is? You can't tell. **SEE 6.33** Because you know how big a playing card actually is, you

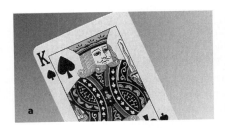
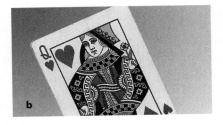
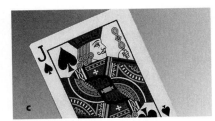

6.33 **Interpreting Object Size: Knowledge of Object**
How big are these playing cards? We don't really know. All we can do is assume that they are the same size.

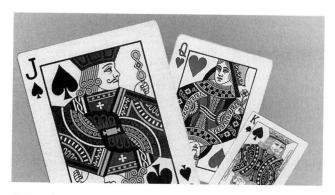

6.34 Comparison to Established Size Standard

Now we know that they are different-sized playing cards. But we still don't know which of the three cards is the normal-sized one.

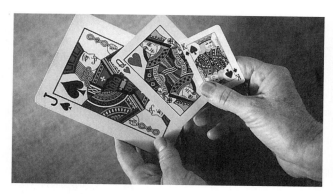

6.35 Size Reference to Human Being

As soon as you see the cards in relation to the universal reference—a human being (or parts thereof, such as these hands)—you can immediately judge the actual size of the objects. The middle card is the normal-sized one.

probably assume that you are seeing close-ups of standard-sized playing cards. Not so. As you can see in the figure, the shots are of cards that differ considerably in size. **SEE 6.34** Which of the three cards is normal size? Although you now know that there are three different sizes of cards, do you know just how big they actually are? You still can't tell for sure. The only sure way of indicating actual size is to put the cards in the context of a universal size reference: a human being. For example, a hand holding the three cards is an immediate and fairly accurate index of the cards' actual sizes. **SEE 6.35**

But we also have other, perhaps more subtle perceptual clues to judging size when objects appear as screen images: knowledge of the object, relation to screen area, and scale.

KNOWLEDGE OF OBJECT

If you are familiar with the object displayed on the screen, you automatically translate the screen image into the known size of the object regardless of whether the object appears in a long shot or a close-up (see figure 6.33).

RELATION TO SCREEN AREA

If we don't know the object on the screen, we tend to judge its size by how much screen area it occupies. If it takes up a large portion of the screen, we perceive it as relatively large. **SEE 6.36** If it covers only a small area, we perceive it as relatively small. **SEE 6.37** But even if we know the object, we tend to feel more graphic weight and, with it, more aesthetic energy when the object is shown in a close-up than in a long shot.

Let's assume for a moment that you are asked by an advertising agency to get a tight close-up of a tiny, powerful new watch battery so that viewers can read the manufacturer's name stamped on it. Would you agree to such a shot? In the light of the theories put forth here, such a close-up would certainly prove counterproductive. A screen-filling close-up of the battery would take up so much of the picture area that we would perceive the battery as both large and heavy.

A relatively simple solution might be to pull back for a long shot so that the battery is quite small relative to the surrounding screen space and then key the name of the manufacturer above or below it. Even more effectively, you could have someone hold it on a fingertip, using the hand as a universal size reference. You could then move in for a tight close-up, because the size relation between

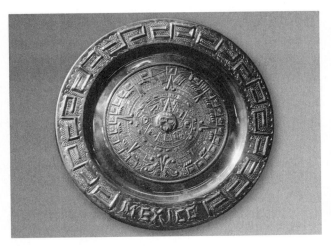

6.36 Screen Area as Size Reference: Close-up

If we don't know the object, we tend to judge its size by how much screen area it occupies. The more it occupies, the larger it seems to be. In this close-up, the disc seems large.

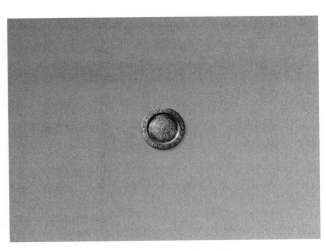

6.37 Screen Area as Size Reference: Long Shot

In this long shot, the disc occupies relatively little screen space, so it appears to be small.

hand and battery is established and will remain largely intact. You can then key into the frame the manufacturer's name.

SCALE

As in our real environment, we make continual judgments about object size by seeing the object on-screen in relation to other (usually known) objects that appear in the same shot. We seem to decide on a size standard against which the other sizes are judged and hierarchically ordered. The convenient feature about scale is that it remains constant, regardless of whether you perceive it on the large movie screen or the tiny mobile video display. To establish a scale, however, we must have some norm, some clue that tells us just what is large and what is small. In the absence of such contextual information, even a comparison of two known objects leaves you in the dark about their actual size. **SEE 6.38**

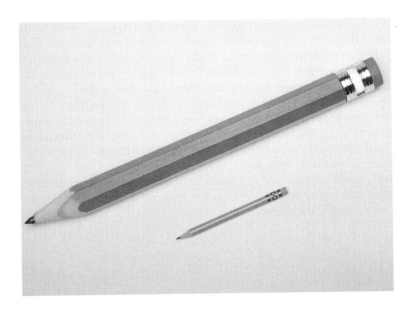

6.38 Screen Frame as Scale Reference

In the absence of more accurate contextual clues, we use the proximity of the object to the frame edge as a clue. The larger pencil is probably shown in a close-up.

6.39 Hand as Scale Reference

As with the playing cards, the hand as a contextual reference helps establish an accurate scale. The large pencil was not a normal-sized one on a close-up but an oversized one on a medium shot.

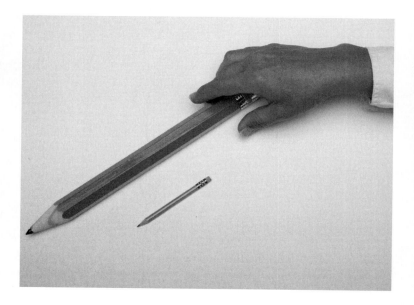

The two pencils obviously differ in size. But how? In the absence of more obvious clues, we try to estimate the apparent distance of an object and then calculate its size.[9] If we assume that the larger pencil is a normal-sized one, it must be on a close-up, and the smaller one must be a little pencil. This stands to reason because we come up against more small pencils than supersized ones. But when we introduce our universal size reference—a hand—we see that we were, indeed, fooled by this shot and that our established scale was based on wrong assumptions. **SEE 6.39**

We usually get a great variety of contextual clues that help us establish a reasonably accurate scale for screen-displayed object size. But if it is contextual clues that prompt us to establish a scale for object size, couldn't we provide false clues that trick the viewers into a fallacious scale so that they perceive small things as large and large things as small? Yes, and we do this every time we use small models for simulating large-scale events or put an event into a computer-generated environment. The real problem, however, is not establishing a scale but maintaining it throughout the screen event. A model of a skyscraper must look big in relation to all contextual event factors, such as people, cars, and trees. The important, and not always easy, additional task is to make the movement of all people and objects fit the established scale. A small model of a large battleship usually bounces much too fast in relation to the real movement of the waves. A model of a spaceship must move extremely slowly if we are to believe that it is huge. Fortunately, today we can manipulate such movement quite easily with digital wizardry.

Cartoons always operate on the contextual principle of scale: the close-up of a foot trampling houses, trees, bridges, and everything else in its way becomes that of a giant if we take the landscape as the norm. But if we take the foot as the standard-sized reference, the landscape becomes small like the one of the unfortunate Lilliputians in *Gulliver's Travels*.

As with the perception of other aesthetic phenomena, our translation of screen images into actual object size is greatly influenced by other contextual clues—in this case, by the framework of the story.

Image Size

Have you ever felt ill at ease when watching a motion picture spectacle on the small video screen or, worse, on the mobile video display? Some motion pictures designed for the large, wide movie screen do not seem to come across as well on a standard-sized television screen.

Despite our hardwired ability to perceive scale as constant regardless of how big the pictures are, physical size still has considerable influence on how we perceive and feel about screen images.

The overwhelmingly large images on the horizontally stretched movie screen present a spectacle, no matter what is shown. People as well as things attain dramatic proportions, not only physically but also psychologically. The landscape aspect of a scene—that is, its physical environment—carries at least as much energy as the people who play in it. On the large movie screen, the simple event of a man walking down a country road becomes a grand act; on the small video screen, it remains a simple gesture.

In a movie about space exploration, the spaceship floating majestically across the giant screen most likely has as much or more impact on the viewer as the fate of the crew. Large HDTV screens favor, similar to the large movie screen, landscape over people. But on the small video screen, the people and their actions command attention and supply the primary energy; the environment remains relatively peripheral if not incidental. Cinema and large-screen video derive their energy from landscape as well as people; in small-screen video, it is primarily people with all their complexity who power a scene, while the landscape aspects take a back seat.

Does this mean that we cannot show landscape-type movies on a mobile video device? Not necessarily. First, the computer interface, which often divides its page into many diminutive pictures and text blocks, has already conditioned us for small-screen static and moving images. Second, it depends on how you are looking at the movie. Trying to watch a complex, full-length film while sitting on a bus would probably not be the most stirring experience, even if the bus ride were fairly long. Although you would be able to follow the plot enough to fear for the hero and loath the villain, the small images and inadequate sound would probably fail to communicate the story's full dramatic impact or give you the gut-level experience of large, high-energy images and sound.

But if your friend sends you the same movie via your mobile video device with a request to analyze the continuity of its editing, the small screen and its tiny images do not present an insurmountable handicap, even while riding on a bus. You no longer are trying to immerse yourself emotionally in the program but are scrutinizing it more intellectually. When you do this, the experience of watching the small mobile video display is not much different from looking at landscapes or portraits in miniature paintings or through the viewfinder of a film or video camera when framing a shot. In either case, the aesthetics of size and the emotional impact on how we perceive screen images of people and their surroundings are no longer an issue.

But how can we optimize the images on the mobile video display, assuming that mobile video is used as a diversion rather than an instrument of analysis or communicating text messages?

MOBILE VIDEO MEDIA AS COMPANION

Much like watching a program on your small television set in the kitchen while doing the dishes, or listening to your iPod while jogging, your mobile video media can be a pleasant companion or an occasional diversion from your primary activity. In this case, you would do much better by choosing a video that has been specifically designed not only for the small screen but also for such viewing conditions. But what are these design factors? Let's have a look at the major ones.

Close-ups Like the standard television screen, the mobile video display requires a predominance of close-ups. On the most basic level, if the shot is too wide and you can't see what it contains, you need to get closer. Long shots are always hard to see on a small screen, and they lack aesthetic energy. In fact, the quickest way to deflate a shot of its energy even on a larger screen is to zoom back from a close-up to a wider shot. On the small screen, you need to use close-ups as much as possible, regardless of whether you show people or environment. Yes, the infamous "talking heads" gain new prominence. In fact, this is one of the prerequisites for presenting interviews. There is literally no room on a mobile video display to have your guests sit comfortably apart from each other on a loose medium shot during the interview or walk side-by-side through a picturesque countryside on a long shot.

Inductive sequencing As you will learn in chapter 11, the inductive visual approach means that you present a story in a series of close-up details rather than move from an establishing long shot to a few eventual close-ups. The shot sequence must be very dense, which necessitates cramming a lot of shots into a relatively short time period, much like commercial spots do. Because inductive sequencing is mostly done with close-ups, it is essential for mobile video.

Brief running times The stories must be told in a very short time span or at least in relatively short segments, from 30 seconds to a maximum of three minutes. If this seems too short to you, just look at the average news story, which rarely exceeds 20 seconds, video clips included. Again, realize that your stories are mostly watched by somebody walking to the subway, riding on a bus or in a car, or sitting in a classroom (before the professor arrives). A series of brief stories that, like soap operas, are self-contained but have a continuing plot are most effective. You can also provide the necessary continuity by using the same character in different stories. A researcher from the London School of Economics calls this "content snacking."[10]

Dense audio track Because of the extremely limited visual space, you need to pay particular attention to the audio track. The audio must not only reproduce what is being said but also provide ambient sounds. These environmental sounds will help expand the screen and convey what is occurring in on- and off-screen space as well as provide much needed aesthetic energy (see chapter 15).

You probably noticed that all these design factors for mobile video are already applied to movie trailers and commercial spots. Despite your best efforts, however, it is virtually impossible to generate the aesthetic energy of large images on the tiny mobile video display. If you try to do it by boosting the audio level—a technique that works well in a movie theater—the sound has a tendency to separate from the picture and take on its own life.

IMAGE SIZE AND RELATIVE ENERGY

Despite our facility for size constancy, image size still influences how we feel about certain screen events. The large images on the panoramic movie screen *feel* more overpowering than a small video image. They are visually "louder" than the pictures on the video screen. When an image is large, it simply has more aesthetic energy than the same image does when small.

Just think of how you felt in the presence of an exceptionally large thing: a huge skyscraper, a giant ocean liner, a crowded football stadium, a towering redwood tree, a majestic mountain, or the Grand Canyon. You may not have felt smaller physically than in any other environment, but the grandiosity of the object probably overwhelmed you somehow. The mere energy of enormousness can inspire awe. Large things do not seem to be as manageable as small things; you have less control over them, which makes them appear more powerful.[11]

When you watch a documentary on a small standard (4 × 3) video screen and then see it on an equally small wide-screen (16 × 9) receiver, you probably notice relatively little energy change. When you switch from the small screen to a large HDTV screen, however, the energy change is readily apparent. This is why some movies that emphasize landscape (from actual landscapes to spaceships or battle scenes) must be seen on the large screen to feel the total impact. Even if you use proper conversion methods for aspect ratios, squeezing such large images into the small video screen reduces not only image size but also, if not especially, event energy. Close-ups, inductive sequencing, and a dense audio track help generate some aesthetic energy on the small video screen, but they cannot compete with the large movie images and high-volume surround sound.

SUMMARY

This chapter explored the two-dimensional field—the area of the video and film screens and some of the basic structural elements and characteristics we confront in this field. The video or film screen provides us with a new, concentrated living space—an aesthetic field in which to clarify and intensify an event. We examined the structural factors of screen space: aspect ratio and the aesthetics of object size and image size.

Contrary to the picture area in painting and still photography, which can have any shape and orientation, the standard video and film screens are rectangular and horizontal. The classic film screen and the standard video screen have a 4 × 3 (1.33:1) aspect ratio: the screen is 4 units wide by 3 units high, regardless of size. This aspect ratio permits easy framing of horizontally as well as vertically oriented objects or scenes. Most HDTV presentations and motion pictures are now shot and projected in a horizontally stretched format. The aspect ratio for HDTV is 16 × 9 (1.78:1); for standard motion picture projection, it is 5.55 × 3 (1.85:1).

Standard video and movie screens are horizontally oriented because our peripheral vision is greater horizontally than it is vertically, and in keeping with our everyday experience of living on a horizontal plane. The aspect ratios of small mobile video displays can be horizontal or even vertical in a great variety of aspect ratios.

There are several, albeit not always satisfactory, solutions to making a standard 4 × 3 presentation fit the 16 × 9 screen and vice versa. Windowboxing is to center the smaller screen within the actual video screen. The window can have any format but is usually 4 × 3 or 16 × 9. Letterboxing is making a 16 × 9 image fit a 4 × 3 screen by masking the unused areas on top and bottom of the screen with horizontal stripes, sometimes called dead zones. Pillarboxing is used to make a 4 × 3 picture fit a 16 × 9 screen, leaving the vertical stripes on either side of the screen.

With digital special-effects equipment in video, we can easily generate secondary frames that have various aspect ratios and configurations. In film we can either black out the sides of the screen to reduce the horizontal stretch or fill in the sides with scenic objects to change the aspect ratio more unobtrusively.

The aesthetics of size includes the perception of object size when shown on the screen. Our perception is guided by size constancy, which means that we perceive people and their environments as normal sized regardless of whether they appear in a long shot or a close-up on a large movie screen or a small video screen, or whether we are relatively close to or far away from the screen. The major clues to the actual size of an object when shown on-screen are knowledge of the object, relation to the screen area, and contextual scale.

When we know an object, we perceive its screen image as actual size. When we don't know the object, we tend to translate the image size into actual object size as perceived on-screen: the more screen area the object takes up, the larger it seems and vice versa. When several objects are shown on-screen, we establish a size standard and judge all other objects accordingly. We also use the perceived distance of an object for establishing scale. The most common size reference for objects is a human being.

When shown on the movie screen, the image size of an object is many times larger than when shown on even a large video screen. Because of size constancy, we perceive the objects as equal in size. Nevertheless, the large movie image usually carries much more aesthetic energy than does the small video image. People as well as things attain spectacular dimensions on the wide screen. On the standard video screen, human actions gain prominence whereas the mere spectacle of things is de-emphasized.

The small display area of mobile video media can show landscape movies but fails to communicate the emotional impact and the aesthetic energy. When a mobile video device is used as a companion, these major aesthetic factors need to be considered in creating content: close-ups, inductive sequencing, brief running times, and a dense audio track. Despite these production factors, however, it is virtually impossible to generate the aesthetic energy of large images on the tiny mobile video display.

NOTES

1. Boris Uspensky, *A Poetics of Composition,* trans. by Valentina Zavarin and Susan Wittig (Berkeley: University of California Press, 1973), p. 143.

2. When you're standing still, your normal peripheral vision is considerably wider on a horizontal plane (about 180 degrees) than on a vertical one (about 70 degrees). Expressed in a rectangular aspect ratio, this comes to approximately 2.53:1. When moving, however, our peripheral vision diminishes rapidly. See Arthur Seiderman and Steven Marcus, *20/20 Is Not Enough* (New York: Alfred A. Knopf, 1990), pp. 112–13, 142–43.

3. Such eyeball jumps are called saccadic movement. James J. Gibson says that it is the combination of saccadic movement and temporary fixation that constitutes the act of scanning. See James J. Gibson, *The Ecological Approach to Visual Perception* (Hillsdale, N.J.: Lawrence Erlbaum, 1986), pp. 211–13.

4. John Belton, *Widescreen Cinema* (Cambridge, Mass.: Harvard University Press, 1992), pp. 15–18. See also Mark Schubin, "Searching for the Perfect Aspect Ratio," *SMPTE Journal* (August 1996): 460–78; and Mark Schubin, "No Answer," *Videography* (March 1996): 18–33.

5. Peter Ward, *Picture Composition for Film and Television,* 2nd ed. (Boston and London: Focal Press, 2003), pp. 90–105. Ward argues eloquently against the "spectacle" idea and considers it a throwback to the 1950s. He suggests that the wider-screen aspect ratio was developed simply "for its ability to engage the audience."

6. Steven D. Katz, *Film Directing: Shot by Shot* (Studio City, Calif.: Michael Wiese Productions, 1991), p. 215.

7. Ward, *Picture Composition,* p. 83.

8. There are several projects under way to develop a technique that can adjust, or "repurpose," video productions and films to fit various screen aspect ratios and sizes. For how aesthetic decisions are made in such a process, see Chitra Dorai and Svetha Venkatesh (eds.), *Media Computing: Computational Media Aesthetics* (Boston: Kluwer Academic, 2002).

9. E. H. Gombrich, *The Image and the Eye* (Ithaca, N.Y.: Cornell University Press, 1982), p. 198.

10. "Content snacking" was coined by Dr. Shani Orgad, a media scholar at the London School of Economics and Political Science. See Shani Orgad, *This box was made for walking: how will mobile TV transform viewers' experience and change advertising?* Nokia Mobile TV report 2006, no. 2519. Available at *www.nokia.com/NOKIA_COM_1/ Press/Press_Events/mobile_tv_report,_november_10,_2006/Mobil_TV_Report.pdf.*

11. See Alva Noë, *Action in Perception* (Cambridge, Mass.: MIT Press, 2004), p. 105.

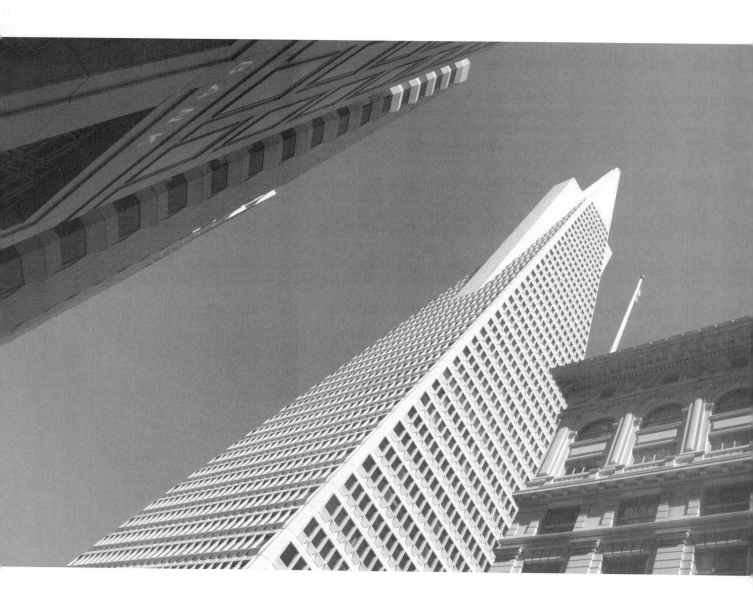

The Two-dimensional Field:
Forces Within the Screen

IN OUR EFFORT TO TAME SPACE AESTHETICALLY, THAT IS, TO CREATE A picture space, you should now consider the video, computer, and motion picture screens a new field of operations. Within this fixed and clearly defined space operate specific field forces that are quite different from those of an undefined space, such as our actual three-dimensional environment. To clarify and intensify events within this new operational field, you must understand these major field forces: main directions, magnetism of the frame, asymmetry of the frame, figure and ground, psychological closure, and vectors.

Main Directions: Horizontal and Vertical

One of the most basic field forces is how we perceive and structure events that occupy primarily horizontal and vertical screen space. Because we ordinarily move about in a horizontal world, and also spend a great portion of our lives in a horizontal position while sleeping, a horizontal placement within the screen, and horizontal lines, seems to suggest normalcy, calm, tranquility, and rest. **SEE 7.1** Vertical space, on the other hand, is harder to manage. Thus vertical lines seem more dynamic, powerful, and exciting than horizontal ones. **SEE 7.2**

These aesthetic principles have been applied throughout civilization. The Gothic cathedral, for example, was built with a vertical orientation to direct the human experience upward, toward heaven and God. **SEE 7.3** Renaissance buildings, in contrast, emphasized the importance of human endeavors and are therefore principally horizontal in orientation. **SEE 7.4**

Today's high-rise buildings operate much in the spirit of the Gothic cathedrals. Though their vertical orientation may have been primarily motivated by the high cost of real estate, they nevertheless reflect the contemporary human spirit—adventurous with an admirable earth-defying dynamism. **SEE 7.5**

Because of gravity and the fact that we are used to standing upright on level ground, we like to see our environment mirror our experience and be portrayed as a stable series of horizontals and verticals. In fact, most of our natural or constructed physical environment is organized into verticals that are perpendicular to the level ground. **SEE 7.6**

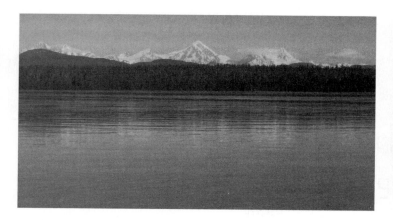

7.1 Main Direction: Horizontal

Horizontal lines suggest calm, tranquility, and rest. We feel normal when operating on this familiar horizontal plane.

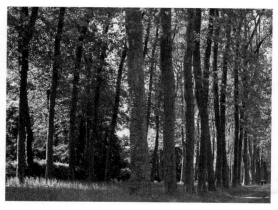

7.2 Main Direction: Vertical

Vertical lines are more powerful and exciting than horizontal ones. Their defiance of gravity charges them with extra energy.

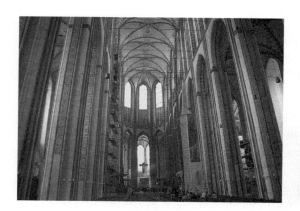

7.3 Vertical Orientation: Gothic Cathedral

The extreme vertical orientation of Gothic cathedrals and their imposing size were designed to remind people of their insignificance relative to God and to direct their spirit upward toward heaven.

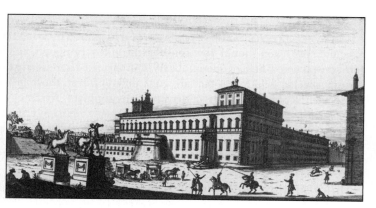

7.4 Horizontal Orientation: Renaissance Building

The horizontal orientation of Renaissance buildings appropriately reflected people's renewed interest in human affairs.

Courtesy of the DeBellis Collection, San Francisco State University.

> In the Gothic period (roughly from 1150 to 1400), life on earth was simply a preparation for the "real life" in heaven. People lived and worked strictly *in dei gloriam*—for the glory of God. The vertical orientation of the Gothic cathedrals reflects this mind-set.
>
> The Renaissance (roughly from 1400 to 1600), with its rebirth of classical Greek architecture, emphasized the importance of humanity. *In dei gloriam* was supplanted by *in hominis gloriam*. Horizontal buildings are in keeping with this new attitude of glorifying the human spirit.

TILTING THE HORIZONTAL PLANE

Our sense of vertical and horizontal accuracy is so keen that we can, for example, judge whether a picture hangs straight or crooked with uncanny precision even without the aid of a level. It's no wonder that when we see a tilt to the horizontal plane within the screen, we become somewhat disturbed if not disoriented. Our normal and hence secure upright position on a level horizontal plane is threatened by what we perceive. As the horizon starts tilting, we lose our usually reliable and stable reference: the earth. When the horizon tilts, we immediately seek a new and more stable reference regardless of whether it makes sense. For example, when sitting in an airplane that banks sharply, we tend to assign stability to our immediate environment—the airplane—and not to the earth. Consequently, the horizon, rather than the airplane, seems to be doing the tilting.

Lacking a new stable reference, such a tilting effect may cause in us considerable psychophysical discomfort. For example, when we

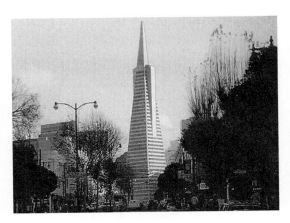

7.5 Vertical Orientation: High-rise Building

Modern high-rises, like their Gothic cousins the cathedrals, are bold and earth defying. They mirror the dynamic spirit of contemporary people.

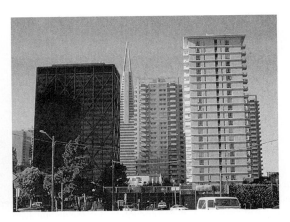

7.6 Horizontal/Vertical Environment

A combination of horizontals and verticals reflects our everyday world. Most of our normal physical environment—the buildings we live in, our furniture, doors, and windows—are verticals perpendicular to level ground.

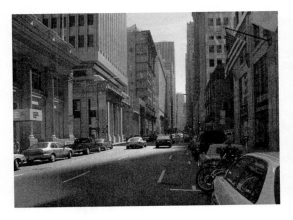

7.7 Level Horizon: Stability

If you want to emphasize stability, conservatism, and reliability, you must show the buildings standing on level ground.

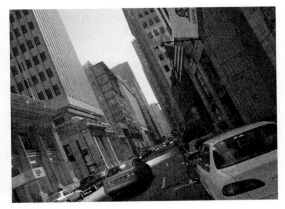

7.8 Tilted Horizon: Dynamism

If you want to suggest energy, activity, and progress, you can render the scene dynamic by tilting the horizontal plane.

sit close to a large movie screen, the tilted horizon effect can, in extreme cases, cause nausea.

Simply by canting the camera and thus tilting the horizontal plane, you can easily destabilize a scene or make an otherwise uninteresting building or object look dynamic. **SEE 7.7 AND 7.8** You can also suggest people's extreme physical or mental stress by having them operate on a tilted horizontal plane. **SEE 7.9**

There is no video of a rock concert that does not have the horizon tilt at least a few dozen times. Because this adds intensity to the already high-energy scene, such an aesthetic device is usually justified. If it is indiscriminately applied to news or documentary productions, however, tilting the horizon often proves counterproductive. A tilted horizon will not liven up a dull interview or help a wooden political candidate get elected.

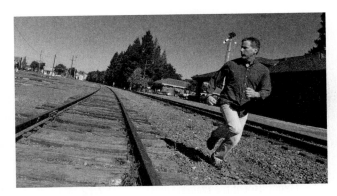

7.9 Tilted Horizon: Stress

By tilting the horizontal plane, you can intensify the feeling of physical or mental stress of someone running from danger.

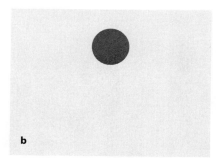
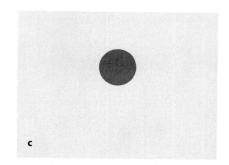

7.10 Magnetism of the Frame: Top

The edges of the screen exert a strong pull on objects near them. The disc in (a) seems to be glued to the top edge despite the normal downward gravitational pull. The pull of the frame is strong enough to hold the disc up even when there is more space between the disc and the edge (b). Only when the distance between the top edge and the disc reaches a certain point does it become so great that gravity takes over (c).

Magnetism of the Frame

The borders of a picture field act like magnets: they have a tendency to attract objects near them. This ***magnetism of the frame*** can be so strong that it counteracts our natural reaction to gravitational pull. **SEE 7.10** Note how the disc seems to be glued to the upper border in figure 7.10a. The gravitational pull comes into play only after the disc is a considerable distance away from the upper border and its magnetic attraction (figure 7.10c).

The sides of the screen also exert a strong pull. **SEE 7.11** As you can see in figure 7.11, the discs do not seem to be pulled down by gravity as you might expect; instead they are attracted by the magnetism of the frame's sides. Because the screen corners combine the magnetism of two sides, they exert an especially strong pull. Obviously, you should avoid compositions whose dominant lines lead directly to the corner of the screen. **SEE 7.12**

The most stable position for the disc is clearly screen-center. Here it is farthest away from the magnetic pull of the edges; and the force of the pull, however weak, is equally distributed. **SEE 7.13**

If the disc is large and wedged into the screen, it is subject to the magnetism of all four edges. We have the feeling that it wants to burst out of the frame's confinement and expand. **SEE 7.14** Of course, the magnetism of the screen edges is

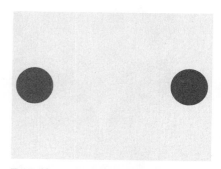
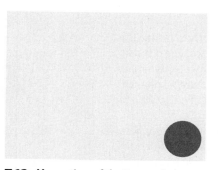
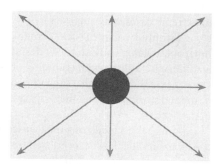

7.11 Magnetism of the Frame: Sides

The pull of the side edges is so strong that it easily overrides gravitational pull.

7.12 Magnetism of the Frame: Corners

The screen corners exert an especially strong magnetic pull.

7.13 Neutralized Magnetism: Screen-center

When the disc is centered within the frame, all magnetic pulls are equalized. The disc is at rest.

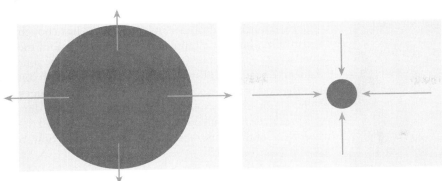

7.14 Large Object: Expansion
When an object is wedged into the screen, it is subject to the magnetism of the entire frame and therefore tends to expand and look unusually large.

7.15 Small Object: Compression
When the object is small enough and relatively far from the screen edges, the magnetism of the frame no longer operates. On the contrary, the space surrounding the object compresses it to make it appear quite small.

not the only reason why we perceive the disc as unusually large. It also occupies a relatively large screen area, which, as discussed in chapter 6, indicates a large object.

Conversely, when the small disc is centered within the picture field and far from the screen edges, it is no longer subject to their magnetic pull. The concentrated "heavy" negative space surrounding the object also seems to compress it, making it appear smaller than it really is. **SEE 7.15** This principle was also applied in figures 6.36 and 6.37.

Let's see how to work with the magnetism of the frame when composing a shot.

HEADROOM

A close-up with too little space between the top of the head and the upper edge of the frame looks awkward. Why? Because the head seems to be glued to the upper screen edge. We are as uncomfortable with such a composition as we are standing up in a room with a very low ceiling. **SEE 7.16** You need to leave some "breathing space," called ***headroom***, to counteract the magnetic pull of the upper screen edge. **SEE 7.17** But if you leave too much headroom, the head is pushed down into the lower half of the frame through the combined forces of gravitational pull and the magnetism of the lower screen edge.[1] **SEE 7.18**

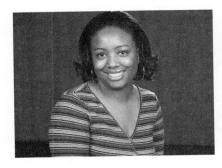

7.16 No Headroom
Without headroom the attraction of the upper screen edge pulls the head firmly against it.

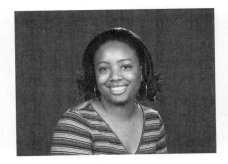

7.17 Proper Headroom
To counteract the pull of the upper screen edge, you must leave enough headroom.

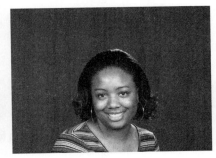

7.18 Too Much Headroom
Here you have too much headroom. The magnetism of the frame has now capitulated to gravitational pull, so the shot looks bottom-heavy.

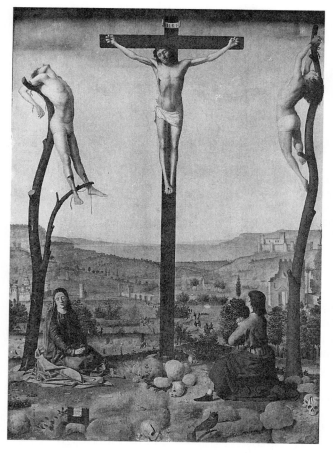

7.19 Using the Pull of the Top Edge

The old masters used the magnetism of the frame to intensify their messages. By reducing headroom to a minimum, the figures seem to be more suspended than if they were lower in the painting.

Antonello da Messina (c. 1430–1479) *Crucifixion.*/Koninklijk Museum voor Schone Kunsten, Antwerp, Belgium/Scala/Art Resource, NY.

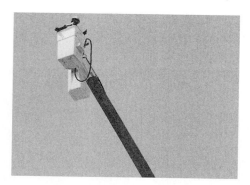

7.20 Lack of Headroom for Intensification

To emphasize the precariousness of somebody working up high, you can use the magnetism of the upper edge to advantage. In this shot the minimal headroom maximizes the pull of the upper screen edge.

How much headroom should you leave? Just enough to neutralize, but not eliminate, the magnetic pull of the upper screen edge. But just where is that? Technically, your headroom framing will be approximately correct if you place the eyes of the person in the upper third of the frame's height. Unfortunately, you will have little opportunity during a production to pull out a tape measure to pinpoint the upper third of the frame. You are better off learning how to judge it intuitively.

PULL OF THE TOP EDGE

Leaving headroom is not mandatory, however. Under certain circumstances you can use the magnetic pull of the upper edge to your advantage. You can learn more about the pull of the top edge of a frame by studying the paintings of old masters. For example, in his painting *Crucifixion,* Antonello da Messina placed the figures, especially that of Christ, so close to the upper edge that its magnetic pull comes into action and heightens the agony of hanging from the cross. **SEE 7.19**

In a similar way, you can emphasize the precariousness of someone operating at uncomfortable heights by deliberately leaving inadequate headroom. This lack of space will pull the person to the upper edge and make him hang in space more than if you had framed him with the customary headroom. **SEE 7.20** You can also stretch aesthetically a fashion model by wedging her between the top and the bottom edges of the frame.

PULL OF THE SIDE EDGES

The major problem that occurs as a result of the magnetic pull of the side edges is that objects that seem normally spaced in a long shot will often look too far apart in a tighter shot. You can see this in an establishing shot of an interview, when the host and the guest seem to be sitting at a comfortable distance from each other. **SEE 7.21** But as soon as you move in with the camera for a tighter shot, the two people now look too far apart, seemingly glued to the left and right edges of the screen. **SEE 7.22** They have become part of the screen edge and created a secondary frame, emphasizing the empty center portion of the picture. This problem is similar to that of framing two people facing each other, as shown in figure 6.17.

When working in the 4 × 3 aspect ratio, this magnetism problem of pulling people apart is ever-present. One way of solving it is to use over-the-shoulder shots or cross-shots for two people talking to each other (see figures 11.22 to 11.25). In the wider 16 × 9 aspect ratio, however, this problem is greatly reduced or even eliminated because you have enough space between the people and the screen edges to neutralize the magnetism of the frame.

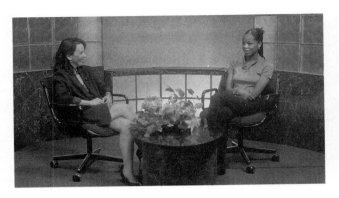

7.21 Normal Distance in Long Shot

In this establishing shot, the people seem to be sitting at a comfortable distance from each other.

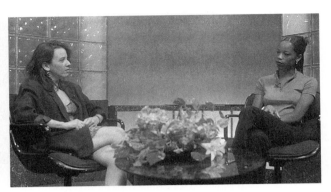

7.22 Edge Pull in Medium Shot

When you move in for a tighter shot, however, the people are pulled apart. The magnetism of the side edges intensifies this separation.

Fortunately, the pull of the sides is not all bad and can work for, rather than against, effective composition. For example, when you want to emphasize the width of an object, the pull of the screen's sides becomes a definite graphic asset. The combined pull of the left and right edges seems to stretch the old road cruiser horizontally, epitomizing the pride of its owner for having such a big car. **SEE 7.23** You can also use the magnetic force of a screen edge to arrest motion and keep someone rooted to the spot. **SEE 7.24**

You encounter a similar problem if you hang pictures at a "normal" distance from one another on a set. The edges of the screen attract the pictures, so they appear pulled apart.

To make pictures look normally spaced in a medium shot, you must crowd them. The attraction of graphic mass among the pictures then counteracts, at least to some extent, the pull of the frame.

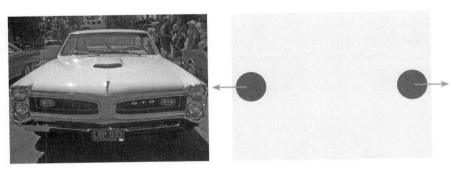

7.23 Positive Pull of Side Edges

When you want to emphasize the width of a large vintage car, the pull of the screen edges becomes a definite graphic asset.

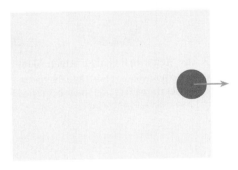

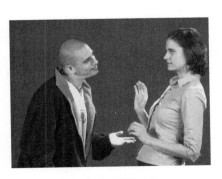

7.24 Positive Pull of Side Edge

Here the pull of the frame works to your advantage. To emphasize visually that the woman has little chance of avoiding this man, she is pinned against the right screen edge.

7.25 Positive Pull of All Screen Edges
The magnetism of all four edges helps emphasize the enormity and the weight of this millstone. It begs to burst out of the confinement of the frame.

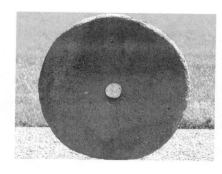

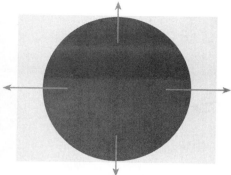

PULL OF ENTIRE FRAME

When an object is wedged into the screen so that all four edges are allowed to pull, the object seems to be as uncomfortable as we are when looking at it. Its confinement makes it look bigger and heavier, which can also be a positive effect. For example, the weight of the millstone in figure 7.25 is properly intensified through its tight framing. **SEE 7.25** A similar thing happens when you frame a close-up of a head in this way. Because of the magnetic pull of the frame, the head seems unusually large, as if it's trying to burst out of the screen. Obviously, you should not frame a head in this fashion.[2] **SEE 7.26**

ATTRACTION OF MASS

All screen images have a certain ***graphic mass***. Usually, larger images with highly saturated colors have a larger graphic mass than smaller ones with less saturated colors. The larger the graphic mass, the greater its ***graphic weight***, that is, the "heavier" (more prominent) the image seems within the frame. Graphic mass attracts graphic mass. The larger the mass, the greater its attractive power. Also, a larger graphic mass attracts smaller ones and not vice versa. Finally, a larger graphic mass is more stable and less likely to move than smaller ones. **SEE 7.27**

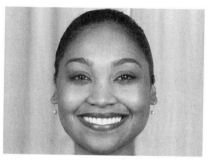

7.26 Negative Pull of All Screen Edges
Wedging this women's head into the frame intensifies the perfect oval shape of the head but also makes it appear bulky.

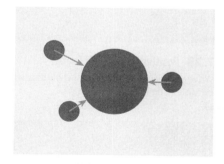

7.27 Attraction of Mass
Graphic mass attracts graphic mass: the larger the mass, the larger its attractive power. The larger graphic mass attracts the smaller one and not vice versa. A large mass is more independent than smaller masses. The larger graphic mass is also more stable (less likely to move) than the smaller ones.

Asymmetry of the Frame

We do not seem to look at the left and right sides of any screen in the same way, nor do we pay equal attention to objects that are located on either half of the screen. We carry this perceptual peculiarity over to the video, film, and computer screens, where we consider it one of the structural screen forces. The two sides of the screen seem structurally unequal. This concept is known as *asymmetry of the frame*.

UP/DOWN DIAGONALS

Take a look at the following figures. **SEE 7.28 AND 7.29** Which of the diagonals seems to go up and which seems to go down?

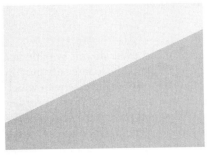

7.28 Diagonal 1
Does this diagonal suggest an uphill or a downhill slope?

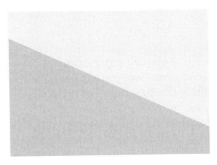

7.29 Diagonal 2
Does this diagonal suggest an uphill or a downhill slope?

Now look at the next set of figures. **SEE 7.30 AND 7.31** Which diagonal do you now perceive to go up and which down?

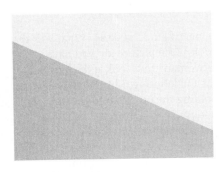

7.30 Diagonal 3
Does this diagonal suggest an uphill or a downhill slope?

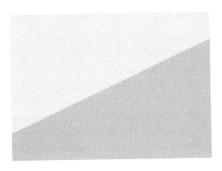

7.31 Diagonal 4
Does this diagonal suggest an uphill or a downhill slope?

You probably chose diagonals 1 and 4 as going up and diagonals 2 and 3 as going down. Why we perceive a specific diagonal as going uphill and another as downhill is anyone's guess. Regardless of whether we learned to write from left to right, right to left, or top to bottom, or whether we are right- or left-handed and right- or left-brained, we seem to "read" the diagonals from left to right.

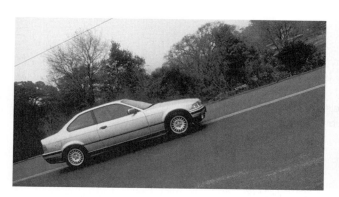

7.32 Uphill Motion Aided by Uphill Diagonal

The uphill diagonal helps pull the car to the top of the hill.

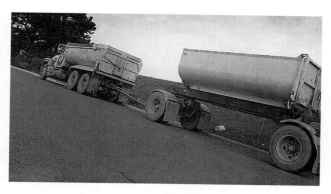

7.33 Uphill Motion Impeded by Downhill Diagonal

This truck has to overcome the graphic down-diagonal, which therefore emphasizes the truck's power.

Although any movement along either slant can override this graphic up/down sensation, you can nevertheless use the up/down slants to intensify motion along the diagonals. For example, if you would like to show the ease with which a car moves up a hill, you should have the car go on a diagonal from lower left to upper right. This way the uphill diagonal helps pull the car to the top of the hill. **SEE 7.32** On the other hand, off-road vehicles, trucks, or bulldozers seem to need more power and effort to climb a hill from right to left than from left to right because they now have to overcome the natural flow of the graphic downhill slant. **SEE 7.33**

If you want to intensify the apparent speed of a runaway truck, have it move along the graphic downhill diagonal (left to right) instead of against the uphill diagonal from right to left. But wouldn't we see the truck race downhill no matter what? Of course, but we are dealing with the finer points of media aesthetics to intensify a scene, however subtle such intensification may be.

SCREEN-LEFT AND SCREEN-RIGHT ASYMMETRY

Quickly glance at the advertisement in the next figure. **SEE 7.34** What was the woman holding? When you take another look at the picture, do you have a tendency to focus more on the product than the woman? Now look at the next figure. **SEE 7.35** Yes, it is a flopped image except for the lettering. But did you now pay just a little more attention to the woman holding the box than to the box itself? If you did, this is a common perceptual response.

Even if the screen is not divided symmetrically, we tend to pay more attention to the right side. Despite the considerable academic controversy surrounding this aesthetic phenomenon,[3] we can use the up- and downhill diagonal as a reasonable explanation of why the right picture area seems to be more conspicuous than the left. In practice this means that if you have a choice, you should place the more important event on the right side of the screen. If, in an interview show, you consider the guest more important than the host, place the guest screen-right and the host screen-left. Most prominent hosts, however, do not want to be upstaged, so they occupy the more conspicuous screen-right position.

Why, then, do we see so many newscasters on screen-left with the less important graphic information of the box on screen-right? Should you not put the primary information source—the newscaster—on screen-right and leave the screen-left side for the computer-generated box? From an aesthetic point of view, the picture is more balanced when the high-energy information source, in this

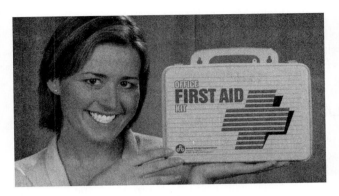

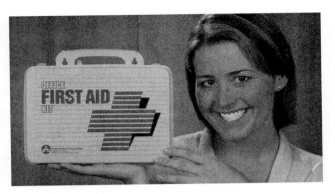

7.34 Emphasis Through Screen Asymmetry

At first glance do you pay more attention to the person or the object?

7.35 Shift of Emphasis

When the picture is flopped, do you still see it in the same way, or has your attention shifted from the object to the person?

case the newscaster, appears on the weaker screen-left side and the lower-energy graphic on the stronger screen-right side. From a communication point of view, however, the primary information source—the newscaster—should definitely be on screen-right, with the illustrative material relegated to the weaker left side. Otherwise we run the risk of having, however subconsciously, the often crude and cryptic graphic representation of the news stories accepted as the primary message rather than the more-detailed accounts by the newscaster.

The asymmetry principle is especially important when designing Web pages. Generally, you should keep the navigation instructions on screen-left and the text (including essential illustrations) on screen-right. Because the navigation information is one of the primary interactive tasks to access the desired content, it does not need to be favored by the right side. The content itself, however, needs to be the focus of attention and is therefore best placed on the stronger screen-right side. **SEE 7.36**

7.36 Asymmetry on Web Page

Because the right side of the screen commands more attention, keep all essential content on the right. Put the navigation information on the less prominent left side.

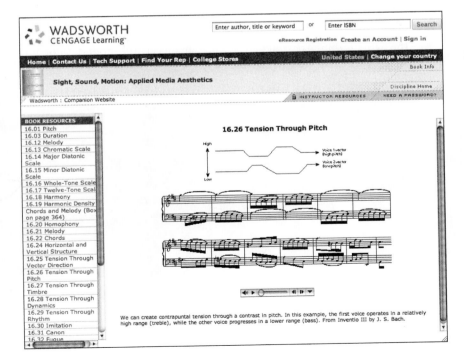

You probably notice that the asymmetry principle is dependent on screen size. On the tiny mobile media display, it does not seem to affect even our subconscious perception whether the newscaster or talk-show host is placed screen-left or screen-right or where the text is placed relative to the navigation instructions.

Figure and Ground

As is our everyday perception, one of the most elemental structural forces operating within the screen is the ***figure/ground principle***. As discussed in chapter 1, our perceptual tendency is to organize our environment into stable reference points (usually the background) against which we can assess the less-stable elements (the figures in front of it). Organizing our environment into a figure/ground relationship is one of our most fundamental perceptual activities and is so automatic that we are usually unaware of it. It helps stabilize our environment and make it manageable.

The letters on this page and the illustrations appear as figures, with the page as the ground. If your book rests on a table, the book becomes the figure and the supporting table is the ground. As you can see, the figure/ground relationship is contextual and hierarchical. Depending on what you determine the figure to be, the ground will change accordingly. Contrary to the static and fixed figure/ground relationship in a painting or still photograph, the on-screen relationship changes, as it does in real life, with the camera's point of view. Thus the figure in a medium shot can become the ground in a close-up. **SEE 7.37 AND 7.38**

FIGURE/GROUND CHARACTERISTICS

What exactly distinguishes a figure from its ground? Look at the well-known figure/ground example on the next page. **SEE 7.39** If you perceive the vase as the figure, the gray area becomes the ground. If you consider the two profiles as the figure, the white area becomes the ground. When you see the vase as the figure, it takes on certain characteristics, as does the gray ground. The characteristics reverse when you perceive the gray profiles as the figure. Here are some of the major characteristics of figure/ground perceptions:[4]

■ The figure is thinglike. You perceive it as an object. The ground is not; it is merely part of the "uncovered" screen area.

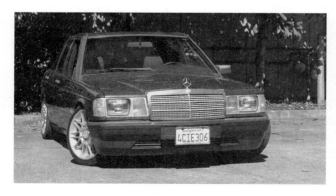

7.37 Figure/Ground Relationship in Medium Shot

With a moving camera or a changing field of view, the figure/ground relationship alters continuously. In this shot the car is the figure and the bushes are the ground.

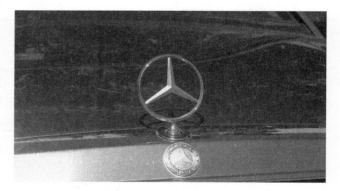

7.38 Figure/Ground Relationship in Close-up

When you move in for a close-up, the hood ornament becomes the figure and the car's hood becomes the ground.

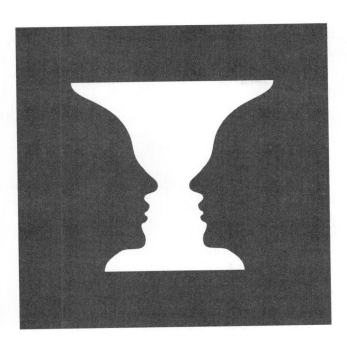

7.39 Figure and Ground

We assign figure and ground depending on what we perceive. For example, if you see a white vase here, the gray area becomes the background. But if you see two gray profiles, the white element becomes the ground. Notice how figure and ground switch characteristics, depending on which you assign to be the figure and which the ground.

- The figure lies in front of the ground. The white vase obviously lies on top of the gray background.

- The line that separates the figure from the ground belongs to the figure, not the ground.

- The figure is less stable than the ground; the figure is more likely to move.

- The ground seems to continue behind the figure.

Unless you possess a Zenlike state of mind that allows you to reconcile opposing elements, you will not be able to perceive figure and ground simultaneously. You must opt to pay attention to either the figure or the ground. At best you can oscillate between one figure/ground structure and the other.

Because of this urge to organize our environment into figure/ground relationships, you can achieve especially startling effects by rendering the figure and the ground purposely ambiguous or by reversing the figure/ground relationship. Some artists, like M. C. Escher, created a great variety of drawings and paintings that play with such figure/ground reversals.[5] Modern designers often come up with similarly startling creations by using a figure/ground reversal. **SEE 7.40**

As you can see, we are coerced by this logo into perceiving parts of the ground as the figure. It is almost impossible not to see the *A* and the *O* as figures

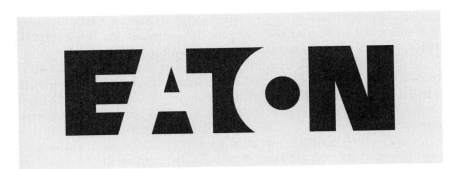

7.40 Figure/Ground Reversal

If the design is simple, a designer can achieve a startling effect by having some of the ground appear as the figure. You will find it hard to consider the *A* and the *O* as the ground rather than a figure.

7.41 **Ambiguous Figure/Ground Relationship**

Through electronic effects, such as this superimposition, you can change the figure/ground relationship in ways that give the image new meaning.

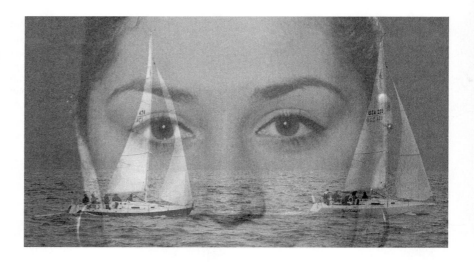

although they are actually parts of the common ground—the white page. The *A* begins to disappear, however, when you cover up the *E*. All of a sudden, a new pyramid-like figure appears that looks more like the top of a sharp pencil than the holes in the letter *A*.

Superimposition too derives its strength from rendering the figure/ground relationship purposely vague. It is often difficult to determine which of the two superimposed images is the figure and which is the ground. It's no wonder that a "super" is such a popular effect when suggesting dream sequences. **SEE 7.41** Through a variety of digital effects, you can reverse the figure and the ground at will and thus create powerful and enigmatic images.

We are so used to seeing moving figures relative to a stable ground that we maintain this relationship even if the ground moves against a stationary figure. We can easily trick the viewer into perceiving a car racing through downtown streets simply by shooting the stationary car against a rear projection or a computer-generated background of moving streets. We discuss this figure/ground reversal more thoroughly in chapter 13.

The figure/ground principle also applies to the structuring of sound. We usually try to establish specific foreground sounds against more general background sounds. Figure/ground relationships in sound structures are explored more fully in chapter 15.

Psychological Closure

In our quest for perceptual sanity, if not survival, we continuously seek to stabilize our infinitely complex and often chaotic environment. One of our built-in survival mechanisms is our tendency to mentally fill in gaps in visual information to arrive at complete and easily manageable patterns and configurations. This perceptual activity is called *psychological closure*, or closure for short.[6]

Take a look at the random shapes on the next page. **SEE 7.42** As soon as you see them, your perceptual mechanism automatically tries to group them into some sort of simple pattern. What patterns do you see in figure 7.42? Don't force yourself—let the pattern come to you. Now use a pencil to trace the most obvious connections.

You probably arrived at a series of relatively simple and stable figures, such as a triangle, a trapezoid, and a line, by taking a minimum number of visual cues and mentally filling in the missing information—by applying closure. **SEE 7.43**

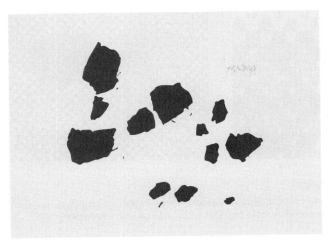

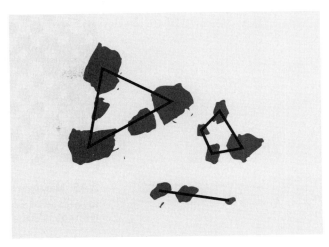

7.42 Perceiving Patterns
Look at these random shapes. You will probably find it hard not to group this random array into some kind of order.

7.43 Psychological Closure: Pattern
Most likely, you organized the shapes into a large triangle at the upper left, a trapezoid at the right, and a line at the bottom.

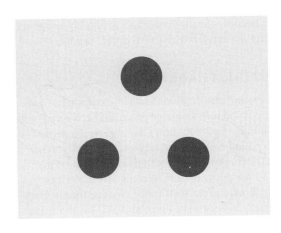

7.44 Psychological Closure: Subjective Completion
Although the page shows only three dots, you must try hard *not* to apply psychological closure and perceive a triangle.

Let's repeat this process in a much simpler visual field. **SEE 7.44** Although the figure shows only three dots, you automatically perceive a triangle; in fact, it takes considerable effort *not* to see a triangle. As you can see, through applying closure you constructed a new stable pattern—a triangle—from a minimum number of clues—three dots.

GESTALT

The pattern that results from applying psychological closure is often called a ***gestalt*** (German for "form," "configuration," or "shape"). A gestalt is a perceptual whole that transcends its parts. As soon as you perceive a triangle (the whole) instead of three dots (the parts), the dots have become part of the gestalt; they are no longer independent elements but have become part of a triangle. This is why *gestalt* is often defined as a whole that is larger than, or at least different from, the sum of its parts.[7] The relationship of the parts to the whole becomes especially apparent in music. Three notes played in sequence sound quite different when played simultaneously as a chord. The individual elements (the three notes) have now been molded into a gestalt (the chord) and have thus surrendered their individual functions to that of the new structure.

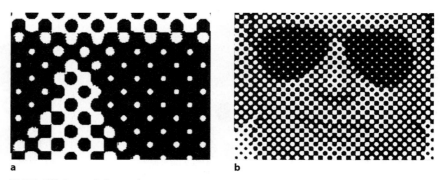

7.45 Minimum Information

You need a minimum amount of information to perceive a meaningful pattern. Notice how the seemingly random dots (a) suddenly make sense when you add enough information (b).

Note that to apply psychological closure we need a minimum amount of information. If the information falls below the required minimum, the stimulus elements remain random, and we cannot perceive a pattern. For example, three dots are the minimum number of elements needed to perceive a triangle. One dot less would produce a line but never a triangle. As soon as we have enough information, however, the pattern becomes immediately and inevitably apparent, and we experience an almost instant switch from chaos to order. **SEE 7.45**

HIGH- AND LOW-DEFINITION IMAGES

A *high-definition* image has more picture information than a low-definition image. **SEE 7.46** Figure 7.46a shows the lowest-definition image of a triangle, figure 7.46b shows a higher-definition image, and figure 7.46c shows the highest. Commercial motion pictures display high-definition images; the large screen lets you see a great amount of event detail, and the film images have high resolution. Similarly, *high-definition television (HDTV)* produces images of remarkable clarity.[8]

A *low-definition* image requires a great deal more closure than a high-definition image to arrive at a gestalt. In contrast to film and HDTV, the images of STV (standard television, with 480 visible scanning lines) are definitely low-definition. First, their picture resolution is low. Second, even a large television

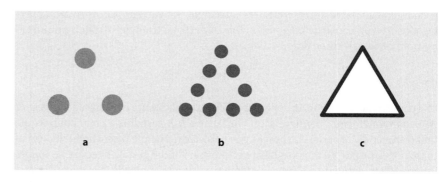

7.46 Low- and High-definition Images

The triangle in (a) has the minimum information: three dots. One dot less and you would perceive a line. The triangle in (b) has more information. You need to apply less psychological closure to arrive at the gestalt of a triangle. The triangle in (c) has the maximum information. You can see its shape without applying any closure.

screen is small compared with a motion picture screen. Third, the contrast ratio—the steps between the lightest and darkest picture areas—is limited. Fourth, to maintain a reasonable level of aesthetic energy, the event details are normally presented as a series of close-ups rather than event overviews, as is frequently the case in motion pictures. Obviously, standard video viewing requires a great deal more psychological closure than watching a film or large-screen HDTV. Because of the miniature screen size, watching video on a mobile media device is unavoidably low-definition, even if the pictures on the small display are touted as high-definition.

Is this innately bad, and should we try to produce images that are maximally high-definition? Not necessarily. Very much like impressionist paintings, standard television derives much of its visual intensity and our perceptual involvement from its low-definition images. Precisely because low-definition images require constant psychological closure, we as viewers are required to *work* with the event—to continuously fill in missing external (form) and internal (story) information to make sense of the picture and story narrative so that we can arrive at the appropriate gestalt. We no longer remain passive spectators but become active, perceptually hardworking participants.[9] Thus the communication is not necessarily inhibited by the low-definition images, which may well result in a desirable intensification of the event.

HDTV practitioners have already discovered that the medium's high resolution is not always a desirable attribute. Especially in intimate scenes, it is often better to soften the image through filters or focus manipulation, very much like the desaturation of color. This participation and intensification aspect of low-definition images has prompted graphic artists to render specific scenes or commercials purposely low-definition. Many television crime series use low-definition effects, such as fast-falloff lighting, color distortion, and especially electronically enhanced high-contrast images, to intensify especially brutal scenes. Some directors soften the sharp "in-the-face" look of HDTV by creating a very shallow depth of field (with long-focal-length zoom positions) or by reducing the saturation of the brilliant HDTV colors, which are otherwise hailed as one of the laudable achievements of high-definition video. Other examples are graphics that carry only minimal information so as to elicit maximum psychological closure. **SEE 7.47** Low-definition fashion drawings may encourage you to project how you would ideally like the clothing to look more than high-definition photographs.

You should realize, however, that the constant mental activity necessary to make sense of a low-definition presentation requires considerable mental effort, however subconscious, on the part of the viewer, which can lead to fatigue. This effort for closure is one of the reasons why you may find it much more tiring to watch a three-hour film on small-screen television than on the large, high-definition screen in a movie theater—even if you have the same amount of popcorn and soft drinks.

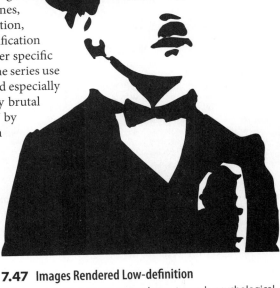

7.47 Images Rendered Low-definition

This low-definition image compels you to apply psychological closure. In fact, you will find it hard *not* to see the line of the right side of the face, although it is not actually present.

FACILITATING CLOSURE

A low-definition image is helpful only if it facilitates, rather than inhibits, closure. When framing a shot, arrange the picture elements in such a way that they can be easily completed in the viewer's mind even in off-screen space; or you can group them into simple figures, that is, into recognizable patterns of basic geometric shapes. This is explored more fully in chapter 8.

We know that people apply psychological closure to formulate specific patterns. But is the process of psychological closure predictable? Can we predetermine the stimuli necessary for someone to perceive a particular pattern? Can we deduce any principles of psychological closure? Yes. Three gestalt psychologists—**Wolfgang Köhler** (1887–1967), **Max Wertheimer** (1880–1943), and **Kurt Koffka** (1886–1941)—helped develop three major principles of psychological closure: proximity, similarity, and continuity.[10]

Proximity When similar elements lie in close proximity to one another, we tend to see them together. Because of attraction of mass, we connect more readily those elements that lie closer together than those that lie farther apart.

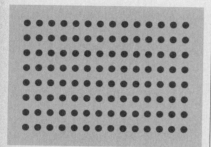

Here we see horizontal rather than vertical lines because the horizontal dots lie closer together than the vertical dots.

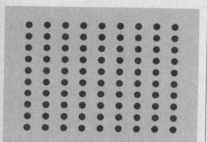

Now we perceive vertical lines because the vertical dots are closer together than the horizontal ones.

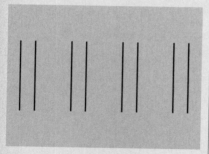

Here we tend to see four narrow columns rather than three fat ones.

Similarity Similar shapes are seen together.

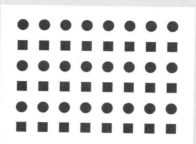

All these dots are equally spaced, yet we see horizontal lines because we tend to see similarly shaped objects together.

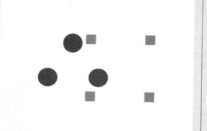

Here the similarity overrides the proximity. We see a triangle and a square intersecting.

Continuity Once a dominant line is established, its direction is not easily disturbed by other lines cutting across it.

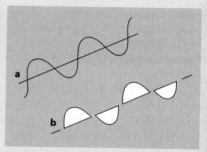

We see a curved line being intersected by a straight line (a) rather than four oddly shaped forms attached to each other (b).

These three principles of psychological closure—proximity, similarity, and continuity—are all based on our desire to establish **visual rhythm**. I propose this overriding perceptual principle:

> We tend to perceive together those elements that are easily recognizable as occurring at a certain frequency (number of similar elements) within a certain interval (distance from one another) or that pursue a dominant line.

Vectors

Probably the strongest forces operating within the screen are directional forces that lead our eyes from one point to another within, or even outside of, the picture field. These forces, called vectors, can be as coercive as real physical forces.[11] Each vector has a certain magnitude, or strength as to directional certainty and power. A **vector** is therefore a force with a direction and a magnitude.[12]

A vector on-screen indicates a main direction that has been established either by implication—such as with arrows, things arranged in a line, or people looking in a specific direction—or by actual screen motion, such as a man running from screen-left to screen-right or toward or away from the camera.

For screen displays, where you must deal with implied as well as real motion, the proper understanding and handling of vectors becomes extremely important.

Once you have grasped what vectors are and how they interrelate and interact with other visual and aural elements, you can use them effectively not only to control screen directions but also to build screen space and event energy within a single frame or over a series of frames. A solid understanding of the vector theory will help you immensely in preproduction placement of cameras and in postproduction editing.

VECTOR FIELD

In structuring **on-screen space**, we no longer work with isolated vectors but instead with a **vector field**: a combination of vectors operating within a single picture field (frame), from picture field to picture field (from frame to frame), from picture sequence to picture sequence, from screen to screen (when you use multiple screens), and from on-screen to off-screen events.

You can also find vectors in color, in music, and even in the structure of a story; in fact, a vector is any aesthetic element that leads us in a specific space/time—or even emotional—direction. More complex vector fields include **external vectors**, which operate within or without the screen, and **internal vectors**, which operate within ourselves, such as feelings and empathetic responses.

For the present, however, let's concentrate on the visual vectors that operate in the on- and off-screen space of film, video, and computers.

VECTOR TYPES

If you carefully examine the various ways that visual vectors operate, you will discover three principal types: graphic vectors, index vectors, and motion vectors.

Graphic vectors A **graphic vector** is created by a stationary element that guides our eyes in a certain direction. It is driven by the principle of continuity. The direction of a graphic vector is ambiguous, however. A simple line is a graphic vector, but we can scan the line from left to right or (with a little more effort) from right to left. When we establish a point of origin for the line, we increase the magnitude of the graphic vector. Its directionality is now determined by a point of origin but is still somewhat ambiguous. **SEE 7.48A AND 7.48B** The pipe structure supporting the roof of a ferry boat pier and the lines of the high-rise building give basic directional orientation, but they do not unequivocally point in a single direction, so their directional magnitude remains relatively low. **SEE 7.49 AND 7.50**

Index vectors In contrast to a graphic vector, an **index vector** is created by something that points unquestionably in a specific direction. Examples are arrows or people pointing or looking in a particular direction. Index vectors also include

7.48 Line as Graphic Vector

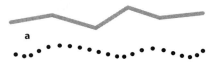

a

A graphic vector is created by a line or by an arrangement of objects that guides our eyes in a certain direction.

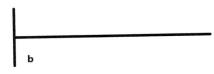

b

This graphic vector (b) has a more definite direction than those in (a), but it is still not unidirectional.

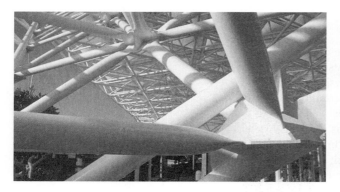

7.49 Graphic Vectors: Roof Structure

This pipe structure that supports a roof generates a multitude of graphic vectors.

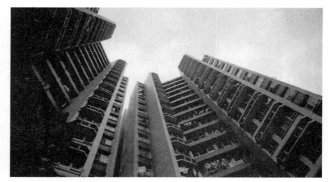

7.50 Graphic Vectors: High-rise Building

The vertical lines of this building create strong graphic vectors. The horizontal lines of the windows are also graphic vectors.

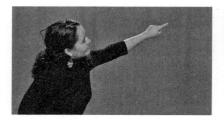

7.51 Index Vector: Pointing

An index vector is created by anything that points unequivocally in a specific direction. Somebody pointing forms a high-magnitude index vector.

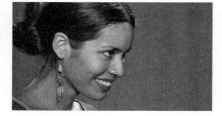

7.52 Index Vector: Looking

Somebody looking in a specific direction forms an index vector.

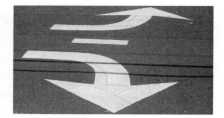

7.53 Index Vector: Arrow

An arrow is a high-magnitude index vector.

7.54 Index Vector: Motorcycle

Note that a still shot of a person or an object in motion is not a motion vector but rather a strong index vector. Even a blurred photo suggesting movement is still an index vector. A motion vector is created only by something that is actually moving or is perceived as moving on-screen.

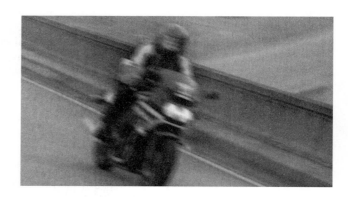

still photographs of runners or somebody riding a motorcycle. SEE 7.51–7.54 Note that in figure 7.54 you don't see the motorcycle actually moving (despite the blur indicating motion), so it is an index rather than a motion vector.

Motion vectors   A *motion vector* is created by an object that is actually moving or seen as moving on-screen. Obviously, a motion vector cannot be illustrated with a still picture in a book. Even if you blur a still photo, as in figure 7.54, or imply motion by keeping the object in focus and blurring the background or foreground, it does not move and is therefore not a motion vector. Imagine that a ladybug has landed on the page you just read and is crawling around figure 7.54. The page with the blurred photo of the motorcycle will inevitably remain the stable ground, and the ladybug is the figure in motion. The importance of this distinction is that motion vectors will command immediate attention, overriding all other vectors.

VECTOR MAGNITUDE

The magnitude of a vector is a product of its relative strength, that is, its directional certainty and perceived directional force. *Vector magnitude* is determined primarily by screen direction, graphic mass, and perceived object speed. Although each vector type can be strong or weak (have a high or low magnitude), motion vectors generally have a higher magnitude than index vectors, which in turn have a higher magnitude than graphic vectors. **SEE 7.55**

Vector magnitude and screen direction   As pointed out earlier, a line indicates a general direction (horizontal, vertical, curved) but is not precise as to its direction. Such a graphic vector therefore has a relatively low magnitude. An index vector that is generated by a one-way-street sign, someone pointing in a particular direction, or a directional arrow in a parking garage has a much higher magnitude. Motion vectors have a relatively high magnitude because their screen direction is most conspicuous.[13]

Something moving or pointing directly toward or away from the camera results in a *z-axis vector*, so called because the vector direction follows the *z-axis*—the virtual line extending from the camera lens to the horizon. Whereas a *z-axis index vector*, such as somebody looking or pointing directly at the camera, has a very low magnitude, a *z-axis motion vector* can have a high or low magnitude. A racecar hurtling toward the camera definitely has a higher magnitude than the first uncertain steps of a child toddling toward the camera (representing Mother's arms). Depending on the context, a fast zoom-in or zoom-out can also produce a high-magnitude z-axis motion vector, although the screen motion is now implied rather than actual.

Vector magnitude and graphic mass   The larger the graphic mass that is in motion, the higher its vector magnitude. As stated earlier, a large graphic mass is less likely to be disturbed in its course than a small one. Because its directionality is more certain, its vector magnitude is higher than for small objects.

Vector magnitude and perceived object speed   The faster the speed of an object, the higher its vector magnitude. This principle applies to all motion vector directions, including vectors that move along the z-axis. A runner or cyclist racing across the screen, a galloping horse, and a skier hurtling down a steep slope—all are strong motion vectors of high magnitude. The image of a racecar roaring down the track makes for a higher-magnitude motion vector than does a couple's leisurely stroll through the park. But like all elements in applied media aesthetics, vectors are context-dependent. For example, if you see the racecar moving across the screen in an extreme long shot, its magnitude is definitely lower than the relatively slow motion of a police officer who walks along the street in a tighter long shot, unaware of the villain who lurks in the shadows.

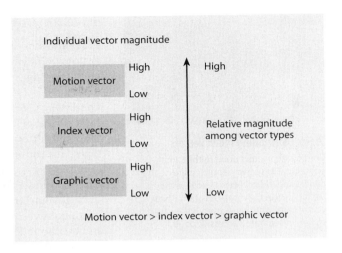

7.55 **Vector Magnitude**

Although each vector type can be strong or weak (have a high or low magnitude), motion vectors generally have a higher magnitude than index vectors, which in turn have a higher magnitude than graphic vectors.

In production you simply estimate the relative magnitude of a vector. Because the context in which you judge vector magnitudes is a given, your estimation of which vector has a higher magnitude, or your efforts to lower or raise a specific vector magnitude, can be fairly accurate. But if you analyze a film or video for the specific magnitudes of its vectors, you may need to develop a more accurate and reliable measuring technique.[14]

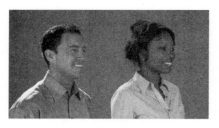

7.56 Continuing Index Vectors

Continuing vectors point in the same direction. These two people create continuing index vectors because they are looking in the same direction. The vectors are continuing, even if they are shown in separate successive shots.

VECTOR DIRECTIONS

Index and motion vectors can be continuing, converging, or diverging. Continuing vectors point in the same direction, converging vectors point toward each other, and diverging vectors point away from each other.

Continuing vectors   When two or more index and/or motion vectors point in the same direction, they are ***continuing vectors***. The continuity can be established by the same vector type (graphic, index, or motion) or by a combination of vector types. The continuity can be established in a single shot or a shot sequence. If, for example, you see two people looking in the same direction in a single shot, their gazes constitute continuing index vectors. **SEE 7.56**

If you show a child watching her balloon escaping into the sky, you have continuous vectors within a single shot. Both the index vector of the child's gaze and the motion vector of the balloon's ascent point in the same direction. These vectors remain continuous even if you show the same event in separate shots. For example, the first shot could show a close-up of the balloon slipping out of the girl's hand and how she looks upward, with the balloon moving out of the frame. The second shot could then show the balloon climbing higher into the sky.

Although graphic vectors have a relatively weak magnitude (their direction is basically ambiguous), they can be continuous, especially in a shot series or in multiple screens. Let's assume that you are shooting a river scene with cliffs as the background. The horizon is a definite graphic vector that cuts across the screen at a particular spot. To ensure the necessary continuity from shot to shot, the horizon should not jump up or down in subsequent shots. The graphic vector (horizon line) must be continuous. **SEE 7.57**

Converging vectors   In contrast to continuing vectors, which support each other in establishing or maintaining a specific single direction, ***converging vectors*** point toward each other either in a single shot or a series of shots. A simple conversation between two people creates converging index vectors whether you show them in a single shot or in individual close-ups. **SEE 7.58–7.60** Two cars racing toward each other represent converging motion vectors. Converging motion vectors are especially useful to increase the aesthetic energy of a high-magnitude event, such as two trains on a collision course.

Diverging vectors   If index or motion vectors point away from each other, they are ***diverging vectors***. Obviously, two people pointing or looking in opposite directions create diverging index vectors. Cars traveling in opposite directions

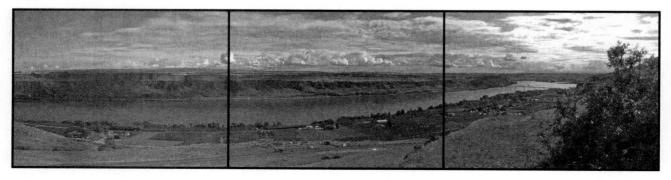

7.57 Continuing Graphic Vectors

Although graphic vectors are low-magnitude, which means that their direction is ambiguous, you can nevertheless see them as continuous. In this three-screen display, the horizon lines must match to form a single graphic vector.

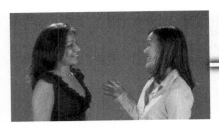

7.58 Converging Index Vectors in Two-shot

Converging vectors point toward each other. These two people looking at each other form converging index vectors.

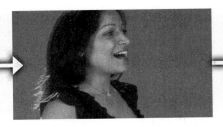

7.59 Index Vector: Screen-right

In a close-up sequence, you need to maintain the same index vectors as in the two-shot. Here the person on the left effects a screen-right index vector.

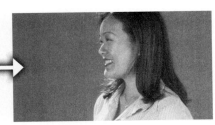

7.60 Index Vector: Screen-left

To make the index vectors converge over the shot sequence, the screen-right person must look screen-left, establishing an index vector that converges with that of the screen-left person.

are examples of diverging motion vectors regardless of whether they appear in a single shot or a shot series. **SEE 7.61**

Whether z-axis vectors (index or motion) are perceived as converging or diverging depends on the event context. For example, if you first see two people looking at each other in a two-shot and then see them in z-axis close-ups, your **mental map**—that is, where you perceive things to be in on- and off-screen space—will most likely tell you that the z-axis index vectors of the close-ups are still converging; you will still see the two people as looking at each other even as they look directly into the camera. If the two-shot shows them looking away from each other, you will most likely see the successive close-ups of the two people looking into the lens as diverging. This time your mental map is set on divergence, and you will perceive the people as looking away from each other even in the separate close-ups. For more examples of z-axis vectors and their behavior, see chapters 8 and 17.

So far we have discussed the basic types of external (screen) vectors and their major attributes—magnitude and continuing, converging, and diverging directions. In the following chapters, you will learn more about how vectors operate within the screen, from shot to shot, and from screen to screen.

The proper manipulation of vector fields is one of the most important aspects of your quest to clarify, intensify, and interpret an event for your viewers.

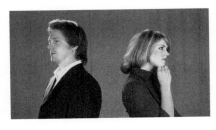

7.61 Diverging Index Vectors in Single Shot

Diverging vectors point in opposite directions. These two people form diverging index vectors by looking away from each other.

SUMMARY

There are six major types of field forces: main directions, magnetism of the frame, asymmetry of the frame, figure and ground, psychological closure, and vectors.

Horizontal lines suggest calm and normalcy. Vertical lines suggest power, formality, and strength. A combination of vertical and horizontal reflects our normal world; it follows the pull of gravity and suggests that we are standing upright on level ground. A tilted horizontal plane implies instability or powerful dynamism in an otherwise stable, or even static, shot.

Magnetism of the frame refers to how the borders of the screen—especially the corners—exert a strong pull on objects within the frame. Moreover, graphic mass attracts graphic mass (all types of screen images). A larger graphic mass (a screen image occupying a relatively large screen area) is usually more stable than a smaller one (occupying a relatively small screen area). The smaller graphic mass is dependent, and the larger is more independent.

A diagonal going from the bottom of screen-left to the top of screen-right is perceived as an uphill slant; a diagonal from top-left to bottom-right implies a downhill slant. This suggests that we tend to start at the left and finish at the right when looking at a picture field. As the destination area, the right side of the screen seems more prominent: we generally pay more attention to an object when it is placed on screen-right.

We always try to organize a picture field into a stable ground against which less stable figures operate. The figure exhibits certain spatial and graphic characteristics, the most important of which is that the figure seems to lie in front of the ground. Certain figure/ground reversals can be distracting but can also contribute to startling and expressive effects.

True to our tendency to stabilize the world we perceive around us, we tend to organize pictorial elements into a pattern of simple geometrical figures, such as triangles, squares, and the like. We can perceive such patterns, even if we have only minimal information, by mentally filling in the missing information—a process known as psychological closure, or closure for short.

The pattern we arrive at through psychological closure is called a gestalt. In a gestalt the parts have assumed a different structural role than when they were independent.

A vector is a force with a direction and a magnitude. All screen events exhibit one or a combination of the three principal vectors: graphic, index, and motion.

A graphic vector is created by simple lines or stationary elements that are arranged so that the viewer sees them as lines. Although graphic vectors suggest a general direction, their actual direction is ambiguous. An index vector is created by an object that unquestionably points in a specific direction. A motion vector is created by an object that actually moves or is perceived as moving on-screen. A still photograph of a moving object, even when blurred, is an index vector, not a motion vector.

Each vector can have a variety of magnitudes (strengths), depending on how conspicuous it is, how emphatically it points in a certain screen direction, its graphic mass, and its perceived object speed. In general, however, graphic vectors have less magnitude than index vectors, which have less magnitude than motion vectors.

Vectors can be continuing, converging, or diverging. Continuing vectors point in the same direction either in the same shot or in a shot sequence. Converging vectors point or move toward each other. Diverging vectors point or move away from each other. How we perceive converging or diverging z-axis vectors depends on the event context.

NOTES

1. Headroom follows the same principles as demonstrated in figure 7.10.

2. See also chapter 8.

3. This asymmetry of screen-right and screen-left—that is, whether one side of the picture draws more attention than the other regardless of picture content—has been a source of confusion and debate for some time. Alexander Dean (1893–1949), who taught play directing at Yale and was quite particular about the asymmetry of the stage, claims that the audience-left side of the stage is "stronger" than the right side because the audience has a tendency to look to the left first and then to the right. Alexander Dean, *Fundamentals of Play Directing* (New York: Farrar and Rinehart, 1946), p. 132.

    Heinrich Wölfflin (1864–1945), a prolific writer on various subjects in art history and theory, claims that the right side of a painting is "heavier" than the left. He says that we have a tendency to read over the things on the left quickly to come to the right side, where "the last word is spoken." He demonstrates convincingly with several illustrations how the character of a painting changes when its sides are reversed. Heinrich Wölfflin, *Gedanken zur Kunstgeschichte* (Ideas for Art History) (Basel: Benno Schwabe, 1940), pp. 82–96.

Rudolf Arnheim speaks of the well-known tendency to perceive the area in the left corner of a visual field as the point of departure and thus the entire picture as organized from left to right. (Rudolf Arnheim, *The Power of the Center* [Berkeley: University of California Press, 1982], p. 37.) But then he goes on to say that "the left side of the field, corresponding to the projection areas in the right half of the brain, is endowed with special weight" and that "objects placed on the left assume special importance." (Arnheim, *Power of the Center*, p. 38.)

In an experimental study, Nikos Metallinos and Robert Tiemens conclude that there is "some evidence that the retention of visual information in a newscast is enhanced when the visual elements are placed on the left side of the screen" but that there is in general "minimal support to the asymmetry of the screen theories." (Nikos Metallinos and Robert K. Tiemens, "Asymmetry of the Screen: The Effect of Left Versus Right Placement of Television Images," *Journal of Broadcasting* 21, no. 1 [1977]: 30.) Very much aware of the contextual nature of aesthetic communication, however, they warn that "no final conclusions can be made on the basis of mere placement of the visual elements" and that "such factors as size, color, shape, vectors (directional forces), and how individual subjects perceive these qualities must also be considered." (Metallinos and Tiemens, "Asymmetry," p. 32.)

More recent eye-tracking experiments are generally inconclusive and demonstrate more the observer's primary interest in the content of the picture than the asymmetry-of-the-screen phenomenon. See Bruce E. Goldstein, *Sensation and Perception,* 7th ed. (Belmont, Calif.: Wadsworth, 2007), pp. 122–31.

4. Goldstein, *Sensation and Perception,* pp. 99–101.

5. Graphic artist M. C. Escher used the figure/ground reversal in a highly inventive and unconventional way. See M. C. Escher et al., *The World of M. C. Escher* (New York: Harry N. Abrams, 1972). See also Bruno Ernst, *De Toverspiegel van M. C. Escher* (The Magic Mirror of M. C. Escher) (Munich: Heinz Moos Verlag, 1978). Even if you don't read Dutch or German, the book contains many of Escher's lesser-known drawings.

6. Wolfgang Köhler, *The Selected Papers of Wolfgang Köhler,* ed. by Mary Henle (New York: Liveright, 1971), pp. 149-65.

7. Max Wertheimer, "Untersuchungen zur Lehre von der Gestalt" (Studies for the Teachings of Gestalt), *Psychologische Forschung* 4 (1923), pp. 301–50. As an eminent member of the Gestalt school, Wertheimer introduced the Law of Prägnanz, which postulates that psychological organization can only be as good as the prevailing conditions allow. *Good* in this case means that the resulting gestalt is often symmetrical, simple, and relatively stable.

8. Although the terms *definition* and *resolution* are frequently used interchangeably, there is an important technical distinction. Definition refers to the perceived sharpness in an image; resolution is the measurement of this sharpness, such as the number of pixels in a specific picture area.

9. Marshall McLuhan, *Understanding Media: The Extensions of Man* (New York: McGraw-Hill, 1964), pp. 312–14.

10. Richard Zakia, *Perception and Imaging,* 3rd ed. (Boston: Focal Press, 2007), pp. 27–53.

11. The term *vector* in a non-science context was first used by Kurt Lewin to refer to psychological forces; it was later used by Andrew Paul Ushenko to mean an aesthetic force. See Kurt Lewin, *A Dynamic Theory of Personality,* trans. by Donald Adams and Karl Zener (New York: McGraw-Hill, 1935); and Andrew Paul Ushenko, *Dynamics of Art* (Bloomington: Indiana University Press, 1953), pp. 60–119.

12. The definition given is an aesthetic one. If you were dealing in physics (the origin of the vector concept), the definition would be that a vector is a physical quantity with both a magnitude and a direction.

13. All vector types are clearly illustrated in the interactive DVD-ROM *Zettl's VideoLab 3.0* (Belmont, Calif.: Wadsworth, 2004). Click on EDITING→ Continuity→ vectors.

14. See Chitra Dorai and Svetha Venkatesh (eds.), *Media Computing: Computational Media Aesthetics* (Boston: Kluwer Academic, 2002).

Structuring the Two-dimensional Field: Interplay of Screen Forces

STRUCTURING THE TWO-DIMENSIONAL FIELD MEANS MAKING THE screen forces work for you rather than against you. This enables you to show events on-screen with clarity and impact. Painters and still photographers strive for a total composition effect in a picture. They try to arrange static pictorial elements so that they look and feel inevitably right. Once such an arrangement is achieved, the composition is finished; it will not change.

Such is not the case in video and film—or even on the computer screen. Most pictorial elements shift constantly within the frame and often change from one picture to the next (from shot to shot, from scene to scene, or during scrolling). You are no longer dealing with structural permanence but largely with structural change.

The old method of composition, that is, the pleasing arrangement of essentially static pictorial elements within a single frame, does not suffice for video and film. You must now think in terms of structuring a dynamic visual field of *on-screen space* and consider visual elements that move about the screen and that need to provide structural continuity between previous and subsequent images. In video and film, the guiding compositional principle is not necessarily the screen space of a frame but of a sequence. For example, the composition of a single shot may look wrong when you examine it by itself, but when you see it as part of a shot sequence its composition becomes perfectly acceptable.[1] **SEE 8.1 AND 8.2**

Structuring the screen space of a Web page presents a unique problem. Often the information does not fit in the relatively small frame of the computer monitor, and the user must scroll up or down and to the sides to reveal pictures and written information. You should therefore consider even a single Web page design not as a static image, similar to a magazine page, but as partial images that maintain their structural integrity when scrolled from one segment to another. In this way their structure is influenced by their sequence much like a brief video scene.

Does this mean that all traditional compositional principles are invalid? Not at all, but they must be adapted so that they fulfill the more complex tasks of structuring static, moving, and sequential images within the two-dimensional field. You must now go beyond the traditional canons of good composition (area proportion, object proportion, and balance) to begin seeing the contextual interaction of the various screen forces, such as the magnetism of the frame, graphic mass, and vectors.

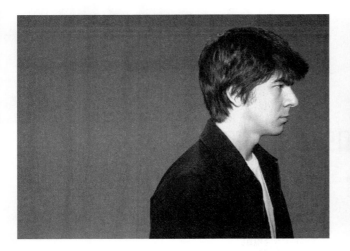

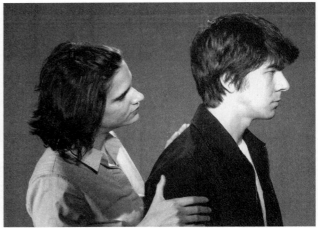

8.1 **Composition in Shot Sequence: Context Lacking**
The composition in this shot is definitely wrong (the man stands much too close to the right side of the frame).

8.2 **Composition in Shot Sequence: Context Provided**
The man's position makes sense as soon as you provide the proper context for such a framing, such as the woman's entering the shot from screen-left.

This chapter explores the interplay of screen forces of the two-dimensional field: stabilizing the field through distribution of graphic mass and magnetic force, stabilizing the field through distribution of vectors, stages of balance, object framing, unusual compositions, multiple screens, and dividing the screen.

Stabilizing the Field Through Distribution of Graphic Mass and Magnetic Force

One of the most basic ways of stabilizing the two-dimensional field is to bring into balance the forces of ***graphic mass*** and the ***magnetism of the frame***. As discussed in chapter 7, every graphic mass operating within a clearly defined two-dimensional field, such as the video, film, or computer screen, carries a graphic weight, which is somewhat akin to the actual weight of an object. ***Graphic weight*** is determined by the dimension of the object (how much area the object takes up relative to the total screen area), its basic shape and orientation, its location within the frame, and its color. **SEE 8.3**

8.3 Factors Influencing Graphic Weight

Factor		Heavy	Light
Dimension		Large	Small
Shape		Simple, geometrically compact	Irregular, diffused
Orientation		Vertical	Horizontal
Location		Corner	Centered
		Upper part of frame	Lower part of frame
		Right	Left
Color	*Hue*	Warm	Cold
	Saturation	Strong	Weak
	Brightness	Dark	Light

A screen object does not, however, have to display all these elements. Object size alone is enough to give an image graphic weight. **SEE 8.4** For example, the disc on the right side of the frame in figure 8.4 is obviously "heavier" (carries more graphic weight) than the one on the left.

If objects are close enough to each other that the attraction of mass comes into play (as explored in chapter 7), we tend to combine the graphic weights of both objects. **SEE 8.5**

The proximity of the object to the screen edges brings another significant graphic force into play: the magnetism of the frame. Obviously, the closer the object is to the edge of the screen, the more powerful the magnetic force will be regardless of its relative weight. A strong index vector, however, can quite easily override the magnetic force of the frame. Let's look at some simple interactions of graphic weight and magnetism of the frame.

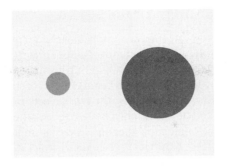

8.4 Graphic Mass and Weight

The larger, darker, and therefore heavier graphic mass on the right side of the screen outweighs the smaller, lighter object on the left.

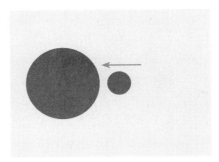

8.5 Mass Attracts Mass

As in physics, in visual design graphic mass also attracts graphic mass. The attracted objects combine into a single, greater mass, which then has greater graphic weight.

SCREEN-CENTER

The most stable position of an object is screen-center. When the graphic mass is located in the center of the screen, the surrounding areas and the magnetic forces of the screen edges and corners are symmetrically distributed. **SEE 8.6**

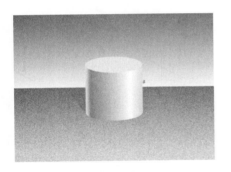

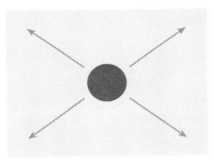

8.6 Screen-center Position

The screen-center position provides maximum stability.

OFF-CENTER

As soon as you move the object to one side, however, the graphic weight increases and the magnetism of the frame comes into play. The more the object moves off-center, the greater its graphic weight—and the attraction of the frame increases. When this happens the picture begins to look unbalanced. But you can certainly use this "wrong" framing to increase the tension in the dynamic picture field. **SEE 8.7**

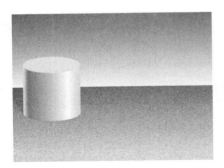

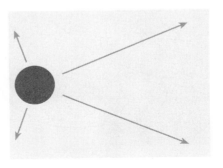

8.7 Off-center Position

When the object moves off-center, its graphic weight increases, and the magnetism of the frame comes into play.

COUNTERWEIGHTING

You can correct an imbalance of graphic weight by centering the object through camera or object movement so that the pull of the frame is neutralized (see figure 8.6) or by counterweighting it with another object or other graphic element (such as lettering or even beam of light) of similar graphic weight. **SEE 8.8** The attraction of mass caused by the two objects makes them gravitate toward screen-center. The closer the objects are to each other, the more apt you are to perceive them as belonging together and having a single graphic weight.

Now let's replace the abstract cylinders with a newscaster. The most stable position for the newscaster is obviously screen-center. Picture stability is important here to signify the newscaster's authority and credibility. **SEE 8.9** Putting the newscaster to one side of the screen makes little sense unless you are making room for a co-anchor or for additional pictorial material, such as the box insert that is customarily placed above and to the side of the newscaster's shoulder. **SEE 8.10**

The graphic weight of the secondary frame obviously provides sufficient graphic weight to balance the off-center newscaster. But when you remove the box during the newscast, you need to once more center the anchor to restore balance. A good camera operator can make this shift so smoothly that most viewers are unaware of this rebalancing act.

8.8 Counterweighting

You can achieve balance by counterweighting an object with another object of similar graphic weight. Note that attraction of mass also operates here.

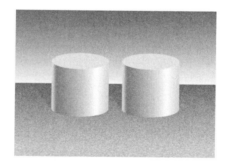
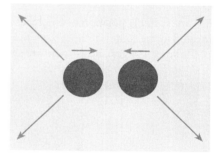

8.9 Newscaster in Screen-center

The most stable and sensible position for a single newscaster is in screen-center because this placement emphasizes the newscaster's credibility.

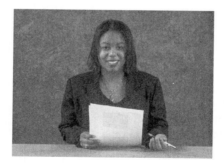
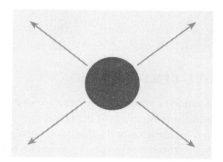

8.10 Off-center Balance with Box

The traditional box insert necessitates the off-center positioning of the newscaster. If the new element has sufficient graphic weight, the shot will remain balanced.

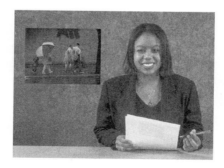
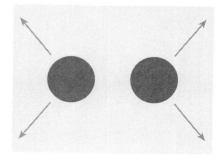

You may, however, want to place titles and other still graphic images off-center to boost the picture's graphic tension and energy. The asymmetrical distribution of graphic mass and vectors is discussed later in this chapter.

Stabilizing the Field Through Distribution of Vectors

When trying to stabilize the two-dimensional field, you need to focus not only on graphic weight but also, if not especially, on the distribution of vectors. They are such powerful structural elements that they usually override the lesser forces of graphic weight and magnetism of the frame.

STRUCTURAL FORCE OF INDEX VECTORS

Take a look at the following figure. **SEE 8.11** You will inevitably perceive the two center discs as belonging together (attraction of mass, see figure 8.8) and the upper-right disc as the isolated one (pull of screen corner, see figure 7.12).

But vectors can easily override these relatively subtle structural forces and cause you to perceive a different pattern. **SEE 8.12** The discs are in the same positions as in figure 8.11, but we have put "noses" on two of them. They have now

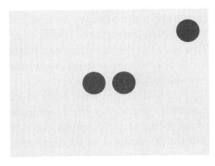

8.11 Structure Through Attraction of Mass

The two center discs attract each other and are seen together. The disc in the upper-right corner is isolated.

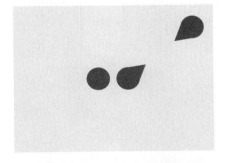

8.12 Structure Through Index Vectors

The converging index vectors now combine the right-center disc and the disc in the upper-right corner. The left-center disc is isolated.

become high-magnitude index vectors that establish a new relationship. Now the right-center disc and the corner disc are strongly connected through their converging index vectors, putting the left-center disc in isolation.[2] The increasing magnitude of index vectors of somebody's turning from a straight-on (z-axis) shot to a profile shot has similar structural consequences.

NOSEROOM AND LEADROOM

Imagine the following figures as a shot sequence. **SEE 8.13** In 8.13a the woman is looking directly into the camera (at you), generating a z-axis index vector. Because this z-axis index vector points directly at you, its magnitude within the screen is practically zero. You can therefore ignore the force of this index vector and stabilize the picture strictly by graphic weight and magnetism of the frame. Putting the subject in the center of the frame (maximum stability of graphic mass) with adequate headroom (neutralizing the magnetism of the upper edge) is the most logical thing to do.

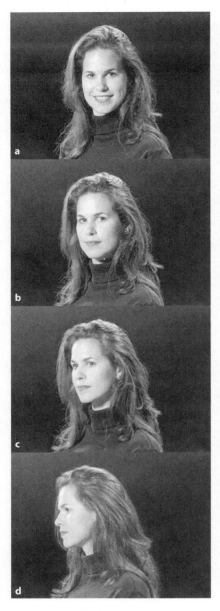

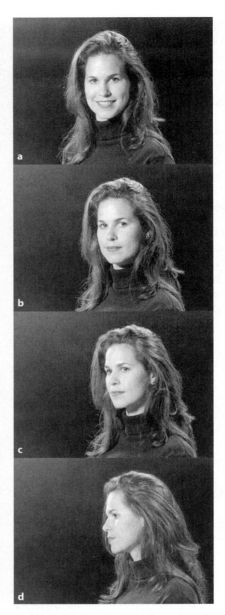

8.13 Force of Index Vector: Lack of Noseroom

The increasing magnitude of the index vector when someone gradually shifts from looking directly into the camera (z-axis vector) to looking to the side will cause the index vector to crash into the screen edge.

8.14 Force of Index Vector: Proper Noseroom

If you compensate for the increasing vector force by pulling the subject back to provide enough noseroom, the vector has enough space to have its force absorbed or comfortably guided through the screen border and into the next shot.

But watch what happens when the woman turns and starts looking at the screen edge (figures 8.13b–d). The more she looks to the side, the greater the magnitude of the index vector and the more the structural force of the vector comes into play. This index vector reaches its maximum magnitude in the profile shot (figure 8.13d). Although she has moved only her head and shoulders and has not changed her basic screen position, in the 4 × 3 aspect ratio the shot looks strangely out of balance. She seems cramped into the screen-left space, with her index vector crashing into the left edge of the frame. Assuming that no other person will walk up behind her to balance the picture through graphic weight (see figure 8.2), you will have to shift the subject more to screen-right to give the index vector enough space to run its course and travel relatively unhindered to, and even through, the screen edge. This space is often called ***noseroom*** for index vectors and ***leadroom*** for motion vectors.[3]

Note that you must leave more noseroom the higher the magnitude of the index vector becomes. **SEE 8.14** The index vector is at its maximum magnitude in the profile shot; therefore, the noseroom has also reached its maximum length (figure 8.14d). This noseroom principle also applies to the 16 × 9 aspect ratio, especially when you frame tighter shots. **SEE 8.15**

But wouldn't the index vector have a better chance of penetrating the screen edge if it originates as close to the edge as possible? Apparently not. When the index vector operates too close to the screen edge, it draws undue attention to the edge itself. As part of a picture frame whose major function is to contain the event, the screen edge acts as the final barrier to the index vector. This "short" vector and the graphic mass of the subject's head fall victim to the magnetism of the frame; both graphic forces are firmly glued to the edge and can no longer penetrate it.

A wider noseroom not only neutralizes the magnetism of the frame but also creates enough space around it to divert our attention away from the edge. Rather than deplete the vector's energy, the noseroom seems to signal clear sailing for the vector, not only through on-screen space but also—through the edge—into **off-screen space**.[4]

You treat motion vectors in the same way. When panning the camera with a moving object, always pan enough ahead to maintain leadroom for the motion vector to play out. If you do not sufficiently lead the moving object, the screen edge toward which the object moves will appear as a formidable barrier. All you see is where the object has been but not, as you should, where it is going. A lack of leadroom will make the motion look cramped and hampered.

Similar to the noseroom of lateral index vectors, lateral motion vectors need the most leadroom. Objects that move at an oblique screen angle need less leadroom, and z-axis vectors don't need any.

CONVERGING VECTORS

You can also balance an index vector with a converging one within the same frame. **SEE 8.16** With two people looking at each other, you achieve balance through the converging index vectors and the almost symmetrical placement of the subjects, whose graphic mass translates into just about equal graphic weight.

GRAPHIC VECTORS

Although graphic vectors as a category have relatively low magnitude, you can nevertheless use them to stabilize the two-dimensional field. **SEE 8.17** The perspective lines of the buildings in the figure produce fairly strong graphic vectors that lead our eyes naturally, though not as directly as an index vector, along the downhill diagonal from screen-left to screen-right. If you want to prevent the vector from plunging through the right screen edge—to contain it properly within the frame—you can do it with other graphic vectors or with graphic mass. In figure 8.17 the downhill vector of the entablature (on top of the columns) is arrested by the horizontal block of the back building.

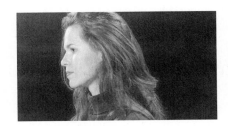

8.15 Lack of Noseroom in 16 × 9 Aspect Ratio

The lack of proper noseroom shows up prominently even in the wider 16 × 9 aspect ratio.

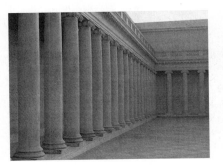
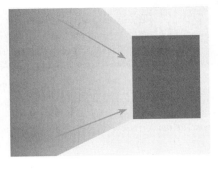

8.16 Converging Index Vectors

Converging index vectors of equal magnitude balance each other.

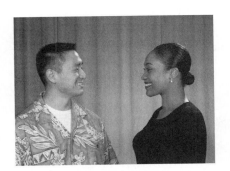
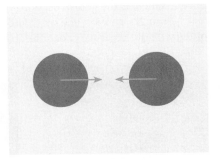

8.17 Distribution of Graphic Vectors and Graphic Mass

You can use graphic vectors and graphic mass to contain other graphic vectors. Here the horizontal and vertical graphic vectors of the back building and the resulting graphic mass block the sloping vectors of the columns.

Stages of Balance

Look back at figures 7.1 through 7.9. You will probably notice that the various structural arrangements in these illustrations do not have the same degree of balance, that is, the same degree of structural stability. Some look more at rest, whereas others appear to have more internal tension—they look more dynamic.

Because our organism strives to obtain a maximum of potential energy and to apply the best possible equilibrium to it, as Rudolf Arnheim points out, balance does not necessarily mean maximum stability within the screen.[5] Rather, **balance** can range from, or fluctuate between, static (stable) and dynamic (unstable) field structures.[6]

STATIC BALANCE

A **static balance** is solid, extremely stable, and not about to move. One extreme form is a symmetrical structuring of visual elements. This means that more or less identical picture elements appear on the left and right sides of the screen. The forces of graphic mass, frame magnetism, and vectors are the same, or at least almost the same, on both sides of the screen. **SEE 8.18**

DYNAMIC BALANCE

In a **dynamic balance,** the graphic elements are asymmetrically distributed. This means that the graphic weight and the various vectors are no longer equal on both sides of the screen. Instead they are engaged in a sort of tug of war with one another that increases dynamic energy. **SEE 8.19**

Golden section   One of the classical ways of creating a dynamic balance is to use the proportions of the **golden section**—a division of the screen (or any other linear dimension) into roughly 3×5 units (or, more accurately, 0.616:1). To achieve a golden section, you divide a given horizontal dimension, such as the width of this page, into a larger part (approximately three-fifths of the total width) and a smaller part (approximately two-fifths of the total width). The point where these portions meet is the golden section.

In such a division, the small and large screen areas are competing with each other, with the larger part not quite able or even eager to outweigh the smaller one.

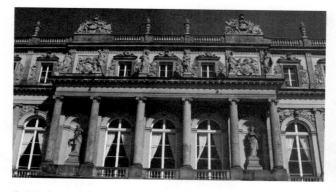

8.18 Static Balance

Symmetrical balance is among the most stable forms of balance. In this picture both sides have identical graphic weights, frame magnetism, and vector distributions. The tension is low.

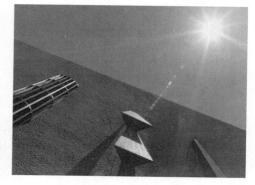

8.19 Dynamic Balance

In a dynamic balance, the aesthetic energy is increased because the asymmetrical distribution of graphic elements and vectors causes some tension.

Also, the dividing line (actual or imaginary) has not given in to the magnetic pull of one or the other screen edge, although one is definitely pulling harder than the other. The result is a less stable structure with increased graphic energy, yet the picture is still balanced. For many centuries this proportion was considered ideal and, at times, even divine. (See more details about the golden section on the next page.)

Although the golden section is rarely applicable when dealing with moving images, it is nevertheless valuable when framing relatively static shots and designing titles and still images for the screen. For example, a title that divides the screen into the golden section proportions often gains dynamism and visual interest compared with one that is centered. **SEE 8.20** Even when using illustrated titles, you may well arrange the major picture elements in proportions according to the golden section. This way the title gains in graphic energy without threatening the overall balance of the screen image.

The golden section division of screen width is especially effective when a vertical element (vertical graphic vector) divides a clean, horizontal vista (horizontal graphic vector). **SEE 8.21**

In a similar way, you can use a relatively uncluttered horizon line (horizontal graphic vector) to divide the screen at approximately three-fifths or two-fifths of its height. Thus, you can place the horizon line in the vertical golden section of the frame. **SEE 8.22**

The golden section division is especially appropriate in arranging a Web page that contains multiple visual elements. By placing the visuals in the golden sections on the screen, you avoid the all-too-common scattered look of the pages without sacrificing their dynamism.

Rule of thirds A variation of the golden section is the ***rule of thirds***, which suggests dividing the screen into three horizontal and three vertical fields. **SEE 8.23** You can always

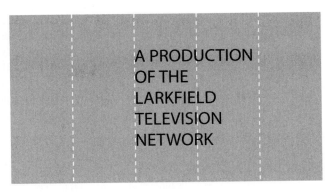

8.20 Golden Section Applied: Titles

The left edge of the text coincides with the golden section, providing increased visual interest. The figure balances the titles through graphic weight.

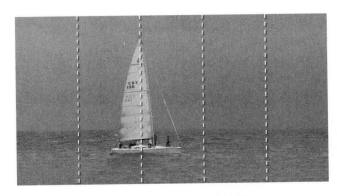

8.21 Golden Section Applied: Horizontal Division

It is especially effective to have a single vertical element divide a clean horizontal graphic vector at the golden section.

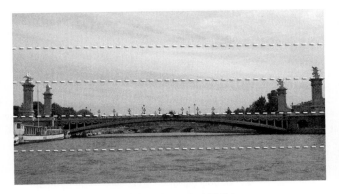

8.22 Golden Section Applied: Vertical Division

You can also use horizontal graphic vectors (such as the horizon line) to divide the screen vertically at the golden section.

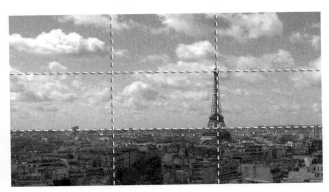

8.23 Rule of Thirds

To achieve a pleasing composition within a frame and placement continuity from shot to shot, divide the screen into thirds. Position the principal subjects where the horizontal and vertical lines intersect.

achieve a fail-safe composition by placing subjects where a vertical and a horizontal line intersect. These fields can help you maintain continuity of subject and object placement when shooting out of sequence and help you, as pointed out earlier, achieve and maintain proper headroom.

Although you may now presume that the golden section or the rule of thirds can provide area proportions that are, indeed, divine, avoid going overboard with them. Think twice before placing the newscaster in the golden section simply

The Modulor   Well-known contemporary Swiss-French architect **Le Corbusier** (Charles E. Jeanneret-Gris, 1887–1965) developed a proportional system that is essentially a refined version of the golden section.[7] His system, which he called *the Modulor*, is also based on the proportions of the human figure, specifically the proportions of a 6-foot man.

All the Modulor proportions are presented in a gradually diminishing scale of numbers. Here, in Corbusier's diagram, all numbers are in centimeters (one one-hundredth of a meter).

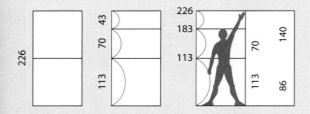

The more exact Modulor dimensions are:

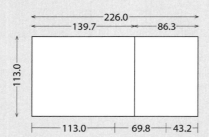

Harmonious Proportions   The question of discovering proper proportions and using them with consistency in the various forms of art has been of major concern to artists for centuries. The Egyptian temples and wall paintings; the Greek and Roman buildings and sculptures; the churches, palaces, and paintings of the Renaissance; the modern skyscraper; magazine layouts; and automobile design— all reveal the human preoccupation with proportional harmony. Amazingly enough, the proportions as revealed by the Egyptian and Greek temples, a Gothic cathedral, or a Renaissance palace still seem harmonious to us today.

Obviously, we have, and always have had, a built-in feeling for what proportion constitutes. But because we are never satisfied with just feeling but also want to know *why* we feel a particular way and what makes us feel that way—mainly to make emotional responses more predictable—people have tried to rationalize about proportional ratios and develop proportional systems. Mathematics, especially geometry, was of great help to people who tried to find the perfect, divine proportional ratio.

One charming illustration of this point is a statement by **Albrecht Dürer**, the famous German Renaissance painter (1471–1528). In the third book of his *Proportionslehre* (Teachings on Proportions), he writes: "And, indeed, art is within nature, and he who can tear it out, possesses it....And through *geometrica* you can prove much about your works."[8]

Golden Section   The most well-known proportional ratio is the golden section, often called the "divine proportion" or the "golden mean." The familiar pentagram, or five-pointed star, contains a series of golden sections, each line dividing the other into a golden section proportion.

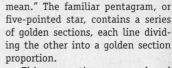

This proportion was produced by calculating minds from ancient Egypt to the Renaissance. Although the Egyptians knew about the golden section proportion and used it extensively in their architecture, sculpture, and painting, the Greeks are usually credited with working out the mathematics of this proportion and relating it to the proportions of the human figure. Later, **Leonardo da Vinci**, the great Italian Renaissance painter, scientist, and inventor, spent much time proving and making public the validity of the mathematical formula of the golden section (0.616:1), worked out by Greek philosopher and mathematician **Pythagoras** as early as 530 B.C.

In the golden section, the smaller section is to the greater as the greater is to the whole. Thus:

$$\frac{BC}{AB} = \frac{AB}{AC}$$

This proportion continues ad infinitum. If you fold the BC section (on the right) into the AB section (on the left), you will again have created a golden section.

$$\frac{AC}{BC} = \frac{AB}{AD}$$

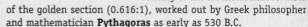

The quickest way to divide a line into golden section proportions is to multiply its length by 0.616. Mark off the line with the resulting length. This point will divide the line into the larger and smaller parts of the golden section.

because you don't like the lost-in-video-space feeling when he or she is centered in the large 16 × 9 screen. Such a maneuver would most likely fail to make the shot more dynamic and keep the viewers watching. If the newscaster lacks dynamism in personality as well as message, even a divine screen placement will fail to improve the communication. Unless the newscaster's shift to the side of the screen is done to accommodate additional visual material, the newscaster will merely look off-center.[9]

Modular units   Architects and scene designers have modified golden section proportions into a modular concept. This means that a piece of scenery or a prefabricated wall can be used in a variety of configurations, with, for example, two or three widths of one scenic or building unit fitting the length of another. This makes the units easily interchangeable. With modular units you can create a great variety of scenic structures without having to build custom sets each time a new environment is required.

PUSHING DYNAMICS

The distribution of graphic weight, frame magnetism, and vectors can be pushed to their structural limit. As viewers we sense that even the slightest change in the field structure would cause a total loss of balance and stability. This instability makes the graphic tension and energy quite high. Note that in video and film, such extreme dynamics are usually temporary, which means that this instability in composition is done to intensify an especially energetic or precarious moment, after which the composition reverts to a more comfortable stasis.

You can achieve such pictorial tension by overloading one or the other side of the screen with graphic weight, by not providing the vectors with enough room to play out, or by constantly having high-energy vectors converge within the shot or in a shot series.   **SEE 8.24**

The easiest way to achieve more tension and move from a static and stable balance to a highly dynamic and *labile*, or unstable, one is to tilt the horizon line. In this way the customary horizontal/vertical equilibrium is disturbed enough to create tension without changing the balance of the other structural forces of graphic mass, frame magnetism, and vectors.   **SEE 8.25 AND 8.26**

Our inborn sense of equilibrium—our desire to see things stand upright on level ground—reacts so strongly to this labile balance that we try almost physically

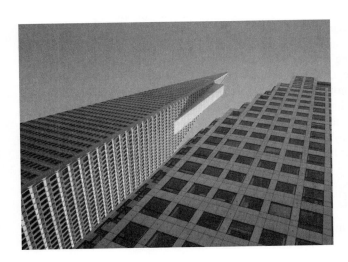

8.24 Labile Dynamics
An extremely dynamic balance may even start out as a temporary imbalance. With the slightest change in the distribution of graphic elements, the vectors would lead to an unbalanced picture field.

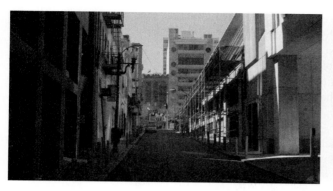

8.25 Static Balance

The straight horizon gives this picture a highly stable balance.

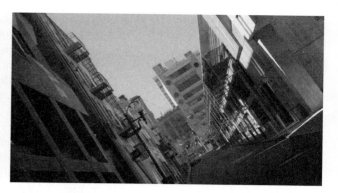

8.26 Dynamic Balance

A heavily tilted horizon gives this picture a labile (unstable) balance.

to keep the objects in the picture from slipping out of the frame and to bring the horizon line back to its normal, level position. Hence we perceive such labile, extremely dynamic types of balance as high-energy.

Whether the balance should be static or dynamic is largely a matter of communication intent and context. As pointed out earlier, if you want to reflect the extreme excitement, tension, or insecurity of an event, the pictorial equilibrium should reflect this instability. You may do well to choose an extremely dynamic, unstable picture balance.

On the other hand, if you want to communicate authority, permanence, and stability, the pictorial arrangement should reinforce and intensify this by means of a static balance. Note that *static* in this context does not mean dull or uninteresting but rather a balance that is solid and stable.

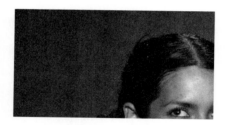

8.27 Imbalance

If the graphic weight and the vectors create a totally lopsided picture, the extreme dynamism has changed into an unbalanced composition. If temporary, it can still serve as a perceptual attention-getter.

UNBALANCED SCREEN SPACE

In an unbalanced composition, there is no longer any aesthetic structure in screen space. Usually, the placement of pictorial elements is arbitrary and uncontrolled. The elements lack deliberate structure and look and feel chaotic. **SEE 8.27** Why talk about unbalanced picture compositions when our goal is to achieve balance in structuring the two-dimensional field? Because in the temporary and transitory moving image of video and film, an unbalanced structure can be so startling as to be an attention-getter (see figures 8.37 to 8.39). You cannot afford to stay with such bad compositions for too long, however, or your intended perceptual jolt will become a perceptual rejection. An unbalanced shot that is not corrected is like a dissonant musical chord that is not resolved.

When looking through the viewfinder of a camera, you must learn to *feel* the proper balance. Especially when working in television news, the constantly shifting events do not tolerate long and careful structural contemplations. Like a ballet dancer or a champion athlete, you should be able to react to the structural demands of the moment both immediately and intuitively. But this type of intuition must grow out of a solid grounding in how to structure the two-dimensional field. Before your reflexes become optimal, you must practice them.

Object Framing

Take a breather from reading for a moment and look around. You'll probably notice that there is no object that you can see in its entirety unless you pick it up and look at it from all sides. When you have to portray this environment within the restricted space of a video or even a film screen, the viewer will see even less. The small video and computer screen, and especially the tiny mobile media display, favor close-ups and close-up sequences, all of which require, as you recall, a great deal of psychological closure, a mental filling in of missing information.

Although closure is an automatic perceptual response, you can nevertheless facilitate it by applying some basic compositional principles when framing a shot; you can inhibit it by ignoring them.

This section provides some answers by discussing closure within a single screen and in the extended two-dimensional field of multiple screens.

FACILITATING CLOSURE

To help you structure the two-dimensional field, try to arrange its visual content so that viewers can group and organize it into easily recognizable patterns of simple geometrical figures. **SEE 8.28–8.30** Even if you encounter visual material that is more complicated to compose than in these illustrations, you can always look for and feature dominant graphic vectors that may give viewers some orientation in the visual jungle and help them apply closure and form a relatively stable gestalt.

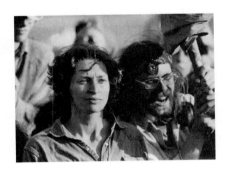
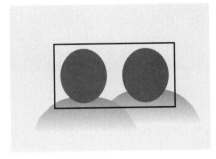

8.28 Closure into Rectangle

The graphic vectors in this picture help form the pattern of a rectangle.

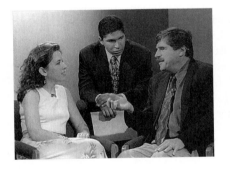
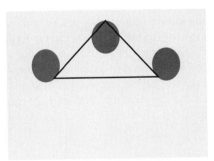

8.29 Closure into Triangle

This composition facilitates closure into a triangle.

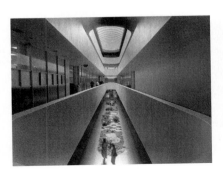
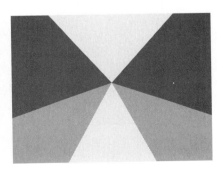

8.30 Closure into Diagonals and Triangles

The strong graphic vectors in this Frank Lloyd Wright building divide the picture into strong diagonals and triangles.

GRAPHIC CUES

When showing only part of an object or a person on-screen, you must frame the subject so that the viewer can easily fill in the missing parts and perceive the whole. In vector terminology this means that you facilitate psychological closure by arranging the vector field within the screen area so that all the vectors (graphic, index, and motion) contribute to the intended stage of balance and especially that they extend easily beyond the screen into off-screen space. **SEE 8.31** In this waist shot, you don't see a picture of a person with the top of the head and the body cut off, or parts of the guitar missing. Instead you automatically perceive a complete person who is seated, playing his guitar. This is primarily because the shot contains enough graphic cues (graphic vectors) to provide psychological closure in off-screen space.

8.31 Closure in Off-screen Space

In this waist shot, we perceive the whole person playing the guitar, although only part of his body and the guitar are visible. Sufficient graphic cues lead us into off-screen space.

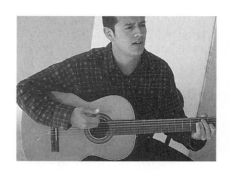
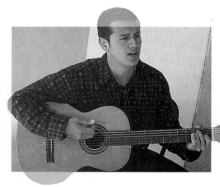

PREMATURE CLOSURE

There are instances, however, in which improper framing can lead to **premature closure**, which occurs when the vector field within the frame entertains such easy psychological closure that the image no longer compels us to extend it beyond the screen. This can happen even if only parts of an object or a person are shown. **SEE 8.32** The head of the subject in figure 8.32 (and in 7.26) is framed in such a way that all necessary conditions for closure exist within the frame; you automatically reduce the head to a simple, self-contained, highly stable gestalt—an oval. Practically no graphic cues lead us beyond the frame. As a result, the head has become an independent unit and so it appears disconnected from its body, resting—like John the Baptist's head on Salome's platter—on the lower part of the screen edge.

8.32 Premature Closure

The shape of the head inevitably leads to closure into an oval. Because an oval is a highly stable and self-contained configuration, you are no longer inclined to project beyond the frame. Hence the premature closure can cause you to perceive the head as disconnected from its body.

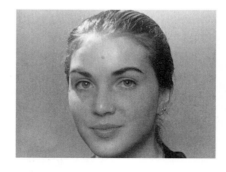
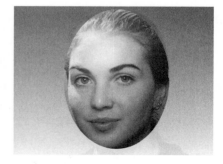

NATURAL DIVIDING LINES

Similar problems of premature closure occur whenever the frame cuts off a person at any of the *natural dividing lines*, such as the eyes, mouth, chin, shoulders, elbows, hemline, and so forth. **SEE 8.33** When framing a shot, do not have these lines coincide with the top or bottom edge of the frame. Always try to frame a person so that the natural dividing lines fall either within or outside the screen edges. That way you give viewers cues to project the image into off-screen space and apply closure to the whole person.

Objects too have natural dividing lines. The principal graphic vectors in the houses in figure 8.34 are the vertical edges of their sides, the V-shaped roof lines, the horizontal belly bands that divide the houses into upper and lower floors, and the fences. If you frame the row of houses so that the side edges of the screen coincide with the outside-wall vectors of two houses, we have no need to project into off-screen space, so we perceive the two houses as a self-contained unit. **SEE 8.34**

But if you crop the picture as in the next figure, we are forced to extend the graphic vectors into off-screen space for proper closure. The outside walls now fall beyond the sides of the screen, and the graphic vectors of the roof lines are added cues that lead into off-screen space. When this happens we are inclined to extend the two houses into a row of houses. **SEE 8.35**

ILLOGICAL CLOSURE

Our need to make sense of the chaotic environmental and perceptual stimulus overload is so strong that we form patterns even when the visual elements that make up those patterns are illogical and obviously do not belong together. Thus we tend to group together in a single structure those visual elements that seem to provide an easy continuation of graphic vectors.[10] Because of the attraction of

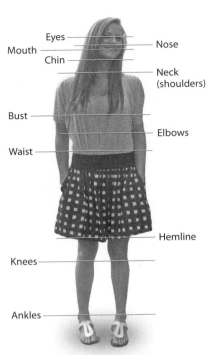

8.33 Natural Dividing Lines in Persons
Premature closure occurs when the upper or lower screen edge coincides with natural dividing lines. You should therefore frame a person so that these lines fall either inside or outside the upper and lower screen edges.

8.34 Dividing Lines Coinciding with Screen Edges
These houses are cut off at their natural dividing lines by the sides of the screen. We cannot tell whether there are only two houses or a whole row.

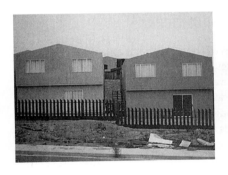

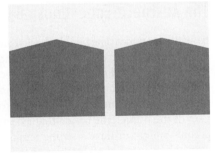

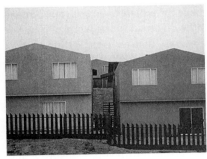

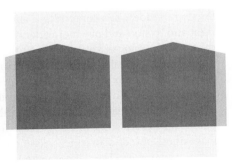

8.35 Dividing Lines Falling Outside the Screen Edges
Now that the edges of the natural dividing lines fall outside the screen edges, you are forced to apply closure in off-screen space; consequently, you are more apt to perceive a row of houses.

8.36 Illogical Closure

If facilitated by the smooth continuity of vectors, we tend to group objects into stable perceptual patterns regardless of whether they belong together. In this case, the field reporter seems to balance a street sign on his head.

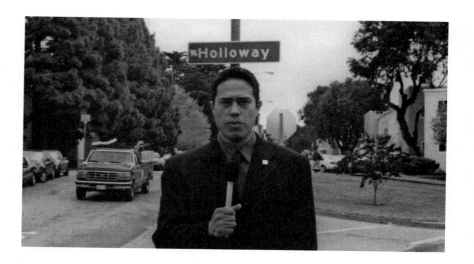

mass and the close proximity of the street sign, we tend to perceive and form a stable configuration even when we know that the field reporter does not balance a street sign on his head. **SEE 8.36**

To avoid this problem when framing a shot, you must learn to look *behind* the main subject to see if possible closure anomalies lurk in the background. Be especially alert when the scene designer puts potted plants behind interview chairs. When the camera is turned on the scene, some of the stems will almost inevitably appear to grow out of people's heads, ears, or shoulders. Similar precautions apply when shooting outside. Look behind the immediate scene you are shooting to see whether any background objects, such as telephone poles or trees, might lead to illogical closure.

The Aesthetic Edge: Unusual Compositions

Now that you have learned the basic rules of composition, it's time to break them. Sometimes, under certain circumstances, unusual compositions will not only startle viewers and make them pay renewed attention but also sharpen the message in a subtle yet compelling aesthetic way. **SEE 8.37**

The woman is almost pulled through the left screen edge by the magnetism of the frame. The bench that extends to screen-right does not carry enough graphic weight or have a strong enough graphic vector to balance the shot. The woman's head is cut off by the upper screen edge just below the nose, preventing us from seeing her eyes—the windows to her personality. But this "wrong" framing increases the weight of the left side of the screen and directs our attention on the dog. Besides, this composition almost begs for a man to enter from screen-right and to stop and pay more attention to the dog than to the woman. You can continue this plot to your liking. Notice, however, that we were setting up this situation aesthetically, through an unusual composition rather than with a wide establishing shot or dialogue.

Other ways of drawing attention to a specific screen area are to place an object way off screen-center or show only part of it on-screen. **SEE 8.38 AND 8.39**

You can see some striking unusual compositions in design books, fashion magazines, and, of course, television commercials and some of the more stylish videos and movies. There is ample room to experiment with your camcorder and still camera. Whatever you do, the guiding principle for such unusual framing must be the intensification of the message, giving it an aesthetic edge, rather than

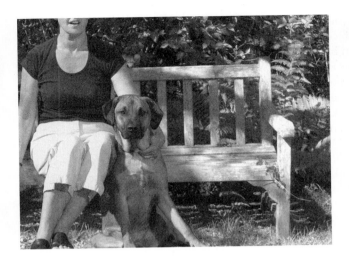

8.37 Emphasis on Dog
Placing the woman at extreme screen-left and having the upper frame cut below her nose puts the emphasis on the dog. We also set up the scene for somebody to enter from screen-right.

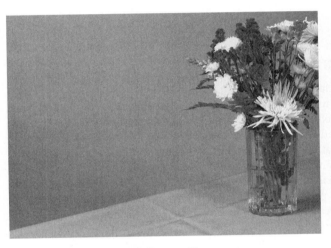

8.38 Emphasis Through Off-center Placement
By placing the vase near the right screen edge, the magnetism of the frame creates an aesthetic discrepancy that draws our attention to the flowers.

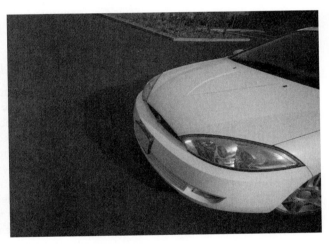

8.39 Emphasis Through Partial On-screen Placement
By showing only part of the car on-screen, we inevitably want the car to drive into on-screen space so that we can get a closer look at it.

making it simply look odd. If overdone, the unusual framing is perceived not as an intensifier but as a mistake; the initial attention-getter becomes an irritant.

Multiple Screens

We live in a world of ever-increasing complexity. Print and electronic media bombard us day and night with significant and not-so-significant information about what is going on in our neighborhood and in the far corners of the world. Instant access to information is no longer a luxury; it has become a necessity and a means of power. We have become information-dependent; that is, we need quick access to a large amount of varied information to function properly in our society. Whether you are shopping in a supermarket or going to the voting booth, you are asked to make choices. To make the right decisions, you need to know about the products or political candidates and be subjected to multiple viewpoints.

Despite its somewhat chaotic nature, the Internet makes information on practically any subject available instantly. Our predicament is not the availability of the information but rather locating what is relevant. Other problems are that much information is drastically streamlined to remain manageable—headline news and sound bites are but two examples—and that the information is still principally delivered linearly, line by line, picture after picture. As a result, the mediated events lack the complexity that you actually experience in everyday life. What is needed is a rethinking of the conventional television, film, and computer display techniques.

There are various ways of coping with this problem. As early as the beginning of the twentieth century, cubist painters, such as Pablo Picasso and Georges Braque, were well aware of the ever-increasing complexity of our existence and let us simultaneously see various points of view of the same event (see figure 12.1). Just a decade later, French film director Abel Gance pioneered the showing of simultaneous **multiple screens** in his film *Napoléon Bonaparte*.[11] His efforts, however, were and remain largely ignored by the film industry.

Today's media are well aware of the need for more efficient and effective communication—the increase of information density while keeping it lucid and understandable.

INCREASED INFORMATION DENSITY

Increased information density is especially noticeable in commercials and newscasts. The average running time of a standard commercial is 30 seconds, in which you may be subjected to 60 different shots. Some newscasts reduce their stories to headlines and sound bites. The more important, and often overlooked, aspect of heightened information density, however, is the increased amount of simultaneous information crammed into a single screen display. Well-known examples are the newscaster who is usually surrounded by a secondary frame—the box—and a variety of unrelated pictures and written information, ranging from the latest acts of inhumanity to weather forecasts, sports, and market results.[12] **SEE 8.40**

The idea behind such a display is to make a variety of information available to viewers and to let them pick and choose. But a newscast is not a newspaper or a magazine or even a Web page, where you are free to scan the information and then go back to the item that interests you. The temporal medium of television

8.40 High-density News Display
This frame from a news presentation shows a high-density information display. The information is not well structured, however, and the individual news items are hard to comprehend.

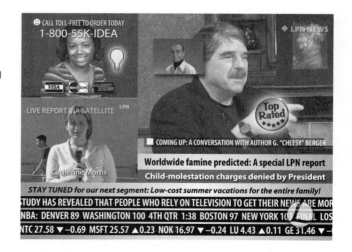

does not allow such scrutiny (unless you have recorded the news). Most often all you can do is take in as much of the information as you can, realizing that you will inevitably miss out on some if not most of it.

One of the problems is that once you have zeroed in on a particular item in a high-density display, your mental operating system tries to save your sanity by blocking out most of the information that is peripheral at that moment. For example, while you are reading a printed news item that is scrolling along the bottom of the screen, you are apt to miss what the anchor is saying and vice versa. Information density on-screen does not guarantee increased information processing by the viewer. In fact, much of the bombardment of simultaneously displayed images not only remains ineffective but often makes the viewer lose interest and tune out completely.

But can't you look at the pictures that relate to the news story while listening to the anchor's commentary? Yes, you can. This indicates that the degree of information density is not a problem so long as it is structured properly. We are now confronted with learning to parlay potential information overload into effective high-density communication. The following points give some guidance on dealing with simultaneously displayed multiple images. You may recall some of the multiple-screen principles from the discussion of aspect ratios in chapter 6.

Dividing the Screen: Graphic Blocks

If you do not have distinct, clearly marked secondary frames within the screen, you must organize the information into discrete information areas, or graphic blocks. Such blocks help the viewer comprehend the information quickly and easily. Once you have assigned the blocks a specific place on the video or computer screen, you should keep the same type of information in the same area in subsequent presentations. For example, if the weather information is in the lower-right corner of the screen, don't move it to the upper-left in the next newscast. Likewise, if you have placed specific navigation instructions for the first part of an interactive module on screen-left, we expect them to be there again for the second part. Such consistency in screen position helps the viewer locate the desired information quickly without having to scan the whole screen. **SEE 8.41**

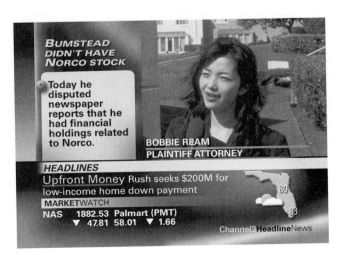

8.41 Use of Information Blocks
Grouping information into multiple frames and text blocks makes it relatively easy to seek out and comprehend the desired information.

Dividing the Screen: Screens Within the Screen

As discussed in chapter 6, we can place a number of secondary frames of various aspect ratios within the primary video screen. To help the viewer assimilate the content of the secondary frames without scrutinizing each individually, you need to be aware of the major aesthetic principles of screens within the screen.

Secondary frame   If you insert a secondary frame on the primary screen, such as the well-known box over the newscaster's shoulder, you need to be especially cognizant of the principal graphic elements operating in this new frame. **SEE 8.42**

Although the field reporter in the secondary frame has proper noseroom according to single-screen standards, her index vector seems blocked by the left edge of the secondary frame and also by the left border of the primary screen. Because her gaze is directed off-screen, she seems oddly disconnected, if not isolated, from the event in the primary screen space (the anchor). Let's reverse the index vector so that the reporter in the box looks toward the inside edge of the secondary frame and see whether this solves the problem. **SEE 8.43** With the woman looking toward the inside (right) edge of the secondary frame, her index vector seems to flow uninhibited through the box and connect with the primary screen event. The anchor's story is now properly supported by the visual structure of the screen display.

Z-axis vectors in split screen   We are accustomed to accepting the sequential z-axis shots of host and guest as converging index vectors. When we see a close-up of the host looking at the camera (and, by extension, at us) followed by a similar close-up of the guest, we have no problem believing that the two people are talking to each other. When they are placed in individual side-by-side boxes, however, such an effect is more difficult to achieve. Unless their original locations (studio for the host and remote for the guest) are clearly established, we may be unsure whether the boxed people are looking at us or at each other.[13]   **SEE 8.44**

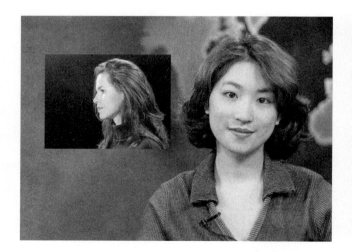

8.42 Isolation Through Index Vector Pointing Outward

In this secondary frame, the index vector points toward the outside (left) edge of the primary screen. Because there is no off-screen space on this side, the woman looks isolated from the news event.

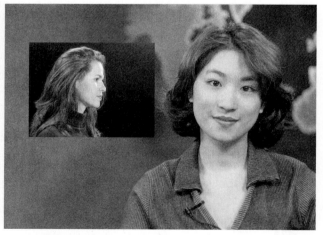

8.43 Connection Through Index Vector Pointing Inward

When her index vector points toward screen-center, the field reporter looks connected to the news event.

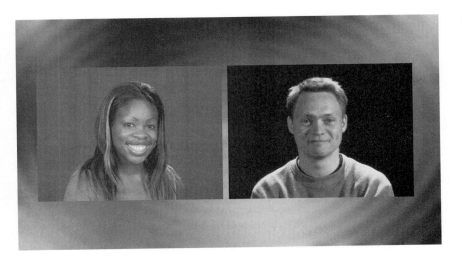

8.44 Split-screen Z-axis Vectors

When two people are isolated in secondary frames, the convergence of their z-axis index vectors depends on context. They can be perceived as talking to each other, to an off-screen person, or to the viewers.

Temporal and spatial contexts   When you use several secondary frames, their structural requirements vary, depending on whether they are used in a temporal or a spatial context.

If you use multiple screens to deal with temporal complexity, for example to indicate simultaneous events that occur at different locations, the graphic weight and the vectors within the secondary frames are of little structural concern. Because the various boxes represent events that occur in widely different locations, their structural separation within the confines of the primary screen may be an asset rather than a handicap. The connection among the frames is strictly temporal—all events take place at the same time. Still, the screen showing the boy running looks better with the motion vector (in this illustration, the index vector) pointing at screen center rather than at the left screen edge. **SEE 8.45**

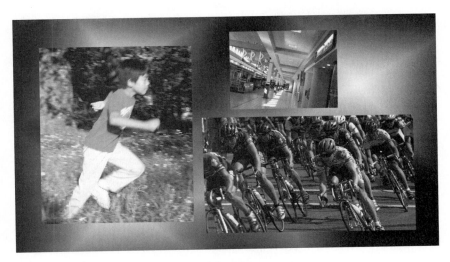

8.45 Distribution of Secondary-frame Vectors in Time Context

When several simultaneous events are shown in separate, isolated secondary frames, the direction of the index and motion vectors within such frames is relatively unimportant.

If the secondary frames are used in a spatial context, such as people in different boxes talking to one another, the placement of the frames in the primary screen space and the direction of the index and motion vectors within each secondary frame become significant structural considerations. Let's assume that you have three equal-sized secondary frames placed side-by-side inside the primary video screen.

In such a three-frame arrangement, only the center frame can project lateral index and motion vectors into the adjacent frames. The two adjacent, or wing, frames on either side of the center frame can project their lateral vectors only toward the center frame but not in the opposite direction. Contrary to a single primary video screen, which operates with off-screen space on all sides, the secondary three-frame arrangement has only limited off-screen space. For example, if a person in the left wing frame looks left, and the person in the right wing frame looks right, we do not project their index vectors into off-screen space. Rather than imply that they are looking at something off-screen, their glance seems to be blocked by the outside frame edges. **SEE 8.46** As soon as the people in the wing frames turn around and look toward the inside edges, however, they connect with the center frame—and even through the center frame with each other. **SEE 8.47**

8.46 Blocked Off-screen Space on Wing Frames

In this three-frame arrangement, we do not project the index vectors of the two outside people into off-screen space. The outside edges of the wing frames seem to block off-screen space to index and motion vectors.

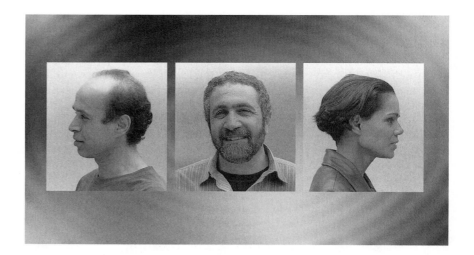

8.47 Connected Frames

When index and motion vectors in the wing frames point toward the center frame, they have no difficulty penetrating the inside edges and even the center frame. The three-frame unit represents a unified space. The focus here is on the center frame.

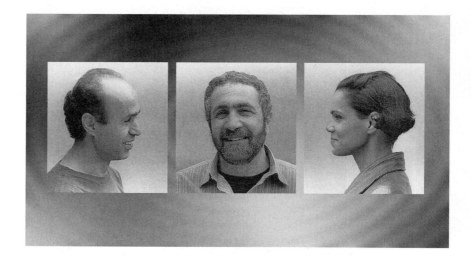

If the persons in the left and center frames look at each other and the person in the right frame looks toward the outside screen edge, the converging vectors connect the left and center screens, but the right screen remains isolated. **SEE 8.48**

When all secondary frames show the people facing the camera and thus projecting z-axis index vectors, the viewer can be persuaded that they are talking to one another if the context suggests a conversation among these people. Such an arrangement is often used when several people report from various locations that would make switching live between action and reaction shots of everybody else extremely difficult. But they also may well talk to the viewer. Such a switch occurs when the newscaster first introduces the field reporters in their remote-location boxes and then, off-camera, asks each individual for specific comments. Their z-axis index vectors are no longer directed toward one another but are intended to converge on the off-screen host. **SEE 8.49**

With individual motion vectors, however, such a convergence switch will not transpire. Just imagine that all three secondary frames show cars speeding along the z-axis toward the camera. You would have a hard time conceiving their motion vectors as converging and that the cars are on a collision course. Despite some credible context, the cars will remain clearly separated.

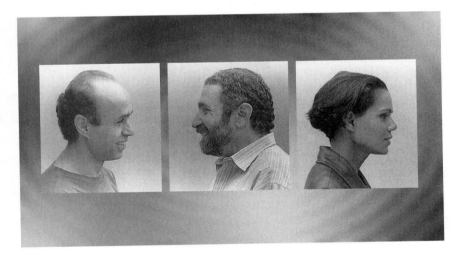

8.48 Isolation Through Diverging Index Vectors

The diverging vectors in the center and right wing frames cause the right frame to become isolated from the other two.

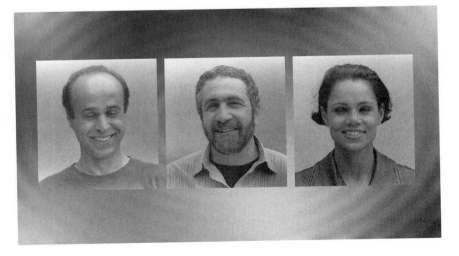

8.49 Triple Z-axis Vectors

When all three frames display z-axis vectors, the target depends on context. If the people in the three frames are in a three-way conversation, it is the audio track that connects the people rather than the index vectors. Their z-axis vectors are more appropriate if they are talking to the viewer or somebody else off-screen.

S U M M A R Y

Structuring the two-dimensional field means making the interplay of screen forces work for rather than against you. The relevant processes and topics include stabilizing the field through distribution of graphic mass and magnetic force, stabilizing the field through vector distribution, stages of balance, object framing, unusual compositions, multiple screens, and dividing the screen.

One of the most basic ways of stabilizing the two-dimensional field is to balance the forces of graphic mass and magnetism of the frame. Each graphic mass (object occupying a certain amount of screen area) has a graphic weight determined by the size of the object, its basic shape and orientation, its location within the frame, and its color.

The magnetism of the frame becomes more powerful the closer an object is to the screen edges. The screen edges attract objects regardless of their size.

The most stable position of an object is screen-center, where graphic weight and frame magnetism are symmetrically distributed. If an object is on one side of the screen, you can balance it with an object of similar weight on the other side.

One of the most important structuring processes is the distribution of vectors. High-magnitude index and motion vectors generally override such forces as graphic weight and frame magnetism. High-magnitude index vectors, as well as motion vectors, require deliberate framing to cope with their structural force and to stabilize the field. You usually do this by giving the vector-producing object enough noseroom (for index vectors) or leadroom (for motion vectors). Although graphic vectors are of relatively low magnitude, you must arrange them so that they do not cause an imbalance in the shot.

There are two basic structural stages of balance: static and dynamic. The most stable form of a static balance is a symmetrical arrangement within the frame. In a dynamic balance, the graphic elements are asymmetrically distributed so that they lead to a higher-energy interplay of forces.

An unbalanced picture lacks aesthetic structure. The placement of all elements within the frame looks arbitrary.

When framing an object so that only part of it can be seen on-screen, you need to provide enough graphic cues to facilitate psychological closure in off-screen space. This enables viewers to mentally fill in the missing parts of the object outside the frame. Premature closure occurs when viewers apply closure to the partial image within the frame without extending the object into off-screen space. This is why you should avoid having the natural dividing lines of a person or an object coincide with the screen edges.

Illogical closure occurs when the visual elements of two unrelated objects provide enough continuation of graphic vectors to be perceived as a single configuration. This visual grouping of continuing vectors is so strong that we tend to group objects that in fact do not belong together, such as seeing a telephone pole as an extension of the person standing in front of it.

Unusual compositions that seem to ignore, or even flaunt, the established rules can be used to emphasize a particular screen area or intensify an event.

The use of multiple screens—or secondary frames within a primary screen—requires additional structural techniques. In contrast to a single screen, which has off-screen space in all directions, the outside edges of secondary frames seem to block index and motion vectors that do not point toward screen-center.

When two people appear in side-by-side boxes, you need to establish that they are talking to each other before the viewer accepts their z-axis index vectors as converging. If you want to show several events that are happening simultaneously in different locations, you can use variously shaped secondary frames within the primary screen. Careful vector continuity is not essential. When multiple screens show people who talk to one another, however, their index vectors must connect so that none of the screens remain isolated.

N O T E S

1. The specific structural principles and demands of a shot series are discussed in more detail in chapters 14 and 17.

2. Credit for the "nose" index vector example goes to my colleague Mike Woal, who used it in his media aesthetics class in the Broadcast and Electronic Communication Arts Department at San Francisco State University.

3. *Leadroom* seems to be a more flexible term than *noseroom*. See Lynne S. Gross, James Foust, and Thomas Burrows, *Video Production: Disciplines and Techniques* (New York: McGraw-Hill, 2005).

4. Vector travel toward or through the screen edge was analyzed by Mark Borden in "On the Problem of Vector Penetration" (Media Aesthetics I, Broadcast and Electronic Communication Arts Department, San Francisco State University, March 1996, unpublished).

5. Rudolf Arnheim, *Toward a Psychology of Art* (Berkeley: University of California Press, 1966), p. 45.

6. The simplification of stages of balance was kindly suggested by William Deering, University of Wisconsin at Stevens Point, Wisconsin.

7. For more information on the Le Corbusier Modulor, see Le Corbusier [Charles E. Jeanneret-Gris], *Modulor,* 2nd ed., trans. by Peter de Francia and Anna Bostock (Cambridge, Mass.: Harvard University Press, 1954); and their *Modular 2* (London: Faber and Faber, 1958).

8. Translation by the author. The original reads: "Dann wahrhaftig steckt die Kunst in der Natur, wer sie herausreissen kann, hat sie.…Und durch die Geometrika magst du deine Werks viel beweisen." In Johnannes Beer, *Albrecht Dürer als Maler* (Königstein i.T, Germany: Karl Robert Langewiesche Verlag, 1953), p. 20.

9. Whereas the golden section or the rule of thirds may be useful for basic shot compositions, both Gerald Millerson and Peter Ward warn against its overuse because such "sameness" of composition may tire the viewer and defeat its intended dynamic tension. See Gerald Millerson, *The Technique of Television Production,* 13th ed. (Boston and London: Focal Press, 1999), pp. 141–42; and Peter Ward, *Picture Composition for Film and Television,* 2nd ed. (Boston and London: Focal Press, 2003). Bruce Block defends it because it helps maintain continuity in relative screen positions. See Bruce Block, *The Visual Story* (Boston: Focal Press, 2001), pp. 141–45.

10. See Irvin Rock, *Perception* (New York: Scientific American Library, 1984), p. 116. Also see Max Wertheimer, "Experimentelle Studien über das Sehen von Bewegung" (Experimental Studies About the Seeing of Motion), *Zeitschrift für Psychologie* 61 (1912): 161–265; and Kurt Koffka, *Principles of Gestalt Psychology* (New York: Harcourt, Brace, and World, 1935), p. 110.

11. In his 1934 film *Napoléon Bonaparte,* Abel Gance (1889–1981) used three 4×3 screens side-by-side to simulate an aspect ratio similar to today's wide-screen format—a process he called polyvision. See William Phillips, *Film: An Introduction* (Boston: Bedford/St. Martin's, 1999), p. 46.

12. Because multiple screens are so rarely seen in film presentations, this discussion is limited to the use of multiple screens in television, although similar multiscreen principles apply to the separate frames in Web page displays.

13. In a study that had three- to five-year-old children react to such second-order frame events, Georgette Communtziz-Page reports that the children were confused with whom the boxed people were communicating. See her "Comprehension of Visual Images in Television" in *Handbook of Visual Communication Research: Theory, Methods, and Media,* ed. by Ken Smith, Sandra Moriarty, Gretchen Barbatsis, and Keith Kenney (Mahwah, N.J.: Lawrence Erlbaum, 2005), pp. 211–23.

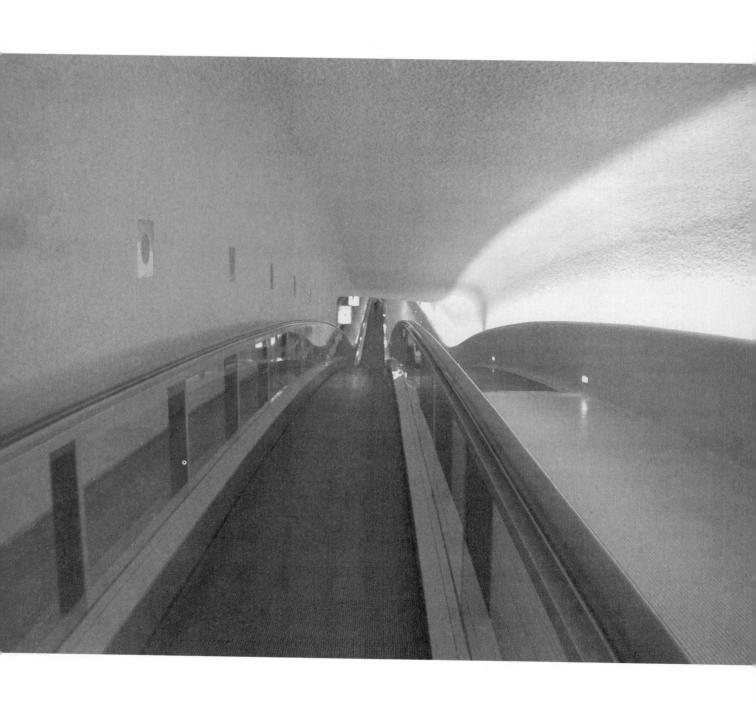

9

The Three-dimensional Field: Depth and Volume

IN VIDEO, FILM, AND COMPUTER DISPLAYS, AS IN PAINTING AND STILL photography, we must project the three-dimensional (3D) world onto a two-dimensional surface. Fortunately, the camera and its single-lens optical system transact such a projection automatically. It is also fortunate that we are willing to accept such a projection as a true representation of all three dimensions: height, width, and depth. **SEE 9.1**

The synthetically constructed images of paintings and computer displays often copy the single-lens-generated depth cues to create the illusion of a third dimension. Although in video and film the camera and the event are often in motion, we can nevertheless draw on the firmly established and proven aesthetic rules of painting to help structure and manipulate this process of projecting a three-dimensional world onto a two-dimensional plane. Note, however, that these techniques do not show us a true stereoscopic projection of the world. Stereoscopy, which is an old technique of displaying the 3D world on a 2D plane, uses two-lens photography or computer programs that simulate our actual two-eyed perception process. Stereoscopic projection is making a comeback in film and has spawned a flurry of activity in video and digital animation.

In this chapter we examine four specific three-dimensional field areas: the z-axis, graphic depth factors, depth characteristics of lenses, and stereoscopic projection.

The Z-axis

As you probably remember from geometry class, the x and y coordinates precisely locate a point in a two-dimensional plane such as the frame of the picture opposite this page, or the video screen. You can describe the width of the screen as the x-axis and the height of the screen as the y-axis. A point within the screen can be assigned an x-value, indicating its relative position along screen width, and a y-value, indicating its position relative to screen height. **SEE 9.2**

In the three-dimensional model, the z-axis is added, which describes depth. The *z-axis* value describes a point located away from the frontal plane—in our case, how far an object seems to be from the camera.[1] You learned about the z-axis in chapter 7 in the context of index and motion vectors that extend from the camera to the horizon and vice versa. **SEE 9.3**

9.1 Projection of 3D Space onto a 2D Plane

In conventional video and film, as in painting and still photography, we project the three-dimensional event onto a two-dimensional surface.

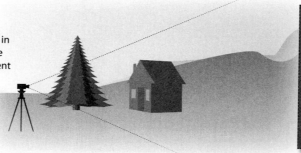

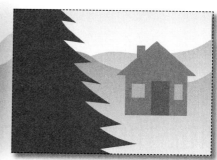

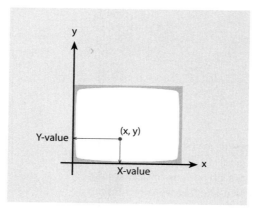

9.2 X and Y Coordinates

The x and y coordinates locate a point precisely within an area, such as the screen. A point within the screen can be assigned an x-value, indicating where it is located on the x-axis (screen width), and a y-value, indicating its position on the y-axis (screen height).

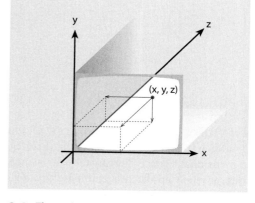

9.3 Three-dimensional Model

To locate a point precisely within a described volume, the z-axis, describing depth, becomes an essential dimension. The z-value describes how far a point is located away from the frontal plane (the screen).

Amazingly enough, the illusory third dimension—depth—proves to be the most flexible screen dimension in film and especially in video. Whereas the screen width (x-axis) and height (y-axis) have definite spatial limits, screen depth (z-axis) is virtually infinite. **SEE 9.4**

Notice that without stereovision or hologram projection (as is the case with all single-lens films, video, and computer displays), we perceive the z-axis

9.4 Z-axis Dimension

Although the z-axis—the depth dimension—is illusory in television and film, it is aesthetically the most flexible screen dimension.

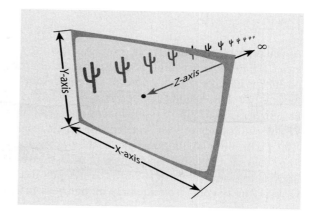

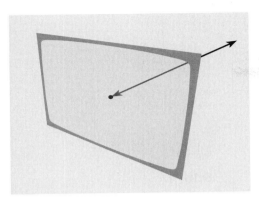

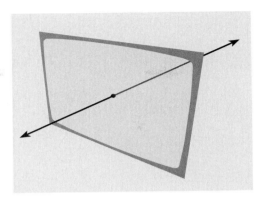

9.5 Z-axis Directions

In normal lens-generated images, the z-axis stretches from the screen (camera lens) to the horizon. The z-axis is bidirectional: movement can occur from camera to horizon or from horizon to camera.

9.6 Z-axis Directions in Stereovision and Hologram Projections

In stereovision or a hologram, the z-axis extends not only from the screen surface back toward the horizon but also through the screen toward the viewer.

as originating from the screen and going backward, from the camera lens to the horizon. The closest object seems to lie on the screen surface; it does not extend toward the viewer. **SEE 9.5**

In stereovision or a hologram, the z-axis extends not only to the horizon but also to the viewer: objects appear to extend out from the screen toward the viewer. We judge their perceived distance relative to ourselves and not to the screen's surface. **SEE 9.6**

As explored in later chapters, the z-axis becomes an important element in structuring screen space and motion.

Graphic Depth Factors

But how, exactly, can we create the illusion of depth on the two-dimensional plane of the screen? **SEE 9.7** Examine the figure and try to identify the many factors that contribute to the illusion of depth on the 2D surface of the page.

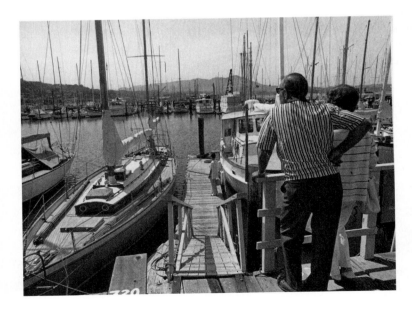

9.7 Graphic Depth Factors

What factors contribute to the illusion of depth in this picture?

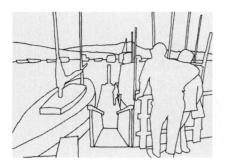

9.8

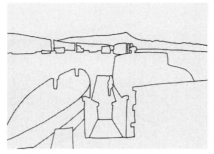

9.9

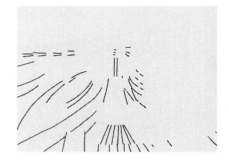

9.10

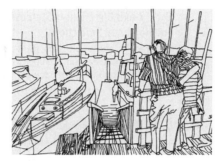

9.11

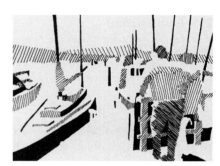

9.12

You probably noticed that some objects are partially hidden by other objects. **SEE 9.8** Also the farther away some objects are (boats, people, hills), the smaller they appear and the higher they seem to be positioned in the picture field. **SEE 9.9** Parallel lines, such as the edges of the boardwalk, appear to converge in the distance. **SEE 9.10** Objects in the foreground are more clearly defined than those in the background. **SEE 9.11** And, finally, the light and the shadows indicate volume, that is, the presence of a third dimension. **SEE 9.12** This section discusses five such *graphic depth factors:* overlapping planes, relative size, height in plane, linear perspective, and aerial perspective.

OVERLAPPING PLANES

The most direct graphic depth cue is an ***overlapping plane***. When you see one object partially covered by another, you know that the one doing the covering must be in front of the one that is partially covered. **SEE 9.13 AND 9.14**

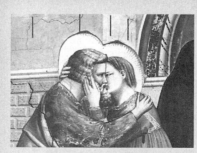

Courtesy of the Museo Civico di Padova.

Medieval painters relied heavily on overlapping planes to indicate depth. In this detail from *The Meeting at the Golden Gate,* one of the many excellent frescoes in the Arena Chapel in Padua, Italy, by Florentine painter and architect **Giotto di Bondone** (ca. 1267–1337), we can see how effectively overlapping planes were used to indicate depth. The only depth confusion arises from the merging halos of Joachim and Anna—caused by the fading of the contour of Joachim's halo at the point of overlap.

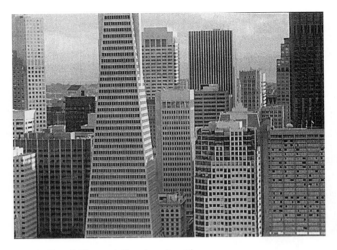

9.14 Depth Through Overlapping Planes
Any object that is partially blocked from our view by another object must lie behind that object. Even with other depth cues missing, we perceive a third dimension by readily assigning partially overlapping objects a "behind" or an "in front of" position.

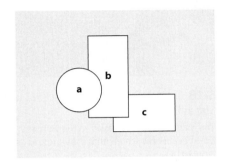

9.13 Overlapping-planes Principle
Object (a) is partially covering object (b), which is partially covering object (c). Although all three figures obviously lie on the same plane (this page), (a) seems to be in front of (b), which seems to lie in front of (c) but behind (a).

RELATIVE SIZE

If you know how big an object is or can guess its size by contextual clues (such as other known objects), you can tell approximately how far the object is from the camera by the *relative size* of the screen image. The larger a subject or an object appears relative to the screen borders, the closer it seems to the viewer. **SEE 9.15** The smaller a subject or an object appears relative to the screen borders, the farther away it seems. This seems to be a hardwired response. **SEE 9.16**

If you know that two objects are similar or identical in size, you perceive the smaller screen image as being farther away and the larger screen image as being closer. **SEE 9.17** In the absence of contradicting contextual clues, we automatically interpret the smaller screen image of the man as being relatively far away from the woman, rather than being unusually small. The more comparable the head sizes, the closer the subjects seem to stand to each other along the z-axis. **SEE 9.18**

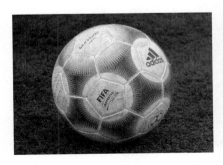

9.15 Relative Size: Close-up
The larger the object or subject appears within the screen—that is, the more area it takes up relative to the screen borders—the closer it seems to us. Appropriately, we call this framing a close-up.

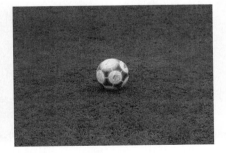

9.16 Relative Size: Long Shot
The smaller the object or subject appears within the screen, the farther away it seems. We call this framing a long shot.

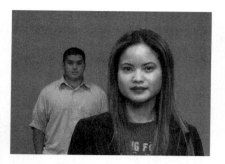

9.17 Interpreting Object Size as Distance: Far

The man seems farther away from us than the woman because his screen image is considerably smaller than hers.

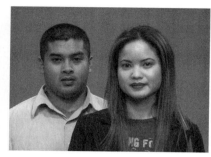

9.18 Interpreting Object Size as Distance: Close

The man seems much closer to the woman now because his screen image is almost as large as hers.

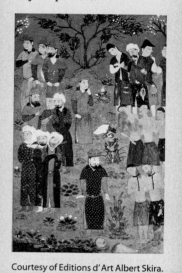

In this sixteenth-century Persian painting, overlapping planes and especially height in plane serve as major depth cues.

Courtesy of Editions d'Art Albert Skira.

HEIGHT IN PLANE

Assuming that no contradictory distance cues are evident and that the camera is shooting parallel to the ground, you will perceive people and objects as being more and more distant the higher they move up in the picture field. This distance cue operates only until they have reached the horizon line. This is known as ***height in plane***. **SEE 9.19** Because of the mobility of the camera, however, which causes the horizon line to shift constantly within a shot or from shot to shot, the height-in-plane distance cue is not always reliable. **SEE 9.20** The fire escape near the top edge of the picture in figure 9.20 seems closer than the high-rise buildings at the bottom edge of the screen. Obviously, the camera did not shoot parallel to the ground. Especially when shooting up or down a large object, the height-in-plane cue is no longer a valid depth indicator.

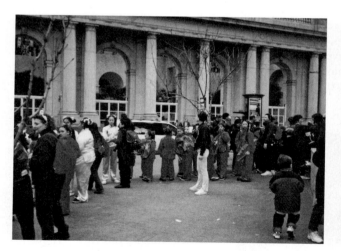

9.19 Height in Plane: Camera Parallel to Ground

In the absence of contradictory distance cues and with the camera shooting parallel to the ground, the people seem farther away the higher up they move toward the horizon in the picture plane. As they line up along the x-axis, they do not move up in the picture plane any longer.

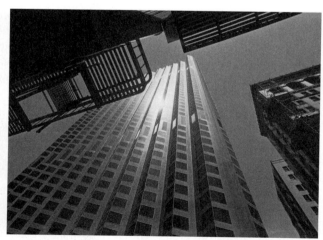

9.20 Height in Plane: Camera from Below

When the camera does not shoot parallel to the ground, height-in-plane distance cues are no longer valid.

LINEAR PERSPECTIVE

This is among the more powerful and convincing graphic depth factors. In a *linear perspective*, all objects look progressively smaller the farther away they are, and parallel lines converge in the distance, with the vertical and horizontal lines becoming more crowded as they move away from the observer (camera). **SEE 9.21**

All parallel lines converge and stop or disappear at the *vanishing point*, which always lies at eye level or camera level on the horizon line. **SEE 9.22**

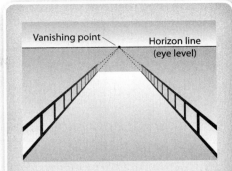

If we look down on an object, the eye (camera) level is above the object. Therefore the horizon line, and with it the vanishing point, lies above the object. We see the object—in this case, the bridge—from above.

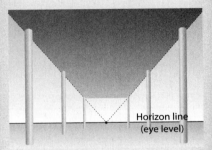

If we are below the object and look up, the eye (camera) level, the horizon line, and the vanishing point lie below the object. We see the object—the bridge—from below.

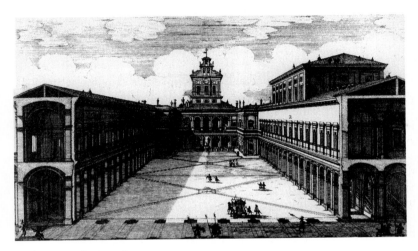

9.21 Linear Perspective

In this architect's drawing of an Italian palazzo, all the prominent horizontal lines (graphic vectors) converge at one point. We call this perceptual phenomenon linear perspective.

Courtesy of the DeBellis Collection, San Francisco State University.

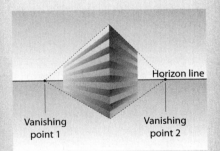

If we see two sides of a building, with one corner closest to us, we perceive two sets of converging lines going in opposite directions. We have, therefore, two vanishing points. But note that the two vanishing points lie on the horizon line; after all, we look at both sides of the building from the same eye level. This is called two-point perspective.

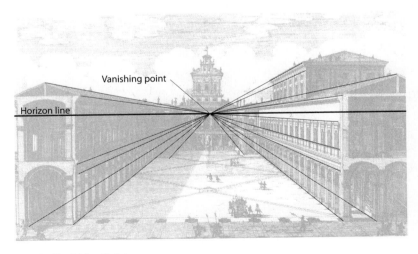

9.22 Vanishing Point

The point at which all parallel lines converge and discontinue (vanish) is aptly called the vanishing point. The vanishing point always lies at eye (or camera) level on the horizon line.

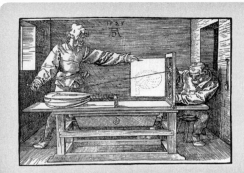

Attempts at using linear perspective to create the illusion of depth on a two-dimensional surface were made by many painters long before the Renaissance, but it was not until the first half of the fifteenth century that Italian artists established scientific laws of linear perspective, such as the horizon line and the vanishing point. With this woodcut one of the masters of the Renaissance, German painter **Albrecht Dürer**, illustrated some of the techniques used by the artist to ensure correct foreshortening (linear perspective).

Taken from *The Complete Woodcuts of Albrecht Dürer,* edited by Dr. Willi Kurth, republished in 1963 by Dover.

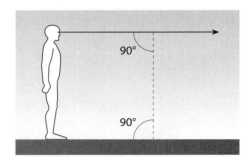

9.23 Horizon Line

The horizon line is an imaginary line parallel to the ground at eye level. More technically, it is the plane at right angles to the direction of gravity that emanates from the eye of the observer at a given place. If you want to find the eye level and the actual horizon line, simply stand erect and look straight forward. The eye level and the horizon line are in the distance where you do not have to look up or down.

To find the **horizon line** and *eye level*, simply stand erect and look straight forward or point the camera parallel to the ground. Assuming your index vector runs parallel to the ground, the horizon line moves up or down with your eyes (camera) regardless of whether you are kneeling on the ground, standing on a ladder, or pointing the camera out a helicopter window. **SEE 9.23**

Now take another look at figure 9.21. Can you tell from which height the artist looked at the palazzo? Was he looking at it from the street level? Sitting in a chair? Standing up? Perhaps from the balcony or window of an unseen building opposite the clock tower?

If you chose the window or balcony, you estimated the artist's correct position. As you can clearly see, the parallel lines converge at a vanishing point that lies above the palazzo near the roofline of the clock tower building (see figure 9.22). The artist must therefore have looked at the building from that position.

Also note that the arches and the windows of the building seem to lie closer together the farther away they are from the observer (see figure 9.21). Many painters have used this crowding effect, or texture, to simulate depth. **SEE 9.24** You can apply this principle just as effectively with computer-generated graphics. **SEE 9.25**

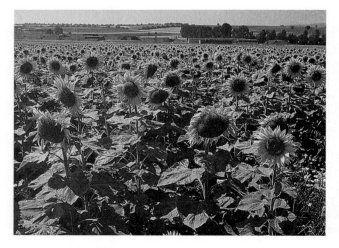

9.24 Crowding Effect Through Texture

Notice how the sunflowers appear more and more crowded the farther away they are from the camera. This crowding effect is an important depth cue.

9.25 Depth Through Crowding

In this computer-generated image, we perceive depth through the crowding effect of distant objects.

Forced perspective Because we tend to interpret image size and convergence of lines with relative distance, we can generate the impression of distance by having parallel lines converge "faster"—more readily—and make distant objects appear smaller than we would ordinarily perceive. Such an artificial forcing of linear perspective is called, appropriately enough, ***forced perspective***. One of the more striking applications of such a forced perspective is the grand staircase in one of Hong Kong's luxury hotels. The wide staircase seems to curve up to the mezzanine in a long, impressive sweep. But when you actually climb the stairs, you will notice that they gradually narrow to less than half of their original width about a third of the way up. As you will discover in this chapter, we can achieve the same effect with the proper choice of lenses.

AERIAL PERSPECTIVE

A certain amount of moisture and dust is always in the atmosphere. We therefore see objects that are close to us somewhat more sharply than those farther away, a phenomenon known as ***aerial perspective***. **SEE 9.26** In fog this difference in sharpness and image density between foreground and background is especially pronounced. Colors also lose their density and become less saturated the farther away they are from the observer (camera). Outdoors, distant colors take on a slightly blue tint.[2]

When creating scenery, for example, you should paint the background objects slightly bluer and less sharp than the foreground objects. This greatly enhances the illusion of depth.

Generally, warm hues seem to advance and cold hues seem to recede. Highly saturated colors seem closer than less saturated colors. Assuming a fairly dark background, the brighter colors (higher position on the brightness scale) seem closer, and the less bright colors (lower position on the brightness scale) seem farther away. We can say that the more the brightness of an object assumes the

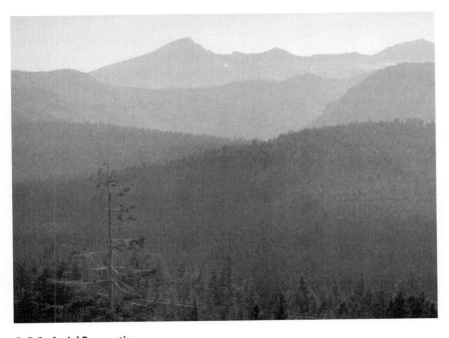

9.26 Aerial Perspective
Notice how the foreground objects in this picture are relatively sharp and dense and that the background objects become progressively less clear and less textured the farther away they are.

9.27 **Aerial Perspective and Color**

So far as aerial perspective is concerned, objects with warm, highly saturated colors that are the opposite of the background brightness seem closer to the viewer than objects with cold, less saturated colors that are similar to the background brightness.

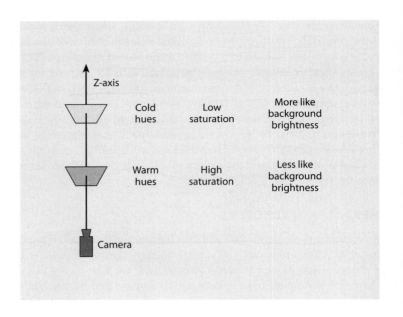

brightness of the background, the farther away from the observer (the camera) it appears. **SEE 9.27**

Depth Characteristics of Lenses

The optical characteristics of lenses can greatly enhance or hinder the illusion of a third dimension on the video or movie screen. Moreover, your choice of lens is important in achieving the certain "feel" of a screen event—whether buildings or objects look squeezed or stretched or whether the z-axis looks compressed or elongated. Synthetic computer images generally simulate the depth characteristics of lenses in their manipulation of the third dimension.

Before discussing the psychological impact of such space manipulation, we will first review the basic depth characteristics of wide-angle and narrow-angle lenses.

Note that our use of the terms *wide-angle* (or *short-focal-length*) and *narrow-angle* (or *long-focal-length* or *telephoto*) lenses includes the wide- and narrow-angle positions of the zoom lens. To put the zoom lens in the extreme wide-angle position, you zoom all the way out. To put it in the extreme narrow-angle, or telephoto, position, you zoom all the way in. The so-called normal lens position is in the middle of the zoom range. For emphasis we concentrate here on the extreme wide-angle and narrow-angle lens positions.[3]

The focal length of lenses influences four principal graphic depth factors: overlapping planes, relative size, linear perspective, and aerial perspective.

OVERLAPPING PLANES: WIDE-ANGLE LENS

Although the wide-angle lens does not rely on overlapping planes as much as the narrow-angle lens does, it can't avoid showing them. Because the objects along the z-axis look more stretched out with the wide-angle lens, it renders overlapping planes less essential as a depth indicator. **SEE 9.28**

OVERLAPPING PLANES: NARROW-ANGLE LENS

The narrow-angle lens does just the opposite of the wide-angle lens, making objects appear closer together along the z-axis than they really are. Because the

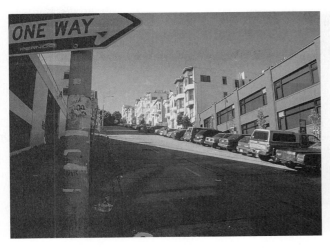

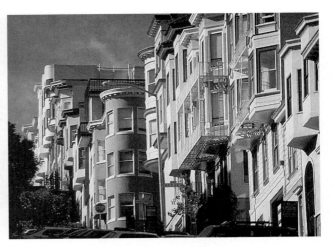

9.28 Overlapping Planes: Wide-angle Lens
Overlapping planes are reduced in prominence, but are not eliminated, with the wide-angle lens.

9.29 Overlapping Planes: Narrow-angle Lens
With a narrow-angle lens, overlapping planes are a major depth cue.

narrow-angle lens enlarges the background objects where things look crowded, foreground and background objects look similar in size. Consequently, they appear closer together than they really are. Objects positioned along the z-axis look squeezed, and the z-axis itself appears shorter than you would ordinarily see.

Because of the similarity in size of foreground and background objects, overlapping planes become a major depth cue for separating one object from another and, ultimately, separating foreground, middleground, and background objects. **SEE 9.29**

RELATIVE SIZE: WIDE-ANGLE LENS

The wide-angle lens greatly exaggerates relative size. Objects that lie close to the camera photograph as relatively large, whereas similar objects positioned on the z-axis only a short distance behind the close object show up in a dramatically reduced image size. **SEE 9.30** The image size of the foreground tugboat is relatively large, and the one just a short distance behind it is relatively small. This great difference in relative size is lessened only at the far end of the z-axis.[4] Because image size is an important distance cue, we interpret this difference as meaning that the background object is farther behind the foreground object than it really is. Thus the wide-angle lens stretches the virtual z-axis.

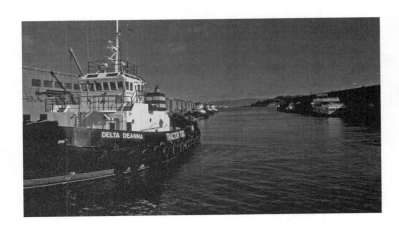

9.30 Relative Size: Wide-angle Lens
The wide-angle lens makes objects close to the camera look relatively large and those just a short distance farther away on the z-axis look relatively small. Because relative size is an important distance cue, the tugboats look farther apart than they really are.

9.31 **Relative Size: Narrow-angle Lens**

The narrow-angle lens enlarges the
background image so drastically that
the tugboats as well as the background
hills seem much closer together than in
figure 9.30, although their actual positions
along the z-axis have not changed.

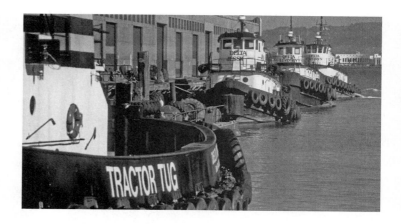

RELATIVE SIZE: NARROW-ANGLE LENS

When the same scene is photographed with a narrow-angle lens, the two boats
seem much closer to each other. **SEE 9.31** This is despite the fact that their actual
distance is identical to that in figure 9.30. You now know why. The narrow-angle
lens enlarges the background, making the second object appear close in size to that
of the foreground object. We translate this similarity in size as relative proximity.
The narrow-angle lens shows objects placed along the z-axis squeezed; the z-axis
therefore appears shortened.

This compression effect of the long (or narrow-angle) lens is very apparent
when you shoot the same row of columns with both a wide-angle and a narrow-
angle lens. Using the wide-angle lens, the columns quickly diminish in size the
farther away they are from the camera; they seem comfortably stretched out.
SEE 9.32 But when you shoot the same scene using a narrow-angle lens, the image size of the background columns is almost the same as that of the foreground
columns. They now seem closer together than they really are; they no longer feel
graceful but instead look massive and crowded. **SEE 9.33**

LINEAR PERSPECTIVE: WIDE-ANGLE LENS

The wide-angle lens accelerates the convergence of parallel lines; that is, they seem
to converge more quickly than when seen normally, thereby giving the illusion
of stretching an object or a building. The z-axis space appears elongated. **SEE 9.34**

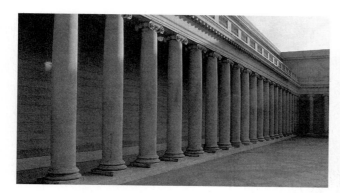

9.32 **Stretching with a Wide-angle Lens**

This row of columns seems quite long, and the columns seem to
be a comfortable distance from one another.

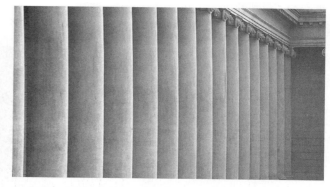

9.33 **Compressing with a Narrow-angle Lens**

With a narrow-angle lens, the columns appear very close together.
The space between them seems squeezed.

LINEAR PERSPECTIVE: NARROW-ANGLE LENS

In contrast, the narrow-angle lens inhibits the normal convergence of parallel lines and thus reduces the illusion of depth through linear perspective. It also squeezes space and makes the doors appear narrower and closer together than they really are. **SEE 9.35**

By now you should have no problem distinguishing between the wide-angle and narrow-angle shots of a piano keyboard. **SEE 9.36 AND 9.37** The wide-angle lens makes the graphic vectors of the keyboard converge much more drastically than when shot with a narrow-angle lens. The "wide-angle" keyboard looks longer, with the keys farther away from the camera looking distinctly smaller. The "narrow-angle" keyboard, on the other hand, does not seem to converge much toward a vanishing point. In fact, the keys farthest from the camera look almost as big as the ones closest to it. This makes the keyboard look short and squeezed. Were you to watch somebody playing quick runs up and down the keyboard, the wide-angle lens would exaggerate such dexterity; the narrow-angle lens would reduce such motion and, with it, the pianist's virtuosity.

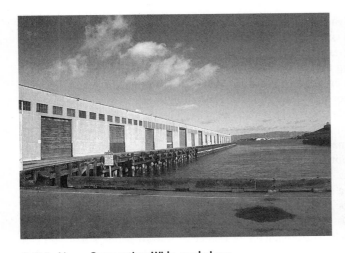

9.34 Linear Perspective: Wide-angle Lens
The wide-angle lens makes parallel lines converge much "faster" (more drastically) than when seen normally.

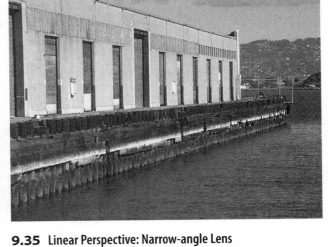

9.35 Linear Perspective: Narrow-angle Lens
The narrow-angle lens "retards" our normal expectations of parallel lines converging. The horizontal lines do not converge as readily as with a normal or a wide-angle lens.

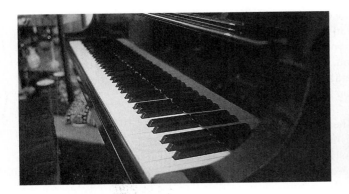

9.36 Piano Keys: Wide-angle Lens
When shot with a wide-angle lens, the piano keys reduce drastically in size the farther they are from the camera.

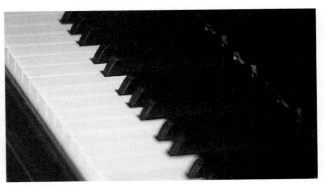

9.37 Piano Keys: Narrow-angle Lens
When shot with a narrow-angle lens, the same keys look squeezed. The piano keys at the far side of the z-axis look almost as big as the ones that are close to the camera.

WORKING WITH AERIAL PERSPECTIVE

You can achieve aerial perspective by manipulating the ***depth of field***—the area along the z-axis that appears in focus—and by making use of selective focus, that is, focusing on only a specific area along the z-axis.

When objects are placed at different distances from the camera along the z-axis, some of them will appear in focus and some will be out of focus. The portion of the z-axis in which the objects appear in focus—depth of field—can be shallow or great. In a shallow depth of field, only a relatively small portion of the z-axis shows objects in focus. In a great depth of field, a large portion of the z-axis shows objects in focus. The depth of field depends on the focal length of the lens, the lens aperture (iris opening), and the distance from the camera to the object.

Assuming that you shoot with a wide-angle lens under normal light levels and do not move the camera extremely close to the target object, the depth of field will be great. A narrow-angle lens gives a shallow depth of field. Generally, wide shots have a great depth of field; close-ups have a shallow one. Take another look at figures 9.36 and 9.37. The wide-angle lens shows the whole keyboard in focus. When shot with the narrow-angle lens, the keys closest to the camera are out of focus because the camera was focused on the middle part of the keyboard.

Aerial perspective: wide-angle lens   Because the wide-angle lens generates a great depth of field, it de-emphasizes aerial perspective. In a great depth of field, most of the articulated z-axis appears in focus. This means you cannot easily focus on only one spot along the z-axis while keeping the rest of the z-axis out of focus (see figure 9.36). A great depth of field is obviously advantageous when covering news, where you normally have little time to achieve optimal focus. Although a misnomer, a great depth of field is also called deep focus.

Aerial perspective: narrow-angle lens   The narrow-angle lens has a shallow depth of field and thus emphasizes aerial perspective. Once you focus on an object using a narrow-angle lens, the areas immediately in front and in back of the object are out of focus. Even a slight position change of camera or object along the z-axis will necessitate refocusing (see figure 9.37).

Although it is difficult to keep a moving object or camera in focus in a shallow depth of field, the advantage of this critical focal plane is that you can use selective focus to emphasize events. You have probably noticed that shooting in a shallow depth of field has become stylish in video and film production. For example, you may see two out-of-focus people walking along the z-axis toward the camera until their images become focused in the depth of field. Such aerial-perspective maneuvers are often accompanied by a similar audio manipulation: when the people are out of focus, you can barely make out what they are saying; but once they are in focus, their dialogue becomes loud and clear. In an over-the-shoulder shot, you may initially see in focus the shoulder and the head of the camera-near person, but the camera-far person, who is facing the camera, is out of focus. The camera will then switch the focus to the camera-far person, with the camera-near person being out of focus.

Selective focus   The technique of ***selective focus*** allows you to choose the precise portion (plane) of the z-axis that you want to be in focus, with the areas immediately in front of or behind the focused object being out of focus. Contrary to a natural aerial perspective that occurs on a foggy day—where only the foreground object is "in focus," that is, more clearly visible than the background objects—the optically induced aerial perspective using selective focus allows you to move the focused plane from the foreground to the middleground or background or the other way around. In the next figure, we start out with the focus on the foreground

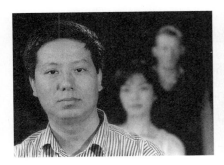

9.38 Selective Focus: Person in Front

A narrow-angle lens is used to create a shallow depth of field that allows selective focus. Note how the focus is on the person closest to the camera, with the people behind out of focus.

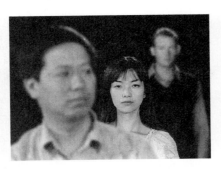

9.39 Selective Focus: Person in Middle

The middleground person is in focus, with the foreground and background persons out of focus.

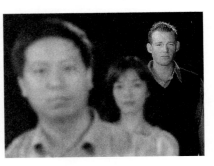

9.40 Selective Focus: Person in Back

The person farthest from the camera is in focus, with the middle and front persons out of focus.

person, with the people in the middleground and the background out of focus. **SEE 9.38** Or you can feature the middleground and leave the foreground and the background out of focus. **SEE 9.39** You can also focus on the background, while the middleground and the foreground remain out of focus. **SEE 9.40**

Rack focus The *rack focus* effect involves changing the focus from one location on the z-axis to another. If, for example, you want to shift the emphasis from a spray can to the person holding it without changing the shot (through a dolly, zoom, cut, or dissolve), you can first focus on the spray can with the person out of focus and then "rack through" the focus range of the lens until the person's face comes into focus, throwing the spray can out of focus. **SEE 9.41 AND 9.42** Obviously, you need a relatively shallow depth of field to accomplish such a rack focus effect, which means that you must use a narrow-angle lens.

If you had a great depth of field (wide-angle lens with a small lens aperture), you could just about rack through the entire focus range without noticeably affecting the focus. A rack focus effect is therefore not possible in this case. With a narrow-angle lens, on the other hand, the depth of field becomes so shallow that even a slight racking of focus shifts the focal plane from one point along the

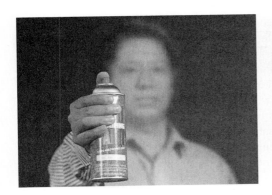

9.41 Rack Focus Effect: Object Emphasized

In this shot the focus is on the spray can. The shallow depth of field renders out of focus the person holding the can.

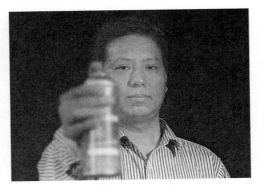

9.42 Rack Focus Effect: Person Emphasized

Emphasis has shifted from one z-axis location (the spray can) to another (the person). Because the depth of field is shallow, we can shift focus from the spray can to the person by changing (racking through) the camera's focus.

9.43 Lens Characteristics and Depth Cues

A + sign indicates that the lens characteristic is facilitating the illusion of depth; a – sign indicates that it inhibits the illusion of depth.

Depth Effects	Lens Position	
	Wide-angle	Narrow-angle
Overlapping planes	–	+
Relative size	+	–
Linear perspective	+	–
Aerial perspective	–	+

z-axis to another. This means that a little adjustment of the focus control shifts the focus from one object to the other, even if they are only a short distance from each other along the z-axis. The table above summarizes how lenses influence our perception of depth. **SEE 9.43**

You can also achieve a type of aerial perspective by using "fog filters" that render portions of the picture out of focus while keeping other portions sharp. Though the filter does not actually distinguish among different z-axis locations, but rather among picture areas that are in and out of focus, we still perceptually interpret this as changes in the picture depth.

3D Stereoscopic Projection

Stereoscopic displays differ technically and aesthetically from the standard representation of a third dimension we have just explored. Whereas the traditional (single-lens) depth cues are contained in the visual representation of a scene, the stereoscopic projection is strictly illusory and exists only in your mind. We can trace and measure the elements of standard 3D clues on a photo (see 9.22), but not the ones of a stereoscopic projection. The stereoscopic effect is truly virtual.

STEREOSCOPIC 3D VERSUS STANDARD 3D: TECHNICAL DIFFERENCE

The basic technical difference between standard 3D and stereoscopic 3D is that standard 3D is based on a single-lens, or one-eyed, view of an event and stereoscopic 3D is based on a dual-lens, or two-eyed, view. Because our eyes are some distance apart, we see an object from slightly different angles; this is called binocular disparity. The easiest way to achieve this disparity with some consistency is to use a two-camera rig, with the two lenses set apart much like our eyes. Some devices use two lenses but only one camera. In this case, the two images are recorded side by side on the same medium. This disparity gives us important distance cues and enables us to engage in stereo vision, provided we have a suitable mechanism that directs one of the two pictures into one eye and the slightly offset picture into the other eye.

Such mechanisms can take various forms and are constantly being refined for film, video, and computer projections. The most basic one is the stereoscope, which was developed in the early 1830s. You have most likely seen or even used

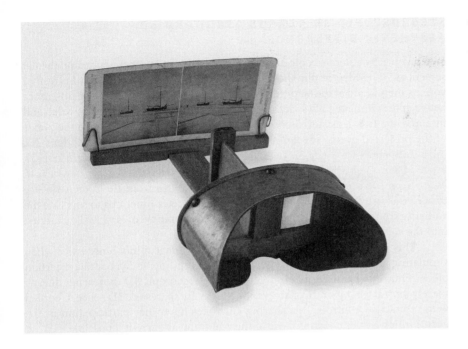

9.44 Stereoscope

In the traditional stereoscope, the viewer directs the left eye to the left-eye photograph point of view of a scene, and the right eye to the right-eye point of view.

one of these contraptions, whereby you look through two different openings dedicated to each of the two slightly differing scenes (usually tinted with monochrome sepia to make them look old). Each eye is blocked from seeing the other's point of view.[5] **SEE 9.44**

This principle of making one of your eyes see an event from one point of view and the other eye from a slightly offset one is still used in the anaglyph process, in which the left-eye image of a scene is given a specific color (usually red), and the right-eye image is given its complementary color (cyan). Both images are slightly offset to simulate the different points of view of each eye. When looking at this double red/cyan image with stereoscope glasses, the left red lens lets you see the red part of the double image with your left eye, but not with the right one, which is blocked by the cyan-filtered image. The right cyan lens, on the other hand, lets you see the cyan-colored image with your right eye, but blocks most of the red image.

You probably noticed that we are dealing here with basic subtractive color mixing: the red filter lets no light of the complementary color pass through and renders the entire cyan part of the stereoscopic image black. The complementary cyan filter does the same thing to the red light, rendering the red part of the double image almost invisible to the left eye. Whatever colors are used in the stereoscopic glasses, they must be complementary to effect subtractive color mixing and, thereby, prevent both images from simultaneously entering either eye. Careful color correction is required for all techniques so that what you see through your rose-colored glasses represents the normally colored world.

There are many other techniques of displaying the two offset images—such as using polarized rather than colored filters, slightly offset fields in interlaced video scanning, or pixels that achieve the binocular disparity through a slight pixel shift[6]—but they all work on the same stereographic principle: to present the same scene in two slightly offset images: one as our left eye would see and the other as our right eye would see. The stereoscopic effect happens not on the screen but in the optical system of your brain.

STEREOSCOPIC 3D VERSUS STANDARD 3D: AESTHETIC DIFFERENCE

When you view a stereoscopic 3D projection, the event is not contained on the flat screen, as with video or film, but comes *toward you*—it seems to float in front of you. As mentioned at the beginning of this chapter, the major aesthetic difference between the simulated 3D space of the standard one-lens projection of video and film and the two-lens stereoscopic 3D projection is how we perceive the z-axis of the projected event (see figures 9.5 and 9.6). In the standard single-lens 3D, the z-axis, and with it the 3D articulation, points from the screen surface back toward the event horizon. In the ***stereoscopic projection,*** the z-axis extends both ways, from the screen surface to the horizon but also from the screen surface toward the viewer. In fact, the screen as such no longer functions to separate the audience from the projected event, and the stereoscopic event is virtually dumped into the viewer's lap.

This phenomenon is, of course, a great advantage, if not a necessity, when simulating an event for students who want to learn how to fly, operate a certain piece of machinery, or perform surgery. With stereoscopic 3D the learner doesn't merely look at a 3D picture of an event but actually shares the 3D space. Coupled with interactive controls, this sharing facilitates his or her participation in the event, which comes about as close to the real thing as currently possible.

But this space sharing of audience and stereoscopic event may also be the deeper cause for the apathy the audience has so far shown toward stereoscopic movies, video, and the holograms of still shots. Even if we can eventually do away with the colored glasses and improve the resolution and the color fidelity of the stereoscopic image, we may still resist, however subconsciously, having our comfort zone invaded by stereoscopic film or video events. The extended z-axis, which hurls the event not only from horizon to the screen but *through* the screen and into our face leaves us psychologically, if not psychophysically, unprotected. We are coerced to confront the event literally head-on and somehow participate in it. Bereft of any aesthetic distance between ourselves and the simulated event, we are no longer comfortable watching violent or intimate scenes from a distance while eating popcorn but have the hero or villain step off the stage and sit next to us in the audience. Even in a holographic still image, such as a postcard from Hawaii, the event is no longer contained within its borders or a picture frame but invades our personal space, clamoring for attention.

The renewed and combined efforts of the entertainment industry and the equipment manufacturers to resurrect stereoscopic movies and video will, at least initially, be most successful if the content is nonthreatening, such as cartoons, or predisposed to participation, such as sports.[7] We will then see whether the new superhigh-definition stereo camera systems can remove "old boundaries, freeing us to take audiences on fantastic adventures and tell incredible stories in a whole new way."[8] But we will have a hard time accepting a character's escaping a highly charged emotional scene by stepping through the screen and walking toward us. **SEE 9.45**

There is also some serious concern about the inevitable eye (and brain) strain resulting from making the two slightly offset images appear as a single 3D image.[9]

What deserves special attention in such stereographic presentations is the audio. So far, the spatial manipulation of stereo audio occurs mostly sideways, along the x-axis, and to a limited extent along the z-axis that stretches from the screen to the horizon. Even 5.1 surround sound has only a limited reach when it comes to extending the z-axis from the screen to the viewer. The sound technique that most successfully defines the z-axis space from horizon to screen and from screen to viewer/listener is binaural audio.

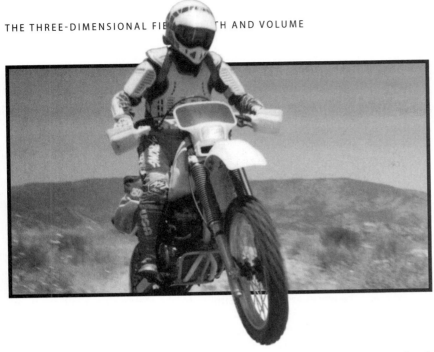

9.45 Invasion of Viewer Space
The stereoscopic 3D event extends from the screen toward the viewer, invading the viewer's space.

Binaural audio is recorded with two microphones stuck in a dummy head, approximately where the ears would be, and is reproduced through headphones (see "Outer Orientation Functions of Sound" in chapter 15). Yes, we used a similar method by using two lenses, separated by the approximate distance of our eyes, when recording video for stereoscopic images. But don't worry. By the time stereoscopic digital cinema and television are in full swing, we probably won't need to wear earbuds in addition to the two-colored glasses every time we switch to a stereoscopic program.

SUMMARY

In video, film, and computer displays, the three-dimensional world must be projected onto the two-dimensional surface of the screen. Although the third dimension (the z-axis) is illusionary, it proves to be aesthetically the most flexible screen dimension.

Three concepts describe the aesthetics of the three-dimensional field: the z-axis, graphic depth factors, and the depth characteristics of lenses.

Whereas the screen width (x-axis) and height (y-axis) have definite spatial limits, screen depth (z-axis) is virtually limitless. The camera is therefore much less restricted in its view and movement along the z-axis than it is either horizontally or vertically. We perceive the z-axis as originating from the screen, extending toward the horizon. In stereovision and hologram displays, the z-axis extends toward the viewer as well.

Graphic depth factors include overlapping planes (objects that partially overlap each other); relative size (an object positioned close to the camera projects a larger screen image than one of similar size that lies farther down on the z-axis); height in plane (assuming that the camera shoots parallel to the ground, we perceive an object that is higher on the screen as farther away from the camera); linear perspective (horizontal parallel lines converge toward a vanishing point at the eye-level horizon line; equally spaced objects appear to lie closer together the farther away they are from the camera); and aerial perspective (the foreground in focus with the background out of focus). More generally, aerial perspective means selected focus on a spot along the z-axis in a shallow depth of field with the surrounding areas out of focus.

The depth characteristics of lenses are significant in the manipulation of the third dimension of a screen image. Wide-angle lenses exaggerate relative size and linear perspective; they de-emphasize overlapping planes and aerial perspective. Narrow-angle (telephoto) lenses exaggerate overlapping planes and aerial perspective, de-emphasizing relative size and linear perspective. Selective focus and rack focus effects are powerful means of articulating the z-axis and drawing attention to a specific plane along the z-axis. They are possible only in a shallow depth of field and therefore with narrow-angle (telephoto) lenses.

A stereoscopic 3D effect differs from the standard 3D representation on a screen in how we perceive the z-axis of picture space. In the standard 3D simulation, the graphic depth factors define the z-axis from the screen back to the horizon; in the stereoscopic projection, the articulated z-axis extends through the screen space toward the viewer. It is generated by a two-lens recording system, whereby the lenses are set apart similar to our eyes; we get a left-eye point of view and a right-eye point of view of the same scene. To show both slightly offset points of view on a single screen, one is colored red and the other is cyan. When the viewer wears glasses with a red lens for the left eye and a cyan lens for the right eye, each eye sees its dedicated point of view. The optical system in the viewer's brain melds the two images into a single three-dimensional projection, which extends through the screen toward the viewer.

N O T E S

1. The x-, y-, and z-axes are used here in the traditional sense of the Cartesian model that quantifies Euclidian space.

2. Although we call both phenomena "aerial perspective," there is a difference between aerial perspective and detail perspective. Detail perspective refers to the gradual diminishing of detail in the distance, whereas aerial perspective refers to the more bluish tint the farther away the object is from the observer.

    Leonardo da Vinci described vividly what happens in aerial perspective:

    > There is another kind of perspective which I call aerial, because by the difference in the atmosphere one is able to distinguish the various distances of different buildings when their bases appear to end on a single line, for this would be the appearance presented by a group of buildings on the far side of a wall, all of which as seen above the top of the wall look to be the same size; and if in painting you wish to make one seem farther away than another you must make the atmosphere somewhat heavy. You know that in an atmosphere of uniform density the most distant things seen through it, such as the mountains, in consequence of the great quantity of atmosphere which is between your eye and them, will appear blue, almost of the same colour as the atmosphere when the sun is in the east. Therefore you should make the building which is nearest above the wall of its natural colour, and that which is more distant make less defined and bluer; and one which you wish should seem as far away again make of double the depth of blue, and one you desire should seem five times as far away make five times as blue. And as a consequence of this rule it will come about that the buildings which above a given line appear to be of the same size will be plainly distinguished as to which are the more distant and which larger than the others.

    Leonardo da Vinci, *The Notebooks of Leonardo da Vinci*, ed. and trans. by Edward McCurdy (Old Saybrook, Conn.: Konecky and Konecky, 2003), p. 880.

3. Herbert Zettl, *Television Production Handbook,* 10th ed. (Belmont, Calif.: Wadsworth, 2009), pp. 97–98.

4. Actually, the narrow-angle lens simply enlarges the end of the z-axis, where even with a wide-angle lens objects look crowded and space is squeezed. This crowding effect is entirely in line with increased density of texture at the far end of the z-axis.

5. The first commercial use of stereoscopic 3D is credited to Sir Charles Wheatstone, who introduced binocular vision and his stereoscope to the Royal Scottish Society of Arts in 1853. During the second half of the nineteenth century, stereoscopy rapidly gained in popularity and became a huge commercial success. Producing stereo photos and viewing them with the stereoscope become a huge commercial success and a popular pastime. For more information about stereoscopy photography, see Ray Zone, *Stereoscopic Cinema and the Origins of 3-D Film 1838-1952* (Lexington: University Press of Kentucky, 2008); and his *3-D Filmmakers: Conversations with Creators of Stereoscopic Motion Pictures* (Lanham, Maryland: Scarecrow Press, 2005), part of the Scarecrow Filmmakers series.

6. Trevor Boyer, "Stereo Hype," *Digital Content Producer* 35, no. 2 (February 2009): 15–18.

7. One of the more obvious examples of rekindling the public's interest in stereoscopic 3D movies was that the 2009 Cannes Film Festival showed as opening film the animated story *Up* by Pixar. There are many consumer products on the market now that encourage the production of stereoscopic video.

8. D. J. Roller, "World's First 4K 3D Cinema Camera System for Studio, Location, and Underwater Filming with RED camera," PRNewswire (March 3, 2009). Available at *http://news.prnewswire.com/DisplayReleaseContent.aspx?ACCT=104&STORY=/www/ story/03-03-2009/0004982328&EDATE=.*

9. Daniel Engber, "The Problem with 3-D," *Slate* (April 2, 2009). Available at *www.slate .com/id/2215265.* See also Bryant Frazer, "How Big Will 3D Be?" *Studio Daily* (April 23, 2009). Available at *www.studiodaily.com/blog/?p=1371.*

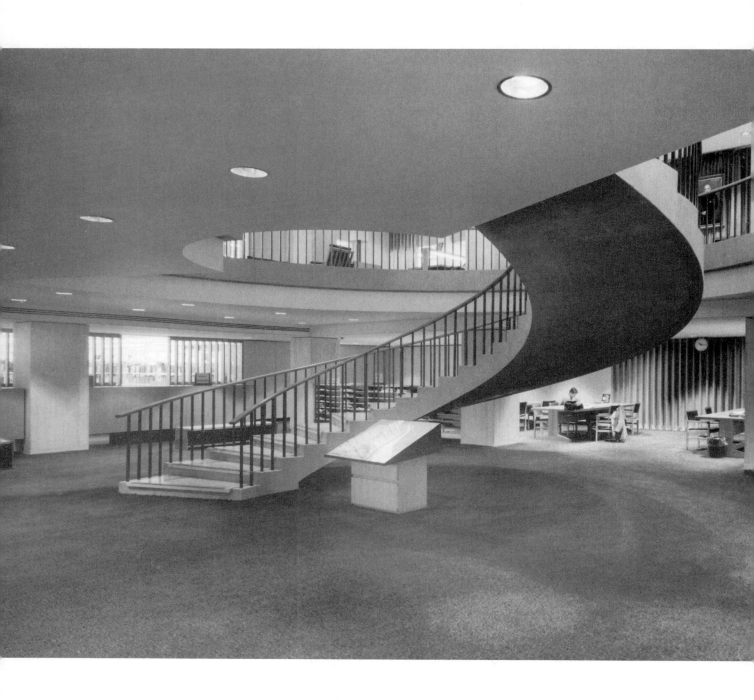

Structuring the Three-dimensional Field: Screen Volume and Effects

S
O FAR WE HAVE DISCUSSED SOME OF THE BASIC PRINCIPLES AND factors that help you project the three-dimensional world onto the two-dimensional video, film, and computer screens and create the illusion of depth. We now examine how to structure the three-dimensional field. We do this principally by manipulating lens-generated space, building computer-generated space, and a combination of both.

Regardless of whether you capture part of the real world through the camera lens or construct an image with 3D computer software, you need to provide distinct depth planes along the z-axis.

The most basic structure of the three-dimensional field consists of a *foreground* (the depth plane closest to the camera, marking the beginning of the z-axis), a *middleground* (the depth plane marking the approximate middle of the z-axis), and a *background* (the depth plane farthest from the camera, marking the end of the z-axis). **SEE 10.1**

When structuring the three-dimensional field, you must—as with most other aesthetic fields—take into account the element of change, that is, the movement of the event itself, of the camera, and of the sequence of shots. A camera that dollies past a row of columns; people dancing; cars moving along the z-axis; a zoom; or a cut from one camera to another—all create a changing structural pattern, a changing three-dimensional field. For example, when the camera is zooming in, the foreground may disappear, the middleground takes on the role of the foreground, and the background becomes the new middleground. Or when you cut from one camera angle to another view, viewers essentially see a new z-axis with its own spatial articulation.

To structure the lens- or computer-generated 3D field, you need to consider three important aspects: volume duality, z-axis articulation, and z-axis blocking. Special effects operate strictly in a virtual volume; that is, they are purposely displayed not as a simulation of real space but as synthetic, constructed *screen space*. Realize that in *stereoscopic projection*, the foreground plane extends toward the viewer and is no longer perceived as part of screen space.

10.1 Depth Planes

This picture is clearly divided into a foreground plane (the tree trunks and the camera-near ground), a middleground plane (the creek bank and the bushes), and a background plane (the mountain). This threefold breakdown represents the most basic structure of the three-dimensional field.

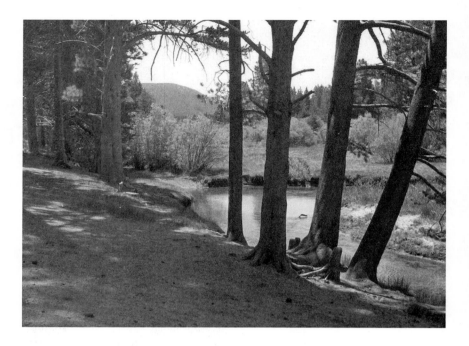

Although the most basic articulation of the z-axis is its division into a foreground plane, a middleground plane, and a background plane, you can divide the z-axis into as many planes as you wish, but such divisions must fulfill some aesthetic purpose; otherwise the z-axis space simply looks cluttered. **Josef von Sternberg** (1894–1969), who directed Marlene Dietrich in the famous 1930 film *The Blue Angel,* was obsessed with articulating the z-axis space in his films with appropriate space modulators and meaningful action to keep "dead" z-axis planes to a minimum. Look for z-axis articulations in the latest dramatic television series.

Volume Duality

When you look at the cloudless sky, you do not experience any depth. Empty space gives no clues as to distance because nothing is either near to or far from you. An extreme long shot looks exactly the same as when you are zoomed all the way in. As soon as you look ahead of you and see the houses, trees, and people, however, you can readily tell which things are near you and which are farther away. The objects help define the space around you and make it possible to perceive the third dimension—depth. We can say that positive volumes (houses, trees, and people) have articulated empty space with a series of negative volumes.

A ***positive volume*** has substance; it can be touched and has a clearly described mass. Positive volumes include such objects as cars, pillars, desks, and chairs as well as people. But a positive volume is also any screen image that has the appearance of substance.[1]

A ***negative volume*** is empty space that is somehow delineated by positive volumes. Unlimited negative space, such as the cloudless sky, constitutes negative space but not negative volume. The interior of a room is a negative volume because it is clearly described by the positive volumes of the walls, ceiling, and floor. The hole in a doughnut is also a negative volume, but the space surrounding the doughnut is not (assuming that we ignore the larger negative volume of the room).

The interplay between positive and negative volumes is called ***volume duality***. The control of volume duality—how the positive volumes articulate the negative space—is an essential factor in the manipulation of three-dimensional space and the illusion of screen depth. Designing scenery for video or film and blocking talent and camera action—all are careful and deliberate manipulations of volume duality. For example, the empty studio represents a clearly defined (by the studio walls) yet unarticulated negative volume—the empty studio. As soon as you put things into the studio, such as scenery and set pieces, you begin to modulate the negative volume of the empty studio with positive volumes, giving each scenic element its specific place and dividing the large negative volume into smaller, organically related negative volumes. Thus the positive volumes act as space modulators.

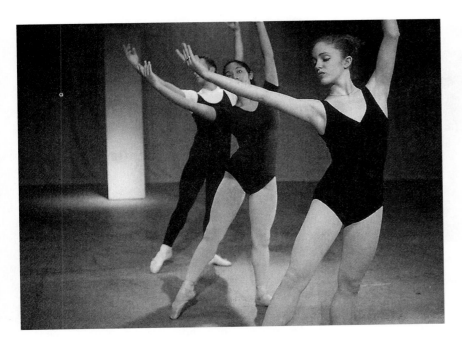

10.2 Creating Volume Duality
The negative volume of the studio space is articulated by the positive volumes of the set pieces, which remain relatively stationary, and the dancers who move around and thereby change the volume duality. The dynamic changing relationships between negative and positive volume is called volume duality.

Volume duality can vary in degree. When people or objects move through the negative volume (such as the studio, for example), they continuously redefine the volume duality. **SEE 10.2**

DOMINANT POSITIVE VOLUME

When you stuff many objects into the studio or any other room, the positive volumes outweigh the negative ones, making the room look crowded. Too much positive volume can confine movement and make you feel restricted or boxed in.

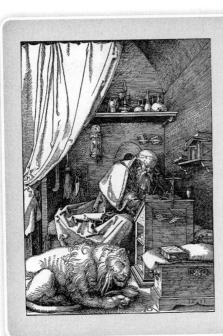

In this medieval chamber, positive volumes overpower the interior's cramped negative volume. Thick walls and solid furniture give the room a heavy, restricted look. One feels boxed in, if not imprisoned.

Taken from *The Complete Woodcuts of Albrecht Dürer*, edited by Dr. Willi Kurth, republished in 1963 by Dover.

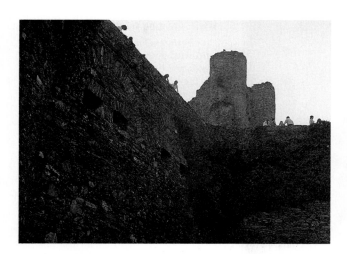
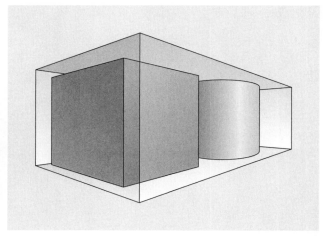

10.3 Preponderant Positive Volume

Volume duality can vary in degree. When using many and/or large space modulators, the positive volume can outweigh the negative volume.

A medieval castle is a good example of a preponderance of positive volume with relatively little negative volume. **SEE 10.3**

Like modern bunkers, the heavy positive volumes protect the restricted living space inside but also inhibit freedom. It's no wonder that medieval knights broke out of this spatial confinement sporadically to beat each other up for no apparent reason! Some modern concrete structures reflect the same confined negative space even if their function is to provide as much negative volume as possible, like a parking garage. **SEE 10.4**

If you want to re-create for the camera this sense of confined space, you need to crowd the negative volume with positive volumes—that is, stuff things into a relatively small space. If, for example, you want to show that a crowded office is difficult to work in, confine the action area—the area in which people can move

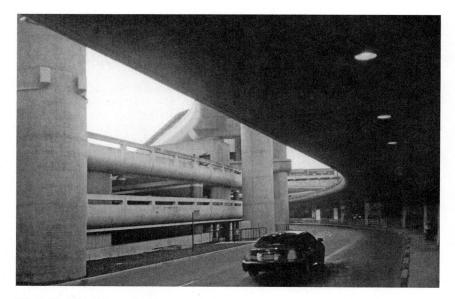

10.4 Restricted Operating Space

The parking garage on the left of this picture has so much positive volume that it looks cramped even if there is ample space inside.

about—by placing lots of desks and file cabinets in close proximity. By using a narrow-angle (long-focal-length) lens and chiaroscuro lighting, you can further intensify such a dominance of positive volumes. If you want to emphasize the potentially explosive situation of a mass political protest, wedge the protesters into a narrow street or intersection rather than show them marching through the wide-open space of the city park. In a similar way, you can intensify the sheer bulk and power of a big person by having him sit on a small chair in a tiny, low-ceilinged room.[2]

DOMINANT NEGATIVE VOLUME

A large, well-articulated negative volume invites mobility. We feel less restricted and can breathe freely and move about easily. **SEE 10.5**

A dominant negative volume isolates us and can make us feel insignificant and humble in the presence of so much emptiness. Much like the huge positive volume of a mountain, a large negative volume, such as an open plaza, an empty stadium, or the interior of a Gothic cathedral, can fill us with awe.[3] **SEE 10.6**

Too much negative volume, however, can promote a certain emptiness wherein we feel alone, cold, isolated, and lost.[4] **SEE 10.7** It's no wonder that people who work in the large, unarticulated space of modern offices put up screens

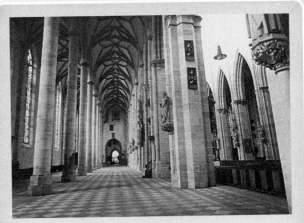

Gothic cathedrals were deliberately built with a maximum of negative volume. The positive space modulators, such as the walls and the pillars, were kept to a bare structural minimum to emphasize the wide expanse of the church interior. Such a vast, vertically oriented interior space contributes greatly to making us feel both reverent and subservient.

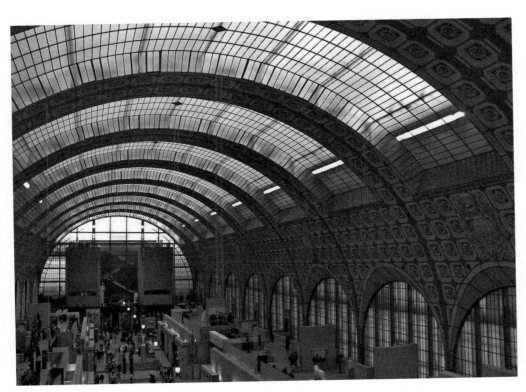

10.5 Dominant Negative Volume
With only a minimum of space modulators, the negative volume remains large though highly articulated. This interior has an open, spacious feeling.

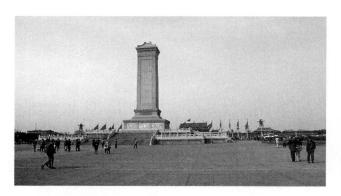

10.6 Feeling Vastness

This plaza has a preponderance of negative volume, which is nevertheless articulated by the people and the monument in the center. Such vast negative volumes can inspire awe. At the very least, we feel dwarfed by the space.

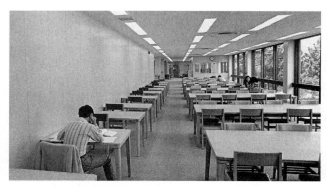

10.7 Lost in Negative Volume

An interior with too much negative space can make us feel isolated and uncomfortable. This library room is anything but cozy.

and partitions or use space modulators such as file cabinets to create a less public and more personal space for themselves.

APPLICATIONS OF VOLUME DUALITY

You can see the most obvious application of volume duality for its own sake in sculptures done primarily to explore the interrelationship of positive and negative volumes. **SEE 10.8**

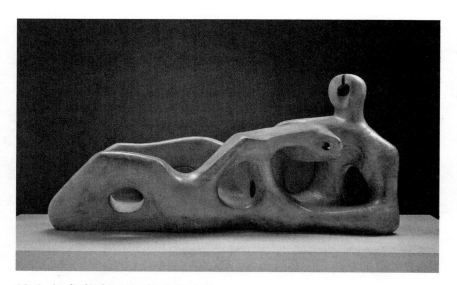

10.8 Applied Volume Duality in Sculpture

This sculpture by the late English artist Henry Moore shows a masterful handling of volume duality. The holes in the sculpture are so well placed and well defined by the positive volumes that they attain positive spatial characteristics. As in a figure/ground reversal, the holes no longer represent nothingness—an absence of something—but rather define a variety of negative volumes that counteract and supplement the positive volume.

Henry Spencer Moore (1898–1986) *Reclining Figure* (1939), elm. The Detroit Institute of Arts, USA/Founders Society purchase with funds from Mr. and Mrs. Charles Theron Van Dusen and Beatrice W. Rogers Fund/ The Bridgeman Art Library/Reproduced by permission of The Henry Moore Foundation.

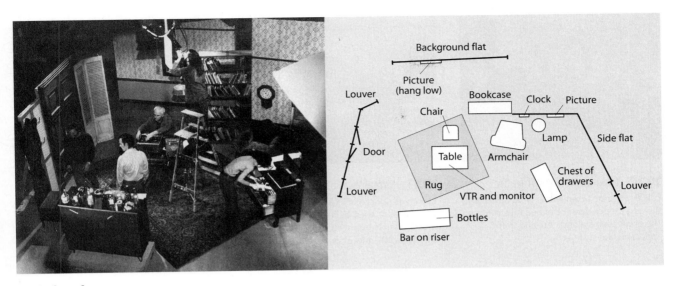

10.9 Open Set

In an open set, we modulate rather than merely describe the negative volume of the studio by the positive volumes of scenery and set properties. Modulating the negative volume means transposing it into an important scenic element. The spaces among the flats are no longer empty holes but rather appear as solid walls much as the positive flats themselves do. Proper lighting is essential to transpose negative space into positive scenic elements.

In scene design volume duality is applied in an open set. ***Open set*** refers not to a set that is open to the public but rather to scenery that is not continuous; the open set is not closed or boxed in by connected walls but instead consists of only the most important parts of a room, for example, a window, some furniture, and a few separate single flats. **SEE 10.9**

The open-set method is particularly effective for a single-camera video production that builds its screen events inductively, bit by bit, close-up by close-up, in a mosaic fashion. So long as your visualization approach is inductive, the open set is even advantageous in multicamera productions; it allows for optimal camera points of view and a more fluid shot sequencing. This is different when shooting "landscape-style" for digital movies or large-screen video. The frequent long shots of large vistas or interiors require a continuous interior and make an open set impractical.

Z-axis Articulation

The z-axis is especially important in structuring video space because the other principal spatial dimensions of the standard video screen—height and width—are limited compared with the larger and especially much wider HDTV or motion picture screen. The camera, very much like the human eye, has no trouble looking along the z-axis all the way to the horizon. It can therefore take in a great number of objects stationed along the z-axis. It can cope successfully with even extremely fast movement without panning (horizontal camera movement) or tilting (camera looking up and down) so long as the objects are placed or move along the z-axis. Vertical and horizontal object motion require a great deal of camera panning and tilting, and this becomes especially difficult for the camera if the object motion is rapid. The articulation of the z-axis is therefore one of the principal factors of spatial and motion control in standard video.

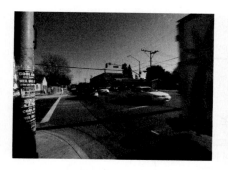

10.10 Wide-angle View of Traffic

This z-axis shot, taken with a wide-angle lens, shows a preponderance of negative volume. The z-axis seems elongated, and traffic appears relatively light.

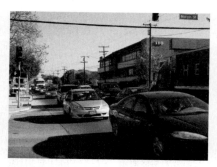

10.11 Normal View of Traffic

Taken with a normal lens (medium zoom lens position), the z-axis now looks slightly shorter than in figure 10.10, and traffic appears a little more congested.

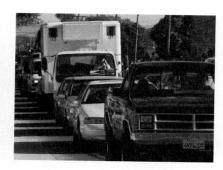

10.12 Narrow-angle View of Traffic

With a narrow-angle lens, the cars look closer together, making the z-axis look compressed.

Articulating the z-axis means to place positive volumes along the z-axis to help the camera distinguish among the depth planes. By placing objects or people at various z-axis locations and by choosing a specific lens (wide-angle, normal, or narrow-angle zoom lens positions), you can make the viewer perceive restricted or open space, with objects being crowded or else comfortably or agonizingly far apart.

Take a look at the three traffic situations in the figures above. **SEE 10.10–10.12** Figure 10.10 shows a long stretch of road with apparently light traffic. In figure 10.11 the traffic seems slightly heavier; in figure 10.12 the traffic appears completely jammed. Actually, all three shots were taken from the same position within seconds of one another, but each was taken with a different lens, that is, with a different zoom lens position. You probably recognized that the shot in figure 10.10 was taken with a wide-angle lens. The resulting volume duality shows preponderant negative volume. The exaggerated convergence of parallel lines and relative size make the cars appear much farther apart than they actually are. The aesthetic effect is that we perceive traffic to be light. The shot in figure 10.11 was taken with a normal lens. The perspective, relative-size factors, and volume duality in this shot appear approximately as you would normally see them. This means that traffic conditions are reflected accurately in this shot. The shot in figure 10.12 was taken with a narrow-angle (telephoto) lens. Here the volume duality shifts to a predominant positive volume. The linear perspective and the relative-size differences are minimized, and the parallel lines do not converge as rapidly as in the other two shots. The cars are reduced in size much less toward the background than in the wide-angle shot. Because they appear similar in size, the z-axis space seems to have shrunk, and the cars appear much more crowded than they actually are; traffic seems heavy.

NARROW-ANGLE LENS DISTORTION

The crowding of objects through a narrow-angle lens can cause a variety of perceptions. **SEE 10.13** By reducing the negative space to a minimum, the signs in figure 10.13 seem right on top of one another. The signs have lost their effectiveness. Instead of being individual carriers of specific information, they have become mass elements of visual pollution.

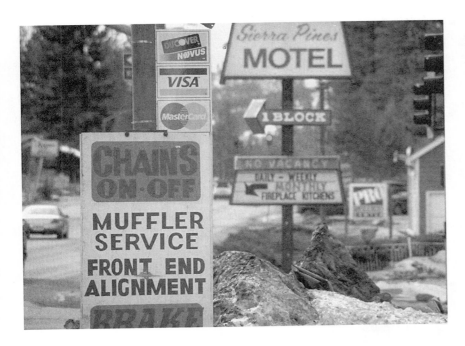

10.13 Sign Pollution
The narrow-angle (long-focal-length) lens not only crowds these signs but also emphasizes the visual pollution.

When spatially condensed by the narrow-angle lens, a row of separate columns becomes a single, massive support. With the reduction of negative space, the volume duality has given way to a mass of positive volume. **SEE 10.14** Similarly, when squeezed by a narrow-angle lens, a row of houses connotes certain psychological and social conditions, such as closeness or crowdedness with little room for expansion. Depending on the overall context, you might also think of fire danger. **SEE 10.15**

Like a military uniform, the narrow-angle lens can rob people of their individuality and suggest sameness of behavior, collective goals, a high degree

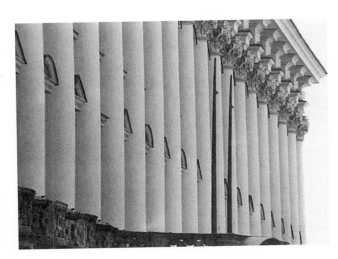

10.14 Massive Columns
When shot with a narrow-angle lens, the columns lose their individuality. We perceive only positive volumes.

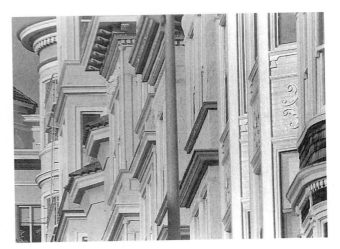

10.15 Cramped Housing
The narrow-angle lens crowds these homes even more than they really are, intensifying their close proximity and suggesting cramped living conditions or fire danger.

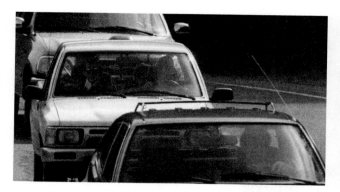

10.16 Tailgating

By reducing the space between the cars to a minimum, the narrow-angle lens intensifies the danger of tailgating.

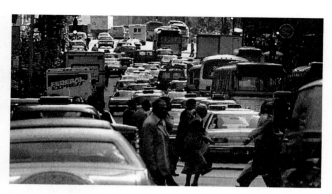

10.17 Rush-hour Traffic

The crowding of the vehicles by the narrow-angle lens intensifies the density of rush-hour traffic.

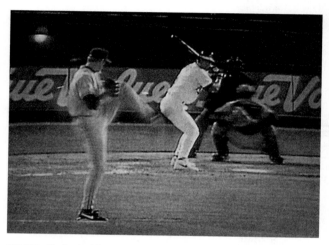

10.18 Undesirable Distortion

Even if we know the actual distance between pitcher and batter (60 feet 6 inches), the long-focal-length lens (extreme narrow-angle zoom lens position) shows the players as standing fairly close together.

of persuadability, or simply raw, irrational power. Extreme closeness can suggest danger, especially when applied to fast-moving vehicles. The precariousness of tailgating is highly intensified by the narrow-angle field of view. **SEE 10.16**

Shooting heavy traffic along the z-axis with an extremely long-focal-length lens (zoomed in all the way to its narrowest-angle position) crowds the vehicles even more than they really are. Such a shot readily communicates the frustration of the people stuck in rush-hour traffic. **SEE 10.17**

As with every aesthetic effect, the depth distortion through a narrow-angle lens can, of course, also work to your disadvantage. You are no doubt familiar with the deceiving proximity of the pitcher to home plate. Because cameras must remain at a considerable distance from the action, the extreme narrow-angle lens used in the reverse-angle shot from pitcher to batter drastically shrinks the apparent distance between the two. In such a shot, we may wonder how the batter could ever hit the ball when the pitcher fires at him from such a close range. **SEE 10.18**

WIDE-ANGLE LENS DISTORTION

The wide-angle lens also exaggerates size relationships. An object close to the camera appears much larger than a similarly sized object placed just a short z-axis distance away (see figure 9.17 in the previous chapter). We automatically interpret this size difference as increased z-axis distance. Depending on the context, however, we can also interpret such a size discrepancy as an exaggeration of object size. Through what Sergei Eisenstein called "conflict of volumes and spatial conflict," such distortions carry not only aesthetic but also psychological messages.[5]

Ordinary shots can become highly dramatic through a wide-angle lens. **SEE 10.19 AND 10.20** For example, the

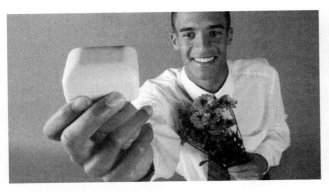

10.19 **Implied Message: Importance**

The distortion of relative size through the wide-angle (short-focal-length) lens implies that the box contains a precious gift.

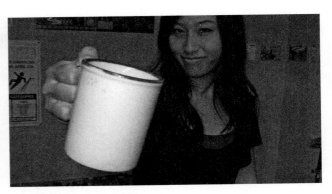

10.20 **Implied Message: Danger**

The wide-angle-lens distortion of this cup implies that the liquid it contains might be dangerous to drink.

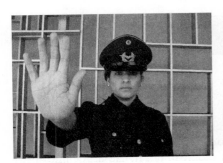

10.21 **Intensified Message: Stop**

The wide-angle-lens distortion of her hand intensifies the guard's stop command.

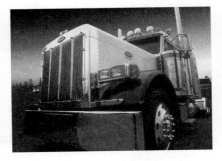

10.22 **Implied Message: Power**

The power of this truck is intensified by the wide-angle-lens distortion.

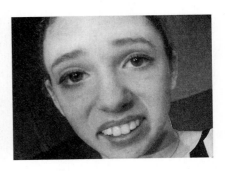

10.23 **Implied Message: Emotional Stress**

Although wide-angle-lens distortions of a face are usually avoided, you can nevertheless use them to intensify extreme emotional stress or unbalance in a person.

wide-angle-lens distortion of the little gift box underscores the importance of the occasion (figure 10.19). On the other hand, the distortion of the cup suggests that it may contain something other than the aromatic coffee that wakes you in the morning (figure 10.20). A gesture signaling a stop is made more forceful and authoritative when shot with a wide-angle lens. **SEE 10.21** The power of huge things, such as trucks, jet planes, or heavy machinery, is also aptly dramatized by the wide-angle shot. **SEE 10.22**

You can also use wide-angle-lens distortion to communicate intense emotional stress in a person. **SEE 10.23** Extreme facial distortions as in figure 10.23 suggest that the woman may be no longer stable or rational. Obviously, such a distortion must operate in concert with other contextual media aesthetic clues.

When you shoot through prominent foreground pieces, the foreground acts as a secondary frame (the primary frame being the video screen), which focuses our attention on the middleground or background objects. **SEE 10.24** Because of the volume conflict (large foreground objects on screen-left) and the relatively small background objects (people), this shot inevitably directs our attention to the main subject—the two boys sitting in chairs. Such implied secondary frames are especially important when composing shots for the wider HDTV or movie screens.

10.24 Secondary Frame

You can focus attention on a scene by shooting through a prominent foreground piece, creating a secondary frame.

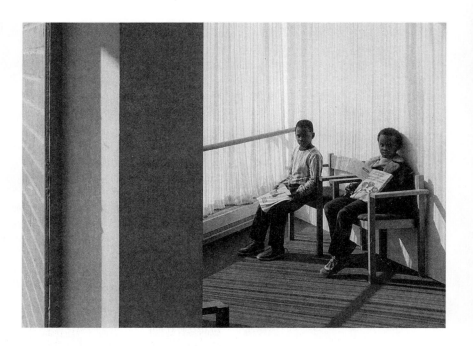

Z-axis Blocking

Z-axis blocking refers to placing people and their movements primarily along the z-axis—toward and away from the camera. Such blocking is one of the major devices for effectively articulating the z-axis, creating a dynamic volume duality and intensifying the illusion of a third dimension on the two-dimensional screen.

When blocking action for the theater stage, we usually rely heavily on lateral or diagonal rather than upstage/downstage (z-axis) motion. In fact, lateral action is generally preferred in theater because the stage is usually wider than it is deep. **SEE 10.25**

The blocking for the wider HDTV screen can be more lateral so long as the video is projected onto a large screen. If a projection is limited to a relatively small HDTV screen, however, you should still block primarily along the z-axis, much as you would for the standard 4 × 3 video screen. The small screen cannot tolerate much lateral action without having the camera pan or truck along with it. Aside from the technical problems of keeping a fast-moving object properly framed, too much lateral action can become distracting and disorienting.

Proper blocking along the z-axis minimizes camera movement and emphasizes object (and people) motion, not camera motion. In fact, high-impact action is often blocked along the z-axis, even in large-screen movies. A person running or an object hurtling along the z-axis toward the camera is usually more dramatic and carries more aesthetic energy than when staged sideways along the x-axis.

10.25 Lateral Action in Stage Blocking

The relatively large lateral space of the theater stage and the wide motion picture screen make lateral action an effective blocking technique in theater and film.

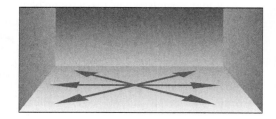

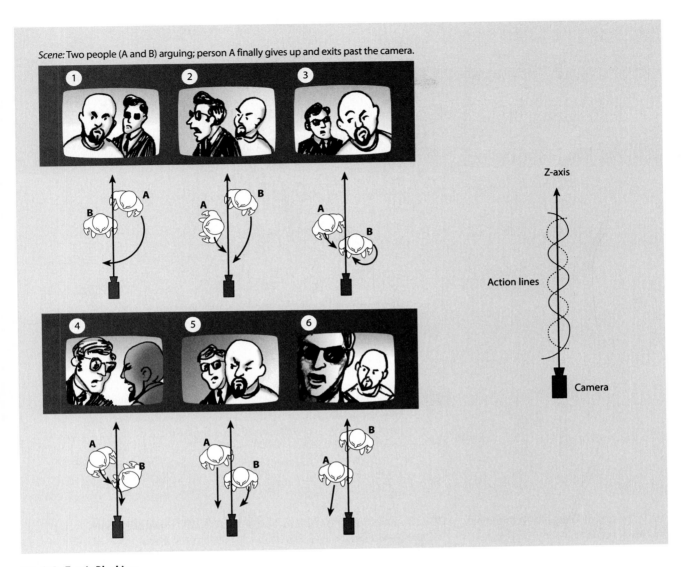

Scene: Two people (A and B) arguing; person A finally gives up and exits past the camera.

10.26 Z-axis Blocking

Because of the limited height and width of the standard video screen or mobile media display, action is most appropriately staged and blocked along the z-axis.

When blocking for television, you can have the action weave toward and/or away from the camera along the z-axis. **SEE 10.26**

Such z-axis blocking for the standard video screen allows you to show a relatively large number of people interacting with one another from a single camera's point of view. **SEE 10.27** For example, you can use z-axis blocking to simulate a crowd scene with just a few people. **SEE 10.28** The same scene shot from another angle reveals how sparse the "crowd" really is. **SEE 10.29**

If, in a multicamera production, you intend to use a second camera for close-ups in such a "crowd" scene, you would need to have the second camera fairly close to the first so that the z-axes of both cameras are practically identical or at least run pretty much parallel to each other. Otherwise the first camera would see the crowd along the z-axis, and the close-up camera would view them along the x-axis (see figures 10.28 and 10.29).

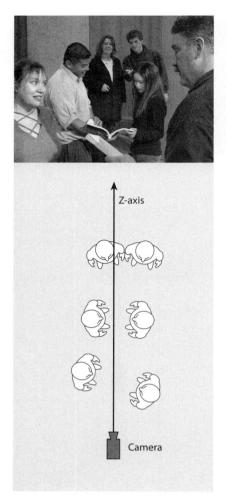

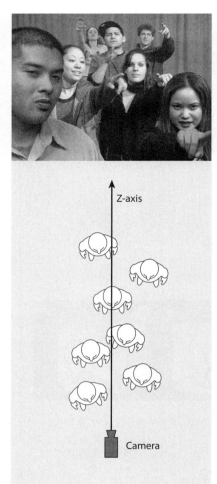

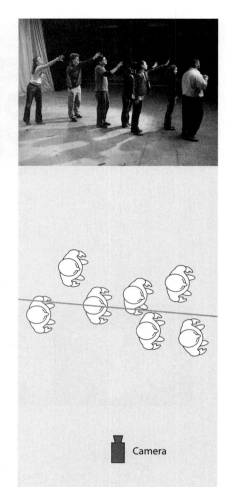

10.27 Z-axis Blocking of Several People

A relatively large number of people can be included in a single shot so long as they are blocked along the z-axis.

10.28 Z-axis Blocking of Crowd

A crowd scene is easily simulated in video by blocking a few people along the z-axis. A wide-angle lens is used to stretch the z-axis.

10.29 Crowd Scene Shot Along the X-axis

When seen from another angle (along the x-axis), these few people certainly don't simulate a crowd. This is one of the reasons why we use so many extras in crowd scenes for the horizontally stretched motion picture screen.

Good blocking for the small screen means staging an event along the z-axis for each camera; this is called ***multiple z-axis blocking***. For example, you can have the camera look down a hallway, such as a hospital corridor, and block the action from the back of the hallway toward the camera (z-axis 1). Have most of the people exit by walking past the camera. Now have the camera pan left and follow someone (perhaps the chief surgeon) walking down another articulated z-axis (z-axis 2). **SEE 10.30** You probably recognize this technique as being used in many serial dramas.

In a typical situation comedy setup with the inevitable couch, you can easily block the action along three articulated z-axes—one for each camera. If done properly, such blocking requires little or no camera movement. **SEE 10.31** Such blocking is desirable regardless of whether the production calls for a single camera or multiple cameras.

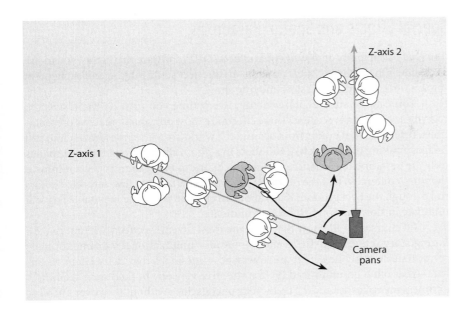

10.30 Double Z-axis
You can block action so that the camera can pan from one articulated z-axis to another in a single shot.

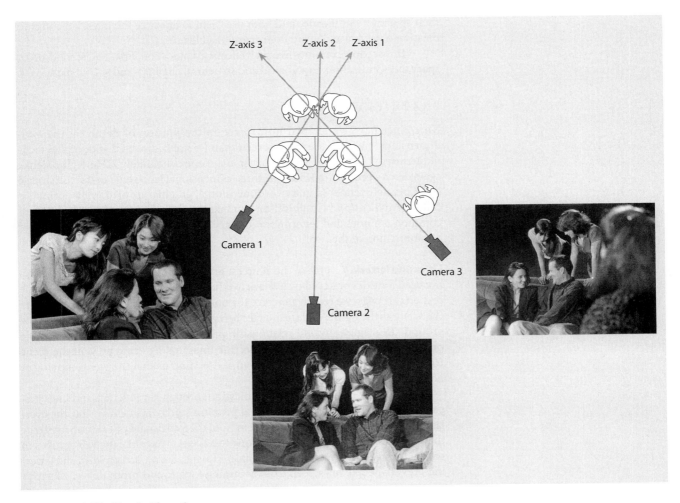

10.31 Z-axis Blocking for Three Cameras
In this setup each camera has its own properly articulated z-axis.

Special Effects and Spatial Paradoxes

The ready availability of **digital video effects (DVE)** software may tempt you to use such effects just to liven things up a bit—to interject some motion and excitement into an otherwise dull and slow-moving show.

You can see such digital wizardry every time you turn on the television, regardless of program content. These effects are most prominent in news presentations. Brief videos of events from around the world are sometimes frozen into still images, making them look like still shots in a photo album or a picture that hangs over the news anchor's shoulder. Sometimes various background effects reinforce the story content. When the news item is about war, tanks in low-saturated colors roll through the background; if it is about an election issue, the inevitable flag will undulate in slow motion behind the candidate.

Of course, we all know that even the most inventive effects will not make a boring story interesting. These effects may also unintentionally or intentionally communicate fairly powerful metamessages—messages that carry latent meanings—that often go unnoticed by less attentive viewers. In fact, such seemingly harmless messages are sucked up by your unconscious without your ever knowing and may well prime your reaction in a predictable way.[6] Knowing some of the aesthetic codes and subcodes that underlie such effects can enable you to identify their semantic significance and both use them to enhance the intended communication objective and avoid their irresponsible use.

This section examines five such effects: graphication, first- and second-order space, personification, topological and structural changes, and spatial paradoxes.

GRAPHICATION

No sooner have we learned how to create the illusion of depth on the two-dimensional plane of the video screen than we are confronted with digital techniques used to render a three-dimensional scene deliberately 2D and graphiclike again. Such a process, in which the three-dimensional lens-generated screen image is deliberately rendered in a two-dimensional, graphic- or picturelike format, is called **graphication**.[7] Graphication can take on many forms, of which the most common are lines and lettering, secondary frames within the video screen, and a combination of the two.

Lines and lettering   One of the simplest graphication devices is lines and lettering used for titles or keyed over the actual full-screen image. Like we perceive the text on this page, we readily perceive the on-screen lines and lettering keyed over the scene as the figure, and the images behind the letters (the actual scene) as the ground. This figure/ground relationship persists whether the ground is a static or a moving three-dimensional scene. The lines and lettering prevent the scene from pushing itself into the foreground and remind us that the scene, moving or not, is merely a picture. **SEE 10.32**

People are not immune to graphication through keyed letters and lines. Regardless of whether people on-screen appear in a studio or a field setting, the overlapping graphics inevitably remove them from the foreground position and relegate them to a lesser space farther back along the z-axis. Much like the velvet ropes in banks, theaters, and hotels that keep us in a queue, the on-screen lines and lettering prevent people on-screen from assuming foreground prominence. **SEE 10.33**

Secondary frames   One of the more popular ways of graphicating a scene is to put it into a secondary frame, such as windowboxing. The digitally generated

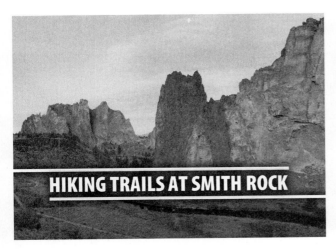

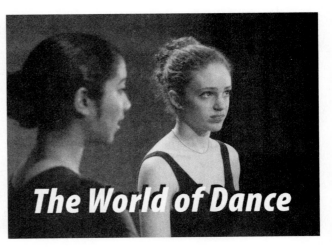

10.32 Graphication Through Lines and Lettering

Lines and lettering superimposed over a video scene become the figure, relegating the actual scene to a ground position. The scene has become picturelike, very much like a photo in a magazine. We call this process graphication.

10.33 Graphication of People

Lines and lettering can also have a graphication effect on people, regardless of whether they are moving.

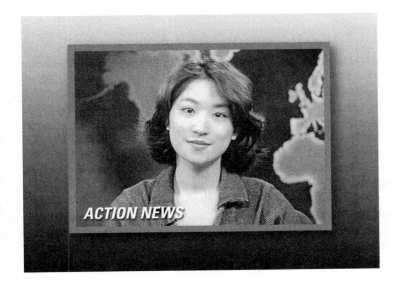

10.34 Graphication Through Secondary Frame

A common windowbox graphication device is the secondary frame within the primary video screen. It contains a scene in much the same way as a picture that hangs on the wall.

box clearly delineates an additional picture area within the borders of the actual primary space of the video screen. This technique renders the event displayed in the secondary frame as a picture similar to the pictures in newspapers and magazines. In fact, we often make the secondary frame look like a picture by giving it a border and setting it off from the background of the primary screen with drop shadows. **SEE 10.34**

FIRST- AND SECOND-ORDER SPACE

When a secondary frame is placed over the newscaster's shoulder, there are two types of screen space: the primary space as defined by the video screen's borders, and the space of the digitally created secondary frame. We call the total screen area *first-order space* and the secondary frame *second-order space*. The anchor

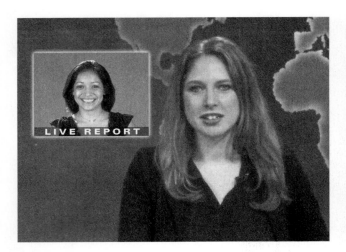

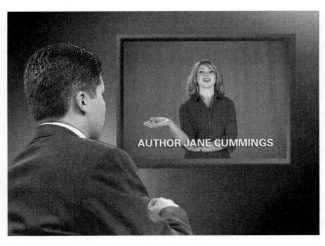

10.35 First- and Second-order Space

The newscaster occupies nongraphicated first-order space. The field reporter appears in a graphicated secondary frame, the so-called box. This box represents second-order space.

10.36 Aesthetic Personification Factor

Persons occupying nongraphicated first-order space experience a higher degree of personification from viewers than people appearing in graphicated second-order space. The host operates in first-order space; his guest appears in the graphicated second-order space.

occupies first-order space; the person or event in the box is in second-order space.[8] **SEE 10.35**

Because the second-order frame is such a strong graphication device, we tend to perceive its content as picturelike, regardless of whether the pictures are static iconic motifs or lens-generated events that move. In contrast to this abstracted space, first-order space seems to be more "real."[9] A strong possibility exists that, under certain circumstances, we may even extend first-order space into our own living space and share our environment. This extension is quite different from a stereoscopic projection because it is a pure psychological phenomenon. At the very least, events in first-order space seem to attain a certain degree of verisimilitude and believability. An example of an extension of first-order space into our living space is when a newscaster, operating in nongraphicated first-order space, first talks to us—the viewers—introducing the guest who is confined in a second-order box. When the anchor then turns toward the secondary frame for the actual interview, we may perceive, at least temporarily, the newscaster sharing our actual environment, interviewing the guest from our—the viewers'—position. **SEE 10.36**

PERSONIFICATION

Such close personal contact, however much imagined, fosters familiarity and trust.[10] Subconsciously, we attribute to the people operating in the extended space the flesh-and-blood qualities of real people—a certain degree of ***personification***.

This personification effect does not seem to take place in second-order space. The abstraction through graphication is so great that viewers inevitably consider the people appearing in second-order space as video images or pictures. Even when the second-order people are occasionally and temporarily "let out of the box" to occupy the full primary screen, we still consider them as occupying second-order space so long as the full-screen display is brief. To make sure that the people appearing in second-order space do not invade first-order space, additional graphication devices in the second-order space, such as name, place, and time superimpositions, are generally used.

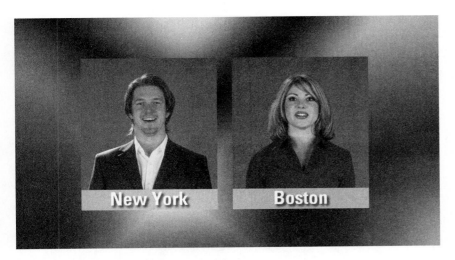

10.37 Host and Guest in Second-order Space

When both the anchor (screen-left) and the guest (screen-right) are confined to secondary frames, the personification factor for both parties is eliminated.

But don't we often see the anchor and the field reporter or guest appear in identical side-by-side boxes? Aren't they now both graphicated and operating in second-order space? The answer to both questions is yes. But, then, aren't we making a mistake by graphicating the anchor in this way? From a personification point of view, yes, we are. With both host and guest confined to second-order space, we inevitably perceive them to be picturelike and equally removed from us. For all practical purposes, the personification effect is lost. **SEE 10.37**

As you recall, this is also a questionable practice from an aesthetic point of view. Despite the context of a two-way conversation, the continuing z-axis index vectors are not necessarily perceived as converging; they may well be seen as continuing, being directed at us, the viewers.

From a production point of view, however, it is a convenient way to show two people talking to each other without the need for frequent cutting between the two close-ups. Such a side-by-side arrangement is especially convenient when the anchor is conversing with four or five guests simultaneously.

In any case, a better solution would be to have the host remain in first-order space, looking with the viewers, at the guest framed in second-order space (see figure 10.36). You can then switch to the secondary frame (or frames, if there are several guests) and have the host ask questions from an off-screen position. The z-axis index vectors of the guests are now directed toward the off-screen host and, at the same time, toward us, the viewers. We are then able to identify with the host, who is temporarily operating from an extended first-order space.

TOPOLOGICAL AND STRUCTURAL CHANGES

Digital video effects enable you to shrink the full-screen video and change its topology—its outer shape—at will. For example, you may see an especially tragic event briefly appear on-screen, freeze, peel off a large stack of snapshots, and flip unceremoniously through video space to make room for a new series of disasters. **SEE 10.38**

10.38 Flips

One of the many digital video effects is a topological change—a manipulation of the outer shape of the video image. In this case, the video image is made to look like a photo that flips through first-order space. Such special effects can carry negative metamessages.

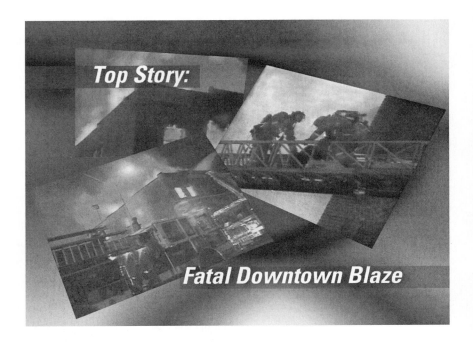

At first glance such effects are relatively harmless attention-getters. On closer examination, however, we discover that such visual acrobatics carry metamessages that, although not consciously perceived by most viewers, can readily change their attitude toward the event itself. The freezing and careless flips of disturbing scenes may convey an I-don't-really-care attitude toward the calamities displayed, making it all too easy for us to remain emotionally uninvolved. What we perceive, however subconsciously, is that we are no longer watching a slice of reality, a documentation of an actual occurrence, but merely some easily deposable pictures. Although we do indeed see only fleeting pictures when watching television, such topological changes to the regular video image become more anomalous the more we believe that the television-mediated event is the real thing. The combination of negative graphication and the often simultaneously displayed irrelevant information, such as sports scores and the weather, provide an easy escape from getting emotionally involved—or even from social responsibility to do something about the displayed human suffering.

The large palette of possible DVE also invites you to change the structure of the image. The mosaic effect as well as images with heightened contrast and color distortions are but two well-known examples. **SEE 10.39** They may be less weighty than the graphication flips, but they nevertheless transform what we normally perceive as a three-dimensional "real" video scene into picturelike abstractions. Most often they simply provide visual interest but can, if appropriate, also intensify the message. Before using any of these effects, however, think carefully about why you would choose a specific effect and what possible metamessages it may carry.

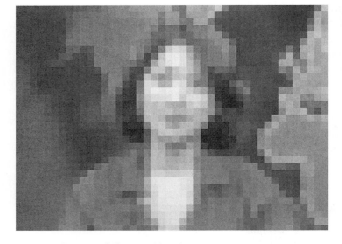

10.39 Structural Change: Mosaic

We can also graphicate an image through a structural change. One popular DVE technique of this sort is the mosaic effect, in which an image is made to break up and look as though it were composed of a series of mosaic tiles.

SPATIAL PARADOXES

Some special effects not only alter the topology or structure of a particular image but also combine pictures to create

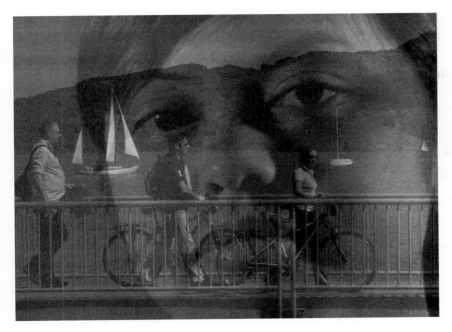

10.40 Spatial Paradox: Superimposition

The super works against our hardwired organization of a figure that lies in front of a background. Its overlapping transparent images confuse the figure/ground principle and suggest event complexity.

spatial paradoxes—arrangements that go against our perceptual habits. Some of these effects help structure and communicate complex messages; others violate our perceptual principles and work against effective communication.

Superimposition   As mentioned in chapter 7, a superimposition leads to an image in which the usual figure/ground relationship and the overlapping planes are largely dissolved into a complex array of intersecting images. By "supering" one image over another, the objects seem to become transparent, eliminating the illusion of depth and volume. The collapsed separate viewpoints or events into a single two-dimensional picture plane change the viewer's normal perceptual expectations and give not only a more complex view of things but particularly deeper insight into the event's underlying complexity. Because of this new structural bond, a *super* can suggest a strong relationship between seemingly unrelated events. Thus we often use the super to create a surrealistic or dreamlike feeling. **SEE 10.40**

Figure/ground paradox   Never mind what the newscaster is saying—all we care about right now is what the newscast looks like or, specifically, how the three-dimensional field is structured in this particular shot. When you see a close-up of the anchor in the foreground and the keyed-in graphicated box over his shoulder, you automatically presume that the anchor is in the foreground, the box behind his shoulder is in the middleground, and parts of the newsroom or news set are in the background. **SEE 10.41**

At first glance we seem to have a classic structuring of the three-dimensional field, with a prominent foreground (the anchor), a somewhat ambiguous middleground (the secondary frame seems to float somewhere between the anchor and the back wall), and a common background (the back wall of the news set). But perceptual problems occur when the anchor shifts his position or the box key is slightly off. In either case, the box may temporarily overlap the anchor's shoulder.

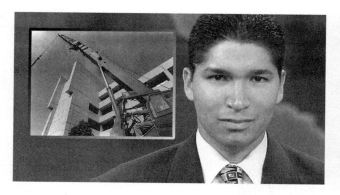

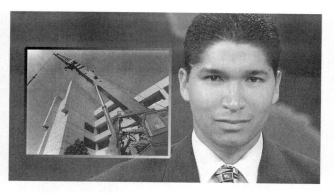

10.41 Figure/Ground Organization in Newscast

In this shot the three-dimensional field is clearly organized into a foreground plane (the anchor), a middleground plane (the graphicated box), and a background plane (the back wall of the news set).

10.42 Figure/Ground Paradox

We experience a structural paradox when the middleground plane suddenly overlaps the foreground plane.

SEE 10.42 According to our normal perceptual expectations, we would expect the box (middleground) to be overlapped by the anchor (foreground). But this basic spatial organization is paradoxically upset: the middleground overlaps the foreground. Will we now perceive the box as being the foreground? Not really. Despite the strong overlapping-planes cue, which clearly puts the box in front of the news anchor, our mental map holds on to the basic organization and tells us that the anchor is still in the foreground.

This problem persists even if the overlap is intentional. In the attempt to make the second-order box a foreground piece, some graphic designers attach it to one of the edges of the first-order primary screen. At times the anchor is overlapped by the box and thus relegated to the middleground of the video space. **SEE 10.43** Despite this deliberate figure/ground reversal, it is difficult for us to go against our hardwired organizational figure/ground principles. First, we still expect the larger image of the anchor to be the foreground figure and the smaller, graphicated second-order box to be somewhere behind the anchor. Second, such an arrangement also works against our psychological organization principle: because the anchor is definitely the primary information source, we expect her to occupy the foreground, and not the middle- or background. A similar problem arises when we reverse the image size between host and guest.

10.43 Intentional Overlap

Even if the second-order frame is purposely placed in the foreground plane, the occasional overlap still represents a spatial paradox.

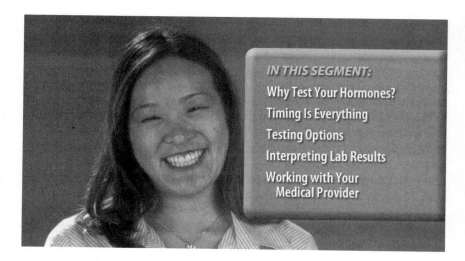

Relative-size paradox   Most likely you have seen interviews in which the studio host (usually one of the anchors) talks to a guest who appears from a remote location in an oversized second-order box on-screen. **SEE 10.44** Considering that we perceive objects as smaller the farther away from us they are, you can probably spot the structural problem right away. According to the relative-size principle, the image of the guest, who appears in the background, should be smaller than that of the host, who is located in the foreground of the first-order space of the news set. This relative-size paradox makes the guest appear oversized if not overpowering. But why would you perceive the guest as too big instead of the host as too small?

First, as relatively similar-sized objects (in this case, heads), the one in the background (the guest's) should look smaller than the one in the foreground (the host's), even if it contains a bigger brain. Second, you have probably appointed the host rather than the guest as the size standard. Now you need to recall the reality aspect of first-order space compared with the graphicated second-order space. Because the host operates in the more "real" first-order space, you will use the host as the size standard rather than the guest, who appears in the picturelike, graphicated second-order space. Compared with the host, who has become your size standard, the guest in the background looks too large. The sheer graphic mass of the guest's image inevitably overpowers the host even if he is functioning in first-order space. Subconsciously, you are inclined to shift the host's authority and credibility to the guest.

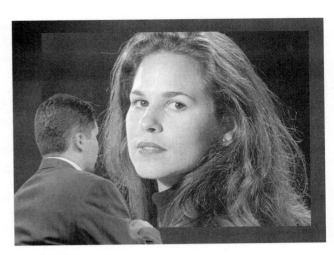

10.44 Relative-size Paradox

In this reversal of the relative-size principle, the background figure is larger than the foreground figure. We perceive the background figure as exceptionally large. This arrangement diminishes the personification of the anchor.

STEREOSCOPIC PROJECTIONS

Even when the z-axis extends in both directions from the screen, the stereoscopic projection does not alter the basic principles of screen volume and their effects. You still need an articulated z-axis to emphasize depth, regardless of whether you look at it with one eye (single-lens 3D volume) or with both eyes (two-lens 3D volume). The difference is, of course, that in stereoscopic projection the z-axis extends from the screen to the horizon as well as through the screen toward the viewer.

SUMMARY

We basically structure the three-dimensional field into various planes, or grounds, indicating z-axis placement or depth: a foreground, a middleground, and a background. To establish such depth planes, we must articulate the z-axis with positive space modulators—people or objects that are placed along the z-axis.

Structuring the three-dimensional field includes creating and controlling volume duality, articulating the z-axis, z-axis blocking, and dealing with spatial paradoxes.

As soon as we put things into an empty studio, we are modulating the negative volume of the studio with positive volumes. Positive volumes define space. We create a volume duality—the interplay of positive and negative volumes. When positive volumes prevail, the space looks and feels crowded. Large, well-articulated negative volumes suggest mobility. They can inspire awe because of their vastness but also suggest isolation and loneliness.

Various zoom lens positions (narrow- and wide-angle) create depth planes that the viewer perceives in specific ways. Generally, narrow-angle (long-focal-length) lenses squeeze space between objects; they shorten the z-axis and make objects look crowded. Wide-angle (short-focal-length) lenses exaggerate the relative size of objects close to the camera and those farther away, creating the impression of increased depth and a lengthened z-axis. Extreme wide-angle-lens distortions carry powerful psychological associations of intense feelings and actions.

Because of the limited width and height (x and y axes) of the standard video screen, action is best blocked along the depth dimension (z-axis). Such z-axis blocking increases the feeling of depth, is relatively easy for the camera to follow, and intensifies the drama and the aesthetic energy of the shots. It is also a powerful blocking device for large HDTV projections and motion picture screens.

Digital video effects (DVE) can create spatial paradoxes that, when used in a proper context, can convey specific meanings. Unintentional spatial paradoxes, however, such as those that violate figure/ground and relative-size principles, can disturb our mental map and upset our perception of the three-dimensional structure, thus reducing the impact of the message.

Special effects often carry powerful metamessages that need to be considered before the effects are used. Graphication is the deliberate rendering of television-mediated events, which appear three-dimensional on the video screen, as two-dimensional images that look like pictures in magazines or newspapers. The major graphication devices are lines and lettering and the creation of secondary frames within the primary screen, such as the box over the newscaster's shoulder.

Such secondary fames divide the screen into first-order space (the actual illusory three-dimensional screen space) and second-order space (the picturelike secondary frame). Personification means that we assign the person operating in nongraphicated first-order space more prominence and, to some extent, the flesh-and-blood qualities of real people compared with those appearing in the highly graphicated second-order space.

Topological changes are images whose shape is digitally manipulated. Structural changes affect the way images are built. Such manipulation may result intentionally or inadvertently in powerful metamessages and therefore must be used with great care.

NOTES

1. László Moholy-Nagy, *Vision in Motion* (Chicago: Paul Theobald, 1947, 1965). Moholy-Nagy discusses in detail the forms and the applications of volume duality, especially in sculpture. He distinguishes between actual positive volumes that have mass and are thinglike, and virtual positive volumes that are created by moving elements, such as a rotating flashlight. In a similar way, the screen images of a person or object can be considered a positive volume.

2. See Steven D. Katz, *Film Directing: Shot by Shot* (Studio City, Calif.: Michael Wiese Productions, 1991), pp. 239–40. Katz refers to the use of a dominating positive volume in the early scenes of Orson Welles's classic film *Citizen Kane:* "In most of these scenes the ceilings are low, and Welles, who actually was tall, seems to dominate his surroundings."

3. A plaza becomes a negative volume because it is bordered by surrounding buildings and/or landscaping. Big plazas were, and still are, a sign of wealth and power. The huge expanse of a plaza is often defined by a positive volume in the middle of it—a fountain, monument, column, or arch. If the positive volume is too big or obtrusive, however, such as the pyramid in the middle of the plaza of the Musée du Louvre in Paris, it defeats rather than accentuates the imposing nature of the plaza's large negative volume.

4. Katz continues to comment on the influence of negative volume: "By the end of the film, Kane, an old man, who has lost much of his influence, is still photographed from low angles, but now the huge spaces of the rooms and halls of Xanadu dominate him and he seems small by comparison." *Film Directing,* p. 240.

5. Sergei Eisenstein, *Film Form and The Film Sense,* ed. and trans. by Jay Leyda (New York: World, 1957), *Film Form,* p. 54.

6. Malcolm Gladwell cites persuasive evidence of how our unconscious can be influenced to prime us for specific behavior patterns and attitudes. See especially the section "Primed for Action" in his book *Blink* (New York: Little, Brown, 2005), pp. 52–61.

7. Herbert Zettl, "The Graphication and Personification of Television News," in *Television Studies: Textual Analysis,* ed. by Gary Burns and Robert J. Thompson (New York: Praeger, 1989), pp. 137–63.

8. Zettl, "Graphication and Personification," pp. 157–61. Compare alienation through graphication with the idea of Bertold Brecht's *Verfremdungseffekte* [alienation effects]. See Bertold Brecht, *Brecht on Theatre: The Development of an Aesthetic,* ed. and trans. by John Willett (New York: Hill and Wang, 1964), pp. 90–99, 101. See also Boris Uspensky, *A Poetics of Composition,* trans. by Valentina Zavarin and Susan Wittig (Berkeley: University of California Press, 1973). Uspensky advances the idea of *ostranenie*—a clear separation of the stage event and the perception of such an event by the audience. This concept was first introduced by Russian theater critic Victor Shklovskij, who called it *priem ostrannenija*—a device for making strange.

9. Belgian painter René Magritte (1898–1967) tried to make us aware of such a switch between first- and second-order space in his witty painting *Les deux mystères* (the two mysteries), in which he shows a large pipe, which Sherlock Holmes would have liked, floating in the upper part of the painting, and an easel with a framed painting of the same pipe on the right half of the primary painting. The small painting on the easel has this caption: *Çeci n'est pas une pipe* (this is not a pipe). Apparently, the mystery is why the larger pipe is more readily perceived as the real thing than the small pipe in the painting on the easel, which he has labeled as not a pipe. If Magritte had read *Sight Sound Motion,* the two mysteries would have been readily solved: the big pipe is like the news anchor operating in first-order space, being "personified" (made more real), and the painting of the pipe on the easel is like the second-order box over the newscaster's shoulder. The graphicated pipe is definitely not the real thing. The caption that the little pipe is only a picture is no longer necessary.

   See John Willats, *Art and Representation: New Principles in the Analysis of Pictures* (Princeton, N.J.: Princeton University Press, 1997), pp. 274–275.

10. Erik Bucy and John Newhagen, "The Micro- and Macrodrama of Politics on Television: Effects of Media Format on Candidate Evaluation," *Journal of Broadcasting and Electronic Communication* 43, no. 2 (1999): 193–210.

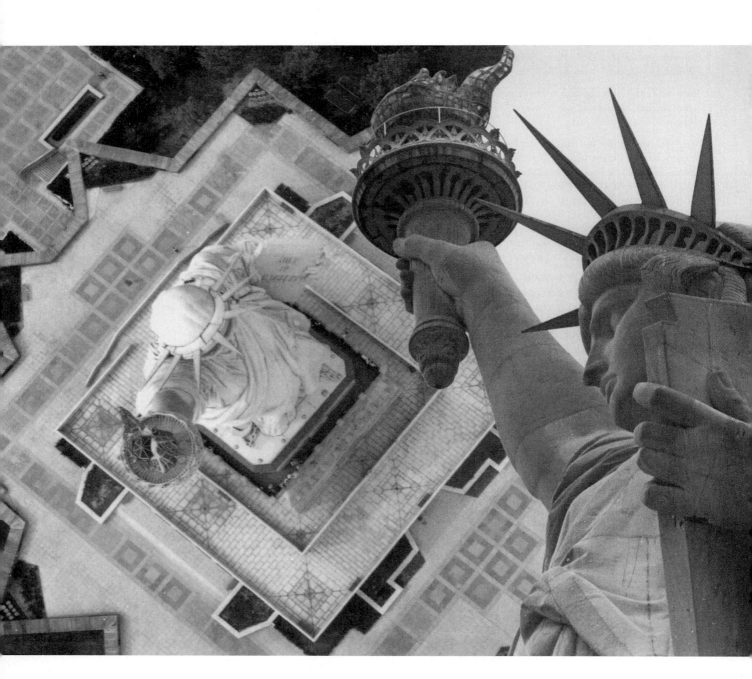

Building Screen Space: Visualization

VISUALIZATION MEANS THINKING IN PICTURES OR, MORE PRECISELY, IN individual shots or brief sequences. It also means thinking about the sounds that go with your video production or film. For example, take a moment and visualize your mother. How do you see her? What is she wearing? What is she doing? What familiar sounds surround her? If she were to appear on television, would you visualize her in the same way? What if she were to appear on a wide motion picture screen? Would you still visualize her in the same way?

Now visualize your favorite car. How do you see it? What color is it? In what environment is it? Is it moving or still? What sounds accompany your visualizations? How would you visualize it for a small video screen or a large motion picture screen? Now do just one more exercise and visualize—that is, see as screen and sound images—the following shot instructions:

Video	Audio
CU (close-up) of car	Tested on the hairpin turns of the Swiss Alps, this sleek beauty holds the road exceptionally well.
CU of car	Be careful, it may be booby-trapped!
CU of car	The minister of foreign affairs has finally arrived and is greeted by the vice president.

Exactly how did you visualize each event? You probably had some trouble actually seeing an image in all its detail, but most likely you had some notion of what the shots should contain and how you would like to see the events appear on-screen. Although the video instructions with each shot read "CU of car," you likely used a different car and a different environment for each shot. Why? Your choice was inevitably influenced by your personal experience, needs, and desires; by the context of the event; and especially by the medium—that is, whether you visualized it for the tiny mobile media display, the standard video screen, the small or large HDTV screen, or the huge screen in a movie theater. Additional factors in your visualization are your medium skill—whether you understand the technical and aesthetic limitations and potentials of the medium (in this case, video or film)—and your personal way of seeing things in general, your personal style.

Whatever prompts you to come up with specific pictures, the overriding guiding principle for any visualization should be to clarify, intensify, and interpret an event for the viewer.

Here is an example of how your visualization of the same object may shift when put into different contexts:

Video	Audio	Visualization
CU of can	Be sure to buy this can with the brand X label	

All you want to do here is show the can as clearly as possible so that the target audience will see what the can and the logo "X" look like and what color the can and the logo have. If the design is distinct enough and appropriate for the product, a little bell will go off in the viewers' memory when confronted by a wider choice of similar products in a supermarket. To this end the can is centered within the screen, and the vector field is stable. The can is close enough that the viewers can read the label even on a small screen. No attempt is made to dramatize the event.

Video	Audio	Visualization
CU of can	Get away from it— it may leak gas!	

In this instance the context demands that you visualize the can in such a way as to reveal its potential danger. To dramatize the shot, load it emotionally, and create immediate impact, you must create a purposely labile vector field: the horizon is tilted, and the mass of the can leans heavily toward the right side of the frame. The vector magnitude is increased by the downhill pull of the slanted horizon line. The can is highly distorted by the wide-angle lens. The distortion of the can and its labile arrangement within the frame reflect and intensify the precariousness of the event. Within its context the shot is properly visualized. Do advertisers really think of all such variables when deciding on product packaging or advertising: definitely yes, and then some.

This chapter explores the basic factors that will help you translate your visualizations into camera shots: deductive and inductive visual approaches, ways of looking, field of view, point of view, angles, and the storyboard.

Deductive and Inductive Visual Approaches

Your visualization depends not only on the context of each shot but also on the overall visual approach—on how you want to tell the story. Whether you use a deductive or inductive visual approach is extremely important when visualizing content that is to be shown on the large video and film screens or on the tiny mobile media display. In fact you may discover that the inductive approach is essential for producing effective video for the small mobile media display.

DEDUCTIVE APPROACH

The ***deductive visual approach*** means moving from the general to the specific (look back at figure 1.10). You can, for example, start with a wide establishing shot and then get progressively tighter through a zoom or a shot series to the final close-up detail. **SEE 11.1** Such deductive sequencing is still the classic narrative movie approach to telling a story. The establishing shot, called the master shot, sets up visually who is where in what situation and thus provides the context for the scene. It is similar to an exposition in good storytelling, during which the characters are introduced and the situation that eventually leads to conflict is presented. This conflict then propels the plot forward.[1] In deductive sequencing we move from long shot to medium shots and from there to close-ups. The close-ups not only provide a closer and more detailed view of the scene but also act as intensifiers.

As you can see, the deductive visual approach is ideally suited to a large, horizontally stretched HDTV or movie screen. On such large screens, a panoramic establishing shot shows vista as well as picture detail and usually carries much greater aesthetic energy than similar shots on a smaller video screen. More than a convenient device to construct a mental map (where you see and remember how things are situated in relation to others), the establishing shot can also grab your attention with powerful landscape images.

Even when shooting for the small standard video screen, however, you can use the deductive approach for setting the scene quickly and effectively. You have undoubtedly seen this well-worn deductive sequence: *Shot 1:* long shot, taxi cab drives up to a restaurant, man and woman get out. *Shot 2:* medium shot, waiter brings the menu to the two people seated at a nice table. *Shot 3:* alternate close-ups of the two people looking tenderly into each other's eyes. *Shot 4:* CU of wine bottle being shown to man and woman for approval.

Commercials use this approach frequently to set the scene more or less instantly: *Shot 1:* extreme long shot of a sports car racing around the tight curves of a wide-open country road. *Shot 2:* medium close-up of car going through a tight turn. *Shot 3:* CU of driver's happy face (at least until the first payment is due).

In general, such small-screen establishing shots can be informative, but they lack the aesthetic impact of the large-screen image. In most cases, the standard establishing shots also fail to provide the essential event context when shown on the small mobile media display. The well-worn but effective long shots of a crowded sports stadium or the playing field get totally lost on the tiny screen. Even if the screen image is high-definition, the shot details, such as the many people in the stands or the players on the field, are simply too small to be seen or to establish such a high-energy event. You may be able to use the audio to reflect, at least to some extent, the prevailing tension of audience and players, but not establishing shots.

Even on a large screen, the customary deductive approach may be perceived as too obvious and trite. The establishing shot reveals, as it should, a great deal of the scene, so the close-ups function more as explanations of what is going on rather than elements for building a scene. We are simply led closer to the event but have no part in discovering or building it. Wouldn't it be better to have the viewers *discover* the event through a series of close-ups rather than have it presented all at once in a single shot? The answer is, of course, yes, and you have undoubtedly seen such a visual sequence many, many times on television and in movies. But that is a case of inductive, rather than deductive, visualization.

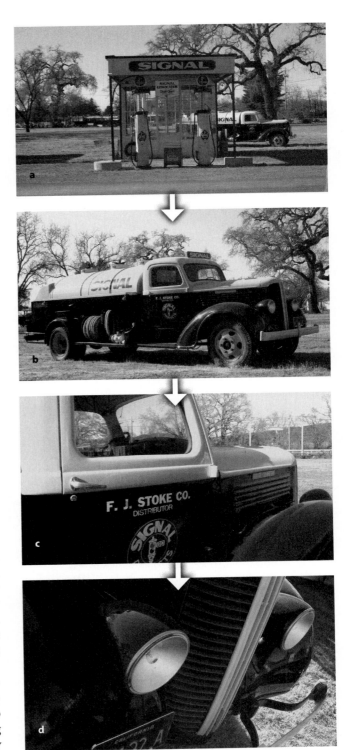

11.1 Deductive Shot Sequence

In the deductive visual approach, we start with a wide establishing shot (a) and move progressively tighter into the event detail (b–d). This approach is especially well suited to the large motion picture screen with its sweeping horizontal expanse.

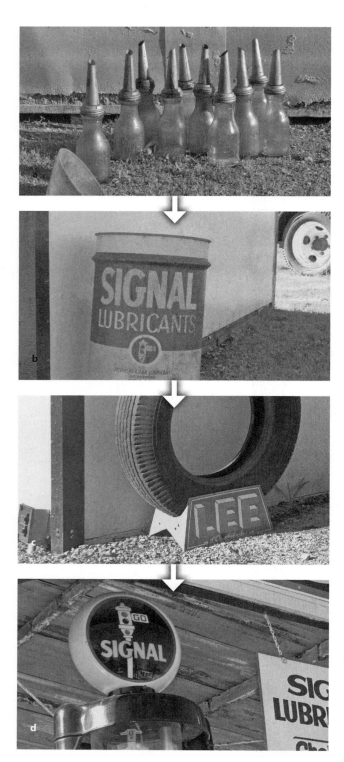

11.2 Inductive Shot Sequence

In the inductive visual approach, we select significant details that are characteristic of a whole event and present them as a series of close-ups. This visualization and sequencing approach is especially well suited to the small video screen.

INDUCTIVE APPROACH

The *inductive visual approach* means that you go from details of the event to a general overview (see figure 1.11). You do not begin a shot sequence with a wide establishing shot but rather with a close-up of a significant detail. Then you follow this close-up with a series of close-up details that best portrays the overall event. To aid the viewer in seeing the close-ups in relation to one another and to provide or reinforce a specific context, you may want to end such an inductive shot sequence with an occasional wider orientation shot. But if you have carefully selected the various close-ups so that they express the essence of the event, you may well be able to dispense with overview shots. If done correctly, the viewer can then structure the close-up series into a sensible event gestalt.[2] **SEE 11.2**

Although not the exclusive province of video, an inductive approach is ideally suited to the relatively small video screen. On the small screen, the close-up has more aesthetic energy than a long shot; it delivers a higher-impact punch irrespective of content. More so, close-ups and medium shots are the only ones that show up reasonably well on the tiny mobile media display. In long shots all small detail gets lost. Even if the close-ups on the mobile media display will never be able to match the high-energy punch of large-screen close-ups, they nevertheless enable you to see what is going on.

Because inductive sequencing provides the viewer with a detailed close-up view of many event details, it remains somewhat impressionistic; but therein lies the very strength of the inductive approach. You as the viewer are now called upon to participate mentally and help build a coherent event sequence, much in the way you would try to make the pieces of a jigsaw puzzle fit together. At the same time, you are coerced to call up your previous experience to make sense out of the whole thing—to construct a meaningful narrative. Thus, the impact of the inductive approach comes not only from a bombardment of high-energy shots but also by participating—however subconsciously and automatically—in the construction of the screen event and its meaning.[3]

One of the liabilities of inductive sequencing is that the close-up sequence may not lead to the desired closure but rather to a fragmented narrative. Such a fragmentation is likely to occur during a live telecast or content streaming of sports. If, for example, you are on a close-up of a particular soccer player or quarterback passing the ball, you may not be able to cut fast enough to a close-up of the player receiving the pass. Even if you can get to the pass receiver on time, you will miss out on seeing the pattern formation of the other players. As you can imagine, ice hockey presents an especially difficult problem because of the speed of the players, the high rate of pattern change, and the difficulty of seeing the puck on the screen. One way to deal with such problems is to have a second unit cover the game entirely with the inductive approach, with a radiolike narration to compensate for the visual discontinuity. In the standard football pickup, the second unit might be able to use the iso (isolated) video feed, which is normally reserved for instant playbacks. As you can see, the mobile media display requires a rethinking and a restructuring of the traditional approaches to sports pickups.

For now let's apply the deductive and inductive principles to video-record a brief automobile race sequence intended for postproduction, first for a wide-screen motion picture and then for the standard-sized video screen. When shooting deductively for film (including large-screen video), you may decide to start with the almost inevitable overhead establishing shot of the racecourse from a helicopter or blimp. Next you might want to show as much of the excited crowd as possible, temporarily obscured by the racecars that roar past them from one edge of the screen to the other. Then you finally move in on a two-shot of the lead car and the one in hot pursuit.

When shooting inductively for normal-sized television screens, this scene might look quite different, especially if you want to reflect the high energy of the event. For example, you could start with a close-up of the lead car's rearview mirror that reveals the desperate passing attempts of the pursuing car. Then you could show extreme close-ups of the lead driver's face, a similar shot of the second car's driver, and then the leading driver's hands on the steering wheel. Next you could do quick close-ups of one or two members of the pit crew, officials, or spectators. Of course, the shot selection—and especially the shot sequence—depends entirely on the communication context, on what you consider to be the essence of the race. In any case, a good sound track with the roaring engines and the cheering crowd will help provide the viewer with the necessary landscape element of the race and aid in combining these individual shots into a high-energy whole.

When you watch car commercials, you will find that almost all of them use the inductive visual approach. You see tight close-ups of the interior or the tail lights, a slow pan along the sleek shape of the fender, and, if at all, the car finally racing through the city or along a country road. Of course, many other types of commercials use this impressionistic approach to let you not only see the product but also feel it at the same time.

Motion pictures have long held on to the classic deductive approach of moving from establishing shot to close-up. But you may have noticed that especially creative movie directors have used the inductive approach, at least for a few scenes or scene openings, for quite some time. Today many directors of large-screen motion pictures favor the inductive visualization approach. They realized that the inductive series of close-ups increased not only the already high energy of the screen images but the emotional participation by the audience as well.

As you will learn in chapters 15 and 16, the sound track becomes an essential element for facilitating closure in inductive sequencing. In fact, I believe that the inductive approach to sequencing in motion pictures was greatly facilitated by the introduction of high-energy surround sound.

Ways of Looking

Another important visualization consideration is deciding as early as possible just how you intend to look at an event—a basic approach to viewing it. You can, for example, merely look *at* an event and report it as faithfully as possible; or you can look *into* an event and try to communicate its complexity and psychological implications. You can also choose to use the technical potential of the medium to create special effects or images that are entirely computer-generated. Examples of creating such unique screen events are the digital video effects (DVE) discussed in previous chapters. Thus you have three basic ways of looking and using the medium for optimal communication: looking *at* an event, looking *into* an event, and *creating* an event. Each of these basic ways of looking can serve as a game plan for your general visualization, your production approach, and, inadvertently, the overall style of your production.

In practice, however, these three basic ways of looking usually—and should—overlap. Even in the live pickup of a football game, where most of the coverage is done within the framework of looking *at*, the extreme close-ups that show the players' tension give you an opportunity to look *into* the event and empathize with the athletes.

LOOKING AT AN EVENT

When you merely want to report an event, use a visualization approach that comes as close as possible to the point of view of an observer of the actual event—someone who watches it more or less objectively from a particular point of view. This we call *looking at* an event. In this visualization framework, you use the camera and the microphones primarily to report what is going on. Most news coverage is looking *at*, as are most shots during a live or live-recording of a sporting event. Looking *at* is done mainly for event clarification. **SEE 11.3**

LOOKING INTO AN EVENT

Looking into an event means to scrutinize it as closely as possible, to look behind its obvious outer appearance, to probe its structure and, if possible, its very essence. Looking *into* means communicating to the viewer aspects of an event that are usually overlooked by a casual observer and providing an insight into the nature and the emotions of the event. If you were to objectively report—look at—two people in a lively conversation, a simple two-shot with an audio track of their dialogue would suffice. But if looking *into* the event, you would use the camera to reveal the psychological implications and the emotional tensions of the conversation; the sound track of the dialogue may well be supported by music or even some sound effects. Looking *into* not only shows what is happening but why. Its main purpose is event intensification. **SEE 11.4**

CREATING AN EVENT

Creating an event means you use the technical devices and the potentials of the medium to build a unique screen event that depends entirely on the medium. You can use a lens-generated event (as seen by the camera) as the basic energy source and manipulate it through DVE, or you can create an event entirely through digital processes. Creating an event does not mean manufacturing it to mislead the public, such as inventing and reporting a big story on a slow news day. Rather it refers to building a screen event synthetically through various electronic and/or optical special effects for event clarification, intensification, and interpretation. **SEE 11.5**

Let's use a simple action, such as placing a telephone call, and visualize the event according to these three principal ways of looking.

Event 1: Looking at　　All you need to do is communicate as simply and accurately as possible the action of placing a phone call. The woman reaches for the phone, picks up the receiver, inputs the number, waits for the other party to respond, and starts the conversation. You could easily cover this sequence with a single camera on a medium shot with a possible zoom-in when she makes the connection to the other party. **SEE 11.6**

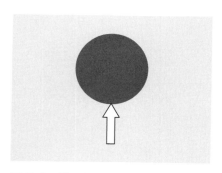

11.3　Looking At

When using the medium for looking *at* the event, we try to assume as neutral and objective a point of view as possible.

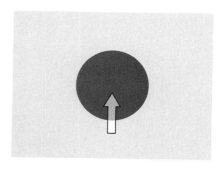

11.4　Looking Into

When using the medium to look *into* the event, we provide a deeper insight into what is going on.

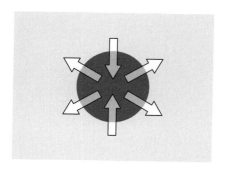

11.5　Creating

In this case, the medium is essential for creating a screen event. The event exists only as a screen image.

Event 2: Looking into   Now the event calls for intensification. You want to communicate the urgency of the call, the emotional state of the caller, and the overall tense atmosphere. The easiest way to fulfill these communication objectives is to use tighter shots. But this means deciding which parts of the event to show. Do you need to show the woman reaching for the phone? Probably not. You can start with a close-up view of her hand inputting the phone number. Under stress, the woman will probably call the wrong number and have to do it all over again. You may not even want to show the second attempt but instead switch to, and stay on, a close-up of her face. By partially blocking her face with the phone, you can suggest the negative nature of the call. As you can see, your choice of shots becomes very important with this approach.   **SEE 11.7**

Event 3: Creating   To show the relative complexity and/or urgency of this event, you may use any one of the many available DVE such as jogging, whereby the motion shows a frame-by-frame advance, or such digital manipulation as solarization or mosaic effects.[4] Such manipulation through digital devices reveals the underlying complexity of the event and greatly intensifies it. The following figure shows how the DVE of jogging (represented here by multiple images) and solarization are media-created images that amplify and interpret the woman's emotional state.   **SEE 11.8**

Note that the series of manipulated images in figure 11.8 exists only as a screen event. Under normal circumstances we do not perceive the world as moving frame-by-frame or in reversed polarity. The event is now created by the medium, using the lens-generated or actual event—the phone call—as raw material.

11.6 Telephone Call: Looking At

Here the woman is simply placing a routine call. We look at it as objectively as possible.

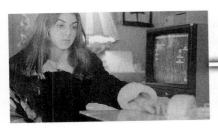

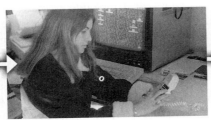

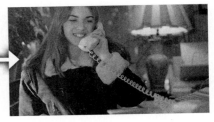

Viewers see her walking up to the phone and sitting down.

She picks up the receiver and inputs a number.

She engages in a simple conversation. The shots for this sequence are not dramatic. They simply show us what is going on.

11.7 Telephone Call: Looking Into

Now the woman is under stress. You need to let the viewer experience the event's intensity and complexity.

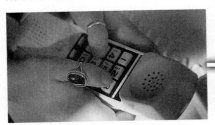

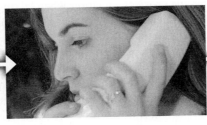

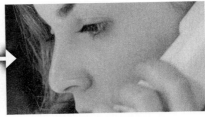

The close-up of the keypad action intensifies the importance of the call.

By partially blocking the woman's face with the phone, you can emphasize the negative aspects of the call.

An even tighter close-up will further intensify the event.

11.8　Telephone Call: Creating

The intensification in this shot series is achieved through selective view, close-ups, and electronic manipulation of the lens-generated image.

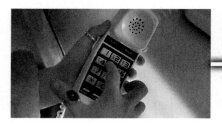

We start out with a normal close-up of the woman's hand making the call.

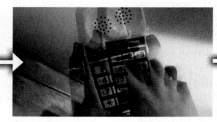

Jogging shows a quick series of still frames in a shot (shown here simultaneously). It reveals the woman's extreme nervousness.

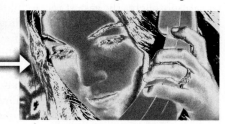

The intensity of the conversation is further enhanced by solarization.

Field of View

Field of view refers to how far away or close we show on-screen an object or a person or how much territory a shot includes. There are five traditional designations of fields of view: *extreme* long shot (ELS), long shot (LS), medium shot (MS), close-up (CU), and extreme close-up (ECU or XCU). **SEE 11.9–11.13**

How much territory should a long shot encompass? What is a medium shot? Exactly how close is a close-up? How big should the steps—the changes in image size—be between an extreme long shot and a close-up? There are no reliable formulas for these shot designations. They are relative and depend, like other viewpoint factors, largely on the context and the interpretation of an event. You will be greatly aided in deciding on the basic field of view by determining as early as possible your principal way of looking—that is, whether you intend to basically look at, look into, or create the event.

Even if you have decided on the primary approach, you can move freely among the three. But an early determination of the principal way of looking will help you establish a basic visual approach. Take another look at figures 11.6 and 11.7; you will notice that in the looking-at approach each individual shot and the progressive steps are considerably looser (wider) than in the more intimate and intense looking-into approach. As you recall, shots are generally wider when looking at an event and quite a bit tighter when looking into one.

Long shots and close-ups differ not only in how big objects appear on-screen (graphic mass relative to the screen borders) but also in how close they seem to us, the viewers. Close-ups seem physically and psychologically closer to us than long shots. Because we seem to perceive variations in field of view as variations of physical and psychological distance, we seem to react to them in the same way we do to the actual distances of people and things in everyday life. In some societies people stand much closer when talking to one another than in other cultures, a phenomenon called proxemics.[5] Similarly, what constitutes a close-up is not uniform throughout the world. For example, the close-ups of newscasters and even actors in dramatic productions are much wider in some parts of the world than in the United States. This pseudo-interpersonal relationship between somebody on television talking to us, named paraproxemics or video proxemics,[6] has become especially important now when we can watch the person addressing the viewer on the large home-theater screen or the tiny mobile media display.

Regardless of the cultural differences of people and their actual proxemics, however, close-ups are perceived to be more intimate, physically closer to the viewer, and of higher aesthetic energy than long shots. News producers in some countries show their anchors in medium shots rather than tight close-ups because

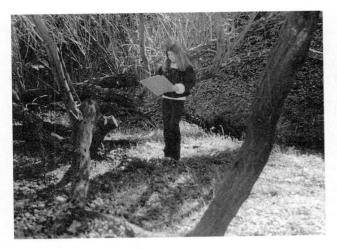

11.9 Extreme Long Shot (ELS)

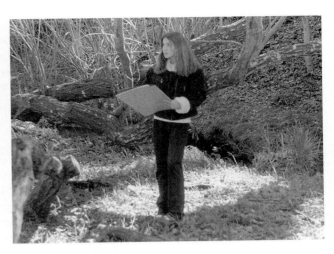

11.10 Long Shot (LS)

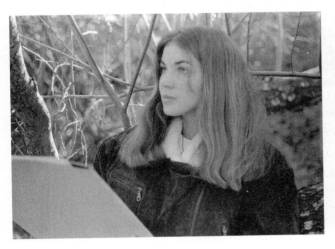

11.11 Medium Shot (MS)

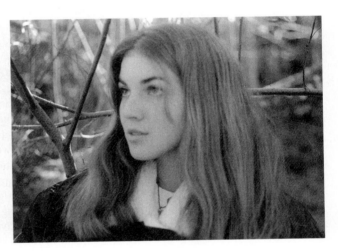

11.12 Close-up (CU)

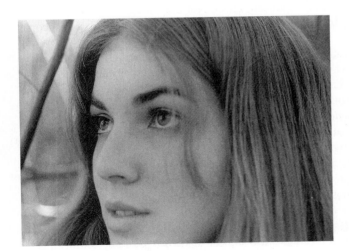

11.13 Extreme Close-up (ECU or XCU)

they want to make the news presentation more objective and less personal. Others feel that the extreme close-up is intruding on the viewer's private space and should therefore be used sparingly.[7] As you can see, your visualization must take into consideration not only the media aesthetic impact of a shot but the paraproxemic impact as well.

Point of View

The term *point of view* has several different meanings, depending on who uses it and the context in which it is used. Basically, **point of view (POV)** refers to the camera's simulating the index vector of a particular person or persons on-screen. But it can also mean what we called ways of looking, or a specific character's perspective. In the famous Japanese film *Rashomon*, the same event is told from four people's differing perspectives—points of view. Visualization can be guided by an internal, psychological rather than an external point of view. And, for good measure, you may detect an author's or a director's point of view—the way the director has the camera look at or into an event. Most often all these point-of-view types, and then some, are intermixed in a single dramatic episode.[8]

Technically, there is a distinction between camera viewpoint and point of view. **Viewpoint** simply refers to what the camera is looking at and from where. Point of view, on the other hand, means that the camera takes on a bias of looking: it no longer describes (looks at) but comments on the event (looks into and interprets). Point of view refers to the camera's narrative involvement. Most often, however, the terms *viewpoint* and *point of view* are used interchangeably, sometimes referring to camera viewpoint (what the lens sees) and sometimes to the camera's narrative involvement. Such a multidefinition of *point of view* is so ingrained that it would prove futile and counterproductive to insist on holding on to these definitions absolutely. Nevertheless, I will observe the distinctions to help explain how point of view operates.

Our discussion of point of view focuses on three major areas—POV: looking up and looking down; POV: objective viewpoint to subjective point of view; and POV: subjective camera.

POV: LOOKING UP AND LOOKING DOWN

For some time kings, preachers, judges, schoolteachers, and gods have known that sitting up high had a significant effect. Not only could they see better and be seen more easily but they could also look down on people—and make people look up to them.

Physical elevation has strong psychological implications. It immediately distinguishes between inferior and superior, between leader and follower, and between those who have power and authority and those who don't. Phrases like *the order came from above, moving up in the world, looking up to and down on* (rather than *looking up and down at*), and being *on top of the world*—all are manifestations of the strong association we make between physical positioning along a vertical hierarchy and feelings of superiority and inferiority.

The camera's viewpoint can evoke similar feelings in an audience. When we look up with the camera (sometimes called a low-angle or a below-eye-level point of view), the subject or object seems more important, more powerful, more authoritative than when we look at it straight-on (normal-angle or eye-level point of view) or look down on it (high-angle or above-eye-level point of view). When we look down with the camera, the subject or object generally diminishes in

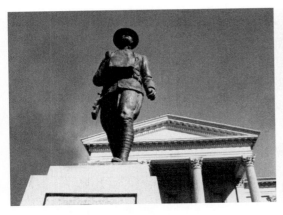

11.14 Prestige Through Looking Up
Statues of influential people and heroes are often put up high so that we have to look up at—or rather up *to*—them.

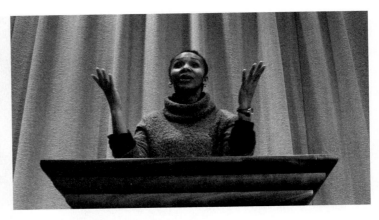

11.15 Power Through Looking Up
Speakers position themselves high enough so that they can see their audience and, more importantly, make the audience look up to them. Such a superior position seems to confirm their authority and power.

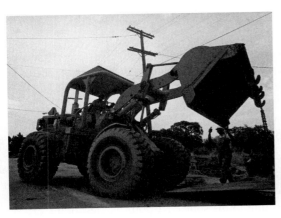

11.16 Intensifying Power of Machinery
Even machines tend to gain in strength when shot from below.

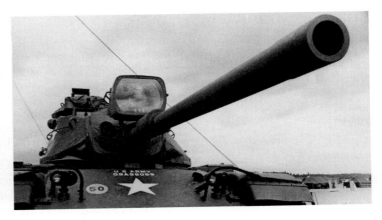

11.17 Intensifying Destructive Power
Machines that are designed primarily for destruction become more menacing and powerful when shot from below.

significance; it becomes less powerful and less important than when we look at it straight-on or from below. As viewers we readily assume the camera's viewpoint and identify with its superior high-angle position (looking down on the object or subject) and its inferior low-angle position (looking up at the subject or object).[9]

Statues of famous people are either huge, such as those of the kings in ancient Egypt, or are put on pedestals to force people to look up at them or, more appropriately, up *to* them, which makes viewers assume an inferior position relative to the statue. **SEE 11.14**

When speakers address large crowds, they usually stand on platforms with the audience looking up to them. If you want to duplicate this effect and intensify the authority and the power of the speaker, have the camera look up at the speaker from a below-eye-level position. **SEE 11.15**

You can emphasize the power of heavy machinery or the menace of machines designed primarily for destruction by looking at them from below. Again, as normal mortals we are put in an inferior position. **SEE 11.16 AND 11.17**

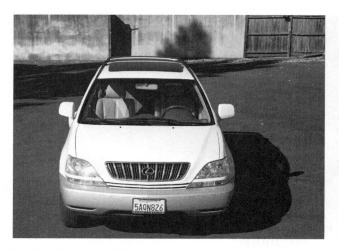

11.18   Point of View from Above
When shot from above, a car seems less dynamic or powerful than when shot from below. A moving car seems to travel at a more leisurely speed when shot from above.

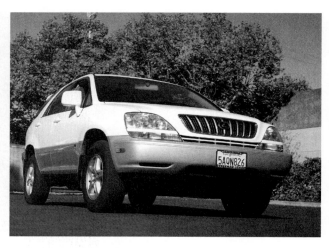

11.19   Point of View from Below
A below-eye-level view of a car makes it look dynamic and powerful. A car seems to move at a higher speed when shot from below than when shot from above.

Even our perception of movement varies with whether we observe the motion from a low- or a high-angle position. When shot from above, a car seems to move more leisurely than when shot from below. **SEE 11.18 AND 11.19**

POV: OBJECTIVE VIEWPOINT TO SUBJECTIVE POINT OF VIEW

The most common way of using point of view is to have the camera first focus on a person looking in a particular direction and then follow with a shot of what the person sees. **SEE 11.20 AND 11.21** As you can see in the shot sequence, we move from a general objective viewpoint to the subjective point of view of the driver. With this follow-up driver's point of view (figure 11.21), you can suggest what the driver of the car is thinking. If you were to emphasize the driver's amusement or shock about the logo of the firm or its telephone number, you could take a closer shot of the back of the truck. If you want to communicate the driver's concern about the speed of the truck that just passed him, you could cut to a close-up of

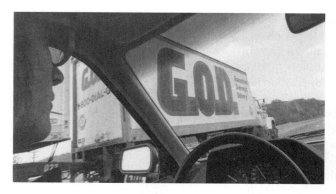

11.20   Establishing Driver's Index Vector
This shot establishes the driver's index vector. We see the driver looking through the windshield of his car. The shot is objective.

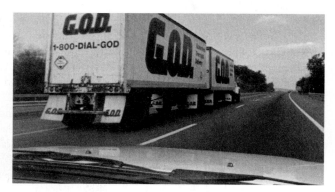

11.21   Switching to Driver's Point of View
This shot shows what the driver sees. We are now looking through the driver's eyes. The shot is now subjective.

the wheels or the swaying trailer. You are obviously no longer looking *at* the situation but *into* it. By switching from an objective viewpoint (seeing the driver look at something) to the driver's subjective point of view, you are now commenting on the event, not just reporting it.

Over-the-shoulder shooting　In *over-the-shoulder (O/S) shooting*, the camera literally looks over the shoulder of the camera-near person at the camera-far person and vice versa.　**SEE 11.22 AND 11.23**　Note that in the reverse-angle shot, the dialogue partners remain in their respective screen-right and screen-left positions.

Cross shooting　In *cross shooting* the camera has moved past the shoulder of the camera-near person to get a tighter close-up of the camera-far person. In each shot the camera-near person has temporarily moved into off-screen space.
SEE 11.24 AND 11.25

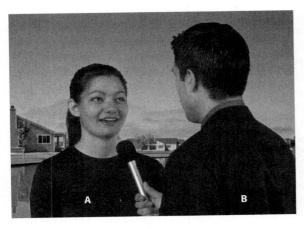

11.22　Over-the-shoulder Shot

This is one of the most common reverse-angle shots when covering a conversation. In this z-axis shot sequence, we alternately see the woman's face (A), with the man's head and shoulder in the foreground (B). In this shot we are looking at the woman (A) over the shoulder of the man (B).

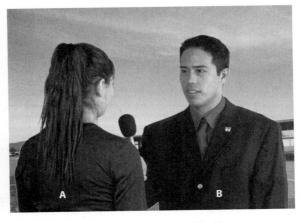

11.23　Reverse-angle Over-the-shoulder Shot

Now we see the man (B) over the shoulder of the woman (A). Note that both people remain in the same screen position despite the reverse angle.

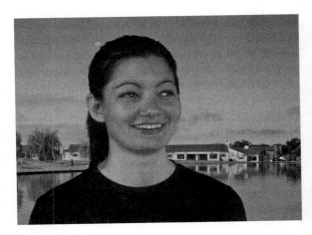

11.24　Cross-shot

In cross shooting we simply move in tighter on the person facing the camera. The man is now out of the shot, and we see only a close-up of the woman looking in his direction.

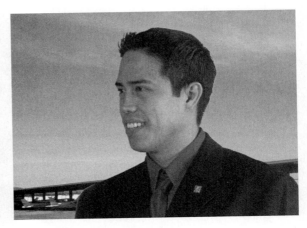

11.25　Reverse-angle Cross-shot

Now we have reversed camera angles to show a close-up of the man looking in the woman's direction.

In both of these reverse-angle shooting techniques, the viewer has no trouble accepting the shifting points of view so long as you keep the dialogue partners in their assigned screen positions and, in cross shooting, give each enough noseroom to facilitate the index vector penetration through the screen edge into off-screen space. We revisit the subject of screen positions in chapter 17 to explain their importance in continuity editing.

Over-the-shoulder and cross shooting are especially advantageous for the small video screen and essential for the mobile media display. In contrast to the large 16 × 9 HDTV screens, the old standard 4 × 3 and small 16 × 9 HDTV video screens are simply not wide enough, and the small mobile media display is not big enough, to block two people laterally along the x-axis. Positioning the two people more or less along the z-axis for over-the-shoulder and cross-shots solves the problem for all aspect ratios and screen sizes.

POV: SUBJECTIVE CAMERA

The ease with which we can have the viewer assume, however temporarily, the screen person's point of view has prompted video and film directors to use the camera in more conspicuously subjective ways. This is known as **subjective camera**—when the camera participates in, rather than merely observes, an event. Most frequently, the camera assumes the role of a screen character, substituting for the performer's eyes and actions. For example, you could show a child running through the woods and then have the camera show what he sees: trees going by and bushes passing left and right and occasionally brushing his face (the camera lens). As viewers we now share the child's (camera's) view of trees and bushes moving past. The idea is to have us participate in the action, even if it is merely illusory. **SEE 11.26 AND 11.27**

A camera can become inadvertently subjective if, for example, the news videographer who is covering an especially dangerous event keeps the camera running while dashing out of harm's way. The precarious context can make such unintentional footage highly dramatic and captivating for the viewer, even if the picture sequence is bouncing up and down and mostly out of focus. You should realize that it is the situation that makes such footage compelling, not the shaky and out-of-focus camera. In a staged event, such a tour-de-force sequence is effective only if properly motivated. Let's look at this point more closely.

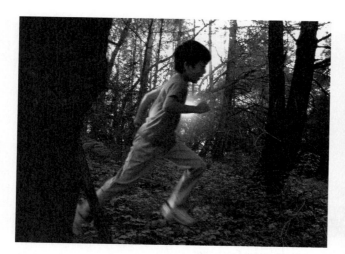

11.26 Camera Viewpoint: Child Running Through Woods

In this shot we see a child running through the woods. The camera provides an objective viewpoint.

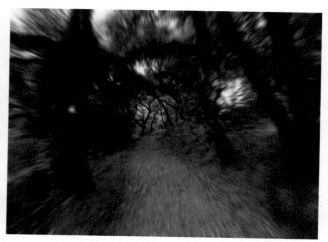

11.27 Child's Point of View: Subjective Camera

In this follow-up shot, the camera becomes subjective. We now look through the boy's eyes and see the trees and bushes go by.

Assuming the character's point of view   Because as viewers we can readily adjust to, and even identify with, the camera's point of view, we should easily be enticed to participate in the screen event through subjective-camera techniques. After all, we do get up and yell during a football game, even if we watch it not from the stands but only on television in the living room. But we still remain very much spectators and not participants.

Unfortunately, the transformation of the viewer from event spectator to event participant rarely occurs, especially if the camera is used to represent the point of view of one of the screen characters. If we see the trees go by and the bushes part, we still have a hard time assuming the role of the child running through the woods. The problem is that, especially when watching a movie, we remain in our seats, observing the screen event from a safe and comfortable position. We do not feel catapulted out of our chairs and onto the screen to mingle with the other characters.[10] Even in virtual-reality screen displays, which shift with our changing viewpoint, we are usually aware that we are not physically moving. The desired dislocation, in which we forsake our own perspective and position for that of the camera, is difficult to achieve and may happen more readily in stereoscopic 3D displays, where the z-axis extends through the screen toward the viewer.

Nevertheless, instances do occur where the subjective camera can persuade us at least to associate closely with the camera's point of view and occasionally with its action. Such involvement depends on the motivation to participate in, rather than merely observe, the event. The three most effective motivational factors seem to be: a strong delineation between protagonist and antagonist so that the viewer can easily choose sides (rooting for your favorite team) or else switch back and forth comfortably between the two; a highly precarious situation including physical danger, discomfort, or psychological stress; and a situation in which the viewer's curiosity is greatly aroused. These are all preconditions for you to participate in an event empathically (feeling part of the event) and occasionally even kinesthetically (reacting physically to the screen event, such as shouting approval, clapping, moving one's arms when watching a boxing match, or having one's leg muscles twitch during a soccer game).

Here is an example of viewers' assuming the role of one of the characters in the screen event: The scene is from a boxer's story. The protagonist, a very likable fellow, is badly beaten by the antagonist, who is a despicable tough guy. When watching such a contest, we will obviously side with the good guy. It is likely that we will become so much identified with the good guy's fate that we may, on occasion, switch from psychological support (hoping he will win after all) to kinesthetic action (rooting for him and even helping him box). Once we reach this perceptual stage, a subjective-camera treatment is more likely to succeed. We will now accept more readily the shift from the objective two-shot of the fighters to the single shot showing the protagonist's point of view, perceiving it as a logical and organic intensification of the event rather than an artificial camera trick. A series of quick cuts, showing the grimacing face looking at us (the lens), the distorted view of the huge boxing glove shooting toward us with lightning speed, and the tilting overhead lights and spectator rows slowly going out of focus. All this is of course accompanied by the crowd noise that goes from exaggerated echo to sudden silence.

Even if we are still perfectly comfortable in our seats, we should now at least feel deeply involved in the protagonist's fate. The next objective-camera shots show our protagonist unconscious on the mat and finally being transported to the hospital. How badly is he hurt? Will he be all right?

Now we should be properly motivated to feel enough empathy for him to accept another subjective-camera scene. We see a gray screen but hear the distorted sounds of the doctors talking. The sounds become clearer as the camera racks slowly into focus, looking up at the happy faces of the medical team. Yes, he has regained consciousness. And, yes, he has a remarkably speedy recovery, as evidenced by the objective-camera shot series that shows him even smiling.

Because of our strong empathic involvement with the protagonist, the subjective camera simply underscores, but does not superimpose, the viewers' event participation.

Popular (yet rarely successful) subjective-camera techniques include mounting a camera behind the driver of a racecar or behind a stunt pilot. The assumption is that this type of subjective camera will make us experience what banking into a high-speed turn with a racecar or performing a series of quick rolls in a stunt plane feels like. Unless we are highly motivated, however, a position switch does not occur. Instead of participating in such screen events, we are more likely to watch dispassionately a racetrack relentlessly rushing toward the screen, with the wall and spectator section slightly tilting, or seeing the back of the pilot silhouetted against the horizon spinning in a clockwise and counterclockwise fashion like a clock gone mad.

So long as the camera is mounted firmly inside the car or cockpit, the camera tilts exactly with the car and the airplane, keeping the car or the airplane upright and steady in the picture frame. Also, our first frame of reference—the visible parts of the racecar and the driver, or the back of the pilot, do not move relative to the screen edges. What is doing the tilting is the environment outside the car and the plane—in this case the racetrack and the horizon. Because we see both the driver and the pilot sitting straight up, firmly glued to their seats, we have a hard time transferring the tilting ground or rotating horizon to the stable figure, let alone feeling like we are driving the racecar or flying the stunt plane.

Being discovered   If, however, the screen action is aimed directly at us in our viewing position, we feel "discovered" and thus inevitably linked with the screen event. Because this subjective-camera technique does not require us to assume a screen position but rather allows us to remain in our seats, we may be more inclined to accept this use of the subjective camera as a direct link between us as the viewers and the screen action.[11] Let's say we see a sniper shooting at anything that moves. The police are inching carefully toward his stronghold. Suddenly, he turns the gun on us (into the camera). This action does not require us to assume the position and the point of view of the police officers; rather, we have become the direct target of the sniper and hence participants in the event.

Direct-address method   The direct-address method of television, in which performers speak directly to us, the viewers, is another form of subjective-camera "discovery." The difference is that this time the television performers do not really discover and surprise us but rather come into our home as invited guests or at least as tolerated communication partners. But as with the direct discovery technique, the communication is aimed from the screen directly at us in our viewing position, without requiring us to assume anyone else's point of view.

Standard television is ideally suited for such a direct-address method of communication. The relatively small screen size permits close-ups that approximate our actual experience when talking with someone. In our culture even a tight close-up of the performer on a standard video screen is not large enough to intimidate viewers. We accept the television medium, and most of its content, as an integral and intimate part of our daily routine. We feel in close communion with our favorite performers and accept them as welcome companions. It seems perfectly natural to us that some of them tell us about the benefits of a certain brand of soap, others about the day's happenings, and still others about their troubles at the office, even if it happens to be the Oval Office at the White House. Good television performers are acutely aware of this close relationship. They do not try to address the millions of viewers "out there in videoland" but instead communicate in a low-key, intimate way with a single viewer—you. In fact, we as viewers are so used to this close relationship with television performers that we even feel free to turn away from the set to do some chores while listening to the performer's stories without feeling we've interrupted the communication, much like if a neighbor drops in for a chat as we are preparing dinner. The television performer's demeanor, rather than a specific production technique, plays a big part in establishing the proper paraproxemics for a variety of direct-address messages.

Film is quite different in this respect. We look up to film actors. They are not a part of our daily lives; they represent something special. They are stars. We do not expect film actors to turn to us from time to time and include us in a conversation they are having with other actors on-screen. Indeed we feel somewhat uncomfortable and jarred out of our fantasies and the security of the darkened, popcorn-flavored environment when such an invasion of our dream world by the screen image occurs. Because as viewers we usually suffer from a slight psychological shock when "discovered" while watching the happenings on the big film screen, we feel more comfortable when the direct-address technique is used for comic, rather than dramatic, reasons. As Woody Allen has demonstrated, however, the screen character can establish a direct dialogue with the audience, even when the dialogue is about deep-seated anxieties and frustrations rather than belly laughs. We have the feeling that he is simply including us in his talking to himself.

Angles

When we shift the camera's viewpoint, we create a variety of **angles**—distinct vector fields that can help us clarify and intensify a screen event. Although we have already explored the aesthetic implications of certain shooting angles (such as the looking-up and looking-down camera positions), we reexamine angles here for their usefulness in building effective screen space: for continuity, multiple viewpoints, event intensification, and style setting.

ANGLES FOR CONTINUITY

When you shoot a scene out of sequence for postproduction, a change of angles between shots will generally facilitate smooth cutting during postproduction editing. **SEE 11.28**

If you do not change the angle between shots, any slight misalignment from shot to shot will show up prominently. The so-called *jump cut*, in which an object seems to jump or jerk from one screen position to another, is a direct consequence

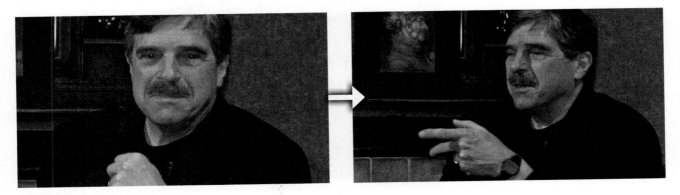

11.28 Angles for Continuity
The most elementary use of camera angles is to avoid jump cuts and to provide smooth continuity in a series of shots.

of slight but significant misalignments of camera to object from one shot to the next. We discuss the jump cut more extensively in chapter 14.

An important use of angles is to maintain the continuity of how and in what direction people are looking. When a tall person (A) talks to a shorter one (B), the tall person obviously looks down at the shorter person, and the short person looks up at the taller one. You will notice, however, that many times the camera angle does not seem to change whether it assumes the point of view of the short or the tall person. Such a discrepancy is especially noticeable in close-ups, where the camera seems to be at the same level, even if the people are at different heights. The following figures (11.29 to 11.31) show the correct camera placement and the general angles of the index vectors of a tall person talking with a shorter person. **SEE 11.29**

When the tall person (A) is shown in a subsequent close-up, the camera should assume the shorter person's (B's) point of view. This means that the camera needs to be adjusted to the eye level of B looking up at A. We see A from below her eye level. **SEE 11.30** When cross shooting to a close-up of B, the camera needs to be adjusted to the higher eye level of A looking down. The camera is now above B's eye level. **SEE 11.31**

ANGLES FOR MULTIPLE VIEWPOINTS

By changing angles from shot to shot, you introduce directional shifts that are perceived as a change in viewpoint rather than positional jumps. Like the cubist painters, you are helping the viewer see an object or event from various positions, thereby providing a more complete and intensified screen space than would be possible without such angles.

The relationship between shifts of viewpoint through camera angles and the variable viewpoints in cubist paintings shows up especially in the display of simultaneous screen space, such as superimpositions, electronic matting, and multiple screens. By showing various angles of an object simultaneously, you create

11.29 Point of View: Converging Index Vector Angles

When a tall person (A) talks to a shorter person (B), the camera needs to be positioned at a height resembling the eye level of the person doing the looking. The camera has to assume A's index vector and, in the reverse angle, B's index vector.

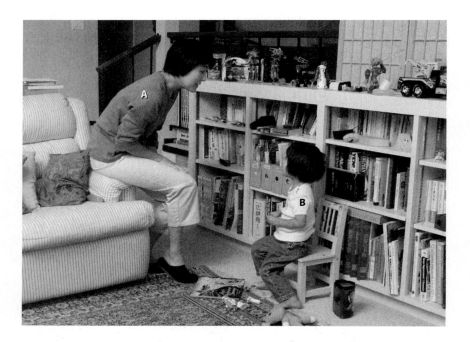

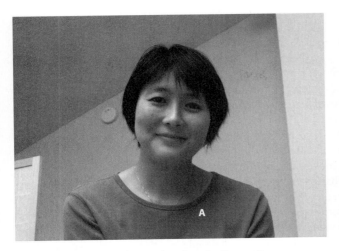

11.30 Point of View: Person A as Seen by Person B

In reverse-angle shooting, the camera height and angle need to be adjusted to the eye level and the index vector of the person doing the looking. When the child (B) looks up at the woman (A), A is seen from a below-eye-level position.

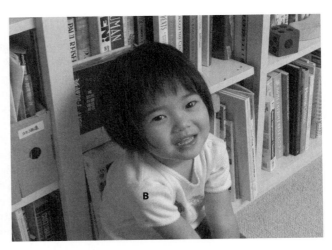

11.31 Point of View: Person B as Seen by Person A

When a close-up of the child (B) is shown, the camera needs to be adjusted to the height and the index vector direction of A. The woman (camera) looks down at the child.

a unique vector field that can exist only as screen space. Because in our real space/time environment we cannot be in two or more places at once, we can observe real events from only one viewpoint at a time. But when you use the unique potentials of the medium, a simultaneous display of various viewpoints provides a new visual reality that permits us to experience the complexity of an event all at once. The new vector structure can transcend the original event, creating a new, synergetic field of experience that, though based on an original event, communicates a greatly increased amount of aesthetic energy.[12] **SEE 11.32**

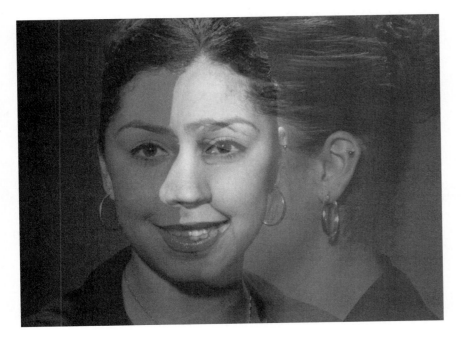

11.32 Simultaneous Angles

When you show the various shooting angles simultaneously, such as in a superimposition, you create a new visual event that lets viewers experience it from various points of view, very much like a cubist painting.

ANGLES FOR EVENT INTENSIFICATION

As with wide-angle-lens distortion, you can use angles to intensify an event or to reveal the underlying feelings of a person in a particular situation. Take a look at the following series of shots (figures 11.33 to 11.35), which are to intensify the dancers' upward movement. When the dancers are in their low starting position, the camera looks down at them. **SEE 11.33** As they begin to rise and reach up, the camera moves to eye level. **SEE 11.34** At the peak of their upward movement, the camera looks at the dancers from a very low position and frames them along the screen diagonal. **SEE 11.35** The camera's point of view and the tilted horizon line make a simple movement look dramatic.

Even if you change the field of view from a medium shot to a close-up, the absence of angles makes the same dance movement less dramatic. **SEE 11.36–11.38**

To demonstrate how you can use camera angles as point of view to reveal and perhaps even intensify a person's attitude and feelings in a specific situation, let's go downtown and observe a variety of people entering an exclusive, expensive department store for women.

Here is what we observe:

Event 1   A woman does some browsing in an expensive department store because she has some time to kill before her champagne luncheon with the other women from her club. She enters the store swiftly and surely, much like entering a supermarket. She knows where to go. She knows that the sales staff is here to serve her.

Event 2   Another woman, who cannot afford to shop in such an expensive store, has saved up some money to buy a present for her friend, who is more impressed by fancy labels than product quality. She enters hesitatingly, does not know what to say to the hostess who greets her at the entrance, and feels quite embarrassed by the cool stares of the salespeople.

Event 3   A little girl wanders into the store. Her mother is busy talking to a friend outside. The girl simply wants to look at all the wonderful things in the store.

Now try to visualize these three events. How do the different attitudes and feelings of the women and the girl influence the points of view? What are the predominant angles? Without telling you specifically how to visualize these three events, let me simply describe one possibility for deciding on camera viewpoints and POV angles.

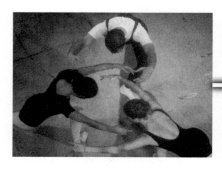

11.33   From Above: High Angle

Angles can intensify an event. In this shot sequence, angles add intensity to the dancers' upward movement. We begin by looking at them from above, emphasizing their low position.

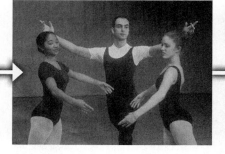

11.34   Eye Level: Normal Angle

This new angle is about at eye level, with the camera anticipating the upward movement.

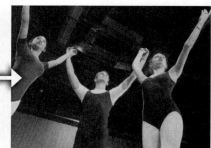

11.35   From Below: Low Angle

Now the camera has a low-angle position, looking up at the dancers and thus intensifying their upward movement.

Event 1   The woman pays the cab driver, walks quickly to the store, and enters without hesitation as though the doors were nonexistent. She gives the hostess (store manager?) a polite smile and proceeds to the elevator. She is obviously doing a routine thing. The shooting angles should therefore comply with the routine character of the event. They too are normal and routine with a minimum of viewpoint shift; the vector field is stable. Angles should contribute more to the clarification than to the intensification of this event. The camera objectively follows the woman's actions; no attempt is made to shift to the woman's POV.

Event 2   This woman walks by the store once or twice before entering, pretending to study the window displays. We see her from inside the store, looking through the window. Even the building appears threatening to her. The camera looks up at the building. She finally gathers enough courage and enters. The door still in hand, she sees the smiling hostess. We see a close-up of the hostess's forced smile from the woman's POV. The camera pans slowly, revealing the huge store (wide-angle-lens distortion) and the other salespeople, all bearing similar forced smiles. Again, this sequence is shot from the woman's POV and approaches a subjective-camera technique. Depending on whether you want her to gradually gain more confidence or become progressively more ill at ease, the angles should either stabilize or become more acute and labile.

Event 3   We see the little girl from above as she walks to the door. From inside the store, the camera watches her try to open the heavy door. She walks inside. Shift to girl's POV (low camera position looking up at people and things). This will emphasize the girl's fascination with the store and its people. Shift back to hostess's POV, looking down at the girl. If the girl becomes more and more captivated by all the wonders in the store, the camera may switch more frequently from the girl's POV to close-ups of her face looking here and there. If the girl becomes frightened, however, the viewpoints would become more and more subjective (the girl's POV) and the angles more acute (tilted horizon line, wide-angle-lens distortion).

One word of caution: avoid becoming angle crazy. If your basic visualization is determined by a simple looking-at context, keep the angles and the points of view to a minimum. There is no need to shoot a newscaster from below eye level, then from above, then from her left, and then from her right, especially if all she is doing is reading the weather report.

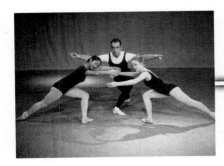

11.36 Long Shot

The lack of different camera angles makes the same dance sequence less dramatic even if we move from an LS to a CU.

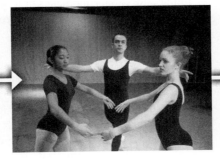

11.37 Medium Shot

Moving in tighter on the action helps viewers see better but does not intensify the upward movement.

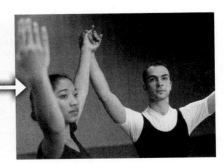

11.38 Close-up

A tight close-up helps viewers associate more closely with the dancers' feelings than with experiencing an intensified upward movement.

A dull, uninteresting speech will not become more exciting by using extremely varied angle shots. As a matter of fact, with your visual acrobatics you will probably destroy the little information the speaker has to give. If, on the other hand, you want to emphasize the menacing power of a demagogue, you may very well want to cover his speech from various extreme angles.

ANGLES FOR SETTING STYLE

Even when the event context, the thematic implications, and the actions and the attitudes of the on-camera people dictate to a large extent the basic use of angles, you still have wide latitude in which angles to use and how to use them. Your visualization is finally determined by your basic aesthetic concept of the event and your knowledge of the technical and aesthetic requirements and potentials of the medium through which you communicate it. While recognizing the usual determinants for camera angles set forth here, you may still choose different angles to satisfy your own sense of style. But as with all good things, your style should remain subtle. It should not draw attention to itself but should become yet another element in the totality of aesthetic communication. Like your handwriting, your shooting angles should not become the communication; instead they should simply be a reflection of your personality and aesthetic sensitivity. As with all other aesthetic variables we have discussed so far, your use of angles should primarily serve the clarification, intensification, and interpretation of the mediated event.

Storyboard

Finally, after working more or less patiently through the many variables of the visualization process, you are ready to get your visualizations out of your head and onto paper. A series of hand- or computer-drawn sketches of key visualizations and audio ideas make up the **storyboard**. The storyboard "frames" show how you would ideally like your visualizations to appear on the video or film screen. The audio information is usually written below the corresponding storyboard frame. To tell a story, a good storyboard will show not only the visualizations of the individual shots but also their sequencing. **SEE 11.39** Computer-generated storyboards are becoming more and more popular, mainly because they are relatively easy to produce.[13]

All commercials are carefully storyboarded before they go into production. Some filmmakers (such as Steven Spielberg and Alfred Hitchcock) are noted for storyboarding each shot for entire films—long before the camera starts to roll. Of course, storyboarding makes little sense if you are capturing a news story or shooting a documentary; in this case, your guiding principle for your shots is not your visualization but the event itself.

SUMMARY

Visualization means thinking in individual pictures or brief shot sequences. It also means thinking about the sounds that go with your video production or film. It refers to imagining how a camera would see a particular event from a specific point of view. Visualization is principally guided by the event context, your personal insight into the event, your skills in using the medium of video or film, and your personal style.

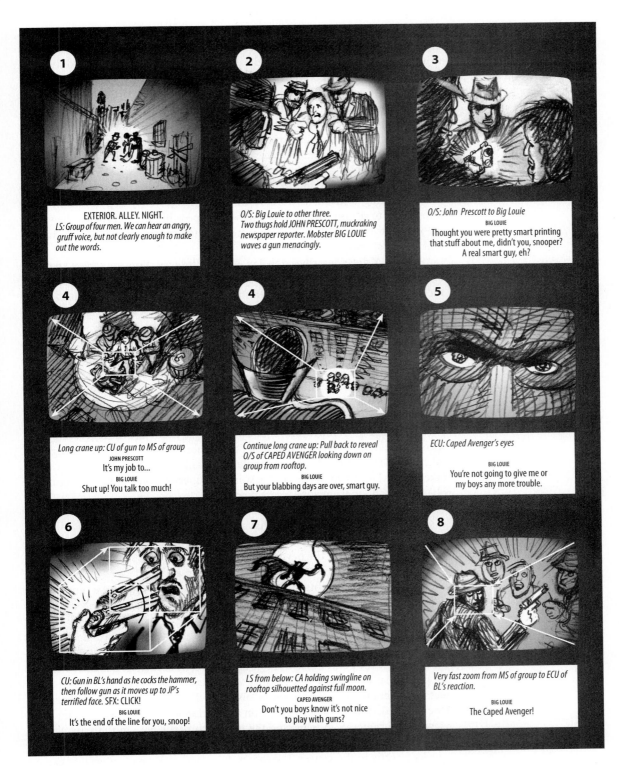

11.39 Storyboard

A storyboard shows the visualizations of key points of view in a progressive manner.

A deductive visual approach to shooting means that we move from the general to the specific or from an overview to event detail. It is the classic approach to a visual narrative in motion pictures. An inductive visual approach to shooting means that we show the event through a series of close-ups. We move from the specific to the general. The inductive method usually has a greater visual impact than the deductive method and is ideally suited to the relatively small video screen. The inductive sequencing of close-up shots is essential for making events visible on the small mobile media display.

The basic visualization factors are: ways of looking, field of view, point of view (POV), angles, and the storyboard.

Ways of looking refers to using the camera to look at, look into, or create an event. Looking at means to observe an event as objectively as possible. Looking into means to scrutinize an event as closely as possible and to provide the viewer with insights into the event. Creating means to use special effects to create images that can exist only as a screen event.

Field of view describes how far away or close we show on-screen an object or a person or how much territory a shot includes. The usual shot designations of the field of view range from an extreme long shot (ELS) to an extreme close-up (ECU). The way a viewer relates to the relative size of the screen image of a person is sometimes described as paraproxemics or video proxemics.

Point of view can mean that the camera substitutes for a character's index vector; it also refers to a camera's bias of looking—the camera no longer describes but comments on the event from a specific perspective. Viewpoint refers to what the camera is looking at and from where. That said, *point of view* and *viewpoint* are normally used interchangeably.

When the camera takes a looking-up position with respect to an object, a person, or an event (sometimes called a low-angle position), the object or person seems to be more powerful than when the camera looks at the event straight-on (at eye level) or from a downward angle (high-angle position). When the camera takes a looking-down position, it assumes a superior point of view, making the object, person, or event appear less powerful.

The most common way of using point of view is to show a person looking at something and then follow up that shot with what the person sees.

In over-the-shoulder shooting, the camera looks over the shoulder of the camera-near person at the person facing the camera. We usually see parts of the shoulder and the head of the camera-near person and the face of the camera-far person. When cross shooting we go to a tighter shot that moves the camera-near person entirely out of the frame and into off-screen space, leaving only a close-up view of the camera-far person.

Subjective camera means that the camera no longer observes an event but participates in it. One subjective-camera technique is to have the camera temporarily assume the point of view of one of the screen characters. Subjective camera supposes that the viewer will identify with this character. Another type of subjective camera is when the viewer is "discovered" by one of the screen characters (the camera). The character's attention and action are then aimed directly at the viewer (the camera), thus forcing the viewer to participate in the screen event.

The direct-address method, in which a television performer or film actor speaks directly to the viewer (the camera), is another form of subjective-camera technique. Although common and readily accepted by the viewer in video presentations, it is not often used in motion pictures.

Angles are useful for facilitating continuity, multiple viewpoints, event intensification, and style setting.

A storyboard consists of a series of sketches that represent visualizations of key camera shots and their intended sequence.

N O T E S

1. For more information on storytelling in the media, see Stuart W. Hyde, *Idea to Script: Storytelling for Today's Media* (Boston: Allyn and Bacon, 2003), pp. 41–64.

2. Revisit chapter 7 for an explanation of psychological closure and gestalt.

3. Marshall McLuhan, *Understanding Media: The Extensions of Man* (New York: McGraw-Hill, 1964), pp. 319–20.

4. See Herbert Zettl, *Video Basics 6* (Boston: Wadsworth, 2010), p. 202.

5. Anthropologist Edward T. Hall catalogued personal distance in various cultures. See Edward T. Hall, *Silent Language* (Garden City, N.Y.: Anchor Press/Doubleday, 1973).

6. The idea of paraproxemics was developed some time ago by Joshua Meyrowitz in his article "Television and Interpersonal Behavior: Codes of Reception and Response," in *Inter/Media: Interpersonal Communication in a Media World*, 2nd ed., ed. by Gary Gumpert and Robert Cathcart (New York: Oxford University Press, 1982), pp. 221–41. At about that time, I was involved in a study that compared the actual distance of people talking to each other in various cultures with the relative closeness of their news anchors. Unaware of Dr. Meyrowitz's earlier work, I had called this phenomenon "teleproxemics."

7. Personal interviews with Professor Dr. Manfred Muckenhaupt, chair, Media Department, University of Tuebingen, Germany, and Professor Tiffany Yeh, Department of Communication Arts, Fu Jen University, Taiwan.

8. The idea of showing varying points of view of the same event is powerfully expressed in the Japanese novel *In a Bush* by Ryunosuke Akutagawa, which was popularized by Akira Kurosawa in his classic 1950 film *Rashomon*. See Michael Rabiger, *Directing the Documentary*, 5th ed. (Burlington, Mass.: Focal Press, 2009), pp. 263–76, for a discussion of the various types of point of view.

9. Although proven successful over many centuries and in various situations by practical application, the psychological implications of looking up and looking down have not been substantiated by early experimental research. Studies in this field are not conclusive and are, in fact, sometimes contradictory. The problem seems to lie more in the measurement tool and the research design than in the existence of the psychological effect. The difficulty of measuring such subtle psychological effects is probably why this kind of study has not been done more frequently.

10. See George W. Linden, *Reflections on the Screen* (Belmont, Calif.: Wadsworth, 1970), pp. 26–27. Linden explains subjective point of view and the problem it presents for the film audience in a highly original and lucid way. Unfortunately, this unique and insightful treatise on the art of film is out of print but is still available from online booksellers.

11. This type of subjective camera was researched and made explicit by Elan Frank, an award-winning documentary filmmaker, while participating in my experimental production seminar.

12. The use of multiple screens in film and television is summarized by Caryn James in "Critic's Notebook: Splitting. Screens. For Minds. Divided," *New York Times* (January 9, 2004). Also see the discussions in this book of extending the field in chapter 8 and of special effects in chapter 10. For my early attempts at grappling with multiple screens, see Herbert Zettl, "Toward a Multi-screen Television Aesthetic: Some Structural Considerations," *Journal of Broadcasting* 21, no. 1 (1977): 5–19.

13. For detailed information about storyboards, how to move from idea or script to image and indicate various camera movements, see Marcie Begleiter, *From Word to Image* (Studio City, Calif.: Michael Wiese Productions, 2001); Francis Glebas, *Directing the Story: Professional Storytelling and Storyboarding Techniques for Live Action and Animation* (Burlington, Mass.: Focal Press, 2008); and Mark Simon, *Storyboards: Motion in Art*, 3rd ed. (Burlington, Mass.: Focal Press, 2007). Various software programs contain a standard vocabulary for storyboard creation.

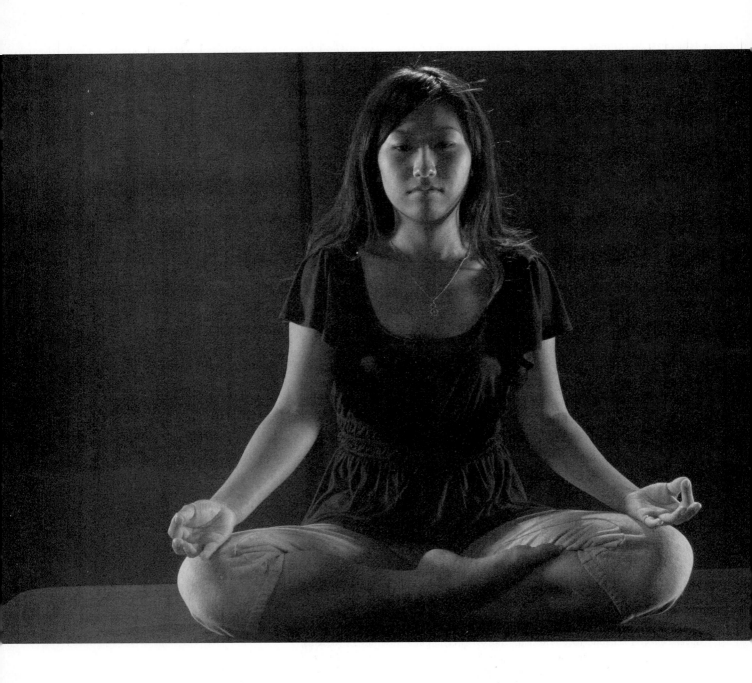

The Four-dimensional Field: Time

HE STUDY OF THE FOUR-DIMENSIONAL FIELD—THE VARIOUS THEORIES and applications of time and motion within the context of new media, such as video, film, and computers—is one of the most important steps in this discussion of various aesthetic fields. After all, the basic structure of video and film is the *moving* image. As in real life, change is the essence of the four-dimensional field. Video and film demand the articulation and the manipulation not only of a spatial field but also of a space/time field.

Structuring the four-dimensional field means achieving a spatial/temporal order. The concept of vectors and vector fields includes the time element. Vector fields in video and film are not static but continually changing either within a shot or from shot to shot. A vector is created not only by a stationary arrow that points in a particular direction but also by one that flies off the bow toward its target.

Let us now lay the groundwork for structuring the four-dimensional field by discussing some of its most basic elements: the theories and modes of time and motion.

The Significance of Time

Humans have always been concerned with time. We are born and die at a certain time. We experience recurring phenomena that suggest the passage of time: day and night, the months, the seasons. We experience periods of activity and inactivity and of bodily wants and needs and their satisfaction. We learn how to record the past, and we live in the present. We try to predict the future and cheat human mortality; at least we try to prolong our life span as much as possible. We construct theories and beliefs that suggest another life after death. In all we seek to manipulate—to control—time.

In our efficiency-oriented society, time has become a significant commodity. It has gone far beyond its former spiritual and ethereal importance and has attained a new existential significance that surpasses the Roman concept of *carpe diem* ("seize the day")—having a good time right now and not worrying too much about yesterday or tomorrow. Time is money. Time salespersons and time buyers bargain shrewdly for segments of broadcast time. They have tables that list the

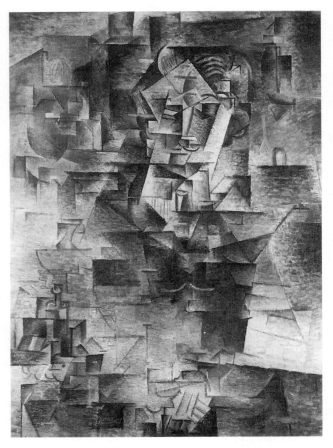

12.1 Time in Cubist Painting

This cubist painting by Picasso shows various sides of the object simultaneously. It implies a shift in viewpoint, that is, the viewer's moving about the object. Also the pattern of this painting suggests a certain rhythm, which we can sense as a type of motion.

Pablo Picasso, Spanish (1881–1973), worked in France, *Daniel-Henry Kahnweiler* (autumn 1910), oil on canvas, 39¹³⁄₁₆" × 28⅞" (101.1 × 73.3 cm). Gift of Mrs. Gilbert W. Chapman in memory of Charles B. Goodspeed, 1948.561. Photograph by Robert Hashimoto. Reproduction. The Art Institute of Chicago/© 2009 Estate of Pablo Picasso/Artists Rights Society (ARS), New York.

price of time. Some of the rate cards for broadcasting time point out that no time is "sold in bulk."

Time is an essential factor in measuring the worth of work. Efficiency is assessed not only by what you do but also by how fast you do it. We build machines that break down or at least become inefficient at a particular time, and we accelerate this carefully calculated obsolescence with periodic style changes. When traveling we are now inclined to measure distances not by spatial units but by units of time: it is six hours to Europe and three days to the moon. Computers that perform the most intricate calculations with incredible speed and various new discoveries in physics and space travel—all have contributed to a new space/time concept.

At the very least, the new media have demanded of us a new, intense, and unprecedented awareness of time. Over the past decade or so, we have graduated from a highly mobile society to an electronic one in which much of the actual movement is carried out not so much by people as by electronically coded information. In fact, new media, such as a computer-video combination operating in real time, allow us a *telepresence*, a term coined by Lev Manovich to describe our ability to view and affect an event without actually being there.[1] We get impatient if our computer takes just a few seconds longer than expected to retrieve a highly specific piece of data from the inconceivably vast information pool on the Internet. In the context of such an electronic society, time and motion have become almost the essence of life.

In any event, it is high time, so to speak, that we learn to function properly and effectively within this new space/time environment and reconcile old values with the new social and psychological requirements of our "now" generation that span from instant pudding to instant information.

Small wonder, then, that the new time concept—this "now" factor—has prominently entered all fields of the arts. We can find artists trying to manipulate time and motion in such nonmotion arts as painting, sculpture, and still photography as well as in the more obviously time-and-motion-based arts of theater, dance, and music.

Painters, for example, cope with this new time/motion dynamism in various ways. As mentioned in chapter 11, the cubists painted a scene from several points of view to create the impression that the observer is moving from one vantage point to another or is viewing the object from various points of view simultaneously. **SEE 12.1** Other painters invite an empathic time response by letting us feel the motion and the force of their brush strokes or by showing us successive "freeze-frames" of a moving object. **SEE 12.2 AND 12.3**

Some painters are so fascinated with time and motion that they create vibrating patterns to simulate movement. Whereas the factors of time and motion in various types of cubistic or abstract-expressionist paintings are relatively hidden, they are unavoidable in paintings designed to directly influence our perceptual mechanism. **SEE 12.4** When looking at figures 12.1 through 12.3, you need to reconstruct the aspects of time and motion cognitively—by thinking about them. But in the paintings that influence your optical perceptual mechanisms, called "op art," the illusion of motion is generated physiologically through a planned disturbance of the eye/brain system.

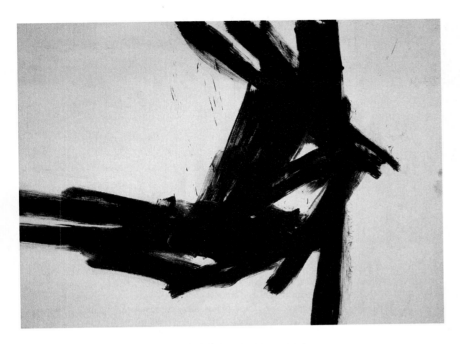

12.2 Implied Motion in Abstract Expressionism

In this abstract-expressionist painting by American painter Franz Kline, we can relive and move with the energy of the powerful brush strokes.

Franz Kline (1910–1962) *Corinthian II* (1961), oil on canvas./Museum of Fine Arts, Houston, Texas, USA/Bequest of Caroline Weiss Law/The Bridgeman Art Library/© 2009 The Franz Kline Estate/Artists Rights Society (ARS), New York.

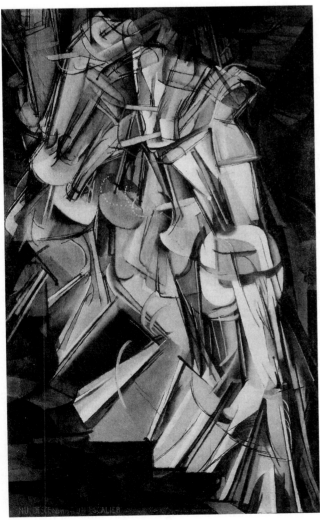

12.3 Simulated Motion Through Multiple Object Positions

French painter Marcel Duchamp shows frozen elements of motion in this painting, which closely resembles time-lapse photography. Indeed, he used himself as a model going downstairs in a time-lapse photo.

Marcel Duchamp (1887–1968) *Nude Descending a Staircase (No. 2)* (1912), oil on canvas, 57⅞" × 35⅛" (147 × 89.2 cm). The Louise and Walter Arensberg Collection, 1950./The Philadelphia Museum of Art/Art Resource, NY/© 2009 Artists Rights Society (ARS), New York/ADAGP, Paris/Succession Marcel Duchamp.

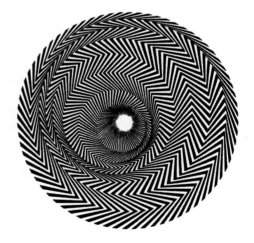

12.4 Simulated Motion Through Optical Vibrations

Some contemporary painters are so time-conscious that they create vibrating patterns that show virtual movement.

Bridget Riley, *Blaze 1* (1962). Courtesy of Richard L. Feigen & Co., New York.

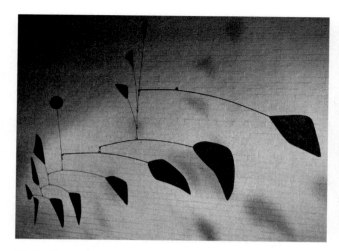

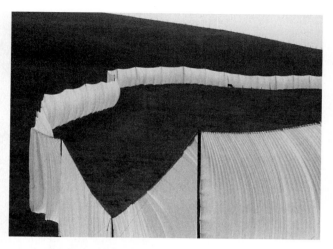

12.5 Kinetic Sculptures

Sculptors, who heretofore simply arrested motion in one immobile pose, are now creating works that actually move. The inventor of kinetic sculpture, Alexander Calder, an American, produced a great variety of mobiles.

Alexander Calder (1898–1976) *Big Red* (1959), sheet metal and steel wire, 74" × 114" (187.96 × 289.56 cm). Whitney Museum of American Art, New York; purchased with funds from the Friends of the Whitney Museum of American Art, and exchange 61.46/Photography by Sandak, Inc./© 2009 Calder Foundation, New York/Artists Rights Society (ARS), New York.

12.6 Time in Conceptual Art

Some artists create events merely to demonstrate the close connection between art and life—to show that art is merely a process (including the fighting of bureaucracy) bracketed by time. Bulgarian-born artist Christo (born Christo Javacheff in 1935) battled numerous county agencies and landowners before he could erect his gigantic 24-mile-long, 18-foot-high *Running Fence* in Marin County, California, only to have it dismantled two weeks later. Christo is especially famous for wrapping buildings, bridges, and even islands with plastic or woven material.

Sculptors, who heretofore simply arrested motion in one still pose, now create works that actually move. Such kinetic sculptures can take many forms, from mobiles or machinelike constructs whose only purpose is to generate motion to contraptions created solely for the purpose of watching them decay. **SEE 12.5 AND 12.6**

Still photographers try to communicate motion through strobe effects or through blurring the moving object. **SEE 12.7 AND 12.8**

Film simulates motion by projecting a number of still photos (24) in a period of time (one second). The ultimate instrument with which to express now-consciousness is video. Even a single video frame is a process image; its picture is in a continuous state of creation and decay. While some pixels of the video display are activated, others are already losing their charge and growing dark. Live television allows for the clarification and the intensification of an event while the event is occurring, and an almost unlimited number of widely dispersed people can experience this clarified and intensified event simultaneously. It's no wonder that this medium holds such a fascination for us.

What Is Time?

We do not know what time is. All we know is how to experience time in various forms, such as duration, change, causality, recurring phenomena, cycles, rhythm, and motion. We can measure time. We live, love, have children, suffer, and die with it and through it, but we do not know exactly what it is. We can live only in the present, but when we try to define the present, we run into all sorts of troubles.[2] We get different answers to the seemingly simple question of what time is, depending on whom we ask. The philosopher gives us one set of answers, the physicist another. Even Albert Einstein believed that "the experience of the Now [*sic*] means something special for man, something essentially different from the

"Space-time stands for many things: relativity of motion and its measurement, integration, simultaneous grasp of inside and outside, revelation of the structure instead of the facade. It also stands for a new vision concerning materials, energies, tensions, and their social implications."[3]

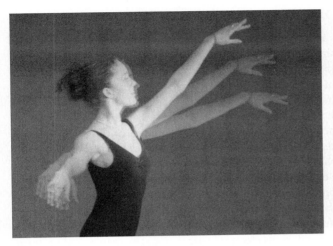

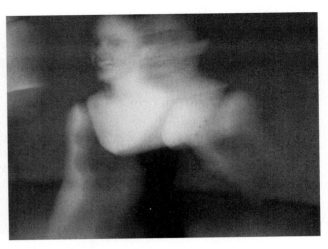

12.7 Simulated Motion Through Successive Positions
In this picture the movement of the dancer is frozen in successive positions by a flashing strobe light, simulating its progression in time.

12.8 Simulated Motion Through Blurring
A slow shutter speed or a zoom with the shutter open causes a moving object to blur. We tend to interpret this blurred image as object motion although the actual photograph shows the object at rest. Note, however, that the blurred photo of the dancer shows not a motion vector but an index vector.

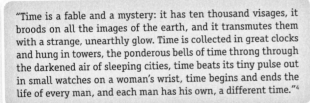

"Time is a fable and a mystery: it has ten thousand visages, it broods on all the images of the earth, and it transmutes them with a strange, unearthly glow. Time is collected in great clocks and hung in towers, the ponderous bells of time throng through the darkened air of sleeping cities, time beats its tiny pulse out in small watches on a woman's wrist, time begins and ends the life of every man, and each man has his own, a different time."[4]

past and the future…" and that "there is something essential about the Now which is just outside the realm of science."[5] J. T. Fraser, who devoted his scholarly career to the study of this subject, still calls time "the familiar stranger."[6]

Artists may be concerned only with the aspect of time that best suits them in their quest to clarify and intensify experience within a specific medium, such as dance, music, or theater. And this is exactly what we will do: select and discuss those aspects of time and motion that seem most relevant to our media—specifically video and film—and that help us best in understanding and structuring the four-dimensional field.

Types of Time

First of all we must distinguish between the time that the clock records and shows and the time that we feel. We have all experienced an interminable five minutes, whereas at other times an hour seemed to pass in seconds. Obviously, the time we feel does not always correspond with the time we measure. The time we measure by the clock is called, appropriately enough, clock time or *objective time*. The time we experience is called psychological time or *subjective time*. A time also exists that regulates our body functions and determines when we feel alert and when we feel tired. This third type is called *biological time*. In structuring the four-dimensional field for video and film, we are primarily interested in the first two types: objective and subjective time.

OBJECTIVE TIME

Objective time is what an accurate clock reports. It is measured by observable change—some regularly recurring physical phenomenon, such as the movement of stars or the revolution of the earth around the sun or of the moon around the earth. Day and night cycles as well as the seasons of the year are also manifestations of objective time. Humans invented more manageable devices to measure objective time, such as the hourglass, whose displacement of sand from top to bottom measures the passage of a certain amount of time, or the clock, which is constructed to produce some kind of regular motion, which is then translated into the spatial displacement of the hands on the analog clock or the readout of the numbers on the digital clock.

Despite Einstein's theory, which holds that even objective time changes depending on how fast clocks travel relative to an observer, in our ordinary day-to-day life the most fundamental conditions of a clock are that its recurring events (the movement of its hands or its electronic oscillations) be regular and uniform. So far the most accurate device we have to measure objective time is the atomic clock, which uses the cesium atom. This atom oscillates 9,192,631,770 times per second, and it does so without losing or gaining time over a long, long period—it is accurate to within a second in about 6 million years.[7] But even objective time is arbitrary. We can decide just what the clock should read, which we do twice a year: once for setting it for what we consider standard time for our time zone and then to move it ahead one hour for daylight saving time.

Objective time regulates the behavior of almost all people on earth. Have you ever counted how often you look at your watch or other time devices during the course of a day? Most of the world's activities would stop if we were to do away with all time-measuring tools.

SUBJECTIVE TIME

Subjective, or psychological, time is "felt time." Regardless of what the clock says, you may experience an activity or event as being short or long. Clock time is a superimposed standard. This standard ticks off units of time regardless of how we feel or what we do. Subjective time, on the other hand, is a personal experience. It depends very much on how you feel and what you do.

Perceived duration　How long or short, then, is an event that you experience? Think of some examples of when you have felt that an event moved quite fast or dragged on for a long period of time, even if both took exactly the same amount of objective time. A 50-minute lecture on time may seem endless, whereas surfing the Internet for the same period may somehow feel much, much shorter to you. To the casual observer, a chess game appears exceedingly slow; but to those playing the game time flies, or rather the flow of time seems peculiarly absent. When waiting for a person we love, time crawls, but when with that person, the point of departure comes all too soon.

Common experience seems to tell us that the more involved we are in an event, the shorter the event's duration seems to be; and the less involved we are, the longer the duration seems to be. But certain controlled studies seem to contradict this theory. For example, when asked to recall the duration of a roller-coaster ride or an especially action-packed segment of a film, subjects of the experiment generally overestimated the actual clock time of the event.[8] You have probably experienced fun-filled weekends that seemed like a week's vacation in retrospect, or else had time stand still during the ecstasy of love, the unreality of death, or in moments of extreme beauty or terror. In such moments we seem to feel the instantaneousness of eternity or, perhaps more accurately, the timelessness of total involvement. How can this be?

Duration as vertical vector   The confusion about the relative length of subjective time, about an experienced duration, is mainly due to our erroneous assumption that it is somehow a subgroup of objective time.[9]

Although we organize our lives by the clock in terms of keeping appointments, getting up at a certain time whether we like it or not, or tuning in to a certain television program, we actually experience time more by the quality of what we do, that is, by whether and how much we are interested in what we are doing and by how much we are affected by what we perceive. We read the clock, but we experience time. The major difference between objective clock time and subjective psychological time is that clock time is measured quantitatively and subjective time is perceived and processed qualitatively.[10]

The clock moves along, measuring recurring periods (hours, minutes, and seconds), independent of how we actually experience the relative intensity of the event or the succession of event details. An appropriate representation of objective time is a horizontal *time vector*. **SEE 12.9**

Subjective time expresses our relative involvement in an event and, with it, our relative awareness of time. Counting the degree of involvement or how much we are aware of a certain duration in seconds, minutes, and hours makes as little sense as using a yardstick to measure the weight of a person. Unfortunately, in our efficiency-oriented society, we seek to measure, rather than to enjoy, quality. We rate the value of a van Gogh painting by how many millions of dollars were spent for its purchase, and we evaluate a woman's beauty on a scale of 1 to 10. It's no wonder that we tend to measure subjective time as though it were clock time. Instead we need to look at subjective time as going into depth rather than progressing horizontally. We can best visualize subjective time as a vertical vector indicating greater or lesser intensity. **SEE 12.10**

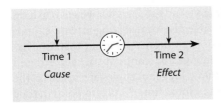

12.9 Objective Time: Horizontal Time Vector

The progression of objective, or clock, time is represented by a horizontal vector. Objective time is quantitative. It goes from time 1 to time 2, from cause to effect.

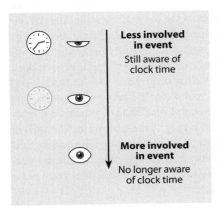

12.10 Subjective Time: Vertical Time Vector

The intensity of subjective time is represented by a vertical vector. This kind of felt time is qualitative.

12.11 Zero Point in Time

When uninvolved in an event, the subjective-time vector runs almost parallel with objective time (a). But the more involved we get in an event, the steeper the subjective-time vector becomes (b). When we are totally involved in an event, the subjective-time vector no longer occupies any space on the horizontal objective-time vector (c). The subjective-time vector has reached a zero point in time.

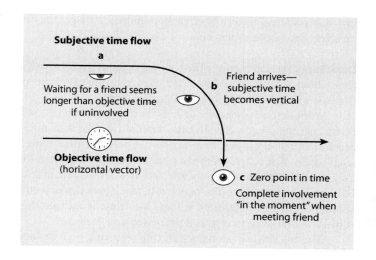

Subjective time flow
a

Waiting for a friend seems longer than objective time if uninvolved

Friend arrives—
b   subjective time becomes vertical

Objective time flow
(horizontal vector)

c Zero point in time
Complete involvement "in the moment" when meeting friend

When waiting, you are usually not highly involved in the act of waiting, which is merely a necessary condition for the anticipated event to occur. Because it is something you would like to have pass as quickly as possible, you probably find yourself looking at your watch frequently. Checking the clock time helps bring structure to the amorphous time experience of waiting. You seek comfort in the regularity of the clock, but in this case the clock is also the bearer of bad news; what felt like a half-hour wait might turn out to be only 10 minutes of elapsed clock time. Because you are so aware of objective time (wishing it to be as short as possible before the anticipated event occurs), the subjective-time vector is no longer vertical but instead runs almost parallel with the horizontal clock time vector.

But when riding a roller coaster, you are probably much more intent on hanging on for dear life than looking at your watch to find out how much clock time it takes from start to finish. Here the time vector has become more vertical and gained considerably in magnitude, indicating that you are involved in riding the roller coaster and less aware of clock time. As indicated earlier we seem to have no perception of either objective time or subjective time during intense experiences. To call such moments "timeless" is more accurate than to say that time has stood still. In such a case, the subjective-time vector stands at true vertical and has gained so much magnitude that its point no longer occupies any space on the horizontal time vector. It has reached a zero point in time. This zero point in time does not denote a durationless instant but rather the absence of time.[11] **SEE 12.11**

Why, then, do studies show that we overestimate the actual duration of an intense or especially crowded event rather than underestimate it? Should not an intense or crowded event seem shorter to us than it really was because of our involvement? Considering the previous arguments, the answer should be yes. The problem seems to arise in our trying to translate subjective time (felt duration) into objective (clock) time after the experience. In remembering our experiences, we are inclined to substitute the horizontal vector magnitude (clock time period) for the perceived magnitude of the vertical vector (intensity of experience). That is, we change the vertical vector into a horizontal one. In this switch we simply use the magnitude, or length, of the vertical vector as the magnitude (length) of the horizontal one. Hence we erroneously interpret the high-magnitude vertical vector of an intense experience as an equally high-magnitude horizontal vector—more elapsed clock time. Thus we remember being on the roller coaster for a longer time than we actually were. **SEE 12.12**

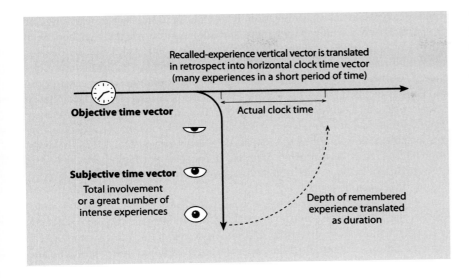

Recalled-experience vertical vector is translated
in retrospect into horizontal clock time vector
(many experiences in a short period of time)

Objective time vector

Actual clock time

Subjective time vector

Total involvement
or a great number of
intense experiences

Depth of remembered
experience translated
as duration

12.12 Remembered Time: Horizontal Time Vector

When asked to estimate the elapsed clock time of an event, we translate the magnitude of the vertical subjective-time vector (degree of event involvement) into an equally strong horizontal (clock time) vector. The deeper the vertical vector, the longer the recalled duration of the event.

What it boils down to is that we experience subjective time in basically two ways: the duration we *experience* during the event and the duration we *remember* of the event. While we experience an event—an event in the process of becoming—we become less aware of passing time the more involved we are. When we are totally involved in the event, we forget time altogether. When we think back to the event or events we encountered, however, our memory places the number and the intensity of events that occurred into an objective-time context. The more we remember having done in a day, the longer the day seemed in retrospect. This type of subjective time is a mental construct and measures principally a reconstructed event; but it is no longer felt time—a primary experience of an ongoing event. It is similar to watching an edited video recording of the event instead of actually experiencing it in real time.

BIOLOGICAL TIME

One type of subjective time operates quantitatively, which means it tells us when to do certain things. All living things seem to have a built-in biological clock. Migrant birds return when their biological clock says it is time to do so, regardless of the prevailing weather conditions back home. Some plants open and close according to their biological-clock time, not because it is night or day or hot or cold.

You probably have awakened many times just before the alarm clock went off. Your biological clock told you when it was time to get up. The biological clock is set by habit. If you gradually change sleeping and waking hours, your biological clock resets itself to the new schedule. But if you change a schedule abruptly, your biological clock keeps ticking faithfully according to the old time schedule. This can be quite annoying or exhausting, especially during travel, when it is commonly referred to as "jet lag." When everyone in the new location is ready for bed, you start feeling wide awake. And when your biological clock tells you that it is the time you normally go to bed, the people in the new location, whose biological clocks are set differently, are eager to start a new day. This type of biological-time upset is called circadian cycle (or rhythm) desynchronization.[12] Fortunately, your biological clock will adjust after a while to the new working and sleeping rhythm.

Although biological time does not directly help structure the four-dimensional field, it nevertheless contributes to the readiness of viewers to respond properly to mediated communication. If they are dead tired when watching our program, we will certainly have a more difficult task arousing their aesthetic sensitivities than if they are wide awake. In television you should at least consider adjusting programming to the general waking and sleeping habits of your audience. You should also be sensitive to the general mood and receptiveness of the audience as dictated by the biological clock. In midmorning, when the audience is wide awake and energized, they may tolerate, if not demand, a higher-energy program than late at night, when the biological clock tells them to relax and be comfortable. Late-night network shows are usually video-recorded in the afternoon rather than the morning, precisely because of the biological clock. The time rhythm of hosts, guests, and studio audience are then more like that of the late-night television viewer.

Before we apply some of these admittedly abstract concepts to video and film, we need to try your subjective-time patience and engage you in a brief theoretical discussion of the direction of time. We do this to lay the groundwork for our later argument about the difference between live and recorded television and between video and classic film. This segment should also clear up some traditional myths about the value of live television.

Time Direction

Everyday experience in life gives us ample evidence that time moves relentlessly forward, that the past precedes the present, and the present, the future. Regardless of whether it is we who are doing the moving rather than time, we experience birth before death, and cause preceding effect. In our world entropy seems to work in only one direction, from an organized system to a loss of organization, from a high information level to a low one.[13] We have therefore come to believe that the flow of time is irreversible, that the "arrow" of time—the horizontal time vector—moves in only one direction.

Live television is inevitably tied to this unidirectional time vector. Once an event is video recorded or filmed, however, you are no longer tied to the past/present/future flow of time nor to the cause/effect principle. You can change the direction of the time vector of the screen event in any way you desire.

To understand the potentials of such time vector shifts, let us now take a brief look at the past/present/future division of time and its relevance to television and film.

PAST/PRESENT/FUTURE

Based on our ordinary experience, we divide the time continuum into the past, the present, and the future. **SEE 12.13**

We remember the past and have proof of it. Historians and archeologists make a profession of verifying the past. We personally have photographs, films, or video recordings of past events or else old letters from Grandmother. We anticipate the future and try to predict it as much as possible. We are eager to know what the weather will be like tomorrow, who will win the election, and how our production will turn out. Both past and future are really addresses in the time continuum: Martin Luther King Jr. was assassinated on April 4, 1968; I will have a dentist appointment on May 21. As you can see, we can accurately pinpoint time in the past and in the future. **SEE 12.14**

The present is more elusive. When is now? Right now! When? Whoops—your "now" just passed. Now you are still thinking about it, but it has not yet come about. Too late, it has again eluded you. Can we pinpoint and freeze the

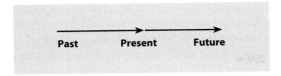

12.13 Past/Present/Future
The time continuum—the arrow of time—is usually
divided into past, present, and future.

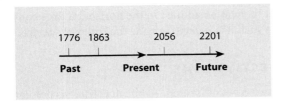

12.14 Addresses in Time
We can accurately pinpoint specific epochs, or addresses,
in the past and the future but not in the present.

now so that it becomes a spot in time, a specific instant in the time continuum?
Or is it something that continuously comes and goes in a constant flux, always
lost somewhere between the "not yet" and the "has been"?

More than 16 centuries ago, Saint Augustine wrote in his *Confessions* that
the rigid division of time into past, present, and future was incorrect because
whenever we speak of the past or the future, we do so in the very present, our
very present, right now. Therefore, he claimed, there can be only a present of
things past, a present of things present, and a present of things future.[14] And yet,
as Augustine points out, "the present has no space," at least not on the normal
horizontal time vector that envisions time as an orderly progression from past
to future.[15] It seems as though the present has no place in our consciousness. But
aren't you reading this sentence right now? Isn't that the present? The paradox
of the present is that it is the only time phase in which we consciously live, yet it
seems to remain outside our cognitive grasp.

This paradox has haunted philosophers ever since.[16] And, for that matter,
media scholars who think about the portended pertinence of live television. Is
the real present an unconscious moment during which our senses receive all the
information around us, which, however, does not reach our consciousness until
later? Or does the real now consist of the memory of what has just passed and the
anticipation of what will come in the next seconds? Or is there another present, a

Saint Augustine (A.D. 354–430), Bishop of Hippo (present-day Algeria), was
a truly original thinker. Throughout his *Confessions*, which he wrote in A.D.
397, he apologizes frequently to God for being so bold as to have his own deep
thoughts about creation and the many aspects of the human condition. Some
think that his insightful writings are his "soul's journey to grace." His analysis
of time and his emphasis of the "now" place him among the very early forerunners of existentialism.

more specious present as some scholars call it, in which we are conscious of what is going on around us, at least for a moment? But how long is this specious present?

As you can see, such arguments can lead us quite readily down a blind alley. What this argument suggests, however, is that we should not try to pinpoint when the present is or how long it lasts—after all, it is right now while you are reading this—but rather *how aware we are of what we are doing.* What we must do is free ourselves from the arrow metaphor and simply observe our awareness of what we are doing and experiencing at a given moment. It is this conscious presence that we need to address when structuring time for optimally effective communication. Most likely, this is the "essential difference" between the now and the past and future to which Einstein was alluding. Whereas past and future are quantitative time concepts (you can pinpoint them as an address in the horizontal time continuum), the now is a quality. As such it is indeed "outside the realm of science."

THE PRESENT AS SUBJECTIVE TIME

We seem to be confronted with two types of "present"—the unconscious present and the conscious one. In the unconscious present, which precedes the conscious one, we are simply bombarded with whatever happens around us. It all enters unfiltered through our eyes, ears, and skin. It all happens continuously, *when,* rather than *where,* the future slips into the past. **SEE 12.15** This tremendously large data input is sorted out and organized an instant later by our cognitive faculties. This sorting results in the conscious present. It is largely determined by the temporary relevance of what we are experiencing. It is further modified by the intensity of the experience and how aware we are of what is happening.[17]

The degree of awareness, this close-up of time, is obviously not a quantitative state but a qualitative one. As part of qualitative time, the present becomes less mysterious. It is simply a mode of subjective time. The conscious present is no longer a state of being, a point in the time continuum, but a process of becoming. Depending on your awareness of what is around you, this process can be very brief (casual observance of an event) or extended (various degrees of consciousness).

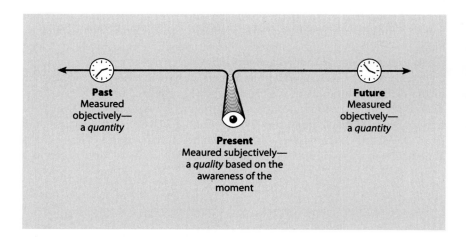

Past
Measured
objectively—
a *quantity*

Present
Meaured subjectively—
a *quality* based on the
awareness of the
moment

Future
Measured
objectively—
a *quantity*

12.15 Present as Zero-time Quality

We cannot pinpoint the elusive present as we can the past and the future. It is more fruitful to consider the present as subjective rather than objective time. As such we experience it qualitatively (according to our relative awareness of the moment) rather than quantitatively (how long the moment is). The conscious present is a process, not an address on the clock time vector.

Such an awareness does not come to you as a gift. You need to work at it. You need to learn to look around you, listen, and feel what is going on so that you can perceive not only the obvious development of the event but also its significant details and essences. You have to learn to look into an event rather than merely at it. This heightened awareness is what separates the artist from the casual observer. The artist can shift to different states of awareness and see event details that usually go unnoticed by most of us, especially if we are in a hurry. You may see a white wall as white, even if there is a shadow falling on it. But when you look closely, you may discover that it also has a multitude of different colors on it: the bluishness of the shadow, the yellows from the nearby flowers, and the red reflection from the car parked nearby.

With a bit of training, you can shift into this close-up-view mode (and with it a close-up of time) even when running after a news story. Like artists in other fields, you can then capture event details that communicate to the audience not only what the event looks like but also how it feels. Such a shift does not necessarily mean that you use extreme angles or a wildly moving camera when shooting an interview. A tight close-up may be all that's necessary to reveal the unease of a guest who is apparently not telling the truth. At other times reaction shots to an event may be more telling than showing its gruesome details. Like a good painter or novelist, you are now helping the audience see and feel the event in a clarified and intensified way.

TRANSCENDING TIME

You may have noticed that the various stages of awareness are close to some prevailing Eastern traditions. Contrary to the Western concept of time, the followers of Eastern spiritual traditions transcend the from/to, cause/effect direction of the time vector into a liberation from time altogether. In this higher state of consciousness, the time vector changes from its horizontal direction to a vertical one; it transcends from a quantitative mode to a qualitative one. As a quality rather than a quantity, time no longer measures cause/effect progression but has given way to the simultaneous coexistence of all events. As such the "flow of time" has lost its meaning.[18] In the absence of meditation, you may experience such an absence of time occasionally through extreme emotional conditions, such as overwhelming love or terror. Paradoxically, each of such timeless moments contains eternity.[19] Because such occasional timeless moments will rarely get the job done, however, a heightened state of awareness—focusing on what is going on and what you have to do—will suffice. In fact, there are some proven techniques with which you can influence the audience's subjective time, that is, make them perceive an event as "long" or "short."

Controlling Subjective Time

The common means to influence subjective time is not by controlling time but by manipulating the event itself and how we experience it. Specifically, you need to consider event density, event intensity, and experience intensity.

EVENT DENSITY

The relative number of event details that occur within a brief clock time period constitutes *event density*. Thus a high-energy event is one in which many things occur within a relatively short time. For example, if you attend a three-ring circus, more things are going on at the same time than you can watch. A movie or video sequence with many brief shots and shifts of point of view, location, or angles is also a high-density event. We tend to interpret such a rapid assault on our senses as event density and are therefore more apt to be stimulated by such a rapid-fire presentation than by a less dense shot sequence. If the high-density event has any kind of beat to it, such as the beat generated by the rhythmic cuts and music in a commercial, we tend to interpret the faster rhythm as faster speed than if the cutting rhythm of a commercial is less dense (and therefore slower), even though the actual running time of the two commercials may be exactly the same.

In applying the concept of event density to the structure of a commercial, a drama, a situation comedy, or even a documentary, you will find that the density concept can take a variety of forms.

Because of their brief running time, commercials try to pack in as many shots as possible. Commercials require that you get the attention of the viewer, tell an interesting story, and show variety yet with enough redundancy to make the product stick in the viewer's mind—all in 30 seconds. A high-density commercial can contain 35 or more shots in its 30-second running time. This translates into an average shot length of less than a second.

In documentaries a rather crude yet effective technique to quickly get from one place to another or to switch from one segment to the next is to show some of the recorded segments in a fast-forward progression with a voice-over narration. If, for example, in a documentary about the new library addition, you need to show a group of deans inspecting the media section, you can show their long walk from the DVD storage room to the computer room in accelerated motion. The voice-over narrator now has time to add some details about the new computers that are housed there. In this way you can increase the density of the event and maintain the energy level of the documentary without spending much time on it.

In a drama the dialogue is usually clipped and kept to short sentences. There are few pauses between the characters' lines, and they frequently overlap (a planned stepping on each other's lines). This is especially (and often painfully) apparent in some crime dramas, when the police and the witnesses all seem to be engaged in "police-speak": "Got there too late. Checked it out. Saw nothing!" The video portion is equally restless: people running, driving, moving through crowds, or talking to each other while moving along the z-axis down a hallway. You are certainly familiar with the routine shot along the z-axis of a hospital corridor, where a gurney with a gravely ill patient is rushed to surgery and a group of nurses is hurrying in the opposite direction while trying to get around a visiting family that is blocking their way.

In a situation comedy, many things can happen at once. Visualize the scene in which the young couple are finally left alone and try to edge a little closer to each other. But there is a knock on the front door and, at the same time, the telephone starts ringing. For good measure the teakettle begins to whistle in the kitchen. As they are bolting from the couch, the girl knocks over Grandmother's favorite lamp, and so forth. You can add your own creative touches to make the situation even denser.

EVENT INTENSITY

Some events seem to carry more energy than others. The relative energy and significance we perceive about an event is a measure of *event intensity*. A herd of stampeding cattle has more energy than a single cow grazing; a person running has more than someone sleeping. Usually, we respond to a high-energy event more readily than to a low-energy event, especially if the event has no specific significance for us. Thus a high-energy event is likely to involve us more than a low-energy event and, consequently, to increase the magnitude of the subjective-time vector. This means that the high energy of an event, regardless of content, can increase event intensity and thereby distance us more from clock time. As a result, we perceive the event as moving faster than a comparable low-energy event.

Action movies thrive on high-intensity events. Spectacular explosions, car chases and crashes, earth-defying leaps from rooftop to rooftop—all are aimed at keeping you awake even if the storyline and the acting are less than spectacular. Such movies or television shows are usually driven by the ***plot***, and characters are clearly divided into protagonists and antagonists. You are supposed to cheer when the good guy survives a spectacular crash and the bad guy doesn't. Of course, there are plot-driven plays that portray or develop high-intensity events in a much more poetic fashion. In such dramas the events lead up to a major crisis that forces the heroes to react and make a crucial choice—a choice that leads to either their salvation or their inevitable doom. Aristotle, as a stout defender of such plot-driven plays, writes in his *Poetics:* "So, plot is the basic principle, the heart and soul, as it were, of tragedy and the characters come second."[20]

But, as you know, many of the modern plays, films, and video dramas are character-driven. The event intensity comes from within rather than from without, from the characters' feelings and actions rather than from their reaction to what is going on around them. Eighteenth-century drama critic Gotthold Ephraim Lessing was an outspoken critic of neoclassic plays that were modeled after the formal plot-driven Greek plays. He advocated that dramatic intensity should spring primarily from the way we experience life, from the way the playwright develops character rather than plot.[21] Ingmar Bergman's *Persona* and Mike Figgis's *Leaving Las Vegas* are good, though disturbing, examples of character-driven high-intensity motion pictures. In video the aesthetic intensity is primarily established and maintained by close-ups and inductive sequencing.

EXPERIENCE INTENSITY

The condition of ***experience intensity*** refers to the number of relevant experiences we go through either simultaneously or in rapid succession and the relative depth or impact such events have on us. You have probably experienced overwhelming moments when, waking up at night, all your problems seem to converge on you at the same time with tremendous intensity.

Experience intensity commonly depends to a great extent on the relevancy of the event: the more relevant the event is for you, the more intense your experience is likely to be. Waiting to see whether your chess partner has discovered the trap you set for her is nothing like the empty waiting period discussed earlier. Because you are now totally involved, waiting for your partner to make her move is a high-intensity experience. Taking an exam or playing in a tennis final are equally involving, high-intensity experiences.

Experience intensity is less dependent on the relative energy or density of the event and more dependent on how much the event means to you. As you recall from the discussion of subjective time, low involvement means more awareness of clock time; high involvement means less awareness of clock time. That we usually experience a high-intensity event as having no time or sometimes as lasting an eternity is one of the paradoxes of subjective time.

A live telecast of an exceptionally horrific disaster or an extremely precarious situation can cause a high degree of involvement, as can sporting events. A live telecast of a sports contest has all the key elements of a dramatic structure. It is clearly divided into protagonists and antagonists and has some sharply delineated heroes and villains. Usually, it is a high-density and high-intensity event. Its plot is straightforward and clearly delineated by certain rules, but it moves constantly from one unpredictable crisis to the next. Its final outcome is known only at the very end of the event. Every single moment of such an event carries the potential of victory or defeat, triumph or disaster for either team.

When you are rooting for your favorite team while watching a live telecast, your experience intensity can, at least to some extent, approach that of attending the event in person. In fact, if the director is doing a good job of looking into, rather than merely at, the event, frequent tight close-ups and inductive shooting may well lead to an event intensification that is even higher than if you were watching the game from way up in the stands. Can we therefore assume that a live pickup and transmission of an event will inevitably lead to a high experience intensity? For example, should we try to do an especially good television play live to achieve a comparably high degree of experience intensity? A quick answer to both questions is no. The following sections on live and recorded television offer some explanation.

Live Television

One of the unique powers of television is that it can capture, clarify, intensify, interpret, and distribute an event to a potential world audience almost instantly while the event is in the process of becoming. We have grown so used to this unique feature of television that we don't consider it anything special to sit in our living room and watch live pictures of traffic backups, a spacewalk by astronauts, a championship game, or even the grim realities of war.

Much of the aesthetic energy seems to come not only from the events themselves but from the knowledge that they are live, happening right now. But aren't most of the programs we see carefully edited video recordings or film? Are there any significant advantages to doing something live, such as television drama? Will such a live presentation increase the experience intensity? Let's find out.

LIVE TELEVISION AND EVENT TIME

The objective time of an actual event and the televised event are inevitably tied to each other when the telecast is live. Live television means that the event and the event telecast are happening simultaneously. Broadcasters refer to such programs as occurring in *real time,* that is, at the time of the actual event. At this point you might argue that technically no true simultaneity exists between the actual event and the televised event. For example, when the television signal is distributed via satellite, we can experience a time delay of almost half a second between event origin and reception.[22] When the picture finally gets from the downlink (the satellite signal receiver on the ground) to the broadcast station, it is briefly stored by a digital synchronization device before transmission.[23]

Aesthetically, however, such minor time delays do not constitute a recording of the event. Even if the televised event is slightly delayed by signal processing and distribution, it cannot free itself from the objective time of the actual event and must follow its flow.

The unique ability of television to be in several places at the same time permits the showing of simultaneous live events even if they are widely dispersed. As you know we can display various points of view of the same action, such as an especially interesting basketball play, simultaneously in digitally created secondary frames. When a host in New York interviews live three guests from Beijing, Paris, and Buenos Aires, we can see all four on a single screen, talking to one another. Satellite transmission and the digital secondary frames make such an experience of simultaneous events almost routine. With a worldwide television system, you can be not only in two places at the same time but in millions of places.

LIVE TELEVISION AND EVENT DEPENDENCY

In the context of objective-time vectors—that is, the clock time of the actual event—the live telecast is totally event-dependent. The only control you have over clock time when originating a live program is the starting and end times of the telecast and when you temporarily cut away for commercials or other announcements. But as much as you may want to know the outcome of a football game, for example, you cannot fast-forward the live event or its live transmission. If you show brief recordings of the live pickup (such as instant replays), or commercials, you will inevitably miss out on the progression of the game during this time period unless you show both events simultaneously on a split screen.

If you choose to have the cameras look at something more interesting than the main event action, such as close-ups of the fans instead of the players on the field, such cutaways will not influence the actual clock time duration of the main event but they will most certainly influence the subjective time of the viewers—how involved they get and how they feel about the game.

In some instances the mere presence of the medium may alter the event. Much as we all take on a slightly different persona as soon as somebody is taking a picture of us, the presence of video cameras inevitably alters an event. Even in sports the medium sometimes dictates the event rather than the other way around. Time-outs in a football game are not always called because the coach wants to give his team new instructions but also because a few commercials have yet to be put on the air. Recall Lev Manovich's idea of telepresence, which describes our ability to use video and computers to affect the reality in a location without having to be at that location.[24]

LIVE TELEVISION AND OPEN FUTURE

The event dependency of live television has interesting aesthetic consequences: the televised event—a soccer championship game, for example—has the same "open future" as the real event. This means that even if the outcome of the real event is predictable, it is not predetermined. As in real life, the unexpected can occur at any time. Such event dependency allows us as viewers to participate in the process of becoming; it involves us in the event and affords us a glance at the continual creation of the world, however humble its scale. Bound by time and closeness to the actual event, the television audience of the live transmission may well lose some of its usual heterogeneity and become a more closely knit social aggregate. Perhaps when many millions of people watch the same live event on television, we may come closer to achieving a true global community than through world politics.

But now we need to return to the question raised earlier: will a live presentation of a television play increase our experience intensity? The reason why we answered negatively is that a well-written play has no open future. The script determines its outcome even before production commences. Any departure from the rehearsed dialogue and action is not a stimulant for higher involvement or an expression of sudden inspiration but simply a mistake. After all, the strength of the well-made play lies in its carefully crafted plot, dialogue, and action. Unless you come up with a ***dramaturgy*** that allows for an open future without sacrificing its artistic control, doing a fully scripted play live makes little sense.

Some attempts have been made with improvisational theater, in which only the theme is given but what the actors do and say is entirely extemporaneous. The "happenings" of the 1960s were the most deliberate attempt to inject an open future into performances. When transferred from stage to screen, the problem is that both the actors and, by necessity, the cameras improvise. Such simultaneous ad-libbing may lead to a heightened experience intensity for the crew but rarely for the viewer.[25] Any program content whose outcome is predetermined by the script has its future closed. A live performance cannot change this condition. All it does is invite a lower-quality product.

Some show formats by their very nature contain elements of an open future. Examples are game shows and interviews. Like sports, a game show has a given approach and certain procedural rules, but a great part of its appeal lies in the unpredictability of the participants' answers. The same goes for the interview format. Whereas the questions may be prepared by the interviewer ahead of time, the answers are usually not. Both formats may benefit from being live.

Video Recording

As soon as an event is video-recorded, it has become a record of the past. As such it is free from the arrow of time. Much like film, most video recording is done for postproduction editing, where you have the opportunity to construct your own event time with its own objective- and subjective-time vectors. Through editing you can put the end of the actual event at the beginning of the screen event, and the middle at the end. You can change an especially slow portion of the actual event into a fast one and vice versa. As you can see, the video or film event is now largely medium-dependent.

Let's see how we use this freedom from the time arrow of the actual event by focusing on the uninterrupted recording of a live event and instant replays.

UNINTERRUPTED VIDEO RECORDING OF A LIVE EVENT

The uninterrupted video recording of a live event, called ***live-recording,*** is usually done for unedited playback at a later time. This technique is almost always used to have the program start at the same hour in different time zones. When done in television, the audience is sometimes told that it is a "live" telecast recorded for delayed playback. But then it isn't really a live telecast anymore because the major criterion—the simultaneity of actual and televised events—no longer exists. Does it matter? What if you don't know that it has been recorded and believe that it is, indeed, a live telecast? We address this tricky subject by looking at the relative magnitude of the subjective-time vector and the factor of aesthetic entropy.

Vector magnitude   If you are totally unaware that the screen event is a delayed version of a live telecast, your involvement may well be as intense as if you were watching a truly live broadcast. Still, because your aesthetic experience is based on a perceptual fallacy, it becomes rather precarious. You are fooled into a pseudo-experience of becoming, of changing with the event, of experiencing the living present when actually you are presented with a record of the past in which the outcome of the event is at this point immutably fixed. As soon as you become aware that the program is a recording, the subjective vector magnitude—your involvement—inevitably decreases. Even if you don't know the outcome and you are still very interested in the event, chances are you now distance yourself from it; you tend to change from a highly involved event participant to a less involved event viewer.

Your relative involvement in the recorded telecast is also greatly affected by knowing the outcome of the actual event while watching it on television. For example, if you heard on the radio the final score of a football game before watching the recorded telecast, you will probably react quite differently to the presentation than your friend, who does not know the outcome of the game. While he may get very excited about a last-second field goal attempt, you may get annoyed by all the media hoopla (close-ups and the announcer's screaming), knowing full well that the kick will fall short and the game will be lost. As you can see, the very same screen action can produce subjective-time vectors of entirely different magnitudes, depending on whether the viewer knows the outcome of the event. Once you know the outcome, you are hard-pressed to maintain interest during the slow periods of the game.

Aesthetic entropy   As soon as you have recorded the present, aesthetic entropy sets in. Even if the recording of the event does not change, it becomes subject to your attitude changes, depending on how far removed in time you are from the event. You will also experience a different degree of involvement if the context in which you review the recording changes. Usually, the subjective vector magnitude gradually decreases in intensity; you become less and less involved in the event. "Time heals" is a clichéd but appropriate interpretation of the entropic process of a particularly unpleasant or sad event.

In video and film, you can combat this energy loss by editing. Condensing an event into its highlights through editing is often a necessary reenergizing procedure when the video-recorded event is replayed at a later date. Because of this entropy factor, there is some justification to the "hot news" concept. With few exceptions news events are important only within their immediate time context. When the recorded news gets communicated as soon as possible after the actual event, the recorded event still lives off the energy of the original event. The longer you wait, however, the less relevant the recorded event becomes and the more rapidly the event energy dissipates.

Does this mean that every recorded video event or every film automatically becomes obsolete with time? What about "classic" movies and television shows? It seems that classic films or video programs—or any other pieces of high-quality art—resist aesthetic entropy because they are packed with so much aesthetic power and density that their entropic atrophy is extremely slow. They also carry universal messages (in both form and content) that are not easily rendered worthless by contextual changes dictated by history or personal attitudes. Thus they remain meaningful to us despite the passage of time.[26]

INSTANT REPLAYS

Instant replays are recordings of event highlights that are played back immediately after they occurred in the actual event. Although instant replays are informative, they nevertheless constitute an aesthetic discrepancy. Because most sports telecasts fulfill a looking-at function—that is, they try to reflect the actual event as much as possible—the rhythm of the screen event approximates that of the actual event. Instant replays, however, interrupt the flow of the actual event and create an event rhythm all their own. They can also prevent the viewer from witnessing a key play live because they occur at exactly the same time, so you must again revert to instant replay to show the missed action. If you are not careful, you may wind up showing more event time as a recording than live.

Despite the possible disruption of the actual event's rhythmic flow and an occasional blocking of key live events, instant replays have nevertheless become an important component in most sports coverage. First, they let the referees and the audience see the action again close-up and usually from a better angle than originally presented. Thus the instant replay can, paradoxically, influence the future. For example, an instant replay during a football game can well reveal a wrong call by the referee and determine who gets the ball or even who wins. Second, and more important, instant replays have coincidentally become a way of revealing the complexity of the moment, permitting a quick view of the immediate past and its consequences for the present. Instead of an interruption of the rhythm of the live game, instant replays have become one of its structural components.[27]

As a viewer you now have digital devices that allow you to perform your own instant replays by recording certain sections and viewing them while the event is under way. Such devices give flexibility in recalling some past portions of the televised event, but they cannot influence either the sequence or the time arrow of the event itself. Even with all the digital wizardry at your disposal, you cannot fast-forward during a live transmission.

Time in Edited Video and Film

The time vectors in edited video are largely independent of the actual event. Through editing you can change the time order of past, present, and future at will and construct your own time arrow. For example, a flashforward will interrupt the normal cause/effect development of a story and provide viewers with a brief glimpse of a future event. The instant replays have triggered a new use of the traditional flashback, which shows brief scenes of past events anytime in the story. A simple conversation between two friends or an interrogation of a suspect might trigger an instant recall, which is then illustrated by a brief, distorted scene, accompanied by various audio effects. These memory flashes have been refined from an occasional intensifier into an important dramaturgical plot accelerant.

Once the actual event is recorded, you can reverse the usual time vector of the screen event altogether and have the effect occur before the cause. For example, when you want to chart the growth of a plant, you will most likely follow the horizontal time vector and show its development from seed to fruit-bearing maturity to decay. After internalizing an event, however, you may no longer see it in quite this order. You might first think of the plant in full bloom, then how the fruit tasted, then how someone prepared the soil and planted the seedling. Obviously, the logical, unidirectional time vector no longer applies. What you are now doing is editing by emotion, that is, creating a high-magnitude vertical vector.[28]

Postproduction editing has drastically altered the classic dramaturgy and storytelling that moves chronologically from the introduction of characters and situation to a variety of crises to a final resolution. Instead of showing how our hero played with model cars as a child, tinkered with motorcycles as a teenager, became a successful racecar driver as a young man, but then was in a horrendous crash, you can alter the sequence of events through flashforwards and flashbacks. You could, for example, start with a hospital scene of the badly injured driver (flashforward, or foreshadowing), then present him on the winner's platform with flashbacks of how he started as a boy playing with cars. In this sequence you could freeze the moment of the crash and show simultaneous yet spatially separated reactions to the horrible accident.

Soap operas show several plots sequentially by interrupting each one from time to time to make room for the others. Some filmmakers manipulate the chronology of events so much that it is hard to make sense of what is going on. Some do this to make us feel the complexity of the moment, others to impress on us that we don't remember or anticipate events in a neat chronological order.

The subjective-time vector yields to equally high manipulation. Through editing you can take an originally high-energy and involving event and render it low-energy and neutral. Or you can take a low-energy event and make it highly dramatic and involving. We take up this subject again in our discussions on structuring the four-dimensional field in chapter 14.

S U M M A R Y

Change is the essence of the four-dimensional field. Structuring the four-dimensional field means achieving a spatial/temporal order.

As in all efficiency-oriented societies, time has attained a new significance. Efficiency is measured not only in what we do but by how fast we do it. The ultimate instrument with which to express now-consciousness is television. Television is unique in that it can capture, clarify, intensify, interpret, and distribute worldwide an event that is in the process of becoming.

We distinguish among three types of time: objective (clock) time, subjective (psychological) time, and biological time. Objective and subjective time are especially important for video and film.

Objective time is what the clock says; it can be measured quantitatively. Subjective time is felt duration; it is perceived and processed qualitatively. Objective time is a horizontal vector that indicates quantity. Subjective time is a vertical vector that indicates our relative involvement in an event and the relative absence of any objective time consciousness. The more involved we are in an event, the less aware we are of clock time passing, which we interpret in retrospect as having a short duration. If we are not involved in an event, we become aware of clock time and tend to interpret such awareness as a long event duration. When we think back and remember a time span in which we did a great number of things, we usually overestimate its actual duration.

Biological time is a subjective time that operates quantitatively. It operates like a not-too-accurate alarm clock, telling us when to do certain things.

In our experience time is unidirectional and irreversible. We cannot have the effect precede its cause. And though we can establish past and future events as "addresses" in the time continuum, we cannot do this with the present.

When we are conscious of the present, it has already occurred or has not yet happened. Aesthetically, we therefore consider the present as belonging to subjective rather than objective time. Subjective time is qualitative rather than quantitative. Thus our perception of the present depends on how aware we are of the moment and what we are doing. A high state of awareness allows us to perceive a close-up of time.

We can control subjective time by manipulating event density, event intensity, and experience intensity, regardless of whether the event is live or constructed from recorded event sections.

Live television means that the actual event and the televised event are happening simultaneously. The televised event is inevitably tied to the objective time vector of the actual event. The live telecast is event-dependent; that is, it is bound by the progression of the actual event. Like the actual event, the televised event has an open future. This means that its outcome is not predetermined by a script. Live transmissions of sporting events are good examples of such open-future characteristics.

As soon as an event is recorded, the screen event becomes medium-dependent. We can build an event and give it its own time, independent of the flow of the original event time. Two recording techniques are still bound to the original event: a live-recording, which is usually done for synchronizing telecasts in different time zones, and instant replays.

Once an event is recorded, it is subject to aesthetic entropy. Although instant replays interrupt the flow of the actual event time, they have become so common that they are now considered part of the very fabric of live sports transmissions.

When an event is recorded for postproduction editing, the screen event is totally independent of the objective- and subjective-time vectors of the original event. The horizontal time vector can be reversed or temporarily interrupted by instant-replay-like memory flashes. The screen event now becomes a new construct with its own objective and subjective times.

N O T E S

1. Lev Manovich, *The Language of New Media* (Cambridge, Mass.: MIT Press, 2002), pp. 162–67.

2. Robin Le Poidevin, "The Experience and Perception of Time," in *Stanford Encyclopedia of Philosophy,* ed. by Edward N. Zalta (August 2000; rev. October 2004); *http://plato.stanford.edu/entries/time-experience.* See also Remy Lestienne, *The Children of Time: Causality, Entropy, Becoming,* trans. by E. C. Neher (Urbana: University of Illinois Press, 1995).

3. László Moholy-Nagy, *Vision in Motion* (Chicago: Paul Theobald, 1947, 1965), p. 268.

4. Thomas Wolfe, *The Web and the Rock* (New York: Grosset and Dunlap, 1938), p. 626.

5. Paul A. Schilpp (ed.), "Carnap's Intellectual Biography," in *The Philosophy of Rudolf Carnap,* Library of Living Philosophers, vol. II (La Salle, Ill.: Open Court, 1963), pp. 37–38. See also John Boslough, "The Enigma of Time," *National Geographic* 177 (March 1990): 109–32.

6. J. T. Fraser, *Time, the Familiar Stranger* (Amherst: University of Massachusetts Press, 1987).

7. John Langone, *The Mystery of Time* (Washington, D.C.: National Geographic, 2000), p. 175. See also Paul Davies, *About Time: Einstein's Unfinished Revolution* (New York: Touchstone, 1996), pp. 21–24; and Boslough, "Enigma of Time," pp. 112–16 and 121–26. Still one of the best popular explanations of Einstein's relativity of time is the chapter on the Einstein revolution in Samuel A. Goudsmit and Robert Clairborne, *Time* (New York: Time-Life Books, 1961), pp. 144–65.

8. Philip Kipper, "Time Is of the Essence: An Investigation of Visual Events and the Experience of Duration." Paper presented at the Conference on Visual Communication, Alta, Utah, 1987.

9. Modern scholars reluctantly admit that measuring experienced duration may involve "some psychological process" that operates within some kind of time memory. See Le Poidevin, "Experience and Perception of Time."

10. Henri Bergson, *Time and Free Will,* trans. by F. L. Pogson (New York: Harper Torchbooks, 1960), pp. 197–98. The difference between quantitative and qualitative time is further discussed in Stephen C. Pepper, *World Hypotheses* (Berkeley: University of California Press, 1970), p. 242. See also Robert M. Pirsig, *Zen and the Art of Motorcycle Maintenance* (New York: William Morrow, 1974).

11. The term *zero time* for a high-magnitude subjective time vector was suggested by my colleague Philip Kipper, Broadcast and Electronic Communication Arts Department, San Francisco State University.

12. *Circadian* comes from the Latin *circa* ("about") and *dies* ("a day"), referring to the approximate day/night cycles of biological clocks.

13. Langone, *Mystery of Time,* pp. 219–26. See also David Park, *The Image of Eternity* (Amherst: University of Massachusetts Press, 1980), pp. 51–53. There is no reason, however, why the arrow of time could not go in the opposite direction. See Davies, *About Time,* pp. 197–232. Also, there are compelling arguments that suggest that time stands still but that it is we and our environment that undergo time-bound change. See Robin Le Poidevin, *The Images of Time* (New York: Oxford University Press, 2007).

14. Saint Augustinus, *The Confessions of St. Augustine,* book XI, sec. x–xxxi (Chicago: Henry Regnery, 1948), p. 196.

15. Saint Augustinus, *Confessions,* p. 196.

16. Le Poidevin, *Images of Time,* pp. 125–40.

17. The unconscious and conscious present are not to be confused with the preattentive and focused stages of visual processing. See Anne Treisman, "The Perception of Features and Objects," in Richard D. Wright (ed.), *Visual Attention* (New York: Oxford University Press, 1998), pp. 26–54.

18. Fritjof Capra, *The Tao of Physics* (Boulder, Colo.: Shambhala, 1975), pp. 185–87.

19. Jürgen Rausch, "Ökonomie unserer Zeit" (Economy of Our Time) in Hans Jürgen Schultz (ed.), *Was der Mensch braucht* (What a Human Being Needs) (Stuttgart: Kreuz Verlag, 1979), pp. 384–94. In the conclusion of his article on the philosophy of time, Rausch says: "It is the mystery of time that eternity can fit into it" (p. 394).

20. Aristotle. *Poetics. 39 b3,* trans. by Gerald Else (Ann Arbor: University of Michigan Press, 1970), p. 28.

21. Gotthold Ephraim Lessing, *Hamburgische Dramaturgie* (Hamburg Dramaturgy) (Hamburg: In Commission by J. H. Cramer, Bremen, 1767–1768). This is a collection of critical essays on a great number of plays performed during this period. Lessing was especially critical of the French formalists (such as Pierre Corneille), who were basing their rather rigid dramaturgy on Aristotle's *Poetics.* Long before the television series *24,* Corneille insisted, for example, that all dramatic events must occur within 24 hours. Lessing advocated a different, more open character-based approach to dramaturgy. In reverence to Aristotle's fame, Lessing claimed that the French dramatists of the neoclassic period probably misunderstood Aristotle in their interpretation of his dramatic rules. But the clear and straightforward style of Aristotle's *Poetics* leaves little room for such misinterpretations.

22. Often a television signal is sent up to and received from two satellite links, traveling a total of 89,200 miles. Even at the speed of light, such travel takes almost half a second (0.4795 second).

23. The device is a frame store synchronizer, which stores in digital form one complete video frame at a time before sending it on to the transmitter. The reason for this temporary storage is to synchronize its scanning cycle with other video sources that are not synchronized. If this synchronization is lost, you may see a picture of a live event temporarily freeze and then continue.

24. Manovich, *Language of New Media,* pp. 167–70.

25. My many attempts to develop a dramaturgy that allowed, at least partially, an open future, have failed. Even if the group of actors knew one another well and were quite successful on-stage, the simultaneous coordination of cameras and audio proved to be an almost insurmountable obstacle. The few times when actors and cameras were, by some miracle, synchronized, the resulting dialogue was unfortunately so banal that it inhibited, rather than facilitated, emotional involvement. Among other things, this proved to me that good dialogue must be carefully crafted and simply cannot be ad-libbed.

26. For a discussion of the seeming discrepancy between entropy in nature and negative entropy in art, see Rudolf Arnheim, *Entropy and Art* (Berkeley: University of California Press, 1971). For the power of universal themes, see Stuart W. Hyde, *Idea to Script: Storytelling for Today's Media* (Boston: Allyn and Bacon, 2003).

27. Philip Kipper calls multiple instant replays "a layering of experience leading to the next live moment rather than some kind of disrupting side trip." Unpublished review of Herbert Zettl, *Sight Sound Motion,* 3rd ed. (Belmont, Calif.: Wadsworth, 2003). See also Philip Turetzky, *Time* (London and New York: Routledge, 1998), pp. 165–68.

28. Walter Murch, *In the Blink of an Eye: A Perspective on Film Editing,* 2nd ed. (Beverly Hills: Silman-James Press, 2001), pp. 17–20.

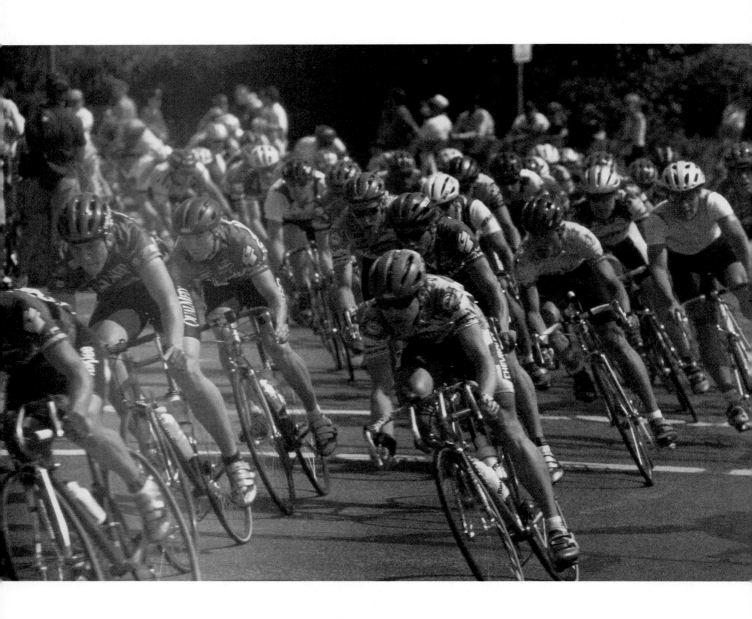

The Four-dimensional Field: Motion

THE PREVIOUS CHAPTER EXPLORES TIME AS AN IMPORTANT ELEMENT IN the four-dimensional field. This chapter takes a closer look at one of the most obvious manifestations of time: motion. It should come as no surprise that motion is an important factor in the art of the moving image of video and film. It is primarily the various aspects of motion that help us define the four-dimensional field in media aesthetics: perceived motion; film motion and its basic structural unit; video motion and its basic structural unit; aesthetic implications: the film look; large-screen digital cinema; motion frames of reference; perceived speed; slow and accelerated motion; and synthetic motion.

Perceived Motion

We ordinarily perceive motion only when something changes its position more or less continuously relative to a more stable environment. We notice a car moving when it gets closer to us or farther away, or a child running after a ball when she passes the swing and the slide on the playground. This holds true when we see the same scene on a movie or video screen although, in a strict sense, screen motion is illusory. The following discussion of the differences between film motion and video motion and the basic structural units of the two media is important even while digital cinema replaces photographic film as a medium. The difference in how the illusion of motion is created is of interest not just historically but also and especially from an aesthetic point of view. The efforts to get video to acquire the enigmatic look of film are just one example.

Film Motion and Its Basic Structural Unit

Much like strobe photography, film photography involves taking a great number of snapshots of a moving object. Each of the snapshots, or frames, shows the object at rest, so when you hold and enlarge a film frame—the basic *structural unit of film*—you cannot tell whether the object was stationary or in motion when the picture was taken. **SEE 13.1**

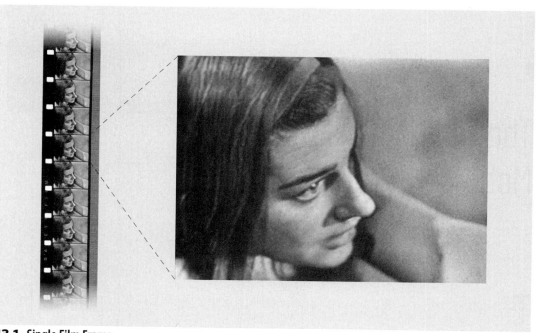

13.1 Single Film Frame

Much like a strobe light, film takes a number of snapshots of a moving object, but each frame shows the object at rest.

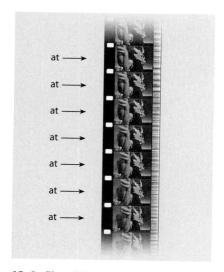

13.2 "At-at" Motion of Film

Each film frame shows a specific "at" position of the object motion.

Film motion is, therefore, an illusion. Film does not move, but it makes us see things move in our minds. The only real motion in film occurs when the projector pulls down frame after frame in front of the light source. During this motion the screen is blacked out, so we do not witness the pull-down of each frame. As soon as a film frame reaches the gate, it stops temporarily and the projector light shines through that frame to project it onto the screen. The projected image is always at rest. The important thing to remember is that the basic structural unit of film—the film frame—shows the object at rest regardless of whether the object was in motion.

Note that we are talking about the basic aesthetic *structure* of film, not how we perceive film motion. Assuming the standard film projection rate of 24 frames per second (fps), we could conceivably use 24 slide projectors and fire them one at a time within one second. The net effect would be exactly the same as that of the "moving" film. Thus, you can think of film as a great number of slides glued together for easier projection. Film motion is created by showing a number of static positions in sequence, each of which is slightly advanced from the previous position. Why we see this position change as movement is based on the apparent motion, or stroboscopic, illusion.[1] Every film frame shows a unique "at" position in the time continuum, a snapshot of part of the motion. In effect, film samples various "at" positions of the motion. **SEE 13.2** But each sampled "at" position shows the object at rest.[2]

Because motion in film is broken down into a series of small, discontinuous, static increments (frames), we can leave them in their original sequence or we can change them around. We can add some, cut some out, or insert some parts from an entirely different event. As you can see, the very nature of the basic structural unit of film courts the building of a screen event—editing.[3]

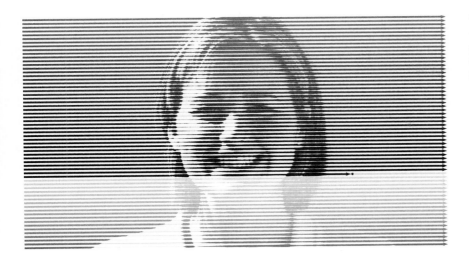

13.3 Process Image of Video
The basic unit of video—the video frame—is not a snapshot of an "at" position in the time continuum like a film frame; it is an image that is continuously renewing itself.

Video Motion and Its Basic Structural Unit

Contrary to the basic unit of film—the frame you can hold, enlarge, reduce, project, and store in a box very much like a slide—the basic **structural unit of video** is always in motion. The video screen consists of millions of pixels (picture elements) that are arranged in horizontal and vertical lines. When activated by a fluctuating electric charge, a certain number of mosaic-like dots of the video screen light up only temporarily in one of the three primary colors (red, green, or blue). The video image is never complete. While some of the screen dots light up, others are already off again.[4] Unlike the frame of an optical film, which you can hold in your hands and examine, the video "frame" (a complete scanning cycle of all horizontal and vertical lines) can be produced only on a video screen. Contrary to the film frame, which is always in a state of being, the video image is always in a process of becoming. The structure of a video frame is a process image.[5] **SEE 13.3**

Aesthetic Implications: The Film Look

Although the stroboscopic effect enables us to perceive motion regardless of whether we are viewing a series of static film frames or the evanescent dots of the video frame, there are some aesthetic implications that may, however subtly and subconsciously, influence how we perceive the difference between film and video.

THE FILM LOOK

Since the advent of digital cinema, which uses video for the entire production process of the screen event, the mysterious and somewhat nostalgic "film look" has become a serious and fervent topic of discussion among filmmakers and video people. Ardent defenders of traditional film insist that film has its own unique aesthetic quality that, according to them, video has yet to achieve. Video people who are engaged in digital moviemaking seem to agree. The producers and users of video equipment have been trying to emulate the film look through adjusting the video frame rate to that of film (24 fps) and with various postproduction software effects.

But what exactly is the film look? Some diehard video people contend that the film look is nothing but a combination of shortcomings of the film medium and that we had better get used to the superior image of high-definition video. Yet when trying to step up to moviemaking, they eagerly embrace a 24 fps frame rate and such crude computer effects as scratches, exaggerated film grain, and emulsion blur to make their videos look like traditional film.

The usual explanations of what the film look is all about are rather vague. They range from "film looks softer," "video has stark colors; colors are less crass on film," "film has more subtle brightness differences," and "film images look more polished" to "video is too sharp and clear" and "film images are less in-your-face."[6]

Although it would be easy to dismiss outright such largely unsubstantiated and intuitive arguments about the film look, in our quest to explore the creative potentials of the relatively new medium of digital cinema we need to take notice of such observations and see what differences, if any, there are between the appearance of film and that of video. Let's take up the above comments one by one.

Film looks softer   This "softer" look of film may be the direct result of the brief blackout periods that occur each time a new film frame is pulled up to the gate to be projected onto the screen. In fact, when you watch a 90-minute movie, you see 36 minutes of black screen.[7] Each time a new film frame is projected, it is cushioned by a brief period of black preceding and following it. Not so in video. The scanning of a complete frame is almost instantly followed by the scanning of the next frame, without any black cushion between them. Thus the change from frame to frame in video is simply a continuation of the scanning process.

Some manufacturers of video cameras claim that the film look in video is primarily the result of the variable frame rate that allows a video camera to switch from the 30 fps of standard video and 60 fps of HDTV to the 24 fps of film. Although it is important when transferring video to film, I doubt that a reduction of the frame rate to 24 fps would make video images noticeably softer. As a matter of fact, European video has always had a frame rate of 25 fps, and it still looks and feels more like the U.S. video than film. More likely, it is a slower shutter speed (below 1/60 second) that helps temper the starkness of the video image.

Some video people experiment with diffusion filters or even gauzelike material in front of the lens to achieve the desired overall softness of the video image. Others rely on postproduction software that introduces an almost imperceptible flicker into the video footage, which emulates the black periods between film frames. This flicker makes some sense because it affects the way we perceive the traditional film image.

Video has stark colors   One reason for this perception is the difference between subtractive and additive color mixing. As you recall from chapter 4, video mixes colors additively, by combining in various proportions the three light primaries of red, green, and blue (RGB). Film, on the other hand, mixes colors subtractively, by filtering out proportions of its subtractive "paint" primaries of cyan (greenish blue), magenta (bluish red), and yellow (see color plates 11 and 15).

Film *projects* colors; video *creates* a color mosaic. You probably notice that when you project video on a regular movie screen, the colors are less "in-your-face" than when you watch them on a video monitor. In video the colors are produced by lighting up the individual, discrete color pixels on the video display; each pixel retains, however temporarily, its assigned additive primary (RGB) and does not mix with the others. The colors of the optical film image are already mixed for each frame when projected onto the screen; in digital cinema projection, the video image still consists of the millions of RGB pixels that are projected onto the screen. Such color generation in video, which is much like that of pointillist painters, produces an especially vivid color palette.

To match the colors of film in digital cinema, you can control the brilliance of video colors by reducing to a certain degree their brightness and especially their saturation. You can also try to add a subtle tint to the video colors. This may, at least to some extent, produce a less conspicuous color palette without doing too much damage to the color fidelity. Also, the more pixels projected, the higher the definition but also the more quickly they mix optically when watching the digital cinema screen.

Film has more subtle brightness differences   This observation is still valid, even if the HDTV systems can technically match those of film. The emphasis here is on the subtle differences in the middle values of the grayscale (luminance scale). This means that the film image has a better overall exposure by limiting extreme highlights without detriment to the subtle middle grayscale steps and transparency in deep shadow areas. In perceptual terms film displays a more pleasing exposure than HDTV. You should realize, however, that much of the subtlety of the brightness steps in film, as well as the more muted color palette, can often be attributed to superior film lighting rather than its inherent number of subtle grayscale steps. This may explain why films, even when projected digitally in theaters, still exhibit the more subtle light and shadow gradations.

Film images look more polished   Again, the polished look of film may be a matter not so much of its inherent aesthetic qualities and potentials as of paying more attention to such production values as lighting, scenery, and set dressings. If you can devote as much attention to lighting, scenery, and camera handling in video production as you do in good films, a properly adjusted high-definition video camera—usually called a digital cinema camera—can produce images that are equal, if not superior, to film. In digital cinema such high production values are certainly not compromised by using an electronic rather than a traditional film camera.

Video is too sharp and clear   The crisp colors, progressive scanning, the high number of scanning lines (720 or 1,080 visible lines), and especially various contour enhancements—all contribute to the "sharp and clear" HDTV image. But the most noticeable factor of the sharp and clear video image is its seemingly great depth of field. Because the high-definition image of digital video is so sharp and clear, we tend to confuse the sharpness of the picture with a great depth of field. Everything along the z-axis appears in focus, even if the middleground and the background are actually slightly blurred. In fact, the depth of field in HDTV is actually quite limited. This combination of an inherently sharp picture and the limited depth of field makes it difficult to focus with a high-definition camera, especially one with a relatively small viewfinder. This is one of the reasons why a focus-assist mechanism has been developed for higher-end video cameras.

It seems ironic that once we have achieved high-resolution video images that rival or surpass those of film, we consider it an aesthetic disadvantage and immediately seek remedies to make the video images less "sharp and clear." A great depth of field—even if it is illusory—lacks aerial perspective. A shallower depth of field helps define the z-axis planes and shows an image that approximates more our normal visual experience; it is therefore often preferred by painters, photographers, filmmakers, and video production people. Fortunately, you can reduce the depth of field through a wider lens aperture, a longer-focal-length lens position (zooming in), moving the camera closer, or actual or electronic filters that soften the image.[8]

Film images are less in-your-face   This comment may be interpreted as being psychologically farther removed from the screen event when watching a film in a darkened movie theater than when somebody is talking to you almost face-to-face in your living room. In paraproxemic terms, film images seem more distant in relation to the viewer than are video images. Traditional motion pictures have a tendency toward external action and spectacle, even if the subject is an intimate and deeply personal one. Video, on the other hand, favors the small gesture rather than the grand act. Video shines with smaller-scale, more people-oriented shows, such as interviews.

This presence and vitality of the video image—this in-your-face quality—may be a function not just of program content but also of the ontological, structural makeup of the video frame. The film frame has a certain historic permanency, much like a painting or a photograph. Scanning, on the other hand, gives the video image an electronic immediacy, an aliveness, regardless of whether it is live or video recorded, analog or digital. An isomorphic relationship, a structural similarity, exists between the evanescence of the scanning process and the fleeting "now" of the present. This in-your-face immediacy can well be one of the assets rather than a detriment of digital cinema.

Large-screen Digital Cinema

Recall the discussion in chapter 6 of some of the effects of the large image size on the aesthetic energy of the screen event. Large-screen digital cinema presents an interesting media aesthetic problem inasmuch as it resembles the motion picture in size but video in basic image structure. What happens if the "small gesture" video events are projected on the large movie screen? Will they become external to the extent that the environment, such as streets, houses, or the furniture in an apartment, becomes as important a dramatic agent as the people operating within it? With this emphasis on environment, the outer action of movies may well influence the basic dramatic structure of traditional television plays.

The large-screen digital cinema projection, with its potential for spectacle, is a constant lure for the writer to create external, plot-oriented stories rather than the more difficult internal, character-motivated ones. After all, a good car chase sequence is more spectacular and easier to write than a high-intensity encounter of two people in crisis. Very much in the tradition of action films and Aristotle's dramaturgy, the characters' actions will be driven by outer circumstances—the environment in which the event takes place—rather than spring from inner conflicts. For example, in digital cinema we might be tempted to show a father mistreating his son after a prolonged visit to the neighborhood bar rather than have the son as an adult confess the abuse to his cell mate, as would be more appropriate for the small or midsized video screen. I think that digital cinema production will not be much different from traditional filmmaking except for some technical adjustments, such as making full use of the high mobility of the digital cinema camera and exploring its specific lighting requirements.

What might get lost in such a projection is television's intimacy—our considering television part of our routine home environment and the typically close personal space that exists between the television performer and the viewer. In the large-screen home theater context, we are more popcorn-eating spectators than involved event participants, regardless of the basic nature of the material presented.

Paradoxically, the very small mobile media display and especially the way we use it—by watching it mostly in public places while on the run—may not fare too well with slow, intimate, internal stories. Mobile media stories may require brief, high-energy scenes. In this context *high-energy* does not mean spectacular explosions or similar effects to keep the story moving. The mini-screen and the mini-sound of mobile media will certainly render even the most powerful movie effect harmless.

The typical on-the-go mobile video viewer, however, has neither the time nor the patience to wait for an internal conflict to arise either through gesture or dialogue. Does this mean that you cannot show intimate stories on the small mobile media display? Not at all. But you will have to develop the internal conflict—and with it the energy of the scene—through plot rather than character, by showing what the people do rather than what they feel. In this respect mobile media might benefit more from aligning itself with cinema than with standard television.

With its potential for showing live events, large-screen digital cinema is a bonanza for sports fans. The large screen, combined with surround sound, can accurately transmit the energy and the spectacle of a sporting event. When the event is transmitted live, we can additionally benefit from each moment's open future. The aliveness of the projected video image adds a presence to the event, rarely achieved by the traditional film medium. In this case, the "in-your-face" quality of video is definitely an asset.

In concert with the large-screen projection, the vitality and the presence of the video image are apt to make digital cinema a unique medium. Digital cinema can do justice to the *landscape* aspect of large-screen motion pictures as well as to the *inscape*—the internal intensity of human relationships.[9] The various aesthetic potentials of large-screen digital cinema and small-screen mobile media and their effective use provide ample opportunities for continued research in this area of media aesthetics.

Motion Frames of Reference

Whenever you perceive motion, you automatically establish a frame of reference by which you judge the direction of the vector and its relative speed. This frame of reference establishes a figure/ground relationship. As explained in chapter 7, the figure is less stable than the background. You normally perceive a moving object relative to its immediately more stable environment. What you do, in effect, is establish hierarchical relationships of dependence.[10]

In video and film, the edges of the screen are the most basic frame of reference. For example, if you see a man walking from screen-right to screen-left against a plain and perfectly smooth background, you perceive the man's movement by where he is relative to the screen borders. **SEE 13.4**

When the background is articulated, such as by a row of houses, the movement of the man is judged no longer by where he is in relation to the screen edges but by where he is relative to the houses. The houses are now the primary stationary reference for the man's motion. **SEE 13.5**

If we now see a fly buzzing around the man's head, we most likely

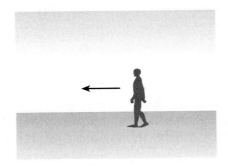

13.4 Screen Frame as Reference
In the absence of other spatial clues, the screen becomes the basic frame of reference for object motion. Thus we judge the man's movement by his position change relative to the frame.

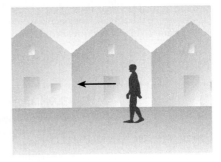

13.5 Houses as Frame of Reference
When looking at a man walking along the street, the houses and not the screen edges become the stable reference against which we judge his motion.

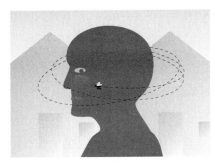

13.6 Person as Frame of Reference

When a fly buzzes around the same man's head, we judge the motion of the fly not against the houses but against the immediately more stable reference—the head.

judge the motion of the fly against the relatively more stable person, even if he is in motion, rather than against the houses. The man, and not the houses, has become the immediate frame of reference for the motion of the fly. **SEE 13.6**

MOTION PARADOX

If you stand still and watch something move, you see it change its location from a "before" to an "after" position relative to you. But if you move with the object at the same speed, you may not perceive any motion at all. For example, if you ride in an airplane, you are in motion relative to the more stable earth; but when wedged into your seat in the center section, you are at rest relative to the plane itself. Such a ***motion paradox*** occurs whenever an object is in motion and simultaneously also at rest. **SEE 13.7** When you walk toward the front of the plane, the motion relationships become more complex. You are moving relative to the people in their seats. You are also moving even faster than the plane relative to the earth as you walk toward the cockpit. **SEE 13.8**

Regardless of how fast a spaceship is traveling relative to the earth, its motion approaches zero relative to another spaceship during docking. **SEE 13.9** The same motion paradox occurs if the camera trucks with a moving object at an identical

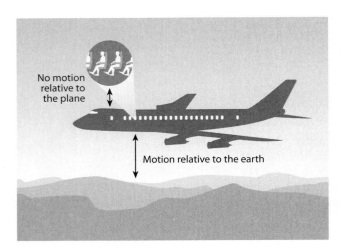

13.7 Motion Paradox: Object at Rest and in Motion

In reference to the airplane, the people seated inside are at rest. But in reference to the earth, the people are in motion.

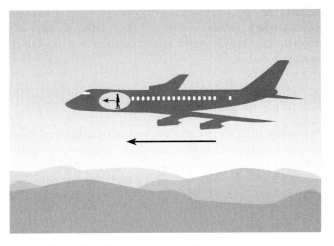

13.8 Motion Paradox: Relative Speed

When walking toward the front of the airplane, the passenger moves relative to the airplane and faster than the airplane relative to the earth.

13.9 Motion Paradox: Zero Speed

Even when moving at great speeds relative to the earth, these spaceships move very slowly; when docked, relative to each other, they don't move at all.

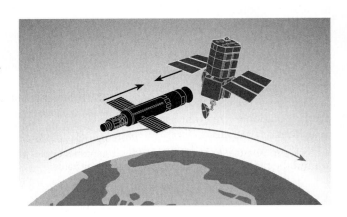

speed. Assuming that the background is unarticulated and that the camera is handled extremely smoothly, you will not notice any object movement on-screen. **SEE 13.10**

This, then, is the motion paradox: an object can be in motion and at rest at the same time. The *aesthetic motion paradox* is that an object can be in motion and perceived at rest, or at rest and perceived in motion.

INDUCED MOTION THROUGH FIGURE/GROUND REVERSAL

Sometimes the motion paradox can play tricks on you, especially when you are confused about which object is doing the moving. Most likely, you have experienced such motion relativity when sitting in a train alongside another train. Instead of seeing the other train as moving out slowly, you may perceive your train, which is still waiting for its departure, as rolling backward. The same figure/ground reversal can occur when you sit in your car next to a large bus, waiting for the stoplight to turn green. When the bus inches forward, trying to get a jump on you, you may feel as though your car is rolling backward even though your foot is on the brake.[11] **SEE 13.11**

Because our figure/ground frames of reference are so strong when perceiving motion, we do not give them up easily. For example, when you pan with a moving car so that the car remains in the center of the screen, the car is in a fixed position relative to the screen borders. What moves on the screen is the background, such as trees that line the road. Similarly, we can simulate object motion on the screen by having the object (figure) remain stationary and the background move (through a rear-screen projection or a chroma key). Because we know from experience that it is more likely for the car to move than the city street, we perceive the street as the more stable ground against which the less stable figure—the car—is moving. **SEE 13.12** In our perpetual quest for a stable environment, we simply cannot admit perceiving the street as doing the moving behind a stationary car.

There are, however, some instances in which we are not willing to let reason overrule perception. Let's revisit the racecar example from chapter 11. With a video camera mounted behind the driver during a race, you don't perceive the car as doing the moving but rather the racetrack. Why? Isn't the racetrack the more stable ground and the car the less stable figure? Yes. This is a perfect example of the motion paradox. Even if the car is traveling at 200-plus miles per hour relative to the racetrack, it is not moving at all relative to the screen borders. All you see is the driver's head bobbing and his arms handling the steering wheel and the gearshift. Because the camera is bolted to the car and immobile in relation to it, its screen image remains equally immobile relative to the screen borders. The relatively immobile image of the dashboard and the windshield, and the driver's head and his hands on the steering wheel, now

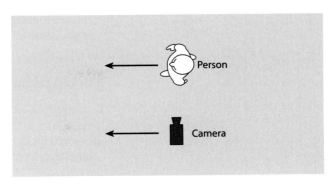

13.10 Motion Paradox: Perceived Zero Speed
When the camera travels at the same speed as the object, we cannot detect object motion in an unarticulated space.

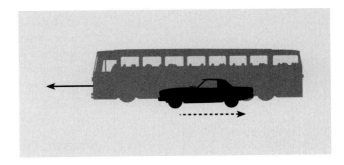

13.11 Perceived Motion Through Figure/Ground Reversal
When both a car and a bus are temporarily stationary and then the bus begins to inch forward, the car's driver may think that the car is rolling backward.

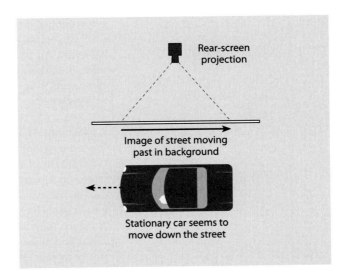

13.12 Induced Figure/Ground Motion Reversal
If you show a car stationary in front of a rear-screen projection or a blue screen (for chroma keying) that displays a moving street, viewers perceive the car (figure) as doing the moving against the seemingly more stable ground (the street) even if they know about the figure/ground reversal.

becomes the stable reference against which you perceive movement, in this case that of the racetrack rushing by.

Perceived Speed

Perceived speed refers to how fast or slowly we sense something moving on-screen. It includes object speed (how fast the object was actually traveling when recorded), the focal length of the lens (a specific zoom lens position), and blocking (the camera's point of view relative to the moving object).

OBJECT SPEED

In an actual environment, we have a built-in sense of what is fast or slow. For example, when standing on a downtown street corner, we can judge quite well whether some people move too slowly across an intersection or if a motorcycle races too fast through a narrow alley. This built-in sense for speed no longer applies when watching screen motion, however. Regardless of the actual speed of an object, we can make the people in the intersection appear to proceed at normal speed and have the motorcycle seem to move cautiously through the alley. In fact, screen motion is almost always manipulated, that is, purposely distorted through lens choice and camera point of view.

LENS CHOICE AND BLOCKING

The perceived screen motion is greatly dependent on the focal length of the lens and where you place the camera in relation to the event.

Lateral motion: long shots and close-ups   Assume, for example, that you video-record your friend riding his new racing bike. You set up your camera on the sidewalk and have him ride past it at various speeds. If you zoom out to a long shot, you will have little trouble following his lateral travel, even if he moves pretty fast. Your visible x-axis is wide enough to see his movement across the screen without his becoming a mere blur. **SEE 13.13**

If you now zoom in to a tighter shot, the same bicycle speed will look lightning fast. All you will probably see is a blur. Because the close-up of the bicycle takes up almost half or more of the visible x-axis, the cyclist seems to fly across the screen. This is why, as a director, you must warn the talent to slow down their actions whenever you are on a close-up. **SEE 13.14**

Z-axis motion and object size   The perceived speed with which an object moves toward or away from the camera along the z-axis is greatly determined by the focal length of the zoom lens position. Recall from chapter 9 that wide-angle (short-focal-length) lenses and narrow-angle (long-focal-length) lenses distort the relative distance of objects to the camera and to one another. A wide-angle lens extends the z-axis and makes objects seem farther apart than they really are. A narrow-angle lens does the opposite: it compresses the apparent length of the z-axis and makes objects seem closer together than they really are. The reason for this perceptual distortion is that the wide-angle lens makes an object look quite large when it is close to the camera but progressively smaller as soon as it is only a short distance away.

Because we are hardwired to perceive a small image of a known object as being farther away than when it has a larger image size, we interpret various shifts in object size not as shrinking or growing but as z-axis motion. If the object does

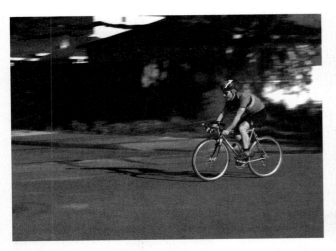

13.13 Long Shot of Lateral Motion
We can frame lateral motion on a small screen so long as the moving object is shown in a long shot.

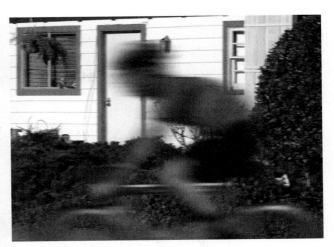

13.14 Close-up of Lateral Motion
On the small screen, a close-up makes fast lateral motion difficult to frame.

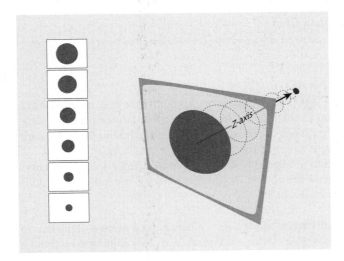

13.15 Induced Z-axis Motion
If these circles were recorded and shown in sequence, we would perceive them not as getting smaller but as a single circle moving away from us along the z-axis. If the recording were shown in reverse, the circle would seem to be moving toward us.

not change very much in image size during its travel along the z-axis, we feel that it is not moving very fast. You can easily re-create such an effect by cutting out a number of cardboard discs that differ in size. When video-recording the discs individually and then playing them back in sequence, the discs that get progressively smaller will not be perceived as shrinking but as receding; when they get progressively larger, they will appear to be moving toward the screen. The ones that differ little in size will seem to move hardly at all. **SEE 13.15** All optical and digital zooms, as well as the z-axis motion in cartoons, are based on this very principle.

Perceived object speed: wide-angle lens   Similarly, a wide-angle lens exaggerates the perceived z-axis speed with which an object appears to move toward or away from the camera (or the camera toward or away from the object). Let's have somebody walk toward the camera. When at the far end of the z-axis, the image of the woman seems to change relatively little. But as soon as she moves closer, her image gets rapidly larger. When close to the camera, the changes of image size

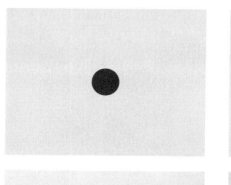
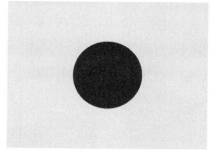
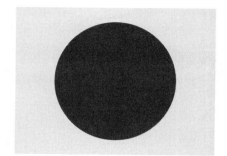
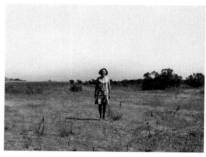
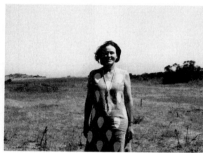
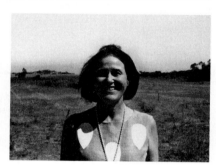

13.16 Z-axis Motion Vector: Wide-angle Lens

When shot with a wide-angle lens, the image size of the woman walking toward the camera along the z-axis changes considerably. We interpret this change as relatively fast movement.

are even more extreme. **SEE 13.16** We interpret this rapid change in image size as a high-magnitude motion vector—her moving rapidly toward the camera. The same process occurs in reverse when she moves away from the camera: the wide-angle lens shows her moving at a rapid pace.

A similar acceleration of perceived speed occurs during a dolly, except now the perspective change of the objects the camera passes is the indicator of dolly camera speed (see figure 14.11).

Perceived object speed: narrow-angle lens　When using a narrow-angle lens to cover the woman's z-axis walk, her image size changes only slightly even though she is covering the same distance at the same speed. We interpret this small change in image size as slow z-axis speed. The z-axis motion vector now has a relatively low magnitude. **SEE 13.17**

When in a very long-focal-length position, the zoom lens can virtually eliminate the feeling of movement along the z-axis. Although structurally different from a slow-motion effect (discussed later in this chapter), it nevertheless has a similar aesthetic result. For example, if you were to place a camera at the far end of the track opposite the starting blocks of a 100-meter sprint, an extremely long-focal-length lens would practically eliminate the z-axis motion of even a world-class runner. You would get an aesthetic incongruity: although you would see the runner's body in full-speed motion, his z-axis progress would appear in slow motion. You have probably seen this lens effect in movies that show someone trying desperately to avert a disaster but despite all efforts moving too slowly to prevent it.

Looking down on, and up at, the moving object　Recall from chapter 11 that moving objects, such as cars or trucks, look more dynamic when photographed from below than from above (see figures 11.18 and 11.19). If you want to make a car appear to move relatively slowly along a country road when it is actually travel-

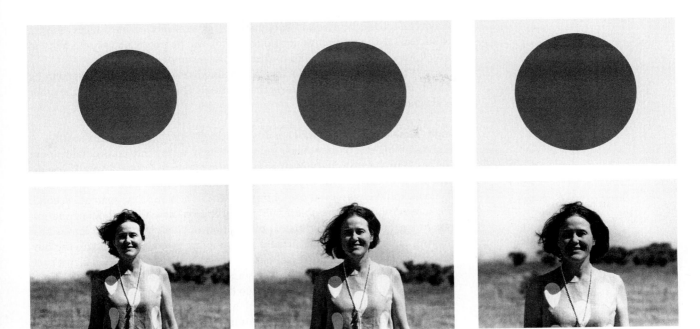

13.17 Z-axis Motion Vector: Narrow-angle Lens
When shot with a narrow-angle lens, the woman's image moving along the z-axis does not change very much in size even though she is covering the same distance at the same speed as in figure 13.16. We perceive this similarity of image size as relatively slow movement.

ing quite fast, shoot from way above eye level and zoom out. The effect is similar to looking at traffic from an airplane that is approaching the runway. When the plane is fairly high, the traffic on the freeway below seems to crawl, regardless of whether the cars are moving at 55 or 95 miles per hour.

To accelerate the perceived object speed, get closer and, if possible, have the camera look up at the moving object.

Slow and Accelerated Motion

Slow and accelerated motion are effective devices for structuring objective and subjective time. Slow motion can give us a "close-up in time," prolonging duration.[12] Accelerated motion can rush us through time and speed up the present. Contrary to slow motion, which may instill in us a feeling of awe, accelerated motion is apt to produce a comic effect by hurling us, roller coaster–like, through the event. Even when used in the context of advancing the story in a documentary, we have a hard time not considering it an amusing rather than a timesaving technique.

Slow and accelerated motions are not simply perceptual manipulations of actual movement through various lenses and camera positions but media-enhanced velocities.[13] They are created in the film or video camera, in the video playback phase, or entirely synthetically through computer animation.

SLOW MOTION

We say an event is in *slow motion* when it appears to be moving considerably more slowly on-screen than it would normally while being photographed. But an object in slow motion does not simply move more slowly than usual; it seems to move through a denser medium than air, which appears to cushion the effect of gravity and make the motion "woolly and soft."[14] Slow motion introduces a feeling of surreality. The motion vector no longer obeys the physical laws of gravity to which we are accustomed, and its direction seems more erratic.

What are the principal factors that distinguish slow motion from something simply moving a little more slowly than normal? One is frame density; the other is absence of gravity.

High frame density   *Frame density* refers to the sampling rate of a motion. A high sampling rate of the actual motion divides an action into considerably more frames than the customary 24 to 30 fps of film and video, respectively. If you divide the shot of a moving object into 24 individual frames during one second of its travel and then project those 24 frames within the same time span of a second, the screen motion of the object will closely approximate the real object motion (assuming that you do not distort the motion optically or through lenses or a moving camera). But if you increase the sampling rate by speeding up the film while photographing the moving object—let's say to 48 fps—and then play it back at the customary 24 fps (or 30 fps for standard television), the object appears to move much more slowly; it now takes up twice as many frames, or twice as long, to get from A to B. **SEE 13.18**

The more frames, or "at" positions in the sampling, you use for the breakdown of a moving object, the smaller the progression of the object's location from frame to frame. And the more minute the object's progression from frame to frame, the slower the object's perceived on-screen motion. In effect, slow motion is induced by a higher frame density. **SEE 13.19**

Freeze-frame   A freeze-frame shows arrested motion, not a picture of no motion. It picks a specific "at" position and repeats it for the duration of the freeze. You can think of a freeze-frame as the ultimate frame density, regardless of whether you use film or video.

Film slow motion   Slow motion in optical film is straightforward: the faster the film runs through the camera, the more frames of the photographed object are exposed per second, the higher the sampling rate, and the slower the motion during the playback standard of 24 fps.

Video slow motion   Slow motion in video is a bit more complicated. It can be induced in two ways: in the playback or in the capture phase.

The traditional way of achieving slow motion in video is in the playback phase. If you slow the speed of the playback recorder, the resulting display of motion slows down. The jogging control on a video recorder, which allows you to advance the recording frame-by-frame, produces such a type of slow motion. In normal slow-motion playback, some of the frames are scanned several times during playback, thus increasing the frame density. There are also software programs that add a number of frames between the sample's "at" positions of the actual motion. The slow motion you see during instant replays in sports is generated by digital systems that make the slow-speed playback relatively smooth.

If you look closely at some video slow motion, however, you may discover that it is not quite as smooth as in film. Unless you use a computer that generates more "at" positions among the original frames, the slow playback of actual motion does not increase the frame density; it simply takes more time and allows you to scrutinize each "at" position. Playback-induced slow motion seems to lack the "woolly" quality of film, which is why some high-end video cameras used for digital cinema have a variable frame rate that can produce slow-motion effects in

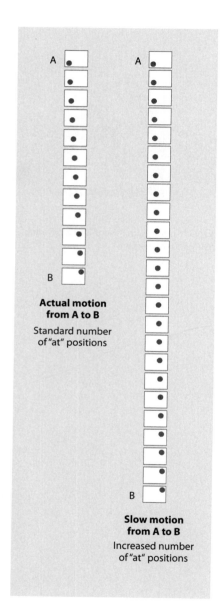

A

B

**Actual motion
from A to B**

Standard number
of "at" positions

A

B

**Slow motion
from A to B**

Increased number
of "at" positions

13.18 Slow Motion

To show an object moving from A to B in slow motion, you must increase the number of "at" positions during the actual filming or video recording. The playback of the increased number of frames takes longer. In video you can also slow down the playback.

the camera rather than during playback. Similar to film, this feature allows you to capture video at the film standard of 24 fps, at a much higher frame rate for slow-motion effects, and at a much lower one for accelerated motion.

Aesthetic effects of slow motion   The most obvious perceptual effect of slow motion is that it allows us to see better. In sports slow-motion replays give the audience and the officials repeated and detailed looks at particular plays. Such slow-motion replays have frequently determined who wins or loses. They have also given scientists an opportunity to observe processes that heretofore were beyond their perception.

Yet one of the most compelling aesthetic effects of slow motion is that it seems to free an object from the force of gravity. Like astronauts in outer space, slow-motion objects appear weightless, and their direction seems unpredictable. A good example of the directional uncertainty of the slow-motion vector is when you watch a slow-motion replay of a fumble during a football game: the ball rolls and bounces agonizingly slowly and without much apparent sense of direction, with the player always just a breath way. This frame-dense atmosphere lets you see, and especially feel, why the player trying to recover the ball has little chance of success. Because the forces of gravity do not seem to operate in slow motion, as viewers we would not be too shocked or even too surprised if, after a bad pass, the ball suddenly floated right back into the quarterback's hands.[15] This absence of gravity can also imply superpowers in people or machines. When seen in slow motion, the hero's jump to the roof of a tall building or his lifting a 3-ton truck isn't too surprising.

Depending on the event context, you may perceive slow motion in various and sometimes contradictory ways. Most often slow motion is used to intensify the agony of getting somewhere. For example, if you try to intensify the last seconds of two people running toward each other for a long-awaited embrace, slow motion can prolong their actual meeting and intensify their anticipation. But you can also use slow motion to signal increased speed. Switching to slow motion during a downhill ski race does not indicate that the champion skier has slowed down but rather exhibits her skill and intensifies her speed.

Slow motion is also used to simulate the moment of total awareness some people seem to experience a split-second before an accident or similar disaster. For example, you can show a driver losing control of a car that is traveling at a high rate of speed. Then, just before the crash, a shift to slow motion will show not only the driver's futile efforts to regain control but also the timelessness of such a moment and the subjective presence of horror.

When used in news events, slow motion can introduce a feeling of menace. To use it to show someone being led into a courtroom implies that the person is guilty. A harmless grin can morph into an eerie grimace.

ACCELERATED MOTION

Like slow motion, *accelerated motion* has its own aesthetic: it shows the object not merely faster than normal but also more erratic, more jumpy. The comic energy of many cartoons and silent movies is based on accelerated motion. For example, accelerated motion can turn a person's normal walk into a jerky, frenzied scurry in which the person seems driven along the street by an unseen force and pulled around the corners as if by a giant rubber band. When shown in accelerated motion, objects sometimes seem self-propelled, shooting unpredictably through the low-density atmosphere that offers little if any resistance.

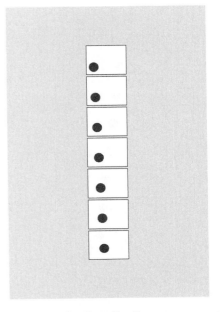

13.19 Higher Sampling Rate: Slower Object Motion

If the "at-at" positions of a moving object differ only a small degree from frame to frame, viewers see the object as moving relatively slowly. The sampling rate is high.

For some reason accelerated motion seems to trigger laughter more often than awe. Perhaps it seems so comic because, contrary to moving slowly, it is far beyond our actual experience.

Low frame density   Like slow motion, accelerated motion is less a matter of relative speed than a function of frame density. In accelerated motion the sampling rate is low; that is, the original event is divided into relatively few "at" positions, each differing considerably from the other.   **SEE 13.20** We sample fewer steps in accelerated motion than in the normal recording of the actual event.

Accelerated motion can be used to show extremely slow processes in a reasonable amount of playback time. Let's assume that you want to show the unfolding of a rose, which takes about 24 hours. To show the process in its normal motion, you would need to run a camera for 24 hours. But you can also decide to sample the total process and have a standard video or film camera take one frame every 5 minutes, leaving out all the intermediate steps. Thus in a 24-hour period, you would end up with 288 frames that show the unfolding of the rose from beginning to end. When played back at regular video speed of 30 fps, the total unfolding process would take only 9.6 seconds. With the 24 fps of the film playback, you would get a 12-second experience of seeing a rose unfold. In this case, the sampling rate was low; that is, relatively few "at" positions of the total process were picked for playback.

In video, accelerated motion is usually generated by a faster-than-normal playback speed or through digital manipulation. Through a fast-forward speed, the action seems propelled by some internal force over which the people on-screen have no control whatsoever and which acts on objects in unpredictable ways. Because some video cameras can lower the frame rate to as much as 4 fps, they can be used to generate accelerated motion that is similar to that of film.

Aesthetic effects of accelerated motion   You can use accelerated motion not only for comic but also for dramatic effects. One of the most striking examples of the dramatic use of low-density accelerated motion appears in Sergei Eisenstein's "Odessa Step Sequence" from his film *Battleship Potemkin*.[16] In a brief scene, he shows the death of a woman fatally shot by advancing soldiers. He intensifies her death by eliminating all nonessential frames from her fall, causing the woman not only an external but also an internal collapse. When she jerks to the ground in this low-density atmosphere, we have no doubt that she has met death.

Velocity change   An effective intensification device is to change abruptly the velocity of an object. For example, you can emphasize the power and the agility of a high-performance sports car by showing it first traveling at normal speed, then having it suddenly lurch forward, then braking for a slow-motion effect, then lurching forward again and skidding to a stop. Such extreme velocity changes intensify the raw power of the car more dramatically than if it were simply accelerating steadily during its travel. This effect is heightened further by appropriate acceleration and deceleration sounds. Aesthetically, we perceive these sudden shifts in velocity as rhythmic jump cuts, very much like a visual jump cut in which an object is jerked from one screen position to another.

Recall the use of accelerated motion as a timesaving device in documentaries to bridge less pivotal events, such as people moving into a courtroom, by simply speeding up the action. You have to be careful using this velocity effect, however. Because of our tendency to perceive accelerated motion as funny, such timesaving bridges may well undermine the seriousness of the documentary.[17]

13.20 Lower Sampling Rate: Faster Object Motion

In accelerated motion the number of "at" positions is lower than that of normal motion. The object seems to leap from one "at" position to the next as though traveling through a thinner atmosphere. The sampling rate is low.

Synthetic Motion

Screen motion, including slow and accelerated motion, can be synthetically generated. In this case, the number of frames and the relative position change from frame to frame are entirely synthetic. In traditional film animation, this process was done by drawing a number of "frames," called cels, each showing the figures and/or the background in a slightly advanced position from the previous one. To increase the frame density for slower motion, a great number of these cels had to be painted. For accelerated motion the number of cels could be considerably reduced. This is one reason for the rapid motion of cartoon characters. Eventually, this exaggerated speed became one of the aesthetic trademarks of cartoons.

When trying to emulate real-life motion through less than high-end computer animation, however, synthetic motion seems somewhat forced and oddly lacking the smoothness and the complexities of real motion. This is not unlike the depersonalized, monotone voices of the first computer-generated speech attempts. But this stiffness of simulated motion can become an asset in slow and accelerated motion, mainly because it accentuates the artificiality, if not the surreality, of such movement.

S U M M A R Y

We perceive motion when something changes position relative to a more stable environment.

The basic structure of a traditional optical film frame is a complete picture that is at rest. When 24 frames that show an object in slightly different positions are shown within a single second, we perceive the object as moving because of the apparent motion, or stroboscopic, illusion.

Video motion also relies on the apparent motion phenomenon, but the structure of each frame is not a picture at rest but an image in constant flux. The pixels on the video screen, which are activated by an electric charge, light up and decay during the scan. The structure of the video frame is a process image.

Because digital cinema uses video cameras for the capture of images, the debate of the traditional film look has become prominent. The film look is attributed to several factors: a frame rate of 24 frames per second (fps) rather than the 30 fps of standard video and the 60 fps of some high-definition systems; a softer image than that of video; softer colors; a wider and more subtle grayscale range; better lighting; and a less "in-your-face" presence. Attempts are made to have the video image attain the film look, especially when video is used for cinematic productions.

Large-screen video may lose the intimacy of television but gain the power of large-screen projection. Digital cinema may be able to do justice to the landscape character of film as well as the inscape character and presence of video.

When perceiving motion we automatically establish a frame of reference: a more stable background against which the less stable figure is moving. This figure/ground relationship is hierarchical.

The motion paradox is that an object can be in motion and at rest at the same time. In a figure/ground reversal, the background moves and the object remains stationary in the frame. If this is done properly, the viewer still perceives the object as moving and not the ground.

Perceived speed refers to how fast we perceive an object to move on-screen. We can influence perceived speed through actual speed changes, by blocking the moving object or person along the x-axis or the z-axis, by showing the object from far away or close-up, and by using various focal lengths of lenses to cover z-axis motion.

Slow and accelerated motion are medium-induced velocities. We achieve slow motion not by moving more slowly but by increasing frame density.

Accelerated motion is also a function of frame density. In this case, it is much less than that for showing normal motion.

There is a technical difference between film and video slow motion. Contrary to film, video can generate slow motion in the playback and the video capture phases. Screen motion can also be synthetically produced entirely by traditional or computer animation techniques.

NOTES

1. Although you may read that film motion is the result of persistence of vision, it is actually caused by the apparent motion, or stroboscopic, phenomenon. When two lights positioned side-by-side each flash at a regular interval, we don't see two lights going on and off at different times but perceive a single light as moving from one position on the x-axis to the other. This was first demonstrated by Sigmund Exner in 1875 and experimentally studied by the Gestalt psychologists in the 1900s. See Max Wertheimer, "Experimentelle Studien über das Sehen von Bewegung" (Experimental Studies About the Seeing of Motion), *Zeitschrift für Psychologie* 61 (1912): 161–265. See also Bruce E. Goldstein, *Sensation and Perception,* 8th ed. (Belmont, Calif.: Wadsworth, 2010), pp. 104, 180–81.

2. The "at-at" motion of film is closely related to the motion theories of the Greek philosopher Zeno of Elea (born ca. 485 B.C.) who, as a disciple of Parmenides, saw motion basically as an infinite number of frozen positions in space, each of which shows the object at rest. Applying rigorous logic, Zeno developed the by-now-famous paradoxes of motion. These paradoxes all try to prove that motion is impossible and only an illusion. Some of the most famous of Zeno's paradoxes of motion are well explained in Robert Audi (ed.), *The Cambridge Dictionary of Philosophy* (Cambridge: Cambridge University Press, 1995), pp. 865–66. The idea of sampling was suggested by my colleague Philip Kipper, Broadcast and Electronic Communication Arts Department, San Francisco State University.

3. Russian filmmaker and theorist Vsevolod Illarionovich Pudovkin (1893–1953) calls editing "the foundation of all film art." See V. I. Pudovkin, *Film Technique and Film Acting,* ed. and trans. by Ivor Montagu (New York: Grove Press, 1960), p. 23.

4. Contrary to Zeno, who saw motion as a series of discrete, static positions and time as a string of discontinuous immobile moments, philosopher Henri Bergson (1859–1941) contends that motion is a dynamic process, a duration with continuous flow of time, which he called *durée.* Bergson argues that motion is not the indivisible, infinite number of static positions as Zeno contends but rather an indivisible, continuous succession of states driven by a neutral (internal) flow. In effect Bergson replaces Zeno's "at-at" theory of motion with a "from-to" theory, which says that the motion of an object simply goes from one point to another at the end of the movement in one uninterrupted sweep. See Henri Bergson, *Creative Evolution,* trans. by Arthur Mitchell (New York: Modern Library, 1944), pp. 324–41.

5. An HDTV (high-definition television) image consists typically of 1,080 horizontal lines stacked vertically, each of which contains 1,920 pixels across. These lines are activated (scanned) one by one from top to bottom. Each complete scanning cycle produces a video frame. Whereas you can record such a frame for playback, its pixels still need to be activated through scanning and displayed on a video screen before you can see it.

6. These comments come from a discussion of the film look in one of my seminars on media aesthetics and experimental production.

7. Assuming a ⅓₀-second pull-down for each frame.

8. Herbert Zettl, *Television Production Handbook*, 10th ed. (Belmont, Calif.: Wadsworth, 2009), pp. 101–2.

9. The term *inscape* was coined by Gerard Manley Hopkins, a British poet (1844–1889).

10. The hierarchical relationships of dependence were researched by Karl Duncker, "Über induzierte Bewegung" (About Induced Movement), *Psychologische Forschung* 12 (1929): 180–259.

11. We are now dealing with induced motion, which means that we perceive something stationary as moving—the car representing the figure (even though something else is doing the moving) and the bus representing the ground.

12. See Pudovkin, *Film Technique,* pp. 174–82.

13. *Velocity* is used here to mean the measurement of an object's rate of change with respect to time and direction.

14. Rudolf Arnheim, *Art and Visual Perception: A Psychology of the Creative Eye, The New Version* (Berkeley: University of California Press, 1974), pp. 372–409.

15. German filmmaker Leni Riefenstahl used this technique decades ago to intensify her highly ideological view of the 1936 Olympic Games in Berlin during Hitler's regime. She showed in slow motion the perfect, birdlike dives of her chosen athletes and then had one go backward, from the water to the diving board. Because the divers seem to defy gravity, the casual observer is hardly aware of this directional switch.

16. See Sergei Eisenstein, *Film Form and The Film Sense*, ed. and trans. by Jay Leyda (New York: World, 1957), *Film Form,* pp. 55–57.

17. Revisit the discussion of this use of accelerated motion in documentaries in chapter 12.

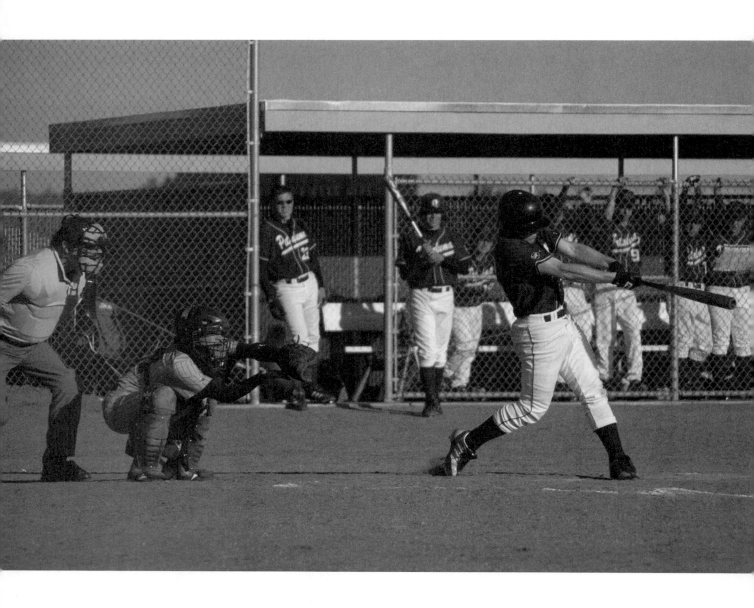

Structuring the Four-dimensional Field: Timing and Principal Motions

14

THE VARIOUS TIME THEORIES DISCUSSED IN CHAPTERS 12 AND 13 ARE not only important for explicating one of the major structural differences between video and optical film, but are also a significant factor in learning and understanding the processes of timing and structuring the three principal motions. This means that after all this time theory, it's time to apply some of it. This chapter explores types of objective time: timing; types of subjective time: pace and rhythm; plot time and character time; and principal motions and their functions.

Types of Objective Time: Timing

Timing usually means the control and the manipulation of objective time and the structuring of subjective time.

Recall from chapter 12 that controlling objective time comprises all clock time events of and within a show, such as how long a film or video production runs, how long the scenes are, and what time span the presentation covers. The structuring of subjective time involves influencing the duration the viewer feels. You will find that objective- and subjective-time manipulations overlap, such as when you shorten a scene here or lengthen one there to establish a specific overall pace and especially an appropriate event rhythm. Or you may have to juggle objective time to speed up the plot but lengthen subjective time to describe the character's confused state of mind. To facilitate timing and the analysis of the four-dimensional field for video and film, this chapter explains the various classifications of objective and subjective time.

To make timing useful in structuring the four-dimensional field, you need to consider six different types of objective time: clock time, running time, sequence time, scene time, shot time, and story time.

CLOCK TIME

Clock time determines the precise "at" position in the objective time continuum. Although all types of objective time are measured by the clock, clock time has come to mean a precise spot—a specific "at" position. Clock time indicates when an event happens. The motion picture you want to see begins at 7:00 p.m. and ends at 9:10 p.m. A program schedule lists the times when the various television programs start, implying when the preceding ones end. A television program log lists the clock times in a second-by-second breakdown. When somebody asks you what time it is, your answer refers to clock time. When the tower clock strikes midnight in a mystery movie, it also designates clock time. As you can see, clock time refers to an "at" position in the time continuum regardless of whether we deal with real time (what your watch says) or fictional time (the pretended clock time in a film or television show). **SEE 14.1**

14.1 Clock Time

Clock time signifies the "at" position of an event in the time continuum.

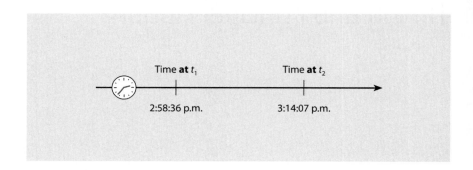

RUNNING TIME

Running time indicates the overall length of a program. For example, this film has a running time of 2 hours, 10 minutes, or this television commercial runs only 10 seconds. **SEE 14.2** Generally, television programs have a shorter running time than motion pictures. The major aesthetic reason for this difference is that watching television is often perceptually more demanding than watching a film, assuming that you are actually paying attention to what is going on rather than simply using the video as a companion during some other activity.

The relatively small screen of standard television plus the typically inductive visual approach require more attention from you and more psychological closure activity than the big-screen, deductively shot motion picture. Video, including television, has less narrative structure than film, which normally tells a story that has a beginning, a middle, and an end. Video is more fragmented; similar to the Internet, it offers a great amount of widely differing information that you can choose. The remote control that invites "channel surfing" only adds to this fragmentation.

Other, more practical reasons for shorter programs are that they allow a greater program variety during a broadcast day and, with it, more commercial advertising than with fewer but longer programs.

14.2 Running Time

Running time indicates a "from-to" position in the time continuum. It specifies the overall length of an event or event segment.

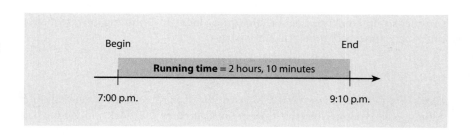

SEQUENCE TIME

A *sequence* is the sum of several scenes that compose an organic whole. Each sequence has a clearly identifiable beginning and end. In a film on the life of Pablo Picasso, for example, his Blue Period from 1901 to about 1904 and his involvement with cubism (1907 to 1921) would be separate sequences. When you start your stopwatch at the beginning of the sequence and stop it at the end, you have the *sequence time*. To keep you properly confused, some people call the clock time duration of a sequence the "running time" of a sequence. **SEE 14.3**

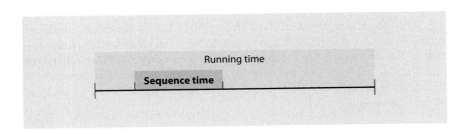

14.3 Sequence Time
Sequence time is a subdivision of running time. It shows the length of an event sequence, which consists of several scenes.

SCENE TIME

A *scene* is a clearly identifiable organic part of an event. It is usually defined by action that plays in a single location within a single story time span. For example, watching Picasso doing some sketches of a bullfight would constitute a scene. *Scene time* is the clock time duration of a scene. **SEE 14.4**

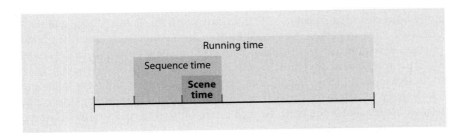

14.4 Scene Time
Scene time shows the length of a scene. It is a subdivision of sequence time.

SHOT TIME

A *shot* is the smallest convenient operational unit in video and film. It is the interval between two transitions, for example, from when you press the *record* button on a camcorder to when you press the *stop* button, or from cut to cut, or the footage between dissolves or other transitions. *Shot time* measures the actual clock time duration of a shot. **SEE 14.5**

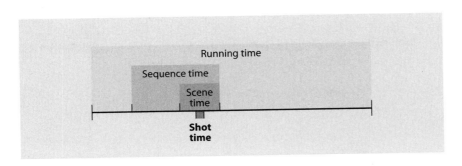

14.5 Shot Time
Shot time is the length of one shot. As a subdivision of scene time, shot time represents the shortest usable objective timing in a television program or a film.

Let's construct a shot sequence for a scene in which we observe Picasso starting a new painting. Note that the sequence is shot inductively for video, which means that we see basically a series of close-ups.

Shot 1: CU of Picasso's hands putting a new, blank canvas on the easel
(shot time: 3 seconds)

Shot 2: CU of his hands squeezing paint onto a palette *(shot time: 2 seconds)*

Shot 3: CU of Picasso's face *(shot time: 5 seconds)*

Shot 4: Tight O/S shot watching Picasso put the first lines on the virgin canvas
(shot time: 4 seconds)

As you can see, the brief scene (total scene time: 14 seconds) comprises a series of shots, each of which has its own time. Can you visualize this sequence—that is, feel its timing? Are the shots too long or too short? With some practice you will find that you can mentally time your shots, scenes, and sequences so accurately that you waste a minimum of your actual working time (clock time) in the editing suite.[1]

STORY TIME

Story time shows the objective time span of an event as depicted by the screen event. For example, if in our video recording on Picasso we depict his entire life from his birth to his death, the story time spans 92 years (from 1881 to 1973). With few exceptions story time and running time are independent of each other. You may, for example, choose to show the first 20 years in Picasso's life in the first 10 minutes of your documentary, but then spend 45 minutes on the three years of his Blue Period. **SEE 14.6**

But it is possible to synchronize running time and story time and depict a one-hour period in someone's life in exactly one hour. If you televise a nonfictional event live or make a live recording of such an event, story time (the period of event development) and running time (the time you devote to its coverage) are synchronous and, therefore, identical. For example, if you devote one hour to the live telecast of the Thanksgiving Day parade, the story time (the floats and bands that pass before the cameras during the hour) and the running time of the telecast are inevitably the same. In such a case, story time and running time are dependent on each other.[2]

14.6 Story Time

Story time is fictional or developmental time. It shows the period of the screen event. Story time usually moves from one calendar date to another or, less often, from one clock time in the story to another. Story time is largely independent of the running time. For example, it could take up to 10 minutes of running time for the 20 years of Picasso's youth, but the remaining 45 minutes of running time could be devoted to the three years of his Blue Period.

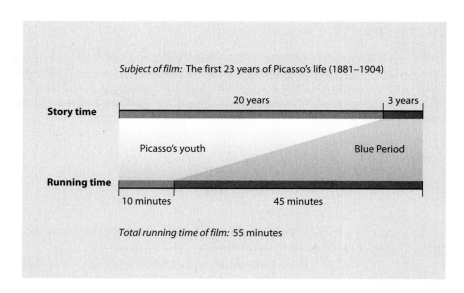

Subject of film: The first 23 years of Picasso's life (1881–1904)

Story time   20 years   3 years

Picasso's youth   Blue Period

Running time

10 minutes   45 minutes

Total running time of film: 55 minutes

Types of Subjective Time: Pace and Rhythm

As discussed in chapter 12, the term *subjective time* contains a paradox. We judge the felt duration of an event not by the clock but by how aware or unaware we are of the passage of clock time during and after the event. Instances do occur, however, in which the manipulation of subjective time requires an acute awareness of objective time. We explore this paradox later in the context of plot time and character time.

Considering the relativity of subjective time, can you ever use it as a reliable element in structuring the four-dimensional field? Yes, but not in a truly scientific way. Because it is more dependent on feeling than measurement, you need to approach the control of subjective time using intuition and educated guesses rather than logic.

Subjective time is usually categorized into pace, tempo, rate, and rhythm. Pace refers to the perceived speed of the overall event, tempo and rate refer to the perceived duration of the individual event sections, and rhythm refers to the flow within and among event segments. At first glance such a variety of subjective-time divisions seems advantageous for managing the perceived duration of a screen event. In practice, however, they prove more confusing and bothersome than helpful. We therefore limit the subjective-time categories here to pace and rhythm.

PACE

As stated, *pace* refers to the perceived speed of an event, that is, whether the event seems to drag or to move along quickly. Different event sections, such as scenes or sequences, can have their own paces, and so can an entire show. We usually consider a fast-paced scene to be one in which many things happen one after the other, with fast dialogue and rapid action. It is a high-density event. A slow-paced event moves less rapidly in story development, dialogue, and action.

You probably wonder at this point whether trimming a few seconds off a dance number in a music video, cutting some lines here and there to render the dialogue a little tighter, or replacing one of the slower songs with a more upbeat number is a manipulation of subjective time (the vertical time vector) or of objective time (the horizontal time vector). Although pace belongs to the subjective-time category because it is not measured by the clock, you can control it by manipulating the horizontal time vector (making an event shorter or longer or increasing its density).

Slow and accelerated motion are especially useful tools in governing pace. Slow motion, as a close-up in time, seems to interrupt pace temporarily rather than slow it down, very much like holding your breath. Accelerated motion does the opposite: it seems to lurch through time, giving pace a temporary push. Pace appears to be out of breath for a while. As you can see, pace does not remove us from an awareness of time. It simply regulates our perception of the flow of time—whether it feels fast or slow, regular or irregular.

RHYTHM

Rhythm refers to the flow within and among event segments (shots, scenes, and sequences) and to a recognizable time structure—a beat. It is determined by the pace of the individual segments and how they relate to one another. Although individual scenes might consist of fast-paced shots, this does not guarantee a smooth flow from one scene to the next.

Very much like the bars in musical notation, the overall rhythm is frequently determined more by the transitions between shots, scenes, and sequences; by the beat created by the shot or scene times; and by the beat of the music than it is by the pace of the individual segments. For example, straight cuts between the shots of a fast-paced car chase will probably produce a much more exciting and appropriate rhythm than would dissolves or fancy wipes. But when establishing a slow rhythm that matches the slow pace of a solemn event, such as a funeral, you may prefer dissolves over staccato-like cuts. Establishing a rhythm is high on the list of priorities for editors.[3] Even if the visual cuts do not establish an obvious rhythm, a rhythmic sound track will provide the necessary beat. The structural function of sound and music is explored in chapter 16.

As with the structuring of the color field, the control of pace and rhythm requires sensitivity and experience. The stopwatch alone should not be your sole guide in assessing pace. But even though we don't have scientifically precise criteria for evaluating pace and rhythm, their role in structuring the four-dimensional field is no less important than that of the clock.

Plot Time and Character Time

There are instances in which you need to juggle the interplay of objective and subjective times on various levels. The story may progress according to a clock time schedule (often marked with the clock times keyed over the action), but the characters may seem to be in a different time zone and marching to a different drummer. **Plot time** consists of the objective and subjective time concerning the story or sequence of events. **Character time,** on the other hand, consists of the objective- and subjective-time elements concerning the character's actions and feelings.[4] When done right the overall effect of a scene can be highly intensified. In music such rhythmic counterpoints happen all the time. You can probably recall a few songs that have a rapid and urgent underlying beat but whose melody seems to float above in a more lyrical way or the other way around. Chapter 16 discusses such tension-building structures.

The difference between plot time and character time is best explained with examples. Visualize this scene: The plot revolves around a young female nurse who is interning in a large-city hospital and her relationship with a male patient who is bedridden with an unbearably painful disease. He can barely move but is very much aware of what is going on around him. He observes the frenetic activity of the nurses and the doctors, who, from his perspective, all seem to move in accelerated motion. At times, when his pain medication kicks in, the accelerated motion changes to slow motion. The camera goes subjective, and we see a distorted close-up of the nurse's face talking to him. Her speech too changes to slow motion. Sometimes the subjective-camera POV (point of view) remains for quite some time on a static shot, such as the curtain that partially hides the neighbor's bed. When the nurse enters the frame and approaches the bed (we see her only from the waist down), she is out of focus and gets progressively more blurred the closer she comes to the patient. During the entire scene, the ambient sounds maintain the frantic pace of the emergency room next door.[5]

As you can see, the plot time (hospital activity) and the character time (man lying in bed) are quite different. The basic pace and rhythm of the hospital are fast and urgent, but the character's subjective time is excruciatingly slow. **SEE 14.7**

In another play the scene may show a simpler plot: three people—a man, a woman, and a four-year-old child—sitting at a table, having lunch. The plot progresses in real time. This means that there is no manipulation of the running time; the scene takes as long as their scripted conversation and actions. However, their not-so-friendly dialogue is intense and fast-paced. Its rhythm is broken from time to time by the child's dropping some food on the carpet, laughing, then climbing off the chair to play with it.

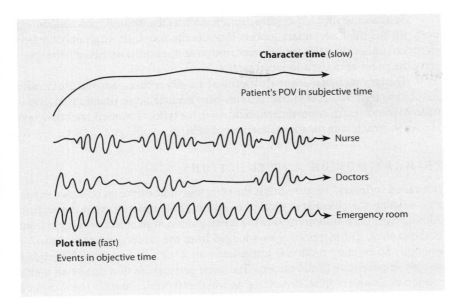

14.7 Fast Plot Time Versus Slow Character Time

The plot time (objective event) is quite fast and hectic and establishes the foundation beat. The subjective character time is seemingly independent and, in this case, much slower.

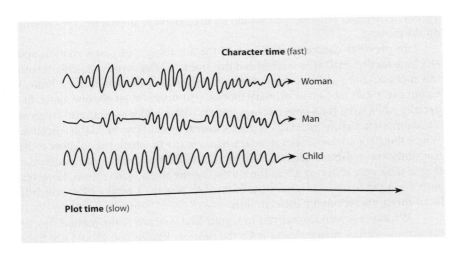

14.8 Slow Plot Time Versus Fast Character Time

The slow plot time (objective event) counterpoints the subjective character time, which is fast and hectic.

Look up for a moment and visualize the lunch scene and especially the dialogue. You cannot help but sense the great differences in pace of plot time and character time. In fact, you could probably intensify the scene by stretching the plot time relative to the staccato conversation. Staying on a close-up of the woman or the man for a relatively long period (and not cutting between their sentences) or watching the child trying to get the spilled food out of the carpet is but one possibility. **SEE 14.8**

Principal Motions and Their Functions

In video and film, we are confronted with many different movements. The performers move about, the camera dollies and trucks along with the action, and the viewpoints shift through cutting. Let's label and order these motions so that you can work with them more easily when structuring the four-dimensional field. There are three principal motions: primary motion, secondary motion, and tertiary motion.

Primary motion is event motion. It always occurs in front of the camera, such as the movements of performers, cars, or a cat escaping a dog.

Secondary motion is camera motion, such as the pan, tilt, pedestal, boom, dolly, truck, or arc. Secondary motion includes the zoom, although only the lens elements, rather than the camera itself, move; aesthetically, we nevertheless perceive the zoom as camera-induced motion.[6]

Tertiary motion is sequence motion. This is the movement and the rhythm induced by shot changes—by using a cut, dissolve, fade, wipe, or any other transition device to switch from shot to shot. All three types of motion are important factors in structuring the four-dimensional field.

PRIMARY MOTION AND FUNCTIONS

It is called "primary" because this is the principal indicator of an object's dynamics—whether the object is in motion or at rest. It is primarily event-dependent. Although primary motion refers to the actual motion of an object or event in front of the camera, its function is always judged from the camera's point of view. For example, no primary motion is intrinsically an x- or z-axis motion. It becomes so only in proximity to the camera. The same primary motion can be an x-axis motion or a z-axis motion, depending on whether it occurs laterally to the camera or toward and away from it. **SEE 14.9**

This motion is primary because it is, and should be, the prevalent motion in a scene. Whenever possible, you should let the person or object, not the camera, do the moving.

In previous chapters we discussed the advantages of z-axis motion and blocking for the small video screen and the dramatic effects you can achieve with this motion.[7] But z-axis blocking does not mean that you cannot use a limited amount of x-axis motion or primary motion that occurs at an oblique angle. Especially when used for a larger-screen format with a wider aspect ratio (such as a wide motion picture or HDTV screen), lateral motion can be highly effective. When shooting a wide-screen movie, a battle scene in which the soldiers come from either side of the screen and clash in the middle is probably more spectacular than if they were charging along the z-axis. On the small video screen, however, such a long shot remains largely ineffective. At best the laterally blocked battle lacks energy; more often it looks foolish.

Whatever screen format you use, your first concern is the natural flow of the action—before manipulating it for the camera. Ideally, you should not force the action to fit the camera position but instead place the camera so that it can capture the natural flow of "event traffic." Nevertheless, you need to adjust the event traffic to fit the camera, especially if you desire a specific intensification effect. For example, you may want to have the actor speed up or slow down for the camera. Close-ups always need a slowdown of the speed with which we normally do things. Trying to follow on a close-up somebody moving the cell phone from pocket to ear can be a frustrating experience unless the whole action is slowed down considerably. You will find that keeping up with lateral action is also difficult, especially on a fairly tight shot.[8]

Although all screen motion is ultimately medium-generated, we seem to sense a difference between event-generated primary motion, such as watching a dancer on-screen, and medium-generated primary motion, such as cartoons or even more-realistic digital video creations of object motion. Somehow, when filming or video-recording actual object motion, the lens-generated motion seems to belong intrinsically to the object. When creating object motion through animation or computer-generated sequences, the motion seems to belong more to the medium; that is, the motion seems to superimpose itself on the object rather than spring from it. Fortunately, overcoming such subtle disparities between lens- and computer-generated fluency have been largely eliminated by computer software.

Another, more obvious timing problem occurs when live action of people and things is coupled with the motion of models. Because models are usually built

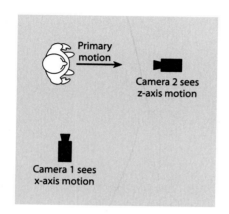

14.9 Primary Motion and Camera Proximity

Depending on the relative camera position, we can see the same primary motion as x-axis movement or z-axis movement.

on a small scale, their speed needs to be adjusted to that of the live action. To get some idea of the problem of matching speeds, hold a pencil vertically on your desk. Pretending that it is a huge redwood tree, let it crash onto the desk. The "crash" took only a fraction of a second; a real tree would certainly take a lot longer to fall. To make the fall of the tree model (the pencil) believable, you obviously need to slow it down. Exactly how much to slow it down requires the synchronization of model and perceived speeds.

SECONDARY MOTION AND FUNCTIONS

Secondary motion—the motion of the camera and the motion created by zooming—is medium-dependent. This means that camera motion is basically independent of event motion. Unfortunately, this independence of primary motion can seduce inexperienced camera operators into believing that it is the moving camera that is primary rather than the moving event. We are all too familiar with the wild and unmotivated camera moves and fast zooms that characterize almost every amateur video or film.

The problem with unmotivated secondary motion is that it draws attention to itself and away from the event. Instead of contributing to the clarification and the intensification of the event, it muddles its depiction. Nevertheless, secondary motion fulfills several important functions: to follow action, to reveal action, to reveal landscape, to relate events, and to induce action.

To follow action   When trying to follow a football player with the camera, you need to pan to keep him in the shot. When a performer stands up while the camera is on a fairly close shot of her, you need to tilt up to keep her in the frame. When you are on a CU of the host and you want to include the guest in a two-shot, you need to dolly or zoom out unless you cut to another shot. Following action is one of the most natural and least obtrusive uses of secondary motion.

To reveal action   A rather dramatic use of secondary motion is to reveal action gradually or to emphasize event detail. For example, you may create considerable tension in the viewer by not showing the accident scene right away but by first showing the horrified face of an onlooker and then, rather than cutting to it, doing a slow pan that traces her index vector to the wreck. Another example of creating tension through revealing action is to follow a skier hurtling down an icy slope (secondary motion to follow action) but then pan ahead to reveal the treacherous crevasse that lies in the skier's path (secondary motion to reveal an event). Will he be able to stop in time once he sees it? (No, but he managed to jump over it.) In this example you used secondary motion as a proven dramaturgical device: to let the audience in on what the hero has yet to discover.

To reveal landscape   A similar application of the revealing function is to show landscape in a dramatic way. For example, you can pan along stopped traffic to show just how long the line of waiting cars is, or tilt up along the awesome height of a skyscraper to discover smoke pouring out of one of the top-floor windows. Showing the line of cars or the high-rise in long shots would be much less dramatic. Sometimes it is more natural to follow some action and, in the process, reveal the desired environment. For example, to show the dilapidated houses and stores of a blighted street, you could pan with a cat prowling along the dirty sidewalk or with a child walking to school. One word of caution: such motivation for secondary motion can be clichéd or, worse, in bad taste. To use a homeless person pushing a loaded shopping cart as a motivating agent would certainly be borderline. On the other hand, having a bicycle messenger weave through the stopped traffic is a perfectly good way of using such an agent for motivating the camera to scan the traffic jam.

To relate events   Through secondary motion you can establish a connection between seemingly unrelated events or draw attention to a specific event detail. Depending on the event context, secondary motion can imply meaning. Let's take a courtroom scene, for example. First we see a close-up of the defendant (a man), who stares at something or someone. Rather than cut to the target of his index vector, the camera quickly pans to it: a woman in the jury box, who meets the defendant's glance ever so briefly, trying to look as inconspicuous as possible. Somehow, they know each other but don't want anyone else to know that. Nevertheless, the secondary motion that followed the man's index vector gave them away and revealed their connection to the viewers. Here the primary function of the secondary motion is not to reveal an event but rather to connect two events—the man and the woman. Such a connection makes the viewers feel good; they've been given a clue to this secret even though the judge, the lawyers, and all the other jurors are not yet aware of such a connection.

You may have noticed that the difference between revealing an event (following an index vector to the accident) and relating events (following the man's index vector to see the woman) is not determined by the pan itself but by the event context. A very fast pan (called a swishpan) from one event to the other, however, usually establishes a relationship between the two events, regardless of the event content. For example, a swishpan from a burning building to the street signs of the nearest intersection will tell viewers where the fire is. You can also use a swishpan to connect two events that are separated by time or location.

To induce action   Sometimes you may want to simulate object motion by moving the camera or zooming on a still picture. In this case, the secondary motion induces a motion vector. For example, by panning in a wavelike motion against the index vector of the picture of a ship, the ship seems to move relative to the screen. The problem with such induced motion is that both the figure (ship) and the ground (sea) move instead of only the figure. Hence, the viewer will usually remain aware of the moving camera and not accept the induced vector as primary motion.

Zooming   We classify zooming as secondary motion, although normally the camera remains stationary during the zoom. The reason for this classification is that, for the inattentive viewer, a zoom looks similar to a dolly. As a matter of fact, there is a tendency even among experienced production people to substitute a zoom for a dolly. Whereas the basic function of the zoom and the dolly may be similar—to change the field of view in a continuous move—there is a significant aesthetic difference between the two motions.

When doing a fast zoom-in and zoom-out, the object seems to hurtle along the z-axis toward the screen or else shoot toward the background as if self-propelled. Fast zooms create induced motion vectors of high magnitude. The reason we perceive the object as flying toward—and sometimes even through—the screen at the viewer is that all space modulators along the z-axis are quickly enlarged. And because we interpret a continuous enlargement of an object not as getting bigger but as coming closer, we see the objects coming toward us during a zoom. When zooming out, the objects get progressively smaller; we perceive them as receding into the background (see figure 13.15). Because the camera does not move during a zoom, there is no perspective change between the various space modulators along the z-axis. The objects seem to be glued together during the entire zoom. **SEE 14.10**

Zooms make us perceive object motion even if we know that the object is stationary. For example, a fast zoom-in on a ringing telephone seems to not only thrust the phone into our lap or face but also suggest the urgency of the call. A dolly-in on the phone would be much too slow to imply such a metamessage.

Because fast zooms are so blatant and can create powerful metamessages, you must be especially careful with their use; viewers can easily become annoyed when bombarded too many times with objects hurtling toward them.

Dollying When dollying, the camera perspective, and with it the volume duality of the space modulators and the spaces between them, changes continuously. The objects close to the camera quickly grow in size when the camera dollies past them, lengthening the apparent distance between the camera-near and the next object, with background objects remaining relatively unchanged. **SEE 14.11**

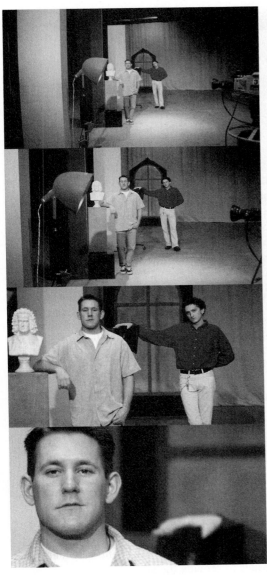

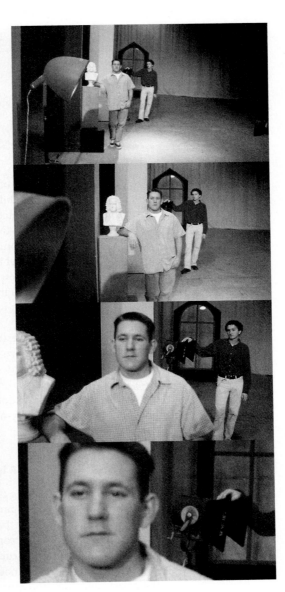

14.10 Perceived Motion During Zoom

A zoom-in seems to bring the object to the screen. Because the camera does not move, the camera perspective remains the same throughout the zoom. Note that the camera-far person's hand does not shift relative to the camera-near person's shoulder.

14.11 Perceived Motion During Dolly

When dollying in we seem to move with the camera into the scene. Because of the moving camera, we experience a continuous changing perspective of the space modulators.

14.12 Zoom Versus Dolly

A zoom-in brings the event toward the viewer; a zoom-out moves the event away from the viewer. A dolly-in takes the viewer to the event; a dolly-out leads the viewer away from it.

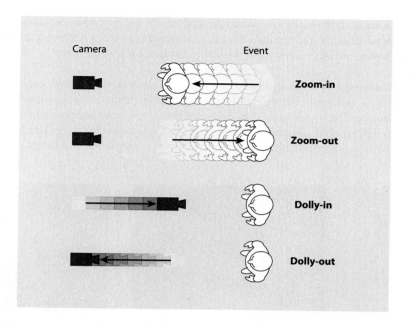

Because this change of perspective is close to what we would see when walking past the space modulators, we tend to identify with the moving camera, perceiving the space modulators as part of the stationary environment. Hence, we seem to be moving into the scene rather than having the scene come toward us, as in a zoom. A dolly-out works on the same principle except that now we are moving out of, instead of into, the scene. Whereas a zoom simulates primary (object) motion with the viewer in a solidly stationary position, a dolly faithfully reflects secondary (camera) motion. It invites the viewer to assume the camera's point of view and walk with it into or out of the scene.

Zoom versus dolly　The aesthetic difference between a zoom and dolly is important enough to emphasize one more time: When zooming in on an event, the event seems to come toward you. When zooming out, the event seems to move away from you. A fast zoom-in hurls the object toward you; a fast zoom-out pulls it away from you. During a dolly-in, you will seem to be moving with the camera toward the event. In a dolly-out, you seem to be moving with the camera away from the event. **SEE 14.12**

TERTIARY MOTION AND FUNCTIONS

Tertiary motion is sequence motion. Through a change of shots, we perceive a progression, a visual development. The important aspect of tertiary motion is not so much the vector field of the individual shot but the moment of change—the relationship of vector fields from shot to shot. As with bars in music, the transition devices act as important structural elements in the overall development of the video production or film without drawing too much, if any, attention to themselves. Their basic and common purpose is to provide the necessary link from shot to shot. Transition devices and the lengths of shots determine the basic beat and contribute to the rhythm of the sequences and the overall pace of the show. They guide the viewer's attention and feelings and supply structural unity.

Digital electronics have provided us with such a great variety of transitional effects that you may well wonder what to do with them all.[9] Many of them are so interesting and so easily produced that it is hard not to use them regardless of their appropriateness. But how can you tell whether a transition device is appropriate? When, for example, should you use a cut rather than a dissolve? What is a good use for a special effect that makes the picture shrink, tumble, and zoom through screen space? Some effects, such as a horizontal wipe, will not be too conspicuous on a small screen but will take on a life of their own when shown on the large and horizontally stretched HDTV screen. There are no simple answers to these questions. Yet by studying the screen presence of the major transition devices—that is, how they look and how we perceive them—you may get a clearer idea of when and how to use them effectively. Let us therefore examine the screen presence and the major aesthetic functions of the following transitions and transition groups: the cut, the jump cut, the dissolve, the wipe, the fade, and special transitional effects.

The cut   The *cut* is an instantaneous change from one image to another. As a transition device, the cut does not exist. Because it occupies neither screen time nor space, it is invisible. We are simply aware of the change itself—that one image has been instantly replaced by another. Cutting most closely resembles changing visual fields by the human eye. Try to scan things in front of you. Notice how your gaze jumps from place to place, neglecting the in-between spaces. You are not smoothly panning the scene but are instead "cutting" from place to place.[10] The filmic cut does the same thing.

Despite its nonexistence we treat the cut as though it were a visible transition device much like the dissolve or the wipe. We speak of a "smooth cut" or a "jump cut" even though we know that it can't be the cut that is smooth or that is doing the jumping. What we really mean by a smooth cut is that the vector fields of the previous and following shots have the expected continuity. The more continuity there is in object direction, speed, color, on- and off-screen location, and general vector magnitude (the perceived intensity), the less aware we are of the cut. When these vector fields are less continuous, we become more aware of the change from shot to shot. **SEE 14.13 AND 14.14** When looking at figures 14.13 and 14.14, try to see them as a sequence of shots rather than simply two adjacent still pictures.

Cutting is the simplest and, when done right, the least obtrusive way of manipulating screen space, screen time, and event density. The principal spatial functions of a cut are: to continue action from shot to shot, to follow or establish a sequence of objects or events, to change viewpoint or locale, and to reveal event detail.

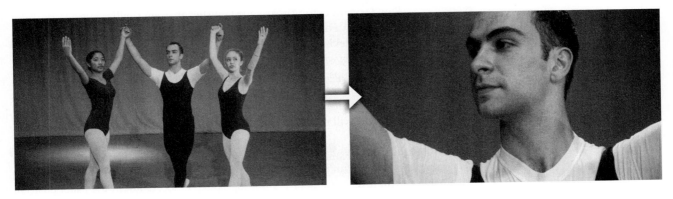

14.13 Smooth Cut
We consider a cut to be smooth if there is continuity in object direction, speed, color, on- and off-screen location, and general vector magnitude between the two shots.

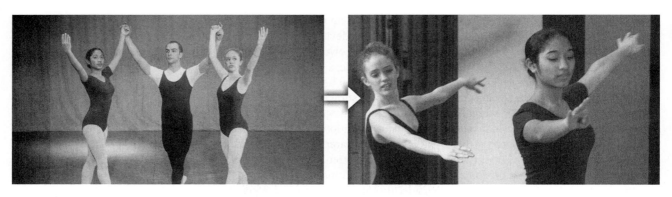

14.14 Bad Cut

This cut is considered bad because the middle dancer has suddenly disappeared and the female dancers have changed positions.

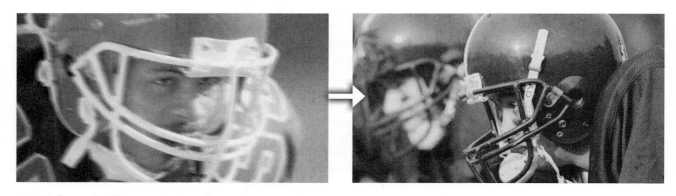

14.15 Converging Vectors to Increase Energy

Cuts between converging vectors can contribute to a high-intensity screen event.

A cut can indicate the passage of time or a change among past, present, and future. It can also indicate simultaneous events. In fact, we have become so accustomed to seeing the cut used to show that events in different locations happen simultaneously that we no longer need the famous "meanwhile-back-at-the-ranch" reminders. Rhythmic cutting can establish a beat, which to a large extent determines the pace of the scene, the segment, or the overall show.

Rapid or slow cutting not only establishes an event rhythm but also regulates the event density. For example, many cuts within a scene increase event density. Thirty-second television commercials that contain more than 30 cuts are good examples. Especially when cutting between converging vector fields and inductively sequenced close-ups, such dense screen events bristle with intensity. **SEE 14.15** Even as seasoned television viewers, we could not take such sensory bombardment for long. Slower cutting between less intense shots and continuing rather than converging vectors will reduce event density and make an event seem more tranquil.

The jump cut When an object jumps from one screen corner to the opposite one during a cut, it is an obvious **jump cut**. You also run into the danger of producing a jump cut if the camera or the photographed object is not in the exact position when repeating a take, especially if the following shot is not sufficiently different in field or angle of view. Such a minor spatial replacement of similar images produces even a more jarring "jump" within the screen. **SEE 14.16**

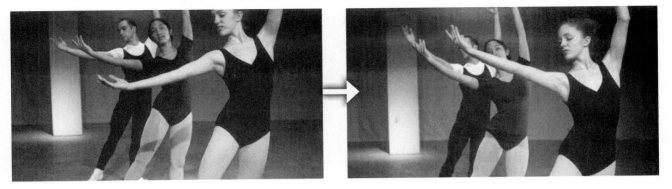

14.16 Jump Cut

In a jump cut, the person seems to jump from one screen location to the next. Though jump cuts are generally undesirable, you can use them to signal a leap in time or extreme emotional stress.

Not too long ago, video and film editors considered a jump cut an aesthetic mistake and immediately discarded it. But now we have accepted the jump cut as part of our aesthetic arsenal. It was made acceptable and even popular by people who edit news interviews. Because of constant deadline pressures and demands for ever-shorter running times for news items, the editors of the news footage eliminated most of a lengthy interview except for a few highlights and then simply strung the remaining shots together without concern for smooth shot continuity. This practice resulted in frequent jump cuts. Eventually, viewers accepted such obvious spatial jumps and translated them accurately into time jumps. After all, the relatively minor positional jumps are manifestations of large "at" position jumps along the horizontal time vector. We are now told indirectly but effectively that there is a jump in time and therefore that part of the interview is missing. To make the jump cut less abrupt and more acceptable to the viewer, some editors use a soft cut as a transitional device. The soft cut is similar to a fast dissolve that briefly overlaps the two images and thus somewhat blurs the jump between the preceding and the following shots.

The jump cut can also function as a powerful intensification device. For example, you can use it in a dramatic scene similar to the jogging device to signal extreme emotional stress (see the discussion of accelerated motion in chapter 13). The cut violates the expected smooth continuity and jolts our perceptual complacency. At the same time, it manifests the character's psychological "jumps" and compels us in a shorthand way to take notice of his or her progressively labile emotional state of mind.[11]

The dissolve The *dissolve* is a gradual transition from shot to shot in which the two images temporarily overlap. In contrast to the cut, which itself is invisible, the dissolve occupies its own screen space and time. **SEE 14.17** A dissolve can be long or short, depending on the time that the images from the preceding and following shots overlap. The dissolve

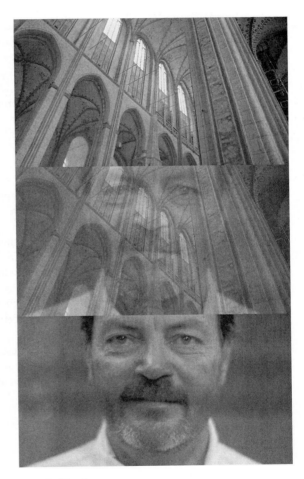

14.17 Dissolve

In a dissolve the image of the preceding shot temporarily overlaps that of the following shot. The dissolve occupies its own screen time and space.

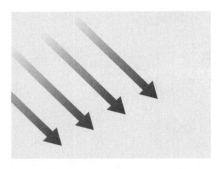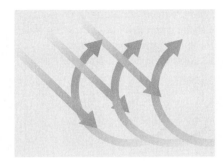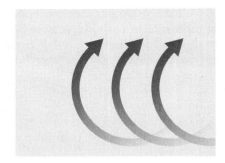

14.18 Temporary Vector Field of Dissolve
In a dissolve the vector fields of the preceding and following shots temporarily overlap, forming a third vector field that occupies its own screen space and time.

has its own visual structure, albeit a temporary one. In a slow dissolve, the visual structure becomes more prominent; in a quick dissolve, the transition has more of the characteristics of a soft cut.

During the overlap, the dissolve creates a new vector field that consists of the vectors of the preceding and following shots. **SEE 14.18** In many cases, this overlap of vectors produces a field in which the direction of the individual vectors is greatly muddled and their magnitude drastically reduced if not eliminated altogether. The temporary directional confusion of the vectors and the resulting reduction of their magnitude make the dissolve appear as a rather smooth, legato transition. A dissolve never ends a shot—it simply blends it into a new one. It's no wonder that the dissolve is such a favorite transition device whenever sequence fluidity is desired.

A dissolve can also cause some confusion about the figure/ground relationship of the overlapping shots; that is, which of the two shots is supposed to be on top and which on the bottom. At the beginning of the dissolve, the first shot maintains its own figure/ground organization. In the middle of the dissolve, both shots surrender their figure/ground organizations to that of the temporal third vector field, which, because of the overlap, remains ambiguous as to which shot is the figure and which is the ground. By the end of the dissolve, the second shot gains control of its own temporal figure/ground organization. This temporary figure/ground confusion makes us take notice and gives the dissolve its high visibility. You have probably figured out that a **superimposition** is simply a dissolve stopped midway.

The main aesthetic functions of the dissolve are to provide smooth continuity, to influence our perception of screen time and event rhythm, and to suggest or establish a thematic or structural relationship between two events.

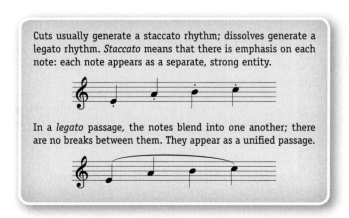

Cuts usually generate a staccato rhythm; dissolves generate a legato rhythm. *Staccato* means that there is emphasis on each note: each note appears as a separate, strong entity.

In a *legato* passage, the notes blend into one another; there are no breaks between them. They appear as a unified passage.

The dissolve aids continuity. Because you create an ambiguous vector field in the middle of a dissolve, you can provide some continuity of shots even if the shots would not cut together well. In an emergency, for example, you can bridge the gap between an extreme long shot and an extreme close-up without losing the viewer's orientation.

A word of warning is in order here: the ready availability of dissolves in video and their ability to camouflage gross sequencing mistakes may entice you to use more dissolves than cuts for every type of show. Resist this temptation. Dissolves may be safer than cuts because they cushion vector discrepancies from shot to shot, and they may feel somewhat smoother, but using too many dissolves is certain to destroy the crisp rhythmic clarity of a sequence. A dissolve should not become a salvaging operation for avoiding jump cuts. Like too much pedal in piano playing, the indiscriminate use of the dissolve muddles the scene. Think of dissolves as a special effect and treat them as such.

The dissolve can also act as a time bridge. Although the cut and even the jump cut have largely replaced the dissolve in indicating a change of locale or a passage of time, dissolves are still an effective and reliable way of bridging time intervals. For example: visualize a lone survivor of a shipwreck, floating in a rubber dinghy; dissolve to a slightly closer shot of the dinghy. This will indicate that some time has passed with no change of circumstances. The dissolve is especially appropriate when you want to show the connection between an event that happened in the past and one that occurred at a later time; for example: a young boy running through his hometown fields; short dissolve to a professor in a large university lecture hall, speaking on the influence of one's youth on adult behavior.

The dissolve greatly influences event rhythm. The legato linkage between shots reduces rhythmic accents and interconnects event details to form a smooth time entity. A slow dance sequence, a religious service, the solemn pace of a funeral—all are probably better served by dissolves than cuts between shots. Dissolves make these events feel less clinical while preserving their emotional intensity.

Dissolves can also suggest thematic or structural relationships, even between two unrelated events. An example of a thematic relationship is a street crowded with people, then a dissolve to a paddock crowded with cattle. An example of a structural relationship is an outfielder jumping to catch the ball, then a dissolve to a leaping dancer.

The wipe In a *wipe* the new image seems to push the old one off the screen, although technically it merely moves aside to reveal the new shot. The wipe has no reverence for vector continuity or structural or thematic relationships. When using a wipe, all you do is have one picture gradually replaced by another, irrespective of whether they have anything to do with each other. **SEE 14.19**

A wipe usually signals a transition between unrelated events—a switch in location or time. Because wipes are not concerned with visual continuity between the previous and the following shots, they become especially conspicuous even on a small screen. On a large, horizontally stretched screen, however, the wipe itself becomes an event. This is why you see very few, if any, wipes in large-screen motion pictures, except perhaps for comic effects. Think twice before using a number of wipes as transitions, especially if your video may be shown on a large screen.

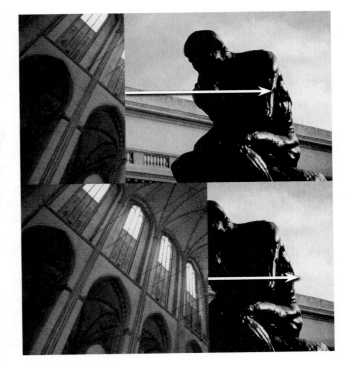

14.19 Wipe
In a wipe the first image yields to the second.

The fade   In a *fade* the picture either goes gradually to black (fade-out) or appears gradually on the screen from black (fade-in), signifying, much like a theater curtain, a definite beginning or end of a sequence. The fade is not a true transition device; rather, it defines the duration (running time) of the individual event sequences or of the event itself. Again, avoid fades between shots unless you want to indicate the end of one event and the beginning of another.

In the early days of television fades were frequently used within shows (such as movies) to signal the beginning and the end of commercials. This is no longer done. To keep the viewer's attention and to maintain the high-energy pace of a show, use cuts rather than fades. (This may lead to some confusion, however, if the commercial has some thematic relevance to what is shown in the program and, therefore, is mistaken as part of it.) Sometimes you may want to use a quick fade-out followed immediately by a fade-in of the next shot—also called a cross-fade or a dip-to-black—as a more obvious indication of a scene or sequence change than a cut would provide.

Special transitional effects   Digital video effects (DVE) provide a great number of transitional choices. The image may flash, freeze, shrink, tumble, stretch, flip, glow—or do all these things and more simultaneously. Still another shot may freeze, expand into a mosaic-like image, undergo an imperceptible metamorphosis, and change into a normal-sized second shot as if nothing had happened. The various special-effects software programs available for desktop computers make such transitional effects readily accessible.

Most of these electronic effects have such an unabashed screen presence that we can hardly call them transitions; rather they are interconnecting shots. Contrary to the cut, such effects operate largely independent of the vector fields of the two shots they connect. The more complex effects may graphicate the images of the previous and/or following shots or create their own images that may or may not be based on the preceding and following shot, scene, or sequence.

Similar to the fade, these obvious electronic effects signify the end of one sequence and the beginning of the next. Unlike the fade, however, they can be more transient. As just mentioned, a wipe does not put a stop to a shot sequence but simply advances it in a rather impudent way. Many digital effects mark—much as space modulators do—the scenes and the sequences of the event. They lead us from one space/time environment to another or, more often, from one event to a quite different one.

Commercial spots perform a similar structural function. In daytime serials, for example, they have become important dramaturgical devices to separate scenes and sequences. When writing for television, you must consider commercial breaks as part of the total show development so that you can use them to function as structural markers and periods of relief, just as the intermission does in a theatrical performance. The trend of joining several commercial spots through cuts rather than more obvious transitions gives the viewers a longer "intermission" without giving much of a chance to exit the program.

The "glow and flow" trend in television, whereby one show or commercial rolls into the next one as seamlessly as possible (to keep its audience), puts emphasis on connecting the show segments not only thematically but also aesthetically.

Because most of these effects are visually exciting, you may be tempted to use them indiscriminately. But don't forgo good content for mere sparkle. Effects can make a message more attractive but also highly objectionable. For example, to freeze the champion ski racer during a high-speed turn and have the graphicated image tumble away toward the snow-covered mountains might be an appropriate way of ending the race coverage, but to use a similar graphication technique for a skier who has been badly hurt would communicate bad taste if not gross insensitivity.

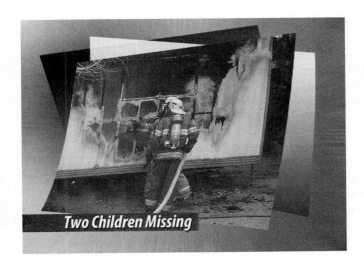

Two Children Missing

14.20 Digital Flips

Digital flips of especially intense scenes may neutralize or even work against the viewer's emotional involvement. The actuality-based event tends to be perceived as a readily disposable photograph.

When digital effects became readily available, many news organizations began using them to embellish their news stories regardless of content. Most of these effects fulfill no communication purpose other than to keep you awake. Some even carry powerful metamessages that may very well have adverse effects on how you perceive and react to the actual news content. An example is the digital flip effects used to visualize headline stories at the beginning of a news segment. The series may open with brief news footage of the terrible aftermath of a suicide bombing, then have one of the more grisly frames freeze and morph into a photolike sheet that flies through first-order video space to make room for a new calamity. **SEE 14.20**

The metamessage of graphicated flips is that they resemble a stack of photos—mere pictures—that we glance at casually before disposing of them. We stop just long enough to mutter how terrible things have become in today's world without getting any more involved. The special effects aid our emotional escape: the shocking reality of such an overwhelming human tragedy has been morphed into disposable pictures.

Enough of effects bashing! The emphasis on the possible misuse of digital effects does not mean that you should not use any of them but rather that you should think twice before using them. The default questions should be: Do I need them? If so, which ones? Does the effect fit the content and the style of the message? Do any of the effects have possible side effects, that is, carry unfavorable metamessages?

SUMMARY

Timing is the control and the manipulation of objective time and the structuring of subjective time in video and film. The control of both objective and subjective time is an essential element in structuring the four-dimensional field.

There are six types of objective time in video and film. Clock time depicts the actual, measurable time when an event happens. The television log lists clock times, that is, the beginning and ending times of shows or show segments. Running time indicates the overall length of a video production or film. You can use it to express the length of a show segment as well. Sequence time is a subdivision of running time that measures the length of a sequence—the organic cluster of scenes. Scene time is a subdivision of sequence time and indicates the length of a scene. Shot time measures the duration of a shot; it is the smallest convenient operational unit in a film or video. Story time is the fictional time depicted by the screen event. If somebody's life is shown from birth to death, the span of this lifetime, rather than running time of the program, is the story time.

The two types of subjective time are pace and rhythm. Pace refers to the perceived speed of an event or an event segment. We speak of the slow pace of a drama or the exceptionally fast pace of a musical. Rhythm refers to the flow within and among the event segments. It is determined by the pace of the individual segments and how they relate to one another. Rhythm provides the underlying beat of the video piece or film.

Plot time and character time can be independent of each other, which requires the control of objective time (usually plot time) and subjective time (character time). Just like the different rhythms among the voices of a musical piece, they often counter each other to clarify, intensify, and interpret the character's feelings and actions.

The principal motions are primary, secondary, and tertiary.

Primary motion includes everything that moves in front of the camera. As such, it is event-dependent. Its function is always judged from the camera's point of view.

Secondary motion is the motion of the camera and the motion simulated by camera zooms. It is medium-dependent. The principal functions of secondary motion are to follow action, to reveal action, to reveal landscape, to relate events, and to induce action.

We define the zoom as secondary motion, although normally the camera remains stationary during the zoom. In a zoom-in, the object gets progressively larger and the camera seems to bring the object toward the screen. In a zoom-out, the object gets progressively smaller and seems to move away from the screen. In contrast, a dolly-in takes the viewer into the scene; a dolly-out takes the viewer away from the scene.

Tertiary motion is sequence motion. It is determined by the specific use of one or several of these transition devices: the cut, the jump cut, the dissolve, the wipe, the fade, and special transitional effects.

The cut is an instantaneous change from one image to another. The cut itself does not exist as it does not occupy its own screen time and space. It is used to manipulate and construct screen space, screen time, and event density. Smooth cuts occur when the vector fields of the preceding and following shots provide continuity.

The jump cut shows the object jump erratically from one screen edge to the other or just a slight yet sudden position change. Both jump cuts are equally startling. You can use this technique to indicate a jump in time or to intensify an especially emotional event.

The dissolve is a gradual transition from shot to shot in which the two images temporarily overlap. The major functions of the dissolve are to provide continuity, influence our perception of screen time and event rhythm, and suggest a thematic or structural relationship between two events.

The wipe is a highly conspicuous effect, especially when shown on a large, horizontally stretched screen. The wipe operates totally independent of content.

The fade is a gradual appearance or disappearance of a screen image. The fade signals a definite beginning or end of a show, sequence, or scene.

Through digital electronics, many special effects are available as transitional devices. Digital video effects (DVE) have such a strong screen presence that they are more like interconnecting shots than pure transitions. Some such effects carry negative metamessages that may run counter to the intended television messages and/or sensitivity of the viewers.

N O T E S

1. Do not confuse the shot time with the length of various "takes." When shooting a scene for postproduction, you will probably do several takes from different angles for the same shot marked in the script. Each of these takes will probably have a slightly different duration (clock time). Normally, the clock times of each take are written down on a field log to aid the director and especially the editor in postproduction editing. Once a specific take is selected and trimmed, it constitutes the shot. The duration of this version is the shot time. See Herbert Zettl, *Television Production Handbook,* 10th ed. (Belmont, Calif.: Wadsworth, 2009), p. 266.

2. Story time and running time are seldom identical in film. One of the more impressive exceptions is the 1958 French film *Rififi* by Jules Dassin, which shows a bold burglary in its actual time from beginning to end. Yes, the culprits get away! Similarly, the television series *24* tried to squeeze an hour of story time, including commercials, into the one-hour running time.

3. In his "Rule of Six" for editing, Walter Murch puts rhythm as third in importance for making a cut. See Walter Murch, *In the Blink of an Eye: A Perspective on Film Editing,* 2nd ed. (Beverly Hills: Silman-James Press, 2001), p. 18.

4. This division was suggested by my colleague Philip Kipper, Broadcast and Electronic Communication Arts Department, San Francisco State University.

5. This scene is loosely based on the by-now-classic 1986 British television series *The Singing Detective.* It was written by the late television dramatist Dennis Potter and serves as an excellent example of the contrapuntal use of plot and character times.

6. Herbert Zettl, *Video Basics 6* (Boston: Wadsworth, 2010), pp. 72–74.

7. Refer to *Sight Sound Motion* chapters 9, 10, 11, and 13 for z-axis explanations and discussions.

8. If they are available, you can set up three monitors side-by-side in multiscreen fashion and connect them to three side-by-side cameras. Have the two wing cameras zoomed out and the center camera zoomed in. When somebody walks along the x-axis of the three cameras, you will see how the close-up view of the center camera dramatically increases object speed.

9. Zettl, *Television Production Handbook,* pp. 459–61.

10. In fact, when you stare at something immobile right in front of you, your eyes will not stand still but will "cut" quickly from one fixation to another. Such fixation shifts are called saccades or saccadic movement. See James J. Gibson, *The Ecological Approach to Visual Perception* (Hillsdale, N.J.: Lawrence Erlbaum, 1986), pp. 212–13. Also see Ann Marie Barry, *Visual Intelligence* (Albany: State University of New York Press, 1997), p. 32.

11. The psychological function of the jump cut is effectively demonstrated by film editor Hank Corwin in Oliver Stone's *U-Turn* (1997).

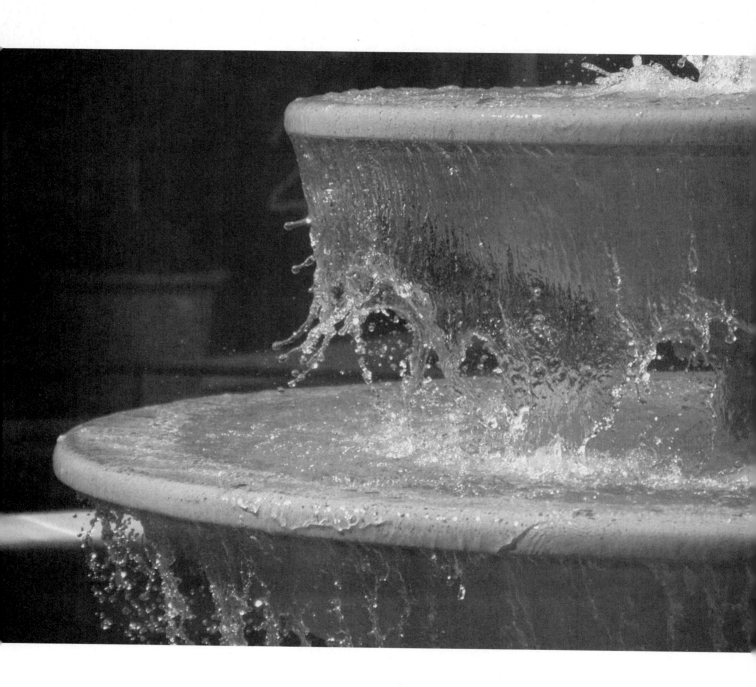

The Five-dimensional Field: Sound

S OUND IN VARIOUS MANIFESTATIONS (DIALOGUE, MUSIC, SOUND effects, and the like) is an integral part of video and film. It represents the all-important fifth dimension in the total field of applied media aesthetics.

For some time sound in film was considered an additional element to an already highly developed, independent visual structure. A considerable amount of time elapsed before the "talkies" were accepted aesthetically as constituting a medium in their own right. Broadcast television and all other forms of video, on the other hand, were born as audiovisual media. Sound is as essential to the video message as the pictures. Unfortunately, the various media terms such as *film, motion pictures, cinema, television,* and *video,* do not incorporate the audio concept. This neglect may have caused some people to believe that sound is a less important or nonessential adjunct of the visual fields of video and film. Far from it. Sound is indispensable to video and film communication.

When large-screen cinema adopted television's inductive visual approach, it could not have done so without an equally high-impact sound system. For example, the 5.1 surround-sound setup not only gives the inductive picture sequence a much-needed structural support but also matches the high aesthetic energy of large-screen images.

In this chapter we consider these major aspects of the five-dimensional field: sound and noise, video and film sound, literal and nonliteral sounds, the information function of sound, the outer orientation functions of sound, the inner orientation functions of sound, and the structural functions of sound. Note again that although the terms *video* and *television* are frequently used interchangeably, *video* here serves as the umbrella term to include all forms of video productions, and *television* is used when the sound requirements are specific to the production or reception of broadcast television.

Sound and Noise

Both sound and noise are audible vibrations (oscillations) of the air or other material. Aesthetically, the distinguishing factor between sound and noise is its communication purpose. **Sound** has purpose; it is organized. **Noise** is essentially random. The same audible vibrations can be sound at one time and noise at another.

Let's assume that you hear a big crash outside while reading this chapter. You run to the window, or outside, to see what is happening. The crash was noise. It happened unexpectedly and interrupted your activities. Now assume that you are working on a sound track. The scene shows a car running a stoplight and crashing into another car. At the precise moment of impact, you use the recording of a crash. What was noise before has now become sound. The crash sound fulfills an important function within the overall structure of your video production or film. In short, it has purpose. Similarly, even your favorite song can become noise if it doesn't fit the pattern of your activities. If, just as you are trying to think of an appropriate musical theme for your video production, a neighbor starts playing the song at full volume, it becomes noise because it interferes with the other melodies you are trying to listen to in your head.

You will find, however, that even some of the critical literature on audio considers all audible vibrations sound regardless of whether they occur randomly or as purposeful communication.

Video and Film Sound

Almost from the very beginning, television sound and pictures were picked up, processed, and broadcast simultaneously. Live television obviously did not permit any postproduction doctoring of sound. But even now, when we have sophisticated digital video and audio postproduction facilities available, we generally record sound and pictures of most routine video productions together. The *sweetening* of sound—improving the quality of the recorded audio mix—or more extensive sound postproduction is done only in larger video projects as part of the total postproduction activities.

In contrast to video, film "learned to talk" much later in its development. By the time sound was added to film, its visual aesthetics had been firmly established and highly refined.[1] It seems natural that for some time respectable filmmakers and theorists believed that sound was a detriment, rather than an asset, to the art of the film.[2] Film, then, was a visual medium, and sound was at that time a foreign element that did not always fit the established visual syntax. Russian filmmaker and theorist V. I. Pudovkin clearly recognized the basic problem of adding sound to a tightly structured visual field: "Usually music in sound films is treated merely as pure accompaniment, advancing the inevitable and monotonous parallelism with the image."[3]

Although the aesthetic sound requirements and production approaches for large-screen HDTV productions, digital cinema, and traditional film are very similar, if not the same, some significant differences remain between traditional small-screen television sound and that of film.

TELEVISION SOUND

You may have heard that television is primarily a visual medium and that you should therefore avoid as much as possible "talking heads"—that is, shots that show people talking instead of illustrating what they are talking about. This is a great misconception. First, television—like all video—is definitely *not* a predominantly visual medium; it is an audiovisual medium. Silent television is inconceivable from an informational as well as an aesthetic point of view. Second, nothing is wrong with "talking heads" so long as they talk well. You will notice that the majority of television programs have people talking.

Let's take a closer look at four major factors of television sound: reflection of reality, low-definition image, production restrictions and technical limitations, and audio/video balance.

Reflection of reality   In broadcast television, sound is a primary, if not an essential, communication factor. Television programming is predominantly reality based. This means that television shows draw on real events, such as news, sports, documentaries, interviews, and talk shows, or on fictional events that reflect some aspect of reality, however distorted such realities may be. All television events happen within a specific sound environment, and it is often the sound track that lends authenticity to the pictures and not the other way around. If, for example, you see a long and barren hallway, all you need to make it into a hospital corridor is the typical loudspeaker sound calling for a doctor. No further props are necessary.

Low-definition image   Even high-definition video is of low definition. This means that the size of the standard video screen is relatively small, the picture resolution of some TV shows is relatively low, and the contrast ratio or color palette is somewhat restricted, especially when compared with digital cinema.[4]

Video normally builds its overview inductively using a series of close-ups. Because the series of close-ups is often not enough to tell the whole story, we need sound to supply important additional information. Just try to follow a television show with the sound turned off. It will be difficult, if possible at all, for you to understand what is going on even though the story may be highly visual. On the other hand, you will have little trouble keeping abreast of what is happening on-screen by listening to the audio portion only.

We also need sound to give coherence and structure to the inductive picture series. For example, we frequently use music not only to establish a specific environment or mood but also to facilitate closure to the picture sequence and make viewers perceive individual shots as a unified whole. The rhythmic structure supplied by editing is not only supported by the beat of the accompanying sound but often dictated by it. If, for example, the tertiary motion rhythm—the rhythm you established through editing the video track—competes with the rhythm of the music, the sound track wins hands down.

Production restrictions and technical limitations   There are still certain production limitations that keep television sound from achieving optimal quality.

First, in many daily routine television productions, the sound is picked up and recorded simultaneously with the pictures, regardless of whether the show is done live, live-recorded, or recorded for postproduction editing. Although technically we have the capability of sound sweetening—stripping the sound off the video recording, improving its quality, and putting it back on again with the picture portion—relatively few routine shows enjoy such a postproduction luxury.

Second, the microphones for a simultaneous sound pickup, such as in daytime serials and situation comedies, are usually suspended from large booms and kept well above the heads of the actors to prevent the mics from showing up in the scene. Consequently, the audio pickup is inherently restricted, even if you use high-quality microphones. The outdoor conditions for electronic news gathering and electronic field production are generally less than ideal for good sound pickup. Indoor locations rarely provide optimal sound environments; and, when shooting outdoors, it is difficult to separate ambient sounds and wind noise from the intended sound. In both cases, the unwanted sounds often get picked up and amplified along with the desired sounds.

Third, the sound reproduction systems in most standard television receivers are severely limited in their frequency and amplitude (loudness) response. The speakers in the television set may even point away, rather than toward, the viewer-listener. It seems likely that any effort to improve the reproduction quality of television sound would be embraced by the public with great enthusiasm, but this has not been the case. Simply improving the quality of the sound without a similar improvement to the picture portion does not lead to an improved viewer-listener experience. The large HDTV flat-panel screens and the 5.1 surround-sound systems of home theater are, of course, the laudable exception. In this case, the high-definition video quality is matched by high-fidelity sound.

Audio/video balance   Have we become so aesthetically insensitive that we accept bad television sound as an inevitable given? On the contrary. It is precisely our aesthetic sensitivity that detects—and rejects—an imbalance between the relatively low-definition video portion and the high-definition stereo audio track and their relative aesthetic energies. You may have heard telecasts of concerts in which the audio portion is transmitted simultaneously with the television pictures via an FM radio channel. The idea is to provide optimal audio quality during the television viewing. Unfortunately, the high-quality sound portion diminishes the small-screen picture portion to the insignificant if not ludicrous. The television screen and its images seem to shrink from the onslaught of the high-energy sound. Like any sensitive viewer-listener, you will probably try to reduce the volume, and perhaps even the frequency response of the sound, to bring it more into balance with the lower-energy images. You may find that, finally, you need to switch back to the low-definition television audio to achieve the proper energy balance between picture and sound.

Such a problem of balancing the picture and sound energies is even more noticeable when watching a video program on the very small mobile media display. The high-fidelity sound that even small earbuds can deliver is likely to usurp the aesthetic energy of the video unless you do a delicate balancing act between the large sound volume and the small video image. Of course, such balancing is not necessary when the audio consists primarily of speech.

As we just mentioned, the large screen and the increased resolution of the high-definition video image require an equally high-definition sound track to achieve the proper audio/video balance. Even if the video is displayed on a relatively small HDTV screen, the sharp pictures no longer tolerate the relatively low-quality sound of standard television. Like film and digital cinema, large-screen HDTV requires high-energy audio. Again, you would be painfully aware of an imbalance of aesthetic energies if the large, high-resolution images of an HD video projection were matched with a single-channel, low-quality sound track.

A high-fidelity 5.1, or any other, surround-sound system, which literally surrounds you with high-quality sound, can provide the necessary energy for balancing the sound track with the large, high-energy video images of HDTV or digital cinema. Such digital sound tracks, however, must be carefully constructed in a relatively complex postproduction process and are therefore reserved for film, digital cinema, and large-scale video productions. I believe that the inductive sequencing we see more and more in major cinema productions is possible only because of the superior-quality and high-energy surround-sound system. **SEE 15.1** Most routine HDTV shows must necessarily do with less complex audio tracks. But in the absence of a 5.1 surround-sound system, even a medium-quality high-fidelity stereo system can provide a satisfactory audio/video balance.

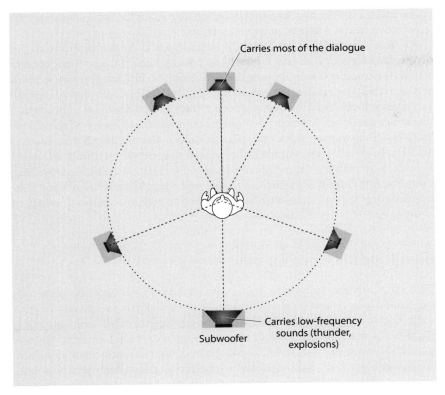

15.1 Standard Surround Sound

The standard 5.1 surround-sound system consists of six speakers: one at front-center; two to the left and right sides of the center speaker; two rear speakers on the left and right sides, and a subwoofer at rear-center, which is the .1 speaker that carries the low-frequency ambient sounds. Because low frequencies are omnidirectional, the subwoofer can be placed anywhere between the 3 o'clock and the 9 o'clock positions.

FILM SOUND

Although film has been firmly established as an audiovisual medium for some time, in many instances the visual field still appears to dominate film presentations. Sometimes the high-definition film image and the deductive sequential structure (moving from overview to event details) are so well suited to tell a story pictorially that the sound can indeed be, as Siegfried Kracauer remarked, occasionally casual and the dialogue embedded in visual contexts.[5]

In landscape films, which emphasize action and environment over complex human emotions, the dialogue is often upstaged by an overwhelming and exciting visual sequence. For example, you can splice in any number of large-screen landscape scenes between the slow-moving dialogue of two cowboys riding through a Montana valley without sacrificing story flow or event energy. But when the same movie appears on small-screen video, the large, high-definition film images are reduced to small, relatively low-definition images. In this transformation the overpowering landscape shots are most susceptible to energy loss. The resulting low-energy landscape shots no longer serve as plausible bridges for the various dialogue lapses. As a consequence we become very much aware of the long pauses among the dialogue elements. Though the slow film dialogue appeared natural in conjunction with the high-energy landscape images on the large screen, on the small video screen it seems spotty and uneven.

Do not be misled into thinking, however, that because the landscape images of film can take over a storytelling function you can neglect the aesthetics of film sound. The contrary is true. Because the high-definition film images carry so much aesthetic energy regardless of content, the sound must be equally high-definition and equally loud. In fact, when watching a high-energy movie in a theater setting with a good sound system, the first few minutes of the film seem exceedingly loud. This high-volume shock, which is especially noticeable after having listened extensively to music and sound on the earbuds of a mobile media device, abates as soon as we perceive the energy of sound and pictures as a single gestalt. Such sound/picture closure in the listener-viewer will occur, however, only if the filmmaker pays at least as much attention to the production and the postproduction of the sound as to the visual portion.

Literal and Nonliteral Sounds

When you listen carefully to the sounds of a television show or a motion picture, you probably hear some form of speech, such as dialogue or narration over a scene, and some *ambient sounds*—the environmental sounds in which the scene plays—such as traffic, the wind, or the pounding of the surf. Inevitably, you will also hear some music and, depending on the story, sounds that are neither speech, music, nor environmental sounds but whose presence inevitably affects how we feel about what we see and hear. Despite the great variety of sounds used in video and film, we can group them into two large categories: literal, or diegetic, sounds and nonliteral, or nondiegetic, sounds.

LITERAL, OR DIEGETIC, SOUNDS

Literal sounds are referential, which means that they convey a specific literal meaning and, in so doing, refer you to the sound-producing source. When, for example, you see a scene of two people talking to each other, you obviously associate the sounds of their conversation with their screen image, even if one moves temporarily into off-screen space. Assuming that you know their language, you also understand the literal meaning of their conversation. When you see the interior of a living room with an open window and hear the sounds of rush-hour traffic, you know that the house is close to a busy downtown street. The traffic sounds are referential inasmuch as they refer you directly to the sound-producing source: buses, cars, motorcycles, and emergency vehicles. In the more complicated world of film theory, they are called *diegetic*, a derivation of the Greek word *diegesis*, which, literally translated, means "telling a story." This terminology implies that these **diegetic sounds** are all part of the story presented on the screen.[6]

Literal sounds can be source-connected or source-disconnected. They are source-connected when you see the sound-producing source while simultaneously hearing its sound. For example, in the first shot we see a two-shot of a mother talking to her child and we hear her at the same time. **SEE 15.2** When you then switch to a close-up of the child while still hearing the mother talk, the literal sound has become source-disconnected. **SEE 15.3** *Source-connected sounds* are on-screen sounds; they emanate from an on-screen event. You see the mother talking to her daughter on-screen. *Source-disconnected sounds* are off-screen sounds; the sound-producing source is located in off-screen space. In the follow-up close-up of the daughter, the mother has moved off-screen but, thanks to our mental map, we still connect her admonition with her image. We instinctively

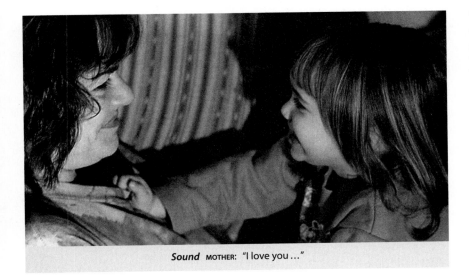

Sound MOTHER: "I love you …"

15.2 Source-connected Literal Sound

When we hear a sound and see the sound-producing source on-screen at the same time, the literal sound is source-connected: we see and hear the woman talk.

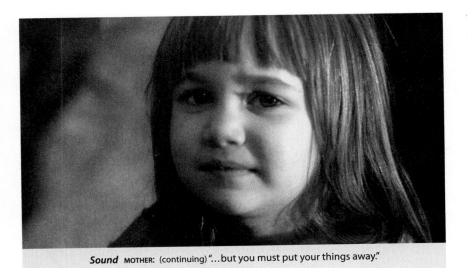

Sound MOTHER: (continuing) "…but you must put your things away."

15.3 Source-disconnected Literal Sound

When we see something other than the sound-producing source, the literal sound is source-disconnected. Here we see the child listening to her mother talk, which means the mother's words (literal sound) are now source-disconnected.

connect a source-disconnected sound with the sound-producing source, in this case, the mother.

NONLITERAL, OR NONDIEGETIC, SOUNDS

Nonliteral sounds are not intended to refer to a particular sound source or to convey literal meaning. They are deliberately source-disconnected and do not evoke a visual image of the sound-producing source. They are also called **nondiegetic sounds**, which implies that they emanate outside the "story space." Nonliteral sounds include the hisses, *boing*s, and *wham*s in a cartoon that accompany the incredible feats of the main character; the romantic music during a tender love scene on the beach; or the rhythmic theme that introduces the evening news. Music is the most frequently used form of nonliteral sound.

But aren't the hisses and whistles of cartoons or the driving, ominous sound rhythms behind a violent scene very much part of the story space? Yes, they certainly are. In fact, cartoon language and the emotional shorthand of crime shows

15.4 Descriptive Nonliteral Sounds

From the following list, choose some factors and try to "listen" to them. Then pick nonliteral sounds (sound effects or music) that best describe each selected item.

Factor	Aspect	Variable
Space	Distance	Far, near, infinite
	Size	Small, large, inflated, huge, microscopic
	Shape	Regular, irregular, round, square, jagged, slender, fat, wide, narrow
	Height	High, tall, low, short
	Volume	Large, small
Time	Seasons	Summer, autumn, winter, spring
	Clock time	High noon, morning, evening, dusk, dawn, night
	Subjective time	Boring, fast, exciting, accelerated
	Motion	Fast, slow, dragging, graceful, clumsy
Light	Sun	Bright, overcast, strong, weak
	Moon	Soft, brilliant
	Searchlight	Moving, blinding
	Car headlights	Passing, approaching, blinding
Quality	Weight	Heavy, light, unbearable, shifting, increasing
	Texture	Rough, smooth, polished, coarse, even, uneven
	Consistency	Hard, soft, spongy, solid, fragile, dense, loose
	Temperature	Hot, cold, warm, cool, heating up, cooling down, freezing, glowing
	Personality	Stable, unstable, cheerful, dull, alive, sincere, insincere, powerful, rough, effeminate, masculine, weak, strong, pedantic, careless, romantic, moral, amoral
	Feeling	Funny, tragic, sad, frightened, lonely, panicky, happy, solemn, anxious, loving, desperate, hateful, sympathetic, mean, suspicious, open, guarded
Event		Sports, church service, graduation ceremony, thunderstorm, political campaign, funeral, death, birth, lovemaking, running, cars in pursuit

live off such nondescript sound effects, and they can have a direct influence on how we perceive the story space. In this respect the term *nonliteral sound* seems much less ambiguous than *nondiegetic*. Nonliteral sound simply means that our recalling its source is irrelevant but not its function to help clarify, intensify, and interpret the story. **SEE 15.4**

LITERAL AND NONLITERAL SOUND COMBINATIONS

Most often literal and nonliteral sounds are combined in the same scene. Assume that we see a mother and her teenage son walking along the beach. We hear their dialogue (literal, source-connected), the pounding of the surf (literal, source-connected), and a jet plane overhead (literal, source-disconnected). When their conversation turns to the son's new girlfriend, a dissonant music theme sneaks in to underscore the sudden tension (nonliteral). Such a mixture of literal and nonliteral sounds communicates what the event is all about and also how it feels. It "shows" the outside and the inside of the event simultaneously.

A mix of literal and nonliteral sounds can also increase the magnitude of the screen event's total vector field, that is, the event energy. For example, the shrill, nervous sounds (nonliteral) that accompany the sounds of squealing tires (literal) of a car that has lost its brakes on a steep, winding road will certainly boost the precariousness of the event. We take up such aesthetic functions later in this chapter.

THE IMPORTANCE OF CONTEXT

You will find that the same sound can be literal or nonliteral, depending on the visual context. Here is the context for a literal sound interpretation: a concert of a difficult contemporary composition. We see close-ups of the conductor, the string basses, and the various percussion instruments that create unusual pounding sounds (literal, source-connected). We see one of the audience members hold her ears as if to protect herself from the relentless rhythms (literal, source-disconnected). We cut back to the conductor, who is accelerating the beat and gesturing for higher-volume sound (literal, source-connected).

Now switch to the visual context of a psychiatric ward. A patient is sitting with the psychiatrist, calmly and intelligently answering a variety of questions (literal, source-connected). But when a particular question triggers something in the patient, we see a close-up of him trying to hide his panic and silently struggling for an answer. During this close-up, we hear music coming up, getting louder, with string basses and percussion instruments creating pounding rhythms. The music is identical to the piece we heard in the concert hall, but now it is nonliteral. In the context of the psychiatric ward, we don't visualize the sound-originating instruments or the conductor but instead perceive the music as a reflection of the patient's state of mind. The different context has changed the function of the sound track. We have moved from an information function (what the new piece of music sounds like) to a purely emotional one (what the patient feels).

Before reading more about the major functions of video and film sound, you should realize that many of these functions overlap and largely depend on the communication intent of a scene and the visual context in which the sounds operate. Like cooking, the treatment of sound depends not only on a good mix of basic ingredients and principles but also to a great extent on an overall feel for balance. Effective sound mixing requires an understanding of, and a sensitivity to, the contextual use of the four other aesthetic fields.

Information Function of Sound

The major information function of sound is to communicate specific information verbally. In our verbally oriented society, a word is often worth a thousand pictures. Just try to use pictures to explain concepts with a high level of abstraction, such as freedom, grammar, justice, process, efficiency, or learning. Or try to express, using just screen images, the following simple communication: telling a friend over the telephone that she should meet you at the library next Wednesday at 9:30 a.m. To get the point across in pictures, you would probably resort to scribbling a message on a notepad by the telephone or using some other ingenious way to display the message in writing. It is certainly easiest to deliver the message by simply saying it.

The forms of speech most often used in television are dialogue, direct address, and narration.

DIALOGUE

A dialogue is a conversation between two or more people. We also use the term *dialogue* if one person is speaking while the other is listening or even when one person speaks to himself. Because thinking out loud is actually conversing with oneself, it is still a form of dialogue, but we refer to it as internal dialogue.

Dialogue in most videos is the chief means of conveying what the event is all about (theme), developing the story progression (plot), saying something specific about the people in the story (characterization), and describing where, when, and under what circumstances the event takes place (environment and context). You may have noticed that the opening dialogue in serial dramas usually recounts what happened previously, tells where the story is now, and suggests where it might be going. This same sequence also introduces new characters. All this information is contained in a few lines of carefully crafted dialogue.

Good dialogue seems to flow naturally. It often sounds like an audio recording of a randomly observed conversation. As most writers will confirm, however, good dialogue is meticulously constructed to sound and feel natural yet communicate a maximum of information. It should make you wish you had said it that way. The most important variables of good dialogue are listed in the dialogue context and variables table. **SEE 15.5**

Samuel L. Clemens (1835–1910), better known as **Mark Twain**, comments on such literary pitfalls in constructing dialogue in his delightful essay on James Fenimore Cooper's literary offenses. He accuses Cooper of having violated in *The Deerslayer* eighteen of the nineteen rules of literary art. Of the eighteen literary requirements, these three are of special interest to us:

> They require that when the personages of a tale deal in conversation, the talk shall sound like human talk, and be talk such as human beings would be likely to talk in the given circumstances, and have a discoverable meaning, also a discoverable purpose and a show of relevancy, and remain in the neighborhood of the subject in hand, and be interesting to the reader, and help out the tale, and stop when the people cannot think of anything more to say. . . .

And:

> They require that when the author describes the character of the personage in his tale, the conduct and conversation of that personage shall justify said description.

Here is how Clemens introduces a dialogue example from Cooper's *The Deerslayer:*

> In the *Deerslayer* story he lets Deerslayer talk the showiest kind of book-talk sometimes, and at other times the basest of base dialects. For instance, when someone asks him if he has a sweetheart, and if so where she abides, this is his majestic answer: "She's in the forest—hanging from the boughs of the trees, in a soft rain—in the dew on the open grass—the clouds that float about in the blue heavens—the birds that sing in the woods—the sweet springs where I slake my thirst—and in all the other glorious gifts that come from God's Providence!" And he preceded that, little before, with this: "It consarns me as all things that touches a fri'nd consarns a fri'nd."[7]

15.5 Context and Dialogue Variables

The important thing to watch in dialogue is that it operates within a fairly consistent pattern.

Context Variables		Dialogue Variables		
Type	**Examples**	**Word Choice**	**Sentence Structure**	**Rhythm**
Education	High	Wide vocabulary range	Precise syntax	Lucid, fluid
	Low	Limited vocabulary	Double negatives	Hesitant, uneven
Occupation	Special	Specialized vocabulary depending on occupation	Involved, depending on occupation (lawyer, college professor)	Flowing
	General	Ordinary vocabulary	Less involved, relatively simple	Staccato
Region	Country	Country-flavor dialect	Simple but can be involved	Relatively slow
	City	Specific city slang		Fast
	Geographic	Southern, eastern		South: legato; East: staccato
Locale	Office	Formal, businesslike	Precise syntax	Fast
	Bar	Informal	Mixed, relaxed structure	Uneven
	Courtroom	Extremely formal	Highly formal and involved	Precise, even for judges and lawyers; uneven for defendants
Time	Period	Vocabulary depending on period (century)	Old-language structure New-language, simpler	
	Morning		Depends on activity	Faster—high-energy
	Night			Slower—low -energy
Partner	Friend	Familiar, less formal	Informal	Relaxed
	Stranger	Formal, general	Formal	Uneven
	Superior	Formal	Formal	
	Employee	Less formal	Less formal	
Situation	Familiar	Common words	Short, relaxed	Even
	Unfamiliar	Formal	Precise	Uneven
	Emergency	Essential words only	Incomplete	Uneven (staccato)
Attitude	Calm	Large vocabulary	Fairly precise	Even, flowing
	Excited	Limited vocabulary	Less precise	Fast, staccato
	Tense	Limited vocabulary	Short	Staccato
	Hysterical	Often nonsensical	Illogical	Uneven

DIRECT ADDRESS

Direct address means that the performer speaks directly to us—the viewers—from her or his on-screen position. We are no longer passive observers but have become active dialogue partners, even if the dialogue is one-sided. The direct-address method provides for optimal information exchange. People on television tell us what to watch, what to buy, what to think, what to feel, and how to behave. We do not think it unusual to have, within a relatively brief time span, a former star athlete tell us about the virtues of a specific fruit juice, an ordinary househusband speak about the power of a new detergent, and the president of the United States describe his difficulty balancing the budget.

Video is ideally suited to the direct-address method. The relatively small screen and the live structure of the image provide the immediacy necessary for such personal "dialogue." What the on-screen dialogue partners say to us is usually of immediate concern. Because this (one-sided) conversation also takes place, at least most of the time, in familiar surroundings—our home—it carries a high degree of intimacy. This intimacy will be preserved even if you are on the run and have this virtual conversation with a partner appearing on the tiny screen of your mobile media device. You are literally holding your conversation partner in your hand, regardless of whether you are in a classroom, riding a bus, or walking from the library to a coffee stand. When listening to the audio with earbuds, you are sufficiently isolated from environmental distractions, so your communication has become acutely private.[8]

Film, on the other hand, lacks this interpersonal aspect. We go to the movie theater, take our place among the other people in an auditorium, and wait until the opening frames reveal a construct of "historical" images—a reconstructed world that moves us one way or another. Marshall McLuhan quite rightly observed that in motion pictures "we roll up the real world on a spool in order to unroll it as a magic carpet of fantasy."[9] We want to look at or be engulfed by the images of film, but we have little inclination to participate in the screen event. This is one of the reasons why the subjective-camera point of view is rarely successful. As spectators we want to remain anonymous. Thus we are apt to become uncomfortable, if not annoyed, when the dream image on the large screen all of a sudden turns around, looks at us, and addresses us directly. We feel discovered, caught in the act of observing. Perhaps worse, the film hero has become mortal, a psychological equal. We are subjected to the painful experience of hearing the emperor admit that he is indeed naked.

All of this does not mean, however, that you cannot or should not use the direct-address method in film; but you must realize that it requires more than just having the actor turn toward the camera for part of the dialogue. The direct-address method in film is a dramaturgical device that requires a specific approach to plot and character and a sensitivity to how audiences react. Woody Allen showed us that it is possible to talk to the movie audience directly and to make it into a silent dialogue partner. But there are few Woody Allens around.

The effect of a direct address by a performer on large-screen video depends on where you watch. If it is in a theaterlike environment, the privacy effect will be the same as watching a movie. If you watch a performer talking to you from a large screen in your home, he or she may seem somewhat intrusive and overpowering, but you will probably not feel uncomfortable or embarrassed by such personal communication. Nevertheless, television news presentations and advertising may, however insidiously, gain in persuasive power. The large screen forces us to look up to, rather than at, the oversized images. The viewer is thus inevitably relegated to an inferior position.

NARRATION

Narration can be on- or off-camera. It is another efficient method of supplying additional information. The narrator usually describes a screen event or bridges various gaps in the continuity of an event. Most video documentaries rely heavily on off-screen, voice-over narration to fill in much-needed information.

Again, the spoken word is frequently more efficient in advancing a story than pictures are. Instead of showing the hands of a clock madly spinning or the clock time keyed into the picture to indicate elapsed time, the narrator can simply say that 20 hours later the situation has not changed. As with direct address, we seem to feel more comfortable with narration in video production than in films. We are psychologically more prepared to have someone talk to us (either on- or off-screen) on video than on film. This is why in film we tend to use written information rather than voice-over narration to indicate extreme changes in time and locale.

Outer Orientation Functions of Sound

The outer orientation functions of sound are similar to those of light. They include orientation in space, in time, to situation, and to external event conditions. As with other elements in the various aesthetic fields, the outer orientation functions of sound often overlap; one sound can fulfill several functions, depending on the event context. For example, a foghorn blowing can tell us that we are near water (location function) and at the same time that it is foggy, requiring the ships' captains to be extracareful (situation). For clarity's sake, however, we discuss each of the major functions separately.

SPACE

Specific sounds can help us reveal and define the location of an event, its spatial environment, and even off-screen space.

Location   Certain sounds identify specific locations, provided the audience is familiar with those environmental sounds. If, for example, you accompany the close-up of a young woman with such literal outdoor sounds as birds singing, a rustling brook, and barking dogs, she is obviously somewhere in the country. You have no need for a cumbersome establishing shot; the sounds will take over this orientation function. Now think of the same close-up accompanied with sounds of typical downtown traffic: car horns, automobile engines, people moving about, a doorman's taxi whistle, and buses pulling up to the curb and moving away. The young woman is now in the city. Specific nonliteral sounds, such as electronic hums and beeps, can even locate her in outer space.

In film and large-screen video, you need to take care that the sound comes from approximately the screen position of the sound-producing source. In 5.1 surround sound, the dialogue is usually carried by the front-center speaker. But if you show a man crying for help from near the left screen edge in an extreme long shot, or establish someone in left off-screen space, you need to have the yelling come from screen-left. Fortunately, stereo sound makes it possible to move the sound anywhere along an on- and off-screen x-axis (horizontal) position. Surround sound extends the sound through a series of speakers to the sides and the back of the audience and, when done well, even occupies limited z-axis positions. All five speakers (except for the .1 rear subwoofer) are responsible for directional sounds. The rear subwoofer, whose low-frequency sounds are basically nondirectional, is especially effective for thunder and explosions. Although these rumbles emanate in the rear, they quickly spread throughout the entire acoustic space. For that reason you can place the subwoofer at the audience sides as well.

For the small, 4 × 3 video screen, a stereo separation of sound is less successful. The built-in speakers are not separated enough to achieve the desired illusion of sonic depth and width. Unless the speakers can be properly separated or you wear earphones or sit in the "sweet spot"—the place where the two channels combine into a three-dimensional experience—you will not be able to tell the direction from which the various sounds are coming. We simply cannot discriminate such minute horizontal sound separations. Even if you achieved the

Not every media theorist is in agreement with the directional function of off-screen sound. For example, **Christian Metz** thinks that a sound source in itself is never "off" because sound is either audible or it doesn't exist. He comments: "When it exists, it could not possibly be situated within the interior of the rectangle or outside of it, since the nature of sounds is to diffuse themselves more or less into the entire surrounding space: sound is simultaneously 'in' the screen, in front, behind, around, and throughout the entire movie theatre." Considering the long history of spatial articulation through stereo sound and, more recently, through surround sound, this argument is surprisingly naive.[10]

proper separation to match the sounds of two people talking to each other from the extreme screen-left and screen-right positions, you would find such an x-axis sound separation unconvincing. Their sounds are now located so far in the left and right off-screen space that they appear separated from their source—the people on-screen. This is why it is the front speaker that carries most of the dialogue in the 5.1 surround-sound system.

The horizontal, x-axis positioning of sound through stereo audio gains importance as soon as the video screen size increases. Large-screen video projections not only benefit from such horizontal sound separation but also demand it for most sound functions. In the treatment of sound, as with other aesthetic elements, large-screen video has very similar requirements to those of film.

Binaural audio, a stereo recording technique that simulates as best as possible how we actually hear, is more accurate in pinpointing x-axis and even z-axis on- and off-screen position.[11] Early television sound experiments have shown that binaural sound is especially effective not only in defining locations along the on- and off-screen x-axis but especially along the on- and off-screen z-axis.[12] You can hear someone walking right through the screen toward you and even past you along the z-axis.

Such 3D sound is essential for stereoscopic 3D video and digital cinema. The ordinary 5.1 surround system is excellent in providing the illusion of 3D space for a standard 2D video and film projection, but it falls short of defining the z-axis space that extends toward the audience. Binaural audio fares much better in this respect, but even then the location of binaural sound along the z-axis must be carefully coordinated with the location of the visual event. Otherwise the sound portion remains oddly removed from the pictures and does not lead to the expected heightened spatial awareness of the audiovisual screen event. The problem with binaural sound is that to benefit from its true effect (extending toward the viewer along the z-axis), you need to wear a headset. There are special speakers that simulate the 3D effect of binaural sound, but they are usually not available on the consumer market. So far, the need to wear earphones makes this audio technique bothersome if not impractical for stereoscopic 3D viewing.

Environment   You can use various sounds to indicate the specific spatial characteristics of an environment. For example, you can indicate whether a person is in the small confined space of a telephone booth or the large space of an empty warehouse simply by manipulating the sound reverberations. More reverb occurs in a large room than in a small one. Outer space is another matter and is usually suggested through novel sustaining, often computer-generated, complex sounds. Simply by switching sounds from expansive to restricted space, you can support or suggest the perceptual switch of what the astronauts see through the porthole to what they feel about their tight living quarters.

You can also comment on the quality of the environment. For example, the excessive clanging of dishes, silverware being dropped, the squeaking of the swinging door to the kitchen, and the yelling of orders by the waiters suggest a different type of restaurant from one in which we hear soft semi-classical piano music, the uncorking of a champagne bottle, and the quiet murmur and occasional laughter of the patrons.

Off-screen space   Sound expands the on-screen event to off-screen space. Staying with the restaurant theme, you can easily suggest the spatial environment of the restaurant through the typical sounds just mentioned even if you show only a tight close-up of two people sitting at a corner table. By hearing a door open and close, we assume that people are either arriving or leaving. When the door is open, you can expand the off-screen space even more by bringing in some traffic sounds. You are now operating with layers of literal off-screen sounds.

To imply that the two people we see talking with each other in the close-up are part of a larger convention group on a lunch break, you can have them wear the traditional name tags and, more important, mix with their dialogue the off-screen ambient sounds of other people talking about the next session, drinking coffee, laughing, and so forth. To make the mix of the various sound tracks convincing, you can occasionally have the ambient sound tracks compete with the major sound track of the main conversation. What you are creating is a sound fabric, a sound impression, of the extended environment.

TIME

Like lighting, sound can be a fairly good indicator of clock time and the seasons. We quite readily associate typical sounds with morning, noon, evening, night, summer, or winter. Try to listen to these sounds. Typical morning sounds are the alarm clock, the shower, or the coffee maker. Outside, the morning sounds may include birds chirping, the newspaper being delivered, a garbage truck pulling up, somebody having trouble getting his car started in the cold morning air, or the first bus rattling by. For a more historical production, you can use a factory whistle to indicate high noon. When appropriate, you can use church bells or the calls for prayer from a minaret to indicate certain clock times. An evening or night in the country inevitably has cricket sounds, the rustling of trees in the breeze, the distant barking of a dog, subdued sounds of a television program, and voices and laughter coming from the neighbors. At night you can add the hooting of an owl for good measure.

Snow acts as an acoustic dampener; everything is quieter when it snows than in summertime. Even if there is no snow, winter sounds are generally more subdued than summer sounds.

SITUATION

Sounds can describe a specific situation. You may, for example, indicate that everything is not going according to plan by accompanying the close-up of the chief surgeon's stoic face with the sound of the patient's irregular breathing. Or, in another event, dogs barking madly outside will indicate that someone is coming. Literal sounds are especially helpful to extend the visual field of the small video screen. If, for example, we see a close-up of a woman telephoning and hear the literal (source-disconnected) sound of a baby crying, we don't have to see the baby to know that it is close by and in need of attention.

Try to listen to the various sounds of specific events and select those that give an event its distinction. A creative sound track contains many universal sounds with which we are all familiar, but it also has sounds that are unique and unexpected. For example, the coffee maker may be so old that it makes a unique hissing sound, the garbage collector may whistle operatic arias while emptying the cans, the office door may squeak in a certain way, and the car radio at the accident scene may still play a romantic love song until overpowered by the siren of the arriving ambulance.

Predictive sound   You can also use literal and nonliteral sounds to forecast an upcoming event. Such **predictive sounds** operate much like predictive lighting to signal an occurrence or a situational change. For example, you can indicate the imminent danger of a forest fire by gradually and softly sneaking in the sounds of fire engines while the video still lingers on the carefree campers preparing to cook their freshly caught trout. Or you may show a successful party with all its laughter, occasional shouts, and serious and not-so-serious conversations. As an additional sound layer, there is party music, which may be perceived as literal (coming from the host's sound system). But suddenly and almost imperceptibly, the music segues to an ominous mood (now it is definitely nonliteral), preparing the audience for a coming mishap during the party.

Leitmotiv   A specific use of predictive sound is the *leitmotiv* (German for "leading motif"), a short musical phrase or specific sound effect that portends the appearance of a person, an action, or a situation. Its basic dramatic function is that of allusion (reference). Like the bell that caused Pavlov's dog to salivate, the leitmotiv "leads" the audience to expect a specific recurring phenomenon. For example, if you hear heavy breathing every time you see the psycho killer, you expect to see the bad guy again when you hear the heavy breathing, even if the story as told by the screen images makes his appearance unlikely. Note that a leitmotiv is effective only if used repeatedly to signal the same event. You need to build up the connection between leitmotiv and event before you can exercise its predictive power.

> The leitmotiv is usually credited to **Richard Wagner** (1813–1883), who used it extensively in his operas. But the leitmotiv had been used successfully before Wagner by many composers, notably by **Wolfgang Amadeus Mozart** (1756–1791) in his opera *Cosi fan tutte* and **Carl Maria von Weber** (1786–1826) in his opera *Der Freischütz*.

EXTERNAL CONDITIONS

Sound can indicate whether something is big or small, smooth or rough, high or low, old or new, fast or slow. Which particular sounds to use depends on the structure of the other aesthetic fields, especially the relative complexity and magnitude of their vector fields. Such audio/video matching tasks are explored in chapter 16.

An example of using nonliteral sounds for describing a certain external event condition is the sudden flooding of a ship's engine room. To convey this dangerous condition in literal sounds, you would probably use engine sounds, the sailors' excited voices, the rushing and gurgling of the water's entering the ship, the shouted commands, and the clanging of tools against the metal hull. Or you may choose such nonliteral sounds as a thumping that gets more and more "squeezed" the higher the water rises, or music that rhythmically and harmonically reflects the rushing and rising water, the desperate pounding of the engines, and the confused panic of the crew.

Creative sound people are ingenious in combining natural and synthesized sounds to get just the right combination to create the appropriate condition. The sound tracks of extraterrestrial stories especially display the virtuosity of such sound designers.[13]

Inner Orientation Functions of Sound

The inner orientation functions of sound include those related to mood, internal condition, and energy.

MOOD

Music is one of the most direct ways of establishing a certain mood. Music can make us laugh or cry, feel happy or sad. It seems to affect our emotions directly without first being filtered through our *ratio*—our rational faculties. This is one of the reasons why we so readily accept music as part of a scene regardless of whether its inclusion makes any story sense. In relation to the visual screen event, music certainly appoints a persuasive context that engenders an audio/video Kuleshov effect (see chapter 18).

Happy music can underscore the overall happy context of the screen event; sad or ominous music will do the opposite. Even if the visual part of a scene expresses a neutral or positive atmosphere, accompanying ominous music will override the visual cues and forewarn the viewer-listener of an impending disaster. As a matter of fact, if you show a relatively neutral scene, such as a mother kissing her children good-bye and then driving off to work, different types of music can shape our perception of this event. With upbeat music we tend to interpret the scene as a happy one; the mother and the children will have a good day. If accompanied by haunting music, we will perceive the identical scene with foreboding and fear that something will happen to either the mother or the children.

Obviously, we can also create or underscore mood with a variety of nonmusical sounds (usually synthesized or otherwise electronically distorted sounds) or a combination of music and nonmusical sounds.

INTERNAL CONDITION

Sounds can express a variety of internal conditions, such as an unstable environment (often in conjunction with the contextual visual clue: the tilting of the horizon line) or a person who feels calm, excited, or agitated. For example, to reveal the fear and the panic of sailors in the flooded engine room, you could put yet another layer of "internal fear" sounds on top of the sounds that depict the squeezing of space. Recall the pounding rhythms that accompanied the scene in the psychiatric ward. This nonliteral use of music intensified the internal condition of the patient.

ENERGY

Music and other nonliteral sounds, such as electronic hisses, whistles, and whines, can provide or increase the aesthetic energy of a scene. Again, the immediate way in which sound affects our emotions is a perfect tool for establishing or supplementing the energy of the screen event. Cartoons, for example, rely heavily on music and sound effects as an energy source. In a cartoon there is no such thing as the villain simply plunging toward the earth; he is literally driven into the ground by the accompanying sound effects. Many crime shows have low-frequency thumps infiltrate most of the dialogue to make sure we understand that there is an impending crisis and to keep our anxiety level high enough so that we won't switch channels. In a similarly unsubtle way, car chases are often energized by frantic music as are scenes in which people run from or toward disaster.

Internal energy is just as easily expressed or supplemented by music. Even if you show a static scene of two people staring at each other, appropriate music will reveal their inner state and the general energy level of the scene.

People have used music and sound effects as energizing elements of the performing arts for quite some time. The high energy of an African dance is primarily dictated and communicated by pounding drums. When the long Greek plays threatened to lose energy and the audience's attention despite the tragic battles of gods and mortals, flute players were called on-stage to keep things moving.[14] Some

"If the music draws away or diverts from the dramatic shape, line, or impulse, it doesn't fit the film. If it understates the case, it will be a disappointment. And if it overstates a particular situation along the way, it will cause a problem of balance or a distortion of the dramatic line. On the other hand, if the music connects with the film in terms of dramatic shape and meaning, bringing out various aspects in a corroborative manner without overdoing it, the music begins to fit the film. How this is done in each situation is the basic question—the most important question for all film music composers."[15]

—**George Burt**, *The Art of Film Music* (1994)

2,500 years later, it is a rare play that does not make some use of music and sound effects not only to underscore the mood of certain scenes but also to add aesthetic energy. The sound effects accompanying video games are based on the same aesthetic principle. You must be careful, however, not to overwhelm the visual with music. After all, the music should be an accompaniment, not the major attraction of the scene. You may also find that *not* using music but only exaggerated literal sounds and long silences in an especially tense scene can be a startling intensifier.

Structural Functions of Sound

One of the most important, though least conspicuous, functions of sound is to help structure the screen event in various ways. The major structural elements are rhythm, figure/ground, sound perspective, and sound continuity.

RHYTHM

You may discover that despite great care your editing has little structural coherence and lacks a precise tertiary motion beat. Such problems frequently occur during continuity editing, when vector continuity rather than rhythm is the major criterion for the cut. In this case, a highly rhythmic sound track will help establish a precise tertiary motion beat even if the visual editing is rhythmically uneven. The sound rhythm acts like a clothesline on which you can "hang" shots of various lengths without sacrificing rhythmic continuity. **SEE 15.6**

When sound rhythms and picture rhythms parallel each other, the total structure becomes unified and stable. **SEE 15.7** Be careful, however, that the beat

15.6 Irregular Picture Sequence Structured Through Sound

In an irregular picture structure, a prominent audio beat will dominate and can, in most cases, make the irregular video rhythm seem structured.

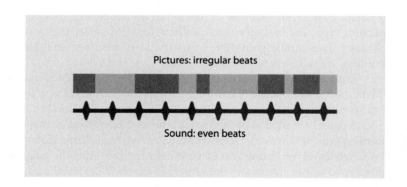

Pictures: irregular beats

Sound: even beats

15.7 Parallel Picture/Sound Structure

In a parallel structure, the tertiary motion of the picture portion (editing beat) is accompanied by an identical beat in the sound portion. The picture and sound rhythms match.

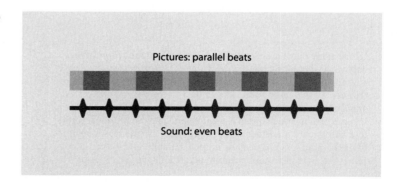

Pictures: parallel beats

Sound: even beats

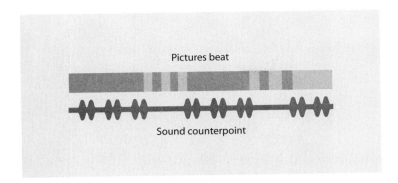

15.8 Picture/Sound Counterpoint

In a picture/sound counterpoint, the rhythm of the video portion (editing beat) relates to the sound rhythm contrapuntally. This can mean that a relatively fast video beat is juxtaposed with a slow sound beat and vice versa.

does not become too regular for too long; this can make the total rhythmic structure monotonous and boring. An interesting rhythm is not one that has parallel tertiary motion and sound track beats but rather one that is slightly syncopated. In such a picture/sound counterpoint, the editing and sound rhythms run parallel for a while but then shift to a contrapuntal structure in which a relatively fast video-editing sequence is juxtaposed with the slow beat of the sound track, or a relatively slow picture sequence is counterpointed with a fast sound rhythm. **SEE 15.8**

This juxtaposition of fast and slow video and audio rhythms is simply another application of the dialectic principle, which is based on putting opposing elements side-by-side (see chapter 18). Sensitively applied, such an audio/video dialectic will increase the complexity of the screen event without impairing its communication clarity. You can also analyze the relative magnitude and complexity of the visual vector field and match it with a sound vector field of similar or opposing characteristics. This aspect of structural matching is discussed in chapter 16.

FIGURE/GROUND

The *figure/ground principle*, according to which we organize our visual environment into a mobile figure and a relatively stable background, also applies to sound.[16] In sound design figure/ground means that you choose the important sounds to be the figure while relegating the other sounds to the background. For example, in a location news report, you need to emphasize the reporter's voice over the ambient sounds of the fire engines and other rescue equipment. The reporter's voice functions as the figure, and the environmental sounds are the ground.

The same figure/ground principle applies when you show two people whispering sweet nothings into each other's ears while standing at a busy downtown street corner. **SEE 15.9** In a long shot, the visual figure/ground relationship between the couple, the other people, and the cars on the street is ambiguous. The visual aspect of cars and people rushing by the happy couple is equally prominent. Consequently, you can mix the couple's voices liberally with traffic and other ambient sounds.

But as soon as you take a close-up of the couple, you establish a much clearer visual figure/ground relationship.

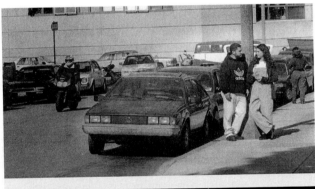

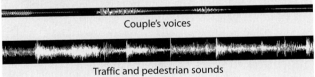

Couple's voices

Traffic and pedestrian sounds

15.9 Figure/Ground in Long Shot

In a long shot, the figure/ground relationship between a prominent foreground sound and ambient environmental sounds is purposely de-emphasized. In this case, the traffic and pedestrian sounds are as audible as the couple's whispers.

15.10 Figure/Ground in Close-up

In a close-up the traffic sounds are relegated to the background, and the couple's quiet whispering is emphasized as the figure (close-up sound).

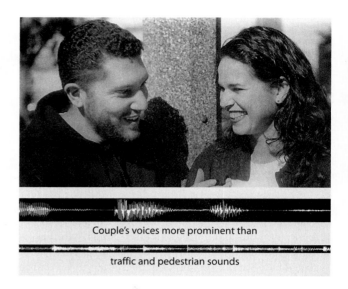

Couple's voices more prominent than

traffic and pedestrian sounds

SEE 15.10 Now the couple stands out as the figure from the partial street background, and viewers expect the sound to follow suit. Regardless of what the actual volume relationship may be between traffic sounds and the couple's voices, their flirtation must now become the sound figure, and the traffic sounds become the ground.

You have surely noticed that this figure/ground principle of sound is identical to that of aerial perspective. In both cases, we "focus" on a particular visual or aural plane while rendering the other picture and sound elements as "out-of-focus" background (see chapter 9). This figure/ground control is possible, however, only if you have separated as much as possible the various sound "planes" during the sound pickup and recorded them on different tracks. In this way the sounds can be remixed in postproduction according to the figure/ground requirements. In critical sound mixing, you may have to record and lip-sync the couple's intimate chatter and mix it with traffic sounds in the studio. Obviously, this technique is much more cumbersome and time-consuming than spending a little more time on the field pickup.

SOUND PERSPECTIVE

Sound perspective means that you match close-up pictures with "close" sounds, and long shots with sounds that seem to come from farther away. Close sounds have more presence than far-away sounds. ***Presence*** is a sound quality that makes you feel as though you are close to the sound source.

Sound perspective also depends on the figure/ground relationship. When we see the happy couple in a long shot standing on a busy street corner, we should hear their voices as coming from equally far away. On a close-up, however, we want their voices to come from a closer distance. The "close-up" sound must have considerably more presence than the sounds in the long shot.

As you have probably noticed, most everyday broadcast television productions, such as news, interviews, game shows, and routine field productions, do not bother with sound perspective. In many cases, the talent wear lavaliere microphones that are fixed to their clothing and therefore do not change the distance from sound source (mouth) to microphone during field-of-view changes (such as a cut from a long shot of all the guests in an interview show to a tight close-up of one of the guests). Because in such cases the perceived distance between long shot and close-up is relatively small (moving, perhaps, from a medium shot to a tight close-up), the lack of sound perspective is not detrimental to the overall effect. If, however, you use lavaliere mics for more ambitious productions, such as dramas or soap operas, the lack of sound perspective becomes painfully apparent. In this case, you need to resort to boom- or fishpole-supported microphones, which can be moved closer or farther away from the sound source for proper sound perspective.[17]

SOUND CONTINUITY

Sound continuity means that the sound maintains its intended volume and quality over a series of edits. As with visual vector or color continuity from shot to shot, we expect a similar continuity of sound vectors. For example, if you cross-cut between close-ups of two people talking with each other, their voices should not change perceptibly in either volume or presence during the cutting sequence. You can achieve continuity most easily by keeping the background sounds as even and continuous as possible. So long as you maintain an even level of ambient sounds, viewers will perceive the foreground sounds as continuous even if they change somewhat in volume, quality, and presence from shot to shot.

Such a technique comes in handy especially when a reporter switches from a low-quality lavaliere mic for the field sound pickup to a high-quality studio mic for the voice-over narration parts once back at the studio.

The same aesthetic principle applies to lighting and color. Despite a cluttered set that has a great variety of brightly colored foreground pieces, you can achieve some sort of visual continuity by keeping the background evenly illuminated and painted with a uniform color of low saturation. As you can see, many of the basic principles apply in some way to all five aesthetic fields; they are, at least to some degree, dependent on one another. This interdependency of aesthetic elements is the main attribute of the various media aesthetic fields.

SUMMARY

The major aspects of the five-dimensional field are: sound and noise, video and film sound, literal and nonliteral sounds, the information function of sound, the outer orientation functions of sound, the inner orientation functions of sound, and the structural functions of sound.

Sound and noise are both audible vibrations of the air or some other material. The difference is that sound has a communication purpose; noise is random and unwanted.

In video, including broadcast television, sound is especially important because much of the programming is reality based, and we experience the world as an audiovisual environment. The low-definition, inductively presented video pictures also need sound as an important informational supplement. Production restrictions, such as low-fidelity speakers and the simultaneous pickup of sound with the pictures, render broadcast television sound usually low-definition. With respect to energy matching between video pictures and sound, the low-definition television sound seems more appropriate to the low-definition image than would high-definition, high-energy sound.

Film and large-screen, high-definition video sound require a higher fidelity than standard television sound, which is important when matching audio and video energies on the large screen. HDTV and certain video programs use postproduction sound techniques that are similar or identical to those of film. The 5.1 surround-sound system is an important feature of large-screen video displays.

Literal sound is referential. It conveys specific meaning and refers to the sound-originating source. Literal, or diegetic, sounds can be source-connected (we see on-screen what is making the sound) or source-disconnected (we see something else on-screen while hearing the sound).

Nonliteral, or nondiegetic, sounds do not carry a particular meaning or point to a sound source. They are deliberately source-disconnected. Some sounds, such as music, can be literal or nonliteral, depending on the visual context.

Video and film sound has four basic functions: information, outer orientation, inner orientation, and structural.

The information function of sound includes all forms of speech, such as dialogue, direct address, and narration. Dialogue is the major form of speech in film, with direct address used only on special occasions. In broadcast television all three forms of speech are common.

The outer orientation functions of sound include orientation in space, in time, to situation, and to external event conditions.

Sound can identify a particular location (downtown, countryside) and the relative position of the sound source on the x-axis of the motion picture or video screen. It can indicate spatial characteristics of an environment (large empty hall, small constricted space) and events that happen in off-screen space. We readily identify specific sounds with a particular clock time or season.

Sound can also give clues about the prevailing situation and reinforce the external condition of an object or event, such as big or small, or fast or slow. Predictive sound means that certain sound changes or repeated sound phrases (leitmotivs) can portend an upcoming event.

The inner orientation functions of sound include mood, internal condition, and energy.

Music is one of the most efficient aesthetic elements to create a specific mood or describe an internal condition. Music and nonliteral sounds are often used to provide additional energy for a scene.

One of the most important structural functions of sound, especially for video, is to supplement the rhythm of the shot sequence or supplement the rhythm of the entire visual vector structure. The rhythm of the sound track can run parallel as a counterpoint to the video rhythm.

Figure/ground in the five-dimensional field means that some sounds are treated as the more prominent foreground sounds (figure) while others are kept in the background (ground).

Sound perspective refers to how close we perceive a sound to be; close-ups should sound nearer than long shots. Sound continuity means that the sound should maintain its intended volume and quality over a series of related shots. This is especially important when different microphones are used by the same talent for on-screen and off-screen comments.

N O T E S

1. See the comments in chapter 18 on the effect of sound on montage.

2. D. W. Griffith was quite despondent about the use of sound in cinema and the resulting loss of power of the montage. He begged to "give us back our beauty." See David Thomson, *A Biographical Dictionary of Film,* 3rd ed. (New York: Alfred A. Knopf, 1994), p. 273. Also note the comments by Rudolf Arnheim, "A New Laocoön: Artistic Composites and the Talking Film," in his *Film as Art* (Berkeley: University of California Press, 1957), pp. 199–230. Also see Elisabeth Weis and John Belton (eds.), *Film Sound: Theory and Practice* (New York: Columbia University Press, 1985).

3. V. I. Pudovkin, *Film Technique and Film Acting,* ed. and trans. by Ivor Montagu (New York: Grove Press, 1960), pp. 310–11.

4. Standard TV here means a 480-line scanning system and a maximum screen size of 26 inches. For a discussion of television as a low-definition media, see Marshall McLuhan, *Understanding Media: The Extensions of Man* (New York: McGraw-Hill, 1964), pp. 311–14.

5. Siegfried Kracauer, *Theory of Film: The Redemption of Physical Reality* (New York: Oxford University Press, 1960), pp. 104–6.

6. Jay Rose, *Producing Great Sound for Film and Video,* 3rd ed. (Burlington, Mass.: Focal Press, 2008). See also Vinay Shrivastava, *Aesthetics of Sound* (Dubuque, Iowa: Kendall/Hunt, 1996).

7. Bernard De Voto (ed.), *The Portable Mark Twain* (New York: Viking Press, 1946), pp. 542–43, 553.

8. Dr. Shani Orgad was one of the first media scholars to write a comprehensive report on mobile TV (cell-phone video); in it she details various business, social, and media aesthetic reasons for its use. See Shani Orgad, *This box was made for walking: how will mobile TV transform viewers' experience and change advertising?* Nokia Mobile TV report 2006, no. 2519. Available at *www.nokia.com/NOKIA_COM_1/Press/Press_Events/mobile_tv_report,_november_10,_2006/Mobil_TV_Report.pdf.*

9. McLuhan, *Understanding Media,* p. 284.

10. Christian Metz, "Aural Objects," in Weis and Belton, *Film Sound,* pp. 157–58.

11. Stanley R. Alten, *Audio in Media,* 9th ed. (Belmont, Calif.: Wadsworth, 2011), pp. 83–84.

12. Benjamin P. Wilson, "The Design, Application and Evaluation of Stereophonic Television: A Production Model." Master's thesis, San Francisco State University, 1980.

13. Some sound designers for major films assign assistants the responsibility for the sounds of a single scene or for a specific type of sounds, such as the flooding of a damaged submarine or all helicopter sounds. Some critics claim that such a method may work against a unified style. See George Burt, *The Art of Film Music* (Boston: Northeastern University Press, 1994). In his highly informative though quite technical book, film composer and teacher Burt demonstrates with a number of examples how a film composer conceives and structures film music.

   On the other side of the fence, Theodor Adorno feels that "despite all the talk, film music has up to now not seen any influx of truly new impulses." Theodor Adorno and Hans Eisler, "Komposition für den Film" (Composition for Film), in Theodor Adorno, *Gesammelte Schriften* 15 (Frankfurt am Main, Germany: Suhrkamp Verlag, 1976), p. 89 (translation by the author). Adorno was clearly caught between his Marxist ideology and his reverence for classical music. Vinay Shrivastava provides a good summary of the Marxist approach to film sound; see his *Aesthetics of Sound,* pp. 177–224.

14. See the delightful description of the role of music in Greek plays as quoted by Ernest Lindgren, *The Art of Film* (New York: Macmillan, 1963), p. 134.

15. Burt, *Art of Film Music,* p. 5.

16. See the discussion of figure/ground in chapter 7.

17. Herbert Zettl, *Television Production Handbook,* 10th ed. (Belmont, Calif.: Wadsworth, 2009), p. 184.

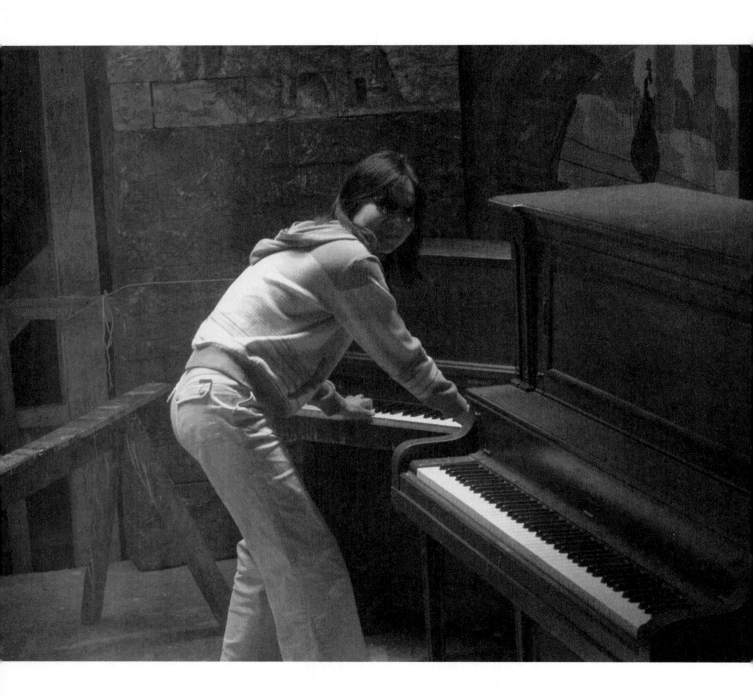

16

Structuring the Five-dimensional Field: Sound Structures and Sound/Picture Combinations

I N THIS CHAPTER YOU WILL ENCOUNTER TERMS THAT ARE QUITE FAMILIAR to musicians and people who deal with music theory but that may be new to you. You may also be somewhat reluctant to make sense of the many examples that use musical notation, much like our tendency to skip examples that contain mathematical formulas. But even if you don't read music, you can understand the examples by simply connecting the notes so that they form vectors. When translated into graphic, index, and motion vectors, musical notation can describe a line, a direction, a movement, and horizontal and vertical structures. Take a moment to look ahead to the figures indicated in the following paragraph.

If the horizontal vectors have an uphill slant, the tune is rising; if they go downhill, the tune gets lower (see figure 16.25). If the vectors go up and down, the melody similarly goes up and down. If the vertical vectors show many notes stacked on top of each other, the chords are dense; if they consist of only two or three notes, the chords are less dense (see figures 16.18 and 16.19). A single note can be subdivided into several shorter notes, which are played faster (see figure 16.3). The basic beat is indicated by the numbers preceding the first note, such as 4/4 or 3/4. The 4/4 has four beats to each unit, called a bar; the 3/4 has three beats to each bar (see figure 16.20).

Now that you have some idea of how to deal with musical notation, I suggest that you listen to the examples by taking the shortcut to the book's Companion Web Site: *www.zettl-ssm.com*. Each track is labeled by figure number as referenced in this chapter. Try to listen to the music while following the notation vectors.

That's all there is to it, at least so far as this chapter is concerned. Even if you don't intend to deal this closely with sound structures, you will nevertheless learn patterns that transfer quite readily to the organization of visual elements.

In this chapter you need to pay particular attention to elements of sound, basic sound structures, picture/sound combinations, and picture/sound matching criteria. When talking about sound, you will have to consider not only its physical characteristics, such as the frequency or loudness of a sound, but also its psychological characteristics, such as how high or low, or how loud or soft we perceive a tone to be. As with color, however, neat physical formulas for sound use do not always translate into equally neat perceptions. Our definitions are therefore often based on perceptual rather than strict physical phenomena and processes. Such perceptions are truly contextual.

Elements of Sound

When you strike a single piano key, blow into a trumpet, or draw the bow across a violin string, you can hear five distinct attributes, or elements, of sound: pitch, timbre, duration, loudness (dynamics), and attack/decay.

PITCH

Pitch indicates the relative highness and lowness of a sound measured against an agreed-upon scale. The pitch of a tone is perceived and measured by its frequency—its vibrations per second. A high-pitched tone vibrates with a higher frequency than a low-pitched tone. The generally accepted pitch standard is the A above middle C, called A4 because it is four octaves above A0, the lowest note of a standard piano. A4 vibrates 440 times per second, which is expressed as 440 Hz (hertz, the international unit of frequency). **SEE 16.1**

TIMBRE

Timbre (rhymes with "amber") describes the tone quality or tone color. The timbre of a tone tells you whether it is produced by a trumpet or a violin. Technically, the timbre of a sound is created by the kind and the relative number of overtones. *Overtones* are a number of frequencies with which a sound-producing source vibrates in addition to its fundamental frequency—the one that we hear as a specific pitch.

All overtones have a higher pitch than the basic tone, although you don't hear the individual overtones as higher pitches in combination with the basic tone. Rather, you perceive the overtones more like a superimposition, as a richer, more complex tone than one without any or with fewer overtones. The figure on the facing page illustrates the formation of overtones. **SEE 16.2**

The point to remember is that a rich, full sound has many overtones; a thin or hollow sound has few overtones. Some instruments, such as the flute, produce sounds with fewer overtones than the violin or cello. The human voice has more overtones than most instruments. When computers were first used to synthesize the human voice, it was the lack of sufficient overtones that gave the voice its robotic monotone "computer-speak" quality.

To listen to the audio files of the music examples in this chapter, take the shortcut to the *Sight Sound Motion* Companion Web Site: **www.zettl-ssm.com**.

16.1 Pitch

You can recognize the pitch of a tone by its relative position on the staff. Note that a higher octave of a tone is exactly twice its frequency; the lower octave is half its frequency.

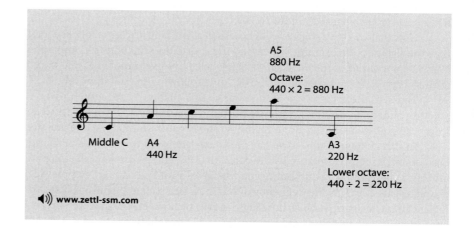

A5
880 Hz

Octave:
440 × 2 = 880 Hz

Middle C   A4
440 Hz

A3
220 Hz

Lower octave:
440 ÷ 2 = 220 Hz

www.zettl-ssm.com

16.2 Timbre

a When you pluck a violin string, it moves back and forth between fixed points (the upper end of the fingerboard and the bridge) in a wavelike pattern. The crest of the wave moves in one direction, and the valley comes back from the opposite direction. Practically, the whole string appears to be moving up and down. The number of such up-and-down movements of the string per second determines its basic frequency (hertz) and pitch. This fundamental frequency is the tone's first harmonic. Because the vibration of the string as drawn in this illustration has no other vibrations superimposed on it, it has no overtones.

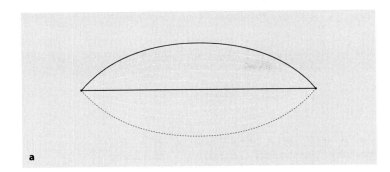

a

b The violin string also vibrates simultaneously in separate sections. In this illustration each half of the string vibrates twice as fast as the total string, which is an exact octave of the basic frequency. This octave is the second harmonic and represents the first overtone.

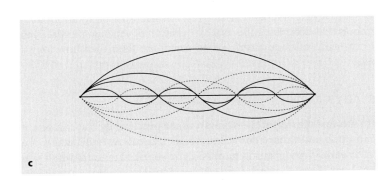

b

c The more sections of the string that vibrate in multiples of the basic frequency, the more numerous and the higher the harmonics become. Although you may not be able to hear each overtone separately, you perceive the sum of these overtones as a richer sound.

c

The frequency of the fundamental tone—and those frequencies that are simple multiples of the fundamental tone, such as double, three times, or six times the frequency of the fundamental—are called *harmonics*. Thus the fundamental tone (the one that determines the pitch) is the first harmonic. The second harmonic may be a frequency twice as high as that of the fundamental. This second harmonic represents the first overtone. Because it has a frequency twice that of the fundamental tone, it is an octave higher. The second and all subsequent harmonics have a progressively higher frequency than the fundamental tone. Let us assume that the fundamental tone (first harmonic) vibrates at a frequency of 440 Hz. You would hear an A4—the normal A you hear when an orchestra tunes up. If the first overtone (second harmonic) vibrates at 880 Hz, which is twice the frequency of the fundamental, you would hear a tone that is an octave higher than the fundamental. If the second overtone (third harmonic) vibrates at three times the frequency of the fundamental, you would have a 1,320 Hz tone (which is a very high E added to the overtones).

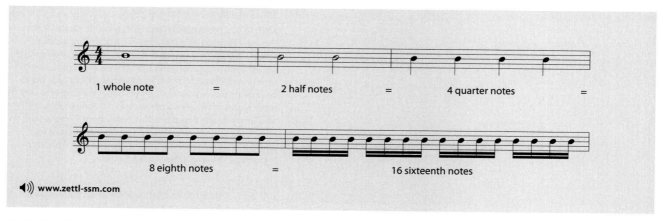

1 whole note   =   2 half notes   =   4 quarter notes   =

8 eighth notes   =   16 sixteenth notes

www.zettl-ssm.com

16.3 Duration

In musical notation the duration of a tone is precisely determined by a specific symbol, such as whole notes, half notes, quarter notes, eighth notes, and so forth. Just how long a whole note is supposed to be when measured by a stopwatch depends entirely on the basic tempo of the piece or section.

DURATION

Duration refers to how long you hear a sound lasting. **SEE 16.3** You may perceive very short bursts of a tone or a long, continuous one. Most musical instruments permit some control of sound duration, like the bow that one pulls across the strings or piano pedals that one depresses or releases. In musical notation there are specific symbols that determine the relative duration of various sounds. Even then different musicians or conductors like to decide on their own how long a note should be.

LOUDNESS (DYNAMICS)

The *loudness* of a tone is its apparent strength as we perceive it. You can play a tone of a certain pitch and timbre either loudly or softly. Essentially, when you have to hold your ears while listening to music, the sounds are loud; when you have to strain to hear them, they are soft. Loud sounds have a high magnitude; soft sounds have a low one. The variations of perceived strength are the *dynamics* of the sound.[1] **SEE 16.4**

f   = forte (loud)

ff   = fortissimo (very loud)

fff = forte fortissimo (extremely loud)

p   = piano (soft)

pp   = pianissimo (very soft)

ppp = piano pianissimo (extremely soft)

16.4 Loudness (Dynamics)

In musical notation the loudness of a tone is indicated by symbols. The electronic volume control on an audio console ultimately affords, of course, more loudness variations.

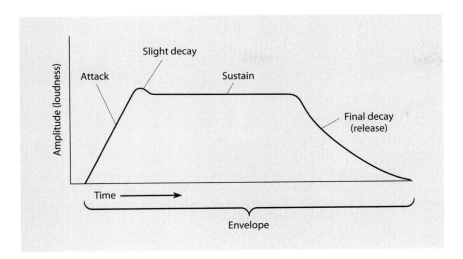

16.5 Envelope

The basic sound envelope consists of attack, initial decay, sustain level, and final release. The time it takes for the release is the final decay of the sound. The length of the release is the decay time.

ATTACK/DECAY

The attack or decay of a sound is part of its dynamics and duration. *Attack* refers to how fast a sound reaches a certain loudness level. After the attack the sound dips a little in volume and then maintains the desired volume level. This steady maximum loudness of a tone is called sustain level. From the point the tone starts to get softer until we can no longer perceive it is called its *decay*. The whole process, from initial attack to final decay, is called the sound envelope or, simply, *envelope*. The envelope represents the total sound duration and not just its sustain level. **SEE 16.5**

To make things even more complicated, there is some confusion among audio experts about just what "decay" means. For some, especially the people who are engaged in synthesized sound, decay refers to the little dip after the attack just before the volume reaches its sustain level and not the fading of the sound volume. What is normally meant by decay, they call "release." For our purposes we will settle on the more common use of *decay*—the fading of the volume until the sound is no longer perceivable.

Both attack and decay can be fast or slow. In vector terminology a fast attack means that the sound vector achieves its maximum magnitude quickly. **SEE 16.6** In a slow attack, it takes the sound vector some time to get up to its maximum strength (loudness). **SEE 16.7**

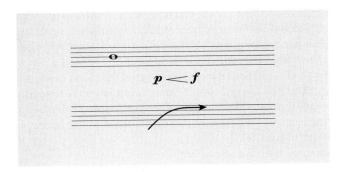

16.6 Fast Attack

In a fast attack, the sound gets loud quickly; the rise time is short. It is a high-magnitude sound vector.

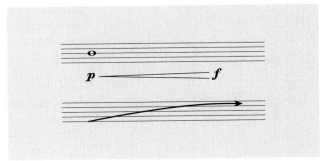

16.7 Slow Attack

In a slow attack, the sound takes a while to reach the desired loudness; the rise time is slow. It is a low-magnitude sound vector.

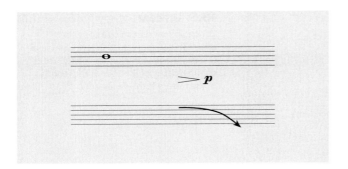

16.8 Fast Decay

In a fast decay, the sound dies quickly. It is a high-magnitude sound vector.

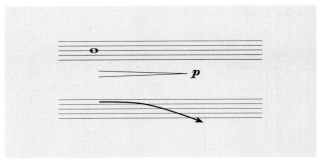

16.9 Slow Decay

In a slow decay, the sound fades more gradually. It is a low-magnitude sound vector.

The sustain level is how long the vector maintains at a relatively steady magnitude. When its magnitude starts to decrease, the sound has entered its decay phase. A fast decay means that the sound vector drops from its high magnitude to zero relatively quickly. **SEE 16.8** When it takes some time for the vector to lose its strength, the sound has a slow decay. **SEE 16.9**

In musical language crescendo stands for a relatively gradual change from soft to loud, and diminuendo is a gradual change from loud to soft. They differ from attack and decay mainly in terms of speed. Even a slow attack is much faster than a crescendo.

Some instruments have by their very nature a fast or slow decay. A drum has a relatively fast decay (thump), and a church bell has a relatively slow one (ring). Much like timbre, the stages of the sound envelope, such as the attack phase, have some influence on how we perceive a specific tone. A fast attack gives the tone a more aggressive edge than does a slow attack.[2]

Not all instruments give you the same control over the sound envelope (duration and dynamics from attack to final decay). As a violin player, for example, you would have maximum control over the attack time, the sustain level, and the decay time. Depending on how you use the bow, you can produce a fast or slow attack, a short or long sustain level, and a fast or slow decay. When playing the piano, however, you have control over the dynamics of the tone (its loudness or softness) but not over its attack and sustain level. The only control you have is over the decay period. When you press the sustain pedal, the sound takes more time to fade; the pedal stretches the decay. The dampening pedal shortens the decay; the tone dies more quickly. When playing the drums, you are at the mercy of the instrument for the entire envelope. You can strike it only softly or hard, to produce a soft or loud bang, but you have no control over attack, sustain level, or decay. The cymbals, on the other hand, give you an almost instant attack but a very slow decay, unless you stop their vibrations with your hand.

The decay of sound is also influenced by the acoustics of the room. In a fairly "live" acoustical environment, the decay is slower (more reverberations) than in a rather "dead" environment (fewer reverberations). When synthesizing sounds and sound combinations, the control of all the major elements of the sound envelope obviously plays an important role.

When you combine picture and sound vectors, you can match the attack and decay variables of both vector types. For example, a visual motion vector can reflect a variety of attack and decay modes, depending on how fast it reaches or loses a specific maximum magnitude. If an object accelerates to a specific speed quickly, you have a motion vector with a fast attack; if it accelerates more gradually, you have a slow-attack motion vector. **SEE 16.10** If the object motion decelerates

16.10 Fast and Slow Acceleration

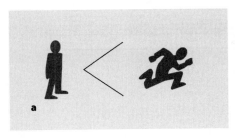

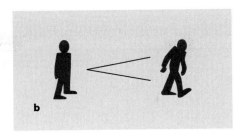

a A fast acceleration (fast attack) creates a high-magnitude vector.

b A slow acceleration (slow attack) creates a low-magnitude vector.

16.11 Fast and Slow Deceleration

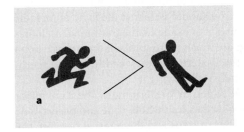

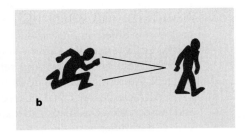

a A fast deceleration (fast decay) creates a high-magnitude vector.

b A slow deceleration (slow decay) creates a low-magnitude vector.

quickly, its magnitude drops equally quickly, and you have a fast-decay motion vector. If it decelerates more gradually, it produces a slow-decay motion vector. **SEE 16.11** The advantage of translating sound into vectors is explored more fully later in this chapter.

Basic Sound Structures

This discussion of sound structures is not meant to be exhaustive but to aid you in dealing effectively with the sound portion of a video or film production. It will help you especially in developing, or deciding on, a sound track that not only supports the video portion but also combines with it synergistically to become an organic, maximally effective whole. To achieve this you should try to translate musical elements and structures into various types of sound vectors whenever possible. As mentioned at the beginning of this chapter, seeing music in terms of sound vectors means you can, for example, deal successfully with the basic notation of a musical piece even if you don't read music. More important, vectors allow you to compare sound with pictures and find relationships between sound and pictures that would otherwise not have been so evident. Vectors convey more readily than any other aesthetic factor the contextual nature of media aesthetics.

Let's now take a closer look at the following basic sound structures: melody, harmony, homophony, and polyphony.

MELODY

A *melody* is a series of musical tones arranged in succession. Like a sequential series of shots, a melody is a sequential series of specific sounds that has a logic in

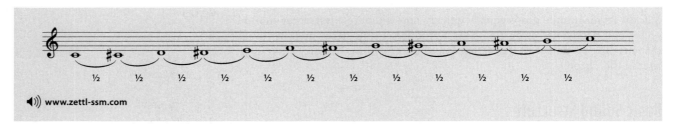

Horizontal sound vector

www.zettl-ssm.com

16.12 Melody

Melody moves as a horizontal sound vector in a linear fashion. Each tone leads to another until they become an entity—a tune.

Composer **Arnold Schönberg** (1874–1951) established the twelve-tone system as a useful compositional device. He taught in Berlin and at the University of California at Los Angeles.

its progression and that forms a tune. Melody can be represented by a horizontal vector. **SEE 16.12**

Like life itself, a melody is constantly progressing and is complete only when it has ended. You experience the various steps of progression, but you can only remember the total melody—the tune. You should note that the logic of melodic progression differs among various cultures. For example, the traditional melodies of Middle Eastern or Far Eastern songs are much more subtle in their progression than are Western melodies. And yet the Eastern cultures readily, if not eagerly, embrace Western music and do extremely well playing it.

All melodies are based on specific scales. In Western music there are major and minor scales, chromatic and diatonic scales, and whole-tone and twelve-tone scales. They differ basically in the number of steps and the interval between the steps within an octave (when the tone repeats itself higher or lower on the scale). **SEE 16.13–16.17**

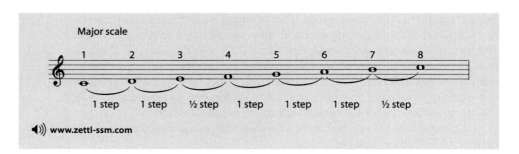

www.zettl-ssm.com

16.13 Chromatic Scale

In the chromatic scale, an octave is divided into 12 equal steps, with the twelfth tone being the octave (double the frequency of the fundamental). It consists entirely of half-tone intervals.

Major scale

www.zettl-ssm.com

16.14 Major Diatonic Scale

In the diatonic scale, an octave is divided into eight steps, with the eighth tone being the octave (double the frequency of the tonic—the first tone). The steps are not equal, with half steps between the third and fourth tones and the seventh and eighth tones. The diatonic scale is what we (in Western music) normally use in melodic and harmonic structures. Generally, a major scale expresses a positive, normal, practical mood.

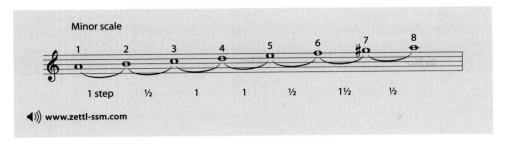

16.15 Minor Diatonic Scale

In the minor diatonic scale, the eight steps are not equal. There is a half step between the second and third tones and the fifth and sixth tones. In the ascending minor scale (which is illustrated here), there is an additional one-and-a-half step between the sixth and seventh tones and a half step between the seventh and eighth (octave) tones. The minor scale reflects a sad, mysterious, haunting, less definite mood.

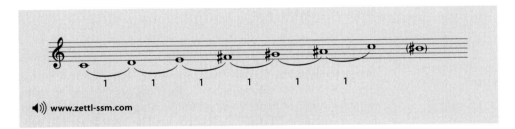

16.16 Whole-tone Scale

The whole-tone scale uses full steps between all seven intervals.

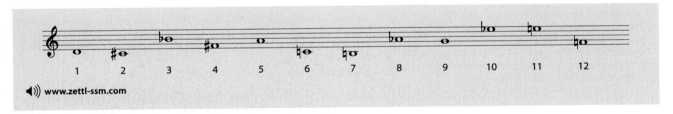

16.17 Twelve-tone Scale

Some composers simply regard the 12 tones of the chromatic scale as equal and arrange these notes in some form regardless of the specific intervals. Because there is a total of 12 notes in a scale before the notes begin to repeat themselves as an octave, the individual row can contain 12 notes. The structuring of such sets of 12 notes has become known as the twelve-tone scale.

HARMONY

Whereas a melody consists of horizontally successive notes, *harmony* is a vertical combination of simultaneously played notes. Melody is linear and sequential; it forms a horizontal vector. Harmony is simultaneous and forms a vertical vector. **SEE 16.18** Contrary to the melody, which you can perceive only incompletely in its development, you can hear harmony in its totality all at once. Melody leads somewhere; harmony is there. It has always arrived. The harmonic combination of two notes is normally called an interval, and three or more notes compose a *chord*.

The magnitude of the vertical sound vector depends on several factors, principally the relative density, or *sound*

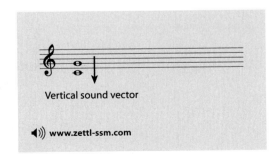

16.18 Harmony

A harmonic structure is created by simultaneous tones. Whereas melody consists of horizontal sound vectors, harmony consists of vertical ones.

16.19 Harmonic Density

Chords can vary considerably in their complexity—their relative chord density, or sound texture. To play this chord on the piano, you would have to press all the white and black keys between the highest and lowest notes of the chord.

From "Pentatonic" by P. Peter Sacco.

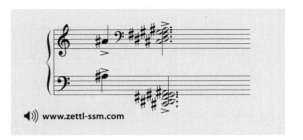

🔊 www.zettl-ssm.com

In traditional music, harmonic structures must adhere to strict rules. The simplest harmonic structure consists of two tones that are played simultaneously. Chords consist of three or more simultaneous tones.

Two simultaneous tones equal an interval.

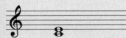

The basic unit of the traditional harmonic structure is the triad, a combination of three tones.

Major Triad

Minor Triad

Vertical harmonic structures are usually built from the same scale in which the melody operates (that is, the chords have the tonality of the melody), but the melody and the chords may also operate in different keys or outside of any predetermined scale (as in twelve-tone structures, for example).

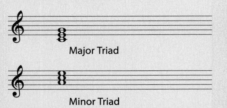

C Major

G Minor

🔊 www.zettl-ssm.com

texture, of the chord (the number of notes in the chord and how close together they are), its perceived tension (consonant, pleasant sounding, or dissonant, consisting of tones that do not blend together well), and its tension relative to the melody. Generally, the higher the chord density, texture, and tension, the higher the vector magnitude. **SEE 16.19**

HOMOPHONY

Homophony means literally "alike sounding" (Greek *homo* means "the same"; *phonos* means "sound"). In music **homophony** refers to the structure in which a single predominating melody is supported by corresponding chords. The chords act like pillars (vertical vectors) that hold up the melody bridge (horizontal vector). **SEE 16.20** In a homophonic structure, the horizontal vector of the melodic line is independent. You can re-create its logic by simply whistling any tune. **SEE 16.21** But the accompanying chords are dependent on the melody; they cannot stand alone—and playing them without the melody would make little sense. The chords by themselves do not lead to satisfactory musical closure. **SEE 16.22**

POLYPHONY

In musical terminology *polyphony* refers to two or more melodic lines that, when played together, form a harmonic whole. Unlike homophonic structures, where a single dominating melody is accompanied by supporting chords, polyphonic structures are composed of multiple, coequal voices (melodies, or horizontal vectors). No single voice is relegated to a subordinate role throughout the piece; each runs its own course, sometimes dominating the other voices and sometimes temporarily assuming a supporting role. When played separately, each voice forms a self-sufficient entity. **SEE 16.23** When played together the various horizontally independent voices form a vertical, harmonic structure. Vertical vectors are formed incidentally through planned juxtaposition and interaction of the horizontal vectors of the various voices. The voices must make sense not only horizontally (melodic development) but also vertically (harmonic development). **SEE 16.24**

Counterpoint   Most polyphonic music is written in *counterpoint*—a specific polyphonic technique in which the individual notes and melodic lines are set against each other. It emphasizes an encounter among the various voices, a vector-against-vector affair. We use counterpoint to achieve a certain structural tension, a high-energy field. By contrasting in a calculated way the various horizontal vectors

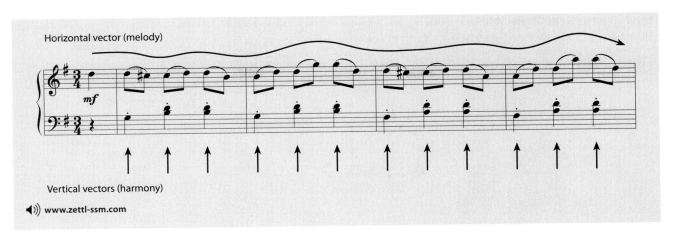

16.20 Homophony

In a typical homophonic structure, the leading melody is supported by a parallel chord accompaniment. When we translate into vectors the written music of this waltz in G major by Franz Schubert, we can see how the horizontal vector of the melody is supported by the vertical vectors of the chords.

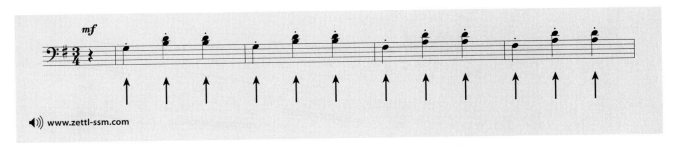

16.21 Melody

In a homophonic structure, the melodic horizontal vectors are independent. The melody can exist by itself.

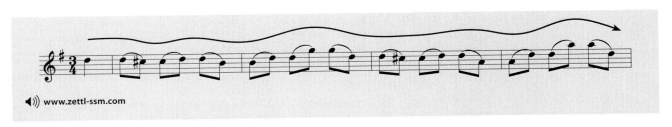

16.22 Chords

In a homophonic structure, the accompanying chords are dependent on the melody. They are dependent vertical vectors; that is, they need the melody to form a gestalt.

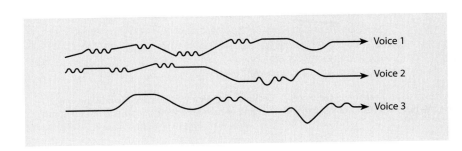

16.23 Polyphony

In a polyphonic structure, each voice (horizontal vector) is basically independent; that is, each voice has its own logical melodic development.

16.24 Horizontal and Vertical Structure

Although in polyphonic music the individual voices are basically independent, they nevertheless connect vertically to form a tight harmonic structure.

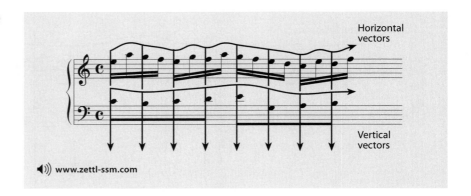

www.zettl-ssm.com

of the independent voices, we also create vertical vectors of varying complexity and magnitude.

Although counterpoint in music is limited to specific melodic and harmonic juxtapositions, for our purposes we can broaden the concept to include techniques for creating tension that involve other aesthetic elements, such as the direction of the voices (melodies) and their pitch, timbre, dynamics, and rhythm. Some of these techniques are similar to those employed in the visual aesthetic fields.

Contrapuntal tension is achieved primarily by having the *direction* of the voices—the melodic lines—go against each other. In the language of media aesthetics, the voices act as converging and diverging vectors. **SEE 16.25**

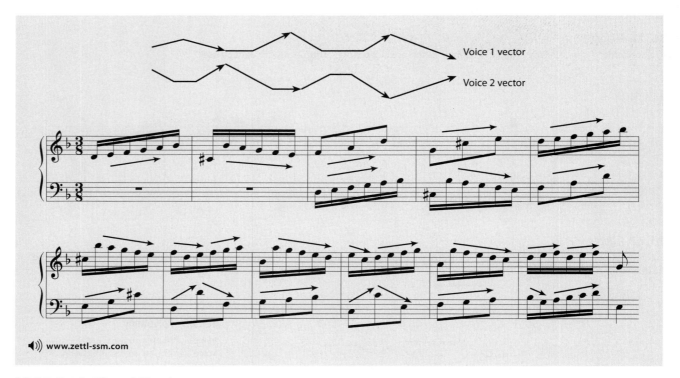

www.zettl-ssm.com

16.25 Tension Through Direction

To achieve the desired contrapuntal tension, we can contrast the direction of the voices—the horizontal vectors. While one melody line (voice) is going down, the other one is going up and vice versa. We have, in effect, converging and diverging vectors (and some continuing ones that run parallel to each other).

From *Inventio IV* by J. S. Bach.

Counterpoint means *punctum contra punctum,* Latin for "point against point." In the first half of the fourteenth century, when the term *counterpoint* first appeared, *punctum* (point) was synonymous with *nota* (note). *Punctum contra punctum* means, therefore, *nota contra notam*—"note against note." In the terminology of media aesthetics, we can define counterpoint as *vector contra vector*—"vector against vector."

You can also contrast the pitch of the various voices. While one voice operates in a relatively high range (treble), the other voice develops in a lower range (bass). **SEE 16.26**

You can achieve a contrast between voices by using timbre. One voice may be played by the violin, the other by the flute. **SEE 16.27**

Contrasting dynamics create various tensions even in a single melody (playing parts of it loudly and others softly), but they are especially effective when they occur between voices. For example, part of the upper voice is loud while the lower voice is soft; then the lower voice is played louder than the upper one. This use of contrapuntal dynamics draws attention to different parts (usually the theme) very much as a close-up does. If you thought that this is like a figure/ground

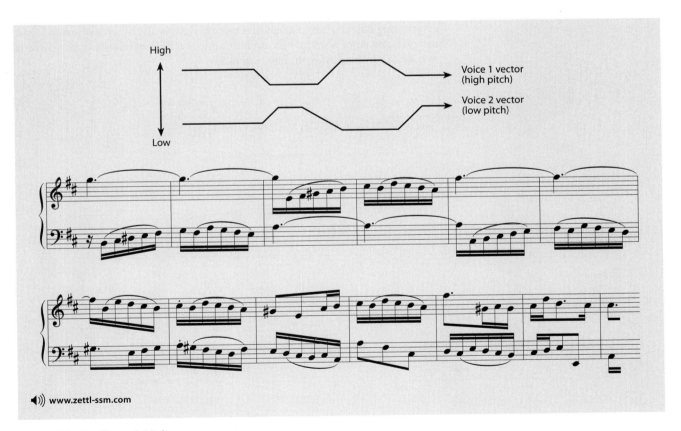

www.zettl-ssm.com

16.26 Tension Through Pitch

We can create contrapuntal tension through a contrast in pitch. In this example the first voice operates in a relatively high range (treble) while the other voice progresses in a lower range (bass).

From *Inventio III* by J. S. Bach.

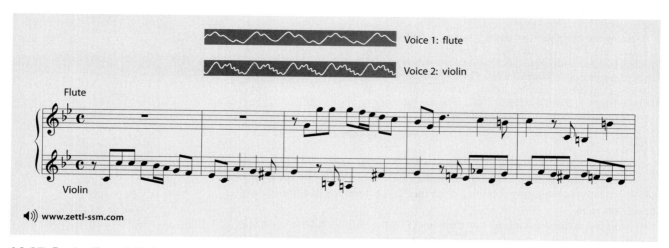

16.27 Tension Through Timbre

We can create contrapuntal tension by giving each voice a distinct timbre. This piece relies primarily on timbre for contrast. One voice is played by the flute, the other by the violin.

arrangement, you are on the right track. Through dynamics one voice can switch between being the figure for a few bars and then serving as background for the other voice. **SEE 16.28**

A rhythmic contrast is similar in effect to a dynamic one. While one voice is progressing quickly, the contrapuntal voice is slow, or the other way around. You can give one voice a sharp staccato beat and set it against another that proceeds in a more continuous legato line. **SEE 16.29**

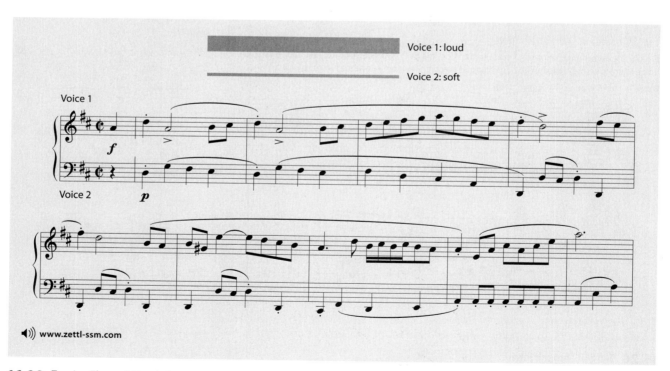

16.28 Tension Through Dynamics

We can create contrapuntal tension by contrasting the dynamics of the various voices. Here one voice (the theme) is rather loud; the other (the counterpoint) is much softer and less obtrusive. In effect there is a juxtaposition of sound vectors of varying magnitudes.

From March in D Major *by J. S. Bach.*

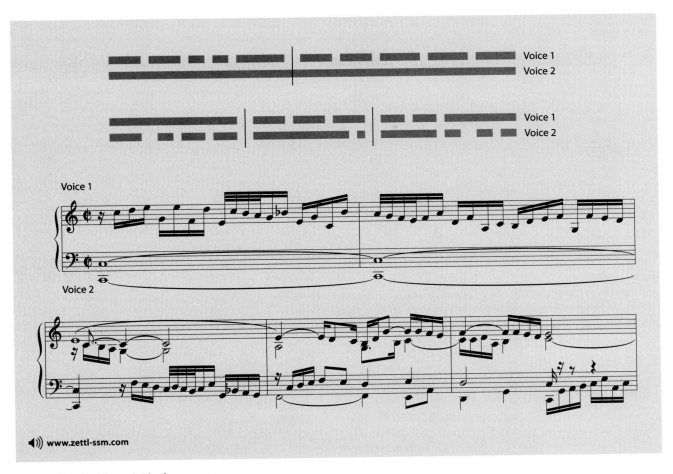

www.zettl-ssm.com

16.29 Tension Through Rhythm

One of the favorite techniques of creating tension in a polyphonic structure is to juxtapose different rhythms among the various voices. While one voice is progressing quickly, the contrapuntal voice is slow; while one has a sharp staccato beat, the other proceeds as a continuous legato line.

From *The Well-Tempered Clavier* by J. S. Bach.

Contrapuntal structures   Widely used contrapuntal structures are imitation, the canon, and the fugue. All these musical forms use the polyphonic principle in which each voice develops independently of the others yet plays against the others in highly calculated ways.

One of the most common elements of contrapuntal structure is *imitation*, wherein a short theme or subject is stated in one voice and then repeated verbatim or in a slightly changed form in the other voice or voices while the first voice continues on its way, providing the counterpoint to the imitated theme. **SEE 16.30** Most contrapuntal structures use some form of imitation.

The *canon*, or round, is the purest and most obvious form of imitation. Not only is the theme repeated verbatim by the other voices but also the entire melody. The harmonic (vertical) structure is created by a phasic shift of the identical melodies; that is, each one starts a little later than the voice immediately above. **SEE 16.31** Familiar canons, such as "Three Blind Mice" and "Row, Row, Row Your Boat," work on the total-imitation principle.

Simple repetitions of the same subject without varying counterpoints can be boring, however, which is why the masters of polyphony, such as Johann Sebastian Bach (1685–1750), vary not only the counterpoint from voice to voice but also occasionally the theme itself.[3]

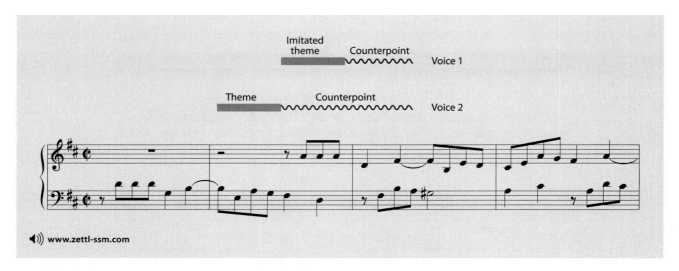

www.zettl-ssm.com

16.30 Imitation

One of the key elements of a polyphonic structure is imitation: a theme or short phrase is repeated verbatim one by one in the other voices. In this example the theme is stated in voice 2 and then imitated in a different pitch in voice 1.

From *The Well-Tempered Clavier* by J. S. Bach.

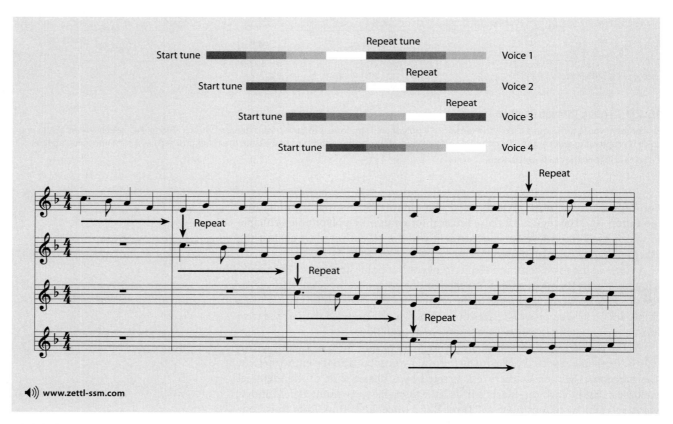

www.zettl-ssm.com

16.31 Canon

In a canon (or round), the complete tune is repeated by phasing. One voice starts the tune, and the others carry the same tune at staggered intervals. Note how the same subject is stated in one voice and then repeated verbatim in the others. The harmonic (vertical) structure is achieved through a phasic shift of the identical melodies.

One of the most intricate contrapuntal structures is the fugue (the word comes from the Latin *fugere*, "to run away, to flee"; and *fuga*, which means "flight"). In a **fugue** a theme or subject is chased and flees from voice to voice throughout the composition. The theme is imitated and expanded in each of the voices, relating vertically at each point to form a complex yet unified whole.

The theme in a fugue is normally introduced all by itself in one specific voice (such as the middle voice), then in another (the top voice), while the middle one proceeds on its own, providing the necessary counterpoint. The theme finally appears in the third voice (the bottom one), with the other two voices continuing on their ways, providing the necessary counterpoint for each other and for the third voice. **SEE 16.32**

> **Johann Sebastian Bach** (1685–1750), German organist and composer, is generally considered the most notable composer of polyphonic music. His *Wohltemperierte Klavier (Well-Tempered Clavier)*, which consists of preludes and fugues for the piano in all 24 major and minor keys, demonstrates the essence of polyphonic music.

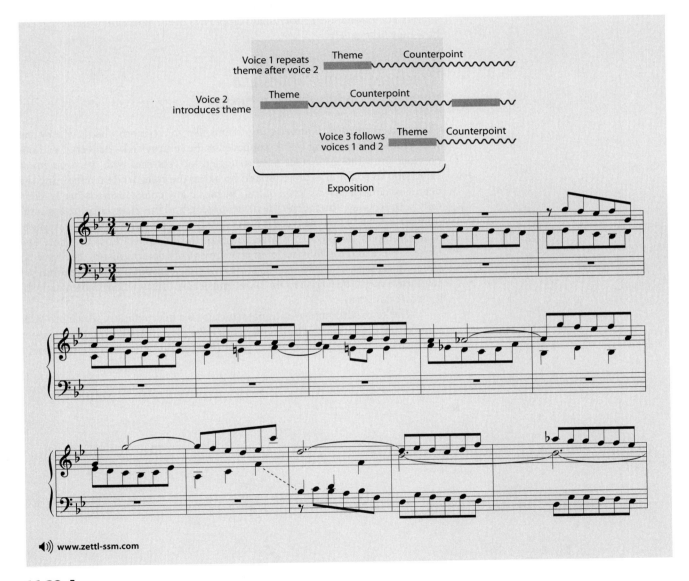

www.zettl-ssm.com

16.32 Fugue

After the theme has been introduced once by all the voices, the exposition is finished. The theme is then imitated, varied, and expanded throughout the voices. This is called an episode. When the theme is clearly introduced again in each voice, we have another exposition. There may be several expositions and episodes in a single fugue. Thus the subject "flees" throughout the composition. In most fugues the theme (subject) is introduced by itself and then repeated in the various voices. In this example the theme is first introduced in voice 2, then imitated in voice 1, and finally repeated in voice 3.

From The Well-Tempered Clavier by J. S. Bach.

When the theme has been introduced once by all the voices, we have the first exposition. The theme is then imitated, varied, and expanded throughout the voices in a free-flowing way. This part, where the composer is showing off, is called the episode. When the theme is clearly introduced again, we have another exposition; and when it is imitated again throughout the other voices, we have another episode. Normally, several expositions and episodes occur in a single fugue.

In the complex fabric of a contrapuntal vector field, the vertical vectors (the harmonic chords as formulated when we read the independent melodic voices vertically at any given point) act as important structural agents. They hold the horizontal voice lines together and give the seemingly independent voices their necessary structural dependence. Essentially, the vertical vectors represent space/time modulators, explicating the spatial (harmonic) as well as the temporal (melodic) relationships and interdependence of the individual voices. The vertical vectors tell us where the individual voices have been, where they are going, and how they fit together.

Structured Improvisations and Notation of Indeterminate Music

The phrase *structured improvisations* seems like an oxymoron because how can you structure something that is supposed to be improvised—delivered without previous preparation? Artists have struggled for centuries with the problem of exercising freedom of expression and breaking the rules while maintaining the degree of control that all art requires. In music any conventional score is like a fully scripted play: the theme, the development, and the final outcome are carefully prescribed before the piece is ever played. The only variable at your disposal is *how* you play the piece, not what you play. In this respect both the score of a musical piece and the fully scripted play are equally deterministic; they have no open future. Even in improvised jazz, the rhythmic conventions and the timing of solos leave very little wiggle room for the musicians. This is where improvisational structure comes in.

The key to this improvisational structure is a new notation, which provides some visual suggestions of how a piece might be played; but it prescribes neither the instruments nor any of the conventional melodic and harmonic sound

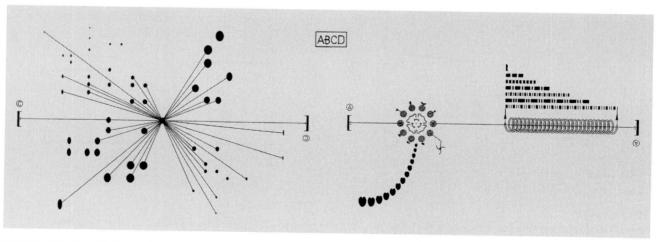

16.33 Notation of Indeterminate Music
This new form of notation offers the musician maximal freedom of expression while retaining some structural control.
From *Medium* for quartet by Mark Applebaum

combinations. There are instances, however, when the musicians are invited to initially interpret the pictographic score on their own, but they must perform it subsequently in exactly the same way, much in the spirit of a piece with standard notation. Although composer Mark Applebaum calls this "notation of indeterminate music," the performance has become very determinate.[4] **SEE 16.33**

Picture/Sound Combinations

Even if you are successful in structuring the picture field and the sound field independently, you cannot expect to arrive at a meaningful audiovisual structure simply by adding the two together. You must combine the video and audio vector fields so that they form a synergistic structure. Such an audio/video combination requires that you *hear* the screen event while visualizing and sequencing it and *see* it while working with the sound. You should try to conceive and develop the video and audio vector fields together as much as possible.

But exactly how should you combine the pictures and the sound so that they form such a synergistic unit, a maximally effective picture/sound gestalt? No easy recipe exists, and each case has its own specific requirements. Nevertheless, homophonic structures and polyphonic structures can act as general guidelines. Additional guidance is derived from the picture/sound matching criteria discussed in the next section.

HOMOPHONIC STRUCTURES

Much like the homophonic structure in music, where a single dominant melody is supported and undergirded by accompanying chords, you can support the video portion step-by-step with appropriate sound or the audio track with appropriate pictures. To accompany the lone cowboy riding through the meadow with the familiar clickety-clack banjo tunes is an example of a well-worn homophonic video/audio structure. A slightly more elaborate example of homophonic video/audio structure is the scene in which a car loses its brakes and is careening down a steep mountain road. The accompanying audio track consists of literal sounds such as squealing tires and nonliteral nervous music. This picture/sound combination represents a typical homophonic structure. The visuals (car without brakes) dominate the scene and tell the principal story. Literal and nonliteral sounds are precisely in step with the visual event, properly intensifying it from moment to moment. **SEE 16.34**

Many music videos illustrate their sound tracks with accompanying pictures in a homophonic fashion. The video shows the singer, band members, dancers, or pictures that support or illustrate the lyrics of the song.

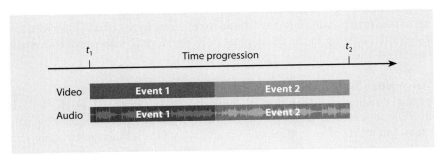

16.34 Homophonic Video/Audio Structure
In a homophonic structure, the audio track (consisting of literal and nonliteral sounds) is in step with the visual event. Each audio event runs parallel to its corresponding video event.

POLYPHONIC STRUCTURES

In a polyphonic picture/sound structure, pictures and sound seem to develop independently as "melodic" lines yet combine vertically into an intensified audiovisual experience. For example, some music videos show pictures that do not in any way parallel the lyrics of the song. The pictures seem to tell their own story (often of the lead singer's psychological frustrations) and are relatively independent of the meaning of the lyrics. While the song proclaims tender love, the pictures may show the singer's first unsuccessful auditions. The vertical structure is achieved through strong parallel rhythms of the pictures (tertiary motion rhythm) and sound.

Four of the more notable polyphonic audiovisual techniques are phasing, transitions, multiple texts, and multiple screens.

Phasing   In *phasing*, the video and audio portions are not tightly synchronized—they are somewhat out of phase. Either the picture precedes the sound event or vice versa, or picture and sound are thematically out of phase, at least for a while. In phasing, the sound is asynchronous to the picture. **SEE 16.35**

Flashbacks are a good vehicle for the phasing technique. Imagine, for example, a mountain climber surprised by a snowstorm on an especially difficult part of the climb. We see him trying to reach a ledge where he can find temporary shelter. We hear the howling storm, the sounds of his crampons, and his labored breathing (homophonic literal sound). Suddenly, these natural sounds switch to a conversation the climber had with his friend before undertaking the difficult climb. The friend warns about the fickle weather and the dangers of avalanches. Then the sounds switch just as suddenly to the laughter of the climber's children. Finally, we switch back to the literal sounds of the climb. While the video tells the story progressively (the climber's efforts to stay alive), the audio is out of phase: it shifts occasionally to the past (friend's warning and children's laughter). Yes, the climber made it back alive, but he had to abandon his solo attempt.

Phasing lends itself especially well to space/time transitions. Here is an example:

Video	Audio
Tight 2-shot: Larry and Barbara in front of the library.	LARRY **Don't you want to go to a movie tonight? You can't study all the time.**
ECU of Barbara.	BARBARA (smiles) **Perhaps.**
Zoom back to reveal entrance to the movie theater. Larry hands her the ticket.	

Now the video has jumped ahead of the audio to the "effect" phase while the accompanying sound (Barbara's reply) still lingers in the "cause" phase. If you now switch the phasing and have the audio progress to the effect phase with the video still lingering in the cause phase, you are dealing with predictive sound (see chapter 15).

Transitions   You can use a type of phasing for transitions from one scene to the next. For example, you can show a couple driving to a rock concert; the woman turns on the car radio and begins to groove with one of the concert band's catchy tunes. *Cut to:* MS of lead singer and bass guitarist of the actual concert scene with the catchy tune now being continued by the band. *Cut to:* CU of woman, now in the audience, moving to the tune the way she did in the car.

Or we may see a young man sitting in a bus, watching the rhythmic play of alternating sunlight and shadows caused by the passing trees. A drumbeat parallels

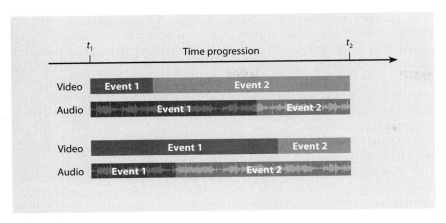

16.35 Phasing

In phasing, the audio track of one scene (as event 1 for example) extends into the next scene (event 2) or changes to the next scene (event 2) while the video portion still shows the previous scene (event 1).

the syncopated rhythm of the sunlight flashes. It increases in volume and texture and carries through the next series of cuts: (1) the young man crossing a busy intersection almost synchronous to the same syncopated beat, (2) rushing to the beat along the crowded sidewalk, (3) entering the backstage door of a concert hall, (4) sitting at the piano, looking at the audition judges, and (5) playing his extemporaneous piece—you guessed it—in the syncopated rhythm of the sunlight flashes of the bus ride.

Of course, you can make the sound track as complex as you want (by adding traffic sounds), but the primary transitional device remains the syncopated beat. In such polyphonic structures, it is the audio that sustains the transitions for the various video scenes.

Multiple texts   The *text* of a story is what a character says and does. A *subtext* is what the character wants to say or do but keeps hidden; it can also refer to the character's psychological makeup. Multiple texts are two or more dialogue tracks that run simultaneously or in a phasing mode. You can use multiple texts for single-screen presentations or, more commonly, for multiscreen productions. The following is an example of multiple texts playing simultaneously with a single-screen scene.

Video	Audio
2-shot of couple.	*Track 1* (main text)
	SHE: **How did it go today?**
	Track 2 (slightly delayed *subtext*)
	SHE: *I don't really care.*
CU of man.	*Track 1*
	HE: **Oh, pretty well!**
	Track 2 (slightly delayed)
	HE: *What do you care, anyway?*
	Track 3 (simultaneous with 2)
	SHE: *Liar!*

As you can see from the multiple dialogue, the two people do not feel as civilized toward each other as they pretend to be in the main dialogue track (track 1). Such a multiple-text technique is an obvious communication device and should be treated with discretion and deftness. Depending on how much of the event complexity you want to communicate, you can emphasize track 1, 2, or 3 or you can play them all together at equal volume. If you play all three tracks at the same time and the same loudness, the audience will no longer be able to follow exactly what is being said. Instead of communicating specific information, you will be providing the audience with a fabric of speech sounds that may reflect the complexity of the moment better than any single track could.

You can also emphasize a specific track by running its volume relatively high while keeping the other tracks at a lower volume. In effect you are applying the figure/ground principle. By emphasizing track 1, you communicate primarily the "outer" event—a woman asking a man about his day. But if you emphasize track 2 or 3, you shift from an outer-event orientation (plot) to an inner one (feeling); you add to the horizontal vector (event progression) a vertical one (event complexity). The advantage of such multiple texts is that you can provide the event complexity through sound while keeping the visual event relatively simple and straightforward.

Multiple screens   You can achieve a truly polyphonic structure by using *multiple screens*. In such a presentation technique, each screen can pursue a different story (voice) that relates to the others thematically or through the interaction of characters. Each screen may have its own sound track, or you can use an identical sound track for all three (or more) screens. Sometimes the various sound tracks get muddled into a dialogue fabric, but they allow the audience to associate with one or another phrase, sentence, or utterance.

If you construct the dialogue tracks of the various screens so that they are sequential rather than simultaneous, the audience will be better able to follow the meaning of each voice. For example, if you have a three-screen setup, the person on the left screen may ask, "How do you feel?" and the person on the right screen may answer "Fine," while the person in the middle screen may simply listen. Thus you can establish a relationship among the three screen events even if the scenes are not connected by event location and event time. Because the dialogue in the three screens is connected through the narrative, we tend to connect the visual events on the separate screens however different they may be.

As with the single-screen presentation technique, there is a limit to how many dialogue tracks we can discriminate among, even in multiscreen presentations. When played simultaneously, the tracks might lose their informational function and yet blend into a sound configuration that serves as a powerful emotional intensification device. You may want to arrange the video and the audio tracks of multiscreen presentations in a fuguelike way in which a particular theme "flees" from screen to screen, with the other screens and especially the other audio tracks providing contrapuntal contexts. Writing for three screens is not easy and requires a nonlinear approach, which means that you must learn to hear in your mind not only the horizontal narrative of the dialogue but also the vertical combined effect of the multiple tracks. You must add to the horizontal narrative vectors more complex vertical ones. You can probably now see the close relationship between such multiscreen structures and the polyphonic musical structures of horizontal melody vectors and the resulting vertical vector chords. **SEE 16.36**

Picture/Sound Matching Criteria

Ideally, you should conceive pictures and sound together as a unit, trying to see and hear the screen event simultaneously as an aesthetic whole. In practice, however,

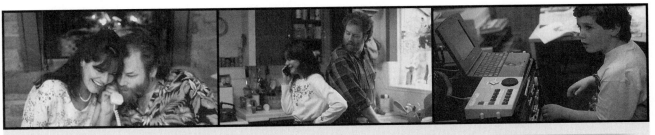

Left screen (present time)   **Center screen** (two years later)   **Right screen** (three years later)

Audio		
Sound: Telephone.	*Sound:* Telephone (slightly later than left screen).	*Sound:* Telephone (slightly later than center screen).
HE: **Hello. Great . . . no this is fine. Yes, I agree . . . Very happy.**	SHE: **Hello. Yes. No. That's OK. Go ahead.**	BOY: **Dad, the phone is ringing.**
SHE: **Who is it, honey? Let me hear it. This is so much fun . . .**	HE *(interrupting):* **Can't you ever ignore that damned phone? Get off the line and give me a hand with these dishes.**	HE: **Let it ring.**
		(She is no longer present.)
		All three sound tracks are phased to overlap to some extent.

16.36 Multiscreen Sound Tracks

In this example of polyphonic dialogue, the three screens display a time shift. The left screen represents the present, the center screen two years later, and the right screen three years later.[5]

such a complete preconception of the whole event is not always possible. Even if the audio portion of your show consists mainly of literal, source-connected sounds, you will most likely need to add some music to intensify the overall screen event.

You probably find that you think in pictures first and then try to locate the appropriate supporting sounds, such as background music. Or you may have a piece of music, such as a popular song, for which you need to find appropriate visuals. But what specific types of music should you use? What if your unfailing instinct fails you just when you need it most? What you obviously need are more reliable criteria for selecting the appropriate music for the more common video events. Although they are hardly foolproof and may even seem offensive to your artistic integrity, you may find some guidance in applying one of the four basic picture/sound matching criteria: historical/geographical, thematic, tonal, and structural.

HISTORICAL/GEOGRAPHICAL

Historical matching means that you pair pictures with music that was created in approximately the same historical period. For example, you would match the picture of a Baroque church with the music of Johann Sebastian Bach; an eighteenth-century scene in Salzburg, Austria, with music by Wolfgang Amadeus Mozart; a scene of 1960s London with music by the Beatles; or the brand-new, supermodern museum building with music by a contemporary composer.

Geographical matching means that you select music that is typical of the geographical area depicted in the scene. You could, for example, match a scene that plays in Vienna with a waltz, a scene in Japan with traditional koto music, or one in the American South with Dixieland jazz.

Once again a word of warning: matching the sights and the sounds of historical periods does not automatically make for effective and smooth picture/sound combinations. For example, the precise, carefully structured music of Bach does not necessarily fit the light, flamboyant Baroque architecture. Also, geographical matching is such an obvious aesthetic device that it might annoy or even insult the sensitive viewer. For example, to introduce an interview show featuring a famous scholar from China with what we consider to be typical Chinese music, or the ambassador from Austria with a waltz, would certainly offend the guests and annoy the viewers. On the other hand, if you do a documentary on Tibet, you might as well have Tibetan music and the sounds of prayer bells under the opening scenes and titles.

THEMATIC

When using *thematic matching* for video and audio, you select sounds that we are accustomed to hearing at specific events or locales. For example, when we see the interior of a church, we probably expect organ music. Or when you show a parade or a football stadium full of people, marching-band music is the thematically correct choice.

TONAL

Tonal matching requires sounds that fit the general tone, that is, the mood and the feeling of the event. If you show a sad scene, the music should be sad, too. Similarly, you can match a happy scene with upbeat sounds. Romantic music that engulfs the lovers' tender moonlit embrace is another familiar example of tonal video/audio matching. The difference between thematic and tonal matching is that in thematic matching you choose music you might hear at a specific event or location; in tonal matching you select music according to how the event feels.

STRUCTURAL

When using *structural matching*, you parallel pictures and sound according to their internal structure. For example, take a look at the following figures and see whether you can "hear" them. **SEE 16.37–16.40**

How did you do with "listening" to these pictures? Could you assign each picture a specific type of music? Did they sound different from one another?

Now go back and try to identify some of the specific pictorial characteristics that prompted you to select a certain type of music. Was it the direction and the arrangement of dominant vectors within the pictures? The relative harshness or softness of the lines? The graphic weight, the degrees of balance, or the relative shadow falloff? Does the picture feel heavy or light? Simple or complex? Which ones were relatively fast or slow? Were you now able to "hear" Applebaum's graphic score?

You probably went more by how the pictures felt to you and whether they were round, soft, hard, brassy, simple, or complex, rather than by a careful vector analysis. Most likely, that was all you needed to accurately match the video and the sound structures. Nevertheless, even with your intuitive approach, you applied—however quickly and subconsciously—a series of vector analyses and comparisons. What you were actually doing was analyzing the visual vector fields and constructing aural vector fields of similar characteristics.

Structural Analysis

Just in case your intuition fails you, or the matching task becomes too complex for quick guessing, you need to apply specific criteria to analyze the video and audio vector fields for compatibility. To isolate the dominant structural element within a picture or picture sequence and to grasp the overall structural tendency

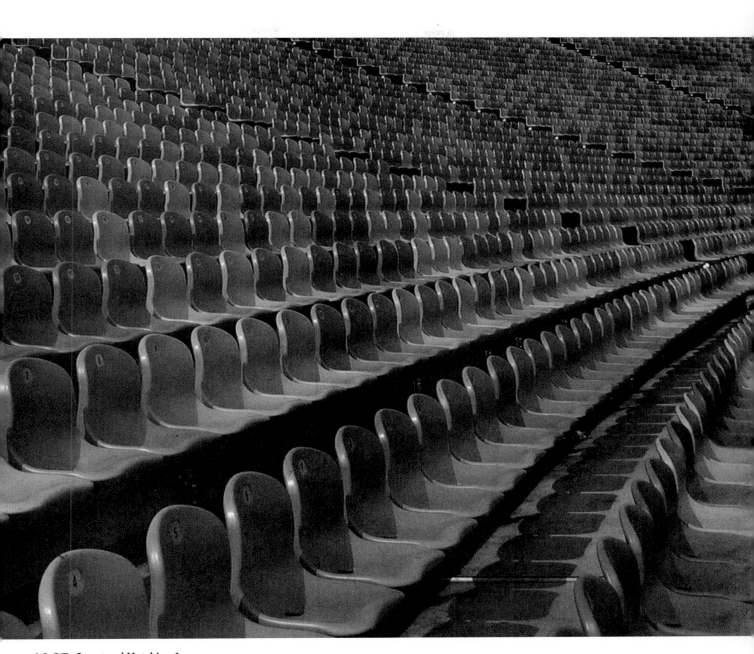

16.37 Structural Matching 1

How does this picture sound? Loud or soft? Fast or slow? Does it have a simple or a syncopated beat?
Is it more polyphonic than homophonic?

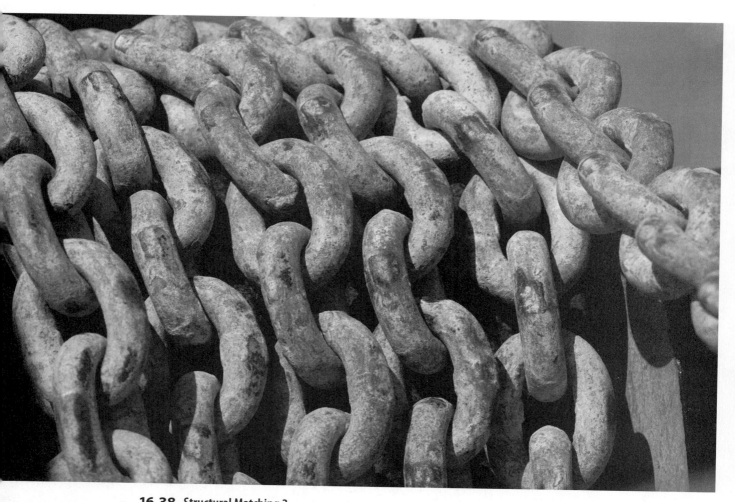

16.38 Structural Matching 2
Compare the sound of this picture to that of figure 16.37. Do you hear a difference? Try to verbalize it.
What audio characteristics can you isolate that are unique to this picture?

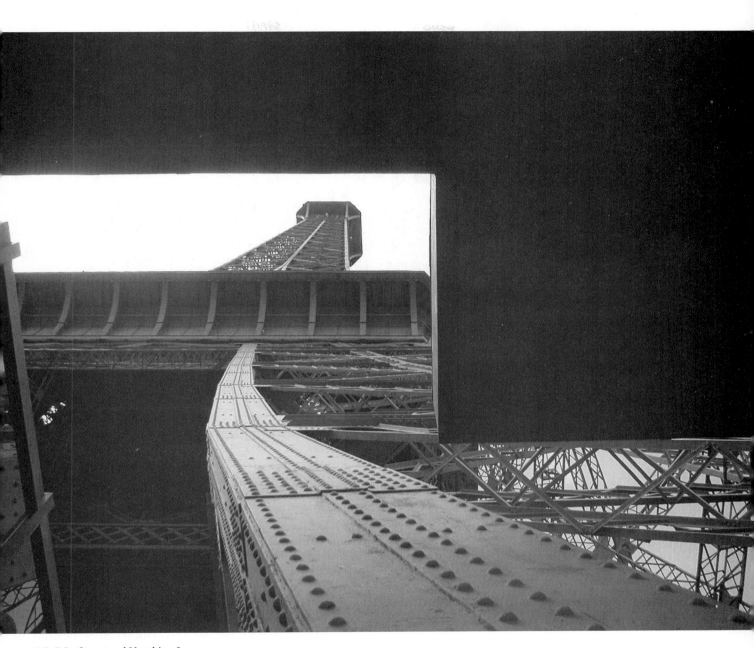

16.39 Structural Matching 3

What specific sound characteristics does this picture have? Does it sound different from figures 16.37 and 16.38? What specific sound vector field would you have to create to match the visual vector field of this image?

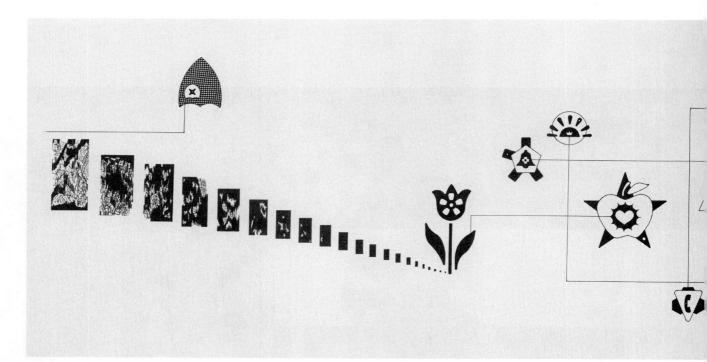

16.40 Structural Matching 4

Try to listen to the pictographic score *The Metaphysics of Notation* by Mark Applebaum. What sounds do you hear? What rhythms do you perceive? How fast or how slow do you perceive the general tempo of the piece to be?

From *The Metaphysics of Notation* by Mark Applebaum

(simple, complex, directional, confused) is not always an easy task. Sometimes a picture or picture sequence just does not seem to "sound" right, or it seems so indistinct that any number of musical structures could fit it equally well or badly. In such a situation, you must be patient enough to analyze the picture sequence step-by-step according to the major aesthetic criteria developed throughout this book: light and color, space, and time/motion. You should then be able to establish primary connections between the major visual vector fields or the dominant aesthetic elements and similar aural ones.

Exactly how does such a structural analysis work? And how can you translate pictorial characteristics into music? There is no single or simple answer. Structural matching, like any other matching criterion, depends on many contextual variables, such as the desired overall effect, what immediately preceded the picture sequence and what follows it, and whether you intend to create montage effects.

The following table shows how you might approach a structural analysis of the video and its translation into musical terminology for audio matching. In fact, this table is an apt summary of the major elements of the five aesthetic fields and how they might relate to one another. **SEE 16.41**

To witness the structural power of music, take any video sequence and run some arbitrarily selected music with it. So long as the tempos of the primary and tertiary motion of the video and the music are similar, you will be amazed at how frequently the video and the audio seem to match structurally. Apparently, we use the tempo—the basic beat—and the relative complexity of the musical piece as the primary reference and expect the video to follow suit. If the visual beats do not match the aural ones, we apply psychological closure and try to make them

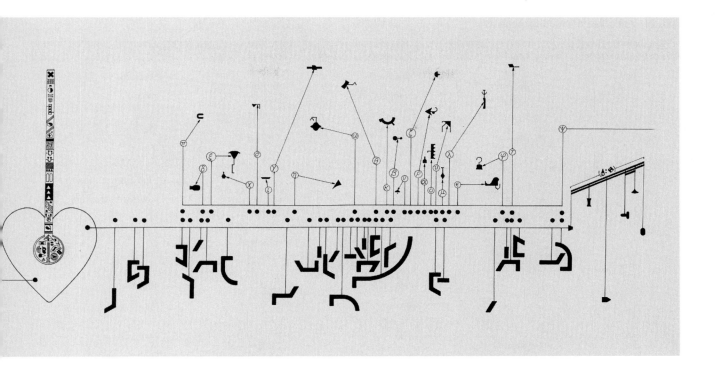

fit until they drift too far apart. Again, the basic beat—the rhythm and the tempo of the music—seems to be the primary agent that determines whether the video portion is a match or a mismatch. Once the tempos are similar, you can look for further matching criteria as indicated in figure 16.41.

When watching a video production or a film without sound, you will become surprisingly aware of the visual structure, especially the tertiary motion. The rhythmic beat of tertiary motion, or the lack of it, shows up with undue prominence without the benefit of the accompanying sound track. When watching the same sequence with sound, however, you may not even be conscious of the tertiary motion employed in the video sequence. Again, the organic structural power of music greatly facilitates the pictorial vector flow. Exactly why will remain as much a mystery as the power of music itself.

SUMMARY

In structuring the five-dimensional field, we concern ourselves with the elements of sound, basic sound structures, picture/sound combinations, and picture/sound matching criteria.

The elements of sound, or basic sound attributes, include pitch, timbre, duration, loudness (dynamics), and attack/decay.

Pitch refers to the relative highness and lowness of a sound measured against an agreed-upon scale; the pitch of a tone is perceived and measured by its frequency. Timbre describes the tone quality or tone color, whether a certain note is played by the violin or the trumpet; timbre depends on the number of overtones that vibrate with the fundamental tone. Duration refers to how long a sound can be heard. The loudness (dynamics) of a tone is its apparent strength as

16.41 Video/Audio Structural Analysis

Aesthetic Field	Video		Audio	
Light	**Type**	Directional / Nondirectional	**Rhythm**	Staccato / Legato
	Mode	High-key / Low-key	**Key**	Major / Minor
	Falloff	Fast / Slow	**Dynamics**	High-contrast (loud/soft) / Low-contrast (even)
Color	**Energy**	High / Low	**Dynamics**	Loud / Soft
	Hue	Warm / Cool	**Key**	Major / Minor
	Saturation	High / Low	**Timbre**	Brass, strings / Flutes, reeds
	Brightness	High / Low	**Pitch**	High / Low
Space	**Screen size**	Large / Small	**Dynamics**	Loud (high-energy) / Soft (low-energy)
	Shot size	Large / Small	**Presence**	Near / Far
	Graphic weight	Heavy (close-ups) / Light (long shots)	**Chords and beat**	Complex (accented) / Simple (unaccented)
	General shape	Regular / Irregular	**Sound shape (timbre, chords)**	Consonant / Dissonant
	Balance of objects within frame	Dynamic (high tension) / Static (low tension)	**Chord tension**	High (dissonant) / Low (consonant)
	Texture	Heavy / Light	**Chords**	Complex / Simple
	Field density (number of elements in single frame)	High / Low	**Harmonic density**	High / Low
	Field density (number of successive elements within given period)	High / Low	**Melodic density**	High / Low

16.41 Video/Audio Structural Analysis *(continued)*

Aesthetic Field	Video	Audio
Space *(continued)*	Field complexity in single frame or shot — High / Low	Harmonic complexity — High / Low
	Field complexity in successive frames or shots — High / Low	Melodic or contrapuntal density — High / Low
	Graphic vectors — High-magnitude / Low-magnitude	Melodic line — Definite / Vague
	Index vectors — High-magnitude / Low-magnitude	Melodic progression — Definite / Vague
	Principal vector orientation — Horizontal (High-magnitude / Low-magnitude) / Vertical (High-magnitude / Low-magnitude)	Sound vector orientation — Melodic (Definite / Vague) / Harmonic (Complex / Simple)
Time/motion	Motion vectors — High-magnitude / Low-magnitude	Volume and tempo — High / Low
	Event rhythm (flow) — Even / Uneven	Sound rhythm — Even / Uneven
	Change in field of view (zooms) — Fast / Slow	Dynamics — Fast crescendo and diminuendo (fast attack and decay) / Slow crescendo and diminuendo (slow attack and decay)
	Vector continuity — Good / Bad	Melodic progression and rhythmic continuity — Even / Uneven
	Transitions (cuts, dissolves) — Seamless / Conspicuous	Modulation (change from one key to another) — Extreme / Conservative
	Rhythm — Complex / Simple	Sound rhythm — Complex / Simple
	Tertiary motion — Fast / Slow	Beat — Fast / Slow
Aesthetic energy	Vector magnitude — High / Low	Dynamics — Loud / Soft
	Vector field energy (total energy communicated) — High / Low	Sound vector field energy — High / Low

we perceive it; you can play a tone either loudly or softly. The variations of loudness are the dynamics of the sound. The attack/decay is a part of the dynamics and the duration of a sound. Attack refers to how fast a sound reaches a certain level of loudness. Decay is the final fading process. The period during which a tone remains at its maximum loudness is called the sustain level. A sound envelope includes the whole tone from initial attack to final release.

The basic sound structures include melody, harmony, homophony, and polyphony. Melody is a series of musical tones arranged in a consequent succession. A melody forms a horizontal vector. Harmony is the combination of simultaneously played notes, which form a vertical vector. Harmonic combinations of three or more tones are called chords.

Homophony refers to a musical structure in which a single, predominant melody is supported by corresponding chords. In a homophonic structure, the melodic line (horizontal vector) can stand alone, but the chords (vertical vectors) make sense only in the presence of the melody.

Polyphony stands for "many voices" and refers to two or more melodic lines (horizontal vectors) that, when played together, form a harmonic whole. When played separately each voice forms a self-sufficient entity. Together they form a vertical harmonic structure. Most polyphonic music is written in counterpoint, which means that the elements of various voices (vector direction, pitch, timbre, dynamics, and rhythm) are countering one another to produce structural tension.

Imitation, a common structural element in polyphony, means that a short theme of one voice is repeated in the other voice or voices. The canon (round) is a direct imitation. The fugue introduces a theme that appears in different voices.

The picture/sound combinations should form a synergistic structure in which picture and sound reinforce each other. In homophonic combinations, the picture dominates and is supported by sound or vice versa. In polyphonic combinations, picture and sound seem to develop independently as melodic lines yet they combine vertically into an intensified audiovisual experience. Multiple texts refer to several sound tracks that are run simultaneously or in a phasing mode.

There are four basic picture/sound matching criteria: historical/geographical, thematic, tonal, and structural. In historical matching you select music that was played in the historical period of the visual event. Geographical matching means that the music chosen has its origin in the geographical area depicted. In thematic matching you select sounds that you expect to hear at a particular event or locale. When using tonal matching, you choose sounds that fit the general mood and feeling of the pictorial event. Structural matching means that we parallel pictures and sound according to the internal structure, that is, their specific vector fields.

Detailed structural analysis involves analyzing the picture sequence according to the major aesthetic criteria of light and color, space, and time/motion. You then establish primary connections between the major visual vector fields or the dominant aesthetic elements and similar aural ones.

N O T E S

1. The background music you often hear in elevators, waiting rooms, and supermarkets has a drastically limited range of dynamics. The music sounds equally soft throughout and is therefore unobtrusive. All other elements (melody, timber, harmony, and rhythm) are kept intact.

2. Stanley R. Alten, *Audio in Media,* 9th ed. (Belmont, Calif.: Wadsworth, 2011), pp. 21–38.

3. Listen to a relatively simple polyphonic composition (such as J. S. Bach's *Two-Part Inventions*) and follow the theme throughout the piece. Note the counterpoint that works opposite the theme or the slight variations of the theme itself when it is reintroduced in each of the two voices. If you are a skilled listener, follow the themes in Bach's *The Well-Tempered Clavier* and in his fugues.

4. "The score, while unconventional, does not invite improvisation; instead, players are charged with the task of predetermining a thoughtful means to sonify (with exactitude) an inferred musicality." From the forward to *Medium* for quartet by composer Mark Applebaum.

5. The basic idea for the telephone conversation was developed by students in my seminar on experimental production.

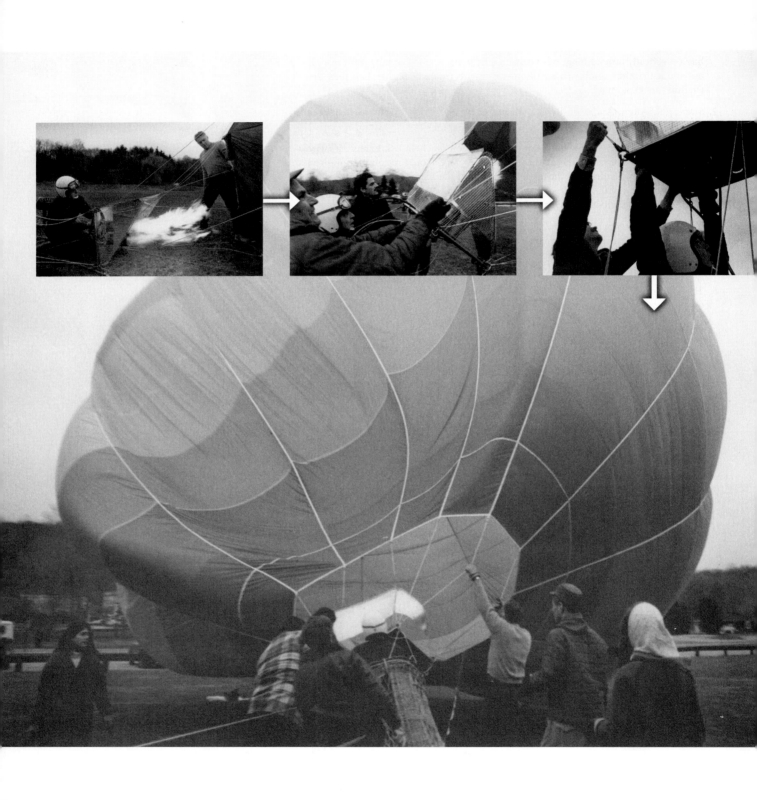

Visual Narrative:
The Syntax of Continuity Editing

YOU HAVE FINALLY ARRIVED AT THE POINT WHERE YOU CAN COMBINE the elements of the five aesthetic fields for the final communication objective: to tell a good story. And just like the literary syntax, which tells us how to form sentences and phrases from words, the ***editing syntax*** prescribes how to arrange individual shots so that they combine into meaningful scenes and sequences. Both types of syntax include the selection of the most appropriate words, or most effective shots, to tell the story. In a broad sense, the editing syntax is a guide to the selection of specific shots and their narrative ***sequencing***. This chapter concerns continuity editing, whose primary aim is the clarification of an event through a smooth visual narrative. The ***syntax of continuity editing*** therefore comprises the editing conventions and techniques primarily used for seamless visual sequences and narrative flow.

Chapter 18 deals with the syntax of complexity editing—the building of an intensified event.

Editing Purpose

Editing involves selecting and sequencing those parts of an event that contribute most effectively to its clarification and intensification. What parts of the event you select and how you tell the story depend on many contextual factors: what you want to say, why and to whom, and especially how. Your decisions about what to use and what to discard, what to emphasize, and exactly how to put everything together for the screen are influenced by your communication intent, the target audience, the medium requirements, the specific visual syntax you choose to tell your story, and your personal style.

INSTANTANEOUS EDITING

Sometimes you will find that you have to make such decisions almost instantly while the television show is under way. Live television, for example, frequently demands immediate decisions and action that, despite careful preproduction preparation, you could not have anticipated. Much of television editing is done in the studio or mobile control room while the show is in progress. Interview shows, sports remotes, and daytime serials—all are shot with a multicamera setup. The editing is done by selecting with a switcher the most effective shots from the continuous video feed of the cameras and the other video inputs, such as video-recorded inserts or computer-generated images. This selecting and sequencing of shots while the televised event is under way is called **switching**, or instantaneous editing.[1]

At other times you will need to deliberate on just which part of the prerecorded material to select and where to place it in the overall show. This more deliberate selection and ordering of prerecorded material is called **postproduction editing**. This process is similar or identical for video and film because all postproduction editing of film is done electronically with nonlinear computer systems.[2] Regardless of whether you are engaged in switching or postproduction editing, for film or video, the aesthetic principles of editing are determined by the established visual syntax.

Visual Syntax of Continuity Editing

Continuity editing concentrates on structuring on- and off-screen space and on establishing and maintaining the viewer's mental map. When driving to a specific location, you are establishing a mental map that you follow on the way back. You do the same when watching video or a motion picture. The **mental map** helps you make sense of where things are, where they are going, or where they are supposed to be in on- and off-screen space. The techniques of vector continuity, discussed later in this chapter, facilitate the establishment and the maintenance of such a mental map. Continuity editing concerns itself primarily, but not exclusively, with the clarification of an event.

When reading and thinking about editing, you should realize that editing procedures are as much audio-dependent as they are video-dependent. This means that you will have to consider sound (dialogue, music, sound effects, and natural environmental sounds) as important an influence on your editing decisions as the pictorial vector field. To keep things manageable, however, we concentrate here on the visual syntax of editing, although you will notice that many of the musical structures also apply to continuity editing.

Specifically, continuity editing is concerned with selecting and putting together shots that have vector continuity and that show objects and people where we expect them to be in on- and off-screen space. You may think that this is a big order to fill—and indeed it is. In film and large video projects, postproduction editing takes longer than the actual recording of the event. Although there is no recipe that guarantees success every time you edit, a thorough knowledge of the basic editing principles will make you secure in your judgment and will ultimately free you to act more intuitively without abandoning artistic control. Now you need to recall the different types of vectors and their continuity principles, as discussed in chapter 7, and apply them. After all, this is what applied media aesthetics is all about. Let's briefly recapitulate these principles and put them into an editing context.

Graphic Vector Continuity Principles

Although **graphic vectors** generally have a low magnitude—which means that they are relatively ambiguous as to specific direction—you must nevertheless consider them when trying to achieve continuity from shot to shot. Especially when shooting a scene with a prominent background line, maintain the horizon at the same screen height in subsequent shots with the same or a similar field of view (see 7.57). In exterior shots, you need to watch that the horizon lines match from shot to shot; in interior shots, watch for such prominent graphic vectors as the back of a couch or a windowsill in the background. Unless you change camera height and angle of view, such lines must continue from shot to shot.

Index Vector Continuity Principles

The continuity principles of *index vectors* apply to on-screen space but also extend into off-screen space. They help establish an important part of the viewer's mental map.[3]

CONTINUING, CONVERGING, AND DIVERGING INDEX VECTORS

As you recall, ***continuing vectors*** point in the same direction, ***converging vectors*** point toward each other, and ***diverging vectors*** point in opposite directions.

Continuing index vectors   Once you show a woman looking left in a medium shot, we as viewers expect her to continue looking left in the succeeding close-up, assuming that she is still focused on the same object. This formation of our mental map is in line with our actual daily experiences and our constant need for a stable environment. **SEE 17.1** The same continuity principle applies if you are showing in the medium shot two people looking screen-right at the same object. If you then cut to individual close-ups, the direction of the index vectors must be maintained for both people. **SEE 17.2**

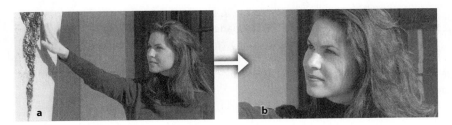

17.1 Continuing Index Vectors
When cutting from a medium shot (a) to a close-up (b), the index vectors in both shots should point in the same screen direction.

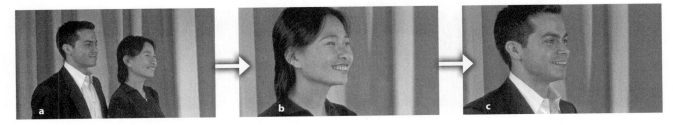

17.2 Continuing Index Vectors: Two-shot
If a two-shot establishes two continuing index vectors (a), the index vectors must continue into the subsequent close-ups (b and c).

Converging index vectors   The continuity principle of continuing index vectors applies in a similar way to converging and diverging index vectors. If in a two-shot you show two people talking to each other, you must maintain the converging index vectors in the following close-ups. Note that there are several possibilities for keeping the index vectors converging. **SEE 17.3–17.5**

17.3 Converging Index Vectors: Two-shot Profile

Index vectors that converge in a two-shot should continue this convergence in subsequent close-ups.

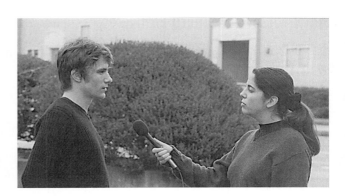

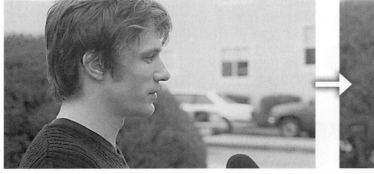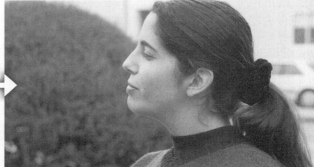

17.4 Converging Index Vectors: CUs of Profile Shots
This close-up series continues the converging vectors in the two-shot in figure 17.3.

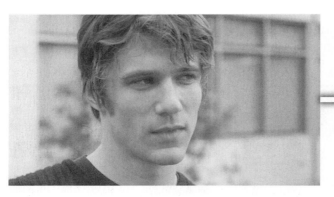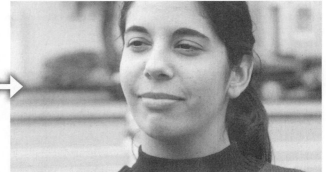

17.5 Converging Index Vectors: Oblique Angles
The convergence of established index vectors can vary from the two-shot. Here the index vectors converge at oblique angles.

When you show medium or close-up shots of a speaker and the audience, you must preserve the original index vector convergence between speaker and audience by having all audience members look in the same direction. **SEE 17.6**

Diverging index vectors   In a similar way, if you establish diverging vectors by having two people look away from each other, you need to carry over the diverging vectors into the succeeding close-ups. **SEE 17.7 AND 17.8**

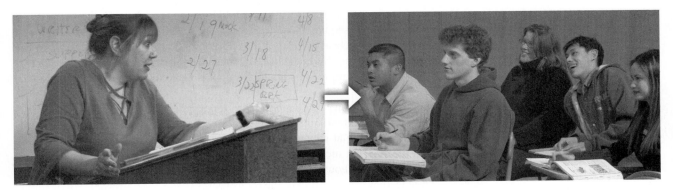

17.6 Converging Index Vectors: Audience and Speaker

Separate shots of a speaker and the audience must produce converging index vectors. As you can see, the converging index vectors in these two shots make the teacher and the students look at, rather than away from, each other.

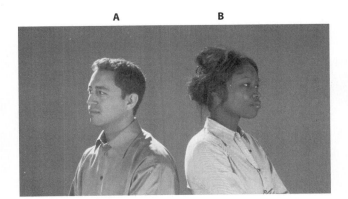

17.7 Diverging Index Vectors

These two people (A and B), who are looking away from each other, form diverging index vectors. These diverging vectors must be maintained in the following close-ups.

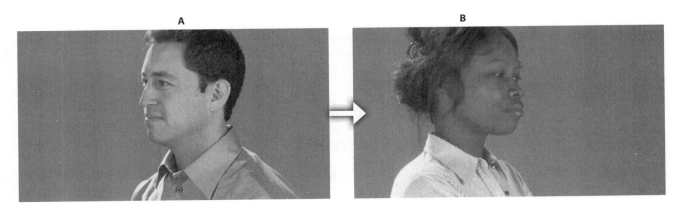

17.8 Diverging Index Vectors: Close-ups

The diverging index vectors of the two people looking away from each other are maintained in the succeeding close-ups.

INDEX VECTOR–TARGET OBJECT CONTINUITY

The continuity of index vector to target object is especially important if you show a person looking at something in one shot and then show the target object in the following shot. As viewers we will remember the direction of the index vector and construct a mental map of where the target object should be positioned relative to the index vector.

On-screen continuity   To maintain the viewer's mental map, you must match in the second shot the camera's viewpoint and the resulting object position of the first shot. For example, if you show a child looking up and screen-right, the target object in the subsequent close-up should be located in the right part of the picture, approximately at the end of the child's index vector. You need to follow the index vector of the child in shot 1 and extend it in the same way into shot 2. This extension leads unquestionably to the upper-right corner of the frame. **SEE 17.9**

Off-screen continuity   The mental map requirements for index vector–target object continuity extend quite readily into off-screen space. If in one shot you show someone looking at something outside the screen, the follow-up shots need to show the object in such a screen position that viewers can perceive the two shots as a single, simultaneous event. The position of the target object is obviously greatly influenced by the direction of the index vector in the previous shot. For example, if in an interview the host looks screen-left in a close-up, we expect the guest to be situated in the left off-screen position. When he looks screen-right, we expect the guest to be in the right off-screen position. **SEE 17.10**

    If you imagined person A to be in the middle, person B at camera left (A's right), and person C at camera right (A's left), you constructed the proper cognitive map of their actual positions. **SEE 17.11**

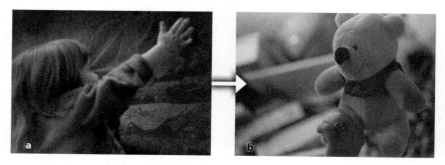

17.9 Index Vector–Target Object Continuity

The strong index vector in (a) influences the screen position of the target object in (b). The girl's index vector leads to the upper-right screen corner in (a). The target object is correctly positioned at the end of the extended index vector in the vicinity of the upper-right corner in (b).

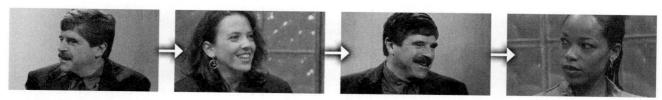

17.10 Index Vectors: Implied Screen Positions

You can use index vectors to help viewers construct a mental map of the off-screen space that shows the positions of people and things.

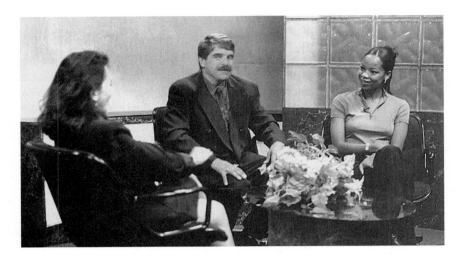

17.11 Actual Screen Positions
The actual positions of the people concur with those implied by the index vectors in figure 17.10.

BAC and ABC positioning   If you were to use the same seating arrangement for an interview, you would run into serious problems maintaining the established screen positions when taking two-shots with the host. With the host (person A) in the middle of the two guests (persons B and C), you switch A's screen position every time you cut to different two-shots during the interview. The host will inevitably jump from one screen edge to the other. **SEE 17.12**

A simple solution to this problem of position continuity is to change the BAC arrangement to an ABC one. By putting the host (person A) on one side and the guests (B and C) on the other, the index vectors between the host and his guests will remain properly converging even in separate close-ups. Host and guests will maintain their screen positions and not upset the viewer's mental map of on- and off-screen space. **SEE 17.13**

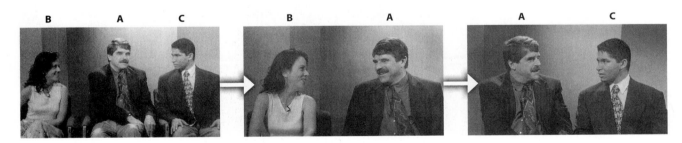

17.12 BAC Positioning
With the host (A) in the middle, cutting to two-shots (BA and AC) will switch the position of the host.

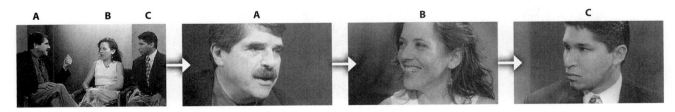

17.13 ABC Positioning
By placing the host (A) to one side of the guests (B and C), the subsequent close-ups maintain the screen positions of host and guests and their converging index vectors.

SUCCESSIVE Z-AXIS INDEX VECTORS

Recall that *z-axis vectors* can point toward or away from the camera. Whether you perceive two successive z-axis vectors as continuing, converging, or diverging depends on context. For example, if you show two people looking at something in shot 1 and then show each person in a z-axis close-up in shots 2 and 3, we perceive them not as looking at us (the viewers) but at the target object. We see their index vectors as continuing in the successive close-ups. **SEE 17.14**

When you have two people talking to each other in shot 1 and then have each one looking directly into the camera to create z-axis index vectors in shots 2 and 3, the converging index vectors are carried over to the successive z-axis close-ups. **SEE 17.15**

If shot 1 now shows the two people looking away from each other, we continue the diverging directions of their index vectors from the establishing shot in the subsequent z-axis close-ups; we perceive them as looking away from each other. **SEE 17.16**

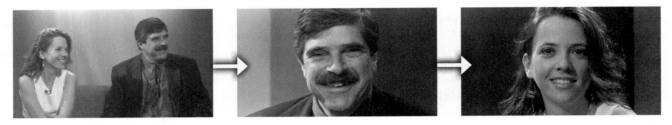

17.14 **Successive Z-axis Vectors: Continuing**

If you establish in a single shot that two people are looking in the same direction (shot 1), viewers perceive successive z-axis close-ups as continuing vectors (shot 2 and shot 3). The two people look at the same target object.

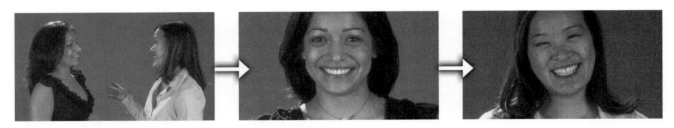

17.15 **Successive Z-axis Vectors: Converging**

When the context establishes converging vectors (shot 1), viewers perceive the successive z-axis vectors as converging (shot 2 and shot 3).

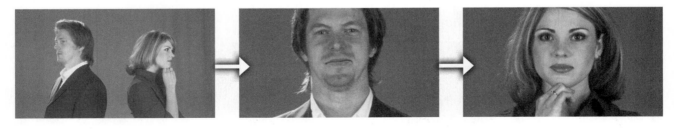

17.16 **Successive Z-axis Vectors: Diverging**

If you establish in shot 1 that two people are looking away from each other, viewers perceive the subsequent z-axis close-ups as diverging z-axis vectors.

INDEX VECTOR LINE AND POSITION CONTINUITY

The *vector line* is important for maintaining the established vector continuity in close-ups and especially for keeping an object in the same screen position from shot to shot. You can establish an index vector line by extending converging index vectors. **SEE 17.17** The vector line—also called the principal vector, the line of conversation and action, the one-eighty, the scene axis, the sight line, the eye line, and, simply, the line—will also aid you in camera placement for proper shot sequencing.

When using a multicamera setup, you will immediately see in the preview monitors when a camera is in the wrong place. But when you shoot with a single camera for postproduction editing, mistakes in camera placement are not so readily apparent and usually show up only during editing, when they may or may not be fixable. Assuming you have a skilled editor who can finesse a workable solution, such mistakes are nevertheless time-consuming and labor-intensive to remedy. "Fixing it in post" should be reserved for unavoidable and unforeseen complications—and not considered a safety net for careless camera placement by a negligent camera operator or director. Observing the rules of the vector line will help you place cameras in optimal shooting positions and avoid such mistakes.

Camera placement for over-the-shoulder shooting   When placing cameras for *over-the-shoulder (O/S) shooting*, you must keep the cameras on the same side of the vector line (camera 1 and camera 2) to avoid a disorienting position switch when cutting from one camera to the other. **SEE 17.18** If you now switch from camera 1 to camera 2, persons A and B will remain in approximately the same screen position relative to the frame, although they change from a camera-near to camera-far point of view. **SEE 17.19**

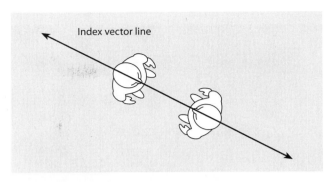

17.17 Index Vector Line

The vector line is created by extending converging index vectors.

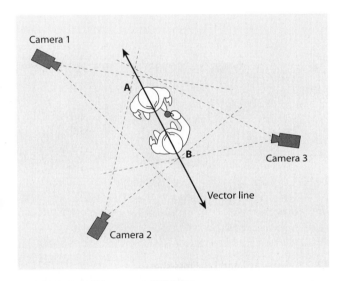

17.18 Camera Placement: O/S Sequence

Which cameras would you use to provide position continuity when cutting from one over-the-shoulder shot to another?

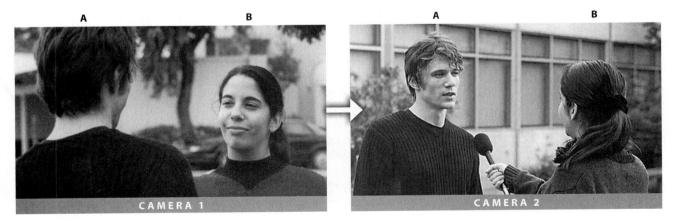

17.19 Cameras 1 and 2: O/S Views

By keeping both cameras on the same side of the index vector line, cameras 1 and 2 provide the proper vector continuity. Both A and B remain in their previous screen positions.

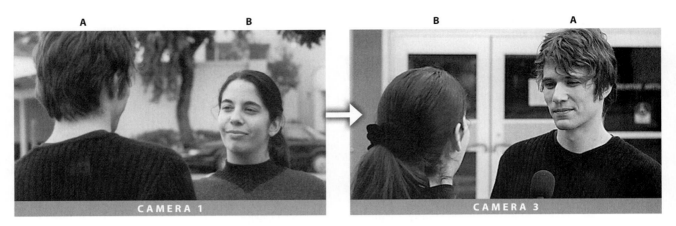

17.20 Cameras 1 and 3: O/S Views
Cameras 1 and 3 shoot from opposite sides of the vector line. As a result, the people switch screen positions during the cut.

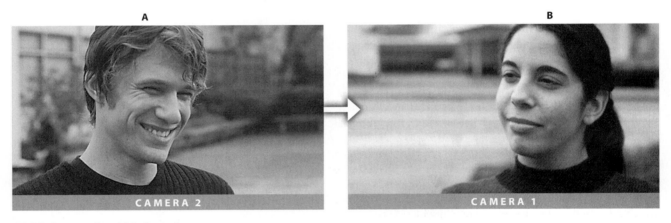

17.21 Cameras 2 and 1 in Cross-shots
As in over-the-shoulder shots, both cameras need to be on the same side of the vector line to maintain converging index vectors.

Visualize, for a moment, how you would see persons A and B in the viewfinders of camera 1 and camera 3 (see 17.18). Yes, placing the cameras on opposite sides of the vector line (cameras 1 and 3), will cause the people to switch positions from one screen edge to the other. **SEE 17.20**

Now try to visualize a cross-shot sequence by zooming in with cameras 2 and 1 on close-ups of A and B (see 17.18). How will you perceive the index vectors of A and B when switching between cameras 2 and 1?

If you predicted that the index vectors of A and B would be converging and make them look at each other, you are correct. **SEE 17.21**

But what if you were to now switch from camera 1 to camera 3? Look again at figure 17.18 and figure out how the direction of the index vectors would change.

Instead of looking at each other, as in figure 17.21, A and B are now looking in the same direction as though they were talking to a third party. The converging index vectors have now changed into continuing ones. **SEE 17.22**

But wouldn't viewers recognize the two people as talking to each other even if they switched screen positions? Of course they would. With the help of the audio track, viewers would probably still believe that A and B are talking to each other even if their vectors are continuing instead of converging. Nevertheless, such a

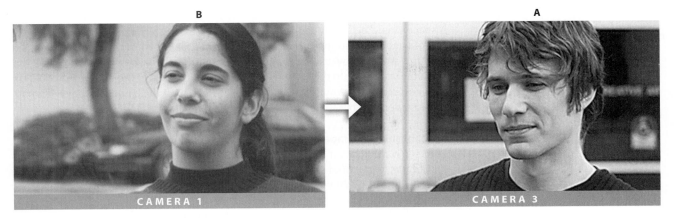

17.22 Cameras 1 and 3: Crossing the Vector Line
Because camera 3 crosses the vector line, the two people seem to be looking away from each other toward someone else. The index vectors are no longer converging but continuing.

position and vector switch would upset a viewer's mental map and require an unnecessary cognitive correction maneuver, however subconscious this might be. Continual corrections of the mental map are not only tiring but may well prevent the viewer from getting emotionally involved.

Z-axis position change: the wedding switch   A similar position switch occurs when you cut from the front to the back of a couple (A and B) standing side-by-side. **SEE 17.23** Although their continuing z-axis index vectors (camera 1) are carried over into the next shot (camera 2), A and B will reverse screen positions.

This problem occurs most frequently when video-recording weddings. It seems appropriate to video-record the couple from the front as they walk down the aisle, and then from the back with the official presiding over the ceremonies in the middle. In doing so, however, you will discover that the bride and the groom switch positions.

Again, we would certainly not confuse the bride and the groom, however often they switch screen positions. Yet the incongruity of where the viewer's

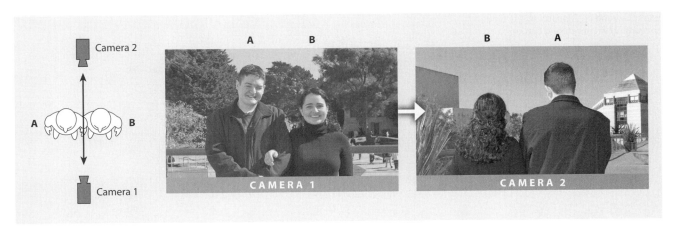

17.23 Z-axis Wedding Switch
When cutting from a front z-axis shot to a back z-axis shot of two people standing side-by-side, the two people will switch positions.

mental map expects them to be and where they really are in on- and off-screen space would definitely reduce the emotional intensity of the event. How can you avoid such a position reversal? One solution is to cut from the z-axis shot of the couple walking toward the camera to a medium shot of the official and show the couple walking into the second shot. The medium shot of the official functions as a good *cutaway*. Another way would be to pan with the couple as they walk past the camera so that the position change occurs within a single shot.

Establishing the index vector line   In certain situations it is not always easy to decide on the vector line or exactly where to place the cameras. In the wedding example, you would think that the z-axis (the aisle) would be the appropriate vector line and that you had your cameras placed at both ends of it but not across it. This is a correct assumption, especially if you place the cameras not at both ends of the z-axis but to the left and right of it. In this case, however, you are no longer dealing with crossing the line but simply with a mirror-like image reversal.

A different but often ignored vector line problem is covering a speaker or an orchestra conductor and getting reaction shots from the audience. Try to imagine the vector line between an audience in a large auditorium and the speaker on-stage (or between a concert audience and the orchestra). Where should the cameras go so that the audience is looking at the speaker rather than away from him? **SEE 17.24**

Which two of the three cameras in figure 17.24 would you use for proper sequencing, that is, for maintaining the converging index vectors between the audience members and the speaker?

If you chose cameras 2 and 3, you are correct. Both cameras are on the same side of the vector line, which runs from speaker's position to the audience and will give you the desired converging index vectors of speaker and audience members. If you were to use camera 1 for audience reaction shots, you would cross the vector line. The close-ups of the audience members and the speaker would show continuing, rather than converging, index vectors, making the audience and the speaker appear to look at a third party rather than at each other. **SEE 17.25**

17.24 Establishing the Vector Line: Speaker

A speaker facing his audience forms a vector line that extends from the speaker to the audience. Which of the three cameras is in the wrong position for maintaining converging vectors during cutting?

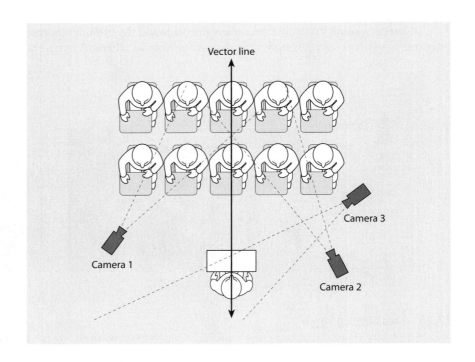

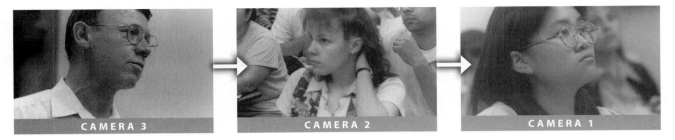

17.25 Camera Views

As you can see, cutting between cameras 2 and 3, the individual close-ups of speaker and audience members, results in converging index vectors—the speaker and the audience are looking at each other. Cutting to camera 1 instead of camera 2 would have them both looking in the same direction. Camera 1 has crossed the index vector line and is in the wrong position.

Motion Vector Continuity Principles

The continuity principles of motion vectors are similar to those of index vectors. Like index vectors, the continuity of motion vectors includes continuing, converging, and diverging vectors and extends into off-screen space.

CONTINUING, CONVERGING, AND DIVERGING MOTION VECTORS

Because of their generally high magnitude, motion vectors play an important role in establishing and maintaining the viewer's mental map. (Remember, we cannot show an actual motion vector in a still photograph. A motion vector is created by a moving object off- and on-screen.)[4]

Continuing motion vectors   As with index vectors, you must continue motion vectors in subsequent shots so that the direction of the moving object is preserved.
SEE 17.26

When you show the traditional yellow cab pursuing the black limousine, for example, their motion vectors must continue in the same direction. If you converge, rather than continue, the motion vectors, viewers will most likely see the two cars as fleeing from or racing toward each other, not one following the other.

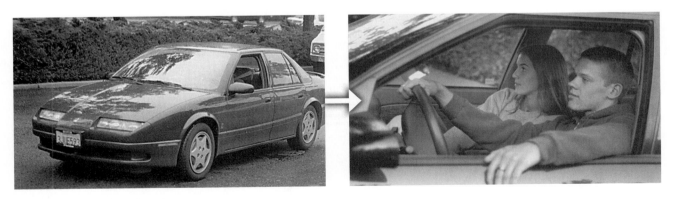

17.26 Motion Vector Continuity

Although you can't show a motion vector on a printed page (motion vectors are created only by a *moving* object or image), you must make sure that the motion vectors are continuing (moving in the same direction) from shot 1 to shot 2.

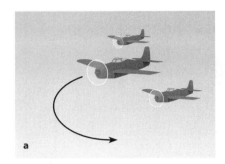
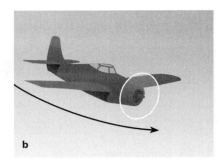

17.27 Directional Change

When the moving object changes its direction within a shot (a), the next shot must show the object moving in the direction it was going at the end of the previous shot (b).

Continuing vectors are also important for preserving a principal direction in subsequent scenes or event sequences. For example, if you show someone driving from San Francisco to New York, the car should continue in the same screen direction after a stopover during the trip, even if you have changed the direction of the motion vector from time to time during the car's actual travel.

If the moving object changes direction within the screen, you need to continue its motion vector in the next shot in the direction it left the screen, that is, at the end of the shot and not necessarily in the direction where it began. **SEE 17.27**

In some cases, you can use converging vectors to indicate continuing motion. Once you have established the travel direction of a prominent, easily recognizable object, such as a train or an isolated person, you can have the motion vectors converge without destroying their continuity. Converging motion vectors often increase the force of the motion (the vectors collide), thereby raising the energy, if not the tension, of the event. **SEE 17.28** But do not use converging vectors to indicate continuing motion of the object if the object is not easily recognizable or if you mix the motion vectors of several objects.

Converging motion vectors   If the context signals disaster, the converging motion vectors of a truck and a bicycle in subsequent shots indicate that they are racing toward each other. **SEE 17.29** (Again, remember that these pictures represent index rather than motion vectors, but with a little imagination you should be able to perceive them as shots in which the objects are moving.)

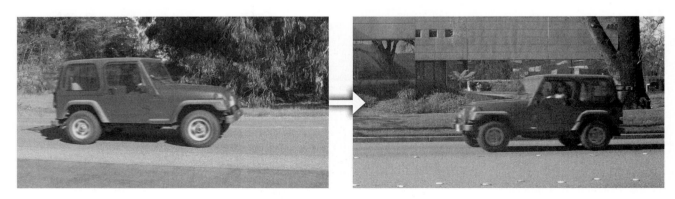

17.28 Converging Motion Vectors Continue Single Direction

If we have an easily recognizable object, we can use converging vectors to intensify its motion. Even though the vectors are converging, we accept them as continuing.

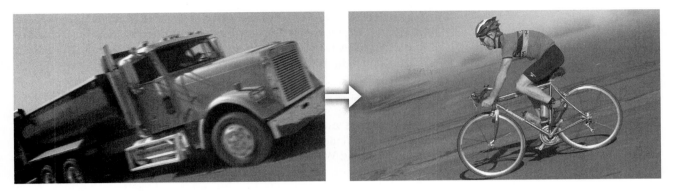

17.29 Converging Motion Vectors Collide
The converging motion vectors of a speeding truck and a bicycle indicate that they are moving toward each other.

If in the context of two people trying to meet, you show a woman walking toward screen-right and, in the next shot, a man walking toward screen-left, we expect the two people to eventually meet. SEE 17.30

Diverging motion vectors Diverging motion vectors operate on the same principle as converging vectors. By simply showing the two people first in the context of bidding good-bye rather than trying to meet each other, we interpret the subsequent shots of the two people walking in opposite screen directions as diverging, rather than converging, motion vectors. SEE 17.31 Note that here we

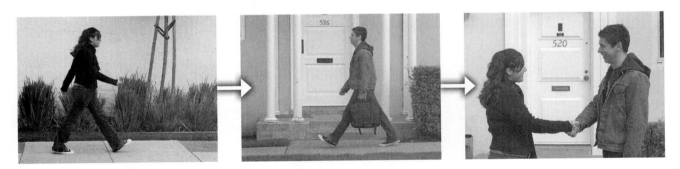

17.30 Converging Motion Vectors: Meeting
If we expect the two people to meet, we interpret the individual motion vectors in separate shots as converging.

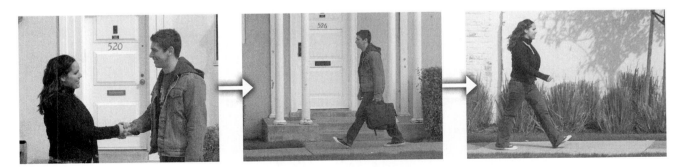

17.31 Diverging Motion Vectors: Departure
If we establish in shot 1 that the two people are saying good-bye, we now interpret the motion vectors of the two subsequent shots not as converging but diverging.

have the same two people in similar shots as in figure 17.30, but the new context forces us to interpret them as walking away from rather than toward each other. This perceptual switch of motion from converging to diverging through context is only a small indication of the manipulative power of editing.

Z-AXIS MOTION VECTORS AND CONTINUITY

Objects that move toward or away from the camera produce z-axis motion vectors. Because they don't move toward a screen edge, they, like z-axis index vectors, have zero directionality. We perceive vector continuity regardless of their direction in the subsequent shot. **SEE 17.32** Figure 17.32 shows cuts from a z-axis motion vector, which has zero directionality, to a screen-left (a–b) and a screen-right (a–c) motion vector as continuing.

   As a matter of fact, you can pretend that the converging vectors of a man in a wheelchair are continuing and pointing in the same direction by placing a zero-directionality cutaway (passersby) between the two shots. **SEE 17.33**

17.32 Z-axis Vector Allows Continuing Motion

If you show a person moving toward the camera, you can cut either to a screen-left (a–b) or a screen-right (a–c) motion vector while maintaining the motion continuity.

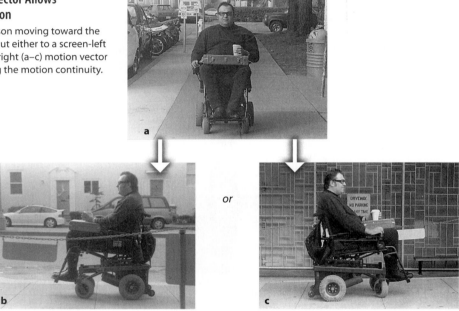

or

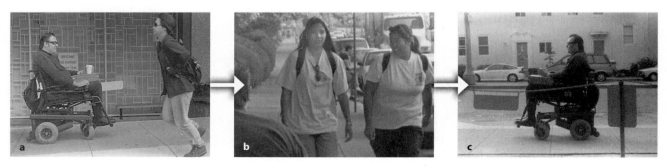

17.33 Z-axis Vector Cutaway

Viewers can perceive diverging index or motion vectors as continuous if a zero-directionality (neutral) image (b) is used as a cutaway—a cut between the vector reversal of (a) and (c).

A cutaway does not have to have a zero directionality to act as a link between shots that otherwise would not cut together well, that is, between shots whose individual vectors are not continuous. But a z-axis motion vector is the most flexible cutaway. Whatever vector direction you choose, the cutaway must be thematically related.

When using a single camera in a production, always video-record or film several such cutaways of sufficient lengths (15 seconds minimum). Your editor will be most grateful when trying to establish continuity between shots whose vectors do not provide the desired continuity.

MOTION VECTOR LINE

The motion vector line is similar in function to the index vector line. Establishing the principal direction of a motion vector helps you place the cameras so that vector continuity is maintained.

Establishing the motion vector line   With the exception of z-axis vectors, all other motion vectors describe a vector line. You achieve motion vector continuity only if you place the cameras on one or the other side of the motion vector line. **SEE 17.34** To maintain the principal motion in a shot sequence, you must place the cameras on the same side of the motion vector. **SEE 17.35**

You may cross the motion vector line if the cameras are placed relatively close together and in such a way that they are practically shooting along the z-axis. By cutting from one camera to the other, you show the moving object from oblique angles (from slightly camera-right to slightly camera-left), but you do not reverse the action. **SEE 17.36**

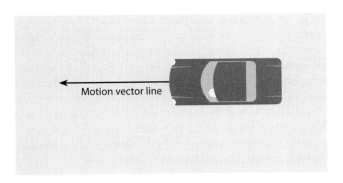

17.34 Motion Vector Line
An extended motion vector forms a vector line.

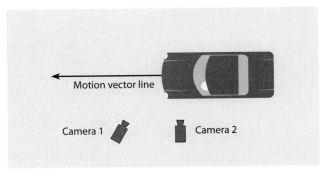

17.35 Camera Placement: Motion Vector Continuity
To maintain the continuity of the motion vector, both cameras must be positioned on one or the other side of the motion vector line.

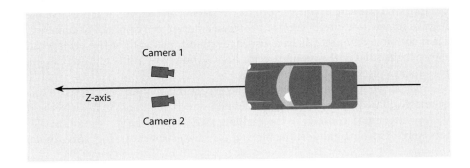

17.36 Camera Placement: Z-axis

The cameras may cross the motion vector line so long as they are close to the z-axis position. The resulting shots merely show the moving object from a slightly different z-axis point of view.

17.37 **Crossing the Motion Vector Line**
Placing the cameras on opposite sides of the motion vector line will reverse the vector direction with each cut.

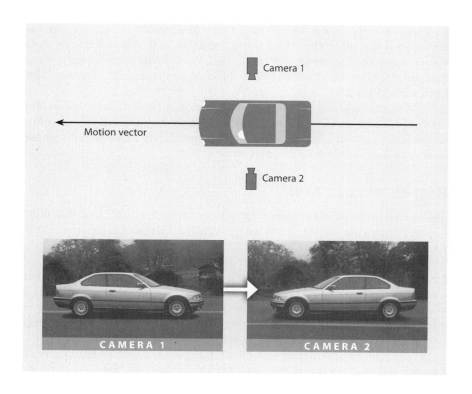

If cameras are placed on opposite sides of the motion vector line, looking at lateral motion, you reverse the motion vector when cutting from one camera to the other. **SEE 17.37**

You may find that in some sporting events, the cameras are placed on opposite sides of the field and so opposite sides of the principal vector line. Cutting to the camera that is across the line reverses the action. Even if such cameras are generally used only for instant replays, the motion reversal is still aesthetically wrong and perceptually confusing. Once viewers have established a screen-right direction for one team and a screen-left direction for the other, however unconsciously, they expect these directions to be maintained in all subsequent shots regardless of field of view. Telling viewers that they are seeing a "reverse-angle shot" may provide them with a rational explanation for the motion vector reversal, but it will not eliminate their mental map confusion.

Motion and index vector lines   Reverse-angle shooting of two people sitting next to each other in an automobile presents an especially tricky vector problem because you have to consider both an index vector line and a motion vector line for camera placement. **SEE 17.38**   If you establish an index vector line along the converging index vectors of the two people conversing and place the cameras accordingly on one side of this vector line (cameras 1 and 2), you will preserve the relative screen positions of the two people in cutting from camera 1 to camera 2. **SEE 17.39**   But in doing so, you have also inadvertently placed these two cameras on the opposite sides of the motion vector line. As you have just seen, such camera placement causes a motion reversal.

Many directors and editors seem to accept this motion reversal as an unavoidable consequence of trying to maintain screen positions of the driver and the passenger. But, contrary to the wedding scene, where the z-axis motion vectors were of zero magnitude, the moving car now establishes a high-magnitude

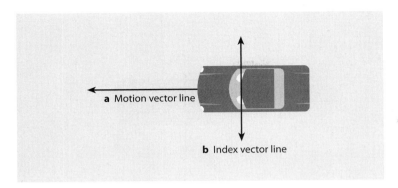

17.38 Index and Motion Vector Lines

When shooting a conversation between the driver and a passenger in a moving car, you must deal with two vector lines: the motion vector line of the car (a) and the index vector line of the two people talking (b).

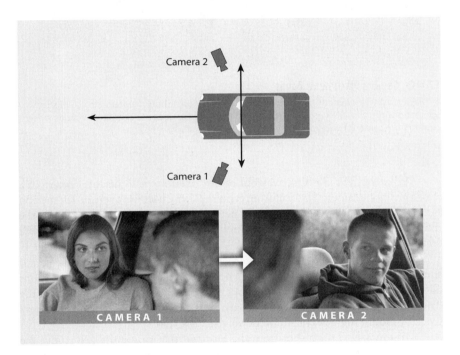

17.39 Camera Placement: Index Vector Line

By keeping cameras 1 and 2 on one side of the index vector line, the positions of the people in the car are preserved, but the car moves in opposite directions each time you switch between the two cameras.

screen-left motion vector. This high-magnitude motion vector should override the principle of screen positions. You should not reverse the direction of the car simply because one or the other person is doing the talking. The usual argument is that, if we can't see much of the landscape rushing past through the car window and keep to a close-up of the two people, their screen direction reversal should not bother us too much. The problem, however, is that even if we can follow the conversation inside the car, our mental map remains confused.

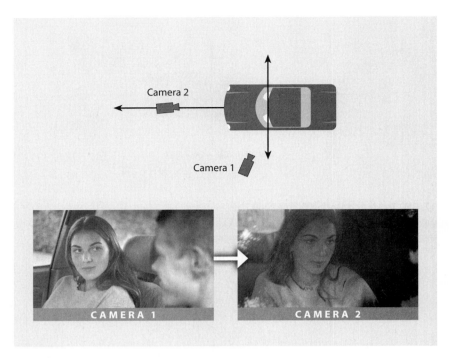

17.40 Camera Placement: Z-axis
By placing camera 2 directly in front of the car, the individual shots maintain the established screen positions as well as motion vector continuity. The car does not change directions when cutting from camera 1 to camera 2.

What can you do? One way out of this dilemma is to place a camera in a z-axis position (camera 2). A cut from camera 1 (which shows a screen-left motion vector) to camera 2 (which shows the neutral z-axis vector) will not reverse the direction of the motion vector, and we will readily accept the second shot as a continuing motion vector. **SEE 17.40**

Better yet, you can place both cameras (1 and 2) in the z-axis position and shoot through the windshield. Such a camera setup maintains the screen positions of the driver and the passenger and looks more realistic than when shot from the driver and/or passenger side. You can have both cameras operate from the camera truck or mount them on the hood of the car.[5] **SEE 17.41**

You may also see a shot from the rear seat that shows the driver and the passenger from the back. This is better than using their index vectors as the guide for camera placement, but the rear-seat shot will still reverse the position of driver and passenger. You can motivate such a shot if one of the actors actually sits in the back seat and enters the conversation.

Additional Continuity Factors

There are some more continuity factors that need attention during the production phase. Observing these will make your postproduction editing much more efficient and enjoyable and will avoid needless headaches and frustration. These factors are continuity of action, subject, color, appearance, and audio.

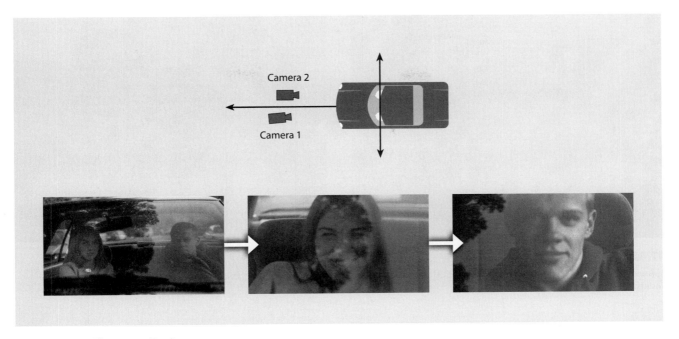

17.41 Camera Placement: Z-axis

By placing cameras 1 and 2 close together in the z-axis position, the through-the-windshield shots provide maximum continuity of screen positions and motion vectors.

ACTION CONTINUITY

To ensure maximum continuity of action, you should try as much as possible to cut *during* the action, not before or after it. When you cut just before or after the action, you accentuate the beginning or end of a motion vector rather than its continuity. For example, if you cut from a shot that shows the hostess getting up from her chair to a medium shot of her standing, you need to cut while she is getting up and not after she is already standing.[6]

When cutting during secondary (camera) motion (pan, tilt, zoom, or the like), you need to continue the secondary motion in the subsequent shot. If you are panning with a moving object, you should have the second camera panning in the same direction before cutting to it. If the camera is not panning during the second shot, the motion vector will look oddly disturbed. Matching the panning speed of both cameras is extremely difficult, however. Don't plan a cut between two moving (panning or tilting) cameras unless absolutely necessary. When cutting from a shot in which the object is at rest to one in which the object is in motion, the object seems to accelerate suddenly and lurch through the frame. When cutting from an object in motion to a shot in which it is at rest, the object seems to have come to a sudden halt as if hitting a brick wall. One way of softening the change from a static to a moving shot or between two moving shots is to do a quick dissolve rather than a cut.

SUBJECT CONTINUITY

If, for example, you cut from an extreme long shot of a group of people to an extreme close-up, the viewer may not be able to tell whether the person shown

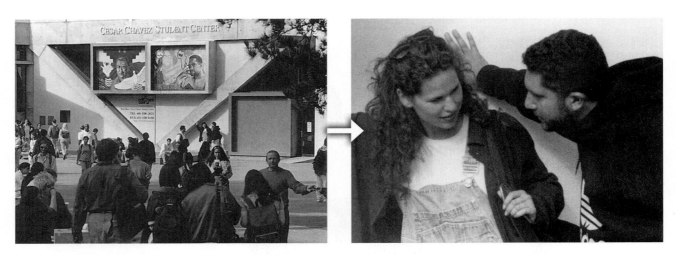

17.42 Subject Continuity
If you cut from an ELS (extreme long shot) to an ECU (extreme close-up), viewers are not always able to verify that the person in the ECU was, indeed, part of the ELS.

in the close-up was indeed part of the original group. **SEE 17.42** You should also avoid extreme angles that do not show any subject relationship between shots.

COLOR CONTINUITY

One of the persistent problems in postproduction editing is maintaining continuity of color. When trying to edit a show, you may suddenly find that the star is wearing a red dress in the long shot but a purple or pink one in the close-up. Obviously, the colors should be continuous unless you change the event to a different time or place. Color matching in postproduction is time- and energy-consuming as well as costly. You can avoid expensive color matching in postproduction by paying particular attention to the lighting and the white balance of the cameras before you record the event or event details.[7]

APPEARANCE CONTINUITY

A scene should reflect the same environment and appearance from shot to shot. For example, if you show an actor in a medium shot just about to sit down in his chair, he needs to wear the same tie in the long shot. Such continuity problems are practically nonexistent in a live coverage or live recording of an event, but when you shoot a scene over a period of time such obvious continuity mistakes can occur quite easily. Make an effort to watch whether the background remains the same during subsequent takes. Little is more annoying than having books disappear or multiply in a background bookcase, or having the scenery change merely because the director, floor manager, or continuity person did not bother to watch the continuity requirements of the background as much as those of the foreground event. When shooting outdoors the changing weather is always a continuity hazard. Having a cloudless sky in a two-shot of people talking but then dramatic cumulus clouds in the subsequent close-ups from the same camera position does not make for good continuity.

Be especially vigilant when you shoot and later edit shots of a scene that contains an activity such as eating, drinking, or building something. Especially when recording over a period of time, make sure that you don't start with a full glass of milk in shot 3 if in shots 1 and 2 the actress had already drunk half the milk. Such seemingly minor details are easily overlooked, but turn out to have dire consequences in the postproduction editing phase.

AUDIO CONTINUITY

Although sound continuity is discussed at length in chapter 15, we list here the aesthetic sound factors that play a major role in aiding the continuity of the visual narrative. As with everything else, paying attention to sound continuity during the production can save you costly postproduction time.

Environment Environmental sounds (traffic, nature, hospital, fire, crowd) must be continuing, even if the scene is shot over a period of time. You cannot have the off-screen sounds of a brook when showing a medium shot of two backpackers at a campfire but ignore the brook sounds during the close-ups that were shot later in the studio. This, of course, is an exaggerated example, but you must always watch that, when reconstructing literal environmental background sounds, they fit the scene and do not change as long as the scene is playing in the same locale.

In fact, it is often the continuous background sounds that give a scene the necessary continuity.

Dialogue What contributes most to dialogue continuity in relation to the video is the relative energy. If the scene is not intended to shift or signal to the audience a forthcoming change, the dialogue must be delivered with the same energy. You cannot have an actress delivering the first part of a scene with high energy early in the day, when she is feeling good, but lower energy in the second part of the scene simply because she's now tired. You need to watch this especially when the talent is doing voice-over narration for a documentary.

Rhythm A music track with a distinctive beat can reinforce, maintain, and even establish the tertiary motion (editing) rhythm. A distinct sound rhythm can even be used as a transitional device from one scene to another.

Perspective and presence If you change from a long shot of a mother calling for her child who has wandered away in a crowded shopping mall to an intimate close-up of her whispering into her child's ear, you also need to change the sound presence from far to near. To maintain a close sound presence for both shots would be as disruptive to the visual narrative as having a far sound presence for both shots.

Dynamics High-energy (high-volume) sounds can maintain that high energy in a scene whose shots vary from fast to slow, brutal to tranquil, or long shots to close-ups. If the overall context is low-energy, a low-energy (low-volume) sound track can maintain that context even if the visuals fluctuate between high- and low-energy.

One of the most obvious continuity mistakes is to have temporary silence at the edit points. Such silences are jarring not only because the sound continuity is interrupted but also because they draw attention to the edit and thus affect the visual continuity. This is why you should always record a good amount of room tone (or specific location sounds) in addition to the intended sound track.

Whereas this chapter was concerned with continuity editing—a visual syntax that helps establish and maintain narrative continuity—the following and final chapter explores complexity editing, a visual syntax that is primarily intended for emotional impact.

S U M M A R Y

The necessary continuity from shot to shot is the task of editing. Editing means selecting those parts of an event that contribute most effectively to its clarification and intensification. The selected parts are then used to build a screen event.

Instantaneous editing, or switching, refers to selecting and combining shots while the televised event is in progress. Postproduction editing means deliberately selecting and sequencing prerecorded material into a unified whole.

The visual syntax suggests some rules for ordering and sequencing shots so that they will tell the intended story. In doing so we establish a visual narrative.

Continuity editing concentrates on structuring on- and off-screen space and on establishing and maintaining a cognitive mental map in the viewer. Specifically, continuity editing is concerned with graphic vector continuity, index vector continuity, the index vector line, motion vector continuity, the motion vector line, and the continuity factors of action, subject, color, environment, and audio.

Graphic vector continuity refers to being aware of prominent lines and having them continue from shot to shot.

Continuity principles apply to continuing, converging, and diverging index vectors in on- and off-screen space. Index vector–target object continuity must be maintained in successive shots. The target object in shot 2 should be placed at the extension of the index vector in shot 1.

BAC positioning, which places the host between two guests, will cause position jumps in subsequent two-shots of host and guest. An ABC arrangement, which places the host at one side and the guests on the other, provides better index vector and position continuity in close-ups.

To preserve converging index vector continuity in over-the-shoulder (O/S) shots or cross-shots of a conversation, the cameras must be kept on the same side of the index vector line. The same camera placement relative to the index vector line is necessary to preserve the subjects' screen positions.

When placing cameras both in front and in back of two side-by-side people, their shots will reverse the people's established screen-left and screen-right positions.

The continuity principles of motion vectors are similar to those of index vectors. Crossing the line with cameras will reverse the motion vector. Z-axis motion vectors provide continuity to any subsequent direction of motion vectors.

A smooth cut requires that you cut during—not after—the action (primary motion) and that when the camera moves in one shot, it must move in the second. Cuts from extreme long shots to extreme close-ups are to be avoided if the subject cannot be recognized in both shots. Continuity in colors and in the general appearance are also important factors to consider.

Preserving narrative continuity is especially important when recording over time and editing a progressive action, such as drinking or building something. The different shots must show the logical progression.

Audio plays a major role in how we perceive the continuity of a visual narrative. Special attention must be given to continuity of environmental sounds, the relative energy of dialogue, rhythm, sound perspective and presence, and dynamics.

N O T E S

1. Herbert Zettl, *Television Production Handbook*, 10th ed. (Belmont, Calif.: Wadsworth, 2009), pp. 268–91.

2. Zettl, *Television Production Handbook*, pp. 420–45.

3. Herbert Zettl, *Video Basics 6* (Boston: Wadsworth, 2010), pp. 282–86.

4. Because we can't show a motion vector in a book, you may want to review the continuity principles of editing on *Zettl's VideoLab 3.0* interactive DVD-ROM (Belmont, Calif.: Wadsworth, 2004). Click on EDITING→ Continuity→ vectors.

5. This is usually done by towing the car with a camera truck and having the camera operators work from the truck's rear platform, or by mounting the camera on the hood of the car. See Steven D. Katz, *Film Directing: Cinematic Motion* (Studio City, Calif.: Michael Wiese Productions, 1992), pp. 69–76.

6. Zettl's VideoLab 3.0, Editing module.

7. See the section on color temperature and white-balancing in Zettl, *Video Basics 6*, pp. 162–65.

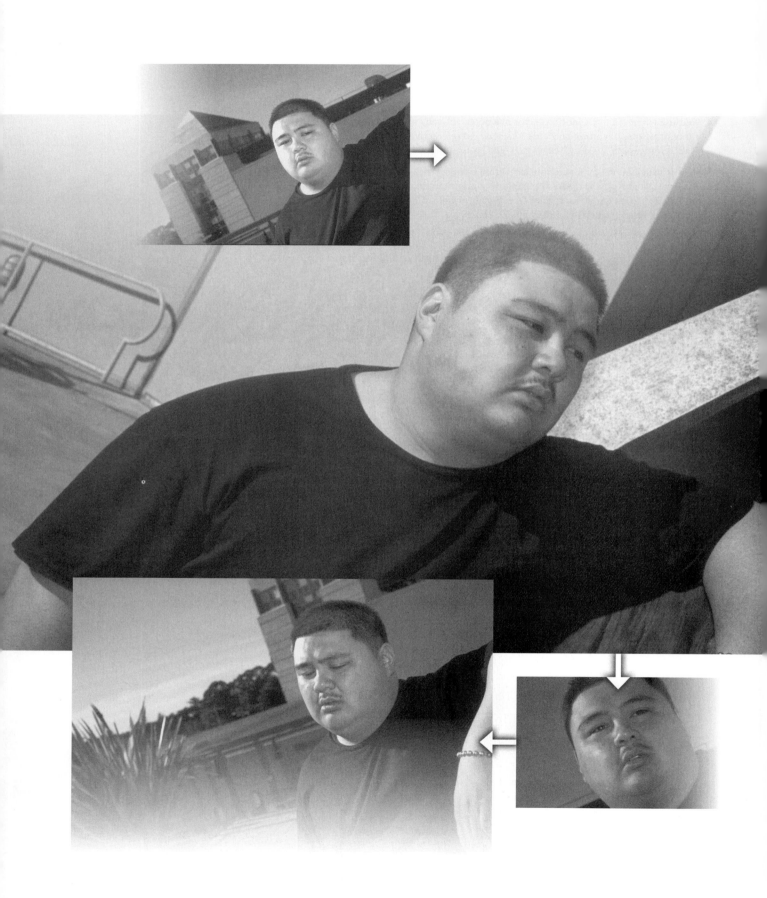

Visual Narrative:
The Syntax of Complexity Editing

COMPLEXITY EDITING IS USED PRIMARILY TO INTENSIFY THE EMO-
tional content of an event and reveal its intricacy. Now you are not so much
concerned with providing continuity as with probing the depth of the event, revealing its complexity, and with doing justice to the emotional intent of the scene. Your
goal in complexity editing is to trigger an empathetic response in the audience.

Complexity editing tends to affect subjective, rather than objective, time.
While progressing by necessity along the horizontal vector of running time,
complexity editing establishes an inner rhythm, a vertical vector. In fact, you are
dealing with inner rather than outer vectors—an emotional rather than a spatial
vector field.[1]

The *syntax of complexity editing*—the selection and sequencing of specific
shots—is based on story and emotion, by what people do, what drives them to do
it, and how they feel about what they do.

Without intending to confuse you, complexity editing may or may not
adhere to the principles of continuity editing. In any case, continuity now takes
a backseat.[2] For example, to show the inner confusion of a troubled person, you
may very well cut between cameras that are positioned on opposite sides of an
index or motion vector. The resulting flip-flop reversal of screen directions is
intended because it represents a visual interpretation of the person's confusion or
labile emotional condition. But the new priorities for an edit do not mean that we
can throw all the principles of continuity editing out the window. Poor continuity
can wreck the intended emotional effect. Whenever possible you should apply the
principles of continuity and keep the viewer's cognitive mental map intact. Yet in
complexity editing, your main focus is establishing and maintaining an affective
map in the viewer.[3]

The basic building block of complexity editing is the *montage*, a term that
literally means "setting together" or "assembling," in our case, of various event
details. In the context of media aesthetics, **montage** is the juxtaposition of two or
more separate event images that, when shown together, combine into a new and
more intense whole—a **gestalt**. Montage is a kind of filmic shorthand that quickly
reveals or creates certain event aspects and ideas. Whereas the classic montage
of the silent film era consisted of a brief series of quick cuts, showing segments
of a single event or of different events, the modern view of montage has become
more inclusive. Today montage implies the construction of a narrative—a brief

story—as well as a series of shots, scenes, or even sequences that create a vertical vector field—a clarification and intensification of emotions. The narrative structure of all types of montage contains some form of conflict.

Although possible montage combinations are numerous, they all seem to cluster into two broad categories: analytical montage and idea-associative montage.

Analytical Montage

In an ***analytical montage***, you analyze an event for its thematic and structural elements, select the essential elements, and synthesize them into an intensified screen event. The two basic types of analytical montage are sequential and sectional. **SEE 18.1**

SEQUENTIAL ANALYTICAL MONTAGE

To achieve a ***sequential analytical montage***, you condense an event into its key developmental elements and present them in their original cause/effect sequence. The sequential montage tells a story in shorthand fashion and moves from event-time 1 (t-1) to event-time 2 (t-2). **SEE 18.2**

One of the characteristics of an analytical montage is that the main event or its major theme is frequently implied but not shown or made otherwise explicit. Take the theme of a small bicycle mishap, for example. **SEE 18.3** We see a girl riding her bike down a driveway toward the street (figure 18.3a). At that very moment,

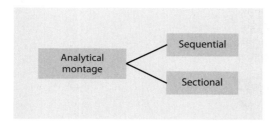

18.1 Analytical Montage

The two types of analytical montage are sequential and sectional.

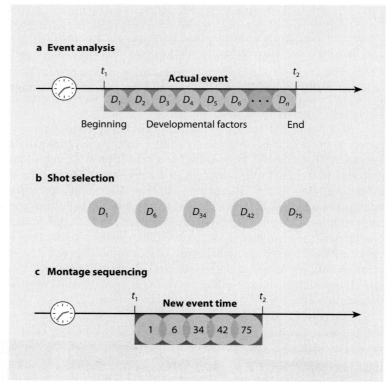

18.2 Sequential Analytical Montage

The sequential analytical montage presents event highlights (developmental elements) in the actual cause/effect sequence of the original event.

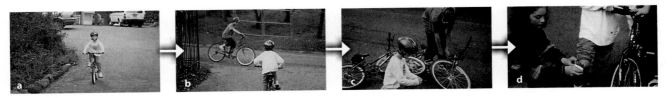

18.3 Main Event Implied

Note that in many sequential montages, the main event or main theme is implied rather than shown. Here the actual accident is not shown; only its development (a–b) and consequence (c–d) are.

another cyclist crosses her path (figure 18.3b). These are the "cause" parts of the montage. The third shot shows the bikes tangled and the little girl holding her knee (figure 18.3c). Fortunately, the collision wasn't serious, and no one was badly hurt (figure 18.3d). The last two shots are the "effect" part of the montage.

Notice that the accident itself is not shown; it is left up to the viewer to imagine. This montage is a type of low-definition rendering of an event that requires the viewer to apply psychological closure to fill in the gaps. Thus you have engaged, if not forced, the viewer to participate in the event—have an empathetic response—rather than merely watch it.

Because the sequential montage is time bound by the cause/effect time vector of the actual event, you cannot reverse or change in any way the time order of the selected event essences. All you can do is condense the event and intensify it through a careful selection of significant details. As you can see, this *t*-1 to *t*-2 sequence is an important element in editing for plot development and continuity of the story narrative.

To impress on you the importance of maintaining the natural order of the event in a sequential montage, let's do some switching of individual elements. **SEE 18.4** The first shot sequence shows montage units in their proper order: proposal, marriage, first baby, second baby. But by placing only a single shot in a different position, we drastically alter the meaning of the montage. Now the story sequence reads: proposal, first baby, second baby, and finally marriage. **SEE 18.5**

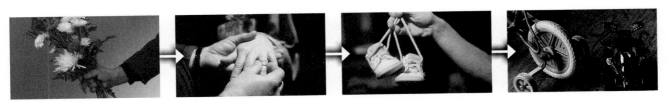

18.4 Cause-to-effect Order of Sequential Montage

Because the sequential montage moves from event-time 1 to event-time 2, the selected shots must be sequenced in the order of the original event. In this montage we imply the logical sequence of proposal, marriage, first baby, and second baby.

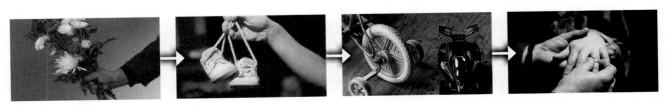

18.5 Changed Plot Through Noncausal Order

The meaning of the montage can change dramatically when the original event sequence is not maintained. Now the sequence suggests a proposal, the birth of the first baby, the second baby, and then marriage.

SECTIONAL ANALYTICAL MONTAGE

The *sectional analytical montage* temporarily arrests the progression of an event and examines an isolated moment from several viewpoints. Rather than moving from t-1 to t-2 to show the cause/effect development, the sectional montage stops the temporary event progression to carefully examine a significant event section or a specific moment. We no longer move along the horizontal objective-time vector but rather along the vertical subjective-time vector. By examining a t-1 to t-1 development, the sectional montage reveals the complexity of the event, that is, the external multi-layeredness and the internal intensity, emotional power, and quality of the moment. **SEE 18.6**

Because the sectional montage is independent of the cause/effect progression of time, shouldn't the order of shots or scenes be of little consequence in telling the basic story? Yes, to a certain extent. For example, if your intent is to show the tension of the moment just before the pitch with the bases loaded, it matters relatively little if you start the series of quick cuts with the pitcher, the batter, or some fans in the stands. The order of shots is important, however, if you want to establish point of view. The first shot or scene in a sectional montage can set the tone of the piece, establish its context, or, at least, suggest the intended emphasis. Both of the following sectional montages tell the same basic story: a teacher trying to communicate information to a less-than-enthusiastic class. **SEE 18.7 AND 18.8**

18.6 Sectional Montage

In the sectional analytical montage, the event sections are not arranged along the horizontal time vector (event progression) but rather along the vertical one (event intensity and complexity).

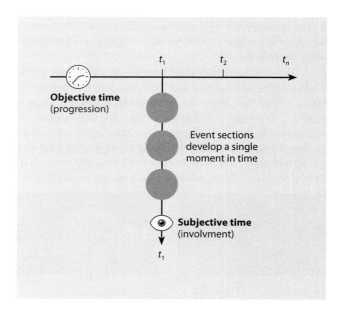

Objective time (progression)

t_1 t_2 t_n

Event sections develop a single moment in time

Subjective time (involvment)

t_1

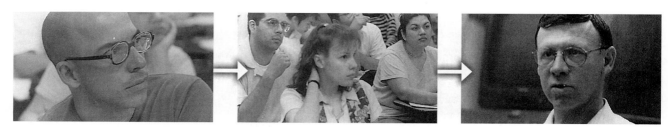

18.7 Sectional Montage Order: Student POV

Because we move vertically rather than horizontally in time, the order of shots does not signify an event development. Starting with the student, however, establishes a student point of view.

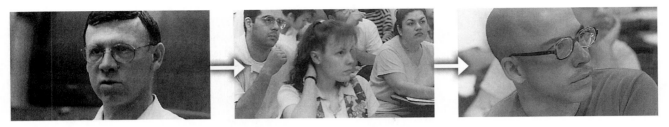

18.8 Sectional Montage Order: Teacher POV
By starting the montage with the teacher, we have now shifted to the teacher's POV.

Now take another look at the montage sequences and try to detect the difference of implied point of view. Even though the three shots in each montage contain admittedly minimal information, you probably notice that in the first sectional montage (figure 18.7) the emphasis is more on the students than the teacher, whereas in the second montage (figure 18.8) it is the other way around. In the first montage, you are more likely to side with the students, who have to suffer a boring lecture. In the second montage, it is the teacher who deserves some sympathy for trying to instill knowledge in students who would rather be doing something else.

In a single-screen presentation, a brief sectional montage is usually presented as a series of rhythmically precise shots. This means that while you aesthetically freeze a moment—remaining at event-time 1 throughout the shot series—you nevertheless take up running time while presenting the sectional montage, shot after shot. The tight rhythm of the shot series indicates to the viewer that you are not just showing a screen version of an actual event but that you have constructed something special, something inherently filmic. We discuss the traditional montage rhythm at the end of this chapter.

Indeed, we often engage in a similar quick scanning of event details in our everyday life. Picture yourself eating alone in a restaurant. Even if you are mainly concerned with your food, every once in a while you will probably glance up and look at various "shots," such as of the waiter skillfully balancing a tray, a couple looking into each other's eyes, people anxious to catch the hostess's attention, and so forth. This series of impressionistic "close-ups" is very similar to a sectional montage, contributing to your perception of the restaurant's ambience.

But isn't such a montage similar to the inductive visual approach to sequencing? Yes, it is. The inductive visual approach, discussed in chapter 11, is merely an extension of the analytical montage. All montage types are basically condensed inductive approaches to sequencing.

Sectional montages that stress the simultaneity of events are sometimes presented as a series of split-screen images or on multiple screens. Because we are dealing with various aspects of a single moment, such simultaneous presentations are actually more appropriate than the sequential presentations of event details.

Although the first attempts at sectional multiscreen montages were unsuccessful in cinema, they definitely fare better in television. It is most often used, or overused, in news presentations, with different field reporters and the locations from which they are reporting appearing in second-order space. Sports telecasts use split screens or multiple secondary frames to show a particular moment from different points of view. But it can also be an effective device in drama to show events that happen simultaneously in different locations.[4]

Why such multiscreen montages are less obtrusive in video than in film may be because, as you remember from chapter 13, the television image is basically

18.9 Multiscreen Sectional Montage
A multiscreen presentation is the ideal vehicle for the sectional montage. The multiple screens display the various event aspects simultaneously.

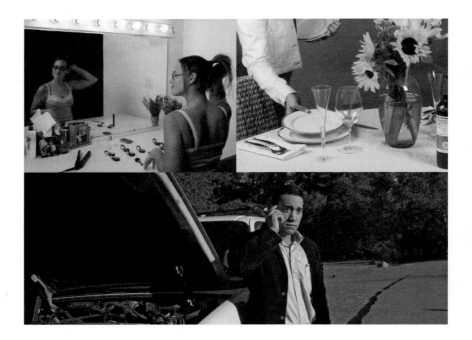

mosaic-like and not as sequential as film. We are also conditioned by the all-too-frequent visual effects during news presentations, which routinely display a great number of screens or information blocks on the video screen.

Digital video effects make it relatively easy to split the primary screen into various secondary frames, each of which can carry an event that happens simultaneously in a different location. For example, in a soap opera segment, one screen could show a woman getting ready for a party; another screen could show the hostess setting the dinner table; and still another could show an invited guest standing by the roadside next to his disabled car, trying to get help.

As you can see, the simultaneity of the three occurrences is no longer implied in a series of quick sequential shots but displayed as authentically concurrent, coexisting events. **SEE 18.9** You could also use multiple video screens side-by-side for the same effect. By extending the mosaic pattern of the single television image, multiple images can, in a sectional montage, reveal the complexity of the moment all at once. Through the simultaneous presentation of event details, you generate the true time structure of simultaneous events and, with it, a new structure—a multifaceted point of view. In a sequential montage, such complexity must be shown sequentially, which even when done well loses the true impact of simultaneity. But as a multiscreen presentation, the sectional montage acts more like a musical chord in which, as you remember, the three notes compose a gestalt that is quite different from playing them one by one.

Idea-associative Montage

The *idea-associative montage* juxtaposes two seemingly disassociated events to create a third principal idea or concept. This montage creates a *tertium quid*—a third something—that is not contained in either of the montage parts. Like the analytical montage, the idea-associative montage has two subgroups: comparison and collision. **SEE 18.10**

The idea-associative montage was created and developed into a high art in the days of silent film to express abstract ideas and concepts that could not readily

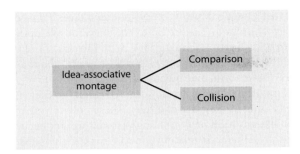

18.10 Idea-associative Montage

The two types of idea-associative montage are the comparison montage and the collision montage.

be shown in a narrative picture sequence. Just think how difficult it would be if you had to communicate a political debate with pictures only. Despite all the sorts of montage effects available, video could not exist without the often-maligned "talking heads." The advent of sound did not really harm the art of film, as early filmmakers and critics claimed, but helped strip the idea-associative montage of its glaring conspicuousness.[5]

COMPARISON MONTAGE

The **comparison montage** consists of succeeding shots that juxtapose two thematically related events to express or reinforce a theme or basic idea. It is also used to generate a specific feeling in the viewer. A comparison montage compares similar themes as expressed in dissimilar events. You could, for example, show in shot 1 a hungry dog digging through a garbage can and in shot 2 a homeless person doing the same thing. The resulting *tertium quid*—the consequent idea or theme—is the desperation and the social degradation of the poor. **SEE 18.11**

Some theories suggest that the comparison montage has an inevitable influence on our perception of the main event, similar to optical illusions. Russian filmmaker and theorist Lev Vladimirovich Kuleshov (1899–1970) conducted several experiments on the aesthetic effects of montage. To demonstrate the power of juxtaposition and context, Kuleshov interspersed the unchanging and expressionless face of the great Russian actor Ivan Mosjukhin with unrelated shots of different emotional values: a child playing, a plate of soup, a dead woman. Through the power of montage, the audience thought they saw Mosjukhin change his facial expression according to the juxtaposed event.[6] The montage had engendered what Kuleshov called an "artificial landscape," a "creative geography."[7]

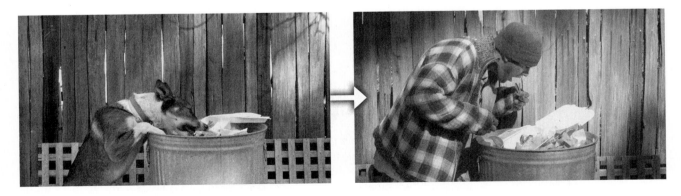

18.11 Comparison Montage

In a comparison montage, we compare thematically related events to reinforce a general theme. In this case, the juxtaposition of a dog scavenging for food among the trash and a homeless person doing the same generates the idea of our neglect to properly take care of the poor.

Video commercials still make frequent use of comparison montages because they must get complex messages across in a short time. You may, for example, see a powerful new sports car racing down a winding road, with the shadow of a jet fighter trying to catch up. The intended theme: the sports car is just about as fast as the jet. Or you may see the graceful and quietly elegant movements of a tiger dissolve in and out of a smoothly running luxury car. The intended theme: the luxury car has the strength, agility, and grace of a tiger. These new comparison montages are no longer a juxtaposition of alternating shots but rather occur within the same shot. It is the close thematic relationship that makes it possible to compare the two principal montage elements within a single shot. The waving flag behind a president rallying his people for support is a well-known and well-worn type of comparison montage.

At this point you may feel that viewers might reject outright such obvious montages as unabashed persuasion devices. If viewers were as knowledgeable as you are about media aesthetics, you would probably be right. But for the casual and uncritical viewer, even such an overt persuasive device may go unnoticed.

COLLISION MONTAGE

In the ***collision montage***, you clash two opposite events to express or reinforce a basic idea or feeling. Thus instead of comparing a hungry man with a hungry animal as in figure 18.11, you would juxtapose the shot of the hungry man looking through a garbage can with a shot of a well-nourished glutton indulging himself. The collision montage is a perfect example of how the complexity syntax uses conflict as a narrative intensifier. **SEE 18.12**

Using conflict as a structural device is nothing new in many areas of aesthetics, including drama, poetry, painting, dance, music, and, as you have seen, video and film. Conflict creates tension—an essential element for any aesthetic experience. The aesthetic use of conflict is closely related to our dualistic existence between life and death or any other process that exists only by oscillating between the absolutes of beginning and end. In the example of the comparison montage, we juxtapose a hungry person with a hungry animal to generate the idea of social degradation. In the collision montage, we collide the hungry person with the glutton to generate an even stronger idea of insensitivity and social injustice.

While the collision montage is a powerful filmic device, it is also an equally conspicuous one, so be extremely careful how and when you use it. If the montage becomes too obvious, you will annoy rather than enlighten or emotionally involve the sensitive viewer.

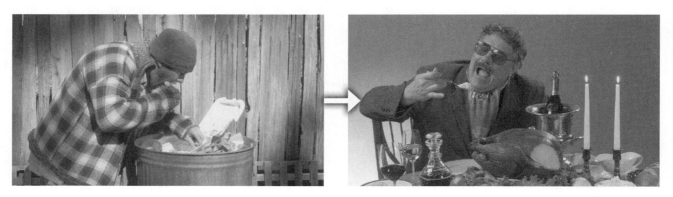

18.12 Collision Montage

In the collision montage, we combine opposing images to generate a new idea. To jolt us into awareness about social insensitivity to the plight of the hungry, the homeless person looking for food is juxtaposed with a well-fed gormandizer stuffing himself during an opulent dinner.

There are techniques you can use to render the collision montage less obvious, however. Let's assume that you've chosen a collision montage to illustrate the idea of environmental awareness, that indiscriminate building of tract houses will destroy the beauty of open spaces. You could juxtapose shot 1, an open field covered with wildflowers, with shot 2, the same space now barren and covered with tightly spaced, look-alike houses. Or, in the same shot, you could show a field with wildflowers and then have a bulldozer enter the shot, ruthlessly plowing the earth and cutting through the flowers with its gigantic blade. For good measure you can accompany the field of flowers and the bulldozer shot with the sounds of frantic building—hammering, buzz saws, trucks, and so forth.

The strength—but also the weakness—of the montage is that it is filmic in nature; that is, it is a purposely synthesized event. This means that idea-associative montages are a deliberate juxtaposition of fixed event elements to produce a specific effect or energy level. It is a deliberate sequencing device very much in line with the basic *"at-at"* structure of film (see chapter 13). Although we usually try to avoid drawing the viewer's attention to the editing process, the montage is meant to be perceived as a medium-induced statement. It is intended to interrupt the natural flow of the event. As you have seen, such event synthesis—Kuleshov's "artificial landscape"—is especially apparent in the two forms of idea-associative montages (comparison and collision) in which two seemingly disassociated, separate events are juxtaposed to generate a *tertium quid*.

In video the idea-associative montage is somewhat of a paradox. At the most fundamental level, the evanescent and fleeting nature of the basic structural unit of video—the video frame—works against the "at-at" juxtaposition of images. When video is used as live television, or in a livelike manner in which the medium is largely event-driven, you can use analytical montages but rarely idea-associative ones. There is usually not enough time or opportunity to look for appropriate shots that, when juxtaposed with the previous one, will generate new meaning. Every once in a while, however, an alert director and camera crew manage to come up with a collision montage even during a live telecast. During a Super Bowl football game, which was decided in the last seconds, one shot showed the defeated quarterback throwing away his towel and leaving the field with his head bowed, and the next shot showed the winning quarterback smiling and pounding his chest. There was no need to comment on the agony of defeat and ecstasy of winning; the quick collision montage said it all.

When video is used in a basically filmic way—that is, when the event details are recorded out of sequence for later postproduction editing—there is no reason why you can't integrate in your production even collision montages. For example, you could use multiple screens to show collision montages that juxtapose such opposites as hot/cold, fast/slow, high-energy/low-energy, color/black-and-white, peaceful/violent, or pristine nature/crowded city.

When using multiple screens, be aware of unintentional collision montages. Such effects can occur quite readily in news, where separate screen areas display different types of information. For example, the primary screen may show explicit footage of a terrible war scene, while the secondary screen areas announce the recipient of the Nobel Peace Prize, the latest football scores, prevailing glorious weather, and the rising stock market. **SEE 18.13**

Similarly, when working on the layout of Web pages, you need to watch that the multiple frames on the computer screen (or the text and the advertising) do not inadvertently create collision montages. The juxtaposition of a close-up shot of a drowning victim with an ad for an ocean cruise would, however incidentally, create a *tertium quid* not conducive to promoting a relaxing time on an ocean liner. The possibility for unintentional collision montages is increased by the necessity to scroll through information. Even if a single Web page displays images that in

Haiku poetry often works on the collision montage principle. In its rigid minimalist structure, it implies a larger picture or concept than its lines actually contain. Here are some examples of Haiku poetry written by Erika Zettl.[8]

*From its small prison
the singing canary holds
its keeper captive*

*Three shiny pebbles
lifted from the crystal creek—
in my hand, dull stones*

*When darkness steals all
color from my roses, their
fragrance comforts me*

*The Golden Gate Bridge
shrouded in ocean-gray fog
spans into nowhere*

18.13 **Unintentional Collision Montage in News**
The multiscreen display of unrelated information in news or Web pages can lead to unintentional collision montages.

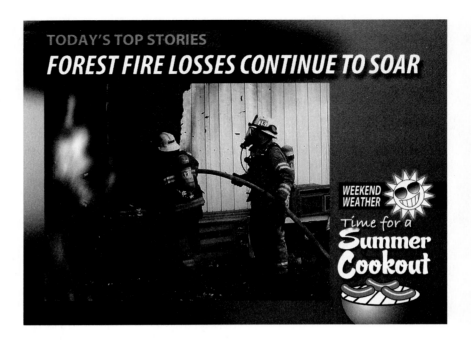

combination are reinforcing the basic message, scrolling may inadvertently "edit" images into a montage that carries an unintended meaning.

Visual dialectic The aesthetic principle upon which the visual conflict of the collision montage is based is called the *visual dialectic*. The concept of dialectic in film and video has been applied not only to the building of collision montages but also to the entire narrative structure of some films and documentaries.

But what exactly is the concept of dialectic?

The ancient Greeks used the dialectical method to search for and, they hoped, find the truth. Through debate and logical argument, they juxtaposed opposing and contradictory statements and ideas to resolve apparent contradictions into universally true axioms—the *dialectic principle*. For example, Greek philosopher Heraclitus (ca. 540–480 B.C.) explained that everything is inevitably undergoing change and that the existence of opposites suggests a universal system in which any changes in one direction are ultimately balanced by similar changes in the other. According to Heraclitus, all existence is based on strife, and unity is nothing more than a temporary balance of opposing forces. You probably notice the similarity between this theory and our vector theory of structuring various aesthetic fields.

Much later German philosopher Georg W. F. Hegel (1770–1831) based his whole theory of idealism on a similar dialectic: every being is juxtaposed by a not-being that resolves itself into a process of becoming. In the spirit of Heraclitus, Hegel considered the ideal as well as the process of life as the result of a continuing "war of opposites."[9]

Specifically, the *Hegelian dialectic* consists of a thesis that is always opposed by an antithesis; this juxtaposition results ultimately in a synthesis. This synthesis, then, represents a new thesis, which, in turn, is opposed by a new antithesis that again results in a new synthesis. This process repeats itself ad infinitum, always striving toward the "ideal," an objective spirit, absolute reason. **SEE 18.14**

Some filmmakers, such as the late Russian film theorist and director Sergei Eisenstein, used the dialectic not only as the basic structural and thematic principle of montage but also as the basic syntax of an entire film. Eisenstein juxtaposed

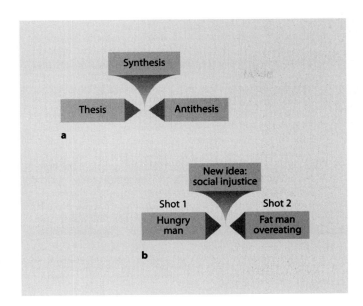

18.14 Dialectic Principle

The dialectic principle as used by **Hegel** states that by juxtaposing a thesis (any statement or condition) with its antithesis (counterstatement or opposite condition), we can arrive at a synthesis in which the two opposing conditions are resolved to a higher-order statement or condition (a). The idea-associative collision montage is a direct application of this dialectic principle (b).

Sergei Eisenstein developed a complex theory of film montage designed to show not only the primary theme and action of an event but also its more subtle overtones. Because of their historical importance, I briefly describe here the major types of Eisenstein's filmic montage. You will notice that I have borrowed or adapted some of Eisenstein's categories for our rhythmic control methods (metric and vectorial, which Eisenstein calls "rhythmic"). Eisenstein describes five basic methods of montage: metric, rhythmic, tonal, overtonal, and intellectual.

Metric montage   The criterion for the metric montage is the "absolute lengths" of the film pieces.

Rhythmic montage   In the rhythmic montage, the content within the frame determines the lengths of the pieces. It is the movement within the frame that impels the montage movement from frame to frame. (In other words, graphic, index, and motion vectors lead to the cut and determine the vector field of the total montage.)

Tonal montage   Here montage is driven by the characteristic emotional sound of the piece—of its dominant. Tonal montage reflects the degree of emotional intensity. For example, the tilted horizon would be part of a tonal montage, indicating the instability of the scene.

Overtonal montage   The overtonal montage derives from a conflict of the principal tone of the piece (the dominant) and the overtones. A comparison or collision montage would fit into Eisenstein's overtonal montage category. The principal tone of the montage (peace; conference table) is juxtaposed with an overtonal concept (war; A-bomb explosion). An overtonal montage also occurs when the basic montage has subtle overtones, such as changes in lighting and the like. For example, the high-key lighting of a happy party scene turns into predictive low-key lighting while the party is still going on. Such predictive lighting is one of the aesthetic factors that can turn a tonal montage into an overtonal one.

Intellectual montage   "Intellectual montage is montage not of generally physiological overtonal sounds but of sounds and overtones of an intellectual sort: that is, conflict-juxtaposition of accompanying intellectual affects."[10] This means that intellectual montage is based on the content—the theme—of the scene. The montage is controlled cognitively. It requires closure by intellect, not just by emotion or intuition.

Eisenstein eagerly took to the Hegelian dialectic because it served not only his aesthetic but also his political and personal aims to have a system that legitimately deals with conflict—that needs conflict for progress. "For art is always conflict," he says, "(1) according to its social mission, (2) according to its nature, (3) according to its methodology."[11]

The dialectical theory was, indeed, applied to social conflict quite successfully by German writer and social philosopher Karl Marx (1818–1883). Marx boldly replaced the Hegelian "idealism" with the more concrete and then-relevant materialism. In his basic theory, Marx states that history is nothing but a continuing conflict among economic groups, notably between social classes. He proposed that the thesis—the bourgeoisie (capitalist class)—must be opposed by the antithesis—the proletariat (workers)—to synthesize the two opposing classes into the ideal classless society in which every single member has, theoretically, equal rights. As we could witness with the breakup of communism, such theories do not always work in practice.

shots in a dialectical manner (colliding opposing ideas to create a *tertium quid*) and also scenes and entire sequences. The whole film, then, represents a complex visual dialectic.[12] But such a formulaic application of the visual dialectic can easily drain the aesthetic energy of the screen event and render it dull and listless. Worse, indiscriminate use of the visual dialectic in film as well as in video can become an aesthetic sledgehammer. The advantage of the vector theory over the dialectic approach to structuring the visual narrative is that to produce energy, vectors need not collide. The vector field is more versatile; it includes a visual dialectic but is not dependent on it.

Metric Montage

What, exactly, distinguishes a montage from simply shots that show different images? Is there still an element in the syntax of complexity editing that marks a series of shots as a montage, however subtle it may be? Yes, there is: it is the tertiary motion rhythm, called metric montage.

The **metric montage,** so named by Sergei Eisenstein, is a rhythmic structuring device.[13] In its purest form, it consists of a series of related or unrelated images that are flashed on-screen at more or less equally spaced intervals. You can create a metric montage simply by cutting the video or film footage to equal, or nearly equal, shot lengths, regardless of content, continuity, or color within the individual shots. This highly precise tertiary motion beat is important to distinguish a montage from an ordinary sequence of shots. The *cut-cut-cut-cut-cut-cut* rhythm will make the various montage shots a structural whole.

A good metric montage should allow you to clap your hands with the rhythm of the tertiary motion. **SEE 18.15**

A variation on the metric montage is the accelerated metric montage, in which the shots become progressively shorter. Your clapping to the cuts becomes progressively faster. You can use the accelerated metric montage to lead up to, or punctuate, a particular high point in a scene. **SEE 18.16**

Of course, you can use the metric montage as a structuring device for all types of editing, but it is especially effective for structuring the sequential and sectional analytical montage types.

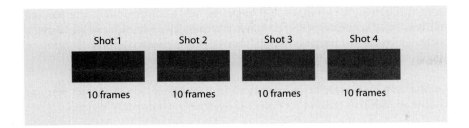

18.15 Metric Montage
In a metric montage, all shots are equally long. A metrically controlled montage provides an even tertiary motion beat.

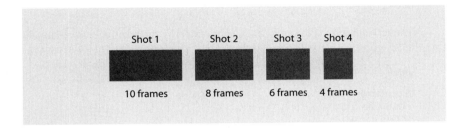

18.16 Accelerated Metric Montage
In an accelerated metric montage, the shots get progressively shorter. The tertiary motion beat accelerates toward the end of the montage.

Audio/Video Montage

Both types of analytical montage (sequential and sectional) and idea-associative montage (comparison and collision) can be created or reinforced by juxtaposing the visual shot sequence with a specific sound track. This is especially advantageous for idea-associative montages. In many cases, you will find it easier to make the comparison and collision montages less glaring but no less effective when using the audio track rather than video as counterpoint.

SEQUENTIAL ANALYTICAL A/V MONTAGE

The sound portion of a visual sequential analytical montage normally consists of literal sounds and/or music that follows the visual sequences. For example, if your sequential montage depicts somebody rushing to the airport, you accompany each shot with its appropriate sound track: traffic, car horns, running and breathing sounds, public-address announcements in the airport terminal, beeps at baggage security, and the roar of a plane taking off. You simply cut from one environmental sound detail to the next. By adding a rhythmically precise music track, you will not only facilitate the visual continuity of the montage but also intensify its rhythmic structure.

Sectional analytical montage   If the sectional analytical montage explores different environments, you can simply cut with the visuals from one sound environment to the next. For example, if you show a quick sectional montage of a young woman exploring downtown shopping areas, you once again accompany each shot with the sound characteristic of the location depicted. As in the sequential montage, you can cut from one sound environment to the next: sounds of a department store, the quiet yet intense sales pitch of a jeweler, and the noisy coffee shop environment. This time the sound is not supporting the progression of the event but rather the mosaic-like environment. The sound portions contribute to the vertical rather than the horizontal vector. You could instead choose to run a continuous sound track of a single event, such as the sounds of the department store, throughout the montage. Although basically a contrapuntal treatment (an uninterrupted sequence of literal sounds versus quick discontinuous visual cuts), such a video/audio juxtaposition can provide much-needed montage continuity. Rhythmically precise music can fulfill the same structural function.[14]

Comparison idea-associative montage   In the comparison montage, you can choose sounds that create a *tertium quid* by allusion (indirect reference).

Video	Audio
LS of red sports car moving through tight turns.	Jet engine of fighter plane.

The *tertium quid* (the implied idea generated by the montage) is obviously that the car goes almost as fast as a jet.

Video	Audio
LS of old man walking with cane on the field of an empty football stadium.	Loud crowd noise.

In this example, the *tertium quid* is to communicate the old man's memories when he was a star quarterback.

In the following example, the A/V comparison montage is used as a predictive device.

Video	Audio
MS of shooting gallery in an amusement park.	Natural, literal sounds.
CU of boy taking aim.	Segue into actual war sounds.

Collision idea-associative montage   In a collision montage, the accompanying sound track is contradictory in meaning and feeling to what you see on-screen. When perceived as a whole, however, the picture/sound combination intensifies the visual scene or produces a *tertium quid* that grows out of the video/audio collision.

For example, to intensify an especially violent scene, you may counterpoint the visuals with soft, romantic music. Or by accompanying an intimate love scene with violent sounds, you may hint at the underlying menace of the relationship. Some audio/video collision montages might look like this:

Example 1:

Video	Audio
CU of slum areas.	Narrator describing the wealth and historical significance of the city.

Example 2:

Video	Audio
Attack helicopter with rockets blazing.	Soft, romantic music.

Example 3:

Video	Audio
Couple drinking coffee in sidewalk café.	Romantic music changing into dissonant chords mixed with synthesized high-pitched hisses.

In the slum montage, the narration will certainly intensify the terrible blight conditions. The overriding message is the blindness of the city council, whose members still don't seem to realize that their city is in deep trouble. In the helicopter montage, the soft, romantic music sharpens the absurdity of war. And in the coffee-drinking scene, trouble is brewing.

The audio/video collision montage can produce comic effects with relatively little effort. All you need to do is use literal sounds that go against our expectations. The sleek racecar that sounds like an old truck, the glamorous soprano who sings her aria in a deep bass voice, or the lion that meows like a kitten—all are collision montage clichés.

Although the A/V collision montage is usually not as blatant as its video-only cousin, you still need to be extremely cautious about how and when to use it. For example, accompanying the news footage of an airline disaster with a Vienna waltz will not contribute to a higher empathetic involvement of the viewers; rather, the *tertium quid* will be the gross insensitivity, if not incompetence, of the news department.

Media Aesthetics and the Human Condition

Finally, here are a few concluding thoughts about applied media aesthetics.

This book was written with one overriding idea in mind: to help you not only cope with and reflect the human condition but also to improve it. By *human condition* I mean how we look at ourselves, portray ourselves in the media, and reinterpret and live in the fragmented, if not fractured, world we have constructed.

As inhabitants of a Western postmodern world, we have shed a considerable amount of cultural baggage yet we've inherited an equal share of troubles. We were finally freed from invariable systems of absolute thought and beliefs but were then promptly dumped into a world of uncertainty, ambiguity, and pliable realities. We are told that there is no longer an immutable reality common to all and that reality depends very much on how and in what context each of us looks at it.[15] The moon presents a different reality in its varying phases and also when you are *on* it instead of looking *at* it. More so, the full moon appears quite different to the scientist who looks for a landing site than to the couple on Lovers' Lane. Different contexts inevitably change how we perceive an event and how we interpret its meaning.

This freedom from absolutes is as liberating as it is demanding. You now have a big stake in the continual re-creation of this world, which mandates responsibility for your actions. You are accountable for the inevitable periodic remaking of you as a person and, as a mass communicator, of society at large. The new insights into the human condition coupled with the digital revolution present great challenges and opportunities.

The challenge is to identify significant events and clarify, intensify, and interpret them through the media for our fellow human beings; the opportunity is to do it imaginatively, creatively, and with style. Applied media aesthetics is intended to help you in this task.

When all is said and done, what we do comes down to good storytelling.

Storytelling has always been concerned with the prevailing human condition, and that has not changed over thousands of years. What *has* changed, however, is how we see the human condition and how we tell the story. Our media, which can instantly transmit big and small events from anywhere to everyone, have drastically changed our worldview but have also made it possible for us to show the human condition as it is, or at least as we think it is, or as it should be to potentially everybody on the planet.

Despite our best intentions, however, this effort will always remain somewhat incomplete. But this incompleteness is very much a part of our daily existence. You always will have left something undone. Don't despair over it because once your life is complete you won't be around to enjoy it. In applying the canons of media aesthetics when telling your story, you will coincidentally discover that they make you inevitably more aware of yourself and the world around you, more tolerant of contradicting viewpoints, and, ultimately, more amenable to temper your enthusiasm with wisdom.

Just one last word of advice: to be creative or to exercise your imagination does not mean that you must always seek the spectacular. Instead you must look closely and compassionately to see the unusual in the usual, the extraordinary in the ordinary. Then you can use the media aesthetic tools to clarify, intensify, and interpret at least some small part of the human condition for your fellow humans.

As the fox in parting reveals his secret to the little prince: "It is only with the heart that one can see rightly; what is essential is invisible to the eye."[16] Your job is to make the invisible visible.

SUMMARY

Complexity editing is used to intensify the emotional content of an event and reveal its complexity and to generate feeling. It affects primarily subjective time. The syntax of complexity editing is based on story and emotion, and the sequencing of shots is principally guided by how to elicit an emotional response in the viewer rather than vector continuity.

The basic building block of complexity editing is the montage. A montage is the juxtaposition of several separate event images that, when shown together, combine into a larger and more intense whole. There are two major montage categories: analytical montage and idea-associative montage.

In the analytical montage, we analyze a single event for its thematic and structural essentials and then synthesize the selected pieces into a brief, rhythmically precise series of shots. There are two types of analytical montage: sequential and sectional.

A sequential analytical montage strings together major developmental factors of an event in their actual event sequence to show, in shorthand style, the cause/effect development of the event.

A sectional analytical montage temporarily arrests the progression of an event and examines an isolated moment from various viewpoints. It explores the complexity of the event.

In the idea-associative montage, we juxtapose seemingly dissociated events to reinforce or generate a new specific idea or overall theme, often called the *tertium quid* (third something), that is not contained in either of its parts. The two idea-associative montage types are comparison and collision.

In the comparison idea-associative montage, we compare two similar themes by juxtaposing images from different events. *Example:* a hungry man going through a garbage can; a hungry dog looking for food. *Theme:* the desperation and social indignation of being poor.

In the collision idea-associative montage, we collide two conflicting themes to create the third idea. The collision montage represents a visual dialectic in which one idea is juxtaposed with an opposing idea. Both ideas are ultimately synthesized into a new idea—the *tertium quid*. The visual dialectic is based on the Hegelian dialectic of thesis-antithesis-synthesis.

The metric montage is concerned with structural techniques rather than thematic juxtapositions. It consists of a series of event images that are flashed on-screen in more or less equally spaced intervals.

The shots of a metric montage are usually structured by a tight tertiary motion beat. This rhythmic framework is especially important for the two forms of analytical montage.

A montage effect can also be achieved by juxtaposing the video sequence with a specific sound track. This is especially effective for idea-associative montages, where the combination of pictures and sound can create a *tertium quid* that may be less conspicuous.

Media aesthetics is designed to clarify, intensify, and interpret an event for a large audience. In so doing it can make us see the world from a new perspective and, hopefully, help improve it.

NOTES

1. The emotional vector field is discussed in different ways and with varying terminologies in various media publications, among them: Michael Rabiger, *Directing the Documentary*, 5th ed. (Burlington, Mass.: Focal Press, 2009), pp. 46–48; Bryce Button, *Nonlinear Editing: Storytelling, Aesthetics, and Craft* (Lawrence, Kansas: CMP Books, 2002), p. 182; and Stuart W. Hyde, *Idea to Script: Storytelling for Today's Media* (Boston: Allyn and Bacon, 2003), pp. 18–40.

2. One of the most striking examples of creative complexity editing is by Dody Dorn in *Matchstick Men* (2003), directed by Ridley Scott. In this film Dorn used multiple jump cuts, double exposures, image squeezing and stretching, and other effects to express the sorry mental state of the lead character. Note that the impeccably placed effects are not used because they were easily available in the nonlinear editing effects arsenal but rather to intensify the scene. See also Walter Murch, *In the Blink of an Eye: A Perspective on Film Editing*, 2nd ed. (Beverly Hills: Silman-James Press, 2001), pp. 15–20, 32–42.

3. Herbert Zettl, "Contextual Media Aesthetics as the Basis for a Media-literacy Model," *Journal of Communication* 48, no. 1 (1998): 81–95.

4. The television drama series *24* makes effective use of the multiscreen sectional montage to show events that occur simultaneously in different locations. It is a relatively quick and easy way to reveal the complexity of the occurrences, summarize the status of the various subplots, and make the viewer tune in again to see how the mess is resolved in the next episode.

5. See the comments by Siegfried Kracauer in his *Theory of Film: The Redemption of Physical Reality* (New York: Oxford University Press, 1960), pp. 102–11.

6. Lev V. Kuleshov, *Kuleshov on Film: Writings by Lev Kuleshov*, select., trans., and ed. by Ronald Levaco (Berkeley: University of California Press, 1974).

7. David Thomson, *A Biographical Dictionary of Film*, 3rd ed. (New York: Alfred A. Knopf, 1994), p. 409.

8. Erika Zettl, *Held Captive* (Forest Knolls, Calif.: Papermill Creek, 2004), pp. 2, 25, 42, 43.

9. Georg W. F. Hegel, *The Phenomenology of Mind*, trans. by F. P. B. Osmaston (New York: Macmillan, 1931).

10. Sergei Eisenstein, *Film Form and The Film Sense*, ed. and trans. by Jay Leyda (New York: World, 1957), *Film Form*, pp. 38–39. Also see the section titled "A Dialectic Approach to Film," pp. 45–63.

11. Eisenstein, *Film Form*, p. 46.

12. One the most concise explanations of the dialectic approach to film—the Marxist narrative—can be found in Vinay Shrivastava, *Aesthetics of Sound* (Dubuque, Iowa: Kendall/Hunt, 1996) pp. 193–209.

13. Eisenstein, *Film Form,* pp. 72–73.

14. During another semester students of the experimental production seminar produced a video essay on the Broadcast and Electronic Communication Arts Department at San Francisco State University called *Impressions.* It was based on the video/audio montage principle in which the quick cuts of the inductive visual sequence (showing student and faculty activities) are supported by a continuous flow of comments by students and faculty about their impressions of the department.

15. For an exceptionally lucid and comprehensive description of the postmodern mind, see Richard Tarnas, *The Passion of the Western Mind: Understanding the Ideas that Have Shaped Our World View* (New York: Ballantine Books, 1993), pp. 395–413.

16. Antoine de Saint-Exupéry, *The Little Prince,* trans. by Katherine Woods (New York: Harcourt Brace Janovich, 1971), p. 87.

Glossary

above-eye-level key-light position The principal light source (key light) strikes from above the object's eye level.

accelerated motion Object motion on-screen appears faster than normal. In film and when digital video is stored on a tapeless device, the division of object motion into relatively few "at" positions, each differing considerably from the other. The frame density is low. In tape-stored video, the videotape moves faster than its normal speed during playback.

achromatic Its basic meaning is "without chroma" (color). Usually, it refers to totally desaturated colors (having no hue) that show up white, black, and various shades of gray (brightness steps). The *grayscale* is an achromatic scale ranging from white to black.

additive color mixing The mixing of colored light. Usually, the mixing of the light primaries—red, green, and blue (RGB).

aerial perspective One of the graphic depth factors: three-dimensional emphasis by means of selective focus in a shallow depth of field. Only a relatively short section of the z-axis is in focus, with everything else out of focus.

aesthetic energy The energy we perceive from aesthetic phenomena, such as color, sound, and motion. Can be expressed as vector magnitudes.

aesthetic motion paradox An object can be in motion and perceived at rest, or at rest and perceived in motion.

ambient sounds Background sounds that normally occur in a specific environment.

analytical montage The selection of key elements of a single event (analysis) and their proper sequencing (synthesis).

angles Variety of camera viewpoints. *Angle* can also refer to a specific approach to a story.

applied aesthetics The branch of aesthetics that deals with sense perceptions and how to influence them through fundamental image elements, such as light and color, space, time/motion, and sound.

applied media aesthetics Same as *applied aesthetics* except that its focus is on video, film, and other electronic audiovisual media.

articulating the z-axis To place objects or people along the z-axis to serve as three-dimensional space modulators.

aspect ratio The relationship of screen width to screen height; 4 × 3 (1.33:1) for the standard video screen; 16 × 9 (1.78:1) for HDTV; and between 1.85:1 (5.55 × 3) and 2.35:1 (7 × 3) for wide motion picture screens. The display screens of mobile video devices range from the standard 4 × 3 aspect ratio to various vertical ratios.

asymmetry of the frame The right and left sides of the video, film, and computer screen are unequal in visual prominence. The right side commands more attention than the left.

"at-at" theory Adapted from Zeno's concept of motion, consisting of a series of static "at" positions in space and time, each differing to some degree from the previous one. Film shows a specific "at" position in each frame.

attached shadow A shadow that is on the object itself. It cannot be seen independent of (detached from) the object. Attached shadows help us primarily with interpreting an object's basic shape and texture.

attack The speed with which a tone reaches a certain (usually maximum) level of loudness. *See also* **decay**.

background A basic structural element of the three-dimensional field—the depth plane farthest from the camera, marking the end of the z-axis.

background light Illumination of the set pieces and backdrops. Also called *set light*.

back light Illumination from behind the subject and opposite the camera.

balance   Relative structural stability of objects or events within the screen. Specifically, the distribution of vectors and graphic weight into *static* (stable and unlikely to change) and *dynamic* (asymmetrical and less stable) pictorial structures.

below-eye-level key-light position   The principal light source (key light) strikes from below the subject's eye level. Also called *horror lighting* and *reverse modeling*.

biological time   An internal clock that tells us when to feel awake or tired. A type of subjective time that is measured quantitatively (when to do certain things).

brightness   The color attribute that indicates how light or dark a color appears in a black-and-white photograph. Technically, brightness is one of the three major attributes of color that indicates how much light is reflected from a colored surface. Also called *lightness* and *value*.

brightness constancy   The stabilization of brightness values by our mental operating system so that we perceive white as white and black as black regardless of the actual reflectance values. Also called *lightness constancy*.

cameo lighting   Lighted objects set off against a plain, dark background. Foreground figures are illuminated with highly directional light, and the background remains unlighted.

canon   The purest and most obvious form of musical imitation. Both the theme and the melody are repeated verbatim by the other voices. Also called *round. See also* **imitation**.

cast shadow   A shadow produced by an object and thrown (cast) onto a surface (part of the object itself or another surface). The cast shadow may be object-connected (shadow touches the object producing it) or object-disconnected (shadow does not touch the object producing it). Cast shadows help us locate an object relative to its surroundings.

character time   The objective- and subjective-time elements concerning the character's actions and feelings.

chiaroscuro lighting   Lighting for light/dark contrast (fast falloff) to emphasize volume and specific areas.

chord   The simultaneous playing of three or more musical tones. Two tones played simultaneously constitute an *interval*. The chord forms a vertical sound vector.

chromatic   Its basic meaning is "with chroma" (color). *Chroma* is another term for the more accurate *saturation,* or color strength.

clock time   The "at" position in the time continuum when an event occurs. *See also* **objective time**.

collision montage   An idea-associative montage that clashes opposite events to express or reinforce a basic idea.

color   Specific wavelengths within the visible light spectrum, which we interpret as various hues.

color attributes   The three color sensations: hue, saturation, and brightness.

color constancy   Perceiving a color as uniform despite variations.

color energy   The relative aesthetic impact a color has on us; the relative energy a color emits within its contextual field.

color harmony   Hues that go well together. Specifically, the balanced energy of colors. Color harmony is most easily achieved with high-energy colors (figure) set off against a low-energy color background (ground).

color model   A graphic representation of the integration of the three color attributes: hue, saturation, and brightness.

color temperature   The relative bluishness or reddishness of white light, measured in Kelvin degrees. Bluish light has a high color temperature; reddish light has a low one. The video camera must be adjusted to the color temperature of the prevailing light. *See also* **white balance**.

comparison montage   An idea-associative montage that compares seemingly disassociated yet thematically related events to establish or reinforce a basic idea.

complexity editing   The building of an intensified screen event from carefully selected event essences. Montages result from complexity editing.

context   The environment in which we perceive and evaluate specific perceptual phenomena. Every aesthetic element operates within, and is dependent on, the context of all others.

contextualism   A branch of philosophy that includes, rather than excludes, the environment (context) in the process of clarifying, intensifying, and interpreting experience.

contextualistic aesthetics   How the various fundamental aesthetic elements (light and color, space, time/motion, and sound) operate in various contexts and in relation to one another. *See also* **contextualism**.

continuing vectors   Vectors that succeed each other in the same direction.

continuity editing   The assembly of shots that ensure vector and vector field continuity. Its principal function is the clarification of an event.

converging vectors   Vectors that point or move toward each other. They usually energize an event.

counterpoint   A specific polyphonic technique in which the various voices (horizontal vectors) encounter each other. In media aesthetics the musical counterpoint of note against note is expanded into vector against vector.

cross shooting   Similar to over-the-shoulder shooting except that the camera-near person is out of the shot. *See also* **over-the-shoulder (O/S) shooting**.

cut   The instantaneous change from one shot (image) to another.

cutaway   A shot of an object or event that is peripherally connected with the overall event and that is (ideally) neutral as to screen direction. Used to intercut between two shots in which the screen direction is reversed.

decay   The speed with which a sound fades to where it can no longer be heard. *See also* **attack**.

deductive visual approach   Moving from an overview to event detail. A deductive method stresses the analysis and the breakdown of a complete video program, film, or computer display into its major aesthetic elements.

depth of field   Area along the z-axis that is in focus. In a great depth of field, most or all objects located along the z-axis at different distances from the camera are in focus. In a shallow depth of field, only objects that lie within a short section of the z-axis are in focus; all others are out of focus. It is dependent on the focal length of the lens, the lens aperture, and the distance from camera to object.

desaturation theory   The more desaturated the colors of a scene, the more internal it becomes and the more the viewer is compelled to participate. Color desaturation renders the scene low-definition.

dialectic principle   The juxtaposition of opposing or contradictory statements or events to resolve the contradictions into universally true axioms or an event synthesis (new event or idea).

diegetic sound   Literal sounds that "occupy story space," that is, are part of the story. *See also* **literal sound**.

digital cinema   Refers mainly to the use of high-definition digital video cameras instead of traditional film cameras for the acquisition of images. Can also refer to the whole electronic production, postproduction, distribution, and projection processes. It differs from HDTV in that it can work with higher-resolution images, such as 4K (4,000) or more pixels per horizontal line.

digital video effects (DVE)   Visual effects created by a computer or other digital video effects equipment.

dissolve   A gradual transition from shot to shot in which the two images temporarily overlap.

diverging vectors   Vectors that point or move in opposite directions.

dramatic agent   Any object or action within a scene that contributes directly to its intensification.

dramaturgy   The art of dramatic narrative and composition. More generally, the whole structure of a play—the total orchestration of dialogue, action, and various aesthetic elements.

duration   The running time of a scene, sequence, or total film or video production. In music, refers to how long we perceive a sound.

dynamic balance   An asymmetrical balance where the graphic weight and vectors are not equal on both sides of the screen. The aesthetic energy is increased because the asymmetrical distribution of graphic elements and vectors causes some tension.

dynamics   The variations of perceived loudness of a sound.

editing   Selecting significant event details and sequencing them into a comprehensive whole—building a screen event.

editing syntax   Prescribes how to arrange individual shots so that they combine into meaningful scenes and sequences to tell a story. *See also* **continuity editing** and **complexity editing**.

encoding   Translating an idea into a message for a specific communication medium.

envelope   The total duration of a tone, from initial attack to final decay. Also called *sound envelope*.

event density   A great number of event details that occur within a specific clock time period. Can also be used to describe the complexity of an event.

event intensity   The relative energy and the relative significance we perceive about a specific event.

experience intensity   The number of relevant experiences to which we are subjected simultaneously or in rapid succession and their relative depths.

external vector   Force with a direction and a magnitude operating outside of us.

eye level   The plane parallel to the ground emanating from the eye of the observer. Eye level and the horizon line lie on the same plane regardless of how high the observer is from the ground.

fade   The gradual appearance of a picture from black or its disappearance to black.

falloff   (1) The brightness contrast between the light and shadow sides of an object. (2) The speed (degree of change) with which the brightest part of an object turns into dense shadow. *Fast falloff* means that the lighted area changes abruptly into dense shadows; the contrast is high. *Slow falloff* means that a very gradual change takes place from lighted area to shadow area or that very low, if any, contrast exists between light and shadow areas. *No falloff* means that there is no contrast—all visible sides are equally illuminated.

field of view   The territory a shot includes, ranging from extreme long shot (ELS) to extreme close-up (ECU).

figure/ground principle   Our tendency to organize a scene into figures that lie in front of a background. In doing this we perceive the ground as being more stable than the figures. In sound design *figure/ground* means that you choose the important sounds to be the figure while relegating the other sounds to the background.

fill light   Additional light on the opposite side of the camera from the key light, used to illuminate shadow areas and thereby reduce falloff. Usually accomplished by floodlights.

first-order space   Video space as defined by the borders of the video screen (x- and y-axes) and the illusory z-axis.

flat lighting   Omnidirectional illumination from no particular single source. The falloff is slow or nonexistent.

forced perspective   An exaggerated linear perspective, making us perceive parallel lines converging more drastically than in normal vision. Wide-angle lenses create a forced perspective.

foreground   A basic structural element of the three-dimensional field—the depth plane closest to the camera, marking the beginning of the z-axis.

frame density   The sampling rate of a motion, that is, the number of "at" positions used to divide a single motion.

fugue   A musical theme or subject stated first in each of the voices (usually four) and then restated verbatim or in a slightly changed form at various times in all voices. The theme is virtually chased from voice to voice throughout the fugue, relating vertically to the counterpoints of the other voices.

geographical matching   Sound and pictures originate in the same geographical area.

gestalt   A complete configuration that we perceive through psychological closure. The perceived pattern is generally different from and often more complete than the sum of its parts. In a gestalt all elements operate in relation to the whole.

golden section   A classical proportional system in which the smaller section of a line is to the greater section as the greater is to the total length of the line. Especially effective when a prominent horizontal line is divided by a vertical one at the golden section point. It creates a dynamic balance.

graphication   The deliberate rendering of a television-mediated event as a two-dimensional, snapshot-like image that assumes the characteristics of a magazine illustration.

graphic depth factors   Features that create the illusion of three-dimensional space on a two-dimensional surface (without the use of motion). The major ones are overlapping planes, relative size, height in plane, linear perspective, aerial perspective, and light and shadow.

graphic mass   A precisely defined screen area—such as a person, an object, or an abstract wipe pattern—that is seen as a figure against a ground. The more screen area the figure occupies, the heavier its graphic mass.

graphic vector   A vector created by lines or by stationary elements arranged in such a way as to suggest a line. Although graphic vectors are ambivalent as to precise direction, they do indicate a directional tendency, such as horizontal, vertical, curved, uphill, or downhill.

graphic weight   The relative lightness or heaviness we perceive from a specific graphic mass; it is determined by the dimension of the object, its basic shape and orientation, its location within the frame, and its color.

grayscale   A series of achromatic steps of gray leading from white to black.

harmonics   Overtones that are simple multiples of the fundamental tone. *See also* **overtones**.

harmony   Elements that go together well. In music, a number of chords or vertical sound vectors.

headroom   The space between the top of the head and the upper screen edge.

Hegelian dialectic   A thesis (basic argument) that is opposed by an antithesis (counterargument), ultimately resulting in a synthesis (resolution or new, more insightful argument).

height in plane   One of the graphic depth factors: assuming that no contradictory distance cues are evident and that the camera is shooting parallel to the ground, we will perceive an object as being more and more distant the higher it moves up in the picture field until it has reached the horizon line. *See also* **graphic depth factors**.

high-definition   A high-resolution picture (consisting of a great number of pixels) or high-fidelity sound.

high-definition television (HDTV)   A video image with an aspect ratio of 16 × 9 that has a much higher resolution (720 or 1,080 visible lines) and color fidelity than the standard television image (in the United States, 525 lines).

high-key lighting   High overall light level; general, nonspecific, bright lighting; slow falloff, usually with a light background. Has nothing to do with the vertical position of the key light.

historical matching   Sound and pictures originate in the same historical period.

homophony   A musical structure in which a single predominant melody is supported by chords. The melody can stand on its own; the chords cannot.

horizon line   The line formed by the actual horizon or an imaginary line parallel to the ground at eye level. More technically, the plane at right angles to the direction of gravity that emanates from the eye of the observer at a given place. The horizon line is always at the eye level of the observer regardless of how high the observer is relative to the ground.

hue   The color attribute that indicates the actual color of an object—red, green, blue, and so on.

hue circle   Colors (hues) arranged in a circle, moving in rainbow order from red to orange, yellow, green, blue, and purple.

idea-associative montage   Juxtaposes two seemingly disassociated images to create a third principal idea or concept. Operates on the dialectical principle in which one idea (thesis) is opposed by another (antithesis), leading to a new idea (synthesis)—a *tertium quid* (third something).

image elements   The fundamental aesthetic elements of video and film: light and color, two-dimensional space, three-dimensional space, time/motion, and sound.

imitation   A short musical theme or subject stated first in one voice and then repeated verbatim or in a slightly changed form in the other voice(s) while the first voice continues.

index vector   A vector created by someone looking or something pointing unquestionably in a specific direction.

inductive visual approach   Moving from event detail to a general overview to create the overall event in the perceiver's mind. The inductive method requires psychological closure. As a theoretical method, it advocates the careful study of each image element without and within its structural field and other contexts .

inscape   Events that characterize an internal condition—how people feel rather than what they do.

instantaneous editing   *See* **switching**

internal vector   Force with a direction and a magnitude operating within us, such as a feeling or an empathic response.

jump cut   An image that jumps from one screen position to another during a cut. It can also mean an illogical or otherwise jarring sequence between two shots.

key light   The apparent principal source of directional illumination falling on an area or a subject. Also refers to high- or low-key lighting (light or dark background).

kicker   Kicker light; directional light that is positioned low and from the side and the back of the subject.

labile balance   A heightened stage of dynamic balance.

landscape   The setting in which the action takes place rather than the people who function in this setting. It may refer to the actual setting—city street, mountains, desert—as well as a broad, outer action, such as a huge battle scene or a space spectacular. It refers to outer events (car chase) rather than inner events (two people expressing their love for each other).

leadroom   The space in front of a person or an object moving toward the edge of the screen. *See also* **noseroom.**

leitmotiv   German for "leading motif," a short musical phrase that denotes a specific event. When repeated it portends an upcoming event. Its basic dramatic function is that of allusion (reference). *See also* **predictive sound.**

letterboxing   Technique for changing aspect ratio to show widescreen material on the standard 4 × 3 video screen by leaving black borders, called *dead zones,* at the top and the bottom of the screen.

light   Radiant energy that behaves commonly as electromagnetic waves.

lighting   The deliberate manipulation of light and shadows for a specific communication purpose.

lightness   How light or dark we perceive various brightness steps.

lightness constancy   *See* **brightness constancy**

limbo lighting   Any set area that has a plain, light background. Often confused with *flat lighting.*

linear perspective   Among the more powerful and convincing graphic depth factors: horizontal parallel lines converge toward the distance at the vanishing point, which lies on the eye-level horizon line. Vertical lines (such as windows) crowd progressively toward the vanishing point. *See also* **graphic depth factors.**

literal sound   Referential sound. It always refers to its originating source (sound of a baby crying alludes to the image and the presence of a baby). Also called *diegetic sound.*

live recording   The uninterrupted video recording of a live event for later, usually unedited, playback.

loudness   The apparent strength of a tone as we perceive it (magnitude of a sound vector). Technically, the amplitude of the sound wave. *See also* **dynamics.**

low-definition   A low-resolution picture (consisting of relatively few pixels) or low-fidelity sound.

low-key lighting   Low overall light level. Selective lighting with fast falloff.

magnetism of the frame   The pull that the frame (screen edges) exerts on objects within the frame (screen).

melody   A series of musical notes arranged in succession, forming a tune. Melody is a horizontal sound vector.

mental map   Tells viewers where things are or are supposed to be in on- and off-screen space.

metric montage   A number of shots of identical or similar length that create a definite tertiary motion beat—a rhythm. The content of the shots is less important than shot length.

middleground   A basic structural element of the three-dimensional field—the depth plane that lies between the foreground and background planes.

mobile video media   Refers to all highly portable devices with a very small viewing screen, such as the iPhone. Can have a variety of aspect ratios. Also called *cell-phone video.*

moiré effect   Color vibrations that occur when narrow, contrasting stripes or intricate patterns interfere with the scanning lines of the video system.

montage   The juxtaposition of two or more separate event details that combine into a larger and more intense whole—a new gestalt.

motion paradox   An object can be in motion and at rest at the same time. Also, the figure is perceived as doing the moving even if it is only the ground that is actually in motion.

motion vector   A vector created by an object actually moving in a specific direction or an object that is perceived as moving on the screen. A photograph or drawing of an object in motion is an index vector but not a motion vector.

multicamera lighting   Lighting for continuous shots from a variety of positions of multiple cameras.

multiple screens   Various-sized second-order screens keyed into the main first-order screen, or separate screens set side-by-side that show different, usually related, scenes.

multiple z-axis blocking   To block the z-axis of each camera with space modulators (people and/or objects) so that when switching from one camera to the next, each shows an articulated z-axis.

natural dividing lines   Graphic vectors that occur at prominent points on a body, such as the horizontal ones formed by the eyes, the bottom of the nose, the mouth, the shoulders, the knees, the waist, and so forth.

negative volume   Empty space that surrounds, or is described by, positive volumes. A definite empty space, such as the inside of a room, that is articulated by positive volumes, such as the walls. *See also* **positive volume.**

noise   Random audible vibrations of the air ("sounds" without communication purpose).

nondiegetic sound   Nonliteral sounds that do not "occupy story space," that is, do not advance the story. *See also* **nonliteral sound.**

nonliteral sound   Does not refer to the sound-originating source. The most common nonliteral sound is music, assuming that the context does not deal with the performance of the music. Also called *nondiegetic sound.*

noseroom   The space in front of a person looking or pointing toward the edge of the screen. *See also* **leadroom.**

objective time　The time measured by the clock. Quantitative measure of time intervals in which observable change occurs. Also called *clock time*.

off-screen space　The space immediately surrounding the video or motion picture screen.

on-screen space　The space actually contained within the borders of the video or motion picture screen.

open set　A set whose background scenery is not continuous. The open set consists of sections of interiors not connected by a common background.

overlapping plane　The most direct of the graphic depth factors: when you see one object partially covering another, you know that the one doing the covering must be in front of the one that is covered. *See also* **graphic depth factors**.

over-the-shoulder (O/S) shooting　The camera looks over the camera-near person's shoulder (shoulder and head included in shot) at another person. *See also* **cross shooting**.

overtones　The number of frequencies with which a sound-producing source vibrates in addition to its fundamental frequency.

pace　The perceived speed of an event: whether the event seems to drag or to move along quickly. Although pace belongs to subjective time, it is treated quantitatively; we speak of slow and fast pace.

pan-and-scan　Technique for adapting a wide-screen presentation to standard television, whereby the more important portions of the wide-screen frame are scanned and made to fit the 4 × 3 aspect ratio of the standard video screen.

personification　To perceive the person (usually a newscaster) operating in first-order space as a real person who shares the viewer's psychological, if not physical, space.

phasing　The sound portion of an event is either ahead of or trails the corresponding picture portion.

photographic principle　The triangular arrangement of key, back, and fill lights, with the back light opposite the camera and directly behind the object, and the key and fill lights on opposite sides of the camera and to the front and the side of the object. Also called *triangle lighting*.

pillarboxing　Technique for changing the aspect ratio to show standard 4 × 3 video material on the 16 × 9 wide screen by leaving empty vertical *side bars* or *dead zones* on the sides of the screen.

pitch　Indicates the relative highness or lowness of a sound, measured by frequency (hertz).

plot　The narrative progression of a story or a sequence of events.

plot time　The objective and subjective time concerning the story or sequence of events.

point of view (POV)　In contrast to viewpoint, point of view has a bias. Usually, the camera simulates the index vector and the field of view of a particular on-screen character. It makes the audience associate with what the character sees and feels. *See also* **viewpoint**.

polyphony　The combination of two or more melodic lines (horizontal vectors) which, when played together, form a harmonic whole (vertical vectors).

positive volume　Objects that have substance and can be touched and weighed. Objects with a certain amount of mass. *See also* **negative volume**.

posterization　Visual effect that reduces the various brightness values to only a few (usually three or four) and gives the image a flat, graphicated look.

postproduction editing　The assembly of recorded audio and video material after the actual production.

predictive lighting　Light changes from one mood to another, signaling an impending occurrence.

predictive sound　Sound change or specific sound combinations that signal an impending occurrence. *See also* **leitmotiv**.

premature closure　Applying psychological closure using on-screen cues that do not project the image into off-screen space.

presence　A sound quality that makes you feel as though you were close to the sound source.

primaries　Basic colors that, when mixed, render almost all other colors. The primaries cannot be achieved by mixing. The additive (light) primaries are red, green, and blue (RGB). The subtractive (paint) primaries are cyan (greenish blue), magenta (bluish red), and yellow (CMY).

primary motion　Event motion in front of the camera.

psychological closure　Taking a minimal amount of clues and mentally filling in nonexistent information to arrive at stable, easily manageable patterns. Also called *closure*.

psychological time　*See* **subjective time**

rack focus　The shift of emphasis from one z-axis plane to another by changing (racking through) optical focus from one object to another in a shallow depth of field.

relative size　One of the graphic depth factors: if you know how big an object is or can guess its size by contextual clues, you can tell approximately where it is located on the z-axis. *See also* **graphic depth factors**.

Rembrandt lighting　A type of chiaroscuro lighting in which only highly selected areas are illuminated while others are kept purposely dark; features fast falloff.

RGB　Stands for *red, green, blue*—the three additive light primaries.

rhythm　How well a scene or show flows. Indicates the pacing of the individual shots and the scene in general and how well the parts relate to one another sequentially.

rule of thirds　A variation of the golden section, wherein the screen is divided into three horizontal and three vertical fields. A fail-safe composition places a subject where a vertical and a horizontal line intersect.

running time　Objective-time measure. Indicates the overall length of a video program or film. It indicates the "from-to" span in the time continuum.

saturation The color attribute that indicates color richness—the strength of the color. Also called *chroma*.

scene A clearly identifiable organic part of an event. It is a small structural (action) or thematic (story) unit, usually consisting of several shots.

scene time The clock time duration of a scene.

screen space The space as contained within the borders of the screen, or the cumulative screen space of a shot sequence or of multiple screens.

secondary motion Camera motion, including pan, tilt, pedestal, crane or boom, dolly, truck, arc, and zoom.

second-order space A clearly defined space within the video screen (such as the box over the newscaster's shoulder), the screen space of a television set within first-order space, or any other clearly defined framed space on the primary video screen.

sectional analytical montage Arrests, temporarily, the progression of an event and examines an isolated moment from various viewpoints. It explores the relative complexity of an event.

selective focus Emphasizing an object in a shallow depth of field through focus while keeping its foreground and background out of focus.

selective perception An automatic reduction of unnecessary details during the perception process.

selective seeing Our tendency to see only such events and event details as we are interested in and/or that seem to confirm our perceptual expectations and prejudices. Often (and inaccurately) called *selective perception*.

sequence The sum of several scenes that compose an organic whole.

sequence time The clock time duration of a sequence.

sequencing Assembling shots so that they form a unified whole. Sequencing is achieved through editing.

sequential analytical montage The sequencing of major event details in the cause/effect order of the actual event.

shot The smallest convenient operational unit in video and film. It is the interval between two distinct video transitions, such as cuts, dissolves, and wipes.

shot time The clock time duration of a shot.

side light Usually directional light coming from the side of the object. Acts as additional fill light and provides contour.

silhouette lighting The background is evenly lit, with the figures remaining unlighted, revealing only their contours.

single-camera lighting Lighting for short-duration shots from a specific camera position. Also called *film lighting* and *film-style lighting*.

size constancy The perception of the actual size of an object regardless of the distance and the angle of view.

slow motion Screen motion that shows the event move more slowly than its actual primary motion. In film, the division of motion into relatively many "at" positions, each differing a little from the next; the frame density is high. In television, it is achieved through slower-than-normal playback speed or digital manipulation.

solarization Visual effect that combines a positive and a negative image of the same subject. The black lines indicate where the two images meet.

sound Purposeful audible vibrations (oscillations) of the air.

sound continuity Maintaining the intended volume and quality of sound over a series of edits.

sound perspective A close-up picture is accompanied by a close-up sound; a long shot is accompanied by a farther-away sound. A close-up picture is accompanied by a sound with more presence (appears to come from nearby) than the sound for a long shot (appears to come from farther away).

sound texture The relative complexity of a harmonic structure (complexity of vertical sound vectors).

source-connected sound Hearing a sound and seeing the sound-originating source at the same time. For example, showing a close-up of a speaker while hearing her speak.

source-disconnected sound Hearing a sound and seeing a picture that shows something other than the sound-producing source.

static balance A stable balance, as in a symmetrical arrangement of visual elements.

stereoscopic projection The z-axis extends not only from screen to horizon but also toward the viewer. The images are no longer confined to the screen space.

storyboard A series of sketches of the key visualization points of an event, with the corresponding audio information given below each visualization.

story time Spans the period of a story told in a video program or motion picture. It moves from a specific calendar date to another or from one clock time to another.

structural matching Pictures and sound are matched according to their internal structure and their dominant vector fields.

structural unit of film The film frame that shows the frozen moment ("at" position) of an event.

structural unit of video A "frame" that is in continuous flow and in the process of becoming and decaying; an image in flux.

subjective camera The camera assumes the role of an event participant; it no longer looks at but rather participates in the event.

subjective time The duration we feel; a qualitative measure. Also called *psychological time*.

subtext What the character wants to say or do but keeps hidden. Can also refer to the psychological makeup of a character.

subtractive color mixing The mixing of color pigments (paint) or filters. The filters subtract (block) certain colors while passing others. Usually, the mixing of paint primaries—cyan (greenish blue), magenta (bluish red), and yellow (CMY).

superimposition The simultaneous overlay of two pictures on the same screen. Also called *super*.

sweetening　A variety of quality adjustments of recorded sound in postproduction.

switching　A change from one video source to another during a show or show segment with the aid of an electronic switcher. Also called *instantaneous editing.*

syntax of complexity editing　Editing conventions and techniques primarily used for heightening emotional impact.

syntax of continuity editing　Editing conventions and techniques primarily used for seamless visual sequences and narrative flow.

tertiary motion　Sequence motion—the editing rhythm (beat) induced by regular shot changes.

tertium quid　The "third something"—a third (new) idea resulting from a montage.

text　What a character says and does. Also, a system of verbal and nonverbal signs. *See also* **subtext.**

thematic matching　The video event is accompanied by sounds we ordinarily associate with the event, such as the interior of a cathedral and organ music, or a football game and crowd sounds.

timbre　Describes the tone quality or tone color. Depends on the amount and the combination of overtones.

time vector　The horizontal direction of time from past to future as we normally experience it.

timing　The control and the manipulation of objective time and the structuring of subjective time.

tonal matching　The video event is matched with sounds that express the general tone or mood of the event, such as lovers and romantic music, or sporting events and cheering.

triangle lighting　The triangular arrangement of key, back, and fill lights. *See also* **photographic principle.**

vanishing point　The point at which all parallel lines seem to converge and discontinue (vanish). The vanishing point always lies at eye (or camera) level on the horizon line.

vector　In media aesthetics, a perceivable force with a direction and a magnitude. Also, any aesthetic element that leads us into a specific space/time—or even emotional—direction. In mathematics, a physical quantity with both a magnitude and a direction.

vector field　A combination of vectors operating within a single picture field (frame), from picture field to picture field (from frame to frame), from picture sequence to picture sequence, from screen to screen (multiple screens), or from on-screen to off-screen events.

vector line　An imaginary line created by extending converging index vectors or a motion vector. To preserve shot continuity, all cameras must be to one or the other side of this line.

Also called *principal vector, line of conversation and action, one-eighty, scene axis, sight line, eye line,* and, simply, *the line.*

vector magnitude　The degree of directional certainty and force of a vector; the amount of energy we perceive. It is determined primarily by screen direction, graphic mass, and perceived object speed. A high-magnitude vector is strong; a low-magnitude vector is weak.

viewpoint　What the camera is looking at and from where. *See also* **point of view.**

visual dialectic　Any juxtaposition of visual opposites; can be opposing aesthetic elements (size, color, vectors), ideas, or conditions.

visualization　Mentally seeing a key image or images in a sequence and, ideally, hearing how it sounds.

visual rhythm　A virtual beat created by distinct visual design elements that pattern themselves at various frequencies and intervals.

volume duality　The interplay between positive and negative volumes. Any articulation of negative space by positive space modulators.

white balance　The adjustment of the three color signals in the video camera to show a white object as white regardless of the relative color temperature of the light that illuminates the object.

wide-screen format　The most common aspect ratio used for wide-screen film—1.85:1. This means that for every unit of screen height there are 1.85 units of screen width. The standard video aspect ratio of 1.33:1 is considerably narrower.

windowboxing　Placing a smaller-sized picture in the center of the actual display screen, with the leftover space of the 16 × 9 frame surrounding it.

wipe　The transition in which a second image, framed in some geometric shape, gradually replaces all or part of the first one.

z-axis　The axis in the coordinating system that defines depth. Also, the imaginary line that extends from the camera lens to the horizon.

z-axis blocking　Arranging the event (people and things) along the z-axis or in close proximity to it.

z-axis index vector　Someone looking or pointing directly at the camera.

z-axis motion vector　Movement along the z-axis (toward or away from the camera).

z-axis vector　An index or motion vector that points or moves toward or away from the camera.

zero time　A high-magnitude subjective-time vector that occupies only a spot (practically zero length) in the objective time continuum.

Bibliography

Books and Journals

Adorno, Theodor, and Hans Eisler. "Komposition für den Film" (Composition for Film). In Theodor Adorno, *Gesammelte Schriften* 15. Frankfurt am Main: Suhrkamp Verlag, 1976.

Alten, Stanley R. *Audio in Media,* 9th ed. Belmont, Calif.: Wadsworth, 2011.

Aristotle. *Poetics. 39 b3.* Trans. by Gerald Else. Ann Arbor: University of Michigan Press, 1970.

Arnheim, Rudolf. "A New Laocoön: Artistic Composites and the Talking Film." In his *Film as Art.* Berkeley: University of California Press, 1957.

———. *Art and Visual Perception: A Psychology of the Creative Eye, The New Version.* Berkeley: University of California Press, 1974.

———. *Entropy and Art.* Berkeley: University of California Press, 1971.

———. *The Power of the Center.* Berkeley: University of California Press, 1982.

———. *Toward a Psychology of Art.* Berkeley: University of California Press, 1966.

Audi, Robert (ed.). *The Cambridge Dictionary of Philosophy.* Cambridge: Cambridge University Press, 1995.

Augustinus, Saint. *The Confessions of St. Augustine,* bk. XI, sec. x–xxxi. Chicago: Henry Regnery, 1948.

Barry, Ann Marie. *Visual Intelligence.* Albany: State University of New York Press, 1997.

Beer, Johnannes. *Albrecht Dürer als Maler.* Königstein i.T., Germany: Karl Robert Langewiesche Verlag, 1953.

Begleiter, Marcie. *From Word to Image.* Studio City, Calif.: Michael Wiese Productions, 2001.

Belton, John. *Widescreen Cinema.* Cambridge, Mass.: Harvard University Press, 1992.

Bergson, Henri. *Creative Evolution.* Trans. by Arthur Mitchell. New York: Modern Library, 1944.

———. *Time and Free Will.* Trans. by F. L. Pogson. New York: Harper Torchbooks, 1960.

Block, Bruce. *The Visual Story.* Boston: Focal Press, 2001.

Borden, Mark. "On the Problem of Vector Penetration." Broadcast and Electronic Communication Arts Department, San Francisco State University. March 1996. Unpublished.

Boslough, John. "The Enigma of Time." *National Geographic* 177 (March 1990): 109–32.

Boyer, Trevor. "Stereo Hype." *Digital Content Producer* 35, no. 2 (February 2009): 15–18.

Brecht, Bertold. *Brecht on Theatre: The Development of an Aesthetic.* Ed. and trans. by John Willett. New York: Hill and Wang, 1964.

Brown, Blain. *Motion Picture and Video Lighting,* 2nd ed. Burlington, Mass.: Focal Press, 2008.

Bruner, Jerome S., and A. L. Minturn. "Perceptual Identification and Perceptual Organization." *Journal of General Psychology* 53 (1955): 21–28.

Bucy, Erik, and John Newhagen, "The Micro- and Macrodrama of Politics on Television: Effects of Media Format on Candidate Evaluation." *Journal of Broadcasting and Electronic Communication* 43, no. 2 (1999): 193–210.

Burt, George. *The Art of Film Music.* Boston: Northeastern University Press, 1994.

Button, Bryce. *Nonlinear Editing: Storytelling, Aesthetics, and Craft.* Lawrence, Kans.: CMP Books, 2002.

Capra, Fritjof. *The Tao of Physics,* rev. ed. Boulder, Colo.: Shambhala, 1991.

Communtziz-Page, Georgette. "Comprehension of Visual Images in Television." In Ken Smith, Sandra Moriarty, Gretchen Barbatsis, and Keith Kenney (eds.), *Handbook of Visual Communication Research: Theory, Methods, and Media.* Mahwah, N.J.: Lawrence Erlbaum, 2005.

Davies, Paul. *About Time: Einstein's Unfinished Revolution.* New York: Touchstone, 1996.

Day, Louis Alvin. *Ethics in Media Communications,* 5th ed. Belmont, Calif.: Wadsworth, 2005.

Dean, Alexander. *Fundamentals of Play Directing.* New York: Farrar and Rinehart, 1946.

DeRose, Keith. *The Case for Contextualism: Knowledge, Skepticism, and Context,* vol. 1. New York: Oxford University Press, 2010.

De Voto, Bernard (ed.). *The Portable Mark Twain.* New York: Viking Press, 1946.

Dobson, Terence *The Film Work of Norman McLaren.* Bloomington: Indiana University Press, 2007.

Dorai, Chitra, and Svetha Venkatesh (eds.). *Media Computing: Computational Media Aesthetics.* Boston: Kluwer Academic, 2002.

Duncker, Karl. "Über induzierte Bewegung" (About Induced Movement). *Psychologische Forschung* 12 (1929): 180–259.

Edman, Irwin. *Arts and the Man.* New York: W. W. Norton, 1928, 1967.

Eisenstein, Sergei. *Film Form and The Film Sense.* Ed. and trans. by Jay Leyda. New York: World, 1957.

Engber, Daniel. "The Problem with 3-D." *Slate* (April 2, 2009). Available at *www.slate.com/id/2215265.*

Ernst, Bruno. *De Toverspiegel van M. C. Escher* (The Magic Mirror of M. C. Escher). Munich: Heinz Moos Verlag, 1978.

Escher, M. C., et al. *The World of M. C. Escher.* New York: Harry N. Abrams, 1972.

Evans, Ralph M. *The Perception of Color.* New York: John Wiley and Sons, 1974.

Festinger, Leon. *A Theory of Cognitive Dissonance.* Evanston, Ill.: Row, Peterson, 1957.

Fraser, J. T. *Time, the Familiar Stranger.* Amherst: University of Massachusetts Press, 1987.

Frazer, Bryant. "How Big Will 3D Be?" *Studio Daily* (April 23, 2009). Available at *www.studiodaily.com/blog/?p=1371.*

———. *Truth and Method.* New York: Seabury Press, 1975.

Gibson, James J. *The Ecological Approach to Visual Perception.* Hillsdale, N.J.: Lawrence Erlbaum, 1986.

Gladwell, Malcolm. *Blink.* New York: Little, Brown, 2005.

Glebas, Francis. *Directing the Story: Professional Storytelling and Storyboarding Techniques for Live Action and Animation.* Burlington, Mass.: Focal Press, 2008.

Goldstein, Bruce E. *Sensation and Perception,* 8th ed. Belmont, Calif.: Wadsworth, 2010.

Gombrich, E. H. *The Image and the Eye.* Ithaca, N.Y.: Cornell University Press, 1982.

Goudsmit, Samuel A., and Robert Clairborne. *Time.* New York: Time-Life Books, 1961.

Gross, Lynne S., James Foust, and Thomas Burrows. *Video Production: Disciplines and Techniques.* New York: McGraw-Hill, 2005.

Hahn, Lewis Edwin. *A Contextualistic Theory of Perception.* University of California Publications in Philosophy, vol. 22. Berkeley: University of California Press, 1939.

Hall, Edward T. *Silent Language.* Garden City, N.Y.: Anchor Press/Doubleday, 1973.

Hegel, Georg W. F. *The Phenomenology of Mind.* Trans. by F. P. B. Osmaston. New York: Macmillan, 1931.

Hyde, Stuart W. *Idea to Script: Storytelling for Today's Media.* Boston: Allyn and Bacon, 2003.

Itten, Johannes. *Design and Form: The Basic Course at the Bauhaus.* Trans. by John Maas. New York: Van Nostrand Reinhold, 1963.

James, Caryn. "Critic's Notebook: Splitting. Screens. For Minds. Divided." *New York Times,* January 9, 2004.

Kandinsky, Wassily. *Point and Line to Plane.* Trans. by Howard Dearstyne and Hilla Rebay. New York: Dover, 1979. (This work was originally published as *Punkt und Linie zu Fläche* in 1926 as the ninth in a series of fourteen Bauhaus books edited by Walter Gropius and László Moholy-Nagy.)

Katz, Steven D. *Film Directing: Cinematic Motion,* 2nd ed. Studio City, Calif.: Michael Wiese Productions, 2004.

———. *Film Directing: Shot by Shot.* Studio City, Calif.: Michael Wiese Productions, 1991.

Kipper, Philip, "Time Is of the Essence: An Investigation of Visual Events and the Experience of Duration." Paper presented at the Conference on Visual Communication. Alta, Utah, 1987.

Koffka, Kurt. *Principles of Gestalt Psychology.* New York: Harcourt, Brace, and World, 1935.

Köhler, Wolfgang. *Gestalt Psychology: An Introduction to New Concepts in Modern Psychology.* New York: Liveright , 1947, 1992.

———. *The Selected Papers of Wolfgang Köhler.* Ed. by Mary Henle. New York: Liveright, 1971.

Kracauer, Siegfried. *Theory of Film: The Redemption of Physical Reality,* reprint ed. Princeton, N.J.: Princeton University Press, 1997.

Kuleshov, Lev V. *Kuleshov on Film: Writings by Lev Kuleshov.* Select., trans., and ed. by Ronald Levaco. Berkeley: University of California Press, 1974.

Langer, Ellen. *Mindfulness.* Reading, N.Y.: Addison-Wesley, 1989.

Langone, John. *The Mystery of Time.* Washington, D.C.: National Geographic, 2000.

Le Corbusier [Charles E. Jeanneret-Gris]. *Modulor,* 2nd ed. Trans. by Peter de Francia and Anna Bostock. Cambridge, Mass.: Harvard University Press, 1954.

———. *Modular 2.* Trans. by Peter de Francia and Anna Bostock. London: Faber and Faber, 1958.

Le Poidevin, Robin. "The Experience and Perception of Time." In Edward N. Zalta (ed.), *Stanford Encyclopedia of Philosophy,* Spring 2002. Available at *http://plato.stanford.edu/entries/ time-experience.*

———. *The Images of Time.* New York: Oxford University Press, 2007.

Lessing, Gotthold Ephraim. *Hamburgische Dramaturgie* (Hamburg Dramaturgy). Hamburg: In Commission by J. H. Cramer, Bremen, 1767–1768.

Lestienne, Remy. *The Children of Time: Causality, Entropy, Becoming.* Trans. by E. C. Neher. Urbana: University of Illinois Press, 1995.

Lewin, Kurt. *A Dynamic Theory of Personality.* Trans. by Donald Adams and Karl Zener. New York: McGraw-Hill, 1935.

Linden, George W. *Reflections on the Screen.* Belmont, Calif.: Wadsworth, 1970.

Lindgren, Ernest. *The Art of the Film.* New York: Macmillan, 1963.

Lowell, Ross. *Matters of Light and Depth.* New York: Lowel-Light Manufacturing, 1999.

Maletzke, Gerhard. *Psychologie der Massenkommunikation* (Psychology of Mass Communication). Hamburg: Verlag Hans-Bredow-Institut, 1978.

Manovich, Lev. *The Language of New Media.* Cambridge, Mass.: MIT Press, 2002.

Mather, George. *Foundations of Perception.* Hove and New York: Psychology Press, 2006.

McCorquodale, Duncan (ed.). *Education and Contextualism: Architects Design Partnership.* London: Black Dog, 2008.

McCurdy, Edward (ed.). *The Notebooks of Leonardo da Vinci.* Old Saybrook, Conn.: Konecky and Konecky, 2003.

McLuhan, Eric, and Frank Zingrone (eds.). *Essential McLuhan.* New York: Basic Books, 1995.

McLuhan, Marshall. *Understanding Media: The Extensions of Man.* New York: McGraw-Hill, 1964.

Messaris, Paul. *Visual Literacy: Image, Mind, and Reality.* Boulder, Colo.: Westview Press, 1994.

Metallinos, Nikos, and Robert K. Tiemens. "Asymmetry of the Screen: The Effect of Left Versus Right Placement of Television Images." *Journal of Broadcasting* 21, no. 1 (1977): 21–33.

Metz, Christian. "Aural Objects." In Elisabeth Weis and John Belton (eds.), *Film Sound: Theory and Practice.* New York: Columbia University Press, 1985, pp. 157–58.

Meyrowitz, Joshua. *No Sense of Place.* New York: Oxford University Press, 1985.

———. "Television and Interpersonal Behavior: Codes of Reception and Response." In Gary Gumpert and Robert Cathcart (eds.), *Inter/Media: Interpersonal Communication in a Media World,* 2nd ed. New York: Oxford University Press, 1982, pp. 221–41.

Millerson, Gerald. *The Technique of Lighting for Television and Film,* 3rd ed. Boston and London: Focal Press, 1991.

———. *The Technique of Television Production,* 13th ed. Boston and London: Focal Press, 1999.

Moholy-Nagy, László. *Vision in Motion.* Chicago: Paul Theobald, 1947, 1965.

Mueller, Conrad, and Mae Rudolph (eds.). *Light and Vision.* New York: Time-Life Books, 1966.

Murch, Walter. *In the Blink of an Eye: A Perspective on Film Editing,* 2nd ed. Beverly Hills: Silman-James Press, 2001.

Noë, Alva. *Action in Perception.* Cambridge, Mass.: MIT Press, 2004.

Orgad, Shani. *This box was made for walking: how will mobile TV transform viewers' experience and change advertising?* Nokia Mobile TV report 2006, no. 2519. Available at *www.nokia .com/NOKIA_COM_1/Press/Press_Events/mobile_tv_re-port,_november_10,_2006/Mobil_TV_Report.pdf.*

Ornstein, Robert. *Multimind: A Way of Looking at Human Behavior.* Cambridge, Mass.: Malor Books, 2003.

Park, David. *The Image of Eternity.* Amherst: University of Massachusetts Press, 1980.

Pepper, Stephen C. *Aesthetic Quality: A Contextualistic Theory of Beauty.* New York: Charles Scribner's Sons, 1938.

———. *The Basis of Criticism in the Arts.* Cambridge, Mass.: Harvard University Press, 1945.

———. *World Hypotheses.* Berkeley: University of California Press, 1942, 1970.

Phillips, William. *Film: An Introduction,* 3rd ed. Boston: Bedford/ St. Martin's, 2004.

Pirsig, Robert M. *Zen and the Art of Motorcycle Maintenance.* New York: William Morrow, 1974.

Pudovkin, V. I. *Film Technique and Film Acting.* Ed. and trans. by Ivor Montagu. New York: Grove Press, 1960.

———. *Directing the Documentary,* 5th ed. Burlington, Mass.: Focal Press, 2009.

Rausch, Jürgen. "Ökonomie unserer Zeit" (Economy of Our Time). In Hans Jürgen Schultz (ed.), *Was der Mensch braucht.* Stuttgart: Kreuz Verlag, 1979.

Rock, Irvin. *Perception,* reprint ed. New York: W. H. Freeman, 1995.

Roller, D. J. "World's first 4K 3D Cinema Camera System for Studio, Location, and Underwater Filming With RED camera." PRNewswire (March 3, 2009). Available at *http://news.prnewswire.com/ DisplayReleaseContent.aspx?ACCT=104&STORY=/www/ story/03-03-2009/0004982328&EDATE=.*

Rose, Jay. *Producing Great Sound for Film and Video,* 3rd ed. Burlington, Mass.: Focal Press, 2008.

Saint-Exupéry, Antoine de. *The Little Prince.* Trans. by Katherine Woods. New York: Harcourt Brace Janovich, 1971.

Schilpp, Paul A. (ed.). "Carnap's Intellectual Biography." In *The Philosophy of Rudolf Carnap,"* Library of Living Philosophers, vol. II. La Salle, Ill.: Open Court, 1963.

Schramm, Wilbur, and Donald F. Roberts (eds.). *The Process and Effects of Mass Communication,* rev. ed. Urbana: University of Illinois Press, 1971.

Schubin, Mark. "No Answer." *Videography* (March 1996): 18–33.

———. "Searching for the Perfect Aspect Ratio." *SMPTE Journal* (August 1996): 460–78. Originally presented as paper no. 137-61 at the 137th SMPTE Technical Conference (1995).

Seiderman, Arthur, and Steven Marcus. *20/20 Is Not Enough.* New York: Alfred A. Knopf, 1990.

Shrivastava, Vinay. *Aesthetics of Sound.* Dubuque, Iowa: Kendall/Hunt, 1996.

Simon, Mark. *Storyboards: Motion in Art,* 3rd ed. Boston: Focal Press, 2007.

Tarnas, Richard. *The Passion of the Western Mind: Understanding the Ideas that Have Shaped Our World View.* New York: Ballantine Books, 1993.

Thomson, David. *The New Biographical Dictionary of Film.* New York: Alfred A. Knopf, 2004.

Treisman, Anne. "The Perception of Features and Objects." In Richard D. Wright (ed.), *Visual Attention.* New York: Oxford University Press, 1998.

Turetzky, Philip. *Time.* London and New York: Routledge, 1998.

Ushenko, Andrew Paul. *Dynamics of Art.* Bloomington: Indiana University Press, 1953.

Uspensky, Boris. *A Poetics of Composition.* Trans. by Valentina Zavarin and Susan Wittig. Berkeley: University of California Press, 1973.

Ward, Peter. *Picture Composition for Film and Television,* 2nd ed. Boston and London: Focal Press, 2003.

Weis, Elisabeth, and John Belton (eds.). *Film Sound: Theory and Practice.* New York: Columbia University Press, 1985.

Wertheimer, Max. "Experimentelle Studien über das Sehen von Bewegung" (Experimental Studies about the Seeing of Motion). *Zeitschrift für Psychologie* 61 (1912): 161–265.

———. "Untersuchungen zur Lehre von der Gestalt" (Studies for the Teachings of Gestalt). *Psychologische Forschung* 4 (1923): 301–50.

Willats, John. *Art and Representation: New Principles in the Analysis of Pictures.* Princeton, N.J.: Princeton University Press, 1997.

Wilson, Benjamin P. "The Design, Application and Evaluation of Stereophonic Television: A Production Model." Master's thesis. San Francisco State University, 1980.

Wingler, Hans M. *The Bauhaus,* reprint ed. Trans. by Wolfgang Jabs and Basil Gilbert. Cambridge, Mass.: MIT Press, 1979.

Wolfe, Thomas. *The Web and the Rock.* New York: Grosset and Dunlap, 1938.

Wölfflin, Heinrich. *Gedanken zur Kunstgeschichte* (Ideas for Art History). Basel: Benno Schwabe, 1940.

Zakia, Richard. *Perception and Imaging,* 3rd ed. Boston: Focal Press, 2007.

Zettl, Erika. *Held Captive.* Forest Knolls, Calif.: Papermill Creek, 2004.

Zettl, Herbert. "Back to Plato's Cave: Virtual Reality." In Lance Strate, Ron Jacobson, and Stephanie Gibson (eds.), *Communication and Cyberspace,* 2nd ed. Creskill, N.J.: Hampton Press, 2003, pp. 99–111.

———. "Contextual Media Aesthetics as the Basis for a Media-literacy Model." *Journal of Communication* 48, no. 1 (1998): 81–95.

———. "Essentials of Applied Media Aesthetics." In Chitra Dorai and Svetha Venkatesh (eds.), *Media Computing: Computational Media Aesthetics.* Boston: Kluwer Academic, 2002, pp. 11–38.

———. "The Graphication and Personification of Television News." In Gary Burns and Robert J. Thompson (eds.), *Television Studies: Textual Analysis.* New York: Praeger, 1989.

———. *Television Production Handbook,* 10th ed. Belmont, Calif.: Wadsworth, 2009.

———. "Toward a Multi-screen Television Aesthetic: Some Structural Considerations." *Journal of Broadcasting* 21, no. 1 (1977): 5–19.

———. *Video Basics 6.* Boston: Wadsworth, 2010.

———. *Zettl's VideoLab 3.0* interactive DVD-ROM. Belmont, Calif.: Wadsworth, 2004.

Zone, Ray. *3-D Filmmakers: Conversations with Creators of Stereoscopic Motion Pictures.* Lanham, Maryland: Scarecrow Press, 2005.

———. *Stereoscopic Cinema and the Origins of 3-D Film 1838–1952.* Lexington: University Press of Kentucky, 2008.

Online Sources

Christopher Dobrian's "Thoughts on Composition and Improvisation": *http://music.arts.uci.edu/dobrian/CD.comp.improv.htm*

Color models: *www.handprint.com/HP/WCL/color7.html* and *http://javaboutique.internet.com/ColorFinder*

Op art: *www.artcyclopedia.com/history/optical.html* and *www.columbusmuseum.org/media/optic*

Works of Mark Applebaum: *www.stanfordalumni.org/news/magazine/2008/mayjun/features/applebaum.html*

Photo Credits

Edward Aiona: p. xxvi, p. 2, p. 18, 2.1, 2.10, 2.12, 2.13, 2.14, 2.21, 2.22, 2.27, 2.28, 2.31, p. 36, 3.1, 3.2, 3.3, 3.4, 3.5, 3.6, 3.14, 3.16, 3.18, 3.19, 3.20, 3.21, color plates 16b, 22, 23, 24, 25, and 26, p. 70, 6.11, 6.12, 6.13, 6.14, 6.16, 6.17, 6.19, 6.20, 6.21, 6.22, 6.24, 6.25, 6.30, 6.31, 6.38, 6.39, p. 102, 7.7, 7.8, 7.9, 7.16, 7.17, 7.18, 7.24, 7.25, 7.26, 7.34, 7.35, 7.41, 7.51, 7.52, 7.56, 7.58, 7.59, 7.60, 7.61, p. 128, 8.1, 8.2, 8.9, 8.10, 8.16, 8.21, 8.24, 8.25, 8.26, 8.27, 8.37, 8.38, 8.39, 8.40, 8.41, 8.44, 8.45, 9.15, 9.16, 9.17, 9.18, 9.20, 10.10, 10.11, 10.12, 10.19, 10.22, 10.27, 10.28, 10.29, 10.35, 10.36 (insert), 10.37, 10.40, 10.43, 11.1, 11.2, 11.15, 11.18, 11.19, 11.22, 11.23, 11.24, 11.25, 11.26, 11.27, 11.28, 11.29, 11.30, 11.31, 11.32, p. 252, 13.3, 13.13, 13.14, p. 272, p. 294, p. 318, 16.38, 17.2, 17.6, 17.7, 17.8, 17.15, 17.16, 17.23, 17.29, 17.30, 17.31, p. 378, 18.4 (left), 18.5 (left), 18.9, 18.11, 18.12

Rudolf Benzler: 16.37

Brand X Pictures/Getty Images: 9.44

Bryan Evans: 9.45, 14.20, 18.13

Jules Frazier/Photodisc: 14.15 (left)

Irene Imfeld: 12.6

MobiTV: 6.23 (inset)

Nokia: 6.23

Gary Palmatier: 6.7, 6.26, 6.27, 6.32, 7.23, 7.37, 7.38, 7.57, 10.32, 17.28

Sherry Ream: 6.6, 7.2, 8.22, 8.23, p. 154, 10.5, 16.39

Steve Renick: 7.20, 8.28, 11.17

Andersen Ross/Photodisc: 14.15 (right)

Chris Rozales: 8.19

John Veltri: 1.7, 1.10 (top photo), 2.11, 2.16, 2.19, 2.29, 2.30, 3.12, color plate 18, p. 80, 6.10, 6.33, 6.34, 6.35, 6.36, 6.37, 7.5, 7.21, 7.22, 7.33, 7.54, 8.13, 8.14, 8.15, 8.29, 8.30, 8.32, 8.42, 8.43, 8.46, 8.47, 8.48, 8.49, 9.14, 9.38, 9.39, 9.40, 9.41, 9.42, p. 176, 10.2, 10.16, 10.17, 10.23, 10.24, 10.31, 10.33, 10.34, 10.36, 10.39, 10.41, 10.42, 10.44, p. 202, 11.6, 11.7, 11.8, 11.9, 11.10, 11.11, 11.12, 11.13, 11.20, 11.21, 11.33, 11.34, 11.35, 11.36, 11.37, 11.38, 12.7, 12.8, 14.13, 14.14, 15.2, 15.3, 15.9, 15.10, 16.36, p. 352, 17.1, 17.3, 17.4, 17.5, 17.9, 17.10, 17.11, 17.12a, 17.12b, 17.13, 17.14, 17.19, 17.20, 17.21, 17.22, 17.25, 17.26, 17.32, 17.33, 17.39, 17.40, 17.41, 17.42, 18.4 (right three photos), 18.5 (right three photos), 18.7, 18.8

Herbert Zettl: 1.1, 1.2, 1.4, 1.5, 2.2, 2.4, 2.5, 2.6, 2.7, 2.8, 2.9, 2.15, 2.17, 2.18, 2.20, 2.23, 2.24, 2.25, 2.26, 3.11, color plate 17, color plate 21, 6.5, 6.8, 6.9, 6.15, 6.18, 6.29, 7.1, 7.3, 7.6, 7.32, 7.45, 7.47, 7.49, 7.50, 7.53, 8.17, 8.18, 8.31, 8.33, 8.34, 8.35, 8.36, 9.7, 9.19, 9.24, 9.26, 9.28, 9.29, 9.30, 9.31, 9.32, 9.33, 9.34, 9.35, 9.36, 9.37, 10.1, 10.3, 10.4, 10.6, 10.7, 10.9, 10.13, 10.14, 10.15, 10.18, 10.20, 10.21, 10.38, p. 181 (cathedral), 11.14, 11.16, p. 228, 13.1, 13.16, 13.17, 14.10, 14.11, 14.16, 14.17, 14.19, 17.37, 18.3

Index